ASPECTS OF LANGUAGE PRODUCTION

Aspects of language production

edited by
Linda Wheeldon
University of Birmingham, UK

Psychology Press
a member of the Taylor & Francis group

First published 2000 by Psychology Press
27 Church Road, Hove, East Sussex, BN3 2FA

http://www.psypress.co.uk

Simultaneously published in the USA and Canada
by Taylor & Francis
325 Chestnut Street, Suite 800, Philadelphia, PA 19106

Psychology Press is part of the Taylor & Francis Group

British Library Cataloguing in Publication Data
A catalogue record for this book is available from the British Library

Library of Congress Cataloging in Publication Data
A catalogue record has been requested for this book

   ISBN 0-86377-882-8 (hbk)
   ISBN 0-86377-883-6 (pbk)

Cover painting: *Three Figures* (Egg Tempera/Collage) by Ian Hopton

Typeset by Graphicraft Ltd, Hong Kong
Printed and bound in the UK by Biddles Ltd, Guildford & King's Lynn

Contents

Contributors

Kathryn J. Bock, Department of Psychology and the Beckman Institute for Advanced Science and Technology, University of Illinois, Urbana, Illinois 61801, USA

Fernanda Ferreira, Department of Psychology, Cognitive Science Program, Michigan State University, East Lansing, MI 48824-1117, USA

Jean E. Fox Tree, Psychology Department Social Sciences II, University of California, Santa Cruz, CA 95064, USA

LouAnn Gerken, Department of Speech and Hearing Sciences, University of Arizona, Tucson, AZ 85721, USA

Zenzi M. Griffin, Department of Psychology, Stanford University, Stanford, CA 94305-2130, USA

David Howard, Department of Speech, University of Newcastle-upon-Tyne, Newcastle-upon-Tyne, NE1 7RU, UK

Glyn W. Humphreys, School of Psychology, University of Birmingham, Edgbaston, Birmingham, B15 2TT, UK

Aditi Lahiri, University of Konstanz, Fachgruppe Sprachwissenschaft, Fach D186, 78457 Konstanz, Germany

Antje S. Meyer, School of Psychology, University of Birmingham, Edgbaston, Birmingham, B15 2TT, UK

Lyndsey Nickels, Macquarie Centre for Cognitive Science, Macquarie University, Sydney NSW 2109, Australia

Diane Ohala, Department of Speech and Hearing Sciences, University of Arizona, Tucson, AZ 85721, USA

Cathy J. Price, The Wellcome Department of Cognitive Neurology, Institute of Neurology, Queen Square, London WC1N 3BG, UK

M. Jane Riddoch, School of Psychology, University of Birmingham, Edgbaston, Birmingham, B15 2TT, UK

Ardi Roelofs, Max Planck Institute for Psycholinguistics, PB310, NL-6500 AH Nijmegen, The Netherlands

Mark Smith, School of Psychology, University of Birmingham, Edgbaston, Birmingham, B15 2TT, UK

Rachelle Waksler, Linguistics Program, San Francisco State University, 1600 Holloway Avenue, San Francisco, CA 94132, USA

Linda Wheeldon, School of Psychology, University of Birmingham, Edgbaston, Birmingham, B15 2TT, UK

Series preface

Over the past 20 years enormous advances have been made in our understanding of basic cognitive processes concerning issues such as: What are
the basic modules of the cognitive system? How can these modules be
modelled? How are the modules implemented in the brain? The book series
"Studies in cognition" seeks to provide state-of-the art summaries of this
research, bringing together work on experimental psychology with that on
computational modelling and cognitive neuroscience. Each book contains
chapters written by leading figures in the field, which aim to provide comprehensive summaries of current research. The books should be both accessible
and scholarly and be relevant to undergraduates, post-graduates, and research
workers alike.

Glyn Humphreys

Studies in Cognition Series
Published Titles

Series Editor
Glyn Humphreys, University of Birmingham, UK

Cognitive Models of Memory
Martin A. Conway (Ed.)
Language Processing
Simon Garrod & Martin Pickering (Eds.)
Knowledge, Concepts, and Categories
Koen Lamberts & David Shanks (Eds.)
Attention
Harold Pashler (Ed.)
Cognitive Neuroscience
Michael D. Rugg
Aspects of Language Production
Linda Wheeldon (Ed.)

CHAPTER ONE

Introduction

Linda Wheeldon
School of Psychology, University of Birmingham, UK

It is usual for the introduction to a volume on language production to begin by bemoaning the lack of relevant research. Traditionally in the field of psycholinguistics, the study of language production has always played the poor relation to research on language comprehension and language acquisition processes. However, happily, I think that this is no longer the case. In terms of research endeavour, language production now boasts a dedicated, imaginative, and highly productive group of researchers, which continues to grow steadily. The first aim of this volume is, therefore, to present readers with a picture of the breadth of current research in the field. To this end, there are chapters investigating all levels of the language production system from the generation of the phonological and phonetic representations of speech to the coordination of spontaneous conversation.

Nevertheless, rather than break with tradition, I do want to start this introduction with a gripe. My complaint is not about the amount or quality of the research in this field but about the acknowledgement of the data and models of language production research in other related fields. Often, a substantial chunk of language production processes is assigned to one output arrow in cognitive models of processes involving speech output. Thus, a second aim of this volume is to draw links between different approaches to language research and to argue the need for the development of models informed by the wide range of language production data that already exists in the literature. In particular contributors have focused on models of visual word processing, aphasic speech, object recognition, and language production in children.

In addition, many chapters highlight the need for psychological models of language production to learn from theoretical linguistics in order to become better informed about the structure of language itself. Indeed, in recent years, psycholinguists have made increasing use of innovations in linguistic theory to explain psychological data. These efforts have met with no little success as a number of the chapters included in this volume will testify. Nevertheless, psycholinguistic models of language processing still have a long way to go before they can provide an account for the complexity of structure and process in the languages of the world. Therefore, this volume also includes chapters written by linguists for psychologists, which serve to remind us of this fact.

My approach to compiling this volume has been simply to invite some of the foremost researchers in the field to write about what they know best. The result is a diverse set of chapters that are representative of the major research issues in language production today. This diversity, while welcome, has foiled all my attempts to impose a clear structure on this volume. However, in general, the chapter topics run from the low level processes of sound form generation and lexical retrieval to high level processes such as the generation of syntactic and conceptual structure and the coordination of conversation. In the rest of this introduction I will attempt to plot a course for the reader through these issues by summarising the chapters in order.

In Chapter 2, Bock and Griffin tackle the lack of acknowledgement of speech production data head on. They argue that the fall of stimulus-response psychology in the early 1960s lead to an implicit avoidance of all processes that result in an overt physical response, e.g., speech. They reevaluate the impressively broad literature on word perception and comprehension in the light of recent advances in the modelling of spoken word production processes. They look at implicit memory, brain imaging, and visual word recognition. In all of these areas data from tasks involving the overt articulation of words have been used to inform models of language comprehension. However, the models that have been developed to explain these data fail to acknowledge the complexity of speech output processes. Bock and Griffin argue convincingly that an acknowledgment of the involvement of production processes in these tasks is not only desirable but essential if comprehension processes are to be accurately modelled and located in the brain. In the chapters that follow, the complexity of the processes by which we generate speech is amply illustrated.

In Chapter 3, Meyer focuses on the generation of the sound form of the words we speak. She describes and evaluates what she terms the "Standard Model" of word-form encoding. The Standard Model incorporates a set of claims that are consistent with most current models of word-form encoding and that have formed the framework for more detailed computational models. The Standard Model can be derived almost exclusively from speech error data. Meyer first reviews the classic speech error data and their standard interpretation. She then evaluates the standard interpretation in the light of new data drawn from both error corpora and experimental studies. What emerges from this exercise is a clear picture of the relative security of the main assumptions that form the foundation of current theories of word-form encoding. A computational approach to some of the same issues is taken by Roelofs in Chapter 4. Roelofs describes WEAVER++, a simulated theory of both lexical selection and word-form encoding. Unlike early models of spoken word production (e.g., Dell, 1986, 1988; Shattuck-Hufnagel, 1987), WEAVER++ has been developed to encode reaction time data rather than speech error generation. Roelofs provides us with a detailed comparison of WEAVER++ and the classical spreading activation model of Dell and colleagues and discusses a wealth of experimental data for which WEAVER++ provides an account.

In Chapter 5, Nickels and Howard examine the role of neuropsychological data has in the development and testing of cognitive models of language production. In particular, they address the relevance of acquired disorders of language production to models of spoken word production concentrating on the level of single word production. They take as their framework Levelt's model of speech production (Levelt, 1989, 1992; Levelt & Wheeldon, 1994; Levelt, Roelofs, & Meyer, 1999; Roelofs, this volume) and examine it step by step, identifying predicted impairments and discussing the limitations of the model in accounting for particular patterns of breakdown. Two things rapidly become clear from this exercise. First, that models of spoken word production can and should be informed by patterns of breakdown in aphasic speech. And second, that detailed models of language production should allow questions concerning impairments in word production to be posed with much greater precision.

In Chapter 6, Humphreys, Price, and Riddoch also focus on the production of single spoken words. They examine one of the most frequently used tasks within speech production research—the naming of pictured objects. In particular, they examine the evidence that early stages of object recognition constrain later word retrieval processes. The evidence they consider is drawn from a wide range of disciplines including experimental and neuropsychology, functional imaging, and computational modelling. They discuss data that demonstrate that name retrieval for objects is strongly influenced by visual differentiation between category exemplars. These data, they argue, present a challenge to discrete stage models of spoken word production (e.g., Levelt, 1989; Levelt et al., 1999; Roelofs, this volume). In contrast, they propose a Hierarchical Interactive Theory of object naming, which allows continuous interaction between different processing levels.

Chapters 7 and 8 signal a complete change of emphasis. These chapters are written by linguists for psychologists and provide a much needed cross-linguistic look at the complexity and diversity of linguistic structures and processes. Lahiri outlines current cross-linguistic generalisations made in phonological theory which relate to the structures and processes required to represent the phonological system of a language. She provides us with a typology of phonological processes and motivates several layers of distinct linguistic constituents. Lahiri argues that an adequate model of language production must be able to provide an account for the cross-linguistic phonological generalisations she describes, and that this will require a more detailed description of phonological representations in the lexicon than exists in current models. Lahiri also discusses these generalisations in the light of current psycholinguistic models of phonological encoding for speech production. The focus is on Levelt and colleagues' incremental model of phonological encoding, which postulates a strict left-to-right build-up of phonological structure with minimal look ahead (Levelt, 1989, 1992; Levelt & Wheeldon, 1994; Levelt et al., 1999; Roelofs, this volume). She presents two tonal phenomena, which require information from further down stream in the utterance than incremental models would allow. Phenomena such as these provide a strong challenge to strict incrementality.

Waksler takes a similar approach to morphological processes. Until recently morphology has received scant attention in production research and the few theories which have modelled the production of complex words are limited to the production of roots with single suffixes or prefixes. As Waksler demonstrates, such forms encompass only a small subset of the morphological structures used in the world's languages. In this chapter we are provided with a typology of the morphological systems in the languages of the world. Waksler then goes on to discuss the potential consequences of different morphological systems for language production models, in particular, the consequences for the representation of lexical entries and for the relationship between semantic, syntactic, and morphological processes.

In Chapters 9, 10, and 11 we are provided with examples of the application of linguistic theory to psychological data. In Chapter 9, I examine the form encoding of connected speech. This chapter describes a wide range of phonological phenomena that occur during connected speech production and argues that some of these phenomena arise during the generation of the prosodic (or rhythmic) structure of an utterance. In the field of linguistics, the theory of the Prosodic Hierarchy divides an utterance into a nested hierarchy of prosodic units, which need not correspond to syntactic constituents. These prosodic units form the domains of application for many phonological rules. I evaluate data relevant to the production of prosody and argue that both psychological and linguistic theory must be combined in order to build adequate models of connected speech production.

Gerken and Ohala also make use of evidence from theoretical phonology to interpret data from child language production studies. To date most studies of child language production have focused on the ways in which child forms deviate from adult forms and thus how the child's production system differs from that of the adult speaker. In contrast, Gerken and Ohala argue that remarkably similar phenomena exist in child and adult speech. They argue that children's deviations do not reflect processes that are specific to immature talkers but are a reflection of certain properties of a single underlying production system. They examine the tendency towards consonant cluster reduction and weak syllable omission in child language production. Their explanation of these phenomena is based largely on evidence from theoretical phonology which points to optimal syllabic and prosodic forms both across and within languages. They show that children's omissions tend to result in forms resembling frequently occurring cross-linguistic patterns. They suggest that adherence to optimal forms may play a role in deviations in both child and adult language (i.e., speech errors or aphasic speech) and argue that we must begin to approach child and adult language production as part of a single developing system.

In Chapter 11, Ferreira reviews the experimental findings relevant to the grammatical encoding of sentences for speech. She introduces an account for these data based on an approach to syntax from the field of computational linguistics. This approach, known as tree adjoining grammars, involves the constrained combination of primitive syntactic trees. Ferreira argues that such an approach can provide an account for the available experimental data. Crucial to her argument is that prototypical trees correspond roughly to a simple clause consisting of a verb and its argument positions. The verbal concept activates its verbal lemma, and all possible elementary trees compatible with a verbal lemma are accessed. Crucially, as Ferreira demonstrates, such theoretical work has a direct relevance to experimental work in speech production in that it naturally suggests a number of testable hypothesis with regard to perennial issues in language production research such as the scope of planning during grammatical encoding.

In Chapter 12, Smith investigates the relation between the conceptual and grammatical structures generated during language production. He begins by analysing rationalist models of speech production (Garrett, 1982; Roelofs, 1992) in which it is claimed that the speaker is compelled to produce a single grammatical structure that precisely replicates both the content and form of the information contained within the conceptual structure. Smith points out some of the theoretical problems entailed by such a view and marshals a broad range of linguistic and psycholinguistic evidence in support of the opposing claim that conceptual and grammatical structures contrast strongly in terms of the information they contain. Smith further argues that this contrast arises because the information within a conceptual structure possesses such a rich, analogue complexity that it cannot be fully preserved within the grammatical structure without incurring excessive formulation costs. On such a view, then, speakers minimise formulation costs by producing grammatical structures that provide only a partial representation of the conceptual structures that underlie them and thus entail much processing effort on the part of the hearer who has to reconstruct something approximating the original conceptual structure on the basis of this incomplete representation.

Finally, in Chapter 13, Fox Tree examines the factors influencing language production during spontaneous conversation. The vast majority of the speech we produce is conversational; however, this form of speech receives scant attention in the production literature. One reason for this is that spontaneous speech is messy—filled with paralinguistic phenomena such as stops and starts, ums, and long pauses. Unlike slips of the tongue, such dysfluencies have been perceived as unfortunate and uninformative elements of the speech stream. In contrast to this view, Fox Tree argues that these phenomena form an integral part of the communicative enterprise. She argues that certain paralinguistic phenomena are used to get around some of the problems inherent to the communication medium of spontaneous speech. They are necessary to coordinate conversation, achieve the grounding criterion, indicate turn units, create a coherent discourse, and warn listeners of upcoming dysfluencies and production trouble.

In summary, the chapters in this volume address a wide range of issues relevant to the cognitive modelling of language production processes. Current theories of phonological encoding, word retrieval, sentence formulation, conceptual structure, and spontaneous speech are evaluated. In addition, the relevance of these models for other areas of language research is addressed, including language comprehension, neuropsychology, language development, and linguistic theory. Finally and most importantly, what emerges from the chapters in this volume is a new set of research questions that should keep us busy well into the third millennium.

REFERENCES

Dell, G.S. (1986). A spreading activation theory of retrieval in sentence production. *Psychological Review, 93*, 283–321.

Dell, G.S. (1988). The retrieval of phonological forms in production: Tests of predictions from a connectionist model. *Journal of Memory and Language, 27*, 124–142.

Garrett, M.F. (1982). Production of speech: Observations from normal and pathological language use. In A. Ellis (Ed.), *Normality and pathology in cognitive functions* (pp. 19–76). London: Academic Press.

Levelt, W.J.M. (1989). *Speaking: From intention to articulation.* Cambridge, MA: MIT Press.

Levelt, W.J.M. (1992). Accessing words in speech production: Stages, processes and representations. *Cognition, 42*, 1–22.

Levelt, W.J.M., Roelofs, A., & Meyer, A.S. (1999). A theory of lexical access in speech production. *Behavioural and Brain Sciences, 22*, 1–75.

Levelt, W.J.M., & Wheeldon, L.R. (1994). Do speakers have access to a mental syllabary? *Cognition, 50*, 239–269.

Roelofs, A. (1992). A spreading-activation theory of lemma retrieval in speaking. *Cognition, 42*, 107–142.

Shattuck-Hufnagel, S. (1987). The role of word onset consonants in speech production planning: New evidence from speech error patterns. In E. Keller & M. Gopnik (Eds.), *Motor and sensory processing in language*. Hillsdale, NJ: Lawrence Erlbaum Associates Inc.

CHAPTER TWO

Producing words:
How mind meets mouth

Kathryn Bock
*Department of Psychology and the Beckman Institute for
Advanced Science and Technology, University of Illinois, USA*

Zenzi M. Griffin
Department of Psychology, Stanford University, USA

INTRODUCTION

One of the premises of contemporary cognitive science is that an organism's response to a stimulus requires sensory, perceptual, and memory processes on an order of complexity unexpected from observations of simple reactions to physical stimulation. It was a touchstone of the cognitive revolution in the late 1950s and early 1960s that these interpretative processes are a proper subject for psychology, setting the goal of explaining how a stimulus is processed through successive mental transformations. In contrast, within behaviourist conceptions that regarded the relationships between stimuli and responses as little more than learned reflexes (Skinner, 1953; Watson, 1913), the role that mental transformations played was on a par with the hyphen in the term stimulus–response (S–R) psychology.

Put into the terms of the theoretical framework that cognitive psychology supplanted, the thrust of the cognitive revolution was therefore directed toward elaborating the S of S–R theories. Cognitive theories have given considerably less attention to elaborating the mental processes by which interpretations or other representations of meaning guide and gain expression in action. There are many reasons for this inattention. First and foremost, action suffered from its associations with behaviour and the eponymous -ism. What behaviourists were seen as neglecting most egregiously were the processes of stimulus interpretation, and those processes justifiably took priority. Second, to begin to explain the cognitive processes that guide action, one must have in hand some framework

7

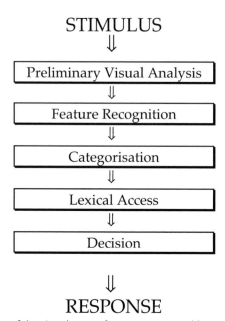

STIMULUS
⇓

Preliminary Visual Analysis

⇓

Feature Recognition

⇓

Categorisation

⇓

Lexical Access

⇓

Decision

⇓

RESPONSE

Figure 2.1.   A caricature of contemporary cognitive models.
Reprinted with kind permission MIT Press from R. Wilson & F. Keil (Eds). MIT Encyclopedia of the cognitive sciencies.

for representing interpretations, because interpretations are the starting point for the formulation of goals. To be firmly grounded, the elements of such a framework should come from theories of stimulus processing. Third, the practical problems of conducting controlled experiments stymied efforts to explore the cognitive precursors of action in many domains, including the psychology of language. And finally, with many experiments requiring only button-press responses, there was little demand for a cognitive theory to explain how the index fingers are controlled.

For all of their merits, these things had an unfortunate by-product. To a considerable degree, cognitive psychology lost sight of the need to explain how actions are guided and how they are learned. Reflecting this, many views of cognition tacitly assume that the essential elements of action comprise its motor components alone. Figure 2.1 caricatures this state of affairs with a cognitive model that includes multiple stages of stimulus processing and no stages of response preparation.

Psycholinguistics is one of the areas that disdained the action side of the cognitive relationship between stimuli and responses, and it is the one that we will highlight in this chapter. Benignly reflecting psycholinguists' neglect of action, in a 1974 review of experimental psycholinguistics, Johnson-Laird defined the field as the study of language comprehension, and with some justification.[1] Little work had been done, explicitly, on language production. This single-minded emphasis on the cognitive processes of interpretation (language comprehension) coupled with the intransigence to experimental investigation of the cognitive processes of expression (language production) led to a marked imbalance in our understanding of adult language use. This distanced the scientific enterprise from the prototype of skill in language, an ability to speak fluently.

There were scattered efforts to change the balance (Carroll, 1958; Deese, 1984; Garrett, 1975; Osgood, 1971), and these efforts have gathered strength and coherence as the problems of language production become more widely recognised (Bock, 1995; Clark, 1996; Dell, 1995; Garrett, 1988; Levelt, 1989). Our goal in this chapter is to broaden this recognition by considering how certain findings from research on language comprehension may bear on our understanding of language production, and vice versa. Our primary focus will be the mechanisms of lexical retrieval. To begin, we sketch how the cognitive processes of expression seem to be organised, in general, and how word production works, in particular. We then contrast the lexical processes of production with the lexical processes of comprehension, revisiting some key claims about word recognition in light of the implications from research on word production.

THE ANATOMY OF LANGUAGE PRODUCTION

The components of the language production system that are directly implicated in the formation of an utterance include a representation of the message, at least two types of lexical retrieval operations, several structural procedures responsible for combining and ordering words and sounds, and all the intricacies of articulatory planning and execution. In Figure 2.2 we offer a rough sketch of this system along with examples to illustrate selected operations that must be implemented to retrieve a single word (rabbit) in the course of creating a spoken utterance (e.g., "There's a rabbit!").

In keeping with our emphasis on lexical processes, we will have little to say about the message apart from assuming that there is one. The key feature of messages is that they stand at the interface between thought and language. They are not verbal or word-based: Messages may be much the same in nature whether the eventual utterance is in English, Guugu Yimithirr, Japanese, or Tzotzil (Potter, So, Von Eckhardt, & Feldman, 1984). In the simple laboratory tasks that are used in most research on word production, a message is rarely more than a single concept. Picture-naming tasks evoke concepts with pictures of concrete objects (like the rabbit in Figure 2.2). In classic Stroop studies, in which speakers are asked to name the colour of the ink in which a word is printed, the concept is evoked by the coloured stimulus (the ink itself or a colour patch; Stroop, 1935). More generally, a message can be viewed as the penultimate link in the traditional information processing chain from sensory processing to output. As such, it is a perceptual or conceptual categorisation of the input.

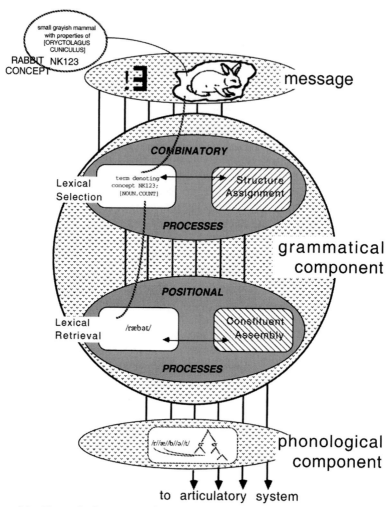

Figure 2.2.   The production processes hypothesised to support retrieval of the word <u>rabbit</u>, in the course of producing the utterance "There's a rabbit!". The rabbit concept includes the speaker's tacit knowledge of what a rabbit is (big ears, burrows in ground, etc.), glossed as the species name in the figure. NK indicates a natural kind concept, and 123 is an arbitrary index (reproduced from Bock, 1999).

Going to the bottom of Figure 2.2, we will also set aside the details of processing within the phonological component, prior to articulation (see the chapters by Meyer and Wheeldon). These phonological encoding processes follow upon the successful retrieval of information about word form. This is the sort of information that might allow one to judge whether the English word for:

rhymes with "Babbitt": It comprises the word's phonological segments and per-haps also its stress pattern and syllabification. Phonological encoding uses this information to smoothly integrate the sound segments for a word (/r/, /æ/, /b/, etc.) into the stream of speech. In connected speech, this means that a phrase such as "another rabbit" may on occasion be uttered by speakers of North American English as "a NOTH er AB bit", combining the /r/ of <u>rabbit</u> and the /r/ of <u>another</u>. This process of *resyllabification* has familiar reflections in children's word play ("I scream, you scream, we all scream for ice cream") and song lyrics ("Mairzy doats and dozy doats and little lamzy divy"), and contributes to one of the central problems in auditory word recognition, the problem of segmenting words (e.g., hearing "The mean of them all" as "The mean of the mall"). For accounts of speaking, the implication is that retrieving the sound form of a word is not sufficient to produce the word, without additional work.

By setting aside the processes of conceptual identification and phonological encoding, we have exhausted almost everything that there is to word production as it is sometimes conceived. But since there is an entire chapter to come, one may suspect that there is more to be said. What more there is comprises the lexical processes that Figure 2.2 depicts as components of grammatical and morphological processing, lexical selection and lexical retrieval.

The motivation for linking lexical selection and retrieval to grammatical processing stems from the kinds of information that words carry about their structural and positional privileges and requirements. In everyday language use, words are rarely produced in isolation. Instead, they occupy places within strings of words, with their positions determined in part by their grammatical categories (e.g., in most English declarative sentences, at least one noun will precede a verb) and with their pronunciations determined in part by their positions (e.g., in many dialects of American English, the definite article <u>the</u> is pronounced "thuh" when it precedes a word that begins with a consonant and "thee" when it precedes a word that begins with a vowel). Thus, in order to create normal utterances, speakers must recover information about the grammatical classes of words and about the words' sounds before phonological encoding can be completed.

Implicit in the architecture of Figure 2.2 is the claim that information about grammatical class is recovered during lexical selection and that information about sound is recovered during lexical retrieval. Selection makes it possible to assign syntactic roles and retrieval makes it possible to inflect word forms appropriately for their positions in an utterance (see Bock, 1995 and Bock & Levelt, 1994, for some of the evidence for these assumptions in the context of sentence production). In the next sections we further detail the processes of selection and retrieval, and then survey some of the reasons for believing that these processes occur not only in connected speech, but even when words are produced in isolation.

Lexical selection and retrieval

Lexical selection involves finding a lexical entry (technically, a *lemma*) that adequately conveys some portion of a message, ensuring that there exists a word in one's mental lexicon that will do the job. A rough analogy is looking for a word in a reverse dictionary, which is organised semantically rather than alphabetically. If the desired meaning is listed in the dictionary with a single word that expresses the sense, there is an appropriate word to be had in the language; if not, the search fails. The mental lexicon is presumably accessible in comparable fashion, permitting speakers to determine whether they know a word that will convey the meaning they intend. Most English speakers, for example, will find at least one lemma for their concept of a member of the family *Oryctolagus cuniculus*.

Locating a lemma yields basic information about how the impending word combines with other words. This corresponds to information about grammatical class (noun, verb, adjective, etc.) and other grammatical features that control a word's combinatorial privileges and requirements (e.g., nouns must be specified as mass or count, and if count, as singular or plural; verbs must be specified as intransitive or transitive, and if transitive, as simple or ditransitive, etc.). The lemma for an instance of *Oryctolagus cuniculus*, for example, is a noun, count, and singular.

Once a lemma is found, the next step is retrieving the word's morphological form (technically, its *lexeme*). In connected speech, this may encompass inflectional processes that adjust a word's morphological structure to its syntactic environment (e.g., making a verb singular or plural). These lexical retrieval processes yield an abstract specification for the morphology of the selected word, a representation suitable for guiding the process of phonological encoding. So, retrieving the lexeme for the singular count noun that denotes a member of the family *Oryctolagus cuniculus* should yield a specification of the morphological structure of /ræbət/.

Two steps to pronunciation?

Contemporary theories of how we produce language are largely agreed on a distinction along the lines of the one we have drawn between lexical selection and lexical retrieval (though see Caramazza, 1997). The distinction can be found in theories that are as different in other respects as those of Butterworth (1989), Dell (1986), Garrett (1975), Levelt (1989), and MacKay (1982). The key feature

TABLE 2.1
Exclusive-OR problem in mapping from conceptual features
to phonological features (Dell et al., 1997)

| Target Word | Conceptual Features | | Phonological Features |
	Female	Parent	Begins with /m/
mother	Yes	Yes	Yes
father	No	Yes	No
woman	Yes	No	No
man	No	No	Yes

is the existence of two lexically specific steps separating meaning from sound: In order to convey a meaning with a word, the speaker must locate both a lemma and a lexeme in the mental lexicon. However, apart from production theories, the need for lexical selection (lemma retrieval) is sometimes disputed (Starreveld & LaHeij, 1996). This warrants consideration of the arguments that motivate the lemma hypothesis.

The first argument is logical, and reflects a basic property of language: The mapping from meaning to sound is arbitrary. This fact has consequences for the representation of words in the mental lexicon (Dell, Schwartz, Martin, Saffran, & Gagnon, 1997). Suppose a speaker wants to produce a word that denotes the concept FEMALE PARENT. This concept is part of a semantic field that includes other concepts like FATHER, MAN, and WOMAN, whose meanings are partially indicated in Table 2.1. Consider the relationship between the matrix in the table and the conditions for an /m/ at the beginning of a word, as an English speaker would utter in expressing the FEMALE PARENT concept with the word mother. For /m/ to be used appropriately in this case, both the FEMALE and PARENT features are relevant. However, if a speaker wishes to express the concept ADULT MALE with the word man, neither the FEMALE nor the PARENT feature is relevant to the utterance of initial /m/. The upshot is that if a single one of the features (FEMALE, PARENT, ADULT, or MALE) is active, initial /m/ should be blocked, but if both FEMALE and PARENT or ADULT and MALE are active, initial /m/ is enabled. This is an instance of exclusive-OR, a well-known computational problem for single-layer associative networks (Minsky & Papert, 1969). Its solution entails that the mapping from meanings to sounds, even for very simple sets of meaning and sounds, includes an additional set of representations. In connectionist frameworks this is a layer of hidden units, and in an interpreted model of language production, it is a layer of lexical entries.

From an empirical standpoint, the most readily appreciated evidence for the lemma hypothesis comes from the universal tip-of-the-tongue experience. This is the familiar frustration of being unable to retrieve the sounds of a word that one knows and—the source of the frustration—knows one knows. This metacognitive awareness is sometimes called a "feeling of knowing". It implicates the identification of an appropriate lemma in the mental lexicon without lexical retrieval, since the phonological form is unavailable.

A concrete link between the tip-of-the-tongue (TOT) state and lemma identification can be found in the kinds of information that are available to speakers in such states. It is common knowledge among psychologists that partial phonological information can sometimes be retrieved: In an early study, Brown and McNeill (1966) discovered that speakers in tip-of-the-tongue states could accurately report the beginnings of otherwise-inaccessible words between 40% and 50% of the time. However, the lemma hypothesis makes the prediction that other kinds of information should be accessible in tip-of-the-tongue states. Specifically, if a tip-of-the-tongue state signals the successful identification of a lexical entry, grammatical information about the word should be available even if phonological information is not.

This proposition has been examined in several studies involving Italian subjects. Like many other languages, Italian has grammatical genders that control (among other things) the determiners that nouns take and the forms of the adjectives that modify nouns—the kinds of information that are needed for a word to combine appropriately with other words. Excepting those few nouns whose grammatical genders reflect biological gender, gender is semantically arbitrary and unpredictable from the word's meaning or reference. These properties were exploited by Vigliocco, Antonini, and Garrett (1997) and Miozzo and Caramazza (1997) in research on the information available to Italian speakers in tip-of-the-tongue states. The results showed that speakers reliably identified the genders of words whose phonological properties were inaccessible, and did so even for words whose phonological forms offer no gender clues (though there are clear phonological correlates of gender in Italian, many words have no overt gender marking or have contrary marking). The rate at which gender was correctly reported was significantly greater than chance—over 80% in Vigliocco et al. (1997) and about 70% in Miozzo and Caramazza (1997).

Interestingly, in Miozzo and Caramazza's research the rates for correct forced-choice identifications of initial sounds were virtually identical to the rates for gender identification. This gives no support to a subsidiary prediction of the lemma hypothesis that grammatical information should be more reliably available than phonological information. Unfortunately, Miozzo and Caramazza's identification test always queried gender before sound, and almost 20% of the initially reported tip-of-the-tongue states were resolved by retrieval of the word during the search for gender information, compared to only 1% during the search for initial phoneme information. It is impossible to tell whether these differential resolution rates affected the results, or how.

In English, the distinction between mass and count nouns has grammatical consequences that require the lexical entries for individual words to indicate whether the word is mass or count. Mass nouns cannot be pluralised (at least not with the same sense as the singular form; compare <u>wheat</u> and <u>wheats</u>), cannot take indefinite articles (compare <u>a bread</u> and <u>a bagel</u>), cannot be used with quantifiers like <u>every</u> (compare <u>every bean</u> and <u>every corn</u>), and so on. Although the grammatical distinction has an obvious semantic basis, it is nonetheless unpredictable: <u>Beans</u> are indistinguishable from <u>corn</u> in most of the ways that matter semantically, but only <u>beans</u> are grammatically count. <u>Noodles</u> and <u>pasta</u> are almost synonymous, yet the former is a count noun and the latter a mass noun. This suggests that the mass/count distinction is a grammatical feature that might be accessible to English speakers in tip-of-the-tongue states, and it is (Vigliocco, Vinson, Martin, & Garrett, 1999).

Perhaps the most striking support for the lemma hypothesis comes from a case report about an Italian anomic aphasic (Badecker, Miozzo, & Zanuttini, 1995). This patient had enormous difficulties naming even common objects. Despite this deficit, his ability to correctly identify the grammatical genders of words that he was unable to retrieve was nearly perfect, even when his performance was at chance on tests of his ability to identify the first sounds in the same words from two alternatives provided. Similar results from a French-speaking aphasic have been reported by Henaff Gonon, Bruckert, and Michel (1989), providing evidence for a lexically specific step of word retrieval that gives access to abstract grammatical information.

Apart from the disorders of aphasia and the disruptions to normal speech caused by tip-of-the-tongue states, there is evidence for the lemma hypothesis from recent studies using an event-related-potential measure called the lateralised readiness-potential. The lateralised readiness-potential (LRP) indexes electrophysiological activity in the brain prior to an overt response. Because the LRP begins to develop as soon as task-relevant perceptual and cognitive information become available to the motor system, it can be used to assess the preparation of the information that guides responding.

Using the lateralised readiness-potential to examine the time course of lexical access, van Turennout, Hagoort, and Brown (1997) asked Dutch speakers to name pictures of common objects. In three experiments, the LRP showed clear evidence of semantic information being activated prior to phonological information. A second series of experiments (van Turennout, Hagoort, & Brown, 1998) tested the lemma hypothesis directly. In these studies, speakers were occasionally cued to judge the grammatical gender or the sound of a Dutch word they were in the process of producing, with the judgements yoked in a way that made it possible to assess the relative time courses for the development of the relevant information. The results showed that grammatical gender was accessible earlier than phonological information, consistent with the lemma prediction.

The implication of these results is that production processes may yield lexically specific information prior to the point at which they achieve access to word forms. In terms of the model in Figure 2.2, lexical selection can be initiated before lexical retrieval, making way for the combinatorial-grammatical properties of words. Among the questions raised by this evidence is whether lemmas (perhaps including grammatical properties) are automatically accessed in the course of producing single words outside of grammatical contexts. These questions have both theoretical and methodological ramifications for accounts of how we recognise and understand words, and in the next section we consider what those ramifications may be.

UNDERSTANDING AND PRODUCING WORDS

The cognitive mechanisms of word production have various counterparts in processes hypothesised to occur during auditory and visual word recognition. This seems only natural. Recognition is logically the reverse of the production mapping from meaning to sound, and speakers and listeners share the same linguistic knowledge if they have the same native language. One consequence of this mirroring is that very similar issues occupy the literatures on word recognition and production. Among these issues there are various matters of experience (how often a word is produced or encountered), lexical organisation (phonological and morphological representation), access paths (what kinds of information are normally retrieved and with what priorities), and the flexibility of access (whether the access to information involves discrete or cascaded stages, whether stages interact, whether all stages are mandatory, whether the system is modular or open to influence from contextual information, and so on).

Despite these broad similarities, there are basic disparities in the processing problems that have to be solved during recognition and production. Production demands the creation or retrieval of different kinds of structures (including the phonological and metrical structures of words) whose properties may not be reconstructed to similar levels of detail during recognition. The production of a word begins with the meaning that the speaker has in mind (a meaning that is unambiguous, at least to the speaker) and proceeds from there through a retrieval process that may allow the simultaneous activation of all of a word's phonological properties, prior to the sequencing of the word's segments. In contrast, the auditory recognition of a word requires the accumulation over time of acoustic cues, segmentation of the word from a continuous stream of speech, and in due course, the recovery of meaning. All of this happens reliably despite some notorious problems with the acoustic signal: The input may be degraded (Samuel, 1981), a partial segment of speech may be momentarily ambiguous (Marslen-Wilson, 1989; Tanenhaus, Spivey-Knowlton, Eberhard, & Sedivy, 1995; Zwitserlood, 1989), or the segmentation cues may be misleading (Cutler & Butterfield, 1992). Even with these hurdles in the speech stream successfully crossed, a correctly segmented and recognised word may remain ambiguous in meaning (Simpson, 1994).

Some consequences of the disparities between word recognition and word production are that the processes almost certainly differ in how they access lexical information (Shallice, McLeod, & Lewis, 1985), in the kinds of lexical information they access (Cutting, 1997), and in how they are affected by repeated use (Cutler, 1995). Other kinds of differences emerge from comparisons of three roughly contemporaneous models of word production (Dell, 1986, 1988), auditory word recognition (Elman & McClelland, 1988; McClelland & Elman, 1986), and visual word recognition (McClelland & Rumelhart, 1981; Rumelhart & McClelland, 1982). Although the models share many basic architectural and processing assumptions (all are connectionist and localist and use spreading activation as a retrieval mechanism), they differ in important respects. The word production model (Dell, 1986) includes syntactic category information as part of each word's lexical entry along with phonological frames ("wordshapes" in Dell, 1988) to order the word's sound segments. Neither of these things can be found in the models of word recognition, which concentrate instead on the identification of individual sounds or letters as the first step toward word identification, and rely on time or space to convey information about order. Although these differences reflect contrasts in emphasis as well as contrasts in principle, they serve to highlight the dissimilarities in theoretical focus that characterise the literatures of word production and word recognition.

The dissimilarities in presumed cognitive mechanisms as well as in explanatory goals make it risky to generalise from how recognition works to how production works, and vice versa. In spite of this, research on word recognition has come to rely on many techniques that have production as their end product, and of necessity incorporate the cognitive processes of production in some form. Since the cognitive processes of production may be fairly complex, as we have argued, the variability that these processes introduce into the data in studies of word recognition may be considerable. Moreover, the variability may be misattributed to processes of recognition.

In the next section we will survey some of the research that has used production tasks to explore recognition processes. Our aim is to disentangle the components of subjects' performance that reflect recognition from those that reflect the cognitive mechanisms of word production.

From recognition to production: One easy step?

Word production is often used in experimental psychology as a task for indexing successful recognition in many kinds of visual and auditory tasks. A few of its applications include assessing the consequences of lexical priming and masking on perceptual identification tasks, indexing the automaticity of visual word recognition with Stroop tasks, as well as straightforward testing of picture, object, and auditory or visual word recognition. In a perceptual identification task, a briefly presented word must be named aloud. In traditional Stroop experiments, the task is to name aloud the ink colour in which a word is printed. In picture- and object-recognition tasks, the name of the depicted object must sometimes be produced aloud. In word-recognition tasks, the word itself may be repeated or pronounced aloud. In each case, the theoretical focus is commonly on the interpretative components of stimulus processing that yield recognition, although the operationalisation of perceptual or cognitive processing necessarily includes the mechanisms of word production. On the occasions when the production components of task performance are taken into account, typical controls include articulation of the word in the absence of the perceptual stimulus or articulation to a cue well after the presentation of the perceptual stimulus (following the procedures inaugurated by Eriksen, Pollack, & Montague, 1970; cf., Balota & Chumbley, 1985). Consequently, any response-specific cognitive components of word production remain in the measure of stimulus processing.

The question is whether there are facets of performance in such tasks that might be more readily explained as cognitive precursors of response preparation— preparation for word production—than cognitive consequences of stimulus processing. To find out, we looked at the contemporary literature in cognitive science and drew a sample of studies that employed word production tasks and measures. In order to explain what we found, we will describe some of the work in detail, although the bulk of the literature in each area will get short shrift.

Perceptual processes in implicit memory

One of the most exciting developments in recent cognitive psychology is the emergence of evidence for two fundamentally different ways in which experience is preserved in the nervous system. One of these is a familiar kind of memory experience that is called *declarative* memory (following Cohen & Eichenbaum, 1993). It is revealed in accurate performance on direct tests of recollection. For example, if a subject encounters a picture of a rabbit, and later recalls seeing the picture or recognises it as something seen before, the subject has a declarative memory for the picture. The second way in which experience is preserved involves *procedural* memory. This kind of retention is revealed in enhanced performance on indirect tests of memory, which tap the same kinds of perceptual or cognitive processes as the original encounter with a stimulus. For example, if the subject who saw the picture of the rabbit fails to explicitly recollect it on a later occasion, but nonetheless perceives the picture itself more quickly than on the first encounter, the subject thereby exhibits procedural memory for the stimulus. One of the empirical signatures of procedural memory is its preservation among anterograde amnesics who may have negligible declarative memory for an event (Cohen, 1997). Schacter (1996) calls this kind of memory *implicit*, and the memory system responsible for it the *perceptual representation system*.

Although the evidence for a procedural or implicit memory system is strong, the assumption that it is entirely perceptual is less compelling. Some of the gaps in the argument can be found in experiments that use word-production measures to assess implicit retention of pictures and words.

Perceptual memory for pictures.   In order to examine implicit retention of pictures, Park and Gabrieli (1995) compared word-to-picture priming with picture-to-picture priming. In the word-to-picture priming condition, subjects pronounced a visually presented word aloud, and later produced the same word when naming a pictured object. In the picture-to-picture priming condition, subjects saw and named the same picture twice. The picture-to-picture condition was designed to promote implicit retention in the form of perceptual priming, which Park and Gabrieli defined as the facilitation from naming the same picture twice. The facilitation was assessed relative to the time needed for naming the pictured object in the word-to-picture condition. By this measure, across experiments there were roughly 94 ms of facilitation attributable to perceptual retention.

The logic of this test assumes that the word-production requirement of pronouncing a visually presented word is equivalent to the word-production requirement of naming a visually presented picture. There are reasons to doubt this: The pronunciation of a visually presented word may not require the selection or retrieval steps shown in Figure 2.2, since skilled readers seem to have the ability to retrieve the sounds of words from their orthography alone (enabling them to fluently pronounce nonwords like zat, for example). Naming a picture, however, demands a more complicated mapping from meaning to sound. In support of this, Wheeldon and Monsell (1992) showed that the production of a picture name is primed more by a prior production of the same name elicited by a definition than by pronunciation of the visually presented word form. Still more striking, the priming is much less likely to be observed when the prime is a homophone of the target word (e.g., the playing-card spade is less likely to prime the digging-tool spade). So, even when the phonological form and articulation of a target word is identical to that of the prime word, the amount of repetition priming can be negligible. The critical component of this lexical repetition priming, Wheeldon and Monsell argue (1992; see also Monsell, Matthews, & Miller, 1992), has a locus after the activation of meaning and before the execution of pronunciation.

This kind of priming is uncontrolled in the experiments by Park and Gabrieli (1995) and in related work on normal (Cave, 1997; Cave, Bost, & Cobb, 1996) and amnesic speakers (Cave & Squire, 1992). It is large in magnitude (ranging from 50 to 120 ms in the experiments by Wheeldon & Monsell, 1992) and long-lasting (persisting over 60 to 120 trials in the conditions of Wheeldon and Monsell's studies). Its contribution to Park and Gabrieli's results can be seen most clearly in their unexplained finding that pictures with low name-agreement produced significantly more repetition priming than pictures with high name-agreement. Name agreement (or codability; Lachman, 1973; Mitchell, 1989) is a factor that affects lexical selection during word production (Griffin & Bock, 1998; Johnson, 1992; Roelofs, 1992; Schachter, Christenfeld, Ravina, & Bilous, 1991). Similar variables have potent effects on name selection in studies of face recognition, and have been identified as components of production (Brédart & Valentine, 1992; Ellis, Flude, Young, & Burton, 1996). In short, some of the effect that has been attributed to implicit perceptual memory in research on picture naming is likely to arise from the overlooked (but perhaps equally implicit) processes of word production.

Perceptual memory for words. A popular task in the implicit-memory literature is word-fragment completion. As commonly implemented, subjects examine a list of words in order to make some judgement about each one (for example, how legible the word is, whether it rhymes with "Babbitt", whether it denotes an animal). Later, subjects are given an ostensibly unrelated test in which words appear as fragments, with several letters replaced by blank spaces (e.g., _a_b_t). A variant of the task is word-stem completion, in which only the final letters are removed (e.g., rab—). By examining how many fragments are correctly completed (assuming that the fragments have unique solutions), or how many are completed with words from the original list rather than with alternative completions (e.g., with rabbit rather than gambit), and comparing this performance to that of subjects unexposed to the original list, a measure of the effect of the initial exposure to the word is obtained. As with other implicit memory tasks, the initial exposure has been found to benefit the fragment-completion performance of both normal and amnesic subjects regardless of whether they can explicitly recollect their previous encounter with the stimulus. So, like picture naming, fragment completion yields dissociations between procedural and declarative memory.

Word-fragment completion incorporates a word-production task, taking it out of the realm of simple perception (cf., Jacoby & Dallas, 1981). Similar arguments can be made about the gating procedure used in studies of spoken-word perception (Grosjean, 1980). The cognitive mechanisms that these tests call upon therefore include production components as well as perceptual processes. Some evidence for this can be found in the kinds of exposure conditions that benefit later fragment-completion performance in the absence of any need to create a visual representation of the word. Komatsu and Naito (1992) found equivalent priming of fragment completion from reading a word and from naming the word given its definition. Likewise, mentally translating words into the language to be used at test produced a large fragment-completion effect (Basden, Bonilla-Meeks, & Basden, 1994). These effects cannot be ascribed to conceptual processing: Basden et al. (1994) showed that imaging the referent of a word at study produced less priming of fragment completion than mentally translating the word did, and Weldon (1991) showed that viewing a picture of the object denoted by a test word is less effective for later fragment completion than mentally generating the word. Moreover, the harder it is for participants to mentally name a picture at study (due to short presentation time or simultaneous shadowing of other words), the smaller the fragment-completion effect becomes (Weldon & Jackson-Barrett, 1993).

The upshot is that implicit memory, certainly as it is measured by picture naming and word-fragment completion, appears to have action components as well as perceptual components. These action components indicate that explanations for implicit memory (and related phenomena such as cryptomnesia; Brown & Murphy, 1989) must go beyond stimulus processing to encompass response preparation.

A related argument against perceptual-priming accounts of implicit memory has been made by Ratcliff and McKoon (1997; Ratcliff, Allbritton, & McKoon, 1997). They attribute implicit-memory effects to a decision bias in memory retrieval. Our contention is that when words constitute the domain of study, the explanation may be more parsimoniously grounded within a specific cognitive system that handles the information processing that people normally engage in when using words in everyday language use. For this kind of account, the implication of research on implicit memory is that the procedures of lexical selection and retrieval can be primed and are likely to be primed by overt and covert word production.

The cognitive neurobiology of perception and word recognition

Another major development in contemporary cognitive science is the increasing use of neurophysiological measures of cognitive processing. Among these measures, neuroimaging techniques such as positron emission tomography (PET), functional magnetic resonance imaging (fMRI), and magneto-encephalography (MEG) have shown great promise for elucidating the brain mechanisms that support human cognition. The interpretation of the results from experiments using these kinds of measures depends critically on cognitive models of the tasks that subjects perform. But here too, the task models often appear to underestimate the cognitive complexities of formulating words for production.

In one of the first groundbreaking efforts to use neuroimaging techniques for localising the brain processes engaged in word recognition, Petersen, Fox, Posner, Mintun, and Raichle (1989) employed positron emission tomography to examine changes in blood flow during the processing of visually presented words. One of their manipulations addressed the semantic processing of words such as hammer by asking subjects to generate and produce words for actions typically carried out with the object denoted by the word (so, the subject would be expected to say "pound"). To isolate semantic processing from the visual and articulatory components of the task, Petersen et al. examined the cortical activation patterns obtained from a control condition. In the control task, subjects saw the stimulus word and pronounced it aloud. These activation patterns were then subtracted from those obtained during the performance of the verb generation task. The reasoning behind the subtraction was that the difference between the two sets of patterns represented semantic processing, with visual processing and articulation stripped away.

Overlooked in this comparison was the nature of the processing that is required to support the voluntary retrieval and phonological assembly of a spontaneously generated word (e.g., <u>pound</u>). These processes include locating the lexical entry for an appropriate verb, retrieving its word form, and carrying out phonological encoding. Because the only one of these processes likely to have been tapped in the word naming task was phonological encoding, the activities associated with the other processes remained in the measure for semantic processing of the stimulus word <u>hammer</u>. It may even be doubted that phonological encoding was controlled for, given that the control word differed from the word articulated during the experimental task (see also Price, Moore, Humphreys, Frackowiak, & Friston, 1996).

The appropriateness of control conditions is essential to the functional localisations that PET research aims for, and Petersen et al. understood the risks of their subtraction approach. In subtracting out the regional activations that stem from incidental components of the task, the aim is to isolate the brain regions that subserve the specific cognitive ability that is the target of study. This demands that the controls be fitting complements for the experimental tasks. Furthermore, for the subtraction logic to work well, it is important at the outset to use a task that produces robust patterns of activation. Word-generation tasks do this, yielding strong signals and broad regions of activation, and for these reasons they continue to be used in PET research. However, the benefits have a number of drawbacks. Different studies find different patterns of activation, in part because of differences in the control conditions, and consequently there is considerable disagreement about the functional interpretations of the observed activity (Friston et al., 1996).

Some of these disagreements arose as an immediate result of efforts to remedy the inadequacies of the word-pronunciation control used by Petersen et al. (1989), and more recent research has begun to move questions about word retrieval toward centre stage (e.g., Warburton et al., 1996). Ironically, however, the complexity of word generation (the very thing responsible for all the blood that the task stirs up) appears capable of threatening simple efforts to control it. There are problem-solving components connected with what we dubbed message generation ("what's the most likely thing to be done with this object?"), unusual metalinguistic judgements about whether or not a retrieved word is of the kind that is supposed to be produced ("is this word a verb?"), as well as uncertainties about the type and the grain of phonological information that is retrieved when generation is silent (as it sometimes is in imaging studies). Although some of these difficulties have been recognised, many have not because word production continues to be viewed as a single simple step from meaning to sound. When its complexities are fully acknowledged, the picture that emerges may be different (Indefrey & Levelt, 1999; Levelt, Praamstra, Meyer, Helenius, & Salmelin, 1998).

Word recognition

The cognitive processes of word production often come into play in more traditional research paradigms in cognitive psychology. Many of these traditional paradigms were developed to study visual word recognition and its interactions with attention, and the results occupy a vast literature (Balota, 1994; Seidenberg, 1995). The central issues in this literature have to do with the perceptual and cognitive pathways that give access to stored lexical information. These pathways have been hypothesised to make use of visual information (in the form of letters), phonological information (as a consequence of recoding letters into sounds), and semantic information (in the form of top-down contributions to perceptual processes). One of the perennial debates is about how to separate the processing events along these access pathways from events that are incidental to or consequent upon contact with lexical information. The debate is reflected in a division of processing effects into *prelexical* and *postlexical*, with postlexical effects deemed irrelevant to most accounts of the recognition process.

Since most of word production is postlexical by necessity, our assessment of relevance is the reverse: Some postlexical effects in word recognition may be straightforward reflections of production processes. The best known of these involve articulation. In delayed pronunciation tasks, visually presented high-frequency words are initiated and completed slightly more rapidly than otherwise comparable low-frequency words. This is not only because they are recognised faster, but also because they are articulated more fluently (Balota, Boland, & Shields, 1989; Balota & Chumbley, 1985). However, some postlexical effects on word recognition may be both more subtle and much larger. This is especially likely when word recognition is assessed in circumstances that tap cognitive components of word production like lexical selection and retrieval.

Identifying these circumstances requires a brief detour into the dual-route theory of word recognition (Coltheart, Curtis, Atkins, & Haller, 1993) and its connectionist competitors (Plaut, McClelland, Seidenberg, & Patterson, 1996; Seidenberg & McClelland, 1989). According to dual-route theories, visual-word recognition can take place in either of two ways: (1) Through the use of grapheme–phoneme correspondence rules that convert print into sound (the *assembled* route); or (2) through an immediate visual route from the word form to its stored lexical entry (the *direct* route). When a word is read orally, the pronunciation may be achieved by either route. In both cases the pronunciation itself comes about through processes such as those of phonological encoding shown in Figure 2.2. However, the assembled route goes from print to phonological encoding, whereas the direct route goes from the visual word form to a whole-word representation. In some theories (see Seidenberg, 1995 for review) the whole-word representation is analogous to the lexeme (the word form tapped during retrieval in production) whereas in others it bears more similarities to an abstract lexical entry (comparable in some ways to the lemma that is tapped during selection in production).

In connectionist frameworks (Plaut et al., 1996; Seidenberg & McClelland, 1989), lexical information is retrieved in the same manner for all words, with different degrees of fluency depending on the frequency with which particular spelling-to-sound correspondences are encountered in reading. However, complete versions of the Plaut et al. model make use of two different kinds of information (semantic and phonological) in arriving at pronunciations, with the division of labour between them trading off in various ways. On this scenario, the circumstances in which semantics weighs more heavily in getting to a pronunciation should be the circumstances that are most likely to make use of existing processes for production, analogous to the use of the direct route in dual-route theory.

In drawing parallels to the cognitive processes of word production, the most relevant recognition results are those that reflect the workings of the direct route or the weights of semantic connections. Consider the standard finding that consistency matters much more for low- than for high-frequency words, with consistent words pronounced faster than inconsistent primarily when the words are low in frequency (see Jared, 1997, for review and qualification). The dual-route account of this interaction involves races between the two routes, and different outcomes depending on word frequency. For high-frequency words, the direct route tends to outpace the assembled route regardless of consistency, but for low-frequency words, the direct route beats the assembled route only when a word's orthography is inconsistent with its pronunciation. In connectionist terms, low-frequency inconsistent words are slow because of the uncertainty of their mapping from spelling to sound, which is a joint consequence of sharing spelling-to-sound correspondences with few other words, of conflicting with many other words in spelling-to-sound correspondences, and occurring infrequently themselves (Seidenberg & McClelland, 1989). In Plaut et al.'s (1996) formulation, inconsistent low-frequency words are also the first to suffer from the withdrawal of a semantic contribution to the spelling-to-sound mapping, as a consequence of the weakness of the phonological mapping route.

With this issue as background, we examined some familiar phenomena for more hints about the workings of word production. Since both of the leading theories of word recognition use interactions with frequency as a litmus test for the involvement of production-relevant representations in pronunciation tasks, our cursory survey of the word recognition literature initially focused on frequency effects. Proceeding in the same vein, we then turned to word-recognition experiments that examined effects of semantic and syntagmatic priming and used tasks likely to tap selection and retrieval processes in word production. Although most of our discussion deals with visual word recognition (because that is what most of the research deals with), we cite related findings from studies of spoken-word recognition where they are available.

Frequency effects in visual-word recognition

Reading skill is normally a product of explicit instruction. Because of this, the ability to read and the corresponding ability to recognise a visually presented word are paramount examples of skills that are learned to variable levels of proficiency depending on specific environmental support and practice. Repeated experience with printed words may be a precondition of acquiring and maintaining the skills. The consequence is that words that are read often are recognised readily, whereas words that are read less often are recognised less readily. Using various estimates of the frequencies with which words are encountered in print, untold numbers of experiments (beginning with Cattell, 1886b) have shown a recognition advantage for words that are likely to be familiar, and the advantage increases with increasing familiarity. Glaser (1992) estimated that increases in the printed frequency of a word speeds its naming by 30 ms for each $\log_{10}$ increment in frequency.

It is harder to make the connection from repeated production of specific words to production fluency for those words. In part, this is simply because of the difficulty of objectively estimating how often speakers produce particular words. But since almost all estimates of spoken-word frequency and familiarity correlate highly with estimates of printed-word frequency and familiarity, investigators have used these measures somewhat interchangeably to assess how frequent use affects word production.

These assessments reveal broadbased similarities between frequency effects in production and recognition. First, just as frequent words are more readily recognised, they are more readily produced, both in terms of speed and accuracy. Speed advantages for frequent words have been observed in experiments on picture naming (usually with controls for the recognisability of the depicted objects; Griffin & Bock, 1998; Huttenlocher & Kubicek, 1984; Jescheniak & Levelt, 1994; Lachman, Shaffer, & Hennrikus, 1974; Oldfield & Wingfield, 1965; Wingfield, 1968), word translation (Cattell, 1887; de Groot, 1992; Jescheniak & Levelt, 1994), and cloze completion (Griffin, in press). Accuracy differences are seen in the incidence of speech errors on high- versus low-frequency words (Dell, 1990; Stemberger & MacWhinney, 1986). Second, the impact on production fluency of frequency differences among words is greater in the lower than in the higher frequency ranges, yielding an inverse logarithmic relationship between frequency and production latencies reminiscent of the inverse logarithmic relationship seen in word recognition, though the slope is much greater. For picture naming, Glaser (1992) estimated the reduction in production latencies with increases in the printed frequency of a word at over 250 ms for each $\log_{10}$ increment in frequency. Finally, frequency effects are likely to be neutralised in strongly supportive contexts, both in word recognition (Becker, 1979; Grosjean & Itzler, 1984; Inhoff, 1984) and in word production (Daneman & Green, 1986; Griffin & Bock, 1998).

Two debates about frequency that are shared between the literatures on word recognition and production have to do with the nature of the experiences that yield frequency effects and the locus of the effects in the perceptual, cognitive, or action systems. These questions about causation and processing locus are tightly linked, inasmuch as any experience with a word has multiple components, and any or all of the components could have consequences for subsequent encounters with the same word.

The traces of what kinds of experience?   The nature of the requisite experience is not well understood, either for recognition or production. Despite the intuitive plausibility of a relationship between the recognisability of a word and the number of times the word is actually encountered in print, the validity of frequency counts as predictors of word recognisability has long been questioned (Gernsbacher, 1984; Howes, 1966). The same is true for word retrievability. One of the variables that seems to do a better job accounting for visual-word naming latencies (e.g., Brown & Watson, 1987; Rubin, 1980) and picture-naming latencies (e.g., Morrison, Ellis, & Quinlan, 1992; Snodgrass & Yuditsky, 1996) is age of acquisition. Age-of-acquisition norms reflect judgements of how early in life a particular word was learned, and they correspond well with empirical observations of word learning in children (Carroll & White, 1973a,b; Gilhooly & Gilhooly, 1980). But because they also correlate highly with measures of word frequency-in-print, separating the contributions is difficult, and it is tempting to view them as interchangeable measures of the same thing: Repeated encounters with words over the lifespan.

Consequently, investigators have been loath to sacrifice widely available frequency norms for a less convenient and seemingly less objective measure, so word frequency has remained the variable of choice for indexing the effects of experience. However, there are good grounds for taking seriously the evidence that age of acquisition particularly affects word production (Gilhooly & Logie, 1980a,b; Morrison et al., 1992; Snodgrass & Yuditsky, 1996). Chief among them are the relationships between age of exposure and language learning itself: No amount of later exposure seems to fully compensate for early deprivation of certain kinds of linguistic experience (Mayberry, 1993, 1994), and the phonology of language may be the most sensitive component (Bahrick, Hall, Goggin, Bahrick, & Berger, 1994; Felge, 1987; Flege, Yeni-Komshian, & Liu, 1999; Scovel, 1989; Snow, 1979). The strong association between accent-free speech and age of exposure to a second language or dialect offers a familiar example of age-dependent effects in language acquisition. Together with evidence that frequency effects in production (probably subsuming age-of-acquisition effects) may be tied to phonological form (Dell, 1990, Exp. 1; Huttenlocher & Kubicek, 1983; Jescheniak & Levelt, 1994), the possibility that phonology has strong age dependencies offers an argument for viewing age of acquisition as an important (and perhaps the most important) index of the accessibility of word forms in adults (Brown & Watson, 1987).

In word recognition, it is less clear how age of acquisition and word frequency-in-print compare as metrics of familiarity for visual word forms, *per se*. Gilhooly and Logie (1980a,b) found frequency-in-print to be a better predictor than age of acquisition for visual recognition thresholds (and for auditory recognition of faint speech), and a worse predictor for naming times. From this they argued that word frequency-in-print may be a better index of visual recognisability, whereas age of acquisition may be a better index of retrievability for production.

Where are the traces of experience to be found in processing?   Gilhooly and Logie's argument makes obvious the connection between the experiential sources of exposure effects and the processing locus for the effects. In line with their hypothesis that word-specific experience can influence the uptake of visual information, there is variability associated with word frequency in the word-fixation times that are measured when monitoring eye movements in reading (Rayner, 1977; Rayner & Duffy, 1986). The story gets more complicated, however, with findings of word-frequency effects for fixation times during reading but not during visual search (Rayner & Raney, 1996), and frequency effects associated with the post-lexical decision component of word–nonword judgements (Balota & Chumbley, 1984; see Figure 2.1). These and similar results have prompted the conclusion that in word-recognition tasks, frequency variations have a greater impact later in processing than they do in the early perception of visual or auditory word forms (Balota, 1994; Cutler, 1995).

In word production, there is mounting evidence that the experience that is indexed by frequency counts (whatever that experience may be) has consequences for the retrieval of phonological word-forms (Dell, 1990, Exps. 1–3; Jescheniak & Levelt, 1994; also see Huttenlocher & Kubicek, 1983). At the same time, Dell (1990, Exp. 4) found one effect that is not easily explained by this view: When sound errors create words, there is no reliable tendency for the words so created to be higher in frequency than the intended words. Dell was able to account for this result as well as all of the other phonological-frequency effects with a computational model in which lexical selection (i.e., the lemma) was the production locus for the impact of frequent use. Because the message conditions for selection vary greatly with the context of speech, one implication of this view is that an effect of frequency is to be found in the mapping from context-specific referential concepts to lemmas (cf., Vitkovich & Humphreys, 1991). Such effects are well known under the heading of codability, name agreement, and typicality (Griffin & Bock, 1998).

It is tempting to look for a resolution to some of the uncertainties about the workings of frequency with a theory that bridges the mechanisms of comprehension and production. Word-recognition tasks that increase reliance on direct or semantic routes to word pronunciation may show the same kinds of frequency effects that picture-naming tasks do (which is to say that they may reflect age of acquisition more than frequency in print; Brown & Watson, 1987), whereas tasks that lean more on spelling-to-sound mappings may show larger effects of visual-word frequency. Some of the frequency biases in lexical decision may ride on the consequences of an operation like lexical selection (Monsell, Doyle, & Haggard, 1989; Paap, McDonald, Schvaneveldt, & Noel, 1987). Of course, if

TABLE 2.2
Sources of data for picture naming, visual-word naming, and
lexical decision response times

Picture Naming	Visual-Word Naming	Lexical Decision
Carroll & White (1973b)	Forster & Chambers (1973)	Fera & Besner (1992)
Griffin & Bock (1998)	Jared (1997)	Forster & Chambers (1973)
Huitema, Griffin, & Bock (1996)	McCann & Besner (1987)	Kelliher & Henderson (1990)
Humphreys, Riddoch, &	Spieler & Balota (1997)	Rubenstein, Lewis, &
Quinlan (1988)		Rubenstein (1971)
Morrison et al. (1992)		
Oldfield & Wingfield (1965)		
Snodgrass & Yuditsky (1996)		

TABLE 2.3
Descriptive statistics for words in the analyses of age-of-acquisition and
frequency as predictors for response times in picture naming, visual-word
naming, and lexical decision tasks

				Mean Normative Values	
Task	Total Number of Words	Mean Response Time	Age of Acquisition	Log Spoken Frequency	Log Written Frequency
Picture naming	675	922	3.31	1.01	1.40
Visual-word naming	804	472	3.33	1.16	1.51
Lexical decision	115	659	3.13	1.11	1.53

our experiences with words have many different facets, each with a proprietary frequency effect, there will be no single cause or processing locus. But for the same reason, distinguishing between the production and comprehension consequences of using words may make it easier to untangle the effects of experience at the same time that it yields an integrated view of language use.

To evaluate the prospects for this kind of integration, we used the existing literature to assess differences between various recognition and production tasks in their susceptibility to age-of-acquisition and frequency effects. From our own normative data and from various manuscripts and published papers (see Table 2.2), we culled average response times for individual words in visual-word naming, lexical decision, and picture naming. For as many of the words as possible, we also obtained age-of-acquisition norms (from Carroll & White, 1973a and Gilhooly & Logie, 1980a) and spoken- and written-word frequencies (from the CELEX database; Baayen, Piepenbrock, & van Rijn, 1993). Table 2.3 gives descriptive statistics for the words in the sample on each measure. For

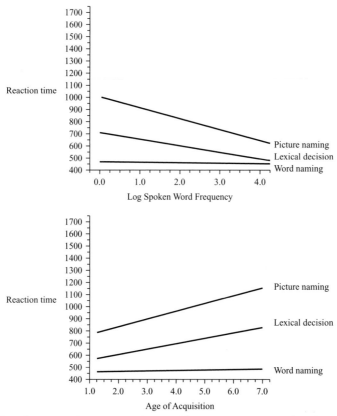

Figure 2.3.   Linear regressions against spoken-word frequency (top) and age of acquisition (bottom) for response times in picture naming, lexical decision, and visual-word naming tasks.

each of the three tasks, Figure 2.3 shows the linear regressions on spoken frequency (top panel) and age of acquisition (bottom panel). The results for written frequency were comparable to those for spoken frequency but generally weaker, so we omitted them for present purposes.

For each of the three task data sets, we performed two separate stepwise multiple-regressions. Age of acquisition and spoken frequency were entered first into alternative analyses, to determine how much residual variance could be accounted for by the unforced variable. For picture-naming times, age of acquisition and spoken frequency each accounted for significant variance regardless of the order in which they were entered, with age of acquisition being a slightly better predictor. For visual-word naming and lexical decision, only age of acquisition reliably predicted response times. So, regardless of whether frequency was entered into the regression before or after age of acquisition, it failed to account for a significant share of the response-time variability across items.

The results for picture naming are generally consistent with previous reports in showing age of acquisition to be the better predictor of naming times (Morrison et al., 1992; Snodgrass & Yuditsky, 1996), although the superiority of age of acquisition over spoken frequency was less pronounced in our item-based analyses. For both of the remaining tasks, age of acquisition was a markedly better predictor than spoken frequency; in fact, it was the only significant predictor of the two. Its predictive power across all three tasks is consistent with there being commonalities that are unlikely to be found in initial processing, since picture naming involves no word display.

Regardless of the impact of early acquisition or frequent exposure on word recognition and production, there are limits to the role that repeated exposure can play in word use. In recognition and production, the magnitude of frequency effects diminishes or disappears entirely when words appear in constraining contexts (Becker, 1979; Griffin & Bock, 1998). For this reason, a great deal of attention has been focused on the question of how supportive contexts facilitate word recognition. The simplest and most-studied contexts are those in which single words are presented in succession or as pairs, in so-called lexical *priming*.

Priming

The several phenomena of priming arise from successive exposures to related words. When the relationship between a prime and a target word happens to be one of identity, the main issues that arise have to do with repetition priming and the procedural/declarative memory dissociation, as described earlier. Here we will restrict our attention to the consequences of exposure to successive words that are related in meaning (semantic priming) or linked by a canonical sequence of syntactic categories that create a grammatically acceptable pairing of words (syntagmatic priming). A prototypical experimental paradigm involves seeing one word, a prime (e.g., *cat*) and then another word, the target (e.g., *dog*) on which some task is performed. The task that we will emphasise is vocal pronunciation ("word naming"), which produces high levels of accuracy but interesting variations in the amount of time required to perform the tasks relative to controls. Ideally, the control conditions include the same target words, but preceded by unrelated primes.

The most common effect of priming is to facilitate recognition of target words, with recognition operationalised as response time in naming and lexical decision tasks,[2] or as accuracy in perceptual identification tasks. However, the explanations for the observed facilitation are points of considerable conjecture and controversy (Balota, 1990; Hodgson, 1991; McNamara, 1992; Neely, 1991; Norris, 1986; Ratcliff & McKoon, 1988; Seidenberg, 1995). To add to the fray, we will consider whether some or even most of the typically observed effects of semantic and syntagmatic priming reflect the cognitive retrieval processes of production.

Semantic priming.   Semantic priming is an effect of semantic relationships between primes and target words. The semantic relationships that figure most prominently in analyses of semantic priming are of two kinds, taxonomic and associative. Taxonomic relationships involve concepts from the same semantic fields or categories, such as types of artefacts (desk–table as items of furniture, shirt–scarf as items of clothing) or natural kinds (dog–wolf as canines, cherry–pear as fruits). Associative relationships have their origins in co-occurrences of words or the objects they denote, and exemplify a motley assortment of meaning similarities. Some associated words are also taxonomic relatives (shirt–tie), whereas others are united by event scripts (milk–cow), by normal predication (milk–white), and so on. The question is whether the recognition of the prime can facilitate the recognition of a semantically related target word by some mechanism specific to the input pathway.

If semantic relationships automatically prime the input pathway, their effects should be observable in recognition regardless of context. So, semantic priming in word recognition should be observable for target words seen in isolation or in sentences. Contesting this, Hess, Foss, and Carroll (1995) and Williams (1988) have convincingly demonstrated that priming effects, which can be readily observed for words in isolation, vanish when the same word pairs are placed into sentence or discourse contexts. Hess et al. (1995) argue that priming comes not from the meanings of words *per se*, but from the contextual predictability or coherence of a word. As contexts change from single-word primes, to sentences, to entire discourses, what is predictable or coherent also changes. After reviewing the evidence, Seidenberg (1995) likewise suggests that whenever semantic priming is observed, it is a consequence of the selective activation of semantic features rather than activation of word meanings as wholes.

Although this kind of contextually modulated meaning activation may have little impact on the recognition of word forms, as Hess et al. suggest, it is central to the selection of words for production. Speakers begin with a nonverbal message that is influenced by the communicative context, and the features of the message reflect the idiosyncracies of particular speakers in particular places and times. As a consequence, messages are unlikely to fully instantiate all of the features of meaning for a single word, but will approximate the conditions for using the word to a greater or lesser degree. The selection of a word indicates only that its conditions (its meaning features) better meet the contextually specific features of the message than do the features of other equally accessible words. Given this, the mechanism responsible for the bulk of semantic priming effects observed in word recognition may be the same kind of lexical selection that precedes word production.

A potential defect in this argument comes from the comparative strength of semantic priming for taxonomic relatives versus associates in word-naming tasks. In naming, taxonomic priming is less likely to be observed than associative priming. But in production, taxonomic relationships are necessarily more central than associations, reflecting the kinds of meaning features that normally drive lexical selection. For example, semantic word substitutions (e.g., saying "your daughter" when "your sister" was intended) typically involve taxonomically related words rather than associatively related words (Hotopf, 1980). If semantic priming in visual-word naming arises from mechanisms that are likewise involved in normal word production, one might expect naming to benefit from selective activation between taxonomically related primes and targets. Yet there is little or no priming between them.

The resolution to this apparent contradiction can be found in research by Wheeldon and Monsell (1994). Wheeldon and Monsell showed that naming a pictured object took more time when the naming episode followed the naming of a pictured taxonomic relative. Interestingly, this effect was slightly (but not entirely) offset by a shortlived facilitation. Thus, the lability of semantic priming between taxonomic relatives in simple word naming may be due to a trade-off between a small and shortlived facilitation that is quickly overwhelmed by the large and long-lasting competition between closely related words. In semantic priming tasks, the presentation of primes and targets activates two conceptually similar words. Since naming requires the selection of just one of the words, this dual activation creates competition. Competition in turn creates errors in speech, and it slows production, as Wheeldon and Monsell's findings attest.

If the appearance of semantic priming in visual-word naming is attributable to events within the production system, one kind of information that should become available as a consequence is information relevant to the target word's syntactic privileges. This would occur if the manipulations that give rise to semantic priming in naming set into motion the selection process for word production. To see if this happens, we turn next to the literature on syntagmatic priming.

Syntagmatic priming.   By syntagmatic priming, we mean a tendency for a word from one grammatical form-class to prime target words that serve as grammatically acceptable successors to the prime. For example, the noun people might serve as a syntagmatic prime for the verb eat, analogous to a kind of response that is sometimes observed in tests of word association (and contrasting with the kind of response called *paradigmatic*, involving words from the same form-class, such as people–animal; Ervin-Tripp, 1961).[3]

There is good evidence for syntagmatic priming in word naming (Boland, 1997; O'Seaghdha, 1997; West & Stanovich, 1986). The syntactic origins of the effect are clear in work by O'Seaghdha (1997) and by Peterson, Burgess, Dell, and Eberhard (in press). O'Seaghdha obtained distinct semantic and syntactic effects on naming times in contexts that varied systematically in semantic and syntagmatic congruence. Peterson et al. presented naming targets to subjects within highly constraining discourse contexts, along the lines of "The man was old and feeble and it was believed that he would soon kick the . . .". At the offset of the context, a word was presented visually that formed a syntactically congruent continuation (e.g., <u>town</u>) or a syntactically incongruent continuation (e.g., <u>grow</u>). Despite the semantic anomaly of both the congruent and incongruent continuations, there was consistent facilitation for the congruent word. Peterson et al. even obtained syntagmatic priming for nonwords that were morphologically marked as nouns (<u>glatter</u>) or verbs (<u>glatted</u>).

On the assumption (common in research on word recognition) that syntactic category information is a by-product of lexical access or morphological analysis, such effects are unlikely to arise from the activation of input pathways during visual or auditory word-perception. In fact, if prime processing is restricted to input pathways, syntagmatic priming in naming may disappear: Sereno (1991) failed to observe it when the primes were presented very briefly and masked.[4]

The constellation of conditions that yield syntagmatic priming in word recognition strongly suggest that when it is seen, it is correlated with the kinds of syntactic information required for production. Specifically, the grammatical category of the prime word becomes available and effective in influencing the response to a syntagmatically congruent target word. As the work by O'Seaghdha (1997) and Peterson et al. (in press) implies, the source of the effect is likely to be the congruence between the syntactic class of the target word and the available slots in a structural frame. One prediction from this explanation is that the effect of syntagmatic incongruence should be inhibitory, and it seems to be: West and Stanovich (1986, Exp. 4; see also Federmeier & Bates, 1997) found that words in syntagmatically congruent contexts were named no faster than the same words in contexts that were neither semantically nor syntactically informative (e.g., <u>The next word is . . .</u>). In syntactically incongruent contexts, the words were named more slowly.

Interference

The complement to priming in word recognition is interference: Sometimes exposure to words retards processing instead of speeding it. The mechanisms of interference are at least as controversial as those of priming, if not more so, and have an even longer history in cognitive psychology by virtue of being intertwined with the operations of selective attention. We will sidestep the attentional issues to focus on the best-known example of an indirect word-recognition test that produces interference, the Stroop naming task.

Stroop interference.   In its most familiar variants, the Stroop task (Stroop, 1935) involves the presentation of words printed in assorted ink colours, and requires naming the ink colours rather than the words themselves. The words, however, denote colours that are congruent or incongruent with the ink colours. For example, the word <u>blue</u> printed in blue ink would be a congruent stimulus (since the correct naming response fits both the ink colour and the word itself), whereas the word <u>red</u> printed in blue ink is incongruent. Ink-colour naming for incongruent stimuli can be dramatically slowed, relative to the naming of congruent stimuli (a comprehensive review of research on the naming of Stroop stimuli can be found in MacLeod, 1991).

The participant's main goal in a standard Stroop experiment is to accomplish the fast and fluent utterance of a word, beginning with the minimal "messages" formed from ink-colour perception. This makes it a task that encompasses the cognitive processing required for word production. However, relatively little attention has been given to where within the production system this occurs. Most of the task's applications have been to questions about attention, visual word-recognition, and the development of word-recognition skills in reading. Since it is normally impossible to avoid recognising the word that constitutes the Stroop stimulus, the interference that arises during ink-colour naming has been used as an index of word recognition.

Yet the locus of much of the interference seems to lie within the production system. One indication is that eliminating the verbal response reduces interference, although competition among lexical entries will remain if lexical selection is needed to mediate a button-press response (Keele, 1972) or typing of the word (Logan & Zbrodoff, 1998). Consequently, Stroop interference can be exploited to gauge the time course of events during word production. One experimental task that does so is picture-word interference.

Picture–word interference. In the picture–word interference paradigm, auditory or visual distractor-words are presented at some point during the naming of a picture, analogous to the combination of word and colour name in the traditional Stroop task. To isolate the source of the interference, the distractors may be semantically related to the picture name, phonologically related, or unrelated. In addition, to determine when the interference occurs during the retrieval and production of the word, the timing of the distractor can be manipulated.

The results from this work have begun to illuminate when during single-word production the information about meaning and sound becomes available. There are two findings of note. First, the effect of a semantic distractor is normally inhibitory, in line with the standard Stroop effect. Inhibition is maximal when an auditory distractor slightly precedes the to-be-named picture, peaking when the distractor precedes picture onset by about 150 ms. At this interval, the distractor appears to disrupt the selection of the lemma for the picture name roughly 300 ms later, or 150 ms *after* picture onset (Levelt et al., 1998). At its peak, the magnitude of the inhibitory effect (relative to an unrelated control condition) is about 30 ms. Second, in contrast to the semantic inhibition effect, phonologically related distractors tend to facilitate picture naming. Maximal facilitation is seen when an auditory distractor and the to-be-named picture have simultaneous onsets, so that the distractor's phonology can facilitate the phonological encoding of the picture name beginning about 300 ms after picture onset. The magnitude of the facilitation is in the neighbourhood of 50 ms (Schriefers, Meyer, & Levelt, 1990).

These parameters are comparable to those for Stroop tasks (Glaser, 1992). In Stroop naming, maximum inhibition occurs when the distractor is presented within a narrow temporal window from 100 ms before to 100 ms after the target. Since Stroop distractors are usually visual (but see Cowan, 1989), the necessary correction for the duration of an auditory distractor in picture-word interference tasks puts the inhibitory effects into the same temporal frame as Stroop tasks. Likewise, the magnitude of Stroop inhibition (relative to an unre-lated distractor) is in the region of 30 to 100 ms depending on the nature of the target, putting picture-word interference in the same range but at the low end (attributable to cross-modal presentation of the distractor). To our knowledge there have been no systematic investigations of modulations of Stroop naming by phonological distractors over time, although picture–word studies consistently show facilitation from graphemically and phonologically related visual distractors (e.g., Lupker, 1982; Rayner & Springer, 1986).

Pursued systematically, these kinds of convergences could serve to clarify the complex empirical picture that surrounds research on Stroop naming in word recognition and attention. The evidence from picture–word interference argues for a contribution to Stroop inhibition from within the word-production system. In that system, there are at least two factors that can influence the magnitude of Stroop effects, stemming from competition for selection and facilitation of phonological coding for speech. There may also be a third factor, to do with the grammatical properties of distractors and targets (Ehri, 1977; Miozzo & Caramazza, 1997; Schriefers, 1993). Although the classic Stroop effect reflects more than disruptions to word production alone, the identification and isolation of the production components of the effect may be prerequisites to an explana-tion of the perceptual and attentional components that have engaged so many cognitive psychologists for so many years.

Summary

Research on word recognition has produced a wide range of results that are relevant to explaining the cognitive mechanisms of word production, as well as to explaining word recognition proper. Although the foregoing survey barely scratched the surface of the literature, it illustrates how the processes of produc-tion can influence performance in many ostensibly perceptual paradigms. These include implicit memory tasks, tasks used for neuroimaging studies, and the traditional tasks of word recognition research, such as visual-word naming, lexical priming, and Stroop naming. In these tasks, the less salutary implications of production processing arise in the absence of adequate controls for the influence of production mechanisms, with the consequence that important experimental results may be compromised. On the positive side, the emergence of a converging body of work on word production raises the prospects for an integrated account of the mechanisms of word recognition and production. We will examine some of these prospects in the next section.

HOW ARE WORD PRODUCTION AND RECOGNITION LINKED?

At least logically, word production and word recognition are mirror-image events. Were they mirror images psychologically, as well, the foregoing exercise in contrast and comparison might have yielded a neater picture. For all the reasons noted earlier, we did not expect to find such neatness, and so its absence is hardly dismaying. What we did find, however, supports some hyptheses about points of convergence and divergence in lexical processing that merit brief mention.

Separate pathways for word recognition and production

Writing in 1987, Monsell argued for separate input and output lexicons, with separate but linked processors for phonological features in recognition and production. This bridge served as an intermediate link between the processing of orthography and the processing of phonology. However, the point of ultimate convergence between lexical input and output was identified as a shared representation of the semantic and syntactic features of words, roughly comparable to the kinds of information that are combined during lexical selection in Figure 2.1. From this view, one would expect certain key effects to emerge from recognition and production tasks that depend on access to a word's semantic and syntactic properties, and different effects to emerge when tasks can be accomplished without tapping information about the meaning or structural privileges of a specific word.

Some direct evidence for Monsell's conception comes from a series of experiments by Cutting (1997). To explore the kinds of processes that are shared by word recognition and word production, Cutting used picture naming coupled with a prime-processing manipulation. To force different ways of processing priming words, subjects were instructed to repeat one word from a dichotically presented two-word prime and to ignore the second word. Words spoken in a female voice were always to be repeated, and words spoken in a male voice were always to be ignored. For example, some participants would hear the words tiger (spoken in a female voice) and sandal (spoken in a male voice) simultaneously, under instructions to repeat only the word spoken in the female voice. Other participants would hear the same two words recorded in different voices (so that they would repeat sandal). Then, 1500 ms later, both groups of subjects would see and name aloud a picture of a lion. The question was whether and how the semantic properties of the primes would influence the time taken to name the depicted object. This influence was assessed relative to the picture naming times after unrelated primes.

Because masked and otherwise unattended words are known to be processed to a level that facilitates subsequent recognition (e.g., Tipper & Driver, 1988), Cutting assumed that the ignored word would traverse perceptual/recognition processes only, whereas the produced word would be processed through the entire comprehension and production system. The hypothesis was that when the semantic relative tiger was to be ignored, it would influence the subsequent production of lion only to the degree that comprehension processes overlap those of production. In other experiments, the phonological properties of attended and ignored primes were manipulated (e.g., liar served as a phonological prime for lion).

Cutting's results showed a clear pattern of priming from semantically related words regardless of whether they were to be repeated or ignored. For phonological primes, however, only produced words had an impact on subsequent picture naming. The same patterns of priming were obtained when the prime words were visually rather than auditorily presented, with the cues to ignore or produce the words conveyed by ink colour. The implication is that the production and comprehension systems share semantic processes but divide phonological processes.

These findings support Monsell's suggestions about the relationships between word production and word comprehension. They argue that recognition tasks with spoken response measures are very likely to call on information that is in the province of language production proper, and that variations in findings across traditional recognition tasks may in part be explainable in terms of which production-relevant processes come into play. In particular, if recognition and production call on different phonological processing systems, whenever recognition is operationalised in terms of spoken-word responses it is likely that some portion of what is measured reflects the processes involved in preparing to talk.

CONCLUSIONS

Talking is a goal-directed action. It is a kind of action that is central to human communication and culture, as well as a kind of action that psychologists exploit for the narrower purposes of research on cognition. Word production is in widespread use as a measure of successful perception, successful word recognition, successful memory, and much more. Although there has been little acknowledgement of the complexity of the high-level preparatory processes that eventuate in the articulation of a word, our survey suggests that these preparatory processes have a great deal in common with the components of normal word production in meaningful, connected speech. If so, much of the research that has been done to uncover the processes of word recognition may ultimately tell us at least as much about how words are retrieved for speaking as about how they are recognised.

Despite the complications that this introduces for current models of word recognition, in the long run it promises a better balanced explanation of language performance. Listeners (and readers) are also speakers, and their ability to do both of these things with their language is the foundation of successful communication. From Cattell (1886a,b) onwards, psychologists have understood that there are significant cognitive events subsequent to perception and recognition. Cattell himself was struck by how much more variability was to be found in the additional time taken for naming something ("will time" in Cattell's terminology) than in the time taken for recognising the same object ("perception time"). A picture of a complex object took little more time to recognise than a simple colour, but considerably longer to name, even with numbers of alternatives equated. Cattell recognised that "will time" includes articulation but also considerably more; what more it includes can begin to be appreciated in light of the cognitive architecture of word production. By putting the pieces of the recognition and production puzzles together, we come closer to achieving the science of cognition that Cattell foresaw as the culmination of studies of naming in psychology.

In retrospect, Cattell's optimism about such matters raises questions about why goal-directed action in general, and word production in particular, have received scant attention in contemporary cognitive psychology. The legacy of behaviourism is surely one culprit, as we noted in the introduction. Watson's original conception of cognition embraced the vaguely lunatic speculation that "thought processes are really motor habits in the larynx" (1913, p. 174), the prototype for what Bock (1996) dubbed the mind-in-the-mouth assumption. The counter-reaction to behaviourist ideas only compounded the problem: Action is behaviour, so cognitive psychology shunned it and thereby overlooked the role of cognition in directing and achieving goals.

One manifestation of this general disdain for action is inattention to how people control their responses within experimental tasks. Task analysis is surely unalluring, and seems especially barren when applied to the kinds of arbitrary responses that psychologists favour. Lever-pulling and button-pressing are used as tasks precisely because of their assumed neutrality with respect to the decisions that motivate them. But recognising the risks of misconstruing how readers carry out the laboratory tasks they are assigned, psychologists have increasingly called for more and better task analysis. This is especially true in research on word recognition (Balota, 1994; Seidenberg, 1995). Balota's work illustrates the importance of task analysis for understanding "the neglected decision stage" (Balota & Chumbley, 1984, 1985) where, one imagines, Cattell's "will time" resides along with the high-level processes of word production.

Word production is different in some fundamental ways from the simpler kinds of decisions that experimental subjects make. It is deeply embedded within an action system that is central to normal human behaviour. The action system is one that we begin to use daily around the age of one and deploy thereafter during almost every waking hour of every day. Ignoring the ecological niche that words normally occupy invites unhappy surprises similar to those that ensued when psychology first confronted the influence of instinctive and prepared action systems on the behaviour of laboratory rats and other animals (Hinde & Stevenson-Hinde, 1973; Marler & Terrace, 1984; Seligman & Hager, 1972). Rats easily learn to run to avoid shock; they resist learning to turn a wheel for the same purpose. Pigeons easily learn to peck a key for food; they resist learning the same action to turn off shock. In short, when natural behaviours are co-opted for the convenience of experimentation without adequate consideration of their normal function for an animal, it can be difficult to understand or fully explain the effects of an experimental manipulation.

Words have typical functions, too. They are selected for their fittingness not only to the context of communication and the intended meaning, but also for the properties that allow them to be woven into connected speech. The combinatorial privileges of words are an integral part of what we know about them, and are crucial to their normal use. Many laboratory tasks nonetheless rely exclusively on the elicitation of single words that are rarely uttered alone. Much can be learned from this work. Much more might be gained by acknowledging the properties of words that are intrinsic to their functions in natural language, and by making allowances for how these properties complicate the journey from mind to mouth. Though logically irrelevant to naming a picture or pronouncing a word, these properties and their associated processes may be no more easily sidestepped for words in the laboratory than for words in the wild.

ACKNOWLEDGEMENTS

The preparation of this paper was supported in part by research and training grants from the National Institutes of Health (R01 HD21011 and T32 MH18990) and the National Science Foundation (SBR 94-11627, 98-73450, and a National Science Foundation Minority Graduate Fellowship). We thank Urbano Chaidez, Todd Reising, and Hilary Silber for their assistance with the frequency and age-of-acquisition analyses, and Linda Wheeldon and two anonymous reviewers for their comments on a previous draft of the manuscript.

NOTES

1. With a bit less justification, Garrod and Sanford (1994) echoed and approved Johnson-Laird's definition.
2. Lexical (word/nonword) decision is a commonly used word-recognition task, but its validity as a test of recognition is suspect. In particular, it is believed to be swayed by postrecognition processes brought into play to make the word–nonword discrimination, such as using apprehended relationships between primes and targets to bias "word" decisions (Balota & Chumbley, 1984). Since unrelated primes and targets by definition lack a relationship, decision times to them may be slow for reasons that have nothing to do with the recognition process itself, and related primes fast, for

similarly irrelevant reasons. Naming, by contrast, is widely viewed as a relatively pure measure of recognition, aside from the minuscule articulatory effects that accompany it.

3. Although syntagmatic priming is known as syntactic priming in the word-recognition literature, this usage invites confusion with a different priming phenomenon from language production (Bock, 1986; Bock & Griffin, in press).

4. Under the same conditions, Sereno did find syntagmatic priming for lexical decisions. This is consistent with other evidence that the locus of syntagmatic priming in lexical decision is different from its locus in naming (compare Goodman, McClelland, & Gibbs, 1981; O'Seaghdha, 1997; Seidenberg, Waters, Sanders, & Langer, 1984; West & Stanovich, 1986; Wright & Garrett, 1984).

REFERENCES

Baayen, R.H., Piepenbrock, R., & van Rijn, H. (1993). *The CELEX lexical database* [CD-ROM]. Philadelphia: Linguistic Data Consortium.

Badecker, W., Miozzo, M., & Zanuttini, R. (1995). The two stage model of lexical retrieval: Evidence from a case of anomia with selective preservation of grammatical gender. *Cognition, 57,* 193–216.

Bahrick, H.P., Hall, L.K., Goggin, J., Bahrick, L., & Berger, S. (1994). Fifty years of language maintenance in bilingual Hispanic immigrants. *Journal of Experimental Psychology: General, 123,* 264–283.

Balota, D.A. (1990). The role of meaning in word recognition. In D.A. Balota, G.B. Flores d'Arcais, & K. Rayner (Eds.), *Comprehension processes in reading* (pp. 9–32). Hillsdale, NJ: Lawrence Erlbaum Associates Inc.

Balota, D.A. (1994). Visual word recognition: The journey from features to meaning. In M.A. Gernsbacher (Ed.), *Handbook of psycholinguistics* (pp. 303–358). San Diego: Academic Press.

Balota, D.A., Boland, J.E., & Shields, L.W. (1989). Priming in pronunciation: Beyond pattern recognition and onset latency. *Journal of Memory and Language, 28,* 14–36.

Balota, D.A., & Chumbley, J.I. (1984). Are lexical decisions a good measure of lexical access? The role of word frequency in the neglected decision stage. *Journal of Experimental Psychology: Human Perception and Performance, 10,* 1340–1357.

Balota, D.A., & Chumbley, J.I. (1985). The locus of word-frequency effects in the pronunciation task: Lexical access and/or production? *Journal of Memory and Language, 24,* 89–106.

Basden, B.H., Bonilla-Meeks, J.L., & Basden, D.R. (1994). Cross-language priming in word-fragment completion. *Journal of Memory and Language, 33,* 69–82.

Becker, C.A. (1979). Semantic context and word frequency effects in visual word recognition. *Journal of Experimental Psychology: Human Perception and Performance, 5,* 252–259.

Bock, J.K. (1986). Syntactic persistence in language production. *Cognitive Psychology, 18,* 355–387.

Bock, J.K. (1995). Sentence production: From mind to mouth. In J.L. Miller & P.D. Eimas (Eds.), *Handbook of perception and cognition: Vol. 11. Speech, language, and communication* (pp. 181–216). Orlando, FL: Academic Press.

Bock, J.K. (1996). Language production: Methods and methodologies. *Psychonomic Bulletin & Review, 3,* 395–421.

Bock, J.K. (1999). Language production. In R. Wilson & F. Keil (Eds.), *MIT encyclopedia of the cognitive sciences* (pp. 453–456). Cambridge, MA: MIT Press.

Bock, J.K., & Griffin, Z.M. (in press). The persistence of structural priming: Transient activation or implicit learning? *Journal of Experimental Psychology: General.*

Bock, J.K., & Levelt, W.J.M. (1994). Language production: Grammatical encoding. In M.A. Gernsbacher (Ed.), *Handbook of psycholinguistics* (pp. 945–984). San Diego: Academic Press.

Boland, J.E. (1997). The relationship between syntactic and semantic processes in sentence comprehension. *Language and Cognitive Processes*, *12*, 423–484.

Brédart, S., & Valentine, T. (1992). From Monroe to Moreau: An analysis of face naming errors.
Cognition, *45*, 187–223.

Brown, A.S., & Murphy, D.R. (1989). Cryptomnesia: Delineating inadvertent plagiarism. *Journal of
Experimental Psychology: Learning, Memory, and Cognition*, *15*, 432–442.

Brown, G.D., & Watson, F.L. (1987). First in, first out: Word learning age and spoken word frequency
as predictors of word familiarity and word naming latency. *Memory & Cognition*, *15*, 1208–1216.

Brown, R., & McNeill, D. (1966). The "tip of the tongue" phenomenon. *Journal of Verbal Learning
and Verbal Behavior*, *5*, 325–337.

Butterworth, B. (1989). Lexical access in speech production. In W.D. Marslen-Wilson (Ed.), *Lexical
representation and process* (pp. 108–135). Cambridge, MA: MIT Press.

Caramazza, A. (1997). How many levels of processing are there in lexical access? *Cognitive Neuropsychology*, *14*, 177–208.

Carroll, J.B. (1958). Process and content in psycholinguistics. In *Current trends in the description
and analysis of behavior* (pp. 175–200). Pittsburgh, PA: University of Pittsburgh Press.

Carroll, J.B., & White, M.N. (1973a). Age-of-acquisition norms for 220 picturable nouns. *Journal of
Verbal Learning and Verbal Behavior*, *12*, 563–576.

Carroll, J.B., & White, M.N. (1973b). Word frequency and age of acquisition as determiners of
picture-naming latency. *Quarterly Journal of Experimental Psychology*, *25*, 1985–1995.

Cattell, J.M. (1886a). The time it takes to see and name objects. *Mind*, *11*, 63–65.

Cattell, J.M. (1886b). The time taken up by cerebral operations. *Mind*, *11*, 220–242, 377–392,
524–538.

Cattell, J.M. (1887). Experiments on the association of ideas. *Mind*, *12*, 68–74.

Cave, C.B. (1997). Very long-lasting priming in picture naming. *Psychological Science*, *8*, 322–325.

Cave, C.B., Bost, P.R., & Cobb, R.E. (1996). Effects of color and pattern on implicit and explicit
picture memory. *Journal of Experimental Psychology: Learning, Memory, and Cognition*, *22*,
639–653.

Cave, C.B., & Squire, L.R. (1992). Intact and long-lasting repetition priming in amnesia. *Journal of
Experimental Psychology: Learning, Memory, and Cognition*, *18*, 509–520.

Clark, H.H. (1996). *Using language*. Cambridge, UK: Cambridge University Press.

Cohen, N.J. (1997). Memory. In M.T. Banich (Ed.), *Neuropsychology: The neural bases of mental
function*. Boston: Houghton Mifflin.

Cohen, N.J., & Eichenbaum, H. (1993). *Memory, amnesia, and the hippocampal system*. Cambridge,
MA: MIT Press.

Coltheart, M., Curtis, B., Atkins, P., & Haller, M. (1993). Models of reading aloud: Dual-route and
parallel-distributed-processing approaches. *Psychological Review*, *100*, 589–608.

Cowan, N. (1989). The reality of cross-modal Stroop effects. *Perception & Psychophysics*, *45*, 87–88.

Cutler, A. (1995). Spoken word recognition and production. In J.L. Miller & P.D. Eimas (Eds.),
Handbook of perception and cognition: Vol. 11. Speech, language, and communication (pp. 97–
136). Orlando, FL: Academic Press.

Cutler, A., & Butterfield, S. (1992). Rhythmic cues to speech segmentation: Evidence from juncture
misperception. *Journal of Memory and Language*, *31*, 218–236.

Cutting, J.C. (1997). *The production and comprehension lexicons: What is shared and what is not*.
Unpublished doctoral dissertation, University of Illinois.

Daneman, M., & Green, I. (1986). Individual differences in comprehending and producing words in
context. *Journal of Memory and Language*, *25*, 1–18.

Deese, J. (1984). *Thought into speech: The psychology of a language*. Englewood Cliffs, NJ:
Prentice-Hall.

de Groot, A. (1992). Determinants of word translation. *Journal of Experimental Psychology: Learning,
Memory, and Cognition*, *18*, 1001–1018.

Dell, G.S. (1986). A spreading-activation theory of retrieval in sentence production. *Psychological Review, 93*, 283–321.

Dell, G.S. (1988). The retrieval of phonological forms in production: Tests of predictions from a connectionist model. *Journal of Memory and Language, 27*, 124–142.

Dell, G.S. (1990). Effects of frequency and vocabulary type on phonological speech errors. *Language and Cognitive Processes, 5*, 313–349.

Dell, G.S. (1995). Speaking and misspeaking. In L.R. Gleitman & M. Liberman (Eds.), *An invitation to cognitive science: Vol. 1. Language* (pp. 183–208). Cambridge, MA: MIT Press.

Dell, G.S., Schwartz, M.F., Martin, N., Saffran, E.M., & Gagnon, D.A. (1997). Lexical access in aphasic and nonaphasic speakers. *Psychological Review, 104*, 801–838.

Ehri, L.C. (1997). Do adjectives and functors interfere as much as nouns in naming pictures? *Child Development, 48*, 697–701.

Ellis, A.W., Flude, B.M., Young, A., & Burton, A.M. (1996). Two loci of repetition priming in the recognition of familiar faces. *Journal of Experimental Psychology: Learning, Memory, and Cognition, 22*, 295–308.

Elman, J.L., & McClelland, J.L. (1988). Cognitive penetration of the mechanisms of perception: Compensation for coarticulation of lexically restored phonemes. *Journal of Memory and Language, 27*, 143–165.

Eriksen, C.W., Pollack, M.D., & Montague, W.E. (1970). Implicit speech: Mechanism in perceptual encoding? *Journal of Experimental Psychology, 84*, 1502–1507.

Ervin-Tripp, S.M. (1961). Changes with age in the verbal determinants of word-association. *American Journal of Psychology, 74*, 361–372.

Federmeier, K., & Bates, E. (1997). Contexts that pack a punch: Lexical class priming of picture naming. *CRL Newsletter* (Vol. 11, No. 2), University of California, San Diego.

Fera, P., & Besner, D. (1992). The process of lexical decision: More words about a parallel distributed processing model. *Journal of Experimental Psychology: Learning, Memory, and Cognition, 18*, 1749–1764.

Flege, J.E. (1987). A critical period for learning to pronounce foreign languages? *Applied Linguistics, 8*, 162–177.

Flege, J.E., Yeni-Komshian, G.H., & Liu, S. (1999). Age constraints on second-language acquisition. *Journal of Memory and Language, 41*, 78–104.

Forster, K.I., & Chambers, S.M. (1973). Lexical access and naming time. *Journal of Verbal Learning and Verbal Behavior, 12*, 627–635.

Friston, K.J., Price, C.J., Fletcher, P., Moore, C.J., Frackowiak, R.S.J., & Dolan, R.J. (1996). The trouble with cognitive subtraction. *Neuroimage, 4*, 97–104.

Garrett, M.F. (1975). The analysis of sentence production. In G.H. Bower (Ed.), *The psychology of learning and motivation* (pp. 133–177). New York: Academic Press.

Garrett, M.F. (1988). Processes in language production. In F.J. Newmeyer (Ed.), *Linguistics: The Cambridge survey: III. Language: Psychological and biological aspects* (pp. 69–96). Cambridge, UK: Cambridge University Press.

Garrod, S.C., & Sanford, A.J. (1994). Resolving sentences in a discourse context: How discourse representation affects language understanding. In M.A. Gernsbacher (Ed.), *Handbook of psycholinguistics* (pp. 675–698). San Diego: Academic Press.

Gernsbacher, M.A. (1984). Resolving 20 years of inconsistent interactions between lexical familiarity and orthography, concreteness, and polysemy. *Journal of Experimental Psychology: General, 113*, 256–280.

Gilhooly, K.J., & Gilhooly, M.L. (1980). The validity of age-of-acquisition ratings. *British Journal of Psychology, 71*, 1105–1110.

Gilhooly, K.J., & Logie, R.H. (1980a). Age-of-acquisition, imagery, concreteness, familiarity, and ambiguity measures for 1,944 words. *Behavior Research Methods & Instrumentation, 12*, 395–427.

Gilhooly, K.J., & Logie, R.H. (1980b). Meaning-dependent ratings of imagery, age of acquisition, familiarity, and concreteness for 387 ambiguous words. *Behavior Research Methods & Instrumentation, 12,* 428–450.

Glaser, W.R. (1992). Picture naming. *Cognition, 42,* 61–105.

Goodman, G.O., McClelland, J.L., & Gibbs, R.W., Jr. (1981). The role of syntactic context in word recognition. *Memory & Cognition, 9,* 580–586.

Griffin, Z.M. (in press). Rating frequency-of-meaning use. *Behavior Research Methods, Instruments, & Computers.*

Griffin, Z.M., & Bock, J.K. (1998). Constraint, word frequency, and the relationship between lexical processing levels in spoken word production. *Journal of Memory and Language, 38,* 313–338.

Grosjean, F. (1980). Spoken word recognition processes and the gating paradigm. *Perception & Psychophysics, 28,* 1267–1283.

Grosjean, F., & Itzler, J. (1984). Can semantic constraint reduce the role of word frequency during spoken word recognition? *Bulletin of the Psychonomic Society, 22,* 180–182.

Henaff Gonon, M.A.H., Bruckert, R., & Michel, F. (1989). Lexicalization in an anomic patient. *Neuropsychologia, 27,* 391–407.

Hess, D.J., Foss, D.J., & Carroll, P. (1995). Effects of global and local context on lexical processing during language comprehension. *Journal of Experimental Psychology: General, 124,* 62–82.

Hinde, R.A., & Stevenson-Hinde, J. (1973). *Constraints on learning: Limitations and predispositions.* New York: Academic Press.

Hodgson, J.M. (1991). Informational constraints on pre-lexical priming. *Language and Cognitive Processes, 6,* 169–206.

Hotopf, W.H.N. (1980). Semantic similarity as a factor in whole-word slips of the tongue. In V.A. Fromkin (Ed.), *Errors in linguistic performance: Slips of the tongue, ear, pen, and hand* (pp. 97–109). New York: Academic Press.

Howes, D. (1966). A word count of spoken English. *Journal of Verbal Learning and Verbal Behavior, 5,* 572–604.

Huitema, J.S., Bock, J.K., & Griffin, Z.M. (1996). *The Huitema collection.* Unpublished picture naming norms, University of Illinois at Urbana-Champaign.

Humphreys, G.W., Riddoch, M.J., & Quinlan, P.T. (1988). Cascade processes in picture identification. *Cognitive Neuropsychology, 5,* 67–103.

Huttenlocher, J., & Kubicek, L.F. (1983). The source of relatedness effects on naming latency. *Journal of Experimental Psychology: Learning, Memory, and Cognition, 9,* 486–496.

Indefrey, P., & Levelt, W.J.M. (1999). The neural correlates of language production. In M. Gazzaniga (Ed.), *The cognitive neurosciences* (2nd ed.) Cambridge, MA: MIT Press.

Inhoff, A.W. (1984). Two stages of word processing during eye fixations in the reading of prose. *Journal of Verbal Learning and Verbal Behavior, 23,* 1612–1624.

Jacoby, L.L., & Dallas, M. (1981). On the relationship between autobiographical memory and perceptual learning. *Journal of Experimental Psychology: General, 110,* 306–340.

Jared, D. (1997). Spelling-sound consistency affects the naming of high-frequency words. *Journal of Memory and Language, 36,* 505–529.

Jescheniak, J.-D., & Levelt, W.J.M. (1994). Word frequency effects in speech production: Retrieval of syntactic information and of phonological form. *Journal of Experimental Psychology: Learning, Memory, and Cognition, 20,* 824–843.

Johnson, C.J. (1992). Cognitive components of naming in children: Effects of referential uncertainty and stimulus realism. *Journal of Experimental Child Psychology, 53,* 24–44.

Johnson-Laird, P.N. (1974). Experimental psycholinguistics. *Annual Review of Psychology, 25,* 135–160.

Keele, S.W. (1972). Attention demands of memory retrieval. *Journal of Experimental Psychology, 93,* 245–248.

Kelliher, S. & Henderson, L. (1990). Morphologically based frequency effects in the recognition of irregularly inflected verbs. *British Journal of Psychology*, *81*, 527–539.

Komatsu, S.-I., & Naito, M. (1992). Repetition priming with Japanese Kana scripts in word-fragment completion. *Memory & Cognition*, *20*, 160–170.

Lachman, R. (1973). Uncertainty effects on time to access the internal lexicon. *Journal of Experimental Psychology*, *99*, 199–208.

Lachman, R., Shaffer, J.P., & Hennrikus, D. (1974). Language and cognition: Effects of stimulus codability, name-word frequency, and age of acquisition on lexical reaction time. *Journal of Verbal Learning and Verbal Behavior*, *13*, 613–625.

Levelt, W.J.M. (1989). *Speaking: From intention to articulation*. Cambridge, MA: MIT Press.

Levelt, W.J.M., Praamstra, P., Meyer, A.S., Helenius, P., & Salmelin, R. (1998). An MEG study of picture naming. *Journal of Cognitive Neuroscience*, *10*, 553–567.

Logan, G.D., & Zbrodoff, N.J. (1998). Stroop-like interference: Congruity effects in color naming with typewritten responses. *Journal of Experimental Psychology: Human Perception and Performance*, *24*, 978–992.

Lupker, S.J. (1982). The role of phonetic and orthographic similarity in picture-word interference. *Canadian Journal of Psychology*, *36*, 1349–1367.

MacKay, D.G. (1982). The problems of flexibility, fluency, and speed–accuracy trade-off in skilled behavior. *Psychological Review*, *89*, 483–506.

MacLeod, C.M. (1991). Half a century of research on the Stroop effect: An integrative review. *Psychological Bulletin*, *109*, 163–203.

Marler, P., & Terrace, H.S. (1984). *The biology of learning*. New York: Springer-Verlag.

Marslen-Wilson, W. (1989). Access and integration: Projecting sound onto meaning. In W. Marslen-Wilson (Ed.), *Lexical representation and process* (pp. 1–24). Cambridge, MA: MIT Press.

Mayberry, R.I. (1993). First-language acquisition after childhood differs from second-language acquisition: The case of American Sign Language. *Journal of Speech and Hearing Research*, *36*, 1258–1270.

Mayberry, R.I. (1994). The importance of childhood to language acquisition: Evidence from American Sign Language. In J.C. Goodman & H.C. Nusbaum (Eds.), *The development of speech perception* (pp. 57–90). Cambridge, MA: MIT Press.

McCann, R.S., & Besner, D. (1987). Reading pseudohomophones: Implications for models of pronunciation assembly and the locus of word-frequency effects in naming. *Journal of Experimental Psychology: Human Perception and Performance*, *13*, 14–24.

McClelland, J.L., & Elman, J.L. (1986). The TRACE model of speech perception. *Cognitive Psychology*, *18*, 1–86.

McClelland, J.L., & Rumelhart, D.E. (1981). An interactive activation model of context effects in letter perception: Part 1. An account of basic findings. *Psychological Review*, *88*, 375–407.

McNamara, T.P. (1992). Theories of priming: I. Associative distance and lag. *Journal of Experimental Psychology: Learning, Memory and Cognition*, *18*, 1173–1190.

Minsky, M., & Papert, S. (1969). *Perceptrons*. Cambridge, MA: MIT Press.

Miozzo, M., & Caramazza, A. (1997). The retrieval of lexical-syntactic features in tip-of-the-tongue states. *Journal of Experimental Psychology: Learning, Memory, and Cognition*, *23*, 1410–1423.

Mitchell, D.B. (1989). How many memory systems? Evidence from aging. *Journal of Experimental Psychology: Learning, Memory, and Cognition*, *15*, 31–49.

Monsell, S. (1987). On the relation between lexical input and output pathways for speech. In A. Allport, D.G. MacKay, W. Prinz, & E. Scheerer (Eds.), *Language perception and production: Relationships between listening, speaking, and writing* (pp. 273–311). London: Academic Press.

Monsell, S., Doyle, M.C., & Haggard, P.N. (1989). Effects of frequency on visual word recognition tasks: Where are they? *Journal of Experimental Psychology: General*, *118*, 43–71.

Monsell, S., Matthews, G.H., & Miller, D.C. (1992). Repetition of lexicalisation across languages: A further test of the locus of priming. *Quarterly Journal of Experimental Psychology: Human Experimental Psychology, 44*, 763–783.

Morrison, C.M., Ellis, A.W., & Quinlan, P.T. (1992). Age of acquisition, not word frequency, affects object naming, not object recognition. *Memory & Cognition, 20*, 705–714.

Neely, J.H. (1991). Semantic priming effects in visual word recognition: A selective review of current findings and theories. In D. Besner & G. Humphreys (Eds.), *Basic processes in reading: Visual word recognition* (pp. 236–264). Hillsdale, NJ: Lawrence Erlbaum Associates Inc.

Norris, D. (1986). Word recognition: Context effects without priming. *Cognition, 22*, 93–136.

Oldfield, R.C., & Wingfield, A. (1965). Response latencies in naming objects. *Quarterly Journal of Psychology, 17*, 273–281.

O'Seaghdha, P.G. (1997). Conjoint and dissociable effects of syntactic and semantic context. *Journal of Experimental Psychology: Learning, Memory and Cognition, 23*, 807–828.

Osgood, C.E. (1971). Where do sentences come from? In D.D. Steinberg & L.A. Jakobovits (Eds.), *Semantics: An interdisciplinary reader in philosophy, linguistics and psychology* (pp. 497–529). Cambridge, UK: Cambridge University Press.

Paap, K.R., McDonald, J.E., Schvaneveldt, R.W., & Noel, R.W. (1987). Frequency and pronounceability in visually presented naming and lexical decision tasks. In M. Coltheart (Ed.), *Attention and performance XII: The psychology of reading* (pp. 222–243). Hove, UK: Lawrence Erlbaum Associates Ltd.

Park, S.M., & Gabrieli, J.D.E. (1995). Perceptual and nonperceptual components of implicit memory for pictures. *Journal of Experimental Psychology: Learning, Memory, and Cognition, 21*, 1583–1594.

Petersen, S.E., Fox, P.T., Posner, M.I., Mintun, M., & Raichle, M.E. (1989). Positron emission tomographic studies of the processing of single words. *Journal of Cognitive Neuroscience, 1*, 153–170.

Peterson, R.R., Burgess, C., Dell, G.S., & Eberhard, K.M. (in press). Dissociation between syntactic and semantic processing during idiom comprehension. *Journal of Experimental Psychology: Learning, Memory, and Cognition.*

Plaut, D.C., McClelland, J.L., Seidenberg, M.S., & Patterson, K. (1996). Understanding normal and impaired word reading: Computational principles in quasi-regular domains. *Psychological Review, 103*, 56–115.

Potter, M.C., So, K.-F., Von Eckhardt, B., & Feldman, L.B. (1984). Lexical and conceptual representation in beginning and proficient bilinguals. *Journal of Verbal Learning and Verbal Behavior, 23*, 23–38.

Price, C.J., Moore, C.J., Humphreys, G.W., Frackowiak, R.S.J., & Friston, K.J. (1996). The neural regions sustaining object recognition and naming. *Proceedings of the Royal Society of London (B), 263*, 1501–1507.

Ratcliff, R., Allbritton, D., & McKoon, G. (1997). Bias in auditory priming. *Journal of Experimental Psychology: Learning, Memory, and Cognition, 23*, 143–152.

Ratcliff, R., & McKoon, G. (1988). A retrieval theory of priming in memory. *Psychological Review, 95*, 385–408.

Ratcliff, R., & McKoon, G. (1997). A counter model for implicit priming in perceptual word identification. *Psychological Review, 104*, 319–343.

Rayner, K. (1977). Visual attention in reading: Eye movements reflect cognitive processes. *Memory & Cognition, 5*, 443–448.

Rayner, K., & Duffy, S.A. (1986). Lexical complexity and fixation times in reading: Effects of word frequency, verb complexity, and lexical ambiguity. *Memory & Cognition, 14*, 1191–1201.

Rayner, K., & Raney, G.E. (1996). Eye movement control in reading and visual search: Effects of word frequency. *Psychonomic Bulletin & Review, 3*, 245–248.

Rayner, K., & Springer, C.J. (1986). Graphemic and semantic similarity effects in the picture-word interference task. *British Journal of Psychology, 77,* 1207–1222.

Roelofs, A. (1992). A spreading activation theory of lemma retrieval in speaking. *Cognition, 42,* 107–142.

Rubenstein, H., Lewis, S.S., & Rubenstein, M.A. (1971). Homographic entries in the internal lexicon: Effects of systematicity and relative frequency of meanings. *Journal of Verbal Learning and Verbal Behavior, 10,* 57–62.

Rubin, D.C. (1980). 51 properties of 125 words: A unit of analysis of verbal behavior. *Journal of Verbal Learning and Verbal Behavior, 19,* 736–755.

Rumelhart, D.E., & McClelland, J.L. (1982). An interactive activation model of context effects in letter perception: Part 2. The contextual enhancement effect and some tests and extensions of the model. *Psychological Review, 89,* 60–84.

Samuel, A.G. (1981). Phonemic restoration: Insights from a new methodology. *Journal of Experimental Psychology: General, 110,* 474–494.

Schachter, S., Christenfeld, N., Ravina, B., & Bilous, F. (1991). Speech disfluency and the structure of knowledge. *Journal of Personality and Social Psychology, 60,* 362–367.

Schacter, D.L. (1996). *Searching for memory: The brain, the mind, and the past.* New York: Basic Books.

Schriefers, H. (1993). Syntactic processes in the production of noun phrases. *Journal of Experimental Psychology: Learning, Memory, and Cognition, 19,* 841–850.

Schriefers, H., Meyer, A.S., & Levelt, W.J.M. (1990). Exploring the time course of lexical access in language production: Picture–word interference studies. *Journal of Memory and Language, 29,* 86–102.

Scovel, T. (1989). *A time to speak: A psycholinguistic inquiry into the critical period for human speech.* Cambridge, MA: Newbury House.

Seidenberg, M. (1995). Visual word recognition: An overview. In J.L. Miller & P.D. Eimas (Eds.), *Handbook of perception and cognition: Vol. 11. Speech, language, and communication* (pp. 137–179). Orlando, FL: Academic Press.

Seidenberg, M.S., & McClelland, J.L. (1989). A distributed, developmental model of word recognition and naming. *Psychological Review, 96,* 523–568.

Seidenberg, M.S., Waters, G.S., Sanders, M., & Langer, P. (1984). Pre- and postlexical loci of contextual effects and word recognition. *Memory & Cognition, 12,* 1315–1328.

Seligman, M.E.P., & Hager, J.L. (1972). *Biological boundaries of learning.* Englewood Cliffs, NJ: Prentice-Hall.

Sereno, J.A. (1991). Graphemic, associative, and syntactic priming effects at a brief stimulus onset asynchrony in lexical decision and naming. *Journal of Experimental Psychology: Learning, Memory, and Cognition, 17,* 459–477.

Shallice, T., McLeod, P., & Lewis, K. (1985). Isolating cognitive modules with the dual-task paradigm: Are speech perception and production separate processes? *Quarterly Journal of Experimental Psychology, 37A,* 507–532.

Simpson, G.B. (1994). Context and the processing of ambiguous words. In M.A. Gernsbacher (Ed.), *Handbook of psycholinguistics* (pp. 359–374). San Diego: Academic Press.

Singleton, D. (1989). *Language acquisition: The age factor.* Clevedon, UK: Multilingual Matters.

Skinner, B.F. (1953). *Science and human behavior.* New York: Free Press.

Snodgrass, J.G., & Yuditsky, T. (1996). Naming times for the Snodgrass and Vanderwart pictures. *Behavior Research Methods, Instruments, & Computers, 28,* 516–536.

Snow, C.E. (1979). Individual differences in second-language ability: A factor-analytic study. *Language and Speech, 22,* 151–162.

Spieler, D.H., & Balota, D.A. (1997). Bringing computational models of word naming down to the item level. *Psychological Science, 8,* 1411–1416.

Starreveld, P.A., & LaHeij, W. (1996). Time-course analysis of semantic and orthographic context effects in picture naming. *Journal of Experimental Psychology: Learning, Memory, and Cognition, 22*, 896–918.

Stemberger, J.P., & MacWhinney, B. (1986). Frequency and the lexical storage of regularly inflected forms. *Memory & Cognition, 14*, 17–26.

Stroop, J.R. (1935). Studies of interference in serial verbal reactions. *Journal of Experimental Psychology, 18*, 643–662.

Tanenhaus, M.K., Spivey-Knowlton, M.J., Eberhard, K.M., & Sedivy, J.C. (1995). Integration of visual and linguistic information in spoken language comprehension. *Science, 268*, 1632–1634.

Tipper, S.P., & Driver, J. (1988). Negative priming between pictures and words in a selective attention task: Evidence for semantic processing of ignored stimuli. *Memory & Cognition, 16*, 1964–1970.

van Turennout, M., Hagoort, P., & Brown, C.M. (1997). Electrophysiological evidence on the time course of semantic and phonological processes in speech production. *Journal of Experimental Psychology: Learning, Memory, and Cognition, 23*, 787–806.

van Turennout, M., Hagoort, P., & Brown, C.M. (1998). Brain activity during speaking: From syntax to phonology in 40 milliseconds. *Science, 280*, 572–574.

Vigliocco, G., Antonini, T., & Garrett, M.F. (1997). Grammatical gender is on the tip of Italian tongues. *Psychological Science, 8*, 314–317.

Vigliocco, G., Vinson, D.P., Martin, R.C., & Garrett, M.F. (1999). Is "count" and "mass" information available when the noun is not? An investigation of tip of the tongue states and anomia. *Journal of Memory and Language, 40*, 534–558.

Vitkovitch, M., & Humphreys, G.W. (1991). Perseverant responding in speeded naming of pictures: It's in the links. *Journal of Experimental Psychology: Learning, Memory, and Cognition, 17*, 664–680.

Warburton, E., Wise, R.J.S., Price, C.J., Weiller, C., Hadar, U., Ramsay, S., & Frackowiak, R.S.J. (1996). Noun and verb retrieval by normal subjects: Studies with PET. *Brain, 119*, 159–179.

Watson, J.B. (1913). Psychology as the behaviorist views it. *Psychological Review, 20*, 158–177.

Weldon, M.S. (1991). Mechanisms underlying priming on perceptual tests. *Journal of Experimental Psychology: Learning, Memory, and Cognition, 17*, 526–541.

Weldon, M.S., & Jackson-Barrett, J.L. (1993). Why do pictures produce priming on the word-fragment completion test? A study of encoding and retrieval factors. *Memory & Cognition, 21*, 519–528.

West, R.F., & Stanovich, K.E. (1986). Robust effects of syntactic structure on visual word processing. *Memory & Cognition, 14*, 1104–1112.

Wheeldon, L.R., & Monsell, S. (1992). The locus of repetition priming of spoken word production. *Quarterly Journal of Experimental Psychology, 44*, 723–761.

Wheeldon, L.R., & Monsell, S. (1994). Inhibition of spoken word production by priming a semantic competitor. *Journal of Memory and Language, 33*, 332–356.

Williams, J.N. (1988). Constraints upon semantic activation during sentence comprehension. *Language and Cognitive Processes, 3*, 165–206.

Wingfield, A. (1968). Effects of frequency on identification and naming of objects. *American Journal of Psychology, 81*, 226–234.

Wright, B., & Garrett, M. (1984). Lexical decision in sentences: Effects of syntactic structure. *Memory & Cognition, 12*, 1931–1945.

Zwitserlood, P. (1989). The locus of the effects of sentential-semantic context in spoken-word processing. *Cognition, 32*, 25–64.

CHAPTER THREE

Form representations in word production

Antje S. Meyer
Max Planck Institute for Psycholinguistics, Nijmegen,
The Netherlands[1]

INTRODUCTION

On most current theories of speaking, the production of an utterance involves three types of processes: conceptualisation, formulation, and articulation (e.g., Bock & Levelt, 1994; Caplan, 1992; Garrett, 1975; Kempen & Hoenkamp, 1987; Levelt, 1989; Levelt, Roelof, & Meyer, 1999; see also Bock and Griffin's chapter in the current volume). Conceptualisation is the generation of a so-called message capturing the speaker's communicative intention. It is a prelinguistic specification of the content of the utterance. Formulation processes take the message as input, access appropriate entries in the mental lexicon, and construct the syntactic and morpho-phonological structures of the utterance. On the basis of this information, articulatory programs can be retrieved and executed.

Lexical access to content words is often taken to consist of two major steps: lexical selection, which takes place during syntactic encoding, and word-form encoding, which takes place during morpho-phonological encoding (e.g., Dell, 1986; Garrett, 1975; Kempen & Huijbers, 1983; Kempen & Hoenkamp, 1987; Levelt, 1989, 1992, 1999; Levelt et al., 1999; Meyer, 1996; Roelofs, 1992, 1993). During lexical selection, a fragment of the message is used to retrieve one or more lemmas from the mental lexicon. On most views, the lemma represents the syntactic properties of a lexical entry, such as its syntactic class and grammatical gender (but see Caramazza, 1997, and Caramazza & Miozzo, 1997, for different definitions of the lexical units involved in language production). Many lemmas have diacritic features (such tense or number), whose values are set based on information included in the message.

Word-form encoding for a single word comprises three major steps: morphological, phonological, and phonetic encoding (Dell, 1986; Levelt, 1989, 1992). The morphological encoder takes a single lemma (for morphologically simple words like "dog"), or a lemma and one or more diacritic values (for instance for plural forms like "dogs" or inflected forms like "writes" or "understanding"), or several lemmas (for instance for particle verbs like "look up" or for compounds like "pet owner") as its input and produces one or more morphemes (see Levelt et al., 1999; Roelofs, 1996a,b, 1997a, for further discussion). Then the phonological encoder generates the corresponding phonological representation. Finally, the phonetic encoder converts the phonological representation into a phonetic representation, which specifies the articulatory commands to be carried out.

The present chapter focuses on word-form encoding, in particular on the properties of the form representations. How these representations are derived is discussed in Roelofs' chapter (see also Roelofs, 1997b,c). The present chapter is organised as follows. The next section introduces a general model of form encoding. Since its central claims are compatible with almost all existing more specific models (e.g., Dell, 1986; Fromkin, 1971, 1973; Garrett, 1975, 1980; Levelt et al., 1999; Shattuck-Hufnagel, 1979, 1983), it will be called the Standard Model. As will be shown, this model can readily be derived from analyses of sound errors. Thus, that section also serves to summarise classic results of speech error analyses and their standard interpretation (see Levelt, 1989; Meyer, 1992, for more extensive reviews of the speech error evidence).

The Standard Model assumes that before articulatory commands for an utterance can be selected and carried out, the stored form representations are decomposed into a set of abstract phonological constituents. This decomposed phonological representation comprises two independent tiers—the segmental and the metrical tier. The following two sections discuss evidence concerning the nature of these representations. Much of this evidence stems again from analyses of speech errors, but there is also a growing body of experimental findings, part of which will be reviewed below. In the penultimate section, the phonetic representation is briefly described. According to the Standard Model, speakers first decompose word form representations into phonological constituents, then reassemble them into larger units, and finally retrieve the corresponding articulatory gestures. One may ask why decomposition and reassembly are necessary and why speakers cannot directly retrieve precompiled motor programs for entire words. These questions are discussed in the final section.

THE STANDARD MODEL OF WORD-FORM ENCODING

Every corpus of speech errors includes sound errors such as "phonological fool" (instead of "phonological rule") and "wish a brush" (instead of "with a brush"[2]), in which the actual utterance differs from the intended one in one or more sounds not corresponding to a complete morpheme. Sound errors demonstrate that word forms are not retrieved from the mental lexicon as units, but are decomposed into smaller constituents. If they were retrieved as units, such errors could not arise. Thus, the occurrence of sound errors is the key observation motivating the assumption of phonological decomposition.

An important property of sound errors is that listeners usually perceive them as phonetically well-formed (e.g., Boomer & Laver, 1968; Wells, 1951/1973). Very few errors have been reported that violate the phonotactic rules of the language (e.g., Fromkin, 1971, 1973; Garrett, 1976, 1980). A classic case illustrating the phonetic well-formedness of errors is the accommodation of the English article occurring, for instance, in "a meeting arathon" (instead of "an eating marathon"). Phonetic accommodation shows that the error cannot arise during the creation of the phonetic representation or during articulation, but must happen earlier, such that phonetic rules can still apply after the error has been committed. Thus, sound errors are typically taken to occur during the creation of a fairly abstract phonological representation.

In most sound errors the intended and erroneous utterance differ by one or two segments. Errors involving individual phonetic features or entire syllables as error units are very rare. Therefore, the main constituents into which stored word forms are decomposed are likely to be phonological segments. Hence, the first processing component in the Standard Model is the retrieval of phonological segments. This process will be called *segmental spellout*.

A particularly revealing type of sound errors are sound exchanges, such as "I have caked a bake" (instead of "baked a cake") and "he caught torses" (instead of "he taught courses"). In these errors, each of the misplaced segments assumes the position meant for the other segment. The standard account of sound exchanges is that there are abstract positions that exist independently of the segments that take them. This explains how each of the misplaced segments comes to occupy the position vacated by the other segment rather than a position elsewhere in the string.

Thus, there appear to be frames with positions to which segments are associated. The frames are commonly assumed to encode the syllabic structure of the utterance because sound errors tend to obey a positional constraint, which Boomer and Laver (1968) described in their classic paper on speech errors as follows: "Segmental slips obey a structural law with regard to syllable-place; that is, initial segments in the origin syllable replace initial segments in the target syllable, nuclear replace nuclear, and final replace final" (p. 7).

There is strong evidence for this syllable-position constraint from analyses of English, German, Spanish, and Dutch error corpora (Fromkin, 1971, 1973; García-Albea, del Viso, & Igoa, 1989; MacKay, 1970; Motley, 1973; Nooteboom, 1969; Shattuck-Hufnagel, 1983, 1987; Stemberger, 1982; but see Abd-El-Jawad & Abu-Salim, 1987, on Arabic and Kubozono, 1989, on Japanese errors). The constraint suggests that the frame positions correspond to syllable constituents. Thus, the second main processing component implicated by analyses of sound errors is the generation of frames representing the syllabic structure of the utterance. In linguistic theory syllable structure is part of the metrical representation of a word. Therefore, I will refer to this component as *metrical spellout*.

The assumption that exchange errors (as well as anticipations such as "taddle tennis", instead of "peddle tennis", and perseveration such as "black bloxes", instead of "black boxes") arise during the assignment of segments to positions implies that segments and metrical frames are initially retrieved independently of each other. According to the Standard Model, speakers first retrieve a set of segments and metrical frames and then combine segments and frames to form a complete phonological representation. This representation must be a fairly abstract characterisation of the word form because misplaced segments phonetically accommodated to their new context. Therefore, there must be a set of phonetic encoding processes that specify the details of the pronunciation of the word.

THE SEGMENTAL REPRESENTATION

The Standard Model makes two important, closely related claims about the units into which word forms are decomposed during segmental spellout, namely, first, that these units have the size of phonological segments, and, second, that they are abstract linguistic entities rather than specifications of motor programs. In this section, the evidence for these claims will be considered.

The assumption that word forms are decomposed into segments, rather than syllables or features, is based mainly on the finding that segments are the most common error units; 60–90% of all sound errors are estimated to be single-segment errors (e.g., Berg, 1988; Boomer & Laver, 1968; Fromkin, 1971; Nooteboom, 1969; Shattuck-Hufnagel, 1983; Shattuck-Hufnagel & Klatt, 1979). However, errors involving other types of units also exist. First, about 10–30% of the sound errors involve sequences of two adjacent segments. An important characteristic of these errors is that the segments constituting the error unit almost always belong to the same syllable constituent, most frequently to the onset (as in "fleaky squoor" instead of "squeaky floor"). MacKay (1972), Shattuck-Hufnagel (1983), and Stemberger (1983) noted that complex syllable constituents more often function as units than breaking apart in errors. Berg (1989) pointed out that German and English complex syllable constituents differ in coherence, depending on characteristics of the included segments, in particular their sonority (see also Kessler & Treiman, 1997). Thus, the coherence of consonant clusters must be represented. One way of doing this is to assume unitary representations for some or all clusters in addition to, or instead of, representations of the individual segments (e.g., Dell, 1986). For a word beginning in a consonant cluster, first an onset cluster and then its constituent segments may be retrieved, and an error may arise during either step.

Occasionally feature errors are observed, such as Fromkin's (1971) often cited "glear plue sky", but these errors are rare. Probably less than 5% of all sound errors are feature errors. However, there is large class of errors in which target and error segments differ by only one feature (as in "Baris" instead of "Paris"; Berg, 1985, 1988; MacKay, 1970; Nooteboom, 1969; Shattuck-Hufnagel, 1986; Shattuck-Hufnagel & Klatt, 1979). MacKay (1970) and Berg (1988) reported that more than 50% of the consonant errors in their German corpora fell into this category. In general, target and error segments are far more similar in their phonetic features than would be expected on the basis of chance estimates. The errors in which the interacting segments differ by only one feature cannot be unambiguously classified as feature or segmental errors. Shattuck-Hufnagel (1983; see also Shattuck-Hufnagel & Klatt, 1979) argued for their classification as segmental errors. She examined those sound exchanges, perseverations, and anticipations in her English corpus that involved target pairs differing in at least two features and computed by how many features the erroneous segments differed from the targets. In 67 out of 70 cases the difference in each half of the error was more than one feature. Thus, these errors were described more parsimoniously as segmental than as feature errors. Hence, Shattuck-Hufnagel proposed that the ambiguous sound errors—those errors where target and error segment differed by only one feature—should also be viewed as segmental errors. This has become the received view in the literature: Phonetic features are "visible" during word-form encoding (which accounts for the phonetic similarity of interacting segments), but they are not the processing units that are independently selected and combined. These processing units are phonological segments.

Roelofs (1999) provided experimental evidence for the claim that word forms are indeed spelled out into segments rather than individual features. He used the so-called implicit priming paradigm. In this paradigm, participants first learn a small set of word pairs (e.g., "hat–cap", "mouse–cat", "bottle–can"). On each trial of the following test block, the first member of a pair (e.g., "hat") is presented as a prompt, and the participants produce the second member, the target ("cap" in the example), as rapidly as possible. Each pair is tested repeatedly within a block. Then the next set of word pairs is learned and tested. The blocks are either homogeneous, which means that the targets are related in phonological form (as in the example, where they share the first two segments) or they are heterogeneous, which means that the targets are unrelated in phonological form. Meyer (1990, 1991) found that the target naming latencies were shorter in homogeneous blocks in which the targets shared one or more word-initial segments than in heterogeneous blocks. She argued that this segmental priming effect was due to the participants' preparation for the utterance (see also Roelofs & Meyer, 1998). In the homogeneous blocks the participants created a partial phonological representation of the targets consisting of the recurrent segments and retained it in working memory. Adding to this representation after prompt presentation took less time than creating a phonological representation from scratch.

In Roelofs' experiments, the targets in homogeneous blocks either shared the onset segment (e.g., they all began in /p/ or they all began in /b/), or they began in one of two segments sharing all features except voicing (i.e., they began, for instance, in /b/ or /p/). In the heterogenous blocks, the initial segments of the targets differed in voicing and place of articulation (i.e., the targets began in /b/, /p/, /d/, or /t/). Roelofs found priming in homogeneous relative to heterogeneous blocks when the targets in homogeneous blocks shared the initial segment, but not when they shared all but one feature. This suggests that the processing units used in this task were complete phonological segments rather than individual features.

Obviously, the task in implicit priming experiments differs importantly from normal speech production. Speakers rarely produce the same set of words over and over again, and they can normally not predict how the next word will begin. However, a large number of implicit priming experiments have shown that speakers can exploit certain types of invariances among the target words but not others (e.g., Meyer, 1990, 1991). A natural account of these pattern is to related them to the way words are normally produced. Thus, the likely reason why the speakers in Roelofs' experiments could use overlap in entire segments but not in several features to prepare for their utterances is that segments, not features, are the units that are selected and combined during word-form encoding.

The second claim about segmental spellout to be evaluated is that the processing units are abstract phonological constituents rather than specifications of motor commands. The most common argument for this assumption is that the error outcomes are usually phonetically well-formed. This shows that the manipulated units cannot be context-dependent allophones or motor programs but must be more abstract form units.

However, not all sound errors yield phonotactically legal sequences. Boomer and Laver (1968) noted that "segmental slips obey phonologically orthodox sequence rules; that is, segmental slips do not result in sequences not permitted by normal phonology . . . This statement is described as a tongue-slip 'law', with 'law' to be understood in a statistical rather than in an absolute sense" (p. 126). Butterworth and Whittaker (1980) and Stemberger (1983) also noted that phonotactic constraints were sometimes violated in errors. Unfortunately, it is difficult to estimate the incidence of phonotactic violations since it is unclear how reliably they would be detected and transcribed. Thus, the often reported phonotactic well-formedness of sound errors is not by itself a compelling argument for the abstractness of the units manipulated during segmental spellout.

Stemberger (1991a,b; Stemberger & Stoel-Gammon, 1991; see also Berg, 1991) argued that the segments retrieved during segmental spellout are not specified for all of their feature values, which implies that they are abstract, as opposed to being complete specifications of motor programs. In phonological theory lexical entries are often taken to specify only those properties of morphemes that are not redundant (e.g., Kenstowicz, 1994). For instance, if in a language all syllable-initial voiceless stops are aspirated, the aspiration of these segments will not be specified lexically. Some theories assume that some non-redundant feature values are likewise unspecified in lexical entries (e.g.,

Archangeli, 1984; Kiparski, 1985). This is possible if all other values are specified. For instance, if voiced segments are lexically specified, voiceless ones need not be specified at all for voicing since the absence of the feature +voiced signals voicelessness. To return to Stemberger's analyses: In general, the segments interacting in errors tend to share more features than expected on the basis of a chance estimate (Fromkin, 1971; García-Albea et al., 1989; Garrett, 1975; Nooteboom, 1969). In extensive analyses of naturally occurring and experimentally induced errors Stemberger showed that those features that can be considered underspecified on the basis of independent linguistic evidence are less influential in determining the likelihood of segments to interact in errors than specified features. Thus, some features appear to be already specified at the moment when most sound errors arise, whereas others are only filled in later. Stemberger (1991a) also showed that asymmetries in segment interactions could be explained by reference to feature underspecification. In general, segments specified for a given feature tend to replace segments unspecified for that feature. This is true even though the segment with the unspecified feature value usually occurs more frequently in the language. Stemberger viewed this pattern as an instantiation of a general "addition bias" in language production, which is based on a processing principle that activated units tend to win in competition against "nothing".

Stemberger's analyses are important for a number of reasons: First, and most importantly for the present discussion, they support the distinction between an abstract form representation in which some features are unspecified and a more detailed representation in which they have been filled in. Second, they show that though segments may be the main units of processing during segmental spellout, the internal composition of segments must be represented—otherwise specified and unspecified features could not differ in their effects. Of course, evidence for the representation of segment-internal structure also comes from the phonemic similarity constraint mentioned earlier; i.e., from the observation that interacting segments tend to share more features than expected on the basis of a chance estimate. Third, though unspecified features are less influential than specified ones, they do play a role in determining which segments interact with each other. This suggests that some sound errors arise at a late moment in processing, after these feature values have been filled in.

Stemberger's arguments for an abstract phonological representation contrast sharply with Mowrey and MacKay's (1990) view, who deny the necessity of assuming abstract sublexical units. They recorded speech motor activity during the production of tongue twisters, such as "Bob flew by Bligh Bay". They determined whether the utterances sounded normal, and whether the patterns of muscle activity were normal. Many utterances were either normal or abnormal in both respects. However, there were also utterances that sounded perfectly normal but showed unusual patterns of muscle activity, which Mowrey and MacKay viewed as blends of the patterns of motor activity typical for different target segments.

Mowrey and MacKay concluded that their data represented a serious threat to the Standard Model, which claims that during speech production discrete linguistic units are selected and combined before motor execution. They argued that on such a view, the motor patterns should always correspond to those typically found for particular linguistic units and should not be blends of such patterns. They note that "the only way to 'save' such models from the evidence is to postulate parallel but independent processing for the two structures which will contribute to the intermediate articulation right down to the level of motor specification, and then 'allow' for simultaneous and graded execution. Unfortunately, 'saving' a model is a far cry from providing support for it" (p. 1310).

Mowrey and MacKay's study is important because it shows that abnormalities can arise during motor execution that cannot be perceived even by the most attentive listeners (see also Nolan, Holst, & Kuehnert, 1996; Stevens, 1989). However, the data do not present a serious challenge for the Standard Model. First, it is unknown how often motor errors similar to those found by Mowrey and MacKay occur in natural speech situations in which speakers do not repeatedly produce tongue twisters but sequences of more dissimilar words, without EMG needles in their tongue and lips. Second, as Fowler (1995) has pointed out, Mowrey and MacKay only recorded speech motor activity at a small number of sites. Hence, it is unclear whether the errors affected only small parts of the motor programs, as Mowrey and MacKay assume, or larger structures, which would imply that at least some of the alleged motor errors could be regarded as feature or segmental errors. Finally, though the EMG data indeed do not provide new support for the Standard Model, they are perfectly compatible with it. The domain of the model is the generation of speech plans, and speech errors analyses have provided ample evidence that these plans can include errors. The speech plans must be executed, and nothing in the model precludes that additional errors can arise during this process. To exclude the existence of abstract linguistic speech plans, it must be shown that all of the evidence usually explained by reference to the properties of these plans can be explained solely by reference to motor variables. There is, so far, no indication that this will be possible.

To summarise, most error units have the size of single phonological segments, and in most cases, the error outcome is perceived as phonetically well-formed. However, there are errors involving smaller error units and errors not resulting in phonetically well-formed utterances, though the frequency of such errors is difficult to estimate. Most likely, there is an encoding process handling phonological segments followed by other processes handling different types of processing units, and errors can arise during each of these processes.

THE METRICAL REPRESENTATION

The Standard Model assumes that in addition to a segmental tier the phonological representations speakers create include a metrical tier. An important claim of the model is that the two tiers are first retrieved independently of each other, and that only later segments are associated to positions in the metrical representation. A second important claim of the Standard Model is that the metrical tier includes a representation of syllable-internal positions or constituents. The discussion in this section will focus on evidence concerning these two claims.

A widely used argument for both claims is the syllable-position constraint—the observation that the interacting segments in sound errors typically stem from corresponding syllable positions. The standard account for this constraint is that there are syllable frames with labelled positions—for example, onset (prevocalic part), nucleus (vocalic part), and coda (postvocalic part)—and that segments are marked with respect to the positions they may take (e.g., Dell, 1986; Shattuck-Hufnagel, 1979, 1983). Segments that can appear in more than one syllable position (which is true, for instance, for most English consonants) must be represented several times with differing positional labels.

There is no doubt that the syllable-position constraint is observed in the majority of the sound errors. However, as Shattuck-Hufnagel (1987, 1992) has pointed out, most of the evidence for this constraint—more than 80% of the relevant cases in the English corpora that have been analysed—stems from errors involving word onsets (see also Garrett, 1975, 1980). Thus, word-onset consonants are particularly error-prone and interact more often with each other than with word-internal consonants (see Wilshire, 1998, and Wheeler & Touretzky, 1997, for reasons why this may be so). This may explain most of the evidence usually taken to support the syllable-position constraint. Vowels show a very strong tendency to interact with each other rather than with consonants. This could be due to a syllable-position constraint, but it could also be due to the general tendency of segments to interact with phonemically similar rather than dissimilar segments. In addition, interactions of vowels with consonants may often lead to sound sequences that violate the phonotactic constraints of the language or cannot be pronounced at all. Consonantal errors not involving word onsets are too rare to be analysed for adherence to a positional constraint. In short, the constraints on segment movements in English corpora do not provide unambiguous evidence for metrical frames representing syllable-internal structure.

García-Albea et al. (1989) reported that in their Spanish corpus the syllable-position constraint was observed in 96% of the cases and that word-internal consonant errors were more frequent than word-initial ones. Thus, the constraint on the landing sites of misplaced segments in this corpus cannot be viewed as a word-onset effect. However, it is not certain that this constraint was a pure syllable-position constraint because the authors do not report how many errors involved consonants and vowels, how many of the interacting segments shared the word position or stress value, and how frequently syllable-initial and syllable-final consonants occurred in the corpus.

Stemberger (1984, 1990) argued for frames of a different type, namely frames encoding the CV structure of the utterance. Such frames have been proposed in autosegmental phonology (e.g., Clements & Keyser, 1983; Goldsmith, 1990; McCarthy, 1981) as an interface between the syllabic and the segmental representation, as each syllable and each segment is associated to one or more of its positions. It captures the number and ordering of vocalic and consonantal elements and their length, with short segments being associated to one position of the CV tier and long ones to two positions. In one study, Stemberger (1984) examined errors involving segments differing in length. If misordered segments typically acquire the length of the segments they replace, length can be argued to be represented independently of segmental content in terms of the number of positions assumed on the CV tier. Stemberger's analyses of small corpora of German and Swedish errors supported this view, as misplaced segments usually acquired the length of the segments they replaced. However, in the English corpus the misplaced segments showed a strong tendency to maintain their original length, which argues against the independent representation of length.

In a second study, Stemberger (1990) examined whether the rate of segmental errors was affected by the degree of similarity in CV structure of the interacting words. Additions to onset consonants (as in "a whole blox of flower" instead of "a whole box of flowers") were more likely when the source word of the added consonant ("flowers" in the example) began with a cluster than when it began with a singleton. Thus, there was a tendency towards increased similarity of the CV-structures of the interacting words. In addition, the likelihood of onset interactions was higher when target and source word had the same number of coda consonants than when they differed in the number of coda consonants. However, whether the words were identical or differed in the structure of their nuclei (V or VV) did not affect the likelihood of onset interactions. Thus, Stemberger's evidence is suggestive but it does not offer strong support for the assumption of an independent CV-structure.

Meijer (1994, 1996) provided experimental evidence concerning the representation of CV structure in Dutch. Native speakers of Dutch with good knowledge of English saw English words, which they had to translate into Dutch. Shortly after the onset of the English word, they heard a Dutch distractor word, which could be phonologically related or unrelated to the Dutch target word. For instance, they saw the English word VALLEY and just before responding with the Dutch translation equivalent "dal", they heard the Dutch word "bus" (bus), which had the same CV structure as the target (CVC), or they heard the unrelated word "bloes" (blouse), which had a different CV structure (CCVC). In two experiments, facilitatory effects of shared CV structure were obtained, but in two other experiments they were absent.

Costa and Sebastian-Gallés (1998) carried out primed picture naming experiments with Spanish speakers. In each of four experiments, picture naming was faster when the primes were related to the targets in CV structure than when they were unrelated. These effects were, however, much smaller than the segmental priming effects obtained in the same study and not always statistically reliable.

Finally, Sevald, Dell, and Cole (1995) used a repeated pronunciation task to study the representation of CV structure in English. They asked speakers to produce alternating sequences of a mono- and a disyllabic pseudoword as often as they could within four seconds. In their first experiment, they found that the sequences were produced faster when the monosyllable had the same CV structure as the first syllable of the disyllable (as in "kil–kil.per" and "kilp–kilp.ner") than when this was not the case (as in "kilp–kil.per" and "kil–kilp.ner"). Importantly, the second experiment showed that this was true even when the two nonwords did not share any segments (as in "kul–par.fen" vs. "kult–par.fen"). Thus, there was a facilitatory effect of shared CV structure. Based on these results, Sevald et al. argued for the representation of CV structure as a skeletal structure to which segments are associated. Note that Sevald et al. measured how many targets participants could produce within a given time period. This makes it difficult to tell how the effect of CV structure arose. It is certainly possible that it arose during the creation of the phonological representation, as Sevald et al. proposed, but it could also originate during the retrieval or execution of motor programs.

So far, the claim has been examined that speakers retrieve metrical representations with distinct positions corresponding to syllable constituents (onset, nucleus, coda) or consonantal and vocalic positions. Levelt (1992, see Levelt et al., 1999) argued for more global metrical structures capturing only the number of syllables and the stress pattern of words but not syllable-internal structure. On this view, segments are directly associated to syllables and thereby acquire syllable positions (i.e., they become the onset, nucleus, or coda of a syllable), rather than being inserted into independently existing subsyllabic positions. The stress pattern of words is assumed to be stored in the mental lexicon because it cannot be reliably derived from segmental or morphological information. But the association of segments to syllables can be derived on the basis of universal and language-specific syllabification rules and therefore need not be stored. (Essentially, each vowel and diphthong is associated to a different syllable, and consonants are treated as syllable onsets unless phonotactically illegal onset clusters arise). On this view, the evidence suggesting that the CV structure of words, or the parsing of syllables into syllable constituents, is in some sense psychologically real can be accounted for by referring to the facts that words with similar CV structures or similar syllable constituents are likely to be syllabified according to similar rules, that in such words the segments in corresponding positions are likely to share phonological features, or that the programs recruited during articulatory programming have similar addresses. Thus, CV structure effects may not be a direct consequence of similarity in stored phonological representations but may be due to similarities in the processes that bind segments to syllables, or the processes that select articulatory commands.

If word-form encoding includes the retrieval of a metrical representation coding the stress pattern of the word, one might expect that occasionally an incorrect metrical representation is retrieved, which could manifest itself in a stress error. Stress errors indeed occur. However, in the overwhelming majority of these errors, the resulting stress pattern is that of a morphologically related word (e.g., "so that we can PROgress" instead of "proGRESS"; Cutler, 1980a,b; Levelt, 1989). Errors resulting in stress patterns not carried by morphological relatives of the target (as in the invented example "BAnana" instead of "baNAna") are extremely rare. This strongly suggests that the observed stress errors are a consequence of errors at the level of morphological encoding.

There is some evidence for stress effects on segmental errors. First, the segments of stressed syllables are more likely to be involved in errors than those of unstressed syllables. Second, in German and English errors, segments move more often to syllables with the same stress value as their source syllables than to syllables with a different stress value (e.g., Berg, 1990; Boomer & Laver, 1968; Fromkin, 1971, 1973; Garrett, 1980; Nooteboom, 1969; Shattuck-Hufnagel, 1983, 1986). Unfortunately, the interpretation of these findings is complicated by the fact that in German and English the syllable carrying the main stress is often the first syllable of the word. Shattuck-Hufnagel (1986, 1992) examined whether segment movements could be better predicted by reference to the word positions or the stress values of the interacting syllables and concluded that for consonant errors word position, and for vowel errors stress was the more influential factor.

Thus, there is some, albeit not entirely convincing, evidence that the stress pattern of an utterance is represented at the moment when most sound errors arise. However, this does not prove that the stress pattern of a word is represented independently of its segmental context. The fact that the error rates differ for stressed and unstressed vowels can either be explained by assuming that segments in certain positions are more vulnerable than segments in other positions, or that certain segments (marked as "stressed") are particularly error-prone. Similarly, the finding that interacting segments typically stem from syllables with identical stress values can either be attributed to similarity of the metrical structures, or to shared diacritics (e.g., "stressed") carried by the segments themselves. Sometimes, exchanges of one stressed and one unstressed vowel occur. In these cases, listeners typically have the impression that the stress pattern of the utterance is maintained (e.g., Shattuck-Hufnagel, 1986). This shows that the segmental content is separated from the metrical structure. However, such errors are rare, and there is, to my knowledge, no objective evidence showing that the constancy of the stress pattern is indeed produced by the speaker rather than arising in the listener's ear (or mind). In sum, speech errors do not provide strong evidence for the hypothesis that stress is represented separately from segmental content.

However, additional evidence supporting this hypothesis comes from recent experiments using the implicit priming paradigm described previously. As noted, Meyer (1991) showed that in this paradigm speakers are faster to produce the target words of a block, when the words share one or more word-initial segments than they have different word onsets. In the experiments by Roelofs and Meyer

(1998), this preparation effect was replicated, but only when the targets in homogeneous blocks shared the stress pattern and the number of syllables in addition to word-initial segments. Constancy of CV structure was not a requirement for obtaining a preparation effect. Thus, the participants had to know the number of syllables and the stress pattern of the entire response word (and not only the stress pattern of the first syllable) to make use of the information that the first two segments were the same for all response words. They did not have to know the CV structure. This suggests, first, that metrical information must be retrieved in order to prepare for an utterance, and, second, that this information is stored and retrieved independently of segmental information. If the stress pattern were coded locally, as diacritics on the vowels, there would be no reason why the participants had to know the metrical structure of the entire response word in order to prepare for its first syllable. Meyer and Roelofs assumed that in the homogeneous condition, participants prepared their utterances before prompt presentation by retrieving the response words' metrical structure and the recurrent segments and associating the segments to the first syllable of the metrical structure. This type of preparation was obviously only possible when the response words shared not only one or more segments but also the metrical structure.

Roelofs and Meyer's findings argue for the assumption of metrical structures capturing only the number of syllables of words and their stress pattern. However, even this information may not be lexically represented for all words. For stress-assigning languages, such as Dutch, English, and German, the stress pattern must be stored for part of the vocabulary because it cannot be reliably derived from segmental information. However, stress assignment in these languages is not random, and stress patterns vary greatly in frequency. Default rules of stress assignment can be formulated which hold for most words. For instance, for Dutch and English, the most frequent stress pattern is to assign stress to the first syllable of the word with a full vowel (e.g., Cutler & Norris, 1988). Levelt et al. (1999; following Schiller, personal communication) estimated that as much as 90% of the word tokens speakers produce may be stressed according to this rule. Deviating from the Standard Model, which assumes that metrical information is stored for all words, they proposed that such information is only lexically represented for those words that deviate from the default stress rule. For all others, the lexical entries only specify segmental information, and the parsing of words into syllables and stress assignment are done by rule. This proposal is compatible with the results obtained by Roelofs and Meyer (1998) because it so happened that in that study only words that deviated from the main stress rule of Dutch were tested. Obviously additional evidence is required to establish that for words obeying the main stress rule of the language the stress pattern is indeed not stored but derived by rule.

To sum up, according to the Standard Model, speakers retrieve a stored metrical representation for each content word they say. Different proposals have been made about the properties of metrical representations; their positions have been proposed to correspond to syllables, syllable constituents, or consonantal versus vocalic positions. Deviating from the Standard Model, Levelt et al. (1999) proposed that metrical information may only be stored for those words that do not obey the main stress rule of the language. For all other words, the stress pattern is computed "on-line" during utterance planning on the basis of segmental information.

THE PHONETIC REPRESENTATION

The final step in word form encoding is the generation of a phonetic representation. The need to postulate this step follows from the abstractness of the phonological representation. In the Standard Model, as in most of linguistic theory (Blumstein, 1991; Keating, 1984, 1990; Kenstowicz, 1994; but see Browman & Goldstein, 1986, 1992a,b for an alternative view), the phonological representation is composed of phonological segments, which are discrete (i.e., they do not overlap on an abstract time axis), static (i.e., the features defining them refer to states of the vocal tract or the acoustic signal), and context-free (i.e., the features are the same for all contexts in which the segment appears). By contrast, the articulatory gestures realising consonants and vowels may overlap in time, the vocal tract is in continuous movement, and the implementation of features is context-dependent.

What are the properties of the phonetic representation? Though speakers ultimately carry out movements of the articulators, the phonetic representation most likely does not specify movement trajectories or patterns of muscle activity but characterises speech tasks (such as lip or tongue closure) to be achieved (see, for instance, Fowler, 1995; Levelt, 1989). Alternatively, the phonetic representation may specify invariant auditory target regions; i.e., they may define the speech sounds to be generated rather than articulatory targets (e.g., Guenther, Hampson, & Johnson, 1998). The main argument for the view that the phonetic representation specifies targets rather than movements is that speakers can realise a given linguistic unit in many different ways. The sound /b/, for instance, can be produced by moving both lips or only one lip and with or without jaw movement. Most speakers can almost without practice adapt to novel speech situations. For instance, Lindblom, Lubker, and Gay (1979) showed that speakers can produce acoustically (almost) normal vowels while holding a bite block between their teeth forcing their jaw in a fixed open position. Abbs and Gracco (1984; see also Folkins & Abbs, 1975) asked speakers repeatedly to produce pseudowords (e.g., "aba" or "sapapple"). On a small number of trials, and unpredictably for the participants, the movement of an articulator (e.g., the lower lip) was mechanically interfered with. In general, these perturbations were almost immediately (within 30 ms after movement onset) compensated for such that the utterances were acoustically almost normal. One way to account for this finding is that the phonetic representation specifies speech tasks, and that there is a neuro-muscular execution system that computes how the tasks are best carried out in a particular situation (see, for instance, Kelso, Saltzman, & Tuller, 1986, and Turvey, 1990, for a discussion of the properties of such systems). In the perturbation experiments, participants maintained constant articulatory task descriptions on all trials, and on each trial the execution system computed the best way to fulfill them. The distinction between a specification of speech tasks and the determination of movements entails that down to a low planning level the speech plan is the same for a given linguistic unit, even though the actual movements may vary.

Levelt (1992, see also Crompton, 1982; Levelt & Wheeldon, 1994) proposed that during phonetic encoding speakers may access a mental syllabary, which is a store of gestural programs for the high-frequency syllables of the language. These syllable programs specify the gestures to be carried out in order to produce specific syllables, such as /ta/ or /bib/. They are to be distinguished from the metrical syllable units discussed earlier. Thus, a word consisting of two high frequency syllables is phonetically encoded by retrieving two syllable programs from the syllabary. The phonetic forms of words composed of low frequency syllables are assembled using the segmental and metrical information provided in the phonological representation. Levelt's proposal is based on the assumption that the main domain of coarticulation is the syllable (as proposed, for instance, by Fujimura & Lovins, 1978, and Lindblom, 1983; see also Browman & Goldstein, 1988; Byrd, 1995, 1996). Coarticulatory effects that cross syllable boundaries (e.g., Farnetani, 1990; Kiritani & Sawashima, 1987; Recasens, 1984, 1987) are attributed to the motor execution system.

The obvious advantage of a syllabary is that it greatly reduce the programming load relative to segment-by-segment assembly of phonetic forms, in particular since the syllables of a language differ greatly in frequency. For Dutch, Schiller, Meyer, Baayen, and Levelt (1996) showed that the 500 most frequent syllable types suffice to construct 85% of all syllable tokens. Similarly, for English, the 500 most frequent syllables suffice to create approximately 80% of all syllable tokens (Schiller, personal communication).

Experimental evidence that is compatible with the notion of a mental syllabary comes from a study by Levelt and Wheeldon (1994), in which a syllable frequency effect was found that was independent of word frequency. Participants first learned to associate symbols with response words (e.g., xxx = apple). On each trial of the following test phase, one of the learned symbols was presented, and the participant produced the corresponding response word as quickly as possible. The speech onset latencies were found to be faster for disyllabic words that ended in a high-frequency syllable than for comparable disyllabic words that ended in a low-frequency syllable. This suggests that high-frequency syllables were accessed faster than low-frequency ones, which implies the existence of syllabic units. In later research by Levelt and Meyer (reported in Hendriks & McQueen, 1996), the syllable frequency effect was not replicated. This does not rule out that speakers retrieve syllable programs, it only shows that the speed of access to these units does not strongly depend on their frequency. The notion of a mental syllabary remains attractive because of the reduction of programming load it implies.

THE NECESSITY OF DECOMPOSED FORM REPRESENTATIONS

The preceding sections showed that during word-form encoding speakers decompose morphemes into sets of segments, assign the segments to syllables, and finally generate a phonetic representation specifying the speech motor tasks to be carried out. This may appear to be a cumbersome process. Why can't speakers directly retrieve motor programs for entire morphemes? The answer is that any morpheme can be pronounced in many slightly different but systematically related ways. The similarities and differences between the surface forms of a morpheme can best be captured by reference to its internal phonological structure (i.e., its segments, features, and metrical structure). Thus, any model of word-form generation in which different pronunciations of a morpheme are generated out of a common base must assume, first, that the stored lexical representation is abstract enough to permit different phonetic realisations, and, second, that during word-form encoding the internal structure of the morpheme becomes visible to the processor and accessible for modification.

As noted in the Introduction, lexical access begins with lemma selection. Each selected lemma in turn selects one or more morphemes, for instance two nouns (as in "photo–copy" or "book–store") or a noun and an affix (as in "book–s", or "book–ing"). The phonological form of a given morpheme often depends on its morphological environment (e.g., Spencer, 1991). Effects of morphological environment are often subtle (compare, for instance, the pronunciation of /n/ in "intolerant" and "incapable", or in "mantrap" and "mankind", or the pronunciation of the plural morpheme in "cats", "dogs", and "horses"), but there can also be substantial changes of base morphemes (compare, for instance, the phonetic realisations of the base in "period", "periodic", and "periodicity" or in "divine" and "divinity"). These differences are systematic, i.e., they occur for all lexical items with certain structural properties and can be described as resulting from the application of certain rules to the base forms. Application of these rules requires the internal structure of the morpheme to be visible to the processor.

Of course, one may want to argue that the mental lexicon includes not only the base forms of individual morphemes, but complete representations for complex words. Whether this is the case is an empirical question in need of further study. Reviewing the relevant speech error evidence, Stemberger and MacWhinney (1986) proposed that the representation of morphologically complex forms may be frequency-dependent: For frequent forms both unitary and morphologically decomposed forms are available, whereas less frequent forms are generated out of their morphological constituents. Experimental evidence (Roelofs, 1996b,

1998) also suggests that certain morphologically complex forms are assembled out of their constituents.

In addition to morphologically conditioned alternations of word forms, there are changes that are conditioned at the phonological level. Some of these alternations are independent of the context in which the word occurs. English examples are schwa deletion (e.g., in "p'lice" for "police"), reduction of full vowels to schwa (e.g., in "potato") and elision ("and" becoming syllabic /n/, "them" becoming "em"; see Giegerich, 1992). The standard linguistic view is that these forms are generated by applying certain postlexical rules to the forms retrieved from the mental lexicon. Very frequent surface forms may be stored in the mental lexicon. However, though alternations are usually described in categorical terms, many of them are gradual, rather than all-or-none, which renders the storage assumption implausible. Thus, these forms must be generated during speech planning.

Some changes of word forms are conditioned by the phonological context in which the words appear. English examples are assimilation (e.g., in "ten pounds", "miss you"), degemination ("call Linda", "weight training"; Giegerich, 1992), and cliticisation ("fish 'n ships", "he'll come"). Though very frequent combinations (like "I've") may be stored in the mental lexicon as units, most context-dependent alternations must be computed on-line.

When morphemes are combined into complex words, they are often syllabified differently than they would be isolation. For instance, "understand" is syllabified as "un.der.stand", but in "understanding", /d/ is the onset of the last syllable, leading to "un.der.stan.ding". The same holds when hosts and clitics are combined. For example, the phrase "understand it" may be pronounced as "un.der.stan.dit" (though "un.der.stand.it" is also perfectly acceptable). In the former case, the two lexical words "understand" and "it" are combined into one phonological unit (a phonological word), which functions as the domain of syllabification. The onset maximisation rule mentioned earlier applies to the entire string of segments within the phonological word and assigns the segment /d/ to the onset position of the last syllable, yielding the syllable "dit".

In linguistic theory, such alternations of syllabification are usually attributed to the application of resyllabification rules (e.g., Booij, 1995; Kenstowicz, 1994; see also Wheeldon's chapter). This implies that morphemes are first syllabified individually and that the syllabification may subsequently be altered depending on the context. By contrast, Levelt (1992, see also Levelt & Wheeldon, 1994; Levelt et al., 1999) suggested that speakers directly create the surface forms: They retrieve all segments of a phonological word and directly associate them to the appropriate syllables. As noted previously, Levelt et al. (1999) do not assume that the syllable structure of words is part of their lexical entries. One reason for this assumption, which has already been mentioned, is that syllabification is rule-based, and that there is therefore no need to store it for each individual item. A second reason is that the syllabification of a morpheme in connected speech often differs from the syllabification of its citation form. Whether Levelt's direct syllabification hypothesis or the traditional resyllabification hypothesis is correct remains to be seen (see Baumann, 1995, for evidence arguing for resyllabification in the case of Dutch cliticisation). Regardless of how syllabification is carried out, it is a fact that in connected speech words are often syllabified differently than their citation forms would be. Therefore, the decomposition of words into segments and the following association to syllables is not a vacuous process but in many cases leads to forms that deviate significantly from the stored ones.

When we speak, we retrieve information about words from our mental lexicon. How a word will be pronounced depends on a variety of nonlinguistic and linguistic variables, some of which have been mentioned earlier. Unless one wishes to store all possible surface forms of each word (or all surface forms a person has experienced), lexical entries must be defined as abstract units out of which different surface forms can be generated by rule. Which rules apply, and how they change a stored form, depends on the phonological structure of the form itself and on its linguistic environment. The decomposition of morphemes into segmental and metrical constituents can be viewed as a way of making phonological structure visible to the processor and amenable to modification.

NOTES

1. A.S. Meyer is now at the School of Psychology, University of Birmingham, UK.
2. All speech errors in this chapter stem from Fromkin's (1973) corpus.

REFERENCES

Abbs, J.H., & Gracco, V.L. (1984). Control of complex motor gestures: Orofacial muscle responses to load perturbations of lip during speech. *Journal of Neurophysiology, 51*, 705–723.

Abd-El-Jawad, H., & Abu-Salim, I. (1987). Slips of the tongue in Arabic and their theoretical implications. *Language Sciences, 9*, 145–171.

Archangeli, D. (1984). *Underspecification in Yawelmani phonology and morphology.* Unpublished doctoral dissertation, MIT, Cambridge, MA.

Baumann, M. (1995). *The production of syllables in connected speech.* Unpublished doctoral dissertation. Nijmegen University, The Netherlands.

Berg, T. (1985). Is voice suprasegmental? *Linguistics, 23*, 883–915.

Berg, T. (1988). *Die Abbildung des Sprachproduktionsprozesses in einem Aktivationsflussmodell: Untersuchungen an deutschen und englischen Versprechern* [The representation of the process of language production in a spreading activation model: Studies of German and English speech errors]. Tuebingen, The Netherlands: Niemeyer.

Berg, T. (1989). Intersegmental cohesiveness. *Folia Linguistica, 23*, 245–280.

Berg, T. (1990). The differential sensitivity of consonants and vowels to stress. *Language Sciences, 12*, 65–84.

Berg, T. (1991). Redundant-feature coding in the mental lexicon. *Linguistics, 29*, 903–925.

Blumstein, S.E. (1991). The relation between phonetics and phonology. *Phonetica, 48*, 108–119.

Bock, J.K., & Levelt, W.J.M. (1994). Language production: Grammatical encoding. In M.A. Gernsbacher (Ed.), *Handbook of psycholinguistics* (pp. 945–984). San Diego: Academic Press.

Booij, G.E. (1995). *The phonology of Dutch.* Oxford, UK: Oxford University Press.

Boomer, D.S., & Laver, J.D.M. (1968). Slips of the tongue. *British Journal of Disorders of Communication, 3,* 2–12.

Browman, C.P., & Goldstein, L.M. (1986). Towards an articulatory phonology. *Phonology Yearbook, 3,* 219–252.

Browman, C.P., & Goldstein, L.M. (1988). Some notes on syllable structure in articulatory phonology. *Phonetica, 45,* 140–155.

Browman, C.P., & Goldstein, L.M. (1992a). Articulatory phonology: An overview. *Phonetica, 49,* 155–180.

Browman, C.P., & Goldstein, L.M. (1992b). Response to commentaries. *Phonetica, 49,* 222–234.

Butterworth, B., & Whittaker, S. (1980). Peggy Babcock's relatives. In G.E. Stelmach & J. Requin (Eds.), *Tutorials in motor behavior* (pp. 647–656). Amsterdam: North-Holland.

Byrd, D. (1995). C-centers revisited. *Phonetica, 52,* 285–306.

Byrd, D. (1996). Influences on articulatory timing in consonant sequences. *Journal of Phonetics, 24,* 209–244.

Caplan, D. (1992). *Language: Structure, processing, and disorders.* Cambridge, MA: MIT Press.

Caramazza, A. (1997). How many levels of processing are there in lexical access? *Cognitive Neuropsychology, 14,* 177–208.

Caramazza, A., & Miozzo, M. (1997). The relation between syntactic and phonological knowledge in lexical access: Evidence from the "tip-of-the-tongue" phenomenon. *Cognition, 64,* 309–343.

Clements, G.N., & Keyser, S.J. (1983). *CV phonology* (Linguistic Inquiries Monographs Series, No. 9). Cambridge, MA: MIT Press.

Costa, A., & Sebastian-Gallés, N. (1998). Abstract phonological structure in language production: Evidence from Spanish. *Journal of Experimental Psychology: Learning, Memory, and Cognition, 24,* 886–903.

Crompton, A. (1982). Syllables and segments in speech production. In A. Cutler (Ed.), *Slips of the tongue and language production* (pp. 109–162). Berlin, Germany: Mouton.

Cutler, A. (1980a). Errors of stress and intonation. In V.A. Fromkin (Ed.), *Errors in linguistic performance: Slips of the tongue, ear, pen, and hand* (pp. 67–80). New York: Academic Press.

Cutler, A. (1980b). Syllable omission errors and isochrony. In H.W. Dechert & M. Raupach (Eds.), *Temporal variables in speech* (pp. 183–190). The Hague, The Netherlands: Mouton.

Cutler, A., & Norris, D. (1988). The role of strong syllables in segmentation for lexical access. *Journal of Experimental Psychology: Human Perception and Performance, 14,* 113–121.

Dell, G. (1986). A spreading-activation theory of retrieval in speech production. *Psychological Review, 93,* 283–321.

Farnetani, E. (1990). V-C-V lingual coarticulation and its spatiotemporal domain. In W.J. Hardcastle & A. Marchal (Eds.), *Speech production and speech modelling* (pp. 93–113). Dordrecht, The Netherlands: Kluwer.

Folkins, J.W., & Abbs, J.H. (1975). Lip and jaw motor control during speech: Responses to resistive loading of the jaw. *Journal of Speech and Hearing Research, 18,* 207–220.

Fowler, C.A. (1995). Speech production. In J.L. Miller & P.D. Eimas (Eds.), *Speech, language, and communication* (pp. 29–61). San Diego: Academic Press.

Fromkin, V.A. (1971). The non-anomalous nature of anomalous utterances. *Language, 47,* 27–52.

Fromkin, V.A. (1973). Introduction. In V.A. Fromkin (Ed.), *Speech errors as linguistic evidence* (pp. 11–45). The Hague, The Netherlands: Mouton.

Fujimura, O., & Lovins, J.B. (1978). Syllables as concatenative units. In A. Bell & J.B. Hooper (Eds.), *Syllables and segments* (pp. 107–120). Amsterdam: North-Holland.

García-Albea, J.E., del Viso, S., & Igoa, J.M. (1989). Movement errors and levels of processing in sentence production. *Journal of Psycholinguistic Research, 18,* 145–161.

Garrett, M.F. (1975). The analysis of sentence production. In G.H. Bower (Ed.), *The psychology of language and motivation* (Vol. 9, pp. 133–175). New York: Academic Press.

Garrett, M.F. (1976). Syntactic processes in sentence production. In R.J. Wales & E. Walker (Eds.), *New approaches to language mechanisms* (pp. 231–256). Amsterdam: North-Holland.

Garrett, M.F. (1980). Levels of processing in sentence production. In B. Butterworth (Ed.), *Language production: Vol. 1. Speech and talk* (pp. 177–210). New York: Academic Press.

Giegerich, H.J. (1992). *English phonology*. Cambridge, UK: Cambridge University Press.

Goldsmith, J. (1990). *Autosegmental and metrical phonology*. Cambridge, MA: Basil Blackwell.

Guenther, F.H., Hampson, M., & Johnson, D. (1998). A theoretical investigation of reference frames for the planning of speech movements. *Psychological Review, 105*, 611–633.

Hendriks, H., & McQueen, J. (1996). *Annual report of the Max Planck Institute for Psycholinguistics*, Nijmegen, The Netherlands.

Keating, P.A. (1984). Phonetic and phonological representation of stop consonant voicing. *Language, 60*, 286–319.

Keating, P.A. (1990). Phonetic representations in a generative grammar. *Journal of Phonetics, 18*, 321–334.

Kelso, J.A.S., Saltzman, E.L., & Tuller, B. (1986). The dynamical perspective on speech production: Data and theory. *Journal of Phonetics, 14*, 29–59.

Kempen, G., & Hoenkamp, E. (1987). An incremental procedural grammar for sentence formulation. *Cognitive Science, 11*, 201–258.

Kempen, G., & Huijbers, P. (1983). The lexicalization process in sentence production and naming: Indirect election of words. *Cognition, 14*, 185–209.

Kenstowicz, M. (1994). *Phonology in generative grammar*. Oxford, UK: Basil Blackwell.

Kessler, B., & Treiman, R. (1997). Syllable structure and the distribution of phonemes in English syllables. *Journal of Memory and Language, 37*, 295–311.

Kiparski, P. (1985). Some consequences of lexical phonology. *Phonology Yearbook, 2*, 83–138.

Kiritani, S., & Sawashima, M. (1987). The temporal relationship between articulations of consonants and adjacent vowels. In R. Channon, & L. Shockey (Eds.), *In honor of Ilse Lehiste* (pp. 139–149). Dordrecht, The Netherlands: Foris.

Kubozono, H. (1989). The mora and syllable structure in Japanese: Evidence from speech errors. *Language and Speech, 32*, 249–278.

Levelt, W.J.M. (1989). *Speaking: From intention to articulation*. Cambridge, MA: MIT Press.

Levelt, W.J.M. (1992). Accessing words in speech production: Stages, processes and representations. *Cognition, 42*, 1–22.

Levelt, W.J.M. (1999). Models of word production. *Trends in Cognitive Science, 3*, 223–232.

Levelt, W.J.M., Roelofs, A., & Meyer, A.S. (1999). A theory of lexical access in speech production. *Behavioral and Brain Sciences, 22*, 1–75.

Levelt, W.J.M, & Wheeldon, L.R. (1994). Do speakers have access to a mental syllabary? *Cognition, 50*, 239–269.

Lindblom, B. (1983). The economy of speech gestures. In P.F. MacNeilage (Ed.), *The production of speech* (pp. 217–245). New York: Springer.

Lindblom, B., Lubker, J., & Gay, T. (1979). Formant frequencies of some fixed-mandible vowels and a model of speech motor programming by predictive simulation. *Journal of Phonetics, 7*, 147–161.

MacKay, D.G. (1970). Spoonerisms: The structure of errors in the serial order of speech. *Neuropsychologia, 8*, 323–350.

MacKay, D.G. (1972). The structure of words and syllables: Evidence from errors in speech. *Cognitive Psychology, 3*, 210–227.

McCarthy, J. (1981). A prosodic theory of nonconcatenative morphology. *Linguistic Inquiry, 12*, 373–418.

Meijer, P.J.A. (1994). *Phonological encoding: The role of suprasegmental structures*. Unpublished doctoral dissertation, Nijmegen University, The Netherlands.

Meijer, P.J.A. (1996). Suprasegmental structures in phonological encoding: The CV structure. *Journal of Memory and Language, 35*, 840–885.

Meyer, A.S. (1990). The time course of phonological encoding in language production: The encoding of successive syllables of a word. *Journal of Memory and Language, 29*, 524–545.

Meyer, A.S. (1991). The time course of phonological encoding in language production: Phonological encoding inside a syllable. *Journal of Memory and Language, 30,* 69–89.

Meyer, A.S. (1992). Investigation of phonological encoding through speech error analyses: Achievements, limitations, and alternatives. *Cognition, 42,* 181–211.

Meyer, A.S. (1996). Lexical access in phrase and sentence production: Results from picture–word interference experiments. *Journal of Memory and Language, 35,* 477–496.

Motley, M.T. (1973). An analysis of spoonerisms as psycholinguistic phenomena. *Speech Monographs, 40,* 66–71.

Mowrey, R.A., & MacKay, I.R.A. (1990). Phonological primitives: Electromyographic speech error evidence. *Journal of the Acoustical Society of America, 88,* 1299–1312.

Nolan, F., Holst, T., & Kuehnert, B. (1996). Modelling [s] to [ʃ] accommodation in English. *Journal of Phonetics, 24,* 113–137.

Nooteboom, S.G. (1969). The tongue slips into patterns. In A.G. Sciarone, A.J. van Essen, & A.A. van Raad (Eds.), *Nomen: Leyden studies in linguistics and phonetics* (pp. 114–132). The Hague, The Netherlands: Mouton.

Recasens, D. (1984). V-to-C coarticulation in Catalan VCV sequences: An articulatory and acoustic study. *Journal of Phonetics, 12,* 61–73.

Recasens, D. (1987). An acoustic analysis of V-to-C and V-to-V coarticulatory effects in Catalan and Spanish VCV sequences. *Journal of Phonetics, 15,* 299–312.

Roelofs, A. (1992). A spreading-activation theory of lemma retrieval in speaking. *Cognition, 42,* 107–142.

Roelofs, A. (1993). Testing a non-decompositional theory of lemma retrieval in speaking: Retrieval of verbs. *Cognition, 47,* 59–87.

Roelofs, A. (1996a). Morpheme frequency in speech production. Testing WEAVER. In G.E. Booij & J. van Marle, H. Baayen, & R. Schreuder (Eds.), *Yearbook of morphology* (pp. 135–154). Dordrecht, The Netherlands: Kluwer.

Roelofs, A. (1996b). Serial order in planning the production of successive morphemes of a word. *Journal of Memory and Language, 35,* 854–976.

Roelofs, A. (1997a). A case for non-decomposition in conceptually driven word retrieval. *Journal of Psycholinguistic Research, 26,* 33–67.

Roelofs, A. (1997b). Syllabification in speech production: Evaluation of WEAVER. *Language and Cognitive Processes, 12,* 657–694.

Roelofs, A. (1997c). The WEAVER model of word-form encoding in speech production. *Cognition, 64,* 249–284.

Roelofs, A. (1998). Rightward incrementality in encoding simple phrasal forms in speech production: Verb-particle combinations. *Journal of Experimental Psychology: Learning, Memory, and Cognition, 24,* 904–919.

Roelofs, A. (1999). Phonological segments and features as planning units in speech production. *Language and Cognitive Processes, 14,* 173–200.

Roelofs, A., & Meyer, A.S. (1998). Metrical structure in planning the production of spoken words. *Journal of Experimental Psychology, Learning, Memory, and Cognition, 24,* 922–939.

Schiller, N., Meyer, A.S., Baayen, R.H., & Levelt, W.J.M. (1996). A comparison of lexical and speech syllables in Dutch. *Journal of Quantitative Linguistics, 3,* 8–28.

Sevald, C.A., Dell, G., & Cole, J.S. (1995). Syllable structure in speech production: Are syllables chunks or schemas? *Journal of Memory and Language, 34,* 807–820.

Shattuck-Hufnagel, S. (1979). Speech errors as evidence for a serial-ordering mechanism in sentence production. In W.E. Cooper & E.C.T. Walker (Eds.), *Sentence processing: Psycholinguistic studies presented to Merrill Garrett* (pp. 295–342). Hillsdale, NJ: Lawrence Erlbaum Associates Inc.

Shattuck-Hufnagel, S. (1983). Sublexical units and suprasegmental structure in speech production planning. In P.F. MacNeilage (Ed.), *The production of speech* (pp. 109–136). New York: Springer.

Shattuck-Hufnagel, S. (1986). The representation of phonological information during speech production. *Phonology Yearbook, 3,* 117–149.

Shattuck-Hufnagel, S. (1987). The role of word-onset consonants in speech production planning. New evidence from speech error patterns. In E. Keller & M. Gopnik (Eds.), *Motor and sensory processes of language* (pp. 17–51). Hillsdale, NJ: Lawrence Erlbaum Associates Inc.

Shattuck-Hufnagel, S. (1992). The role of word structure in segmental serial ordering. *Cognition, 42*, 213–259.

Shattuck-Hufnagel, S., & Klatt, D.H. (1979). The limited use of distinctive features and markedness in speech production: Evidence from speech error data. *Journal of Verbal Learning and Verbal Behavior, 18*, 41–55.

Spencer, A. (1991). *Morphological theory: An introduction to word structure in generative grammar.* Cambridge, MA: Blackwell.

Stemberger, J.P. (1982). The nature of segments in the lexicon: Evidence from speech errors. *Lingua, 56*, 43–65.

Stemberger, J.P. (1983). The nature of /r/ and /l/ in English: Evidence from speech errors. *Journal of Phonetics, 11*, 139–147.

Stemberger, J.P. (1984). Length as a suprasegmental: Evidence from speech errors. *Language, 60*, 895–913.

Stemberger, J.P. (1990). Wordshape errors in language production. *Cognition, 35*, 123–157.

Stemberger, J.P. (1991a). Apparent anti-frequency effects in language production: The addition bias and phonological underspecification. *Journal of Memory and Language, 30*, 161–185.

Stemberger, J.P. (1991b). Radical underspecification in language production. *Phonology, 8*, 73–112.

Stemberger, J.P., & MacWhinney, B. (1986). Form-oriented inflectional errors in language processing. *Cognitive Psychology, 18*, 329–354.

Stemberger, J.P., & Stoel-Gammon, C. (1991). The underspecification of coronals: Evidence from language acquisition and performance errors. *Phonetics and Phonology, 2*, 181–199.

Stevens, K.N. (1989). On the quantal nature of speech. *Journal of Phonetics, 17*, 3–45.

Turvey, M.T. (1990). Coordination. *American Psychologist, 45*, 938–953.

Wells, R. (1973). Predicting slips of the tongue. In V.A. Fromkin (Ed.), *Speech errors as linguistic evidence* (pp. 82–87). The Hague, The Netherlands: Mouton. (Original work published 1951)

Wheeler, D.W., & Touretzky, D.S. (1997). A parallel licensing model of normal slips and phonemic paraphasias. *Brain and Language, 59*, 147–201.

Wilshire, C. (1998). Serial order in phonological encoding: An exploration of the "word onset effect" using laboratory-induced errors. *Cognition, 68*, 143–166.

CHAPTER FOUR

WEAVER++ and other computational models of lemma retrieval and word-form encoding

Ardi Roelofs
Max Planck Institute for Psycholinguistics, Nijmegen,
The Netherlands

INTRODUCTION

A basic skill of speakers is the access of words in memory. In producing utterances, speakers call on many facets of their stored knowledge about words,
including their meaning, syntactic properties, morphological composition, and
sound structure. Lexical access is the process by which this information about
words is retrieved from memory in order to map a lexical concept onto an
articulatory program. The access consists of two major steps: lemma retrieval
and word-form encoding (cf., Levelt, 1989; but see Caramazza, 1997). In lemma
retrieval, a lexical concept is used to retrieve the lemma of a corresponding word
from memory. A lemma, as the term is used in this chapter, is a memory
representation of the syntactic properties of a word, crucial for its use in sentences
(Roelofs, 1992a, 1993). For example, the lemma of the Dutch word *sigaar*
(*cigar*) says that it is a noun and that its grammatical gender is non-neuter. In
word-form encoding, the lemma is used to retrieve the morpho-phonological
properties of the word from memory in order to construct an articulatory program.
For example, for *sigaar* the morpheme <sigaar> and the segments /s/, /i/, /ɣ/, /a/,
and /r/ are retrieved and a phonetic plan for [si.'ɣar] is generated.

   In this chapter, I provide a detailed comparison of the two most widely
discussed computational models of lemma retrieval and word-form encoding:
the classical spreading-activation model of Dell and colleagues (Dell, 1986,
1988, 1990; Dell & O'Seaghdha, 1991, 1992; Dell, Schwartz, Martin, Saffran, &
Gagnon, 1997; Peterson, Dell, & O'Seaghdha, 1989) and the WEAVER++ model

(Levelt, Roelofs, & Meyer, 1999a,b; Roelofs, 1992a, 1993, 1994, 1996a,b,c, 1997a,b,c, 1998, 1999; Roelofs & Meyer, 1998; Roelofs, Meyer, & Levelt, 1996, 1998), which has been developed within Levelt's (1989, 1992) general theoretical framework for speech production. The Dell model and WEAVER++ each have been designed to account for a wide variety of findings (see Levelt et al., 1999a, for a recent review of WEAVER++ applications). Unfortunately, the trend in the word production literature has been away from trying to simultane-ously account for a lot of data in favour of a focus on one or two findings (e.g., Caramazza, 1997; Cutting & Ferreira, 1999; Harley, 1993; Schade & Berg, 1992; Starreveld & La Heij, 1996). Occasionally, I make reference to these more limited models, some of which have not been computationally implemented (e.g., Caramazza, 1997).

Dell's model has been designed to account for speech errors, which con-stitute the traditional database for production research and modelling (e.g., Harley, 1993; Schade & Berg, 1992). In recent years, however, researchers have started to use chronometrical techniques and have collected production latency data. The WEAVER++ model recognises the key insights from speech errors, but has specifically been designed to provide a unifying account of the increasing body of chronometrical data. I start by describing Levelt's (1989, 1992) general the-oretical framework for lexical access. Next, I review the Dell model and its application to speech errors. Finally, I explain WEAVER++. I show that this latter model accounts for production latency data and that it is compatible with findings on speech errors.

Role of lexical access in speech production

Figure 4.1 illustrates the three major types of processes that underlie speaking: conceptualisation, formulation, and articulation. Conceptualisation processes generate so-called messages, that is, conceptual structures to be verbally ex-pressed. In WEAVER++, messages are specified in terms of lexical concepts. Messages may, for example, be derived from external scenes via object per-ception. Formulation processes take the message, access appropriate words (i.e., nouns, verbs, adjectives, etc.) for the lexical concepts, and build a syntactic structure and a morpho-phonological structure. The result is a phonetic plan (articulatory program) for the utterance. In WEAVER++, the phonetic plan makes explicit motor programs for the syllables in the utterance. Finally, articulation processes execute the articulatory program, resulting in overt speech.

As indicated, lexical access consists of lemma retrieval and word-form encod-ing, which are stages of access that are part of the formulation stages of syntactic and morpho-phonological encoding, respectively. In lemma retrieval, a lexical concept is used to retrieve a lemma from memory, which is a representation of the syntactic properties of a word, crucial for its use in sentences. Lemma retrieval makes these properties available for syntactic encoding processes (e.g.,

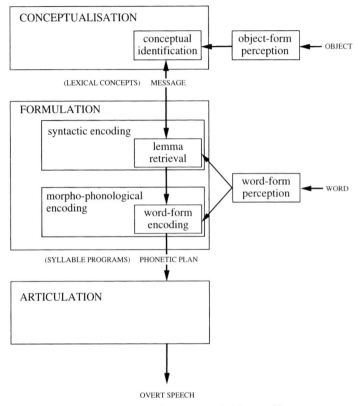

Figure 4.1.   Types of processes underlying speaking.

Kempen & Hoenkamp, 1987). Furthermore, lemmas contain slots for the specifica-tion of abstract morpho-syntactic parameters such as mood (e.g., indicative), tense (e.g., past, present), number (i.e., singular, plural), and person (i.e., first, second, third). In word-form encoding, a lemma and its parameter values are used to recover the appropriate morpho-phonological properties from memory in order to construct a phonetic plan. Lexical access may be initiated by a message, but also by a perceived spoken or written word. WEAVER++ assumes that a perceived word activates lemmas and word forms in parallel (see Figure 4.1).

Stages of lexical access

Figure 4.2 illustrates the further division of stages of access in WEAVER++. Assume a Dutch speaker sees a cigar and wants to name it. Lexical access consists of mapping the lexical concept CIGAR(X) onto the articulatory program for *sigaar*. First, the lemma retriever takes CIGAR(X) and delivers the lemma

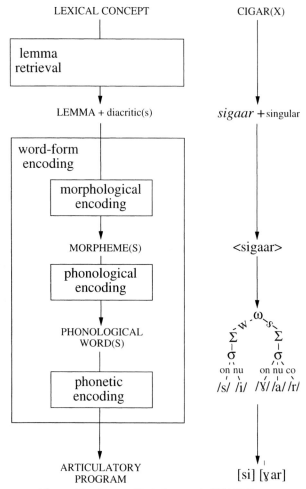

Figure 4.2.   Stages of lexical access in WEAVER++.

of *sigaar*. That is, it makes available the syntactic class "noun", grammatical gender "non-neuter", and so forth. To derive the appropriate word form, singular [si.'ɣar] instead of plural [si.'ɣa.rə], the word's number has to be specified. Therefore, the lemma retriever has to inspect the message for number information and to set the lemma's number parameter. The lemma plus number diacritic are then input to word-form encoding. The articulatory program is derived in three major steps: morphological encoding, phonological encoding, and phonetic encoding (cf., Dell, 1986; Levelt, 1989). The morphological encoder takes the lemma of *sigaar* plus the parameter value "singular" and produces the stem morpheme <sigaar>. The phonological encoder takes this morpheme, spells out its segments, syllabifies them, and assigns a stress pattern. Thereby it produces a so-called phonological word representation. This representation describes the singular form of *sigaar* as a phonological word (ω) consisting of two feet (Σ), one metrically strong (s) and the other weak (w). The first syllable (σ) has /s/ as onset and /i/ as nucleus. The second, stressed syllable has /ɣ/ as onset, /a/ as nucleus, and /r/ as coda. Finally, the phonetic encoder takes this phonological word representation, accesses a syllabary of learned motor programs for syllables (Levelt & Wheeldon, 1994), and delivers the corresponding articulatory program for [si.'ɣar].

Although this functional architecture has been developed on the basis of behavioural evidence (e.g., Levelt, 1989; Levelt et al., 1999a; Roelofs, 1992a, 1997c), it is receiving increasing support from studies such as MEG (magnetoencephalography: Levelt, Praamstra, Meyer, Helenius, & Salmelin, 1998), LRP (lateralised readiness potentials: Van Turennout, Hagoort, & Brown, 1997, 1998), PET (positron emission tomography), and fMRI (functional magnetic resonance imaging). Recently, Indefrey and Levelt (2000) performed a meta-analysis of 58 brain imaging studies in the literature, which anatomically located this functional architecture in the brain. As can be expected from the classical neuropsychology literature (e.g., Wernicke, 1874) and most later studies, the system is basically located in the left hemisphere. Visual and conceptual processing appears to involve the occipital, ventro-temporal, and anterior frontal regions of the brain; the middle part of the left middle temporal gyrus seems to be involved with lemma retrieval (the activity in these areas occurs within the first 275 ms after a to-be-named object is presented). Next, activation spreads to Wernicke's area, where the phonological code of the word appears to be retrieved; activation is then transmitted to Broca's area and the left mid superior temporal lobe for postlexical phonological processing such as syllabification (taking some 125 ms). Finally, phonetic encoding takes places (for the next 200 ms), with a contribution of the supplementary motor area (SMA) and the cerebellum, while the sensory-motor areas control articulation.

Classical support for the stages

The classical behavioural support for a distinction between lemma retrieval and word-form encoding comes from speech errors. A lemma level of encoding explains the different distribution of word and segment exchanges. Word exchanges such as the exchange of *roof* and *list* in "we completely forgot to add the list to the roof" (from Garrett, 1980) typically concern elements from different phrases and of the same syntactic category, here noun. By contrast, segment exchanges such as "she is a real rack pat" for "pack rat" (from Garrett, 1988) typically concern elements from the same phrase and do not respect lexical category. This finding is readily explained by assuming an exchange of lemmas during syntactic encoding and an exchange of segments during word-form encoding.

Speech errors also provide support for a morphological level of form encoding that is distinct from a lemma level with abstract morpho-syntactic parameters. Some morphemic errors appear to concern the lemma level, whereas others involve the form level (e.g., Dell, 1986; Garrett, 1975, 1980, 1988). For example, in "how many pies does it take to make an apple?" (from Garrett, 1988), the interacting stems belong to the same syntactic category (i.e., noun) and come from distinct phrases. Note that the plurality of *apple* is stranded, that is, it is realised on *pie*. Thus, the number parameter is set after the exchange. The distributional properties of these morpheme exchanges are similar to those of whole-word exchanges. This suggests that these morpheme errors and whole-word errors occur at the same level of processing, namely when lemmas in a developing syntactic structure trade places. Similarly, errors such as "I'd hear one if I knew it" for "I'd know one if I heard it" (from Garrett, 1980) suggest that syntactically specified lexical representations (lemmas) may trade places independently of their concrete morpho-phonological specifications. By contrast, the exchanging morphemes in an error such as "slicely thinned" (from Stemberger, 1985) belong to different syntactic categories (adjective and verb) and come from the same phrase, which is also characteristic of segment exchanges. This suggests that this second type of morpheme error and segment errors occur at the same level of processing, namely the level at which morphemes and segments are retrieved and the morpho-phonological form of the utterance is constructed. The errors occur when morphemes in a developing morpho-phonological structure trade places.

THE CLASSICAL SPREADING-ACTIVATION MODEL: DELL (1986, 1988)

The model of Dell (1986, 1988) assumes stages of access similar to those of WEAVER++ described earlier, but there are also some important differences. For example, the Dell model does not make the claim that the output of phonological encoding is a phonological word representation and it does not assume a syllabary.

Basic tenets

Dell (1986, 1988; Dell & O'Seaghdha, 1991, 1992) assumes that the mental lexicon is a network that is accessed by spreading activation. Figure 4.3 illustrates the lexical entry of *sigaar*. The nodes in the network are associated to each other by equally weighed bidirectional connections. The network contains nodes for conceptual features (e.g., MADE-OF-TOBACCO(X), IS-FOR-SMOKING(X), etc.), lemmas (e.g., *sigaar*), morphemes (e.g., <sigaar>), syllables (e.g., si and ɣar), segments (marked for syllable position, e.g., /onset s/, /nucleus i/, /onset ɣ/, /nucleus a/, and /coda r/), and phonological features (e.g., voiced). Phonological feature nodes are left out of the figure for reasons of simplicity. Furthermore,

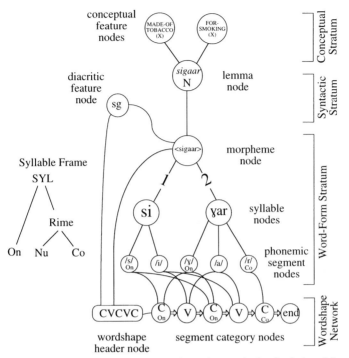

Figure 4.3.   Representation of the Dutch word *sigaar* in the classical model.

there are wordshape header nodes and segment category nodes, specifying the abstract CV structure of a word (Dell, 1988).

Lexical access starts by supplying a jolt of activation to the set of conceptual features making up the intended thought. Activation then spreads through the network following a linear activation function with a decay factor. Lemma retrieval, morphological encoding, and phonological encoding are accomplished by successively selecting the most highly activated lemma node, morpheme nodes, and segment nodes at certain moments in time. The time interval between the successive selections has a constant duration whose value depends on the speech rate. Selected nodes are serially ordered by inserting them into slots of independently created frames (i.e., syntactic, morphological, and syllable frames). For example, the /onset s/ node is inserted into the onset slot of the first syllable frame of *sigaar*. To prevent that, for example, the /onset ɣ/ of *sigaar* or the onset of another morpheme or word is inserted, lemmas, morphemes, and syllables making up an utterance are serially encoded. The serial encoding of the syllables of a polysyllabic word such as *sigaar* is achieved by invoking a procedure that temporarily increases the spreading rate r between the morpheme node <sigaar> and the syllable node for the first target syllable (i.e., si) and decreasing it for the other one (i.e., ɣar), and vice versa for the encoding of the second syllable.

Although the model includes a level of phonological feature nodes, it does not specify how phonetic encoding is accomplished.

Accounting for speech errors

The classical spreading-activation model has been designed to account for facts about speech errors: the kind of errors that occur and the constraints on their form and occurrence. Errors occur when, due to noise in the system, another node than the target is the most highly activated node and gets erroneously selected. The model accounts for a large variety of findings about speech errors. I mention a few major accomplishments (following Dell, 1986).

First, the model accounts for error biases such as the so-called phonological facilitation of semantic substitution errors (Dell & Reich, 1981). When *cat* is intended, the substitution *rat* for *cat* is more likely than *dog* for *cat* (if error opportunities are taken into account). Semantic substitution errors are taken to be failures in lemma node selection. The word *rat* shares segments with the target *cat*. So, the lemma node of *rat* receives feedback from these shared segments (i.e., /nucleus æ/, /coda t/), whereas the lemma node of *dog* does not. Consequently, the lemma node of *rat* will have a higher level of activation than the lemma node of *dog*, and *rat* is more likely to be involved in a lemma selection error resulting in a word substitution. Errors such as substituting *rat* for *cat* are called "mixed" errors because the erroneous words share both semantic and phonological properties with the target.

Second, the model accounts for lexical bias, that is, for the fact that speech errors tend to yield real words rather than nonwords (again, if error opportunities are taken into account). For example, in producing *cat*, the error /h/ for /k/ is more likely than /j/ for /k/, because *hat* is a word but *jat* is not. Again, this bias is due to feedback, now from shared segment nodes to morpheme nodes (e.g., from /nucleus æ/ and /coda t/ to <cat> and <hat>) and from these morpheme nodes to other segment nodes (i.e., from <cat> to /onset k/ and from <hat> to /onset h/). This will not occur for nonwords, because there are no morpheme nodes for such items in the network (i.e., there is no node <jat> to activate /onset j/).

Third, the model accounts for the relative frequencies of segmental substitution errors. Anticipations are more likely than perseverations, and exchanges have the lowest probability (Nooteboom, 1969). For example, the anticipation error <u>s</u>ed sock for red sock is more likely than the perseveration red <u>r</u>ock, which is in its turn more likely than the exchange <u>s</u>ed <u>r</u>ock. The anticipation bias is a built-in feature of the model: Upcoming words also receive a jolt of activation (less than the target). In the model, exchanges occur the least because they are double errors involving both an anticipation and a perseveration. It should be mentioned, however, that some researchers have argued that it is not clear that anticipations are more common than exchanges, since interrupted errors (by far the most numerous form) could have been either. Shattuck-Hufnagel (1987) argued that exchanges are not simply a concatenation of an anticipatory and a perseveratory substitution, but occur under different conditions.

Finally, the model accounts for effects of speech rate on error probabilities. Errors are more likely when one speaks faster. It takes time for activation to spread through the network. At high speech rates, activation levels of nodes at the time of selection are not so high yet, so the system is more vulnerable to selection errors due to small random fluctuations of activation levels. Furthermore, if speech rate decreases, the likelihood of exchange errors decreases too (Dell, 1986). For an exchange to occur, first an anticipation error has to be made, /onset s/ for /onset r/ (yielding _sed_ instead of _red_), and next the /onset r/ still has to be available for selection, /onset r/ for /onset s/ (yielding _sock_ instead of _rock_). This is more likely at high speech rates, because the time interval between the successive selections is then small so that the activation of /onset r/ has not been decayed yet.

In summary, the model of Dell does a good job in accounting for many facts about speech errors, such as the statistical overrepresentation of mixed errors, lexical bias, the (presumed) relative frequency of segment anticipations, perseverations, and exchanges, and effects of speech rate on these errors. A number of problems with the model, however, have motivated the development of WEAVER++.

PROBLEMS WITH THE CLASSICAL SPREADING-ACTIVATION MODEL

Convergence

In the classical spreading-activation model, lemmas are retrieved on the basis of sets of conceptual features (cf., Bierwisch & Schreuder, 1992). This confronts the model with a number of computational issues concerning convergence that have not been appropriately dealt with yet within the classical framework (see Levelt, 1989, and Roelofs, 1992a,b, 1993, 1996a, and especially 1997a, for extensive discussion). The convergence problem consists of a number of sub-problems: (1) How to correctly dissect a thought into lexical concepts during message encoding, (2) how to avoid retrieving hyponyms or hyperonyms along with or instead of the intended words, and (3) how to correctly retrieve a single word instead of several words for a synonymous phrase.

Conceptually driven word retrieval does not appear to proceed by trial-and-error. Word meanings typically evade definition (e.g., Fodor, Garrett, Walker, & Parkes, 1980), but speakers seem to know exactly what conceptual information to prepare to access words efficiently. The dissection problem (Levelt, 1992) concerns the issue of how the message encoder knows which sets of conceptual feature nodes correspond to lexical concepts. For example, the thought MALE PARENT (i.e., FATHER) constitutes a lexical concept but the thought YOUNG

PARENT does not. But only lexical concepts can be verbalised by a single word. Furthermore, in the classical model, the lemma of *sigaar* is retrieved by activating features such as MADE-OF-TOBACCO(X), IS-FOR-SMOKING(X), and so forth. In the traditional view, the set of features of a more specific word such as *Havanna* (*Havana cigar*) contains those of its hyperonyms *sigaar* (*cigar*) as a proper subset (i.e., *Havanna* has all the features of *sigaar* plus some extra ones such as ORIGINALLY-FROM-CUBA(X)). The classical model fails to explain how the system knows which subset of features of a word corresponds to the meaning of its hyperonyms. That is, which features should be given a jolt of activation in retrieving a word. The model has to be changed to solve this problem, perhaps by embedding the conceptual feature nodes in a constraint satisfaction network (cf., the model of Harley, 1993). Lexical concepts may then correspond to stable states of the network.

The words *parent* and *father* may refer to the same person. The hyponym problem is the question of how to avoid retrieving the hyponym *father* along with or instead of the hyperonym *parent*. The node of the conceptual primitive PARENT(X,Y) is linked to the lemma nodes of *parent* and *father*, so both lemmas will attain the same level of activation. This problem may perhaps be solved by giving up the notion of a general spreading rate r and tuning the weights on the links (e.g., by a learning process). The feature PARENT(X,Y) should be strongly connected to *parent* but weakly to *father*.

The word *father* and the phrase "male parent" may refer to the same person. The synonymy problem concerns the issue of how to avoid retrieving *father* along with or instead of *male* and *parent* for the phrase "male parent", or vice versa. Tuning weights is insufficient to solve this problem, because the same primitives are involved in producing the single word and the phrase. Perhaps this problem may be solved by sequentially activating the conceptual primitives in producing a phrase. However, there is empirical evidence that suggests that lemmas making up a phrase are planned in parallel (Meyer, 1996).

In summary, the conceptually decomposed retrieval of lemmas in the classical model confronts it with a number of convergence problems concerning the dissection of messages, hyponymy, and word-to-phrase synonymy. Perhaps, each of these problems may be solved within the model in one way or another, but the solutions are ad hoc. What is lacking is a principled solution to the class of convergence problems as a whole.

Binding and latencies

The binding problem is the issue of how to correctly retrieve the lemmas, morphemes, and segments of a word in the context of the activation of the lemmas, morphemes, and segments of another word. That is, how to keep the planning of a word insulated from interfering cross-talk, for example, from the concurrent planning of other words in connected speech or from seeing words or hearing words spoken by an interlocutor (see Roelofs, 1997c, for an extensive discussion). In the classical spreading-activation model, binding is achieved by imposing severe temporal constraints on the planning process. Suppose that a Dutch speaker wants to produce the utterance "haal eens wat sigaren" ("just get me some cigars"). In order to produce this utterance, the speech segments of the morphemes <wat>, <sigaar>, and <en>, among others, have to be retrieved from memory. In retrieving the segments and assigning them to the correct production slots, the speech production system has to keep track of what goes with what. That is, it has to know that the /onset s/ is retrieved for <sigaar> and the /onset w/ for <wat>. Otherwise, the /onset w/ and /onset s/ may trade places and "<u>s</u>at <u>w</u>igaren" might be produced instead of "wat sigaren". To avoid this indexing problem and the resulting segmental errors, the classical model assumes that only one morpheme is spelled out at a time. That is, during the encoding of <wat>, only /onset w/, /nucleus ɑ/, and /coda t/ are available, so the /onset s/ of <sigaar> will not become selected. This may be called "binding by timing". Binding by timing is at the heart of the classical account of speech errors. Errors occur during the rare event that, due to noise in the system, a segment of another word is the highest activated one and gets erroneously selected. For example, an error occurs when during the encoding of <wat>, the /onset s/ of <sigaar> has a higher level of activation than the /onset w/, and the /onset s/ gets selected as the onset of <wat>.

However, Meyer and Schriefers (1991) have shown that speakers do not make large numbers of errors when several words are available simultaneously under experimental conditions. For example, if Dutch speakers have to name a pictured object (e.g., a cigar) and they hear a word sharing some of its final segments (e.g., /ɣi.tar/, *guitar*), this perceived word helps (i.e., speeds up) naming the object instead of causing trouble in selecting the correct segments. Simulations by Peterson et al. (1989) have shown, however, that the classical model predicts massive amounts of errors. In a priming situation with high-frequency targets and distractors, the probability of selection of a critical target segment (at a time step determined by the lemma's activation level) was $p = .45$. However, in picture–word interference experiments the error rate is about 5% rather than the 50% predicted by the classical model. Similarly, producing the hyperonym of the name of a picture (e.g., saying *furniture* to a table) is speeded up by a semantically related distractor word (e.g., *chair*). And the distractor *chair* inhibits the production of *table*, without yielding massive amounts of errors (e.g., Glaser, 1992; Glaser & Düngelhoff, 1984). In the classical model selection takes place on an ordinal basis as the most highly activated node is selected. So, priming may affect levels of activation, but it will not affect latencies. When it comes time to select nodes, the target node is either the most highly activated node and gets selected (priming will not affect this) or it is not the most highly activated node (due to priming of another node) and an error occurs. So, the low error rate and the latency effects are not to be expected.

In summary, the Dell model attributes speech errors to sporadic interference from the concurrent planning of other words or the hearing of words spoken by interlocutors. However, when multiple words are activated under experimental conditions, planning times are affected but almost no errors are made. Yet, the Dell model predicts massive amounts of errors but no latency effect, exactly contrary to the empirical findings. This suggests that some other mechanism than timing solves the binding problem.

Syllabification and phonetic encoding

The task for a binding mechanism is often even more complex than keeping the segments of different words apart, because binding may be context dependent. That is, sometimes the binding of segments to slots has to ignore morpheme and word boundaries in that a segment of one morpheme or word has to be bound to another morpheme or word. This occurs in the production of polymorphemic words and connected speech. By rigidly storing words as sequences of syllable nodes and storing each consonant as an onset or coda, models such as that of Dell (1988) and Schade and Berg (1992) have a difficult time dealing with the context-dependence of syllable membership (see Roelofs, 1997b, for an extensive discussion).

Consider the production of the plural form *sigaren* of the word *sigaar*. The plural *sigaren* is created by adding <en> ([ə]) to the stem <sigaar>. The resulting form is syllabified as $(si)_\sigma (\gamma a)_\sigma (r\partial)_\sigma$. Thus, juxtaposing *–en* changes the syllabification of /r/. This segment occupies a coda position in *sigaar*, syllabified as $(si)_\sigma (\gamma ar)_\sigma$, but an onset position in *sigaren*. Or consider the production of connected speech involving clitics. Clitics are forms of function words such as pronouns, determiners, particles, auxiliary verbs, prepositions, and conjunctions that are phonologically dependent on a host (e.g., Booij, 1995; Levelt, 1989). For example, the reduced form *'s* [əs] of the Dutch adverb *eens* (*just*) cannot stand alone. In producing "probeer die sigaar 's" ("just try that cigar"), *'s* is adjoined to *sigaar*. This yields the new phonological word *sigaar 's*, which is syllabified as $(si)_\sigma (\gamma a)_\sigma (r\partial s)_\sigma$. In the classical model, segments are marked for syllable position, so we have /coda r/ in the network for *sigaar*. The selection rule in this model prohibits selecting this coda node for the onset slot of a syllable frame, which would be required for the production of *sigaren* and *sigaar 's*.

Word-form encoding does not end with syllabification. The generated phonological representation has to be mapped onto a context-dependent phonetic representation that can guide articulation. But the classical model does not have a phonetic level of encoding and therefore does not account well, for example, for assimilation and allophonic variation of speech segments. Although the model has a level of phonological feature nodes connected to segment nodes, it does not say much of anything about phonetic encoding.

In summary, syllabification across morpheme and word boundaries poses difficulty to the classical model. This is because the model stores each word as a sequence of syllable nodes and each consonant as an onset or coda. Furthermore, the classical model lacks a level of phonetic encoding. In the remainder of this chapter, I first explain the WEAVER++ model and show how it solves the problems and how it accounts for production latencies. Next, I review several empirical tests of the model concerning production latencies. Finally, I show that WEAVER++ is compatible with speech error data. The WEAVER++ model has limitations (see Levelt et al., 1999a,b, and commentaries), but I believe it is a step towards a psychologically and computationally correct model of lexical access in spoken word production.

THE WEAVER++ MODEL

Over the past several years, a computational model has been developed on the basis of insights obtained with a chronometrical approach rather than the traditional approach of speech error analysis (e.g., Levelt, 1989, 1992; Levelt et al., 1991; Levelt & Wheeldon, 1994; Meyer, 1990, 1991; Meyer & Schriefers, 1991; Roelofs, 1992a, 1993, 1994, 1996a,b,c, 1997a,b,c, 1998, 1999; Roelofs & Meyer, 1998; Roelofs et al., 1996, 1998). The word-form encoding part of this model is called WEAVER (an acronym standing for Word-form Encoding by Activation and VERification) and the full model including lemma retrieval is called WEAVER++. As the classical spreading-activation model, WEAVER++ assumes that the mental lexicon is a network of nodes and links that is accessed by spreading of activation. In order to deal with the issues discussed earlier, a few new assumptions have been made.

The WEAVER++ model handles the dissection problem, the word-to-phrase synonymy problem, and the other convergence problems by assuming that each lexical concept is represented in the network by an independent node (cf., Collins & Loftus, 1975). For example, the network contains the nodes CIGAR(X) and TOBACCO(X) connected by a link labelled IS-MADE-OF. The node CIGAR(X) is connected to the lemma node for *sigaar*. Lemmas are accessed from the lexical concept nodes (cf., Fodor et al., 1980) rather than directly from sets of conceptual feature nodes. Since lexical concepts may differ between languages, this view entails that message encoding includes some form of "thinking for speaking". That is, speakers engage in language-specific thinking while they are speaking. I refer to Levinson (1997), Roelofs (1992b, 1997a), and Slobin (1996) for an extensive discussion of this view and its empirical justification.

The WEAVER++ model handles the binding problem, first, by assuming that the relationships between nodes are explicitly coded in the network by labels on the links (e.g., the link between <sigaar> and /s/ says that /s/ is the first segment of <sigaar>), and second, by assuming that the links are verified by the access algorithm. This allows the algorithm to keep track of what goes with what, without the need for special temporal restrictions and without the need to change spreading rates.

The model handles the problem of syllabification across morpheme and word boundaries by assuming that syllable positions are not stored with words in memory as in the classical model (e.g., there are no /onset r/ and /coda r/ nodes), but that syllable positions are assigned on-line by a syllabification process (Levelt, 1992). The assignment of segments to syllable positions takes neighbouring morphemes and words into account. Syllable positions of segments are computed for phonological words rather than for lexical ones.

The model handles the problem of phonetic encoding by assuming that speakers have a syllabary, a store of motor programs for syllables, which is accessed on the basis of the phonological syllables constructed as part of phonological word representations (Levelt & Wheeldon, 1994). The programs make explicit the gestural scores for the articulatory movements (cf., Browman & Goldstein, 1986). The syllabary does not have to contain many programs. Statistical analyses have revealed that 500 different syllables already cover about 85% of the Dutch syllable tokens (cf., Levelt et al., 1999a). Since not all instances of a given syllable are articulated in exactly the same way, some further articulatory programming may be needed once the programs are retrieved from the syllabary (see Levelt, 1989), but this programming is limited.

The WEAVER++ model integrates a spreading-activation based network with a parallel object-oriented production-rule system (Levelt et al., 1999a; Roelofs, 1992a, 1994, 1996c, 1997c). The type of system is a mix of traditional AI, connectionism, and traditional cognitive modeling (cf., Anderson, 1983). Words are not planned by a central agent that overlooks the whole process but by teams of production rules (condition-action pairs) that work in parallel on small parts of the word (like several spiders making a single web). The production rules are stored with the nodes and have a limited overview only. Activation of nodes in the network triggers production rules that choose lemmas and incrementally build phonetic plans by selecting and connecting nodes. Upon activation of a node, a production rule verifies the link between the node and the selected nodes one level up in the network. Syntactic production rules select the lemma node linked to the target lexical concept node. Morphological production rules select the morpheme nodes that appropriately encode a selected lemma node and its tense, agreement, and mood parameters. Phonological production rules select the segments linked to the morpheme nodes and prosodify the segments in order to construct phonological word representations. And finally, phonetic production rules select the syllable program nodes that appropriately encode the constructed phonological syllables, and access the corresponding syllable programs in the syllabary.

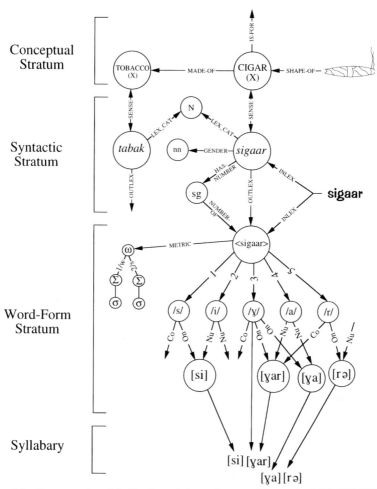

Figure 4.4.   Representation of the Dutch word *sigaar* plus part of the word *tabak* in WEAVER++.

Network structure

Figure 4.4 illustrates the structure of entries in WEAVER++'s lexical network, in particular, the memory representation of *sigaar* plus part of the representation of *tabak* (*tobacco*). A lexical network with nodes and labelled links is connected to a syllabary with learned motor programs for syllables. The lexical network consists of three major strata: a conceptual stratum, a syntactic stratum, and a word-form stratum. The conceptual stratum contains concept nodes and labelled conceptual links. Each lexical concept in the language, for example CIGAR(X), is represented by an independent node. The links specify conceptual relationships, for example, between a concept and its properties such as TOBACCO(X). The syntactic stratum contains lemma nodes (*sigaar*), syntactic property nodes and labelled links (gender: non-neuter; lexical category: noun), and slots for the specification of parameters (number: {singular, plural}). The word-form stratum contains metrical structure, morpheme, segment, and syllable program nodes and links. Morpheme nodes are connected to a lemma and its diacritics. The links between morphemes and segments specify the serial position of the segments. The links between segments and syllable program nodes specify possible—as opposed to actual—syllabifications. The word-form stratum is connected to a syllabary, storing ready-made motor programs for syllables. I now explain the lexical access algorithm. First, I review WEAVER++'s assumptions about lemma retrieval and some applications of the model, and next the assumptions about word-form encoding and some applications.

Lemma retrieval

Basic tenets

A basic theoretical claim implemented in WEAVER++ is that lemmas are retrieved in a conceptually non-decomposed way, that is, for example, the noun *sigaar* is retrieved on the basis of the chunk CIGAR(X) instead of features such as MADE-OF-TOBACCO(X), IS-FOR-SMOKING(X), and so forth. Each lexical concept in the language is represented by an independent node in the network. Retrieval starts by enhancing the level of activation of the node of the target lexical concept. Activation then spreads through the network, each node sending a proportion of its activation to connected nodes. The most highly activated lemma node is selected. For example, in verbalising the thought CIGAR, the activation level of the lexical concept node CIGAR(X) is enhanced. Activation spreads through the network, whereby the lemma nodes *sigaar* and *tabak*, among others, will be activated. The *sigaar* node will become the most highly activated node, because it receives a full proportion of the activation of CIGAR(X), whereas *tabak* and other lemma nodes receive a proportion of a proportion of the activation of CIGAR(X). Upon verification of the link between the lemma node of *sigaar* and CIGAR(X), this lemma node will be selected. Roelofs (1997a) gives a mathematical convergence proof for this retrieval algorithm.

The equations that formalise WEAVER++ are given in Roelofs (1992a, 1993, 1994, 1996c, 1997c). There are simple equations for the spreading of activation and the instantaneous selection probability of lemma and syllable program nodes, that is, the hazard rate of the lemma retrieval and word-form encoding process. The selection probability of a lemma node (syllable program node) equals the ratio of its activation and that of all the other lemma nodes (syllable program nodes). Given the selection ratio, the mathematical expectation of the retrieval (and encoding) time can be computed.

Some applications

SOA curves of semantic effects.   The retrieval algorithm explains, among other phenomena, the classical SOA curves of the semantic effects of picture and word distractors in picture naming, picture categorising, and word categorising. The basic experimental situation is as follows. Participants have to name pictured objects while trying to ignore written distractor words superimposed on the pictures. For example, they have to say *chair* to a pictured chair and ignore the word *bed* (semantically related) or the word *fish* (semantically unrelated). There is also a so-called stimulus onset asynchrony (SOA) manipulation. The written distractors are presented 400, 300, 200, 100 ms before (called negative SOAs), simultaneously with, or 100, 200, 300, 400 ms after picture onset (called positive SOAs). The classical finding is a semantic inhibition effect in a small SOA window ranging from −100 to +100 ms.

Panel A of Figure 4.5 gives the SOA curves. I have plotted the semantic effect (i.e., the difference between the naming latencies with related and unrelated distractors) against SOA. Thus, a positive difference indicates a semantic inhibition effect. The real data are from Glaser and Düngelhoff (1984). Semantic inhibition is obtained at SOA −100, 0, and 100 ms. The predictions by WEAVER++ are also indicated. As can be seen (and has been shown by a stringent statistical measure of fit), the model fits the data.

How does WEAVER++ explain these findings? I illustrate the explanation using the miniature network given in Figure 4.6. The figure illustrates the conceptual stratum and the syntactic stratum of two semantic fields: furniture and animals. Thus, there are lexical concepts nodes (e.g., BED(X)) and lemma nodes (e.g., *bed*). Pictures have direct access to the conceptual stratum and words have direct access to the syntactic stratum (see Figures 4.1 and 4.4). Assume *chair* is the target. Distractors are names of other pictures in the experiment. In the case of a pictured chair and distractor *bed*, activation from the picture and the distractor word will converge on the lemma of the distractor *bed*, due to the connections at the conceptual stratum. In the case of the unrelated distractor *fish* there will be no such convergence. Although the distractor *bed* will also activate the target *chair*, the pictured chair will prime the distractor lemma *bed* more than *bed* will prime the target lemma *chair* due to network distances: three links versus four links (pictured chair → CHAIR(X) → BED(X) → *bed* versus word bed → *bed* → BED(X) → CHAIR(X) → *chair*). Therefore, it will take longer before the activation of *chair* exceeds that of *bed* than that of *fish*. As a consequence, *bed* will be a stronger competitor than *fish*, which results in the semantic inhibition effect.

In WEAVER++, competition in lemma selection is "dynamic" rather than "hard wired". That is, in lemma retrieval a shortlist of target lemmas can be defined depending on the task that is set for the retrieval system (e.g., in a categorisation task the response set consists of hyperonyms such as *furniture*,

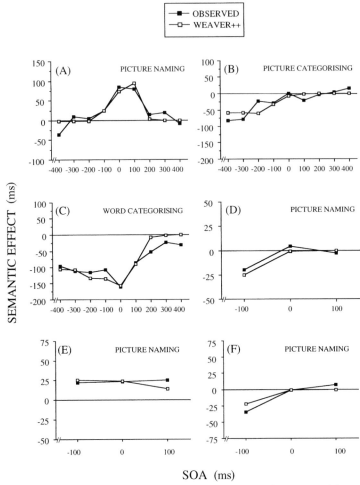

Figure 4.5. SOA curves of the semantic effects for picture naming, picture categorising, and word categorising: Empirical data (A, B, C: Glaser & Düngelhoff, 1984; D: Roelofs, 1992a; E, F: Roelofs, 1993) and predictions by WEAVER++.

animal, etc.). Competition is restricted to these shortlisted lemmas. The assumption is that speakers set up the shortlist before an experiment when they receive a booklet with the pictures and names to be used. Thus, in the model, only potential target responses will compete for selection. In case of picture or word categorisation, *furniture* and *animal* are the targets and will compete, but *chair*, *bed*, *fish*, and *dog* will not. The distractor *bed* superimposed on a pictured chair will activate the target *furniture* via the conceptual network, but *bed* will not be a competitor for *furniture* because *bed* is not a permitted response in the experiment. By contrast, *fish* on a pictured chair will activate *animal*, which is a

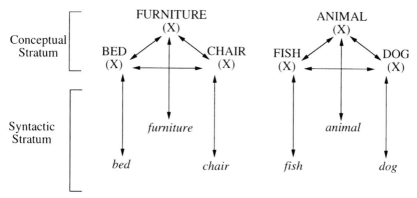

Figure 4.6.   Miniature network for furniture and animals in WEAVER++.

competitor of the target *furniture*. Thus, semantic facilitation is predicted and this is exactly what is empirically obtained.

Panel B of Figure 4.5 gives the results for picture categorising, for example, when participants have to say *furniture* to the pictured chair and ignore the distractor word. Again, the semantic effect is plotted against SOA. A negative difference indicates a semantic facilitation effect. The real data are from Glaser and Düngelhoff (1984). WEAVER++ fits the data. The same prediction holds for the same reasons for word categorising, for example, when participants have to say *furniture* to the word *chair* and ignore the distractor picture. Panel C of Figure 4.5 gives the results for word categorising. Again, WEAVER++ fits the data.

The prediction of semantic facilitation also holds for picture naming with hyperonym, co-hyponym, and hyponym distractors that are not part of the response set. For example, in naming a pictured chair (the only pictured piece of furniture in the experiment), the distractor words *furniture*, *bed*, or *throne* are superimposed. Semantic facilitation is indeed what is obtained (Roelofs, 1992a). Panel D of Figure 4.5 plots the semantic facilitation against SOA. The semantic effect was the same for hyperonym (*furniture*), co-hyponym (*bed*), and hyponym (*throne*) distractors, so the curves represent means across these types of word.

The WEAVER++ model is not restricted to the retrieval of noun lemmas. Thus, the same effects should be obtained in naming actions using verbs, for example, when participants have to say *drink* to a drinking person and ignore *eat* or *laugh* (names of other actions in the experiment). Indeed, again semantic inhibition is obtained, as shown in Panel E of Figure 4.5 (Roelofs, 1993). Facilitation is also predicted for hyponym distractors, for example, when participants have to say *drink* to a drinking person and ignore *booze* or *whimper* (not permitted responses in the experiment). Again semantic facilitation is obtained, as shown in Panel F of Figure 4.5 (Roelofs, 1993).

The finding of semantic facilitation from hyponyms excludes one type of solution to the hyperonym problem in lemma retrieval. Bierwisch and Schreuder (1992) have proposed a model in which the convergence problem is solved by inhibitory links between hyponyms and hyperonyms (i.e., words inhibit all their hyperonyms). For example, in producing *chair*, activating the lemma of *chair* leads automatically to inhibition of the lemma of its hyperonym *furniture*. However, the existence of such inhibitory links predicts semantic inhibition from hyponym distractors (e.g., distractor *throne* should inhibit target *chair*), but facilitation is what has been empirically obtained. As we saw, distractor *throne* facilitates the production of *chair* (see Figure 4.5 panels D and F). Also, the finding of semantic facilitation in picture and word categorising refutes such an inhibitory link between words and their hyperonyms (e.g., between *chair* and *furniture*). In general, the semantic facilitation effects pose difficulty to models in which lemma selection is achieved by hardwired lateral inhibition among lemmas, as in the models of Cutting and Ferreira (1999), Schade and Berg (1992), and Stemberger (1985). Semantic facilitation is difficult to explain if all activated lemmas always compete, that is, if *furniture* and *chair* always compete due to their inhibitory links. Instead, the facilitation suggests that in lemma retrieval, a shortlist of target lemmas can be defined depending on the task set for the retrieval system (e.g., in a categorisation task consisting of hyperonyms such as *furniture*, *animal*, etc.), with competition restricted to these shortlisted lemmas.

The semantic effect is obtained for nouns, verbs, and adjectives (e.g., colour, which is related to the classical Stroop effect) in producing words (Glaser, 1992; Roelofs, 1992a, 1993), but also for lexical access in producing phrases and sentences, as has been shown by Meyer (1996) and Schriefers (1993). Furthermore, Schriefers obtained interference effects due to the selection of grammatical gender (a particular type of lemma information) in producing phrases.

Computing agreement in producing phrases.   Schriefers (1993) asked Dutch participants to describe coloured objects using phrases. For example, they had to say "de groene tafel" ("the green table") or "groene tafel" ("green table"). In Dutch, the grammatical gender of the noun (*table*) determines which definite article should be chosen (*de* for non-neuter and *het* for neuter) or the inflection on the adjective (*groene* versus *groen*). On the pictured objects, written distractor words were superimposed that were either gender congruent or incongruent with the target. For example, the distractor *muis* (*mouse*) takes the same gender as the target *tafel*, namely non-neuter, whereas distractor *hemd* (*shirt*) takes neuter gender.

Schriefers obtained a gender congruency effect, as predicted by WEAVER++. Smaller production latencies were obtained when the distractor noun had the same gender as the target noun compared to a distractor with a different gender (see also Van Berkum, 1997). According to WEAVER++, this gender congruency effect should only be obtained when agreement has to be computed, that is, when the gender node has to be selected in order to choose the appropriate definite article or the gender marking on the adjective. It should not be obtained when participants have to produce bare nouns, that is, in "pure" object naming. WEAVER++ makes a distinction between activation of the lexical network and the actual selection of nodes. Lemma nodes point to grammatical gender nodes, but there are no backward pointers (see Figure 4.4). Thus, boosting the level of activation of the gender node by a gender-congruent distractor will not affect the level of activation of the target lemma node and therefore will not influence the selection of the lemma node. Consequently, priming a gender node will only affect lexical access when the gender node itself has to be selected, for example, when the gender node is needed for computing agreement. Thus, the gender congruency effect should only be obtained in producing gender-marked utterances, not in producing bare nouns. This corresponds exactly to what is empirically observed (Jescheniak, 1994; La Heij, Mak, Sander, & Willeboordse, 1998).

Interaction between semantic and orthographic factors.   Starreveld and La Heij (1995, 1996) observed that the semantic inhibition effect in picture naming is reduced when there is an orthographic relationship between the target and distractor word. Damian and Martin (1999) observed the same for spoken distractors. For example, in naming a pictured cat, the semantic inhibition was less for distractor word *calf* compared to *cap* than for distractor word *horse* compared to *house*. According to Starreveld and La Heij, the interaction suggests that lemmas do not exist or that there is feedback from the output morpho-phonological level to the lemma level (as in the models of Dell, 1986, 1988, and Harley, 1993), contrary to the claim of WEAVER++ that the output morpho-phonological network contains forward links only. However, as argued by Roelofs et al. (1996), in deriving their predictions Starreveld and La Heij did not take into account that printed words may activate their lemma nodes and output morpho-phonological nodes in parallel (see Figure 4.1). In the lexical network of WEAVER++, the orthographic input stratum is connected to both the lemma level and the output morpho-phonological level (see the links labelled INLEX in Figure 4.4). Thus, printed words may affect lemma retrieval directly, and there is no need for backward links in the output morpho-phonological network. Computer simulations (reported in Roelofs et al., 1996) showed that WEAVER++ predicts that in naming a pictured cat, the semantic inhibition will be less for distractor *calf* compared to *cap* than for distractor *horse* compared to *house*, as empirically observed. Thus, WEAVER++ captures the interaction.

Summary and discussion

I have tried to show that WEAVER++ does a good job in accounting for the time course of semantic inhibition and facilitation effects of distractors in picture naming, picture categorising, and word categorising. Furthermore, it accounts for the gender congruency effects and the interaction between semantic and form factors in picture naming. Other models in the literature have been less successful. For example, Starreveld and La Heij (1996) developed a new computational model without lemmas that was specifically designed to account for the interaction between semantic and form effects of distractors in picture naming. As its stands, their model can handle picture naming, but there is no provision in the model to deal with picture categorising and word categorising. And for picture naming, it incorrectly predicts semantic inhibition only, but, as we saw, semantic facilitation has also been obtained (Roelofs, 1992a, 1993). Also, there is no specification of syntax in the model of Starreveld and La Heij, and therefore the gender congruency effects fall outside the model. Moreover, by assuming a direct mapping of concepts onto word forms, the model fails to account for the speech error evidence for a lemma level of representation, namely the two types of morphemic errors discussed earlier. And by the direct mapping, the model predicts phonological activation of semantic relatives of a target (i.e., in planning the word *cat*, the form of *dog* should also become active), contrary to the empirical findings (Levelt et al., 1991; Peterson & Savoy, 1998). The empirical data suggest that during the planning of the word *cat*, the lemma of *dog* also becomes active but *not* its form. This suggests that lemma retrieval and word-form are not only distinct but also discrete processes (i.e., only the form of a *selected* lemma becomes encoded), which is an assumption that has been implemented in WEAVER++ (see Levelt et al., 1999a,b, for an extensive discussion).

Word-form encoding

Basic tenets

A basic theoretical claim implemented in WEAVER++ concerning word-form encoding is that lemmas are mapped onto learned syllable-based articulatory programs by serially grouping the segments of morphemes into phonological syllables. These phonological syllables are then used to address the programs in a phonetic syllabary.

Figure 4.4 illustrates the form representation of *sigaar* in WEAVER++. The non-metrical part of the form network consists of three layers of nodes: morpheme nodes, segment nodes, and syllable program nodes. Morpheme nodes stand for roots and affixes. Morpheme nodes are connected to the lemma and its parameters. The stem <sigaar> is connected to the lemma of *sigaar* and "singular". A morpheme node points to the segments that make up its underlying form, and, for some words, to its metrical structure. For storing metrical structures, a principle of economy applies. WEAVER++ assumes that the main accent of Dutch words is on the first syllable containing a full vowel (which holds for more than 90% of the word tokens), unless the lexical form representation indicates otherwise (Levelt et al., 1999a). Thus, for polysyllabic words that do not have main stress on the first stressable syllable, the metrical structure is stored as part of the lexical entry, but for monosyllabic words and for all other polysyllabic words, it is not. For example, the metrical structure for *sigaar* [si.'ɣar] is stored, but for *tafel* ['ta.fəl] it is not. Stored metrical structures describe abstract groupings of syllables (σ) into feet (Σ) and feet into phonological words (ω). Importantly, it is not specified which segments make up the syllables nor is the CV pattern specified. The links between morpheme and segment nodes indicate the serial position of the segments within the morpheme. Possible syllable positions (onset, nucleus, coda) of the segments are specified by the links between segment nodes and syllable program nodes. For example, the network specifies that /r/ is the coda of [ɣar] and the onset of [rə].

Encoding starts when a morpheme node receives activation from a selected lemma. Activation then spreads through the network in a forward fashion. The form encoders follow simple selection criteria. Attached to the nodes in the network, there are production rules that verify the links between the nodes and target nodes one level up. Production rules are triggered when the activation levels of their nodes exceed threshold. The production rules may be triggered and may fire in parallel.

The morphological encoder selects the morpheme nodes that are linked to a selected lemma and its parameters. Thus, <sigaar> is selected for *sigaar* and "singular". The phonological encoder selects the segments and, if available, the metrical structures that are linked to the selected morpheme nodes. Next, the segments are input to a prosodification process that associates the segments to the syllable nodes within the metrical structure (for "exception" words) or constructs metrical structures based on segmental information. Thus, when stored, metrical structures are retrieved and woven into the speech plan, otherwise they are constructed on the spot. Like weaving a fabric, the process has a certain direction. The prosodification proceeds from the segment whose link is labelled first to the one labelled second, and so forth. In the prosodification, syllable positions (onset, nucleus, coda) are assigned to the segments following the syllabification rules of the language. Essentially, each vowel and diphthong is assigned to a different syllable node and consonants are treated as onsets unless phonotactically illegal onset clusters arise. In the encoding of <sigaar>, the /s/ is made syllable onset and the /i/ nucleus of the first syllable, and the /ɣ/ onset, the /a/ nucleus, and the /r/ coda of the second syllable. The prosodification process provides for cross-morpheme and cross-word syllabification. In planning polymorphemic words or connected speech, the structures of adjacent morphemes or words may be combined (provided that certain phrase-structural conditions are satisfied, see Levelt, 1989, for discussion). This leads to new phonological words. For example, WEAVER++ may syllabify <en> with <sigaar> for the plural *sigaren* or it may prosodify the stem <sigaar> and the reduced form of <eens> together for the cliticisation *sigaar 's*. Then, following the maximal onset principle in syllabification (e.g., Goldsmith, 1990), /r/ will be made onset of the third syllable instead of coda of the second syllable, yielding $(si)_\sigma(\gamma a)_\sigma(r\partial)_\sigma$

and $(si)_\sigma(\gamma a)_\sigma(r\partial s)_\sigma$. In this way, WEAVER++ achieves syllabification across morpheme and word boundaries.

The phonetic encoder selects the syllable program nodes whose labelled links to the segments correspond with the syllable positions assigned to the segments. For example, [ɣar] is selected for the second phonological syllable of *sigaar*, because the link between [ɣar] and /ɣ/ is labelled onset, between [ɣar] and /a/ nucleus, and between [ɣar] and /r/ coda. Similarly, the phonetic encoder selects [ɣa] and [rəs] for the cliticised form *sigaar 's* and [ɣa] and [rə] for the plural form *sigaren*. Finally, the phonetic encoder addresses the syllable programs in the syllabary, thereby making the programs available to the articulators for the control of the articulatory movements (following Levelt, 1992; Levelt & Wheeldon, 1994). The encoder uses the metrical representation to set the parameters for loudness, pitch, and duration (see Levelt, 1989, for a discussion of the role of phrase-level prosody in setting the parameters). After programming some further articulatory adjustments, the phonetic plan will govern articulation.

In sum, word-form encoding is achieved by a spreading-activation based network with labelled links that is combined with a parallel production-rule system. WEAVER++ also provides for a suspend/resume mechanism that supports incremental generation of phonetic plans. Incremental production means that encoding processes can be triggered by a fragment of their characteristic input (Levelt, 1989). The three processing stages compute aspects of a word form in parallel from the beginning of the word to its end. For example, syllabification can start on the initial segments of a word without having all of its segments. Only initial segments and, for some words, the metrical structure are needed. When given partial information, computations are completed as far as possible, after which the computed representations are buffered and the process is put on hold. When given further information, the encoding processes continue from where they stopped.

Some applications

SOA curves of form effects. Meyer and Schriefers (1991) examined the effect of spoken distractor words on word-form encoding in object naming. The experiments were conducted in Dutch. The target and distractor words were either monomorphemic monosyllables or disyllables. The monosyllabic targets and distractors shared either the syllable onset and nucleus (begin related) or the nucleus and coda (end related). For example, participants had to name a pictured bed (i.e., they had to say *bed*, [bɛt]), where the distractor was *bek* ([bɛk], begin related; *beak*), *pet* ([pɛt], end related; *cap*), or there was no distractor (silence condition). Recombining pictures and distractors created unrelated control conditions. The disyllabic targets and distractors shared either the first syllable (begin related) or the second syllable (end related). For example, the participants had to name a pictured table (i.e., they had to say *tafel*, ['ta.fəl]), where the distractor was *tapir* (['ta.pir], begin related; id.), *jofel* (['jo.fəl], end related; *pleasant*), or there was no distractor. The distractors were presented just before (i.e., −300 or −150 ms), simultaneously with, or right after (i.e., +150 ms) picture onset.

The presentation of spoken distractors yielded longer object naming latencies compared to the situation without a distractor (cf., Glaser, 1992). The naming latencies were prolonged less with related distractors than with unrelated ones. Thus, a facilitatory effect was obtained from word-form overlap relative to the non-overlap situation. The difference between begin and end overlap for both the monosyllables and the disyllables was in the onset of the facilitatory effect. The onset of the effect in the begin condition was at SOA = −150 ms, whereas the onset of the effect in the end condition was at SOA = 0 ms. With both begin and end overlap the facilitatory effect was still present at the SOA of +150 ms.

According to WEAVER++, both begin-related (e.g., first-syllable) and end-related (e.g., second-syllable) spoken primes yield facilitation, because they will activate segments of the target word in memory and therefore speed up its encoding. Simply put, the onset difference between begin and end overlap reflects the rightward prosodification of segments. Computer simulations showed that WEAVER++ accounts for the empirical findings (Roelofs, 1997c). With begin overlap, the model predicts for SOA = −150 ms a facilitatory effect of −29 ms for the monosyllables (the real effect was −27 ms) and a facilitatory effect of −28 ms for the disyllables (real: −31 ms). In contrast, with end overlap, the effect for SOA = −150 ms was −3 ms for the monosyllables (real: −12 ms) and −4 ms for the disyllables (real: +10 ms). With both begin and end overlap the facilitatory effect was present at the SOAs of 0 and +150 ms. Thus, the model captures the basic findings.

Implicit priming.   Meyer (1990, 1991) examined the planning of word forms using the so-called implicit priming paradigm. This paradigm involves producing words from learned paired-associates. The big advantage of this paradigm compared to the more widely used picture–word interference paradigm is that the responses do not need to be names of depictable entities, which puts less constraints on the selection of materials. Roelofs (1999) showed that word production from paired associates and picture naming yields equivalent outcomes. In Meyer's experiments, participants first learned small sets of prompt-response pairs such as {*blad–tafel, dier–tapir,* etc.} ({*top–table, animal–tapir,* etc.}). After learning a set, the production of the response words was tested in a block of trials. On each trial, one of the prompts (the first word of a pair) was visually presented on a computer screen. The order of prompts across trials was random. The task for a participant was to produce the second word of a pair (e.g., the response *tafel*) upon the visual presentation of the first word (the prompt *blad*). The instruction was to respond as quickly as possible without making mistakes. The production latency (i.e., the interval between prompt onset and speech onset) was the main dependent variable. In the experiments there were homogeneous and heterogeneous response sets. In a homogeneous set, the response words shared part of their form and in a heterogeneous set they did not. For example, the responses shared the first syllable (*ta* in *tafel*, *tapir*, etc.) or the second syllable (*fel* in *tafel*, *jofel*, etc.) or they were unrelated (*tapir*, *jofel*, etc.). The same prompt-response pairs were tested in the homogeneous and heterogeneous conditions; only their combinations into sets differed. Therefore, all uncontrolled item effects were kept constant across these conditions. Each participant was tested on all sets.

Meyer found shorter production latencies in homogeneous than in heterogeneous sets. However, this difference was dependent on serial order in that it was only obtained when the response words in homogeneous sets shared one or more word-initial segments, but not when they shared word-final segments. Thus, a facilitatory effect was obtained for the set that included *tafel* and *tapir* but not for the set that included *tafel* and *jofel*. Furthermore, facilitation increases with the number of shared segments. This holds not only for overlap within syllables but also across syllable and word boundaries, as shown by Roelofs (1998).

According to WEAVER++, the seriality phenomenon reflects the suspend-resume mechanism that underlies the incremental planning of an utterance. Assume the response set consists of *tafel*, *tapir* and so forth (i.e., the first syllable is shared). Before the beginning of a trial, the morphological encoder can do nothing, but the phonological encoder can construct the first phonological syllable $(ta)_\sigma$, and the phonetic encoder can recover the first motor program [ta]. When the prompt *blad* is presented, the morphological encoder will retrieve <tafel>. Segmental spellout makes available the segments of this morpheme, which includes the segments of the second syllable. The phonological and phonetic encoders can start working on the second syllable. In the heterogeneous condition (*tapir*, *jofel*, etc.), nothing can be prepared. There will be no morphological encoding, no phonological encoding, and no phonetic encoding before the beginning of a trial. In the end-homogeneous condition (*tafel*, *jofel*, etc.), nothing can be prepared either. Although the segments of the second syllable are known, the phonological word cannot be computed because the remaining segments are to the left of the suspension point. In WEAVER++, this means that the syllabification process has to go to the initial segments of the word, which amounts to restarting the whole process (like unravelling a woven fabric). Thus, a facilitatory effect will be obtained for the homogeneous condition relative to the heterogeneous condition for the begin condition only.

Computer simulations of these experiments supported this theoretical analysis (Roelofs, 1994, 1997c). Advance knowledge about a syllable was simulated by completing the phonological and phonetic encoding of the syllable before the beginning of a trial. For the begin condition, the model yielded a facilitatory effect of −43 ms (real: −49 ms, collapsed across trochaic feet and iambs), whereas for the end condition it predicted an effect of 0 ms (real: +5 ms). Thus, WEAVER++ captures the empirical phenomenon.

Implicit versus explicit priming.   The results of implicit and explicit priming are different in an interesting way. In implicit priming experiments, the production of a disyllabic word like *tafel* is speeded up by advance knowledge about the first syllable (*ta*) but not by advance knowledge about the second syllable (*fel*), as shown by Meyer (1990, 1991). In contrast, when first-syllable or second-syllable spoken primes are presented during the production of a disyllabic word, both primes yield facilitation (Meyer & Schriefers, 1991). Only the onset of the facilitation differs. As we saw, WEAVER++ resolves the discrepancy. According to the model, both first-syllable and second-syllable spoken primes yield facilitation, because they will activate segments of the target word in memory and therefore speed up its encoding. Implicit priming reflects the rightward prosodification of segments. Thus, later syllables cannot be prepared before earlier ones.

New experiments (cf., Roelofs, 1997c) tested WEAVER++'s prediction that implicit and explicit primes yield independent effects. In the experiments, there were homogeneous and heterogeneous response sets (the implicit primes) as well as form-related and form-unrelated spoken distractors (the explicit primes). Participants had to produce single words such as *tafel*, simple imperative sentences such as "zoek op!" ("look up!"), or cliticisations such as "zoek 's op!" ("just look it up") where the reduced form *'s* [əs] of *eens* is attached to the base verb. In homogeneous sets, the responses shared the first syllable, (e.g., *ta* in *tafel*), the base verb (e.g., *zoek–look* in "zoek op!"), or the base plus clitic (e.g., *zoek 's* in "zoek 's op!"). The spoken distractors consisted of the final syllables of the utterances, either a target syllable (e.g., *fel* for *tafel* or *op* for "zoek op!", the related condition), a syllable of another item in the response set (the unrelated condition), or there was no distractor (the silence condition). The homogeneity variable (implicit) and the distractor variable (explicit) yielded main effects and the effects were additive (see Figure 4.7). Furthermore, as predicted by

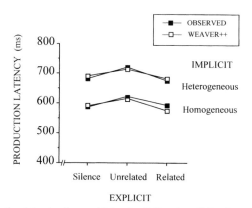

Figure 4.7.   Production latencies for combining implicit and explicit primes: Empirical data (cf., Roelofs, 1997c) and predictions by WEAVER++.

WEAVER++, the effects were the same for the production of single words, simple imperative sentences, and cliticisations. Recall that the prosodification of these three types of utterance proceeds in the same manner in the model.

Rightward incrementality and morphological decomposition.   It is not only characteristic of WEAVER++ that its encoding algorithm operates in a rightward incremental fashion (like in weaving a fabric, the process goes from side to side), but also that it requires morphologically decomposed form entries. Morphological structure is needed, because some morphemes (e.g., prefixes) define independent domains of syllabification (cf., Booij, 1995). For example, without morphological structure, the /r/ of the prefix *ver–* of *vereisen* (*demand*) would incorrectly be syllabified with the base *eisen*, following the maximal onset principle.

Roelofs (1996c) tested effects of rightward incrementality and morphological decomposition using the implicit priming paradigm. WEAVER++ predicts that a larger facilitatory effect should be obtained when shared initial segments constitute a morpheme than when they do not. For example, the preparation effect should be larger for sharing the syllable *bij* in response sets including Dutch compounds such as *bijrol* (morphemes <bij> and <rol>, *supporting role*) than for sharing the syllable *bij* in sets including simple words such as *bijbel* (morpheme <bijbel>, *bible*). For sets with monomorphemic words like *bijbel* consisting of the morpheme <bijbel>, sharing the first syllable *bij* allows phonological preparation only. In contrast, for sets with polymorphemic words like *bijrol* consisting of the morphemes <bij> and <rol>, additional morphological preparation is possible.

When the monomorphemic word *bijbel* is in a homogeneous condition where the responses share the syllable *bij*, the phonological syllable $(bɛi)_\sigma$ and the motor program [bɛi] can be planned before the beginning of a trial. The morpheme <bijbel> and the second syllable *bel* will be planned during the trial itself. In a heterogeneous condition where the responses do not share part of their form, the whole monomorphemic word *bijbel* has to be planned during the trial. When the polymorphemic word *bijrol* is in a homogeneous condition where the responses share the syllable *bij*, the first morpheme <bij>, and the phonological syllable $(bɛi)_\sigma$ and the motor program [bɛi] may be planned before the beginning of a trial. Thus, the second morpheme node <rol> has to be selected during the trial itself, and the second syllable *rol* has to be encoded at the phonological and the phonetic level. In the heterogeneous condition, however, the initial morpheme node <bij> has to be selected first, before the second morpheme node <rol> and its segments can be selected so that the second syllable *rol* can be encoded. Thus, in case of a polymorphemic word such as *bijrol*, additional morphological preparation is possible before the beginning of a trial. Consequently, extra facilitation should be obtained. Thus, the facilitatory effect for *bij* in *bijrol* (consisting of the morphemes <bij> and <rol>) should be larger than the effect for *bij* in *bijbel* (<bijbel>).

The outcomes confirmed the predictions by WEAVER++. In producing disyllabic simple and compound nouns, a larger facilitatory effect was obtained

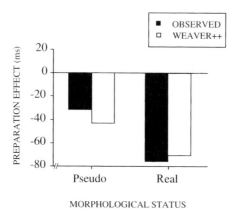

Figure 4.8.   Preparation effects for pseudo and real morphemes: Empirical data (Roelofs, 1996c) and predictions by WEAVER++.

when a shared initial syllable constituted a morpheme than when it did not (see Figure 4.8). For example, the effect was larger for *bij* in *bijrol* (<bij> and <rol>) than for *bij* in *bijbel* (<bijbel>).

The outcomes of further experiments supported WEAVER++'s claim that word forms are planned in a rightward fashion. In producing nominal compounds, no facilitation was obtained for non-initial morphemes. For example, no effect was obtained for <rol> in *bijrol*. In producing prefixed verbs, a facilitatory effect was obtained for the prefix but not for the non-initial base. For example, a facilitatory effect was obtained for the prefix <be> of *behalen* (*to obtain*), but not for the base <halen>.

According to WEAVER++ morphological complexity can play a role in form planning without having a synchronic semantic motivation. As indicated, some morphemes, such as prefixes, indicate domains of syllabification and this is independent of semantic transparency. For example, the /r/ of the opaque prefixed verb *verijdelen* (*frustrate*) is syllabified with the prefix and not with the base as the maximal onset principle would predict. Indeed, Roelofs and Baayen (cf., Roelofs, 1996b) obtained the effect of morpheme preparation for semantically opaque compounds like *bijval* (<bij><val> *applause*). In producing simple (*bijbel* <bijbel>) and compound nouns (*bijrol* <bij><rol> and *bijval* <bij><val>), a larger preparation effect was obtained when a shared initial syllable constituted a morpheme than when it did not, replicating Roelofs (1996c). Importantly, the size of the morphemic effect was identical for semantically transparent compounds (*bijrol*) and opaque compounds (*bijval*), which suggests that morphemes are present in the memory representations of opaque words. These findings support WEAVER++'s modular view of form planning in which morphology operates "by itself" (cf., Aronoff, 1994). Garrett (1980) arrived at a similar conclusion on the basis of speech error analyses, arguing for the representation of "pseudomorphs" in the mental lexicon.

Metrical structure. In developing WEAVER++, a specific role has been assigned to metrical structures in syllabification (see Roelofs & Meyer, 1998). For words like the trochee *tafel*, metrical structures are computed on-line, but for words like the iamb *sigaar*, metrical structures are stored. By contrast, Levelt (1992) does not make this differentiation. The stored metrical structures specify the number of syllables and the stress pattern, but not the precise CV structure of the syllables as the CV headers of Dell (1988) do. The prosodification process in WEAVER++ associates segments to the syllable nodes within the metrical structure for "exception" words (e.g., *sigaar*) or constructs syllable and metrical structures based on segmental information (e.g., for *tafel*). Roelofs and Meyer (1998) conducted a number of implicit-priming experiments designed to test this view on phonological encoding.

On each trial, participants had to produce one Dutch word out of a set of three, or four, as quickly as possible. In homogeneous sets, the responses shared a number of word-initial segments, whereas in heterogeneous sets they did not. As we saw, earlier research has shown that sharing initial segments reduces production latencies (Meyer, 1990, 1991; Roelofs, 1996c). The responses shared their metrical structure (the constant sets) or they did not (the variable sets).

A first series of experiments (Roelofs & Meyer, 1998) tested predictions of WEAVER++ about the role of metrical structure in the production of poly-syllabic words that do not have main stress on the first stressable syllable, such as *sigaar*. According to the model, the metrical structures of these words are stored in memory. WEAVER's view of syllabification implies that preparation for word-initial segments should only be possible if such response words have an identical metrical structure. If the responses in a set have different metrical structures, segment-to-frame association cannot take place before the beginning of a trial, and no preparation effect should be obtained. This prediction was tested by comparing the preparation effect for response sets with a constant number of syllables such as {*manier* (*manner*), *matras* (*mattress*), *makreel* (*mackerel*)} (all two syllables) to that for sets having a variable number of syllables such as {*majoor* (*major*), *materie* (*matter*), *malaria* (*malaria*)} (respectively, two, three, and four syllables). In the example, the responses share the first syllable *ma*. Word stress was always on the second syllable. As predicted, facilitation was obtained for the metrically constant sets but not for the variable sets. The same predictions were also tested by comparing the preparation effect for response sets with a constant stress pattern such as {*marine* (*navy*), *materie* (*matter*), *malaise* (*depression*), *madonna* (*madonna*)} (all responses having stress on the second syllable) to that for sets having a variable stress pattern such as {*marine* (*navy*), *materie* (*matter*), *manuscript* (*manuscript*), *madelief* (*daisy*)} (the first two responses having stress on the second syllable and the last two responses having stress on the third syllable). All response words were trisyllabic. Again, as predicted, facilitation was obtained for the constant sets but not for the variable sets.

The results of the experiments already suggest that constancy in CV structure is not necessary to observe a preparation effect, because in none of the homogeneous sets of these experiments was this structure identical across response words (though one could perhaps argue that the response words in the metrically constant sets were more similar in CV structure than those in metrically variable sets). Results obtained by Meyer (1990, 1991) and Roelofs (1996b,c, 1997b, 1998) also suggest that implicit priming effects can be obtained for homogeneous sets with variable CV structures. However, though constancy in CV structure does not appear to be necessary for obtaining a facilitatory effect, it is still possible that stronger effects arise for sets with constant than with variable CV structure. This is not predicted by WEAVER++, but, as explained earlier, other computational models such as those of Dell (1988) and Schade and Berg (1992) asssume an explicit representation of CV structure. Therefore, we tested whether the size of the preparation effect was affected by the constancy versus variability of the CV structure of the response words. We compared the effect of segmental overlap for response sets having a constant CV structure such as {*bres* (*breach*), *bril* (*glasses*), *brok* (*piece*), *brug* (*bridge*)} (responses all CCVC) to that for sets having a variable CV structure such as {*brij* (*porridge*), *brief* (*letter*), *bron* (*source*), *brand* (*fire*)} (responses respectively, CCVV, CCVVC, CCVC, CCVCC). In the example, the responses share the onset cluster *br*. Facilitation from segmental overlap was obtained for both the constant and the variable sets. The size of the preparation effect was the same for both types of set.

These results suggest that the exact CV structure is not stored, thereby refuting the CV headers of the Dell model. With constant CV structure, the system might select a header (i.e., CCVC) and work its way through the sequence of segment categories corresponding to the shared segments. After the last shared category node has been reached and the corresponding segment has been selected, the encoding process is suspended. The process is resumed when the first non-shared segment has been made available by the morpheme that is derived from the prompt. With variable CV structure, however, the system cannot select a header and work its way through the sequence of segment categories corresponding to the shared segments. For example, suspension in a CCVV sequence leads to wrong results if it turns out that a CCVVC word has actually to be produced. But empirically the same amount of facilitation from segmental overlap was obtained for the constant and the variable sets.

WEAVER++ explains why preparation for word-initial segments is only possible for response words with identical number of syllables and stress pattern, and why an identical CV structure is not needed. Figure 4.9 gives the results of simulations comparing the effect of segmental overlap for response sets with a

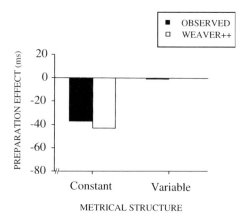

Figure 4.9.   Preparation effects for metrically constant and variable response sets: Empirical data (Roelofs & Meyer, 1998) and predictions by WEAVER++.

constant number of syllables such as {*manier, matras, makreel*} to that for sets having a variable number of syllables such as {*majoor, materie, malaria*}. Varying the place of stress while keeping the number of syllables fixed gives the same results. As can be seen, WEAVER++ accounts for the key empirical finding concerning metrical structure. In contrast, if metrical structures are not involved in advance planning or if metrical structures are computed on-line on the basis of segments for these words, sharing metrical structure should be irrelevant for preparation. Then, preparation (i.e., on-line computing the syllable *ma* before the beginning of a trial and computing the remainder of the word form during the trial itself) should be possible for both the metrically constant and variable sets.

We also tested predictions of WEAVER++ about the role of metrical structure in producing monosyllabic words and polysyllabic words whose main stress is on the first syllable like *tafel* (see Levelt et al., 1999a). According to the model, the metrical structures of these words are computed on-line by the prosodification process. That is, syllabification and stress assignment (i.e., footing) is done on the basis of retrieved segments. Consequently, implicit priming of initial segments should now be possible for both metrically constant and variable sets. This prediction was tested by comparing the preparation effect for response sets with a constant number of syllables such as {*borstel* (*brush*), *botsing* (*crash*), *bochel* (*hump*), *bonje* (*fight*)} (all disyllables stressed on the first syllable) to that for sets having a variable number of syllables such as {*borstel, botsing, bok* (*goat*), *bom* (*bomb*)} (two disyllables stressed on the first syllable and two monosyllables, respectively). In the example, the responses share the onset and nucleus *bo*. As predicted, facilitation was obtained (in an equal amount) for both the constant and the variable sets. The same result is predicted for varying the number of syllables of polysyllabic words with an unstressable first syllable (i.e., words with a schwa as the first vowel) and stress on the second syllable. This was tested by comparing the preparation effect for such words in response sets with a constant number of syllables such as {*gebit* (*teeth*), *gezin* (*family*), *getal* (*number*), *gewei* (*antlers*)} (all disyllables having stress on the second syllable) to that for sets having a variable number of syllables such as {*geraamte* (*skeleton*), *getuige* (*witness*), *gebit, gezin*} (two trisyllables stressed on the second syllable and two disyllables stressed on the second syllable, respectively). As predicted, facilitation was obtained (in an equal amount) for both the constant and the variable sets.

Finally, we tested predictions of WEAVER++ about the production of cliticisations and suffixed forms. According to Levelt (1992), cliticisations like *sigaar 's* (e.g., "probeer deze sigaar 's", "just try this cigar") are produced by first combining the retrieved metrical frames for *sigaar* and *'s*, followed by segment-to-frame association. By contrast, WEAVER++ has implemented the claim that first *sigaar* is syllabified and later *'s* is adjoined (Roelofs, 1997b). The same holds for the production of the plural form *sigaren*: First the stem *sigaar* is syllabified, and later the plural suffix *–en* is attached and prosodified. These different views were tested by comparing the effect of segmental overlap for response sets that combine disyllabic nouns (e.g., *dozijn–dozen*) with disyllabic verb stems (e.g., *doneer–donate*) to that of sets combining the disyllabic nouns with trisyllabic cliticised forms of the verbs (*doneer's*) or with trisyllabic infinitival forms of the verbs (*doneren*). If metrical frames are combined before segment-to-frame association, then the sets with the cliticisations (e.g., the set including disyllabic *dozijn* and trisyllabic *doneer 's*) and the sets with the infinitives (e.g., the set including disyllabic *dozijn* and trisyllabic *doneren*) would be metrically variable, and preparation should not be possible. According to WEAVER++, however, all three types of set are metrically constant, because the clitic and the plural suffix are metrically independent elements that are adjoined after syllabification of the verb stem. The outcomes of the experiment supported the predictions of WEAVER++. The sets with the cliticisations (e.g., the set including *dozijn* and *doneer 's*) and the sets with the infinitives (e.g., the set including *dozijn* and *doneren*) yielded an equal amount of segmental facilitation, and the size of the facilitation was the same as that for the sets including the disyllabic verb stems (e.g., the set including *dozijn* and *doneer*).

In summary, I have reviewed empirical evidence that supports the claim (implemented in WEAVER++) that syllable structure is computed on-line and in a left-to-right fashion (Levelt, 1992). The evidence suggests that syllable structure is computed by associating retrieved segments to the syllable nodes within retrieved metrical frames for polysyllabic words that do not have main stress on the first stressable syllable (which holds for roughly 10% of the words) and by constructing syllable and metrical structures based on segmental information for monosyllabic words and for all other polysyllabic words (the remaining 90% of the words). Furthermore, I reviewed evidence that supports the claim that syllabification across morpheme and word boundaries is achieved by adjoining a suffix or clitic to an already partly syllabified base rather than by first combining the metrical frames for the base and for the suffix or clitic followed by segment-to-frame association.

Frequency effects.   WEAVER++ can capture frequency effects in word production. Frequency effects in the model originate from differences in the speed of production-rule application. Speed depends on frequency of usage (more experienced spiders work faster in making a web).

Experiments by Jescheniak and Levelt (1994; Jescheniak, 1994) have shown that when lemma information such as grammatical gender is accessed, a frequency effect is obtained. For example, Dutch participants had to decide on the gender of a picture's name (e.g., they had to decide that the grammatical gender of *tafel* is non-neuter), which was done faster for high-frequency words than for low-frequency ones. The effect disappeared over repetitions, contrary to a "robust" frequency effect obtained in naming the pictures.

Jescheniak and Levelt (1994) provided evidence that the locus of the robust frequency effect is the form level. When participants had to respond to an English probe word by producing its Dutch translation equivalent, the production latency of a low-frequency homophone was determined by the sum frequency of that word and its high-frequency counterpart. For example, participants had to produce the Dutch word *bos* in response to *bunch* (low-frequency reading). The production latencies for these homophones were compared to the latencies for two types of other words. First, there were low-frequency control words whose frequency was matched to that of the low-frequency reading of the homophone. The low-frequency control for *bos* was *hok* (*kennel*). Second, there were high-frequency control words whose frequency was matched to the sum frequency of the low-frequency reading (i.e., *bunch*) and high-frequency reading (i.e., *forest*) of *bos*. The high-frequency control for *bos* was *hoek* (*corner*). Producing the homophones (*bos*) in their low-frequency reading went as fast as producing the high-frequency controls (*hoek*), and it went faster than producing the low-frequency controls (*hok*). A low-frequency homophone inherits the frequency of its high-frequency counterpart. In WEAVER++, homophones share their form nodes in common but not the lemma (Dell, 1990 and Jescheniak & Levelt, 1994 also take this point of view). By sharing form nodes, a low-frequency homophone inherits the frequency properties of its high-frequency counterpart. This explains the homophone effect observed by Jescheniak and Levelt.

WEAVER++ predicts also an effect of morpheme frequency for the constituents of polymorphemic lexical items. This was tested by Roelofs (1996b, 1998) using the implicit priming paradigm. High-frequency morphemes are retrieved faster from memory than morphemes of low frequency, so the benefit from preparation should be larger for low-frequency morphemes than for high-frequency ones. This prediction was empirically confirmed. For example, in producing compounds (Roelofs, 1996b), the facilitatory effect was larger for response sets sharing a low-frequency morpheme like <bloem> (*flower*)—as in *bloemkool* (*cauliflower*)—than for response sets sharing a high-frequency morpheme like <bloed> (*blood*)—as in *bloedspoor* (*trace of blood*). Also, in producing particle verbs (Roelofs, 1998), the facilitatory effect was larger for *veeg* (low frequency) in "veeg op!" ("clean up!") than for *geef* (high frequency) in "geef op!" ("give up!").

Finally, Levelt and Wheeldon (1994) observed that in word-form encoding an effect of syllable frequency is obtained that is independent from the word-frequency effect. Furthermore, in producing disyllabic words, the syllable-frequency effect was confined to the second syllable. Again, if a selection procedure for a syllable program node is run faster for a high-frequency syllable than for a low-frequency one, then the finding of an independent effect of syllable frequency is readily explained. Furthermore, during the encoding of disyllables, the encoding of the first syllable will have a head-start as a result of the left-to-right prosodification of segments. Thus, according to the model, the second syllable typically sets the pace of the encoding of the whole word form. Therefore, one expects the syllable-frequency effect to be confined to the second syllable, as is observed by Levelt and Wheeldon.

The syllable frequency effects obtained by Levelt and Wheeldon (1994) were very small. Furthermore, in some experiments, syllable and segment frequency were correlated. In recent experiments by Levelt and Meyer (reported in Meyer, 1997) that controlled for a number of possible confounds, effects of syllable, and segment frequency were not obtained. Clearly, the speed of accessing syllables does not depend very much on their frequency.

Simulations showed that WEAVER++ captures the word-frequency effects (obtained by Jescheniak and Levelt), the small syllable frequency effects (obtained by Levelt and Wheeldon), and their independence. In the earlier simulations, the frequency of the targets was held constant in the model. In the current simulations, frequency was explicitly manipulated by varying verification times as a function of the frequency of the item, so that different items took different periods of encoding time within the network. For example, in producing the word *wortel* (['wɔr.təl], *carrot*), doubling the duration of the selection procedure of the first syllable [wɔr] increased the word-form encoding latency by +6 ms (Levelt & Wheeldon observed a non-significant frequency effect for the first syllable of −3 ms), whereas doubling the duration of the procedure of the second syllable [təl] increased the encoding latency by +19 ms (real: +12). This difference between first-syllable and second-syllable frequency was independent of the effect of word frequency. For example, tripling the duration of a morpheme test increased the word-form encoding latency by +25 ms, but the frequency-effect difference between the first syllable and the second syllable remained the same.

Segments and features.   According to WEAVER++, preparation in an implicit-priming experiment critically depends on shared segments rather than shared articulatory movements or phonological features. In support of this, it has been shown empirically that preparation requires that the responses share their initial segments fully and that sharing features only does not allow for preparation (Roelofs, 1999). For example, the initial segment of the words *boat, bird*, and *boy* is the same, whereas the initial segment of the words *paint, boat*, and *bird* is the same except for one feature, namely voicing (i.e., /b/ is voiced, /p/ is voiceless). However, a preparation effect was only obtained for the sets with full segment overlap, but no effect was observed at all (not even a reduction of latencies) for the sets with feature overlap. The same result has been obtained in comparing sets of disyllabic words sharing the first syllable fully (e.g., *te* in *tennis, terrace, teddy*) and sets of disyllabic words whose first syllable differs in one feature only (e.g., *devil, tennis, teddy*). Although syllables were shared except for one feature in the first segment, this feature difference completely blocked preparation. Also, the same results were obtained when words were produced in response to pictured objects, and when place of articulation rather than voicing was manipulated (e.g., /m/ versus /n/).

To conclude, the special status of identity suggests that segments are planning units independent of their features. The findings support segmental models such as WEAVER++, but they argue against models without an explicit representation of segments, such as the PDP model proposed by Dell, Juliano, and Govindjee (1993).

Summary and discussion

I have reviewed empirical evidence for the claim that lemmas are mapped onto syllable-based articulatory programs by serially grouping the segments of morphemes into phonological syllables, after which these phonological syllables are used to address the programs in a syllabary. In agreement with the speech error evidence, the chronometrical findings (i.e., Roelofs, 1996b,c, 1998) support, among other things, the assumption that there is a level of concrete morphemes in addition to the level of syntactically specified lemmas. By contrast, Caramazza (1997) proposed a model with only a single, syntactically specified level intermediate between concepts and segments (the model of Starreveld & La Heij, 1996, is similar to that of Caramazza but contains no syntax).

There are several problems with Caramazza's proposal that a single lexical level suffices. First of all, by assuming just one lexical level, his model fails to account for the speech error evidence that suggests two types of morpheme error (Dell, 1986; Garrett, 1975, 1980, 1988). Furthermore, Caramazza's model has difficulty accounting for the observation that low-frequency homophones inherit the frequency properties of their high-frequency twins (Jescheniak & Levelt, 1994). The Caramazza model assumes separate lexical nodes for homophones of different syntactic classes, so *more* (adjective) and *moor* (noun) each have their own lexical node, which fails to explain why low-frequency *moor* behaves like high-frequency *more*. To save the model, Caramazza and Miozzo (1998) have suggested that feedback from segments to lexical nodes may give rise to the inherited effect (cf., Dell, 1990). However, this is no option for their model, because it contains no backward links. Also, since syntactic properties and segments are accessed through the same lexical node, the model cannot explain the dissociation between the frequency-effect in gender decision and in picture naming. If the frequency effect resides at the lexical node, the effect should be robust both in picture naming and gender decision, contrary to the empirical findings. For an extensive discussion of these and other issues, refer to Roelofs et al. (1998) and Caramazza and Miozzo (1998).

Speech errors

Although WEAVER++ has not been designed to account for speech errors, it can be shown that the model is compatible with speech error data (see Roelofs, 1997c). Here, I briefly indicate how the model copes with the error data reviewed in discussing the Dell model. I address the relative frequencies of segmental substitution errors (e.g., the anticipation error *sed sock* for *red sock* is more likely than the perseveration *red rock*, which is in its turn more likely than the exchange *sed rock*), effects of speech rate on error probabilities (e.g., more errors at higher speech rates), the phonological facilitation of semantic substitution errors (e.g., *calf* for *cat* is more likely than *dog* for *cat*), and lexical bias (i.e., errors tend to be real words rather than nonwords).

In WEAVER++, phonological errors may be due to indexing failures by the phonetic encoder. For example, in the planning of "red sock", the production rule of [sɛd] might find its condition satisfied. It wants to have an onset /s/, a nucleus /ɛ/, and a coda /d/, which is present in the phonological representation. The error is of course that the /s/ is in the wrong phonological syllable. If the production rule of [rɛd] does its job well, there will be a race between [rɛd] and [sɛd] to become the first syllable in the articulatory program for the utterance. If [sɛd] wins the race, the speaker will make an anticipation error. If this indexing error occurs, instead, for the second syllable, a perseveration error will be made, and if the error is made both for the first syllable and the second one, an exchange error will be made. Errors may also occur when WEAVER++ skips verification to gain speed in order to obtain a higher speech rate. Thus, more errors are to be expected at high speech rates.

Figure 4.10 gives some simulation results concerning segmental anticipations, perseverations, and exchanges. The real data are from the Dutch error corpus of Nooteboom (1969), which are typical. As can be seen, WEAVER++ can capture some of the basic findings about the relative frequency of these types of substitution errors in spontaneous speech. The anticipation error *sed sock* for *red sock* is

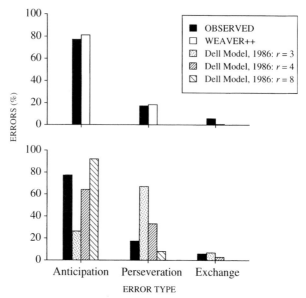

Figure 4.10.   Percentage of segmental anticipations, perseverations, and exchanges: Empirical data (Nooteboom, 1969) and predictions by the Dell model and by WEAVER++.

more likely than the perseveration *red rock*, which is in turn more likely than the exchange *sed rock*. The model predicts almost no exchanges, which is, of course, a weakness of the model. However, comparison of WEAVER++'s performance with the error-based model of Dell (1986) shows that WEAVER++ does not behave poorly. At a low speech rate ($r = 8$), the Dell model predicts no exchanges and at high speech rate ($r = 3$) the model predicts incorrectly more perseverations than anticipations.

Lexical bias has traditionally been taken as an argument for backward links in a lexical network. Backward links are present in the classical model (Dell, 1986) but absent in WEAVER++. Segmental errors tend to create words rather than nonwords. For example, the selection of /h/ resulting in *hat* for *cat* is more likely than the selection of /z/ resulting in *zat* for *cat*. In the classical model, lexical bias is a result of feedback from segment nodes to word nodes (i.e., lemma nodes or morpheme nodes) and from word nodes back to segment nodes. Strings of segments that make up words receive feedback from word nodes but nonword strings do not. So, /h/ receives feedback from *hat* but /z/ not from *zat*, because the latter is not part of the lexicon. Reverberation of activation in the network takes time, so lexical influences on errors take time to develop, as empirically observed (Dell, 1986).

The classical account of lexical bias meets, however, with a difficulty. In this view, lexical bias is an automatic effect. The seminal study of Baars, Motley, and MacKay (1975), however, has already shown that lexical bias is not a necessary effect. When all the target and filler items in an error-elicitation experiment are nonwords, word and nonword slips occur equally often. Only when some words are included as filler items does the lexical bias appear. The account of Baars et al. of lexical bias was in terms of speech monitoring by speakers. Just before articulation, speakers monitor their phonetic plan for errors. If an experimental task exclusively deals with nonwords, speakers do not bother to attend to the lexical status of their phonetic plan. As proposed by Levelt (1989), the monitoring may be achieved by feeding the phonetic plan to the speech comprehension system. On this account, there is no direct feedback in the output form lexicon, but only indirect feedback via the speech comprehension system. Feedback via the comprehension system takes time, so lexical influences on errors take time to develop.

Similarly, the phonological facilitation of semantic substitutions may be a monitor effect. The target *cat* will be in the comprehension cohort of *calf* but not of *dog*. Consequently, it is more likely that *calf* will pass the monitor than that *dog* will. There exists also another potential error source within a forward model such as WEAVER++. Occasionally, the lemma retriever may erroneously select two lemmas instead of one, the target and an intruder. This assumption is independently motivated by the occurrence of blends such a *clear* combining *close* and *near* (Roelofs, 1992a). In WEAVER++, the selection of two lemmas instead of one will lead to the parallel encoding of two word forms instead of one. The encoding time is a random variable, whereby the word form that is ready first will control articulation. In WEAVER++, it is more likely that the intruder wins the form race when there is phonological overlap between target and intruder (i.e., when the form of the target primes the intruder) than when there is no phonological relation. Thus, WEAVER++ predicts that the substitution *calf* for *cat* is more likely than *dog* for *cat*, which is the phonological facilitation of semantic substitution errors. This also explains the syntactic category constraint on substitution errors, that is, like in word exchanges, in substitution errors the target and the intruder are typically of the same syntactic category.

Wider implications for understanding speech production

The basic design feature of WEAVER++ that gives rise to its psychologically and computationally desirable properties is the integration of a spreading-activation based lexical network with a parallel production-rule system embodying linguistic rules or constraints. Words are not planned by a central agent that overlooks the whole process but by teams of production rules that work in parallel on small parts of the word. The production rules are stored with the relevant data structures and have a limited overview only. Retrieval and encoding in the model are lexically driven, that is, production rules operate on the basis of information stored with individual words in the lexicon.

These design features of WEAVER++ are similar to those of the algorithm that Kempen and Hoenkamp (1987) proposed for the planning of syntactic structures. A retrieved lemma (e.g., a noun lemma) triggers procedures that build the appropriate syntactic environment for the word (e.g., an NP, S, etc.). Syntactic encoding in their model is lexically driven, that is, it operates on the basis of information stored with individual words in the lexicon. Also, there is no central agent that overlooks the whole process, but syntactic encoding is achieved by a team of expert procedures which work in parallel on small parts of the sentence. To conclude, lexically driven production systems are, in many ways, beginning to form a coherent theoretical paradigm for understanding the planning of speech, both at the syntactic and the word-form encoding level.

WEAVER++ uses production rules in addition to spreading activation. Back in the dark days of behaviourism, any reference to mental notions was considered to be unscientific. Nowadays, in some circles it is held that theorising may involve connectionist notions only and that production rules are forbidden. Usually, this conviction remains operative in the background but sometimes it is publicised. For example, in their peer commentaries on a BBS target article explaining WEAVER++ (Levelt et al., 1999a), Santiago and MacKay (1999) called production rules "homunculi", others held that production rules involve "unnatural computation" (Roberts, Kalish, Hird, & Kirsner, 1999), or that they are "too declarative" for the brain (O'Seaghdha, 1999). The problem with these criticisms is that our knowledge of how the brain works is still so rudimentary that is seems premature to ban any reference to production rules and other symbolic entities. Moreover, these criticisms overlook that the line between production rules and many connectionist constructs is rather thin. For example, production rules without variables can easily be implemented using a connectionist network. Furthermore, proposals have been made for how a connectionist system may achieve variable binding (e.g., Shastri & Ajjanagadde, 1993; Touretzky & Hinton, 1988), in effect implementing productions rules with variables. Production rules mean nothing more than the operations that they specify. Crucial for the issue of "neural plausibility" is whether we can exclude that the brain performs such operations—and the criticisms do not bring forward evidence against that.

There is no direct way to observe how lexical access happens in the mind of speakers. We can only make use of indirect evidence coming from behavioural and neural studies. In the present chapter, I evaluated existing evidence from behavioural studies. On the basis of these data, I made a case for the WEAVER++ model. This does not mean that other models are by necessity fatally flawed. Models in cognitive science are moving targets and it remains to be seen whether the problems that confront other models can ultimately be solved, which is just another way of saying that more research needs to be done.

REFERENCES

Anderson, J.R. (1983). *The architecture of cognition.* Cambridge, MA: Harvard University Press.

Aronoff, M. (1994). *Morphology by itself.* Cambridge, MA: MIT Press.

Baars, B.J., Motley, M.T., & MacKay, D. (1975). Output editing for lexical status from artificially elicited slips of the tongue. *Journal of Verbal Learning and Verbal Behavior, 14,* 382–391.

Bierwisch, M., & Schreuder, R. (1992). From concepts to lexical items. *Cognition, 42,* 23–60.

Booij, G.E. (1995). *The phonology of Dutch.* Oxford, UK: Clarendon Press.

Browman, C.P., & Goldstein, L. (1986). Towards an articulatory phonology. *Phonology Yearbook, 3,* 219–252.

Caramazza, A. (1997). How many levels of processing are there in lexical access? *Cognitive Neuropsychology, 14,* 177–208.

Caramazza, A., & Miozzo, M. (1998). More is not always better: A response to Roelofs, Meyer, and Levelt. *Cognition, 69,* 231–241.

Collins, A.M., & Loftus, E.F. (1975). A spreading-activation theory of semantic processing. *Psychological Review, 82,* 407–428.

Cutting, C.J., & Ferreira, V.S. (1999). Semantic and phonological information flow in the production lexicon. *Journal of Experimental Psychology: Learning, Memory, and Cognition, 25,* 318–344.

Damian, M.K., & Martin, R.C. (1999). Semantic and phonological codes interact in single word production. *Journal of Experimental Psychology: Learning, Memory, and Cognition, 25,* 345–361.

Dell, G.S. (1986). A spreading-activation theory of retrieval in sentence production. *Psychological Review, 93,* 283–321.

Dell, G.S. (1988). The retrieval of phonological forms in production: Tests of predictions from a connectionist model. *Journal of Memory and Language, 27,* 124–142.

Dell, G.S. (1990). Effects of frequency and vocabulary type on phonological speech errors. *Language and Cognitive Processes, 5,* 313–349.

Dell, G.S., Juliano, C., & Govindjee, A. (1993). Structure and content in language production: A theory of frame constraints in phonological speech errors. *Cognitive Science, 17,* 149–195.

Dell, G.S., & O'Seaghdha, P.G. (1991). Mediated and convergent lexical priming in language production: A comment on Levelt et al. (1991). *Psychological Review, 98,* 604–614.

Dell, G.S., & O'Seaghdha, P.G. (1992). Stages of lexical access in language production. *Cognition, 42,* 287–314.

Dell, G.S., & Reich, P.A. (1981). Stages in sentence production: An analysis of speech error data. *Journal of Verbal Learning and Verbal Behavior, 20,* 611–629.

Dell, G.S., Schwartz, M.F., Martin, N., Saffran, E.M., & Gagnon, D.A. (1997). Lexical access in aphasic and nonaphasic speakers. *Psychological Review, 104,* 801–838.

Fodor, J.A., Garrett, M.F., Walker, E.C.T., & Parkes, C.H. (1980). Against definitions. *Cognition, 8,* 263–367.

Garrett, M.F. (1975). The analysis of sentence production. In G.H. Bower (Ed.), *The psychology of learning and motivation* (pp. 133–177). New York: Academic Press.

Garrett, M.F. (1980). Levels of processing in sentence production. In B. Butterworth (Ed.), *Language production: Speech and talk* (Vol. 1, pp. 177–220). London: Academic Press.

Garrett, M.F. (1988). Processes in language production. In F.J. Newmeyer (Ed.), *Linguistics: The Cambridge survey* (Vol. 3, pp. 69–96). Cambridge, MA: Harvard University Press.

Glaser, W.R. (1992). Picture naming. *Cognition, 42,* 61–105.

Glaser, W.R., & Düngelhoff, F.-J. (1984). The time course of picture-word interference. *Journal of Experimental Psychology: Human Perception and Performance, 10,* 640–654.

Goldsmith, J. (1990). *Autosegmental and metrical phonology.* Cambridge, MA: Basil Blackwell.

Harley, T.A. (1993). Phonological activation of semantic competitors during lexical access in speech production. *Language and Cognitive Processes, 8,* 291–309.

Indefrey, P., & Levelt, W.J.M. (2000). The neural correlates of language production. In M. Gazzaniga (Ed.), *The new cognitive neurosciences* (2nd ed., pp. 845–865). Cambridge, MA: MIT Press.

Jescheniak, J.-D. (1994) *Word frequency effects in speech production*. Unpublished doctoral dissertation. Nijmegen University, The Netherlands.

Jescheniak, J.-D., & Levelt, W.J.M. (1994). Word frequency effects in speech production: Retrieval of syntactic information and phonological form. *Journal of Experimental Psychology: Learning, Memory, and Cognition, 20*, 824–843.

Kempen, G., & Hoenkamp, E. (1987). An incremental procedural grammar for sentence formulation. *Cognitive Science, 11*, 201–258.

La Heij, W., Mak, P., Sander, J., & Willeboordse, E. (1998). The gender-congruency effect in picture-word tasks. *Psychological Research, 61*, 209–219.

Levelt, W.J.M. (1989). *Speaking: From intention to articulation*. Cambridge, MA: MIT Press.

Levelt, W.J.M. (1992). Accessing words in speech production: Stages, processes and representations. *Cognition, 42*, 1–22.

Levelt, W.J.M., Praamstra, P., Meyer, A.S., Helenius, P., & Salmelin, R. (1998). An MEG study of picture naming. *Journal of Cognitive Neuroscience, 10*, 553–567.

Levelt, W.J.M., Roelofs, A., & Meyer, A.S. (1999a). A theory of lexical access in speech production. *Behavioral and Brain Sciences, 22*, 1–38.

Levelt, W.J.M., Roelofs, A., & Meyer, A.S. (1999b). Multiple perspectives on word production. *Behavioral and Brain Sciences, 22*, 61–75.

Levelt, W.J.M., Schriefers, H., Vorberg, D., Meyer, A.S., Pechmann, T., & Havinga, J. (1991). The time course of lexical access in speech production: A study of picture naming. *Psychological Review, 98*, 122–142.

Levelt, W.J.M., & Wheeldon, L.R. (1994). Do speakers have access to a mental syllabary? *Cognition, 50*, 239–269.

Levinson, S.C. (1997). From outer to inner space: Linguistic categories and non-linguistic thinking. In J. Nuyts & E. Pederson (Eds.), *Language and conceptualization* (pp. 13–45). Cambridge, UK: Cambridge University Press.

Meyer, A.S. (1990). The time course of phonological encoding in language production: The encoding of successive syllables of a word. *Journal of Memory and Language, 29*, 524–545.

Meyer, A.S. (1991). The time course of phonological encoding in language production: The phonological encoding inside a syllable. *Journal of Memory and Language, 30*, 69–89.

Meyer, A.S. (1996). Lexical access in phrase and sentence production: Results from picture-word interference experiments. *Journal of Memory and Language, 35*, 477–496.

Meyer, A.S. (1997). Word form generation in language production. In W. Hulstijn, H.F.M. Peters, & P.H.H.M. van Lieshout (Eds.), *Speech motor production and fluency disorders*. Amsterdam: Elsevier.

Meyer, A.S., & Schriefers, H. (1991). Phonological facilitation in picture-word interference experiments: Effects of stimulus onset asynchrony and types of interfering stimuli. *Journal of Experimental Psychology: Learning, Memory, and Cognition, 17*, 1146–1160.

Nooteboom, S.G. (1969). The tongue slips into patterns. In A.G. Sciarone, A.J. van Essen, & A.A. van Raad (Eds.), *Nomen: Leyden studies in linguistics and phonetics* (pp. 114–132). The Hague, The Netherlands: Mouton.

O'Seaghdha, P.G. (1999). Parsimonious feedback. *Behavioral and Brain Sciences, 22*, 51–52.

Peterson, R.R., Dell, G.S., & O'Seaghdha, P.G. (1989). A connectionist model of form-related priming effects. *Proceedings of the 11th annual conference of the Cognitive Science Society* (pp. 196–203). Hillsdale, NJ: Lawrence Erlbaum Associates Inc.

Peterson, R.R., & Savoy, P. (1998). Lexical selection and phonological encoding during language production: Evidence for cascaded processing. *Journal of Experimental Psychology: Learning, Memory and Cognition, 24*, 539–557.

Roberts, B., Kalish, M., Hird, K., & Kirsner, K. (1999). Decontextualised data in, decontextualised theory out. *Behavioral and Brain Sciences, 22*, 54–55.

Roelofs, A. (1992a). A spreading-activation theory of lemma retrieval in speaking. *Cognition, 42,* 107–142.

Roelofs, A. (1992b). *Lemma retrieval in speaking: A theory, computer simulations, and empirical data.* Unpublished doctoral dissertation, NICI Technical Report 92–08, University of Nijmegen, The Netherlands.

Roelofs, A. (1993). Testing a non-decompositional theory of lemma retrieval in speaking: Retrieval of verbs. *Cognition, 47,* 59–87.

Roelofs, A. (1994). On-line versus off-line priming of word-form encoding in spoken word production. In A. Ram & K. Eiselt (Eds.), *Proceedings of the 16th annual conference of the Cognitive Science Society* (pp. 772–777). Hillsdale, NJ: Lawrence Erlbaum Associates Inc.

Roelofs, A. (1996a). Computational models of lemma retrieval. In T. Dijkstra & K. De Smedt (Eds.), *Computational psycholinguistics: AI and connectionist models of human language processing* (pp. 308–327). London: Taylor & Francis.

Roelofs, A. (1996b). Morpheme frequency in speech production: Testing WEAVER. In G.E. Booij & J. van Marle (Eds.), *Yearbook of morphology 1996* (pp. 135–154). Dordrecht, The Netherlands: Kluwer Academic Publishers.

Roelofs, A. (1996c). Serial order in planning the production of successive morphemes of a word. *Journal of Memory and Language, 35,* 854–876.

Roelofs, A. (1997a). A case for nondecomposition in conceptually driven word retrieval. *Journal of Psycholinguistic Research, 26,* 33–67.

Roelofs, A. (1997b). Syllabification in speech production: Evaluation of WEAVER. *Language and Cognitive Processes, 12,* 657–693.

Roelofs, A. (1997c). The WEAVER model of word-form encoding in speech production. *Cognition, 64,* 249–284.

Roelofs, A. (1998). Rightward incrementality in encoding simple phrasal forms in speech production: Verb-particle combinations. *Journal of Experimental Psychology: Learning, Memory, and Cognition, 24,* 904–921.

Roelofs, A. (1999). Phonological segments and features as planning units in speech production. *Language and Cognitive Processes, 14,* 173–200.

Roelofs, A., & Meyer, A.S. (1998). Metrical structure in planning the production of spoken words. *Journal of Experimental Psychology: Learning, Memory, and Cognition, 24,* 922–939.

Roelofs, A., Meyer, A.S., & Levelt, W.J.M. (1996). Interaction between semantic and orthographic factors in conceptually driven naming: Comment on Starreveld and La Heij (1995). *Journal of Experimental Psychology: Learning, Memory, and Cognition, 22,* 246–251.

Roelofs, A., Meyer, A.S., & Levelt, W.J.M. (1998). A case for the lemma-lexeme distinction in models of speaking: Comment on Caramazza and Miozzo (1997). *Cognition, 69,* 219–230.

Santiago, J., & MacKay, D.G. (1999). Constraining production theories: Principled motivation, consistency, homunculi, underspecification, failed predictions, and contrary data. *Behavioral and Brain Sciences, 22,* 55–56.

Schade, U., & Berg, T. (1992). The role of inhibition in a spreading-activation model of language production: II. The simulational perspective. *Journal of Psycholinguistic Research, 21,* 435–462.

Schriefers, H. (1993). Syntactic processes in the production of noun phrases. *Journal of Experimental Psychology: Learning, Memory, and Cognition, 19,* 841–850.

Shastri, L., & Ajjanagadde, V. (1993). From simple associations to systematic reasoning: A connectionist representation of rules, variables and dynamic bindings using temporal synchrony. *Behavioral and Brain Sciences, 16,* 417–494.

Shattuck-Hufnagel, S. (1987). The role of word onset consonants in speech production planning: New evidence from speech error patterns. In E. Keller & M. Gopnik (Eds.), *Sensory processes in language.* Hillsdale, NJ: Lawrence Erlbaum Associates Inc.

Slobin, D.I. (1996). From "thought and language" to "thinking for speaking". In J.J. Gumperz & S.C. Levinson (Eds.), *Rethinking linguistic relativity* (pp. 70–96). Cambridge, UK: Cambridge University Press.

Starreveld, P.A., & La Heij, W. (1995). Semantic interference, orthographic facilitation, and their interaction in naming tasks. *Journal of Experimental Psychology: Language, Memory, and Cognition, 21*, 686–698.

Starreveld, P.A., & La Heij, W. (1996). Time-course analysis of semantic and orthographic context effects in picture naming. *Journal of Experimental Psychology: Learning, Memory, and Cognition, 22*, 896–918.

Stemberger, J.P. (1985). An interactive activation model of language production. In A.W. Ellis (Ed.), *Progress in the psychology of language* (Vol. 1, pp. 143–186). Hove, UK: Lawrence Erlbaum Associates Ltd.

Touretzky, D.S., & Hinton, G.E. (1988). A distributed connectionist production system. *Cognitive Science, 12*, 423–466.

Van Berkum, J.J.A. (1997). Syntactic processes in speech production: The retrieval of grammatical gender. *Cognition, 64*, 15–152.

Van Turennout, M., Hagoort, P., & Brown, C.M. (1997). Electrophysiological evidence on the time course of semantic and phonological processes in speech production. *Journal of Experimental Psychology: Learning, Memory, and Cognition, 23*, 787–806.

Van Turennout, M., Hagoort, P., & Brown, C.M. (1998). Brain activity during speaking: From syntax to phonology in 40 msec. *Science, 280*, 572–574.

Wernicke, C. (1874). *Der aphasiche Symptomenkomplex*. Breslau, Poland: Cohn & Weigert.

CHAPTER FIVE

When the words won't come: Relating impairments and models of spoken word production

Lyndsey Nickels
Macquarie Centre for Cognitive Science, Macquarie University, Sydney, Australia

David Howard
Department of Speech, University of Newcastle-upon-Tyne, UK

INTRODUCTION

Models of spoken word production have been developed using evidence from two primary sources—speech errors and experimental techniques. Probably the most influential in the early development of these models was speech error data. Slips of the tongue made by speakers were examined in terms of types of error that did and did not occur, and the kinds of factors that influenced their occurrence. From these data inferences were drawn regarding the component processes of word production (although the same data could lead to different inferences; contrast, for example, Dell, 1986, and Shattuck-Hufnagel, 1979). The second main approach that has been used is experimental, where the factors that affect subjects' performance (error rates, error types, or reaction times) are studied. Meyer (1992) suggests that experimental procedures have played a relatively minor role, at least in the development of models of phonological encoding. She argues that "detailed and comprehensive models . . . cannot be developed solely on the basis of error analyses [and that] future research should directly investigate the normal process of phonological encoding" (p. 181). Since Meyer made this point, experimental investigations of speech production with normal subjects have become a primary source of data in developing theoretical models (e.g., Levelt, Roelofs, & Meyer, 1999a). Beyond this, however, we would assert

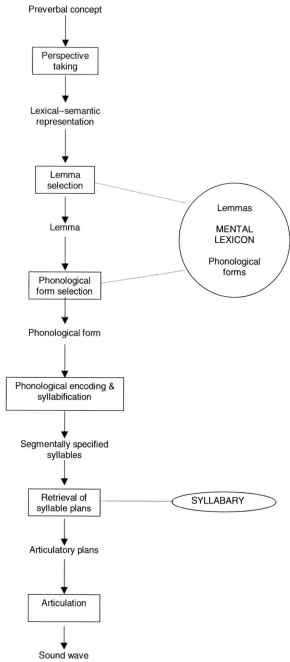

Figure 5.1. An outline sketch of the processes involved in speech production, based on Levelt et al. (1999a).

that models of speech production must also be developed in the light of neuro-psychological data from language impaired (aphasic) subjects.

Cognitive neuropsychology has a reciprocal relationship with cognitive and psycholinguistic models of language. It both aims to use these models to help explain the symptoms observed in neuropsychological patients, and to use the symptoms as tests of the models (Coltheart, 1987; Ellis, 1985). If a model of spoken word production is accurate and adequately specified, then it should be able to describe not only the normal production of words (and the occasional errors that occur in that process) but also the patterns of speech production that occur under conditions of damage.[1] This chapter aims to examine this issue, concentrating on the production of single words and excluding sentence production disorders and problems of connected speech.

As the framework for the discussion, we will use one of the most highly specified models of the (relatively) complete process of spoken word production from "intention to articulation", that of Levelt (1989, 1992; Levelt & Wheeldon, 1994; Levelt et al., 1999a). We shall first outline briefly the major components and processing assumptions of the most recent version of this model, as sketched in Figure 5.1 (the reader is referred to Levelt et al., 1999a, for a full description of the current version, and Levelt, 1989, for an extended discussion of the frame-work). Then we will focus on a number of issues: (1) What might we expect from impairments at each level? (2) How well can this model deal with impaired performance? (3) What commonly observed impairments might the model need to account for that it can't in its current form? These issues will be addressed by examining the model step by step, identifying predicted impairments and discuss-ing the limitations of the model in accounting for particular patterns of breakdown. As and when appropriate we will discuss other theoretical models which may account for some patterns of breakdown in a different way (e.g., Dell, 1986, 1989).

LEVELT'S MODEL OF SPOKEN WORD PRODUCTION

The starting point in the production of a spoken word is the "intention" to produce a word. We will not consider here quite what this might involve, except to say that at some point the conceptual representation of the word must be activated in the preverbal semantic system (see Figure 5.1). This representation then attempts to retrieve a lexical concept. This process will not always find a single lexical concept for a message. Although [male duck], [male swan], and [male crow] are equally plausible prelexical concepts, the first two can be satis-fied by a single lexical concept (DRAKE and COB respectively), but the third will have to be expressed as a phrase (MALE CROW). This is the problem of "lexicalisation". The second kind of indeterminacy in this mapping is that a single prelexical concept can be legitimately referred to in a variety of ways;

for instance, a dog might equally happily be referred to as ANIMAL, DOG, ALSATIAN, ROVER, or HE. Which of these lexical concepts will be activated depends on the pragmatics of the context, which Levelt et al. refer to as "per-spective taking". This lexical-semantic representation then "triggers" lexical items into activity. That is to say, activation of a particular lexical concept (e.g., DOG) will in turn activate the lexical item associated with that concept (e.g., the word "dog"). Levelt's theory, in common with most current psycholinguistic accounts, incorporates two stages in lexical access. The first stage in this process he terms "lexical selection" (Levelt, 1992)—retrieval of the appropriate word given the lexical-semantic representation. This results in retrieval of a "lemma", which makes available the syntactic information associated with that lexical item (necessary for grammatical encoding and sentence planning). The lemma in turn activates the corresponding phonological representation for that lexical item. The retrieval of this phonological form is the starting point of the second stage of lexical access—"phonological encoding". This takes the stored phonological form of a word and produces a phonetic plan which is the input to the final (articulatory) stage of speech production. The phonological form contains suffi-cient information to specify both the segments of a word (phonemes) and the metrical structure (number of syllables and their weight or stress); the metrical structure, however, is only specified where the correct structure cannot be gen-erated on the basis of the phoneme string—in English when the stress does not lie on the first "heavy" syllable.[2] Thus, as far as possible, the metrical frame is computed rather than retrieved from the lexicon. Phonological encoding then requires the segments and the (computed or retrieved) metrical frame to be combined to yield a set of syllable specifications.

At first sight this process is obtuse. Why take a specification of a word's phonology, decompose it, and then recompute it? The answer, Levelt et al. argue, lies in the observation that we do not speak word by word or morpheme by morpheme, but in syllables which do not necessarily respect word or morpheme boundaries. For example, "Hard answer" is produced as the syllables "har-dan-swer" (/hɑ-dɑn-sɜ/). This seemingly convoluted system is necessary to handle this process of resyllabification.

The syllables that result from phonological assembly are then used as addresses for stored phonetic syllable templates. Levelt suggests that these are motor plans for complex articulatory gestures ("gestural scores" in Browman & Goldstein's, 1992, terminology). Frequently used syllables will be stored but rare or novel syllables may still be computed on-line.

LEVELS OF DEFICIT

It is a core assumption of cognitive neuropsychology that brain damage can selectively impair specific components of a processing model.[3] Hence, there are clearly many different possible loci of damage to the model of speech production we have just outlined. We will now work through the model, discussing each level of possible breakdown in turn together with the kinds of disorders that might be (and have been) attributed to these levels of deficit. During the course of this discussion we will focus on the characteristics of single deficits. It is, of course, entirely possible that many aphasic subjects have multiple levels of breakdown, and it is clear that different subjects can have different deficits. The primary source of evidence that we will be considering, therefore, is detailed case studies of brain-damaged subjects with impairments of word production.

Impairments in conceptualisation

The level of preverbal concepts in the model in Figure 5.1 is explicitly non-verbal. Degradation of representations at this level should then result in semantic problems both in tasks of understanding and producing language and in tasks that probe conceptual knowledge in nonlinguistic ways. Patients with a progress-ive disorder known as semantic dementia appear to show a deficit of just this kind. These patients are usually first seen complaining of a difficulty in word retrieval. On testing they are found to perform poorly in a range of tasks probing knowledge of the meanings of words and of objects. Patients perform badly in word-to-picture matching where the distractors are drawn from the same category as the target. With both words and pictures, they make errors in sorting tasks which probe accurate semantic knowledge, for instance in deciding if an item is a British or foreign animal; sorting into more general categories, for instance deciding if an item is an animal or an object, may be performed relatively accurately (Hodges, Patterson, Oxbury, & Funnell, 1992; Warrington, 1975). In naming pictures they make errors where typically they offer the name of the category (e.g., DONKEY → "animal but I don't know which one"), or make semantic errors substituting another item from the same category (e.g., BULL → "cow"). Knowledge of higher frequency items is usually better preserved than lower frequency items. As the disorder progresses, patients become less accurate in sorting and comprehension tasks, and in naming failures to produce any can-didate name come to predominate over superordinate and coordinate semantic errors (Funnell & Hodges, 1991).

The difficulties of these patients are clearly semantic in that their pattern of performance is consistent with the relative preservation of general category in-formation and poorer performance in tasks that require access to item-specific semantic attributes. Their difficulty is also not confined to language: Sorting of pictures is usually as impaired as sorting of words, and the patients also perform poorly in semantic tasks involving only pictures—for instance, in the Pyramids and Palm Trees test where subjects have to decide if a picture of pyramids is associated with a palm tree or a pine tree (Howard & Patterson, 1992). The deficit can be seen as progressive underspecification of conceptual semantics: As knowledge of specific semantic attributes is lost, word retrieval is driven by conceptual representations that are no longer detailed enough to specify the precise target word. Instead, patients substitute superordinates or, where there is activation of a field of semantically related items, the most easily retrieved of the set of semantic coordinates.

In aphasic patients there is also a strong correlation between the incidence of semantic errors in word comprehension and semantic errors in picture naming (Butterworth, Howard, & McLoughlin, 1984; Gainotti, Miceli, Caltagirone, Silveri, & Masullo, 1981; Nickels & Howard, 1994); there are also individual subjects who make high rates of semantic errors in all tasks involving language comprehension and production—for example, the patient KE reported by Hillis and Caramazza (1995). This might be taken as evidence of impairment to central conceptual-semantic representations for these subjects. As Butterworth et al. (1984) point out, it is not clear that this conclusion can be justified. Many aphasic subjects perform poorly in nonverbal semantic tasks, such as associative picture matching. However there are examples of subjects who perform poorly in all semantic tasks involving words, but show wholly normal performance in nonverbal semantic tasks—for instance, TRC reported by Nickels (1992a) and Nickels and Howard (1994). It is then tempting to distinguish between conceptual and verbal semantic systems, with patients like TRC having impairments only in the verbal semantic system (cf., Beauvois, 1982; Warrington, 1975). The difficulty here is that this pattern of impairment is also compatible with a single conceptual-semantic system, with TRC having a difficulty in access to this and output from it from all verbal modalities but not from nonverbal (e.g., Riddoch, Humphreys, Coltheart, & Funnell, 1988). Deciding between these possibilities then raises the question of how to distinguish between corruption of semantic representations and deficits in the procedures involved in access to them. Shallice (1987) proposed a set of criteria that could be used to distinguish between access and storage deficits. Although these criteria have been widely criticised on both empirical and the-oretical grounds (e.g., Howard, 1985; Rapp, Hillis, & Caramazza, 1993; Riddoch et al., 1988), no serious alternative proposals have been made. Recent evidence shows that semantic deficits in severe aphasia and degenerative neurological disorders may have very different properties (Warrington & Cipolotti, 1996), although whether these are best captured as access and storage disorders or as two different kinds of impairment to semantics remains an open question.

There is an obvious relationship here between deficits in lexical semantics and conceptual semantics, and Levelt et al.'s (1999a) distinction between the same two levels. In Levelt's system the two systems could have very differently organised semantic representations. Verbal semantic representations consist of item concept nodes linked by labelled relations. So both CAT and RABBIT are linked to ANIMAL by <IS A>, and to TAIL by <HAS A>. CAT but not RABBIT is linked to WHISKERS, and so on. CAT and RABBIT are not linked directly. Errors can occur through spreading activation within this system result-ing in the wrong node being selected. Given that, on average, apart from the target the most active nodes will be those with a single linkage, errors will be likely to be superordinates (e.g., animal) or associates such as properties (e.g., tail, whiskers). Coordinate items will be activated via two links and will be correspondingly less likely to occur. There is some indication that semantic errors by aphasic speakers conform to this kind of pattern. Both "shared feature" (i.e., superordinates, coordinates, and, much more rarely, subordinates) and "associative" (e.g., parts, properties, locations) occur with almost all aphasic patients (e.g., Butterworth et al., 1984; Nickels, 1997, etc.). An impairment to a lexical-semantic system organised in this way provides a natural explanation of why these two error types typically co-occur.

Levelt et al. (1999a) make no strong claims about the nature of preverbal conceptual representations. One possibility is that, in contrast to the localist representation in the lexical-semantic system, there is a distributed feature-based semantic representation. Within such a system, when some of the features are lost—or degraded—the remaining representation will contain elements of the original representation. This should then result, almost exclusively, in "shared feature" errors, typically coordinates and superordinates of the target. This seems to relate rather closely to descriptions of naming errors in patients with semantic dementia, who rarely, if ever, make associative errors (see Hodges, Graham, & Patterson, 1995, for a detailed analysis).

Impairments in lemma retrieval

How might a patient with no deficit at the conceptual level, but with an impairment at the level of lemma retrieval, behave? Answering this question depends critically on whether the lemma level is involved only in language production or in comprehension as well. Butterworth (1980; Butterworth et al., 1984) suggests that the lemma level (which he calls a semantic lexicon) is involved in both production and comprehension. He argues that difficulties at this level will result in semantic errors in both comprehension and production. The co-occurrence of these errors in patients, such as TRC, without impairment at a conceptual level can then be understood as a consequence of a single lemma-level lesion. Levelt et al. (1999a) also suggest that lemma representations are activated when a word is heard, implying a role in both production and comprehension.

Howard and Orchard-Lisle (1984) describe a woman, JCU, with a severe global aphasia. Although her spontaneous naming was almost totally abolished, she could retrieve around 50% of picture names correctly given the first phoneme of the word as a cue. When she was cued instead with the initial phoneme of a semantically related word (e.g., picture TIGER cue /lə/), she produced 35% semantically related errors. JCU also made high rates of semantic errors in both spoken and written word comprehension, but was within the normal range in associative picture matching (the "Pyramids and Palm Trees Test"; Howard & Patterson, 1992). Howard and Orchard-Lisle argue that this pattern of performance is consistent with JCU using partial, underspecified semantic representations in both word production and word comprehension. This pattern could be due to a lemma level deficit. If, however, there are separable verbal and conceptual semantic systems, JCU's performance might instead be due to a selective impairment to verbal semantics.

Studies of the facilitation of aphasic naming support the view that the lemma level is involved in both word comprehension and word production. Howard, Patterson, Franklin, Orchard-Lisle, and Morton (1985) showed that comprehension of a word in a spoken word-to-picture matching task resulted in improved naming of the treated items that lasted for at least 24 hours. This effect was found with a variety of different comprehension tasks involving both spoken and written words, including spoken word-to-picture matching, written word-to-picture matching, and semantic judgements on spoken sentences. Although all these tasks clearly involve access to conceptual semantics, there are a number of reasons for not locating the priming effect at this level. First, the effect was equivalent for patients with good performance in the Pyramids and Palm Trees test—and therefore good access to conceptual semantics for pictures—and those with poor performance on the test (Howard et al., 1985). Second, there is no effect of priming of semantic neighbours: There is no benefit to the patient's naming of DOG from previously matching the word "cat" to its picture with the picture of a DOG as one of the distractors (Howard et al., 1985). Third, priming by semantic judgements shows no effect of the depth of a semantic judgement; Barry and McHattie (1991) showed that there was equal priming from questions involving superficial category knowledge (e.g., answering the question "Is a duck or a train a living thing?") and those requiring more detailed semantic information (e.g., "Is a swan or a duck a water bird with webbed feet and which quacks?"). Fourth, access to the semantics without hearing the target word form has no effect: Le Dorze, Boulay, Gaudreau, and Brassard (1994) found that there was no priming from matching a description to a picture (e.g., "Show me a mollusc with long arms"), but there was priming when the target word was used (e.g., "Show me an octopus"). And, finally, there was a smaller priming effect for "conduction" aphasics, whose characteristic errors in naming are phonologically related to the target, and so arise at a post-lemma level, than other patients with more central impairments in word retrieval (Howard et al., 1985).

These facilitation effects are also unlikely to be due to priming at a level of phonological word forms. Word repetition, which involves both spoken word recognition and spoken word production, results in much more short-lasting priming of picture naming than tasks involving semantic access (Barry & McHattie, 1991; Patterson, Purell, & Morton, 1983). Phonemically cueing a patient to produce a picture name, by giving them the initial segment(s), has similarly short-lasting effects on naming (Patterson et al., 1983).

The natural explanation of these facilitation effects is that they are located at the lemma level. Access to conceptual semantics in the priming tasks results in priming of the lemma; this makes the lemma easier to access when the same item is presented for picture naming. This account, although attractive, is not easily reconciled with investigations of lemma priming in normal subjects. Wheeldon and Monsell (1994) showed that if a semantic coordinate (a potential competitor) had been produced shortly beforehand, naming was slowed. This inhibition effect, which Wheeldon and Monsell attribute to competition between a partly activated lemma from the previous naming attempt and the target lemma, was found only with short lags between the priming trial and target naming. Why only short-lasting effects are found on normal subjects' latencies, and long-lasting effects on aphasic patients', naming accuracy is still unclear.

Failures of access to phonological word forms

Butterworth (1980) argued that distinguishing between two stages in word retrieval could account for two distinct types of normal speech errors. When the incorrect lemma was retrieved, a semantically related real word would result. When there was misaddressing of the phonological word-form level, a phonologically related real word ("formal paraphasia" or "malapropism") would result.

When a formal paraphasia is produced, however, it has two potential sources. It could be the result of misaddressing of phonological word forms, but it might instead be due to a phonemic error in the production of a correctly accessed phonological word form—in Butterworth's (1979) term a "jargon homophone". These jargon homophones are likely to be particularly frequent with short target words. Consider for example the target "cat". An error on one of the phonemes of this will frequently produce another real word—for instance "fat", "rat", "hat", "cot", "cut", "cap", or "can"—and only rather rarely a nonword, such as "jat" or "ket". With longer words fewer of the phonological neighbours (words sharing all but one phoneme with the target) will be real words; "elephant", for example, has only two real word phonological neighbours—"elegant" and "element".

To show, therefore, that genuine formal errors are occurring it is important to demonstrate that the proportion of real words is greater than might be expected by chance. This is termed a "lexical bias". There is some controversy on the extent of lexical bias in naturally occurring speech error corpora. Garrett (1976) found no lexical bias, Stemberger (1984) a weak bias, and Dell and Reich (1981) a stronger one. As Stemberger (1985) argues, these differences may depend both on the method used to calculate chance levels, and on biases in the collection of the corpora. A stronger lexical bias may be found in elicited speech errors (e.g., Baars, Motley, & MacKay, 1975; Dell, 1990), but, as Levelt (1989) points out, the degree of bias depends on the experimental conditions and may reflect the use of a selective pre-articulatory monitor.

Most aphasic subjects who make phonologically related errors in their speech production show little or no lexical bias in these errors. Nickels and Howard (1995) investigated 15 such patients. Of their phonologically related responses, on average 23% were real words. The proportion of real words was greater with shorter targets—exactly the pattern that would be expected if the real words were real words by chance. With one-syllable targets 41% of phonological errors were real words, and this fell to 15% for two-syllable and 10% for three-syllable targets. When chance levels were assessed by randomly generating pseudo-errors that shared exactly the same number of segments with the target as the real errors, no patient produced more real-word errors than would be expected by chance.

There are, however, three case reports of subjects who make high rates of formal paraphasias in naming. The proportion of phonologically related errors that were real words were 49% for NC, reported by Martin, Dell, Saffran, and Schwartz (1994), 58% for RB, reported by Blanken (1990), and 61% for MF, described by Best (1996). By generating a corpus of pseudo-errors, Best shows that for her subject only 32% of his errors would be real words by chance, and concludes that MF is making genuine formal errors. Unlike the subjects reported by Nickels and Howard, there was no tendency for formal errors to occur more frequently with shorter targets. The formal errors made by these patients could be explained as misaddressing of the phonological word-form level by the lemma level. One should note, however, that all of the patients appear to have had additional deficits: All of them made semantic errors (although for RB there were few of these), and all produced many phonologically related nonword errors. Typically these nonword responses shared more phonemes with the target words than did the formal paraphasias, suggesting that a different mechanism, probably located beyond the phonological word-form level, was responsible for them.

When a lemma is successfully accessed, a variety of kinds of syntactic information is made available, including those that are important for guiding the generation of a syntactic structure. This includes (in languages that mark gender) the target word's grammatical gender. Badecker, Miozzo, and Zanuttini (1995) report an Italian subject, Dante, who on about one-third of occasions could not retrieve the spoken form of a target word in sentence completion or picture naming. On 95–97% of these failed naming trials, Dante was able to give the correct gender of the target items. Grammatical gender in Italian is partly determined by semantics—*padre* (father) is masculine, and *madre* (mother) is feminine—but such information does not determine gender for many items. More informative is phonological form; most words ending in /o/ are masculine, and most ending in /a/ are feminine. There are, however, numerous exceptions to this, so both *casa* (house) and *mano* (hand) are masculine, and *caso* (fate) and *problema* (problem) are feminine. Badecker et al. are careful to show that Dante's ability to access gender information was just as good for items whose gender was not accurately predicted by their semantics or their phonological form, as those with predictable gender. Moreover, Dante was at chance on questions probing his knowledge of the target's phonological form, including aspects such as the item length, and the initial or final letters. This is persuasive evidence for a failure to access the target's phonological form at the phonological word-form level with correct retrieval of gender information from the lemma level. Dante does not seem to have lost phonological forms; his accuracy in naming items that he had, on a previous occasion failed to name was not significantly worse than on an unselected set.[4]

This inconsistency in Dante's word retrieval can be contrasted with the patient EE reported by Howard (1995). EE was very consistent in the items he could name correctly, even when the confounding effects of the lexical variables affecting his naming were partialled out. Furthermore with an initial phoneme cue, or extra time EE could never name items that he consistently failed to name without such help. His errors consisted almost entirely of omissions and descriptions of the items. His naming was unaffected by both phonological factors such as target length, and semantic properties such as target imageability, but was affected by target frequency (with rated familiarity the best predictor of his success). Although it is impossible to show conclusively that lexical items have been lost, rather than being present but consistently unavailable, Howard argues that the pattern of EE's performance is best described as lost or permanently and consistently inaccessible lexical items, affecting primarily those of lower frequency. EE's comprehension of the same words which he could not produce as names was unimpaired. If, as has been suggested by Butterworth, the lemma level is involved in both word comprehension and word production, EE's problem cannot be at this level; his problem must then be due to a deficit at the phonological word-form level.

The tip-of-the tongue state and aphasia

When asked to retrieve very low-frequency items, normal subjects will often feel that the word is "on the tip of their tongue" (TOT). When in this state, subjects can often retrieve similar sounding words (for instance retrieving "secant" for the target "sextant"), and can often supply partial information about sound pattern of the word, including its initial letter (or sound—few attempts have been made to disambiguate these), its syllable length, and its metrical pattern (see Brown, 1991; Brown & McNeill, 1966). Subjects can typically retrieve phonological information of this kind on around two-thirds of occasions when they are in the TOT state.

How can one account for this state where partial phonological information has been retrieved without the full phonological form? Garrett (1976) suggested that the partial phonological information was deducible from the linking address retrieved from the lemma level and used to retrieve the phonological word-form information (cf., Butterworth, 1992; Levelt et al., 1999a). Thus, when the lemma had been correctly accessed, but the phonological form was unavailable, subjects could often guess general features about its form.

When aphasic subjects fail to produce a word, they will often volunteer that "I know the word, but I can't say it". Could such people be in a TOT state? Goodglass, Kaplan, Weintraub, and Ackerman (1976) found that, with the exception of "conduction" aphasics, aphasic subjects were no better than chance in indicating the length of words they could not retrieve. And, given that many of the patients diagnosed as having conduction aphasia have post-phonological word-form deficits in phonological encoding (Caplan & Waters, 1992; Kohn, 1992), this is no evidence for access to lemmas without retrieval of the phonological form. Supporting this view, Feinberg, Rothi, and Heilman (1986) showed that some conduction aphasics were good at judging whether pictures had homophonous names even though they could not produce the names accurately. Whereas most aphasic patients know little of the length of target words they cannot produce, in the Goodglass et al. study they were above chance, although very poor at indicating the initial letter of the word. Bruce and Howard (1988) showed that many subjects who could indicate targets' initial letters with above-chance accuracy had no knowledge of the relationships between letters and sounds. They argued that, in such patients, the ability to indicate initial letters reflects access to orthographic information without partial information about the phonological form of the target word.

We have suggested that both the patient Dante, and normal subjects in a TOT state, have accessed the lemma without retrieving the corresponding phonological word form. Yet there is an obvious difference: Subjects in the TOT state have partial information about the target's phonological form, whereas Dante had no phonological information. This difference can be explained if we postulate different kinds of failures in these subjects. Dante has accessed the correct lemma, which makes syntactic information about the item available, but fails to retrieve from the lemma the address of the phonological word form. In the TOT state, in contrast, subjects have accessed the appropriate lemma, and retrieved the phonological word form's address in phonological space but access to the target phonological word form is blocked.

If syntactic information about a target, including its gender, is stored with the lemma, whereas form information requires an activated lemma to address the phonological word form, in the TOT state subjects should only be able to access form information when correct gender information is available. However, several recent experiments with normal Italian subjects show that access to form information is no better when subjects have the correct gender than when they do not (e.g., Caramazza & Miozzo, 1997; Vigliocco, Antonini, & Garrett, 1997). This finding suggests that syntactic information is not stored with the lemma. Rather the lemma points to both syntactic features and phonological form; in the TOT state access to each of these is independent. Dante, whose access to phonological form is blocked, can nevertheless retrieve the target item's gender.

Although longer words should be more susceptible to error in the processes of postlexical phonological encoding, there is a variety of reasons for thinking that access to the phonological form may be easier for long words than short words. Butterworth (1989) suggests that the lemma yields an address to the phonological level, which is organised in terms of a multidimensional phonological space. Where there is a small error in the address with a short word, which typically has many phonological neighbours, an incorrect phonological word form may be retrieved. Longer words have fewer neighbours and inhabit less densely populated regions of phonological space. A corrupted address may still serve to identify the appropriate phonological word form, particularly if phonological word forms are surrounded by attractor basins within the phonological space (see Hinton & Shallice, 1991, for a discussion of attractor basins). Recent connectionist models seem to make a similar prediction. Plaut and Shallice (1993) show that after lesioning there is better retrieval of information for items that are more richly and distinctively represented within a domain. We would emphasise, however, that no current connectionist models of phonological word-form retrieval have manipulated word length; without implementation it is impossible to be sure how the models will behave.

A recent case study, by Best (1995), reports a subject, CGJ, whose naming is more accurate for pictures with long names than short names. He had excellent word and picture comprehension, and showed improved naming with a phonemic cue, suggesting that the phonological form of lexical items has not been lost. On the accounts we have suggested we might anticipate that reverse length effects would be associated with formal paraphasias, when the wrong phonological word form has been addressed. However, CGJ made very few phonologically related responses; his most frequent errors were omissions, and semantically related responses, which may reflect provision of related information in the absence of the target phonological form. One might speculate that he is using his good comprehension abilities to monitor, and edit out, formal paraphasias before they are articulated, but there is no positive evidence in favour of this.

In Butterworth's account, at least, the reverse length effect is, in essence, an effect of the density of lexical items in phonological space and not a true length effect. The length effect should then disappear when the effects of number of phonological neighbours is controlled. However, precisely the opposite pattern is shown by CGJ. Best reports that when word length is controlled there is a trend towards a beneficial effect of the number of neighbours. Why a beneficial effect of both length and neighbours should co-occur is not easily understood.

Phonological encoding deficits and deficits in retrieval of stored syllable plans

As discussed in the Introduction, accessing the phonological form of a word results in three kinds of information being activated—the word's morphological make-up, its metrical shape, and its constituent segments (phonemes). For each morpheme (and this chapter restricts itself to considering monomorphemic words) the segmental and metrical information is "spelled-out". Stored metrical information consists of the number of syllables and position of main-stress syllable. However, this is only stored for words that do not have "regular" stress (in

English, when main stress does not fall on the first full vowel). Spelled-out segments are successively inserted into the metrical template, forming phonological syllables. If no stored metrical template is available then syllables are generated from the segmental information alone, following universal and language specific rules. These syllables then address the stored articulatory plans (in the syllabary).

What are the possible types of breakdown that might occur during this process of phonological encoding? In this discussion we will primarily address the computational version of Levelt et al.'s (1999a) theory—WEAVER++; although this differs in some details from the descriptive theory, the level of specificity of the latter is insufficient to enable clear predictions to be derived (for an illustration of this problem see e.g., Nickels, 1997; Nickels & Howard, 1999).[5] At present, there are several key areas of the descriptive theory that WEAVER++ does not implement. For example, Levelt et al. are clear that syllabification occurs in a left-to-right manner with "lookahead" to determine whether there is a following vowel (and hence a subsequent syllable) that may affect syllabification. However, there seems no such mechanism explicitly implemented in WEAVER++. Likewise, for morphemes with non-default metrical structure there must be a mechanism to use stored metrical information when syllabifying the morpheme —WEAVER++ has no such system. Furthermore, WEAVER++ is designed to account for reaction-time data from normal subjects, consideration of how the model might produce errors (and hence for our purposes the likely effects of damage) is little more than a promissory note. Once again, this makes deriving predictions difficult.

WEAVER++ includes a verification procedure: "Attached to each node in the network, there is a procedure that verifies the label on the link between the node and a target node one level up. Hence, an active but inappropriate node cannot become selected" (Levelt et al., 1999a, p. 23). Thus, for any errors to occur presumably this procedure must fail. Levelt et al. make it clear that verification is not obligatory: "WEAVER++ skips verification to gain speed in order to obtain a higher speech rate. Thus, more errors are to be expected at high speech rates."

The segmental errors made by normal subjects are generally attributed to segmental selection errors when inserting segments into (metrical) frames (Dell, 1986; Shattuck-Hufnagel, 1979). These errors tend to preserve syllable position of the interacting segments. In WEAVER++, selected segments are not marked for syllable position. Therefore, errors made during the construction of phonological representation would not necessarily maintain syllable position. Thus, Levelt et al. (1999a; Roelofs, 1997) argue that the source of these errors is indexing failures in the device that maps syllabified phonological representations onto a mental syllabary. In other words the perceived segmental errors are actually a result of selecting the wrong syllable (rather than the wrong segment). As these errors are the result of syllable selection errors, the more syllables there are to select the greater the likelihood of an error occurring—thus length effects would be predicted in terms of number of syllables (but no effect of number of phonemes within a syllable[6]).

Although this is the only error source discussed by Levelt et al. (1999a) clearly there are a number of other potential sources of error within WEAVER++'s phonological processing system, as follows.

Problems related to activation of the segment nodes:

- Too little activation: If either decay of activation is too fast or the spreading rate too slow (equivalent to low connection strength) then there will be difficulty achieving sufficient activation of phoneme nodes.
- Too much activation: If the decay rate is too slow or rate of spread of activation too fast, then activation will build up across the phoneme nodes with many phonemes becoming active.
- Noise added to resting levels of activation: Random variation in the resting levels of activation of phoneme nodes could lead to the wrong phonemes becoming active.
- Loss of connections: Clearly if a connection or set of connections is lost then the particular phoneme node affected cannot become active as a result of this link.
- Problems with the "numbering" on the connections between the morpheme and segment nodes: In WEAVER++ the serial order of phonemes is marked by numbering the connections, which would seem to be a possible source of impairment. However, it is not at all clear how this numbering is achieved, and therefore predicting the results of disrupting this mechanism is not possible.

The consequences of these impairments are difficult to predict. However, many of the problems would appear likely to result in the "wrong" segment node being most active. Thus, the incorrect phoneme node might be selected for production resulting in substitution errors. However, for some problems (too little activation and loss of connections) it is possible that omissions may occur when the correct phoneme fails to be activated. With longer words more nodes will need to be correctly activated (in the right order) to drive successful production. More connections will be involved, and so we would anticipate that errors should be more likely with words containing more phonemes.

Loss of stored syllable plans. Levelt (1989, 1992) suggests that syllable plans could be computed on-line for less common syllables; under conditions of loss or damage every syllable might then have to be computed. This would not necessarily, therefore, result in any overt errors although there conceivably could be a delay in reaction time. Alternatively, when one plan is unavailable, the most active alternative syllable might be retrieved. In other words, a syllable with a similar structure and phonemes will be retrieved as these will be receiving some degree of activation. Thus, errors that should occur with this level of deficit are syllable substitutions (as with the syllable selection errors described previously). These might, in practice, be difficult to distinguish from phoneme substitution errors arising from earlier levels of deficit, except perhaps by the degree of similarity between target and error. Errors resulting from retrieval of syllable plans from similar addresses (to the target) might be more similar than syllables resulting from substitution of a phoneme. This is because phoneme substitutions at earlier levels of deficit are not necessarily governed by the phonological characteristics of the segments, but syllable plans that are co-active will have similar phonetic structure.

Deficits in syllable plan assembly.   Levelt suggests that low-frequency syllables probably aren't stored and therefore have to be assembled for output. If these assembly procedures were impaired then errors or omissions would be expected but only for low-frequency syllables. There is a tendency for low-frequency syllables to be more complex than high-frequency syllables; as a result, syllable phoneme length will tend to be confounded with syllable frequency. Nevertheless, the relationship between syllable phoneme length and frequency is modest, and it would be possible to match high- and low-frequency syllables for length.

Patient data

So, what do we find when we look at the phonological errors aphasic patients make? First we will discuss two features that have been addressed in the previous discussion (error types and effects of word length) and will then turn to two other factors that influence phonological errors in aphasia but are not as naturally accounted for in WEAVER++ (phonotactics and sonority, and similarity of target and error).

Error types.   The predictions derived earlier suggest that substitutions should be the most common error type observed. This appears to be the case. Blumstein (1973) analysed the phonological errors of 17 aphasics and found that as a group they made more substitution errors (48.5% of errors) than additions or omissions. Niemi, Koivuselka-Sallinen, and Hanninen (1985) also found that each of their three (Broca's) aphasic patients had a higher proportion of substitutions (52% or more). However, each of these three patients also made addition and omission errors. Other patients have been reported who produce more similar proportions of error types. For example, CM (Kohn, 1989) produced 41% consonant omissions, 38% substitutions, and 22% additions. Pate, Saffran, and Martin (1987) report a patient who seems more unusual in producing substantially more omission errors (56%) than substitutions (24%; with 14% additions).

There is clearly no simple division between those patients that make substitution errors and those that make omission (and addition) errors. At present all the patients reported seem to make both types of error. It would appear that breakdown resulting in phonological errors rarely (if ever) results in only one type of error—clearly the model needs to simulate this result.

Length effects.   Length effects are very common in aphasia, indeed, it is more remarkable for a patient to make phonological errors and NOT show a length effect. Nickels (1995) found that 9 of the 14 aphasics who produced phonological errors in her study showed significant effects of word length. However, whereas length effects have been widely reported measured either in terms of number of syllables (e.g., Friedman & Kohn, 1990; Kay & Ellis, 1987) or number of phonemes (e.g., Howard, Patterson, Franklin, Morton, & Orchard-Lisle, 1984), few studies have attempted to disambiguate the two effects. The different deficits discussed earlier suggest that it may be possible for effects of number of syllables and number of phonemes to dissociate. A deficit affecting syllable plan retrieval might be expected to result in an effect of number of syllables (the more syllables a word has, the greater the probability of a spell-out error occurring), whereas a deficit in activating phoneme nodes would be more likely to result in an effect of the number phonemes.

In contrast to the majority of studies, Caplan (1987) does disambiguate the source of the length effect in his patient RL. RL was tested on four-phoneme words of one, two, or three syllables. He showed an effect of the number of syllables even in this test when the number of phonemes remained constant. We have also examined this issue (Nickels, 1997; Nickels & Howard, 2000) by comparing the ability of patients to repeat words that varied in either number of syllables or number of phonemes (but not both). We found patients that showed significant effects of number of phonemes (when number of syllables was held constant). However, no patient showed an effect like that of RL—worse performance on words with more syllables when number of phonemes was held constant. Indeed, three patients showed the reverse effect—better performance on two-syllable than one-syllable words with the same number of phonemes. We would suggest that this is because of the inevitable confound between complexity of syllabic structure and number of syllables when the number of phonemes is held constant—a one-syllable four-phoneme word will contain at least one consonant cluster (i.e., CCVC, e.g., skill, or CVCC, e.g., paste), whereas two-syllable four-phoneme words will often only have single consonants (i.e., CVCV, e.g., hobby, or VCVC, e.g., urban). This hypothesis was supported in a separate task where the patients who showed the reverse syllable length effect were found to be worse at repeating words that contained consonant clusters than a matched set of words that did not contain clusters.

Thus, independent effects of the number of syllables and the number of phonemes in the target can be found and may relate to different levels of deficit in the model, as described previously.

Phonotactics and sonority.   A number of authors have noted that the phono-logical errors aphasic patients produce, like normal speech errors, almost always obey the phonotactic rules of the language (e.g., Blumstein, 1978; Buckingham & Kertesz, 1974). Christman (1994) argues that sonority is also an important factor and that many studies have failed to distinguish between effects of sonority and phonotactics. Sonority refers to the perceptual prominence of one phoneme relative to another. Phonemes obey a hierarchy from least to most sonorant for the initial half of the syllable (to the vowel) and reversed for the final half, together with the language-specific phonotactic constraints. Christman examines the phonological errors of three aphasics and argues that phoneme substitutions are constrained by sonority independent of phonotactics (although this also played a part). She suggests that sonority is a constraint on the default generation mechanism.

Levelt et al. (1999a) are explicit that the syllabification process that generates the syllable structure given the segments of a morpheme, follows universal and language-specific rules including those of sonority. However, it is unclear quite how such a mechanism might work as this has yet to be implemented in WEAVER++.

Similarity of target and error.   Green (1969), amongst others, notes that the target and the error phoneme that replaces it tend to be articulatorily and acoustically similar. Blumstein (1973) divided errors into those that differed from their targets by one distinctive feature and those that differed by more than one. She found that there were significantly more errors that differed by only one distinctive feature than would be expected by chance. However, other authors have not found this pattern. Kohn and Smith (1990) observed that the majority of targets and errors shared none or only one distinctive feature. Similarly, Miller and Ellis (1987) found that target and error phonemes shared no more distinctive features than a randomly generated pseudo-corpus of error phonemes. Both real and pseudo-errors tended to differ from their targets by only one or two distinctive features.

It is unclear, therefore, whether aphasic phoneme substitution errors are related to their targets in terms of distinctive features. This problem is exacerbated because, in different studies, the number of distinctive features are counted in quite different ways, varying from simple voice/manner/place feature descrip-tions to the complex feature sets of Chomsky and Halle. It may be the case that some aphasic individuals do show an influence of the target phonology on the error. If so then this will need to be incorporated into the model. In Dell (1986) there is a featural level which would make substituting phonemes more likely to share distinctive features with the targets (by feedback to the phoneme level). Although no such mechanism is currently implemented in WEAVER++, Roelofs (1997) states that features are part of the phonetic syllabary. He suggests that both segment nodes and syllable programme nodes point to their features, and that indexing (verification) failures may be more likely when segments and syllables point to the same features.

Other authors have used different ways to describe the same data. For example, Béland, Caplan, and Nespoulous (1990) use a model where stored representations are abstract and highly underspecified "essentially consisting of non-redundant phonological features, [and therefore] word sound planning must consist of something very much like the phonological derivations described by linguists. These would add and change many segmental features and add supra-segmental values to the accessed phonological representation of a word" (pp. 126–127). They account for the errors made by their patient, RL, in terms of errors in applying the phonological rules that lead from underlying representations to surface representations (and difficulties with the representations themselves).

Buffer deficits

It is fairly well accepted that there is a need for some kind of holding device or buffer in speech production. Speech errors demonstrate that there is more than one word available at any one time. If this were not the case then anticipatory errors where phonemes are exchanged between words (e.g., "fish and chip" → "chish and fips") could not occur. The exception to this is in interactive activation models such as those of Dell (1989) where these errors can possibly be accounted for by (partial) activation of up and coming words within the network. In non-interactive models, however, buffers are generally incorporated to account for these phenomena. Roelofs (1997) discusses a "suspend/resume mechanism" by which WEAVER can carryout partial phonological encoding of a word and put on hold (buffer) this partial representation until the missing segments are available and syllabification can continue.

What would we predict as the result of damage to this buffer? Once again we come up against the problem that little is known of the properties of this buffering mechanism. However, one possible effect of damage is consistent with the properties generally attributed to memory stores: abnormally rapid decay of information held in the buffer.

A characteristic of buffers (and of WEAVER++ in general) is that information held in them decays over time. If this process is more rapid than usual, the information contained in the buffer may no longer be available when the syllabification process continues. Clearly the longer an item is in a buffer the more likely it is to be subject to the effects of decay. Thus this deficit will also predict an effect of length but with no necessary distinction between syllable and phoneme length. What should occur is a serial position effect—more errors would be expected later in the word as the later segments will have to be held in the buffer resulting in either substitution or omission of later portions of words.

A number of authors have examined whether their patients show a serial position effect in error production. Miller and Ellis (1987) found no effect of serial position for their patient (RD), whereas Kohn and Smith (1994a,b, 1995; Kohn, 1989) report several patients who show increasing numbers of phoneme errors later in the word. They find that these patients produce more errors in later syllables in polysyllabic words and more errors on final phonemes than initial phonemes within a syllable. They too suggest that because of the serial left-to-right nature of phonological encoding that later phonemes are going to be more susceptible to the effects of decay and therefore more likely to result in errors. They do not suggest that this is necessarily due to pathologically rapid decay, but as this pattern is the reverse to that found in "normal" speech errors (where word initial consonants are more susceptible to error; Shattuck-Hufnagel, 1987), it seems likely that some impairment must be involved.

The buffering mechanism suggested by Roelofs (1997) seems to reflect more of a "suspension" of processing at the segment level rather than one where information is "held" in a separate store. However, other models have suggested this type of buffer. In this case, a different type of deficit might apply: Information held in the buffer may fail to decay normally. One possible consequence would be perseveration of phonemes from one response into subsequent responses, or possibly even perseveration of whole responses. Shattuck-Hufnagel has argued that when items are copied into the metrical frame from the buffer they should be "checked off" as having been used. A failure to check items off correctly will result in segmental information persisting inappropriately within the buffer, resulting in segmental perseveration.

Perseveration of erroneous phonemes is commonly observed in the sequences of responses produced in so-called "neologistic jargon aphasia". These are sequences of responses that are phonologically unrelated to their targets—for example, one patient we have studied (RK, Nickels 1992b) when trying to name a picture of a clown said "harrow, herrow, berrow, barrow, harrow". However, although persisting activation (insufficient decay) of phonemes in the buffer could account for these sequences of related responses it could not account for the fact that often these responses are interspersed with other (non-perseverative) responses. For example, Butterworth (1985) reports a patient (KC) who in spon-taneous speech produces similar errors separated by other words ". . . and my /zɒp/ stuff, my bit of /zɒplɪn/ . . . But he liked it. He's so /zɛplɪn/ to a yards . . . and yet after about two /lɛklɪn/ I had from that man . . ." (p. 88; see Bucking-ham, 1985 for further extensive examples). If the source of the perseveration is the persisting activation in the buffer then all sequential responses should be affected; clearly this is not always the case. Thus, this level of deficit cannot account for this type of perseveration. Butterworth (1979) does suggest that the source of these perseverations is a slowly decaying representation in a buffer, but not in a buffer at the level of phonological encoding. He suggests that when there is a failure of lexical retrieval, a "neologism generating device" is used.

This selects phonemes at random, combines them in a phonotactically regular way, and then stores them in a buffer until required for production after which they will slowly decay. If a second failure of lexical retrieval occurs and the device operates again, (some of) the phonemes used in the previous generation may still be available in the buffer (having not decayed completely) and will be incorporated into the next error. How might this device and buffer be related to Levelt et al.'s model of word production? Butterworth (1992) incorporates control processes or "default mechanisms" into the model of spoken word production. These processes are used to generate segments or metrical structure when there is missing information. These processes can be seen as a natural implementation of the earlier neologism generating device and can be considered to have the same properties with regard to perseverations. However, they have the additional advantage that they can account for perseverations in target-related responses as well as in unrelated responses (as they "fill in" for partial loss of representations as well as for completely missing representations; Buckingham, 1985, interpreted the original neologism generator as being used for filling of partial gaps in representations).

Execution of articulatory gestures

The final level at which a deficit might occur within Levelt et al.'s model of speech production would be after the retrieval of the stored syllable plans. These are motor plans for the execution of sequences of articulatory movements. Levelt (1989, p. 421) suggests that these plans must be unpacked making available a hierarchy of plans prior to their execution. Thus, it is possible that deficits could occur to either of these processes. What might the consequences of such deficits be? Levelt suggests that more complex motor units will involve more unpacking. This would suggest that an unpacking deficit might result in more errors on articulatorily more complex phonemes and phoneme sequences (e.g., fricatives and consonant clusters). Difficulties executing the plans might result in articulatory distortions and slowed speech if targets are not reached or the sequence of commands is slow to be executed. It is also possible that execution of more complex commands will be more error prone than execution of simple commands, leading to the same effect of articulatory complexity as a deficit in unpacking the commands.

Traditionally, the disorder that has been associated with deficits in motor planning and execution is apraxia of speech. This was defined by Darley (1969, cited in Rosenbek, Kent, & LaPointe, 1984) as "an articulatory disorder resulting from impairment . . . of the capacity to program the positioning of speech musculature and the sequencing of muscle movements for the volitional production of phonemes. The speech musculature does not show significant weakness, slowness or incoordination when used for reflex and automatic acts." Apraxia of speech has been the source of much controversy in the literature and differential diagnosis (from aphasia and dysarthria) is difficult to achieve. However, a key feature of the disorder is an effect of articulatory complexity and Darley (1982) also reports a number of studies which argue for articulatory distortions (resulting from missing targets). It seems likely that the difficulty in defining the features of apraxia of speech could be a consequence of attempting to include in the same syndrome symptoms which are the result of different levels of deficit. Thus, we have suggested that both an unpacking and an execution deficit could result in an effect of articulatory complexity, but they may yet predict different co-occurring features. It may also be the case that other, earlier, levels of deficit may also result in this same symptom. Consider, for example, a deficit in assembling syllable plans which we argued would affect low frequency syllables (as these are not stored); this too should be more error prone the more complex the plan was that had to be assembled.[7]

Given that some of the features associated with apraxia of speech might occur as a result of deficits at a number of levels in speech production, it is no wonder that there has been considerable controversy regarding the features of the disorder and indeed whether it exists independently from aphasia. These seem to be the wrong questions to be asking; instead what is needed is a way of distinguishing the possible levels of deficit that can lead to the different features of the disorder and how they co-occur.

CONCLUSIONS

The last 20 years have seen enormous progress in our understanding of the processes involved in speech production, from the concept at a message level to the realisation of a sequence of articulatory gestures. Over the same time, we have acquired much deeper knowledge of the ways in which these processes can be affected by brain damage, and of the ways in which these impairments can be analysed. In particular, we are now able to distinguish a series of stages in the processes of speech production, and to a considerable extent distinguish the characteristics of breakdown at these stages.

Nevertheless, the degree to which we can explain different characteristics of aphasic disorders of production is limited by the current underspecification of the theoretical accounts of the operation of the stages. The very process of attempting to determine the effects of breakdown within these models highlights the extent to which the assumptions are unclear regarding the nature of both representations and processing. In this respect connectionist models are clearly an improvement—in order to run a computer simulation the architecture has to be very clearly defined. Clearly, then, WEAVER++ is a welcome step in the right direction. However, not only does it differ in several important way from the descriptive model of Levelt et al. (1999a) but also the behaviour of this model (and all connectionist models) under conditions of damage is hard to establish. It is particularly difficult to identify the kinds of pathological data which might be incompatible with—and so potentially falsify—a connectionist account (Nickels & Howard, 1995).

Two decades ago, the general assumption was that aphasic subjects from the classical diagnostic categories (Broca's aphasics, Wernicke's aphasics, conduction aphasics, and so on) would have similar deficits in the processes of word production. As we have seen, such assumptions are clearly not tenable. For instance, patients with deficits at any level from lexical phonological representations to the assembly of an articulatory programme could all legitimately be described as reproduction conduction aphasics (cf., Kohn, 1992; Shallice & Warrington, 1977), and yet they might have very different kinds of impairments within these processes. In recent years, the performance of individual patients has been much more carefully characterised, using experimental manipulation of the factors affecting their accuracy, as well as analyses of the properties of their errors. However, both of these sources of evidence are, at least partly, ambiguous. Variables can have their effects at many different levels; for instance, as we have seen, decreasing accuracy with increasing stimulus length—a characteristic feature of reproduction conduction aphasia—is a natural prediction of every postlexical production impairment. Speech errors from both normal subjects and patients are similarly overdetermined; as Cutler, Howard, and Patterson (1989) note, many "errors are 'imperfect' by virtue of having more than one possible source" (p. 70).

Much of the patient data currently available is not of the right sort to test the predictions from models of speech production. For example, Butterworth (1992) argued that there is no case in which there is data that clearly distinguishes between disorders of lexical phonological representation and deficits in the processes of output from this level. The techniques for making this distinction are available—by determining, for example, whether the same words result in errors on different occasions, or whether subjects can access phonological word-form information in tasks that do not require overt speech production (as in picture homonym judgement)—but have rarely been used.

It is clear, however, that the advances in theoretical understanding of the last 20 years will allow us to pose questions concerning the nature of impairments in word production with much greater precision. We are now in a position to analyse patients' difficulties in much greater detail. The task for the next 20 years is to develop theories that account, at a more detailed level, both for the properties of normal performance, and the range of patterns of impairment found in brain-damaged people.

ACKNOWLEDGEMENTS

This chapter was prepared whilst the first author was supported by a Wellcome Trust Fellowship and an ARC QEII Fellowship. The second author was supported, in part, by the Medical Research Council. Thanks to two anonymous reviewers for helpful comments during the production of this chapter.

NOTES

1. Levelt et al. (1999b, p. 68) appear to disagree with this widely held view. They state that: "we feel it as (sic) a bridge too far to expect a patient's behaviour to conform to our theory", continuing: "there is little reason to suppose that an impaired system performs according to an intact theory. The real theoretical challenge is to create and test a theory of the impaired system (as is done, e.g., by Dell et al., 1997)". We dispute this point of view. Furthermore, we note that the example they give (Dell et al., 1997) is in fact a theory that was developed to account for intact performance (Dell, 1986) and then lesioned to demonstrate that it can account for aphasic data. This is exactly the approach we advocate and that Levelt et al. seem to be arguing against. In other words, as Ellis (1985, p. 108) states: "by a continuous process of refining and retesting, neuropsychological evidence can help improve cognitive theories in just the same way that data from laboratory experiments can".
2. A heavy syllable is one with a long vowel or at least one consonant in the coda.
3. This is not to say that damage to one component will not have an effect on other processes within that model. The extent of top-down and bottom-up influences of a particular locus of damage will depend on the particular architecture of the model concerned. For example, in an interactive activation model such as that of Dell (1986, 1989) where activation feeds both forward and back through the model, a deficit at one level can have widespread effects throughout the model.
4. One aspect of the results that Badecker et al. report sits uncomfortably with this analysis. The items that he named correctly were both more frequent and shorter than those he could not name. An item's length is only available at the phonological word-form level, and so could not determine a failure to access phonological word forms. However, Badecker et al. made no attempt to disentangle the effects of frequency from those of length, and it is at least possible that the length effects are due to a confounding with frequency.
5. The treatment of phonological encoding by WEAVER++ (Levelt et al., 1999a; Roelofs, 1997) is broadly similar to that of Dell (1986, 1989), with a key difference being that WEAVER++ is feedforward, as opposed to the interactive activation of Dell's model.
6. In contrast, models that explain perceived segmental errors as errors in segment selection (e.g., Dell, 1986; Shattuck-Hufnagel, 1979) predict effects of number of phonemes but not necessarily the number of syllables.
7. Whiteside and Varley (1998, p. 229) propose a similar explanation for apraxia of speech. They suggest that when the syllable plans "are either difficult to access or disorganised, the speech production mechanism has to rely on an indirect phonetic encoding route, which involves more on-line computation and therefore greater cognitive load. This, therefore, results in a system with greater degrees of freedom and the speech characteristics typically exhibited in AOS, such as increased utterance durations, greater variability and inconsistency."

REFERENCES

Baars, B.J., Motley, M.T., & MacKay, D. (1975). Output editing for lexical status from artificially elicited slips of the tongue. *Journal of Verbal Learning and Verbal Behaviour*, *14*, 382–391.

Badecker, W., Miozzo, M., & Zanuttini, R. (1995). The two stage model of lexical retrieval: Evidence from a case of anomia with selective preservation of grammatical gender. *Cognition*, *57*, 193–216.

Barry, C., & McHattie, J. (1991, September). *Depth of semantic processing in picture naming facilitation in aphasic patients.* Paper presented at the British Aphasiology Society conference, Sheffield, UK.

Beauvois, M.-F. (1982). Optic aphasia: A process of interaction between vision and language. *Philosophical Transactions of the Royal Society of London, B298,* 35–48.

Béland, R., Caplan, D., & Nespoulous, J.-L. (1990). The role of abstract phonological representations in word production: Evidence from phonemic paraphasias. *Journal of Neurolinguistics, 5,* 125–164.

Best, W. (1995). A reverse length effect in dysphasic naming: When elephant is easier than ant. *Cortex, 31,* 637–652.

Best, W. (1996). When racquets are baskets but baskets are biscuits, where do the words come from? A single case study of formal paraphasic errors in aphasia. *Cognitive Neuropsychology, 13,* 443–480.

Blanken, G. (1990). Formal paraphasias: A single case study. *Brain and Language, 38,* 534–554.

Blumstein, S.E. (1973). *A phonological investigation of aphasic speech.* The Hague, The Netherlands: Mouton.

Blumstein, S.E. (1978). Segment structure and the syllable in aphasia. In A. Bell & J.B. Hooper (Eds.), *Syllables and segments.* Amsterdam: North-Holland.

Browman, C., & Goldstein, L. (1992). Articulatory phonology: An overview. *Phonetica, 49,* 155–180.

Brown, A.S. (1991). A review of the tip-of-the-tongue experience. *Psychological Bulletin, 109,* 204–223.

Brown, R., & McNeill, D. (1966). The "tip-of-the-tongue" phenomenon. *Journal of Verbal Learning and Verbal Behaviour, 5,* 325–337.

Bruce, C., & Howard, D. (1988). Why don't Broca's aphasics cue themselves? An investigation of phonemic cueing and tip-of-the-tongue information. *Neuropsychologia, 26,* 253–264.

Buckingham, H.W. (1985). Perseveration in aphasia. In S.K. Newman & R. Epstein (Eds.), *Current perspectives in dysphasia.* Edinburgh, UK: Churchill Livingstone.

Buckingham, H., & Kertesz, A. (1974). A linguistic analysis of fluent aphasia. *Brain and Language, 1,* 43–61.

Butterworth, B. (1979). Hesitation and the production of verbal paraphasias and neologisms in jargon aphasia. *Brain and Language, 8,* 133–161.

Butterworth, B. (1992). Disorders of phonological encoding. *Cognition, 42,* 261–286.

Butterworth, B. (1985). Jargon aphasia: Processes and strategies. In S.K. Newman & R. Epstein (Eds.), *Current perspectives in dysphasia.* Edinburgh, UK: Churchill Livingstone.

Butterworth, B.L. (1980). Evidence from pauses. In B.L. Butterworth (Ed.), *Language production: Vol. 1. Speech and talk.* London: Academic Press.

Butterworth, B.L. (1989). Lexical access in speech production. In W. Marslen-Wilson (Ed.), *Lexical representation and process.* Cambridge, MA: MIT Press.

Butterworth, B.L., Howard, D., & McLoughlin, P.J. (1984). The semantic deficit in aphasia: The relationship between semantic errors in auditory comprehension and picture naming. *Neuropsychologia, 22,* 409–426.

Caplan, D. (1987). Phonological representations in word production. In E. Keller & M. Gopnik (Eds.), *Tutorials in motor behaviour.* Hillsdale, NJ: Lawrence Erlbaum Associates Inc.

Caplan, D., & Waters, G.S. (1992). Issues regarding the nature and consequences of reproduction conduction aphasia. In S.E. Kohn (Ed.), *Conduction aphasia.* Hillsdale, NJ: Lawrence Erlbaum Associates Inc.

Caramazza, A., & Miozzo, M. (1997). The relation between syntactic and phonological knowledge in lexical access: Evidence from the "tip-of-the-tongue" phenomenon. *Cognition, 64,* 309–343.

Christman, S.S. (1994). Target-related neologism formation in jargonaphasia. *Brain and Language, 46,* 109–128.

Coltheart, M. (1987). Functional architecture of the language-processing system. In M. Coltheart, R. Job, & G. Sartori (Eds.), *The cognitive neuropsychology of language*. Hove, UK: Lawrence Erlbaum Associates Ltd.

Cutler, A., Howard, D., & Patterson, K.E. (1989). Misplaced stress on prosody: A reply to Black and Byng. *Cognitive Neuropsychology, 6*, 67–83.

Darley, F.L. (1969). *The classification of output disturbance in neurologic communication disorders.* Paper presented at the American Speech and Hearing Association convention, Chicago.

Darley, F.L. (1982). *Aphasia*. Philadelphia: W.B. Saunders.

Dell, G.S. (1986). A spreading activation theory of retrieval in sentence production. *Psychological Review, 93*, 283–321.

Dell, G.S. (1989). The retrieval of phonological forms in production: Tests of predictions from a connectionist model. In W. Marslen-Wilson (Ed.), *Lexical representation and process*. Cambridge, MA: MIT Press.

Dell, G.S. (1990). Effects of frequency and vocabulary type on phonological speech errors. *Language and Cognitive Processes, 5*, 313–349.

Dell, G.S., & Reich, P.A. (1981). Stages in sentence production: An analysis of speech error data. *Journal of Verbal Learning and Verbal Behaviour, 20*, 611–629.

Dell, G.S., Schwartz, M.F., Martin, N., Saffran, E.M., & Gagnon, D.A. (1997). Lexical access in normal and aphasic speech. *Psychological Review, 104*, 801–838.

Ellis, A.W. (1985). The production of spoken words: A cognitive neuropsychological perspective. In A.W. Ellis (Ed.), *Progress in the psychology of language, Vol. 2*. Hove, UK: Lawrence Erlbaum Associates Ltd.

Feinberg, T., Rothi, L., & Heilman, K. (1986). Inner speech in conduction aphasia. *Archives of Neurology, 43*, 591–593.

Friedman, R.B., & Kohn, S.E. (1990). Impaired activation of the phonological lexicon: Effects upon oral reading. *Brain and Language, 38*, 278–297.

Funnell, E., & Hodges, J.R. (1991). Progressive loss of access to spoken word forms in a case of Alzheimer's disease. *Proceedings of the Royal Society of London, 243*, 173–179.

Gainotti, G., Miceli, G., Caltagirone, C., Silveri, M.C., & Masullo, C. (1981). The relationship between type of naming error and semantic-lexical discrimination in aphasia. *Cortex, 17*, 401–410.

Garrett, M.F. (1976). Syntactic processes in sentence production. In R.J. Wales & E. Walker (Eds.), *New approaches to language mechanisms*. Amsterdam: North-Holland.

Goodglass, H., Kaplan, E., Weintraub, S., & Ackerman, N. (1976). The tip-of-the-tongue phenomenon in aphasia. *Cortex, 12*, 145–153.

Green, E. (1969) Phonological and grammatical aspects of jargon in an aphasic patient: A case study. *Language and Speech, 12*, 103–118.

Hillis, A.E., & Caramazza, A. (1995). The compositionality of lexical semantic representations: Clues from semantic errors in object naming. *Memory, 3*, 333–358.

Hinton, G.E., & Shallice, T. (1991). Lesioning an attractor network: Investigations of acquired dyslexia. *Psychological Review, 98*, 74–95.

Hodges, J.R., Graham, N., & Patterson, K.E. (1995). Charting the progression in semantic dementia: Implications for the organisation of semantic memory. *Memory, 3*, 463–495.

Hodges, J.R., Patterson, K.E., Oxbury, S.M., & Funnell, E. (1992). Semantic dementia: Progressive fluent aphasia with temporal lobe atrophy. *Brain, 115*, 1783–1806.

Howard, D. (1985). *The semantic organisation of the lexicon: Evidence from aphasia*. Unpublished PhD thesis, University of London.

Howard, D. (1995). Lexical anomia (or the case of the missing lexical entries). *Quarterly Journal of Experimental Psychology, 48A*, 999–1023.

Howard, D., & Orchard-Lisle, V.M. (1984). On the origin of semantic errors in naming: Evidence from the case of a global aphasic. *Cognitive Neuropsychology, 1*, 163–190.

Howard, D., & Patterson, K.E. (1992). *The pyramids and palm trees test*. Bury St Edmunds, UK: Thames Valley Test Company.

Howard, D., Patterson, K.E., Franklin, S.E., Morton, J., & Orchard-Lisle, V.M. (1984). Variability and consistency in picture naming by aphasic patients. In F.C. Rose (Ed.), *Advances in neurology: Vol. 42. Progress in aphasiology*. New York: Raven Press.

Howard, D., Patterson, K.E., Franklin, S.E., Orchard-Lisle, V.M., & Morton, J. (1985). The facilitation of picture naming in aphasia. *Cognitive Neuropsychology, 2*, 41–80.

Kay, J., & Ellis, A.W. (1987). A cognitive neuropsychological case study of anomia: Implications for psychological models of word retrieval. *Brain, 110*, 613–629.

Kohn, S.E. (1989). The nature of the phonemic string deficit in conduction aphasia. *Aphasiology, 3*, 209–239.

Kohn, S., & Smith, K.L. (1990). Between-word speech errors in conduction aphasia. *Cognitive Neuropsychology, 7*, 133–156.

Kohn, S., & Smith, K.L. (1994a). Distinctions between two phonological output deficits. *Applied Psycholinguistics, 15*, 75–95.

Kohn, S., & Smith, K.L. (1994b). Evolution of impaired access to the phonological lexicon. *Journal of Neurolinguistics, 8*, 267–288.

Kohn, S., & Smith, K.L. (1995). Serial effects of phonemic planning during word production. *Aphasiology, 9*, 209–222.

Kohn, S.E. (Ed.). (1992). *Conduction aphasia*. Hillsdale, NJ: Lawrence Erlbaum Associates Inc.

Le Dorze, G., Boulay, N., Gaudreau, J., & Brassard, C. (1994). The contrasting effects of semantic versus a formal-semantic technique for the facilitation of naming in a case of anomia. *Aphasiology, 8*, 127–141.

Levelt, W.J.M. (1989). *Speaking: From intention to articulation*. Cambridge, MA: MIT Press.

Levelt, W.J.M. (1992). Accessing words in speech production: Stages, processes and representations. *Cognition, 42*, 1–22.

Levelt, W.J.M., Roelofs, A., & Meyer, A.S. (1999a). A theory of lexical access in speech production. *Behavioural and Brain Sciences, 22*, 1–38.

Levelt, W.J.M., Roelofs, A., & Meyer, A.S. (1999b). Multiple perspectives on word production. *Behavioural and Brain Sciences, 22*, 61–75.

Levelt, W.J.M., & Wheeldon, L.R. (1994). Do speakers have access to a mental syllabary? *Cognition, 50*, 239–269.

Martin, N., Dell, G.S., Saffran, E.M., & Schwartz, M.F. (1994). Origins of paraphasias in deep dysphasia: Testing the consequences of a decay impairment to an interactive spreading activation account of lexical retrieval. *Brain and Language, 47*, 609–660.

Meyer, A.S. (1992). Investigation of phonological encoding through speech error analyses: Achievements, limitations and alternatives. *Cognition, 42*, 181–212.

Miller, D., & Ellis, A.W. (1987). Speech and writing errors in "neologistic jargonaphasia": A lexical activation hypothesis. In M. Coltheart, R. Job, & G. Sartori (Eds.), *The cognitive neuropsychology of language*. Hove, UK: Lawrence Erlbaum Associates Ltd.

Nickels, L.A. (1992a). The autocue? Self-generated phonemic cues in the treatment of a disorder of reading and naming. *Cognitive Neuropsychology, 9*, 155–182.

Nickels, L.A. (1992b). *Spoken word production and its breakdown in aphasia*. Unpublished PhD thesis, University of London.

Nickels, L.A. (1995). Getting it right? Using aphasic naming errors to evaluate theoretical models of spoken word production. *Language and Cognitive Processes, 10*, 13–45.

Nickels, L.A. (1997). *Spoken word production and its breakdown in aphasia*. Hove, UK: Psychology Press.

Nickels, L.A., & Howard, D. (1994). A frequent occurrence? Factors affecting the production of semantic errors in aphasic naming. *Cognitive Neuropsychology, 11*, 289–320.

Nickels, L.A., & Howard, D. (1995). Phonological errors in aphasic naming: Comprehension, monitoring and lexicality. *Cortex, 31*, 209–237.

Nickels, L.A., & Howard, D. (1999). Effects of lexical stress on aphasic word production. *Clinical Linguistics and Phonetics, 13*, 269–294.

Nickels, L.A., & Howard, D. (2000). Dissociating effects of number of phonemes, number of syllables and phonological complexity on aphasic word production. *Manuscript in preparation.*

Niemi, J., Koivuselka-Sallinen, P., & Hanninen, R. (1985). Phoneme errors in Broca's aphasia: Three Finnish cases. *Brain and Language, 26,* 28–48.

Pate, D.S., Saffran, E.M., & Martin, N. (1987). Specifying the nature of the production deficit in conduction aphasia: A case study. *Language and Cognitive Processes, 2,* 43–84.

Patterson, K.E., Purell, C., & Morton, J. (1983). The facilitation of naming in aphasia. In C. Code & D.J. Muller (Eds.), *Aphasia therapy.* London: Arnold.

Plaut, D.C., & Shallice, T. (1993). Deep dyslexia: A case study in connectionist neuropsychology. *Cognitive Neuropsychology, 10,* 377–500.

Rapp, B.C., Hillis, A.E., & Caramazza, A. (1993). The role of representations in cognitive theory: More on multiple semantics and the agnosias. *Cognitive Neuropsychology, 10,* 235–249.

Riddoch, M.J., Humphreys, G.W., Coltheart, M., & Funnell, E. (1988). Semantic systems or system? Neuropsychological evidence re-examined. *Cognitive Neuropsychology, 5,* 3–25.

Roelofs, A. (1997). The WEAVER model of word-form encoding in speech production. *Cognition, 64,* 249–284.

Rosenbek, J.C., Kent, R., & Lapointe, L. (1984). Apraxia of speech and overview and some perspectives. In J.C. Rosenbek, M. McNeil, & A. Aronson (Eds.), *Apraxia of speech: Physiology, acoustics, linguistics and management.* San Diego: College Hill Press.

Shallice, T. (1987). Impairments of semantic processing: Multiple dissociations. In M. Coltheart, R. Job, & G. Sartori (Eds.), *The cognitive neuropsychology of language.* Hove, UK: Lawrence Erlbaum Associates Ltd.

Shallice, T., & Warrington, E.K. (1977). Auditory-verbal short term memory and conduction aphasia. *Brain and Language, 4,* 479–491.

Shattuck-Hufnagel, S. (1979). Speech errors as evidence for a serial order mechanism in sentence production. In W.E. Cooper & E.C.T. Walker (Eds.), *Sentence processing: Psycholinguistic studies presented to Merrill Garrett.* Hillsdale, NJ: Lawrence Erlbaum Associates Inc.

Shattuck-Hufnagel, S. (1987). The role of word-onset consonants in speech production planning: New evidence from speech error patterns. In E. Keller & M. Gopnik (Eds.), *Motor and sensory processes of language.* Hillsdale, NJ: Lawrence Erlbaum Associates Inc.

Stemberger, J.P. (1984). *Lexical bias in errors in language production: Interactive components, editors and perceptual biases.* Unpublished manuscript, Carnegie-Mellon University, Pittsburgh, PA.

Stemberger, J.P. (1985). An interactive activation model of language production. In A.W. Ellis (Ed.), *Progress in the psychology of language, Vol. 1.* Hove, UK: Lawrence Erlbaum Associates Ltd.

Vigliocco, G., Antonini, T., & Garrett, M.F. (1997). Grammatical gender is on the tip of Italian tongues. *Psychological Science, 8,* 314–317.

Warrington, E.K. (1975). The selective impairment of semantic memory. *Quarterly Journal of Experimental Psychology, 27,* 635–657.

Warrington, E.K., & Cipolotti, L. (1996). Word comprehension: The distinction between refractory and storage impairments. *Brain, 119,* 611–625.

Wheeldon, L.R., & Monsell, S. (1994). Inhibition of spoken word production by priming a semantic competitor. *Journal of Memory and Language, 33,* 332–356.

Whiteside, S.P., & Varley, R.A. (1998). A reconceptualisation of apraxia of speech: A synthesis of evidence. *Cortex, 34,* 221–231.

CHAPTER SIX

On the naming of objects: Evidence from cognitive neuroscience

Glyn W. Humphreys
Cognitive Science Research Centre, School of Psychology, University of Birmingham, UK

Cathy J. Price
Wellcome Department of Cognitive Neurology, Institute of Neurology, London, UK

M. Jane Riddoch
Cognitive Science Research Centre, School of Psychology, University of Birmingham, UK

In normal circumstances, our ability to put names to objects is strikingly efficient. We can find the name for perhaps some thousands of objects within only a few seconds, and name retrieval for familiar objects can take place well within that time. Yet, in naming an object, the brain needs to pass through a number of processing stages. To begin with, early visual processes must encode the shape and possibly also the surface details of the object (its colour, texture, and so forth). After this, the encoded perceptual information must be matched to memory. Different forms of stored memory may also need to be accessed: knowledge about the form of the object (its stored structural description), about its functional and associative properties (its semantic description), and its name (perhaps in an abstract form, perhaps even its phonological description). Access to the various knowledge forms can be thought of as constituting different stages in the naming process. Here we ask how the "object" part of object naming—including the processes involved in accessing structural and semantic memories—constrains the "naming" part—the processes involved in finding a unique name and eventually a unique phonological description for a stimulus. Is the stage of name

143

retrieval in object naming the same as that involved in naming other stimuli (printed words, descriptions, sounds), or are name retrieval processes fashioned by the nature of preceding visual recognition processes required for objects? To answer such questions, we will first consider how the processing stages in object naming might operate, before going on to evaluate how visual recognition processes impact on name retrieval. Our answers are based on converging evidence drawn from experimental and neuropsychology, functional imaging, and computational modelling.

PROCESSING STAGES IN OBJECT NAMING

Some of the strongest evidence for the involvement of identifiable processing stages in object naming comes from neuropsychology. Impairments in knowledge about the visual properties of objects are demonstrated when patients with good early visual processing are impaired at "object decision" tasks, which require familiarity discriminations between pictures of real objects and nonobjects generated by combining parts of different real objects. Poor performance on object decision tasks can be accompanied by good performance on difficult tests of high-level perception, such as matching objects shown in unusual views (e.g., Gainotti & Silveri, 1996; Sartori & Job, 1988). The same patients can also show associated deficits such as (1) poor drawing from memory, and (2) impaired answers to questions stressing the visual properties of objects, consistent with a deficit in long-term visual knowledge about objects irrespective of whether that knowledge is accessed from vision or from other modalities (audition, when definitions stress visual properties of objects). The problem also need not impinge on long-term knowledge about the functional and associative properties of objects, since the patients may be good at naming to verbal definitions that stress these last properties.

In other patients, access to stored visual knowledge can take place but this is dissociated from access to semantic knowledge. Access to stored visual knowledge can be established through intact performance on object decision tasks (Hillis & Caramazza, 1995; Humphreys & Riddoch, 1999; Riddoch & Humphreys, 1987b; Sheridan & Humphreys, 1993). However, despite this, the patients may be impaired at matching tasks that tap semantic knowledge (e.g., match a hammer to a nail or a screw), as well as at object naming. In some of these cases, good performance has been shown when tests require access to semantic knowledge from audition—as with associative matching to the names of objects and with naming to verbal definition. Thus, poor object naming cannot be attributed to general deficits in semantic knowledge, but rather to impaired visual access to semantic knowledge following intact access to stored visual knowledge. Such patients indicate the existence of a system supporting long-term visual knowledge about objects that can be isolated from functional and associative semantic knowledge.

In other patients, there appears to be good access to both long-term visual and semantic knowledge about objects and there is instead a deficit that seems linked to name retrieval. For instance, patients may be able to make accurate judgements about the visual, functional, and associative properties of objects (in object decision and associative matching tests; Kay & Ellis, 1987), but they remain poor at retrieving phonological information.

These neuropsychological studies are consistent with there being separate stages of object naming involving the retrieval respectively of long-term visual, semantic, and name information about objects. Given this, we can ask how information is accessed at these different stages. Is information accessed sequentially, in a purely bottom-up manner (e.g., Levelt, 1989), or is it accessed in a more continuous fashion, so that semantic and even name information is activated before earlier processing stages are complete? The answer to this question is of some importance for the issue of whether object recognition processes constrain name retrieval. If information is transmitted continuously between levels, then variations in the efficiency of accessing an early stage (e.g., the stored structural descriptions) will subsequently impact on the activation of semantic and name information. If many structural descriptions are activated by an object, then there will increased competition in name retrieval. Also, models with continuous transmission of information would allow for top-down as well as bottom-up effects on naming—for instance, if visual knowledge has to be interrogated at more length for naming to take place. We return to the issue of top-down effects after considering evidence from normal observers on information transmission in object naming.

CONTINUOUS PROCESSES IN NORMAL OBJECT NAMING

Consider how identification may be affected by perceptual overlap between objects. Studies using object decision times as a measure of access to structural descriptions show that performance is slowed if an object is perceptually similar to other objects from the same category, relative to when an object belongs to a category with perceptually distinct exemplars (Lloyd-Jones & Humphreys, 1997; Vitkovitch & Tyrrell, 1995). Presumably, it takes longer to access unique structural information, to make the object decision, if objects belong to categories which have perceptually similar exemplars. In a model assuming serial stages in object naming, several predictions follow. One is that the advantage for stimuli from categories with perceptually dissimilar exemplars should be maintained when tasks tap later stages of processing, providing there is not an equal and opposite advantage for perceptually similar items at these later stages. This prediction does not hold. Using a task that may be assumed to tap semantic knowledge, superordinate classification (is the stimulus living or nonliving?), Riddoch and Humphreys (1987a) found that reaction times (RTs) were faster to objects from categories with perceptually similar members (e.g., animals) than to objects from categories with dissimilar members (e.g., vehicles). That is, the difference between stimuli from categories with perceptually similar and perceptual dissimilar exemplars is reversed. Now part of this reversal may be that semantic information is more securely associated with categories with perceptually similar exemplars (typically living things); Job, Rumiati, and Lotto (1992), for instance, reported an advantage for living over nonliving stimuli in superordinate classification even when the stimuli were the names of objects. However, this advantage is even larger when pictures rather than words are presented (see Riddoch & Humphreys, 1987a), even though access to individual structural knowledge is slower for pictures from perceptually similar categories. Hence there seems to be a differential facilitation in access to superordinate knowledge for objects (relative to words), if the objects come from categories with perceptually similar members. These reversed effects of perceptual overlap (and the increased advantage for pictures relative to words in superordinate classification) should not occur if processing at a structural level (tapped using object decision) had to be complete before semantic knowledge could be accessed (tapped using superordinate classification). Slow access to structural knowledge should generally result in slow access to semantic knowledge.

The contrasting effects of perceptual overlap in object decision and superordinate classification fit with a rather different account of object recognition and naming, in which activation is transmitted continuously between processing levels. In such a model, semantic information can be activated before processing at a structural level is completed (even though structural processing must be initiated first). Objects from categories with similar members produce a spread of activation across the structural descriptions of perceptual neighbours, and this slows the time for object decision. On the other hand, activation across a number of category members is useful if passed forward (continuously) for superordinate categorisation, since this extra activation provides consistent evidence for the target's category. The net effect will be slow object decisions but fast superordinate classification responses.

A second prediction from a serial account is that variables that affect different stages of naming should combine additively on naming times (cf. Sternberg, 1969). Effects of perceptual overlap, reflecting access to structural descriptions, should be additive with effects of a second variable that affects a later processing stage, such as name frequency. Evidence for frequency affecting a later stage of name retrieval comes from studies showing that the frequency of an object's name influences naming time but not the time to assign an object to a semantic category (Morrison, Ellis, & Quinlan, 1992; Wingfield, 1968). In a discrete model the effects of name frequency on name retrieval should be equal for objects from perceptually similar and dissimilar categories, since name retrieval will only begin after access to structural descriptions has been completed. The advantage for perceptually dissimilar objects should simply add to any advantage for objects with high frequency names. Against this, Humphreys, Riddoch, and Quinlan (1988; see also Snodgrass & Yuditsky, 1996) found an interaction between perceptual overlap and name frequency. Frequency effects were larger for objects from categories with perceptually dissimilar members. In a model with continuous processing stages, this can be explained if a delay in accessing stored structural descriptions allows there to be activation of name representations whilst processing at a structural level is being completed. This produces more competition than would otherwise be the case for high-frequency names, attenuating the name frequency effect.

Other data favouring a continuous processing account come from naming errors. One class of error reflects both semantic and phonological similarity between the target and the (incorrect) name; so-called "mixed" errors (*cat* → rat). In a serial model the probabilities of semantic and phonological errors occurring should be independent of one another; it follows that the probability of "mixed" errors should simply be the sum of the probability of each error in isolation. However, "mixed" errors occur more frequently than this (Dell & Reich, 1981; Martin, Weisberg, & Saffran, 1989). There seems to be an interaction between semantic and phonological information in name retrieval.

VISUAL CONSTRAINTS ON NAME RETRIEVAL IN NORMAL OBSERVERS

There is evidence, then, for information being passed continuously between processing stages in object naming. The data on the effects of perceptual overlap are consistent with the idea that this continuous transmission of information operates at least up the process involved in selecting a specific name for an object. In terms of theories of name production, this name-selection process may be at the level of the "lemma" (cf., Levelt, 1989), which is not phonologically coded but nevertheless provides a unique label for an object, or at a phonological level. The evidence on "mixed" semantic and phonological errors suggests that there is continuous transmission of information even to a phonological level (see Dell, 1988), though serial accounts of object naming have attributed combined semantic + phonological errors to a failure in error monitoring following incorrect name selection at a lemma level. For example it might be that, at different times, both "dog" and "rat" are selected incorrectly in place of the name "cat". However, an error monitoring process fails to detect the error "rat" because it is close to the phonological target; in contrast "dog" is detected and edited out as an error (see Levelt, Roelofs, & Meyer, 1999). On this account there may be continuous feed-forward of semantic information to influence name selection, but the effect of phonological similarity arises at a later stage.

As noted previously, one consequence of information being transmitted continuously for name selection is that factors that determine object recognition should also impinge on name retrieval. However, this is difficult to determine using simple measures of naming time. Because object naming contains a number of stages, a variable can affect performance by influencing earlier recognition processes as well as naming processes. Procedures are needed to try to isolate the name retrieval stage. One such procedure is "naming to deadline". Vitkovitch and Humphreys (1991; Vitkovitch, Humphreys, & Lloyd-Jones, 1993) had subjects name to a response deadline that was some 200 ms or so slower than the standard naming time to objects. Perhaps not surprisingly, increased errors result. One type of error involved making a perseverative response by giving the name of a previously named object that was related to the target—a "related perseverative error" (e.g., giving the name "cat" to a picture of a mouse, having seen and named cat in an earlier "prime" block of trials). "Related perseverative errors" occurred when the primes were pictures that participants named but not when either (1) subjects categorised rather than naming the prime pictures (e.g., where the task in trial block 1 was living vs. nonliving decision, whilst in block 2 it was naming to deadline), or (2) the primes were printed words that subjects read aloud (trial block 1, read words aloud; trial block 2, name objects to deadline). Thus these errors reflect a process used in object naming but not in either object categorisation or word naming. Object naming involves mapping from a semantic representation of an object to its name ("semantic name retrieval"), whereas this is not the case for word naming or for object categorisation. Word naming can operate nonsemantically (Van Orden, 1987), whereas object categorisation demands access to semantic information but not to the names of objects (Potter & Faulconer, 1975). Since perseverations only occur when object naming is the priming task, and not with either word naming or picture categorisation, it follows that these errors specifically reflect a bias in mapping from semantic to name representations, so that this bias favours previously named objects. Vitkovitch and Humphreys accounted for the results by arguing that a target related to a previously named object reactivates the original (biased) mappings, leading to a perseverative error (production of the prime's name). Related perseverative errors enable us to study the nature of semantic name retrieval isolated from other stages of object naming.

Interestingly, Vitkovitch et al. (1993) found that related perseverations were *always* semantically and visually related to target objects; they were never purely semantically related. This indicates that name retrieval is constrained by a combination of visual and semantic similarity between objects. Visual information from objects biases name selection to a set of items that share visual as well as the semantic features of the target. A consequence of this is that name selection can be more difficult for objects that share perceptual features with other objects from their category. As we shall now review, this consequence is also apparent in neuropsychological studies of patients with deficits in object recognition and naming.

NEUROPSYCHOLOGICAL IMPAIRMENTS OF OBJECT NAMING

Impairments in object naming can arise at different processing stages (see earlier), and, as with normal subjects, the evidence suggests that information is transmitted continuously to the processes involved in name selection. Caramazza and Hillis (1990, 1991), for example, report dissociations between the errors generated when patients use different responses, such as speaking versus writing the names of objects. Some patients tend to produce semantically related errors in writing (e.g., *carrot* → onion), but not in naming (when the correct response is made); others show the opposite pattern of deficit. In such cases, there seems to be access to the correct semantic information about the object, since the correct response occurs in one modality. However, in the other modality some form of postsemantic deficit seems to give rise to semantic errors, consistent with postsemantic processes dealing with a number of semantic candidates, activated continuously by the object. For one modality only, there is a deficit in dealing with these candidate responses so that semantic errors result.

How do factors affecting the visual processing of objects impact on name retrieval in neuropsychological populations? During the 1990s, a substantial number of reports have been presented of patients with deficits in naming animate objects relative to inanimate, artefactual objects (e.g., see De Renzi & Lucchelli, 1994; Forde, Francis, Riddoch, Rumiati, & Humphreys, 1997; Sartori & Job, 1988; Warrington & Shallice, 1984), though there are also reports of patients with the opposite pattern of deficit (Hillis & Caramazza, 1990; Sacchett & Humphreys, 1992; Warrington & McCarthy, 1983, 1987). For patients with problems in identifying animate things, the evidence suggests that there can be breakdowns at different stages of object naming (see Humphreys & Forde, in press). For instance, some patients are impaired at object decision tasks for stimuli from the affected categories (Sartori & Job, 1988), whereas others can perform well at object decision but remain impaired at retrieving semantic information for the affected items (Sheridan & Humphreys, 1993). For the former patients, a deficit within the structural description system may be suspected, whereas for the latter there appears not to be a problem at the structural level but rather a semantic problem affecting certain categories of item (see also Caramazza & Shelton, 1998). In other patients, the impairment seems to affect even later stages in object naming, such as name retrieval. Farah and Wallace (1992) and Hart, Berndt, and Caramazza (1985), for example, have both reported cases where the patients seemed able to derive a good deal of information about animate things but remained impaired at naming them. From this it might be concluded that, in some way, name retrieval itself is categorically organised, so that there is a functional subdivision between the processes involved in name retrieval for animate and inanimate objects. An alternative view, though, is that at least some of the effects of animacy may be due to animate objects belonging to categories with physically similar exemplars, and that perceptual overlap within a category has consequences for name retrieval. Our own work points to this last factor. To illustrate this, we consider cases of two patients with apparent name-finding problems for animate objects.

IMPAIRED VISUAL KNOWLEDGE AND NAME RETRIEVAL: TWO CASES

SRB and DM are two patients in whom impaired object naming could be linked to deficits in perceptual knowledge (see Forde et al., 1997; Humphreys, Riddoch, & Price, 1997). At the time of testing SRB was 38 years old, and some 3 months earlier he had suffered an intracerebral haemorrhage from an arteriovenous malformation (AVM). DM was a 44-year-old woman who 3 months before testing had a brain abscess evacuated when multiple AVMs in her lungs due to hereditary telangiectasia tracked to her brain. Both patients had right homonymous hemianopias and were alexic; their damage was in the left medial and inferior occipito-temporal region.

SRB and DM presented with clinical problems in naming animate objects along with a relatively preserved ability to name artefacts. For example, when presented with standardised line drawings of animate and artefactual objects, matched for their name frequencies (taken from Humphreys et al., 1988), SRB named 37/38 (95%) of the artefacts but only 28/38 (71%) animate objects. DM named 57/76 (75%) of the artefacts but only 35/76 (46%) animate objects, when tested on two occasions. Name frequency did not affect performance.

Interestingly, many of their naming errors involved semantic circumlocutions. For example, SRB responded to a picture of some *celery* with: "it is green and you have it as a main course, I dip it in salt"; for a *lemon* he said "bitter . . . an orange . . . no". To *lemon* DM said "sour and you have it with . . . you make them in a pan, put milk and eggs and whisk them with this other stuff in a frying pan . . . pancakes!" (pancakes are frequently eaten with lemon juice in the UK). Such errors suggest that the patients entered "tip-of-the-tongue" states when naming animate objects. Semantic access was tested using the associative matching task from the BORB battery (Riddoch & Humphreys, 1993) and the pyramids and palm trees task (Howard & Orchard-Lisle, 1984). In the associative matching task, the patient is given a target picture (e.g., a screwdriver) and has to decide which of two reference pictures (e.g., a screw and a nail) is most associated with it. The pyramids and palm trees test requires a similar decision concerning which of two reference pictures (e.g., palm tree and a fir tree) is most related to a target picture (e.g., a pyramid). In each test, items that are matched are not visually related. SRB scored 29/30 (97%) and 48/50 (96%) correct on the associative match and pyramids and palm trees tests and DM scored 27/30 (90%) and 45/50 (90%). A control score on each task is respectively around 96%. Clearly SRB scored at the control level; DM was just below but at most there was only a mild impairment.

This pattern of good performance on measures of semantic matching was not simply due to the tests involving mainly inanimate stimuli. In semantic tests using only animate items, both patients again performed well. From vision SRB made 18/20 (90%) correct categorisation responses to fruits and vegetables (when he was asked to decide whether an object was a fruit or vegetable—though he named only 13 correctly) and when required to perform an associative matching task using only animate items he scored 37/40 (93%) correct. DM categorised all of the fruits and vegetables correctly (naming only 13 correctly) and she was at ceiling on the animate–associative task. The two errors that SRB made with fruits and vegetables also occurred when he was given the object names, so this was not a specific visual impairment but reflected poor semantic knowledge about the status of a few items. His score on the animate–associative matching task, though slightly below the control level (mean 39/40, SD = 0.84), also revealed no major impairment. The results may be taken to indicate that both patients could access semantic information from objects.

However, more detailed tests revealed that, in contrast to the previous conclusion, both SRB and DM had deficits in stored perceptual knowledge, particularly for animate objects. For example, on a simple test of drawing from memory, both SRB and DM generated poor representations of animate objects (tending not to represent the main features of the objects), whereas their drawings of artefacts were good (see Figure 6.1). In fact the patients were poor at drawing the same objects that they also failed to name, linking a possible problem in stored perceptual knowledge to the naming defect. This was explored further using object decision tests and tests using definitions that stressed either the visual or the functional associative properties of objects (what is the name of an orange, cone-shaped vegetable vs. what root vegetable is said to help you see in the dark?). It was assumed that tests of visual knowledge about objects would require access to stored structural knowledge, even from the object names; in contrast, functional and associative knowledge may be retrieved from a semantic knowledge store. On an object decision task (Riddoch & Humphreys, 1993) the patients both scored 27/32—above chance but more than 2 standard deviations below control subjects (mean 29.8, SD = 1.2, over 30 elderly subjects). With functional definitions both patients performed well. SRB scored 70/76 (92%) and DM 68/76 (89%); the control mean was 71 (SD = 2.1). In contrast the patients were impaired with perceptual definitions. SRB named 39/76 (51%) correct and DM 32/76 (42%) correct; the control score was 56/76 (74%) (SD = 4). The patients were able to retrieve the appropriate names for functional definitions, but they were relatively poor at naming to perceptual definitions (see also Gainotti & Silveri, 1996).

These results with drawing and naming to definition suggest that the problem is not a general one of name retrieval, but rather it occurs when visual properties of objects must be used to derive the name (e.g., as when naming to perceptual definitions, but not when naming to associative definitions). Against this, it

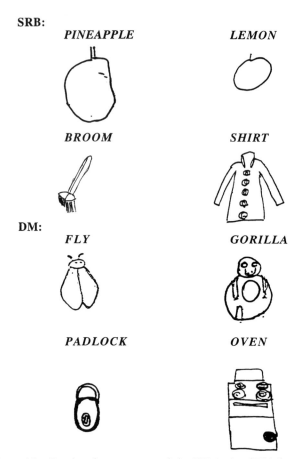

Figure 6.1.   Drawings from memory made by SRB (top) and DM (bottom).

could be that the patients just show strong effects of task difficulty. For controls, perceptual definitions are on average more difficult to name than associative-functional definitions, and animate stimuli tend to be more difficult to draw too, so overall effects of task difficulty should lead to poor drawing of animate items and poor naming of perceptual definitions. Is task difficulty crucial? We suggest that it is not. Perceptual definitions, though difficult for control subjects, tend to be easier for animate than for inanimate objects (31 vs. 25/38), perhaps because animate items are often represented in terms of their perceptual features (Farah & McClelland, 1991). SRB and DM showed the opposite effect, scoring 16 vs. 23/38 and 13 vs. 19/38 respectively on perceptual definitions for animate and inanimate objects. Thus, even though animate objects are easier for the controls, they are more difficult for these patients. There appears to be a specific deficit in using perceptual information to derive the name of animate objects (and also in retrieving stored visual knowledge to draw the same items from memory).

From these cases it appears that impaired retrieval of stored perceptual knowledge does not necessarily preclude access to quite detailed semantic knowledge from taking place (judged from the patients' semantic matching and categorisation performance). SRB and DM are impaired primarily when tasks depend on stored perceptual knowledge to generate a unique response to an object—as in drawing from memory or naming a perceptual definition, or indeed in naming an object from vision. Despite this, they are able to derive sufficient information to be able to perform semantic matching judgements at a control level. From this we conclude that more detailed visual information needs to be derived from objects for a naming task than it does for semantic matching and categorisation tasks, even though access to name information only seems to take place after access to semantic information from objects (Potter & Faulconer, 1975). In this way, visual processing (and in these patients, impaired retrieval of detailed perceptual information) constrains name retrieval.

VISUAL DEGRADATION IMPAIRS NAME RETRIEVAL

Further evidence on the impact of visual processing directly on name retrieval comes from studies showing that degrading visual input can impair naming in neuropsychological patients. This was first reported by Bisiach (1966), who tested a group of dysnomic patients on the naming of real objects and line drawings. He found that, in terms of gesture and circumlocution responses, the patients were equally good with both types of stimulus but that the naming of real objects was superior to that of line drawings. Since gesture and circumlocution responses were about equal for the two types of stimulus, access to semantic information appeared to be equally good, so the problem was more one of naming; real objects seemed to have more influence on name retrieval than line drawings.

We have followed up this finding with DM, using more formal tests of semantic access than those used by Bisiach. She was given target line drawings with a set of irrelevant overlapping circles over them, and she was asked either to name the drawings or to make an associative match decision (she had to point to which of two accompanying pictures was associated to the degraded target). In a baseline (nonoverlapping) condition, DM named 26/30 pictures and matched them all correctly (30/30). With overlapping circles she again matched them all correctly, but now only named 12/30. For 12 items DM made what appeared to be "tip-of-the-tongue" errors (e.g., *camel*—it's in the desert, can go for ages without water, they use them to transport goods and people, like a caravan . . .). This result again suggests that degradation of a visual stimulus can affect name retrieval more than semantic access, consistent with naming depending on finer visual differentiation.

The evidence with DM, then, suggests a mild deficit in stored perceptual knowledge about stimuli, which affects name retrieval more than access to semantic knowledge and which is exacerbated by degrading the input (e.g., with overlapping figures). It may be that any initial "noise" in retrieving stored perceptual information is carried through to the name retrieval stage and blocks that process when there is abnormal perceptual competition. Name retrieval is more affected than semantic matching because name retrieval requires individuation of activation from a target item. In addition to this, naming may not only require bottom-up activation of visual knowledge but also top-down feedback in order to differentiate activation generated by a target object from that of perceptually and semantically similar neighbours. This need for top-down activation may be more pronounced for naming than for semantic matching, and more for animate objects which belong to categories with perceptually similar exemplars. In a patient such as DM, there may be some impairment in using top-down feedback to facilitate the naming process (see Humphreys et al., 1997, for this argument), and this leads to a name retrieval problem that is most profound for animate objects.

One alternative account for the neuropsychological data is that it reflects a disconnection between right hemisphere recognition processes (intact in patients such as SRB and DM) and processes in the left hemisphere concerned with object naming (cf. Coslett & Saffran, 1989; Geschwind, 1965). On this account we may suppose the existence of separate routes for object processing, one to semantic knowledge (that is intact in the patients) and one to phonological retrieval (that is impaired). However, this account fails to explain why naming disorder can be most pronounced for animate objects. As we review later, name retrieval for both artefacts and animate objects is associated with left hemisphere activation (Martin, Wiggs, Ungerleider, & Haxby, 1996; Perani et al., 1995). Consequently a left hemisphere disconnection should affect both classes of object alike. The data contradict this.

Rather than a disconnection account, then, we favour a view in which visual processes directly determine object naming, in part by requiring top-down modulation when objects have many perceptually similar neighbours within their category. Other evidence consistent with a role of top-down feedback comes from studies of the functional anatomy of object naming, which we now consider.

THE FUNCTIONAL ANATOMY OF OBJECT NAMING

Positron emission tomography (PET) techniques measure changes in regional blood flow associated with different cognitive tasks. ^{15}O, administered intravenously as radiolabelled water, will be utilised to varying degrees in contrasting brain areas and the total count per voxel (volumetric element) provides an estimate of regional blood flow in the brain. Using this technique to assess the neural areas involved in object identification, Martin et al. (1996) had subjects either (1) name line drawings of animals or tools silently, (2) view drawings of structurally plausible nonobjects, or (3) view random noise patterns. When compared with viewing the noise patterns (the baseline condition), viewing the nonobjects led to bilateral activation in the fusiform gyri and the inferior gyri of the occipital lobes. This suggests that these areas may be involved in encoding the structural properties of objects, since these properties were shared with the nonobjects (see also Kanwisher, Woods, Ioconi, & Mazziotta, 1997; Schacter et al., 1995, though in both of the latter studies, the areas activated were somewhat more anterior to those reported by Martin et al., 1996; we note here that such differences likely reflect the baselines used in the different studies, and the extent to which the baseline stimuli contained similar features to those in the critical conditions). When compared with viewing the plausible nonobjects, Martin et al. found that object naming produced increased activation bilateral activity in the temporal lobes; this activity overlapped with but was anterior to the areas activated by the nonobjects. There were also differences in the areas activated when naming animals and tools. When animals were named, relative to when tools were named, there was increased activation in left medial occipital lobe, centred on the calcarine sulcus. In contrast, for the naming of tools, relative to animals, there was increased activation in the left premotor area and the left temporal lobe (though in an area more dorsal to that activated by animal naming). Damasio, Grabowski, Tranel, Hichwa, and Damasio (1996) had subjects name animals and tools, but their baseline condition required subjects to say the word "up" or "down" to upright or inverted faces. Relative to this baseline, tool naming activated the middle and inferior temporal gyri, whereas animal naming activated medial and inferior regions of the posterior temporal lobe (though somewhat anterior to the area highlighted by Martin et al.). Perani et al. (1995) reported similar data using a task in which subjects had to judge whether two pictures had the same name. Relative to a baseline in which two random shapes were matched, animals activated the inferior temporal lobes bilaterally and artefacts activated the lingual, the parahippocampal, and the middle occipital gyri and the dorsolateral frontal cortex of the left hemisphere. These results indicate that different brain regions mediate name retrieval with animals and artefacts, though there are some discrepancies in the areas highlighted by different studies. However, all the studies have shown that there is activation of relatively posterior neural regions when animals are named. These regions are usually thought to be involved with high-level visual processing. The data suggest that the naming of these objects involves additional activation of perceptual representations, relative to the naming of artefacts.

We (Moore & Price, 1999; Price, Moore, Humphreys, Frackowiak, & Friston, 1996) too have assessed the neural areas involved in object naming using PET methods. In Price et al., subjects saw coloured pictures of objects or nonobjects (equated in complexity to the real objects). A factorial design was used in which subjects: (1) named the real objects; (2) said "yes" to the occurrence of the objects; (3) named the colour of the nonobjects; and (4) said "yes" to the occurrence of the nonobjects. The naming tasks to objects and to colours (1 and 3) both required the retrieval of learned phonological labels associated with visual stimuli. The "say yes" tasks (2 and 4) required visual analysis and articulation, but not the retrieval of associated phonological labels. Subtraction of the "say yes" conditions from the naming conditions reveals the neural areas that are linked to name retrieval from visual stimuli. The neural areas for processing object shapes are revealed by subtracting the images with nonobjects (3 and 4) from those with objects (1 and 2). Further, the factorial design enables us to test for an interaction between naming and object recognition. This is revealed by the differences between (a) activation in the object naming condition (1) relative to its non-naming baseline ("say yes" to objects, condition 2), and (b) activation in the colour naming condition (3) relative to its nonnaming baseline ("say yes" to nonobjects, condition 4). This interaction highlights the neural areas that are more activated in name retrieval for objects than in other visual name retrieval tasks (in this case colour naming).

The main effect of object recognition (taking the two tasks with objects, relative to the nonobject baselines) was associated with activation of the ventral and dorsal middle occipital cortex, the left mid inferior temporal lobe, the right anterior temporal lobe and the left cerebellum. The inferior temporal activation is quite similar to that found in previous studies (e.g., Kanwisher et al., 1997). Name retrieval (taking the object and colour naming tasks together, relative to their baselines) activated the left inferior occipital gyrus, the left lingual and mid fusiform gyri, the left middle frontal lobe, the left thalamus, the left caudate, and the right parahippocampus. However, for our present purposes the most important finding concerned the interaction between object naming (relative to its baseline) and colour naming (relative to its baseline). Areas more activated in object naming (relative to its "say yes" baseline), when compared with colour naming (relative to the "say yes" baseline with nonobjects), reflect processes mediating name retrieval for objects. These "object naming areas" included: the medial anterior temporal lobes (bilaterally), the left superior temporal sulcus, the left posterior inferior temporal lobe, the left anterior insula, and the right cerebellum.

This study, unlike prior functional imaging studies of object naming, used the same visual stimuli in the naming and baseline conditions. Even so, activation was increased in the inferior occipital lobe and the lingual gyrus: areas linked to early visual processing of shape and colour (Humphreys & Riddoch, 1993; Zeki et al., 1991). From this it appears that there is some modulation of early form and colour processing when object and colour naming is required. Particularly for areas in the left posterior inferior temporal lobe, object naming also generated larger increases in activation than colour naming. Thus, the left posterior inferior temporal lobe is implicated specifically in object identification tasks.

Moore and Price (1999) used either coloured or black and white line drawings of both animate objects and artefacts. The objects were also either visually
complex (animals and multicomponent artefacts) or simple (fruits, vegetables,
and artefacts with simple shapes). Behavioural studies with normal observers
show that, particularly for animate objects, coloured drawings are named faster
than line drawings (Price & Humphreys, 1989). This is presumably because
colour facilitates the process of differentiating between perceptually overlapping
neighbours. Consistent with this last proposal, Moore and Price found that
activation levels in object recognition areas (Price et al., 1996) were reduced for
coloured drawings relative to line drawings. With coloured images, these areas
seem to have to do "less work" for recognition to take place.

In addition to these points, activation in the left medial occipital lobe reflected
the visual complexity of the items. Complex artefacts and animals generated
increased activation levels relative to the visually simple artefacts and fruits and
vegetables. From this it appears that visual processing is more engaged by
complex relative to simple objects, a factor that can also contribute to category
differences with unmatched stimuli.

In both of the last studies (Moore & Price, 1999; Price et al., 1996), relatively
posterior areas of cortex, in the medial occipital lobe and the inferior posterior
temporal lobe, are activated in object naming, and more so by animate than
inanimate objects. We suggest that this increased activation is related to the
greater visual differentiation needed for naming compared to recognition tasks,
and to the greater visual differentiation required when animate objects are named.
It may well be that, compared with recognition tasks, these relatively posterior
areas are activated in a top-down fashion in naming, to enable the visual differentiation necessary for individual identification to take place.

MODELS OF OBJECT NAMING

The evidence we have reviewed, on experimental, neuropsychological, and imaging studies of object naming, have indicated that: (1) information is transmitted
continuously between at least some of the stages involved in object naming;
(2) name retrieval is constrained by visual as well as semantic information
derived from objects; (3) deficits in retrieving detailed visual information from
long-term memory can precipitate naming impairments in patients; and (4) object
naming is mediated by increased activation in relatively posterior regions of the
inferior temporal lobe. These results can be captured by models in which:
(1) different processing stages are specified (e.g., for accessing structural knowledge, semantic knowledge, and name information), (2) activation is transmitted
in cascade between processing levels, and (3) there is feedback of activation to
enhance the process of differentiation between representations for different
objects. Feedback may be more crucial for object naming than for superordinate
categorisation, because only naming requires differentiation of individual object

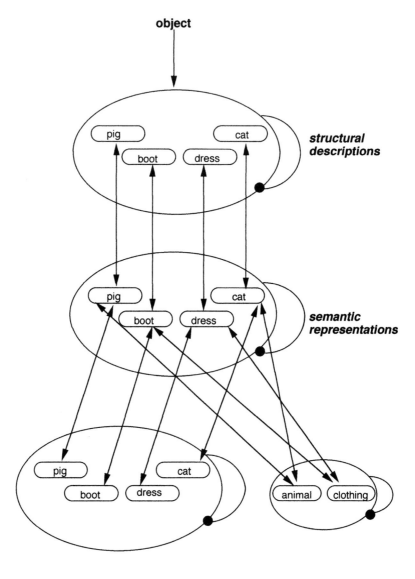

object

structural
descriptions

semantic
representations

name representations   superordinate units

Figure 6.2. The HIT account of object recognition, implemented in an interactive activation and competition framework by Humphreys, Lamote, and Lloyd-Jones (1995). → indicates excitatory connections and —● indicates inhibitory connections (between-level connections not shown).

representations. These three assumptions are captured in the Hierarchical Interactive Theory of object recognition (HIT; see Humphreys & Forde, in press). The architecture of this theory is set out in Figure 6.2.

An implementation of the approach was carried out by Humphreys, Lamote, and Lloyd-Jones (1995), who used an interactive activation and competition framework. This model had three main levels of stored representation: structural descriptions, semantic units, and name units (with separate pools for individual object names and for superordinate category names). Units at each level had excitatory connections to related units at the next level and inhibitory connections to unrelated units. In addition, there were inhibitory connections within each level, so that one unit competed with the others to "win" access to the next level (or to "win" the competition for the response, at the name level). Activation at one level was passed on continuously (in cascade) from level to the next, and also back down the model in an interactive fashion.

Perceptual overlap between objects was simulated by having an input vector, representing each object, reflect the rated similarity[1] between the target object and the other objects "known" to the model. Thus, a given animal would activate to some degree the representations of all other animals, whereas an artefact would generate less activity in the structural descriptions of other atrefacts. Object naming times were based on the activation of individual name units; semantic classification times were based on the activation of superordinate category units. Consistent with the data from normal human subjects, naming times were slower to objects from perceptually similar categories, whereas classification times were faster. This occurred because perceptual overlap led to competition for individual name selection, whereas it enhanced the activation of superordinate classification units. Also, the effects of overlap on naming moderated the influence of name frequency. Name frequencies were manipulated by varying the strength of the connections between semantic and name units. When this was done, name frequency effects were greater on perceptually dissimilar than on perceptually similar objects; with perceptually similar objects, there was greater opportunity for low-frequency names to compete for name selection, reducing the effects of frequency on naming time. This held across a number of different response threshold settings (see Humphreys et al., 1995). Again this mimics the findings with people (Humphreys et al., 1988).

The effects of brain damage were simulated in the model by adding noise onto the weights connecting units at the different levels, or by adding noise to the input activations. When this was done, performance became more impaired on objects from categories with perceptually similar exemplars than on objects from categories with perceptually dissimilar exemplars—similar to neuropsychological patients who find it particularly difficult to identify animate objects. The impairments were greater on naming than semantic classification, since only naming demanded differentiation between category exemplars. This occurred even with damage to relatively "early" stages of processing in the model, when noise was added to the structural descriptions of the stimuli. Again these results concur with the human data, where, as we have shown, impaired perceptual knowledge may underlie a naming problem for some categories of item. We also found that removing top-down feedback, from the semantic level back down to the structural level, disrupted living things more than nonliving things (see Humphreys & Forde, in press). This provides converging evidence for the role of top-down feedback in the identification of objects belonging to categories with structurally similar exemplars, as predicted by the HIT account.

Of course, these simulations may only capture part of the "neuropsychological picture". In the section dealing with neuropsychological studies, we pointed out that some patients can be better at identifying animate relative to inanimate objects; this result cannot be attributed to abnormal increases in noise within a model that, even in normality, favours inanimate objects (from categories with perceptually dissimilar neighbours). These deficits may instead reflect damage to specific representations for inanimate stimuli (e.g., loss of functional knowledge at a semantic level; see also Farah & McClelland, 1991).

These results provide an existence proof that a hierarchical model, operating interactively between processing levels, can simulate data showing that name retrieval is constrained by the visual processing of objects. Within this model, objects from categories with perceptually similar exemplars are subject to more competition for response, and may require more top-down modulation, for name selection to operate. This latter proposal fits with the results on functional imaging, which show increased activation in areas associated with high-level visual processing when naming rather than recognition responses are required.

This model has most in common with interactive theories of speech production, such as that proposed by Dell (1986, 1988), which propose that activation is transmitted continuously between different levels of representation in name production. However, theories such as Dell's emphasise the processes involved in going from a semantic representation of a stimulus to retrieval of a phonological form, for speech; in contrast, HIT emphasises name retrieval for single objects and it does not specify the nature of the name representation involved. Thus it may be that phonological retrieval requires a serial step following parallel selection of an object name at a more abstract level. Serial models of phonological retrieval remain popular for speech production (see Levelt et al., 1999). For HIT, the important point is that visual properties of object constrain the retrieval of semantic knowledge, and that there are consequent effects on both (1) the efficiency of name retrieval for different objects and (2) the brain regions most strongly activated during the retrieval process.

CONCLUSIONS

We have presented data from experimental studies with normal observers, neuropsychological studies with patients with naming deficits, and studies using functional imaging, which converge on the view that name retrieval for objects is strongly influenced by visual differentiation between category exemplars. This differentiation may also involve top-down modulation of earlier visual processes. Naming involves dynamic interactions between different knowledge sources, consistent with interactive models of human information processing.

ACKNOWLEDGEMENTS

The research was supported by grants from the Economic and Social Research Council and the Medical Research Council, UK, to the first and third authors, and from the Wellcome Trust to the second author. We thank members of the University of Birmingham cognitive neuropsychology group, and members of the Wellcome Department of Cognitive Neurology, for discussions concerning the ideas in this chapter and for their contributions to the work.

NOTE

1. Ratings were generated by independent subjects who were given the names of the objects and asked to rate how similar each object was relative to the other objects in the set.

REFERENCES

Bisiach, E. (1966). Perceptual factors in the pathogenesis of anomia. *Cortex, 2*, 90–92.

Caramazza, A., & Hillis, A.E. (1990). Where do semantic errors come from? *Cortex, 26*, 95–122.

Caramazza, A., & Hillis, A.E. (1991). Lexical organization of nouns and verbs in the brain. *Nature, 349*, 788–790.

Caramazza, A., & Shelton, J.R. (1998). Domain-specific knowledge systems in the brain: The animate–inanimate distinction. *Journal of Cognitive Neuroscience, 10*, 1–34.

Coslett, H.B., & Saffran, E.M. (1989). Preserved object recognition and reading comprehension in optic aphasia. *Brain, 112*, 1091–1110.

Damasio, H., Grabowski, T.J., Tranel, D., Hichwa, R.D., & Damasio, A.R. (1996). A neural basis for lexical retrieval. *Nature, 380*, 499–505.

Dell, G.S. (1986). A spreading-activation theory of retrieval in sentence production. *Psychological Review, 93*, 283–321.

Dell, G.S. (1988). The retrieval of phonological forms in production: Tests of predictions from a connectionist model. *Journal of Memory and Language, 27*, 124–142.

Dell, G.S., & Reich, P.A. (1981). Stages in sentence production: An analysis of speech error data. *Journal of Verbal Learning and Verbal Behavior, 20*, 611–629.

De Renzi, E., & Lucchelli, F. (1994). Are semantic systems separately represented in the brain? The case of living category impairments. *Cortex, 30*, 3–25.

Farah, M.J., & McClelland, J.L. (1991). A computational model of semantic memory impairment: Modality-specificity and emergent category-specificity. *Journal of Experimental Psychology: General, 120*, 339–357.

Farah, M.J., & Wallace, M.A. (1992). Categories of knowledge: Unfamiliar aspects of living and non-living things. *Neuropsychologia, 30*, 609–621.

Forde, E.M.E., Francis, D., Riddoch, M.J., Rumiati, R.I., & Humphreys, G.W. (1997). On the links between visual knowledge and naming: A single case study of a patient with a category-specific impairment for living things. *Cognitive Neuropsychology, 14*, 403–458.

Gainotti, G., & Silveri, M.C. (1996). Cognitive and anatomical locus of lesion in a patient with a category-specific semantic impairment for living things. *Cognitive Neuropsychology*, *13*, 357–390.

Geschwind, N. (1965). Disconnexion syndromes in animals and man. *Brain*, *88*, 237–294, 585–644.

Hart, J., Berndt, R.S., & Caramazza, A. (1985). Category-specific naming deficit following cerebral infarction. *Nature*, *316*, 439–440.

Hillis, A.E., & Caramazza, A. (1990). Category-specific naming and comprehension impairment: A double dissociation. *Brain*, *114*, 2081–2094.

Hillis, A.E., & Caramazza, A. (1995). Cognitive and neural mechanisms underlying visual and semantic processing: Implications from "optic aphasia". *Journal of Cognitive Neuroscience*, *7*, 457–478.

Howard, D., & Orchard-Lisle, V.M. (1984). On the origin of semantic errors in naming: Evidence from the case of a global aphasic. *Cognitive Neuropsychology*, *1*, 163–190.

Humphreys, G.W., & Forde, E.M.E. (in press). Hierarchies, similarity, and interactivity in object recognition: On the multiplicity of "category specific" deficits in neuropsychological populations. *Behavioral and Brain Sciences*.

Humphreys, G.W., Lamote, C., & Lloyd-Jones, T.J. (1995). An interactive activation-competition approach to object processing: Effects of structural similarity, name frequency and task in normality and pathology. *Memory*, *3*, 535–586.

Humphreys, G.W., & Riddoch, M.J. (1993). Object agnosias. In C. Kennard (Ed.), *Bailliere's clinical neurology* (pp. 339–360). London: Bailliere Tindall.

Humphreys, G.W., & Riddoch, M.J. (1999). Impaired development of semantic memory: Separating semantic from structural knowledge and diagnosing a role for action in establishing stored memories for objects. *Neurocase*, *5*, 519–532.

Humphreys, G.W., Riddoch, M.J., & Price, C.J. (1997). Top-down processes in object identification: Evidence from experimental psychology, neuropsychology and functional anatomy. *Philosophical Transactions of the Royal Society London*, *B352*, 1275–1282.

Humphreys, G.W., Riddoch, M.J., & Quinlan, P.T. (1988). Cascade processes in picture identification. *Cognitive Neuropsychology*, *5*, 67–103.

Job, R., Rumiati, R., & Lotto, L. (1992). The picture superiority effect in categorization: Visual or semantic? *Memory and Cognition*, *18*, 21–38.

Kanwisher, N., Woods, R.P., Ioconi, M., & Mazziotta, J.C. (1997). A locus in human extrastriate cortex for visual shape analysis. *Journal of Cognitive Neuroscience*, *9*, 133–142.

Kay, J., & Ellis, A.W. (1987). A cognitive neuropsychological case study of anomia: Implications for psychological models of word retrieval. *Brain*, *110*, 613–629.

Levelt, W.J.M. (1989). *Speaking: From intention to articulation*. Cambridge, MA: MIT Press.

Levelt, W.J.M., Roelofs, A., & Meyer, A.S. (1999). A theory of lexical access in language production. *Behavioral and Brain Sciences*, *22*, 1–38.

Lloyd-Jones, T.J., & Humphreys, G.W. (1997). Perceptual differentiation as a source of category effects in object processing: Evidence from naming and object decision. *Memory and Cognition*, *25*, 18–35.

Martin, A., Wiggs, C.L., Ungerleider, L.G., & Haxby, J.V. (1996). Neural correlates of category-specific knowledge. *Nature*, *379*, 649–652.

Martin, N., Weisberg, R.W., & Saffran, E. (1989). Variables influencing the occurrence of naming errors: Implications for a model of lexical retrieval. *Journal of Memory and Language*, *28*, 462–485.

Moore, C., & Price, C.J. (1999). A functional neuroimaging study of the variables that generate category-specific object processing differences. *Brain*, *122*, 943–962.

Morrison, C.M., Ellis, A.W., & Quinlan, P.T. (1992). Age of acquisition, not word frequency, affects object naming, not object recognition. *Memory and Cognition*, *20*, 705–714.

Perani, D., Cappa, S.F., Bettinardi, V., Bressi, S., Gorno-Tempini, M., Matarrese, M., & Fazio, F. (1995). Different neural systems for the recognition of animals and man-made tools. *NeuroReport*, *6*, 1637–1641.

Potter, M.C., & Faulconer, B.A. (1975). Time to understand pictures and words. *Nature, 253*, 437–438.

Price, C.J., & Humphreys, G.W. (1989). The effects of surface detail on object categorisation and naming. *Quarterly Journal of Experimental Psychology, 41A*, 797–828.

Price, C.J., Moore, C.J., Humphreys, G.W., Frackowiak, R.S.J., & Friston, K.J. (1996). The neural regions sustaining object recognition and naming. *Proceedings of the Royal Society, B263*, 1501–1507.

Riddoch, M.J., & Humphreys, G.W. (1987a). Picture naming. In G.W. Humphreys & M.J. Riddoch (Eds.), *Visual object processing: A cognitive neuropsychological approach* (pp. 107–143). Hove, UK: Lawrence Erlbaum Associates Ltd.

Riddoch, M.J., & Humphreys, G.W. (1987b). Visual object processing in optic aphasia: A case of semantic access agnosia. *Cognitive Neuropsychology, 4*, 131–185.

Riddoch, M.J., & Humphreys, G.W. (1993). *BORB: The Birmingham Object Recognition Battery.* Hove, UK: Lawrence Erlbaum Associates Ltd.

Sacchett, C., & Humphreys, G.W. (1992). Calling a squirrel a squirrel but a canoe a wigwam: A category-specific deficit for artefactual objects and body parts. *Cognitive Neuropsychology, 9*, 73–86.

Sartori, G., & Job, R. (1988). The oyster with four legs: A neuropsychological study on the interaction of visual and semantic information. *Cognitive Neuropsychology, 5*, 130–152.

Schacter, D.L., Reiman, E., Uecker, A., Polster, M.R., Yun, L.S., & Cooper, L.A. (1995). Brain regions associated with retrieval of structurally coherent visual information. *Nature, 376*, 587–590.

Sheridan, J., & Humphreys, G.W. (1993). A verbal-semantic category-specific recognition impairment. *Cognitive Neuropsychology, 10*, 143–184.

Snodgrass, J.G., & Yuditsky, T. (1996). Naming times for the Snodgrass and Vanderwart pictures. *Behavioral Research Methods, Instruments and Computers, 28*, 516–536.

Sternberg, S. (1969). Memory scanning: Mental processes revealed by reaction time experiments. *American Scientist, 57*, 421–457.

Van Orden, G.C. (1987). A ROWS is a ROSE: Spelling, sound and reading. *Memory and Cognition, 15*, 181–198.

Vitkovitch, M., & Humphreys, G.W. (1991). Perseverative responding in speeded naming to pictures: It's in the links. *Journal of Experimental Psychology: Learning, Memory and Cognition, 17*, 664–680.

Vitkovitch, M., Humphreys, G.W., & Lloyd-Jones, T.J. (1993). On naming a giraffe a zebra: Picture naming errors across different categories. *Journal of Experimental Psychology: Learning, Memory and Cognition, 19*, 243–259.

Vitkovitch, M., & Tyrrell, L. (1995). Sources of disagreement in object naming. *Quarterly Journal of Experimental Psychology, 48A*, 822–848.

Warrington, E.K., & McCarthy, R.A. (1983). Category-specific access dysphasia. *Brain, 106*, 859–878.

Warrington, E.K., & McCarthy, R.A. (1987). Categories of knowledge: Further fractionation and an attempted integration. *Brain, 110*, 1273–1296.

Warrington, E.K., & Shallice, T. (1984). Category-specific semantic impairment. *Brain, 107*, 829–853.

Wingfield, A. (1968). Effects of frequency on identification and naming of objects. *American Journal of Psychology, 81*, 226–234.

Zeki, S., Watson, J.D.G., Lueck, C.J., Friston, K.J., Kennard, C., & Frackowiak, R.S.J. (1991). A direct demonstration of functional specialisation in human visual cortex. *Journal of Neurology, 11*, 641–649.

CHAPTER SEVEN

Phonology: Structure, representation, and process

Aditi Lahiri
University of Konstanz, Germany

INTRODUCTION

It is not entirely transparent where a theory of phonology should fit in within a psycholinguistic theory of language production. Following Levelt (1989) and Wheeldon and Lahiri (1997), if we accept that the planning process is incremental and the linguistic unit of consequence is a "phonological word" (which is often larger than a syntactic word, incorporating content words with clitics), we need to ask whether the internal structure of such a unit is relevant in a psycholinguistic model. If we assume that linguistic theory is a theory of the underlying knowledge of native speakers, and if we also assume that a general theory of language embodies a system of representations as well as a system of well-formedness principles, rules, and constraints, then a precise phonological characterisation should be relevant for language production. The goal of a theory of language production is to account for how linguistic knowledge is mentally represented, accessed, and ultimately produced. Since the goal of phonological theory is to provide a characterisation of the sound structures found in the languages of the world, valid linguistic generalisations must play a role in constructing a psycholinguistic theory of production. The aim of this chapter is to provide an outline of the crosslinguistic generalisations made in phonological theory concerning the structure of the phonological system of a language, representations, and process. When appropriate we have made direct reference to what consequences phonological generalisations may have for a psycholinguistic model, particularly in the context of incremental planning as assumed in Levelt (1989).

This chapter is organised as follows. We first distinguish between various types of phonological processes, their morphological status and their phonological properties. While providing a typology of phonological processes, we next discuss several issues on phonological representations. Finally, we conclude by referring to certain phenomena which could be interpreted as "action-at-a-distance", and therefore a potential problem for incremental processing.

LEXICAL AND POSTLEXICAL PROCESSES

Sound structure (the domain of phonology) is not just concerned with words but also with smaller units, namely morphemes. Typically, a morphologically complex word consists of a pivotal morpheme combined with a collection of other morphemes. A word like *distrustful*, contains the central morpheme *trust*, which can stand in isolation as well ("free" morpheme), and two other "bound" morphemes, *dis* and *ful*. A morpheme is a minimal unit in word structure, but it does not necessarily have any consistent meaning, or in fact, any meaning at all (cf., Aronoff, 1976). For instance, the bound morphemes {cede}, {mit}, or {tain} can occur with prefixes like {con-} and {re-}. Although no specific meaning can be assigned to these forms, the phonological shape of the morpheme {cede}, [sid], will change to [sɛʃ] when followed by the suffix {-ion}: *concession, recession*. Similarly, [mɪt] changes to [mɪs] when followed by the morpheme {-ive}: *remissive*. This does not happen to any other random word ending with [mit] such as *hermit*, but only to the morpheme {mit}. Hence, this morpheme is a valid linguistic constituent.

Our concern here is the sound structure of words. If we assume words consist of one or more morphemes, we need to distinguish between various degrees of sound alternations in morphologically related words: purely phonologically governed, phonologically related under specific morphological conditions, and those where the alternations have little phonological connection. Following the model of Lexical Phonology and Morphology (LPM) (Kiparsky, 1982, 1985, 1996) we will assume a three-way distinction between (a) morpheme specific alternations (negotiated in the morphology), (b) lexical phonology, and (c) postlexical phonology.

In many instances the three-way division is unproblematic or at least un-controversial. An example of a purely morpheme-specific alternation is *go~went*; such an alternation is suppletive. Our focus will be on morphophonemic processes which deal with phonological alternations which occur only in particular derivations such as *keep~kept, sincere~sincerity*; and alternations such as *lock[s]~log[z]*, where the alternation is phonologically conditioned. This picture is further enriched by the postulation of additional rule types and more fine-grained distinctions among lexical morphophonological rules (cyclic and word-level rules) and among postlexical phonological rules (allophonic rules, rules of phonetic implementation). In the following subsections we will first draw a quick outline of the various phonological domains and their properties, and then discuss several processes that draw the distinction between these levels of morphology–phonology interaction.

Phonology in diverse domains

The degree of phonological variance between two morphologically related words is supposed to indicate whether the words are morphophonologically related or only morphologically related. For example, the phonological relationship between *good–better* is disparate enough to assume that there is no obvious phonological conditioning. However, the relationship between *think–thought* is not so straight-forward. We will not go into various linguistic controversies regarding purely phonological approaches and morphological approaches—for reviews and discussions, see Carstairs (1987), Carstairs-McCarthy (1992), and Spencer (1991). Instead, we will concentrate on fairly standard assumptions concerning lexical phonological and postlexical phonological processes. The model of Lexical Phonology and Morphology (LPM) assumes the following structure.

(1)   Lexical Phonology (based on Kiparsky, 1985)

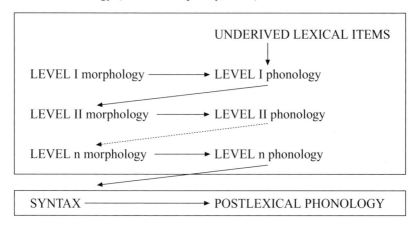

The basic assumption is that at each lexical level, the phonology interacts with the morphology. Each level is associated with a set of phonological rules, which apply after every morphological process. For example, a suffix like {-ity} is added in Level I, after which the regular stress rules of English apply. Depending on the number of syllables of the stem morpheme, the stress may or may not be on the same syllable of the related words: *sincere–sincerity*, but *timid–timidity*. In contrast, suffixes like {-ness} are added in Level II, where there are no stress rules and a suffixed word does not differ from the stem: *happy–happiness*. Consider also an example with prefixation. There are two, phonetically very similar, negative prefixes in English: {un-} and {in-}. The prefix {in-} is added in Level I and triggers place assimilation: *illicit* is derived from {in+licit}, and *irregular* from {in+regular}. This is not true for {un-} which is a Level II prefix: *unlikely*, *unreliable*, and not **ullikely*. Postlexical phonology comes into effect on the syntax level. On this level, there is no conditioning of particular morphological affixation—the context is entirely phonological.

A consequence of level ordering is that it straightforwardly accounts for several generalisations. For example, all Level II affixes are added after Level I affixes. For instance, one might come up with a word like *un-incompatible* but it would be quite impossible to say *in-unregular*. That is, a Level I prefixed word, may get another level of affixation, but no vice versa. The strong prediction is that Level n affixation and the Level n phonological rules should precede Level n+1 morphology and phonology. Kiparsky (1985) claimed that irregular inflection like *foot–feet* were in Level I, compounding in Level II, and regular inflection in Level III. As a result, it is possible to get *teethmarks*, but not **clawsmarks*; one can get irregular plurals in compounds since they are available from Level I inflection, but not with Level III inflection.

We will discuss the properties of the different types of rules in more detail in the following sections. In this model, it is important to emphasise that all phonological rules, lexical or postlexical, are phonological in nature. That is, even though the phonological processes may appear to be morphologically governed, they are really phonological in nature and conditioned by phonological principles. For instance, the stressed vowel in *sincere* is shortened and lax in *sincerity*. Although, such a shortening applies in the context of a limited number of suffixes, the alternation is govenerned by regular metrical structure. These assumptions are crucial for a processing model. For instance, it could be the case that there is morphological decomposition in the mental lexicon, only if there is no phonological alternation between the morphologically related words. Under this assumption, only morphologically related words like *happy–happiness* would be decomposed in the lexicon, while *sincere–sincerity* would be listed as full words. That is, Level I phonology is considered to be fossilised, but Level II phonology is accepted as an active process. In the next two subsections, we discuss in detail properties of lexical and postlexical rules.

Lexical phonological alternations or morphophonology

We first turn to alternations which appear to be morphological, but are not morpholexical alternations. Rather they are morphophonological alternations governed by lexical phonology. We now turn to a class of alternations (morphophonemic) which appear to be morphologically conditioned, but are truly phonological alternations. Most of these processes were historically overtly phonologically conditioned. Due to historical change these alternations can be viewed as being morphologically conditioned and indeed, some researchers have claimed that they are morpholexical rather than phonological. We will first discuss some of the basic tenets of LPM and then show how lexical phonological rules interact with morphology.

The fundamental idea is that phonological rules appear at two distinct points in the grammar: in the lexicon and in the syntactic or postlexical phrasal component. Here we discuss certain properties of lexical rules. A basic concept of LPM is Structure Preservation. Grammars choose certain underlying contrastive segments (the phonemic inventory) and, according to structure preservation, within the lexicon, representations can only make use of these contrasts. Thus, if any phonological rule introduces noncontrastive features (like English aspiration), they must by default be postlexical. Second, lexical phonological rules interact with morphological word formation rules such as affixation. Postlexical rules are insensitive to the internal structure of the word, and in fact can apply across words on the phrasal level.

The basic proposal is that word formation rules and lexical phonological rules are grouped together in several levels (see (1)). For instance, in English, "primary" inflection and derivation is added at Level I, where the rules of stress and shortening apply. Thus, alternations like *foot–feet* (by umlauting), ablaut alternations like *ride–rode*, inflectional suffixes like the past tense [-t] of *keep–kept*, and nominal suffixes like [-ity] of *sincere–sincerity*, are dealt with in Level I. In Level II, other derivations like [-ness] are added and compounding take place, along with the assignment of compound stress rules. In Level III, other inflectional suffixes are added like the regular past tense of *wait–waited*, *dance–danced*, and the plural in *bat–bats*, or *witch–witches* along with the relevant phonological rules. Thus, the phonological rules are restricted to each level.

Some lexical rules like stress assignment in English may be cyclic; that is, they may apply in the lexicon after each word formation rule. A classic case of cyclicity is seen in the difference between the stress contours and reduction of the words *còmp[ə]nsátion* and *cònd[ɛ]nsátion*. The difference lies in the fact that *cònd[ɛ]nsátion* derives from *condénse*, whereas *còmp[ə]nsátion* derives from *cómpensàte*. The derivations with some simplifications are given next.

(2)   Derivations of *cònd[ɛ]nsátion* and *còmp[ə]nsátion*

	[condens]ation	[compensat]ion
First cycle	[condense]	[compensate]
Stress	condénse	cómpensàte
Second cycle	[condéns]ation	[cómpensàt]ion
Stress	condènsátion	còmpensátion
Later rules		
Vowel reduction	—	còmp[ə]nsátion
Stress shift	cònd[ɛ]nsátion	—

The stress rules have to apply cyclically to ensure that the vowel in *condénse* is stressed on the previous cycle which prevents it from reduction later.

We began this subsection by claiming that phonological rules that apply in the lexicon are indeed phonological and not morphological, although they may be subject to particular types of affixation. Since the organisation of the grammar in LPM permits us to divide up suffixation in different levels, the phonological nature of these rules becomes more obvious. We will discuss two such Level I phonological rules, closed syllable shortening with the past tense suffix [-t] and trisyllabic shortening, both of which we touched on earlier.

The alternations between *keep–kept* are accounted for by the fact that in Level I, English constrains monosyllables with long vowels to have only one consonant which is marked extrasyllabic (see p. 192 onwards; cf., Myers, 1987). The verb *keep* is analysed as [kee<p>] where the extrasyllabic consonants are put within angled brackets. When the past tense suffix [-t] is attached, the final [p] is no longer at the edge and loses its extrasyllabic status. The word *kept* is analysed as [keep<t>], with the final [t] being extrasyllabic. Since in Level I a long vowel may only be followed by a single consonant in the syllable, a shortening rule applies leading to [kep<t>]. Verbs ending in [-d] or [-t] also show shortening along with final degemination, a familiar constraint in English which does not allow final geminated consonants. Thus, the *shoot–shot* alternation is derived from [shoot<t>], which leads to shortening of [shot<t>] and finally, the degemination of the final [tt] cluster. Compare also *feed–fed*, *meet–met*, etc. This process accounts also for alternations like *wide–width*, *deep–depth*, etc. Our point is that this rule is by no means morphological although it is restricted to certain suffixes. For instance, the alternative past tense of *dream* (other than *dreamt*), which is formed by the regular suffix [-ed] in Level III, keeps its long vowel in *dreamed*. The phonological nature of the rule is obvious in its structural description and structural change. The target is a phonologically defined segment, namely a vowel. The change is the assignment of a phonological property which is shortening. The context is phonological, that is a closed syllable. In the next example on trisyllabic shortening, we have further support from the fact that the rule is fed by other phonological rules in the preceding cycle.

Trisyllabic shortening (TSS) accounts for alternations like *nation~national*, *sincere~sincerety*. The triggering context is in part phonological, i.e., there is no shortening before a stressed syllable (cf., *titánic*, *gradátion*, etc.). Since TSS is triggered by a specific set of suffixes, it is often assumed to be a morphological rule. However, it is not the suffix per se that triggers TSS, but rather the interactions of cyclic stress and extrametricality, both of which are phonological conditions. The conditions under which TSS applies, are the following: (a) the shortened vowel must be in a stressed syllable; and (b) the following syllable must be unstressed. The explanation could either be a version of closed syllable shortening following Myers (1987), or foot-based (see Lahiri & Fikkert 1999). In the closed syllable shortening analysis, the onset of the second syllable closes the preceding syllable which leads to trisyllabic shortening. Either way, it is metrically conditioned.

(3) Trisyllabic shortening as a phonological process
   (a) *nátion, nát·onal*
       sincére, sincérity
   (b) *cone, conic*
       metal, metallic
   (c) *cycle, cyclic, cyclicity*
       globe, global, globality

In English, final syllables in derived adjectives and nouns are generally extrametrical. In (3a), the vowel in *nation* remains long since the final syllable is extrametrical and does not count for stress. In the adjective *national*, the final syllable is also extrametrical, but here the second syllable remains unstressed and the onset of this syllable closes the preceding syllable leading to closed syllable shortening. An alternative view is that the initial syllable is shortened to construct a maximal foot, and the foot can then span both syllables.[1] In any event, the interaction of extrametricality and TSS is clearly evident in (3b) and (3c). Stress facts show that the suffix *-ic* is not extrametrical. Hence, it does count for stress and footing, leading to TSS. Thus, we get the alternation between *globality* and *cyclicity*.

Processes such as TSS are not therefore morphological, but are purely phonological rules restricted to the lexical phonology. This rule obeys all phonological locality conditions. Its context is partly phonologically derived since the shortening never applies before another stressed syllable. In addition, TSS is fed by other lexical phonological rules, specifically stress. No matter what formulation TSS is given (whether syllable based or foot based), the stress condition holds. Thus, processes such as these are purely phonological rules and must be distinguished from the morpholexical types.

Before ending this subsection, we will once more refer to the property of structure preservation, which is crucial for lexical phonological processes. Thus, these rules do not introduce new contrasts. Phonological processes lead to neutralisations when the relevant segments are part of the lexical phonology. In English, the suffix *-ive* can be added to a verb to make an adjective. When the suffix is added to a [d], it is changed to a fricative [s] bringing about alternations such as *extend~extensive, deride~derisive*, etc. The segments [d] and [s] are neutralised in the context of this suffix, which is attached in Level 1. Both segments are, however, part of the phonemic inventory and the rule does not violate structure preservation. In contrast to such neutralisations, postlexical processes, to which we now turn, may or may not be neutralising and can introduce segments that are not part of the underlying phonological inventory.

Postlexical phonological processes

Postlexical processes apply outside the lexicon and are therefore not subject to any morphological conditions. In fact, at this level, there is no evidence of any morpheme internal structures. Thus, postlexical processes are solely triggered by phonological structure and do not have lexical exceptions. Many of such processes operate within words but also frequently across word boundaries. A standard postlexical process is that of affrication in English, where coronal obstruents such as [t, d, s, z] become palatoalveolar affricates when followed by a front glide.[2]

(4)   English affrication
    (a)   *Did you* like it?   [dɪʤuː]
    (b)   *What you* see in the distance . . .   [wɔʧuː]
    (c)   *Pass your* . . .   [paʃʃɔː]
    (d)   *Does your* . . .   [dʌʒʒɔː]

Postlexical processes are often bound by specific domains of the prosodic hierarchy. It has been assumed that surface syntactic structure is mapped onto phonological units, which are constituents in this hierarchy, like phonological phrases and intonational phrases. For instance, one of the most frequent postlexical assimilation processes, regressive voicing assimilation, applies optionally in Bengali polymorphemic words as well as across word boundaries but not across phonological phrases. An example of this can be seen in focused phrases where the end of the focused material marks the right edge of a phonological phrase.

(5)   Bengali regressive voicing assimilation
    (a)   Object–Verb structures, no voicing assimilation
        (bʰu[t])ₚ (dækʰɑ)ₚ   ghost see
    (b)   N–V complex predicates, voicing assimilation
        (bʰu[d] dækʰɑ)ₚ   ghost see = "to be surprised"

When *bʰut* is focused, it is always in a separate phonological phrase and regressive voicing assimilation is blocked. However, when the noun and verb behave as a complex verb which is reflected in the meaning, the two words belong to a single phonological phrase and voicing assimilations applies across the word boundary.

    As we mentioned earlier, postlexical processes are not required to be structure preserving. The non-structure-preserving status of postlexical processes can be seen in the case of Dutch regressive voicing assimilation, where stops pass on their voicing to the preceding obstruent (Trommelen & Zonneveld, 1979).

(6)   Dutch voicing assimilation

	SING.	PLURAL	GLOSS	COMPOUND	GLOSS	
(a)	knoop	knopen	"button"	knoopdoek	scarf	[bd]
(b)	maat	maten	"measure"	maatbeker	measuring cup	[db]
(c)	zak	zakken	"bag"	zakdoek	handkerchief	[gd]

Dutch contrast labial and dental voiced and voiceless stops ([b]~[p], [d]~[t]) but has only a voiceless velar stop [k]. In (6a) and (6b), voicing assimilation neutralises the underlying contrast between the voiced and voiceless stops. In contrast, in (6c), since there is no *g* phoneme in the language, there is no neutralisation of a contrast but a new segment is introduced. This process of voicing assimilation is thus not a structure preserving rule, and applies only on the postlexical level.

Allophonic rules, that is phonological rules that introduce a new contrast, are definitely postlexical. Thus, two languages may have two similar sounds, but their phonological status would be different. For instance, both English and Bengali have an alveolar/dental [s] and a palatoalveolar [ʃ]. In Bengali, the [s] occurs only after dental consonants and [ʃ] elsewhere. One hypothesis could be that a purely allophonic contrast may be phonetically not as distinct as a real phonological contrast. However, at least insofar as these two consonants are concerned, Evers, Reetz, and Lahiri (1998) show that the phonetic distinction is maintained irrespective of the phonological contrast. We will discuss well-known examples of English flapping and aspiration in detail in a later section, since these are prosodically conditioned.

Summary

We have distinguished between purely morphological alternations from phono-logically governed processes which may be lexical or postlexical. Lexical phonological alternations may superficially look as if they are morphologically governed, but are not. They observe phonological locality, are fed by other phono-logical rules, obey structure preservation and are phonologically conditioned. We have argued that although there are degrees of phonological variance between morphophonologically related words, if the alternations are governed by lexical phonological rules then the alternations are phonological and not morphological. Postlexical rules, on the other hand, are phrasal rules where structure preservation does not play a role, and no morphological conditioning is applicable.

PHONOLOGICAL PROCESSES AND REPRESENTATIONS

Although we have mentioned several different phonological processes, we have not as yet provided a typology of phonological processes. The most frequent types of phonological processes can be characterised as (a) assimilation, (b) dissimilation, (c) deletion, (d) insertion, (e) shortening, and (f) lengthening. The last four types of process are usually prosodically conditioned, and we will deal with them in the next section. All of these processes may be either lexical or postlexical depending on their obligatory and structure preserving properties. As we have shown earlier, postlexical processes may be optional and can introduce new contrasts, and therefore are not structure preserving. Lexical processes, in contrast, are obligatory and are strictly structure preserving. It is possible that the processing system treats these differently. In this section, we will discuss assimilation and dissimilation phenomena, elaborating on the consequences they may have in the phonological system. The focus in this section is not on the phonological processes themselves, but rather they are introduced to argue for particular phonological representations.

Assimilations

Assimilations can be regressive (anticipatory) or progressive (perseveratory). Examples of regressive assimilation involving consonants were given in the preceding section. Vowel assimilations are equally frequent. Most commonly in vowel harmony languages such as Finnish, Turkish, etc., certain features of the root vowel are progressively spread to the suffixes. In Turkish, for instance, the suffix vowels alternate as in *-lar/-ler* (PLURAL) or *-in/-un/-ün/-ın* (GENITIVE) depending on the quality of the stem vowel. The examples are from Halle and Clements (1983).

(7)   Turkish vowel harmony

	NOM. SG.	GEN. SG.	NOM. PL.	GEN. PL.	GLOSS
(a)	ip	ipin	ipler	iplerin	rope
(b)	kız	kızın	kızlar	kızların	girl
(c)	yüz	yüzün	yüzler	yüzlerin	face
(d)	pul	pulun	pullar	pulların	stamp
(e)	el	elin	eller	ellerin	hand
(f)	čan	čanın	čanlar	čanların	bell
(g)	köy	köyün	köyler	köylerin	village
(h)	son	sonun	sonlar	sonların	end

In the second column, the vowel in the genitive suffix, which is always high, assimilates to the stem vowel both in the front/back dimension as well as in rounding. Comparing the genitive singular forms in (7g) and (7h), we can see that the genitive suffix [ü] is both round and front because of the stem vowel [ö] giving the surface form [köyün], but in [sonun] the suffix is back and round corresponding to the stem vowel [o]. In the third column, the vowel in the plural suffix alternates between [a] and [e]. Thus, the plural suffix is always non-high and unrounded, but assimilates to the front/back property of the stem vowel. That the suffix vowels borrow the features of the immediately preceding vowel can be seen when the plural suffix is added first in the examples in the fourth column. The vowel of the genitive suffix takes the features front and unrounded, not from the stem vowel, but from the preceding plural suffix [ler], leading to the surface form [köylerin] and not *[köylerün] in (7g). Although the vowel harmony effects appear to be "action-at-a-distance", the assimilation process is local and takes place between vowels in adjacent syllables.

Until now, although we have mentioned qualities of segmental structure such as voicing, rounding, etc., we have not formally discussed their status. While discussing assimilations (particularly vowel harmony), it becomes obvious that the elements that are passed on to following or preceding segments are certain attributes or features and not the entire copy of the segment. The evidence for the organisation of phonological features rests mainly on assimilations and hence we now turn to the representations of features and segments.

Features and segments

Phonology does not assume that segments are unstructured wholes but that they are made up of a number of phonological features. A consonant [p] is an obstruent, a plosive, and it is voiceless. There are two unfortunate assumptions made in the psycholinguistics literature which should be clarified. First, it is often assumed that a feature is a "smaller" unit than a segment. This is an inaccurate description. A feature represents a natural class of segments. The feature [nasal], for instance, characterises not just the segment [m] in English but also [n] and [ŋ]. In Bengali, which has nasal vowels as well, [nasal] would characterise all the nasal segments, vowels and consonants: [m n ŋ ã æ̃ õ ẽ ũ ĩ]. The second misleading impression rests on the connection between segments and features. There is a tendency to believe that if one has features in the lexical representation, there are no segments and vice versa. This again is an inaccurate point of view. A segment is a composite of many features, and a feature represents a class of segments.

It is not possible to give a complete account of all the phonological features since the literature is vast. Rather, this section will focus on some important classifications of features based on phonological processes and their organisation. We will also draw attention to two controversial aspects of feature representations: the distinction between binary and privative features, and the assumption that consonants and vowels may share place features.

Phonological features are abstract entities with both acoustic and articulatory correlates. Phonological processes, however, do not distinguish a segment depending on its phonetic correlate. In earlier generative models, segments have been assumed to be made up of unorganised feature bundles. This is clearly not the case. Certain features group together more frequently than others. If there is homorganic place assimilation, then nasality does not play a role. To represent natural feature groupings and restrictions on feature combinations, there have been various proposals on the hierarchical organisation of features sometimes informally characterised as the feature tree. In general, the major class features like [consonantal] and [sonorant] are assumed to form the root of the tree. The root node represents the abstract segment node. The laryngeal features [voice] and [aspiration/spread glottis] are often grouped together. Next come the place features like [labial], [coronal], etc. Here there is considerable controversy. In

Chomsky and Halle (1968), all features were binary. This is not a general assumption in the recent literature. Clements (1985) assumes all features to be
binary. Others have assumed the opposite, namely that all features are privative
or monovalent (cf., Rice, 1996; van der Hulst, 1989). The third possibility, that
the major class features and some dependent features are binary and that other
features, particularly place features, are privative or monovalent, has also been
considered (cf., Lahiri & Evers, 1991).

The arguments for and against these three views principally rest on evidence
from assimilation. For instance, if we assume [voice] is a privative feature, then
segments are either marked for [voiced] or nothing. The class of segments which
would be marked [−voice] under the binary hypothesis should not behave as a
natural class in phonological processes. Thus, [−voice] should not spread or
should not provide a context for a phonological process (see Cho, 1990 and
Lombardi, 1991).

There is more consensus concerning the place features which most researchers
now assume to be monovalent. The uncontroversial places of articulation are
[labial], [coronal] (tip and blade of the tongue), and [dorsal] (back of the tongue).
However, within the [coronal] and [dorsal] place nodes, there is considerable
disagreement concerning the status of palatals. Some researchers have assumed
that they are [coronal] (cf., Clements, 1985; Lahiri & Evers, 1991), whereas
others have assumed they are both [dorsal] and [coronal] (cf., Gussenhoven &
van de Weijer, 1990; Keating, 1991). A further assumption has been that the place
node is divided up into [coronal] versus a peripheral node (Rice, 1996), where
the peripheral node includes [labial] and [dorsal]. This is reminiscent of the feature
[grave] of Jakobson, Fant, and Halle's (1952) feature [grave]. On the opposite
end, Clements and Hume (1995) proposed a [lingual] node combining [coronal]
and [dorsal], separating them from [labial].

The evidence again rests on assimilation, which again is connected to the
representation of vowel and consonantal place features. There are two schools of
thought. Following Sagey (1990), many scholars assume that the vowel features
[high], [back], and [low] are all under the dorsal node, which also includes the
velar consonants. Clements (1985) and Lahiri and Evers (1991) assume that the
vowels and consonants share place features (following Jakobson et al., 1952).
Thus, front vowels are [coronal], whereas back vowels are [dorsal]. Clements
assumes a separate level for the vowels that include place features as well as
the features [high], [back], and [low], whereas Lahiri and Evers hold that the
main articulator node splits up into a place node and a tongue height node,
and the latter includes the height features. Again the evidence that is invoked
to support one representation from another relates to assimilation processes
such as palatalisations where vowel features spread to consonants. Moreover,
vowel alternations themselves have now been shown to support such an organisation (Ghini, in press; Lahiri, 1999). We will assume the feature organisation
given in (8).

(8)   Organisation of features (based on Ghini, 1999; Lahiri, 1999; Lahiri & Evers, 1991)

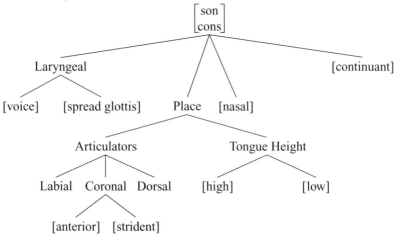

One fact that is clearly demonstrated in all the representations is the notion of dependency. Although details differ, most phonologists agree that there are dependency relations between some of the features or feature groups. For instance, in (8) [anterior] is dependent on Coronal, which means that this feature is only relevant for coronal consonants. This also suggests that if the [anterior] feature is represented, it necessarily follows that the place node Coronal should be present as well. We will discuss this in the subsection on underspecification.

A feature organisation of this sort suggests that assimilation can be seen as establishing an association between two nodes. We now return to assimilations and discuss the concept of extending features in a nonlinear representation.

Assimilation as spreading

In our earlier discussion of assimilations we have only discussed partial assimilations where features are distributed or passed on to neighbouring segments. We can now represent Turkish vowel harmony in terms of feature associations or feature spreading. Since the suffix vowels invariably obtain the features from the stem, we can assume that these are not fully specified for all features. Assuming partial feature specification, the suffixes can be represented underlyingly as /In/ and /IEr/, where /I/ stands for a [high] vowel with no other features specified, and /E/ is specified only for height. The vowel features followed by the application of the vowel harmony rule is shown below, where only the relevant vowel features are indicated.[3] Vowel harmony, under these assumptions, fills unspecified slots by spreading the features of the preceding vowel. Although the feature Coronal is indicated for certain vowels, we assume that it is not marked in the underlying representation. This will be discussed more in the next subsection.

(9)   Turkish vowel harmony as spreading of features: Feature filling

Vowel features

	i	ɨ	u	ü	e	o	ö	a
Coronal	✓			✓	✓		✓	
Dorsal		✓	✓			✓		✓
Labial			✓	✓		✓	✓	
High	✓	✓	✓	✓				
Low					✓			✓

Underlying suffixes: /Vn/   /lVr/

```
                        TH        A              TH
                        |        / \             |
                      [hi]    Lab  Dor         [low]
```

Constraint: *V

```
                              TH        A
                            [low]      Lab
```

(a)   (i)   [kɨzɨn]

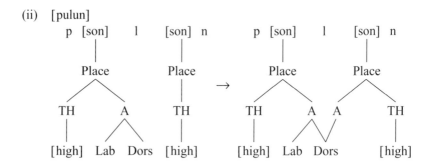

(ii)   [pulun]

(b) (i) [kɨzlarɨn]

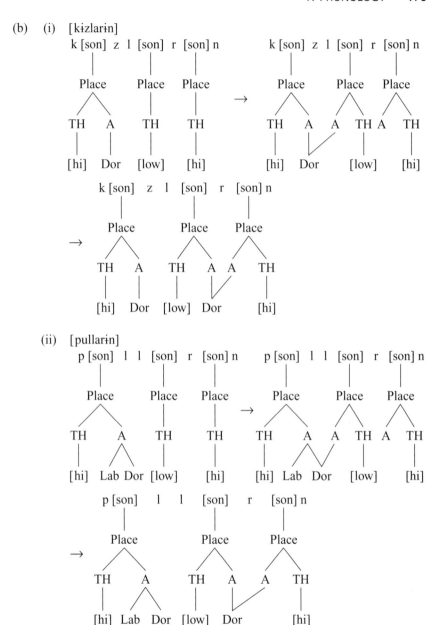

In (9a ii), the Articulator node including Labial and Dorsal spread to the following vowel which has only a Tongue Height feature. The genitive suffix therefore surfaces as [u] in [pulun]. Similarly for [kɨzɨn], the Articulator node spreads Dorsal to the suffix vowel which then also becomes [ɨ]. When the root vowel is

[a] which is also Dorsal, but [low], the suffix vowel again surfaces as [ɨ] because it is already specified for height and the height of the root vowel does not matter.

However, when the plural suffix intervenes, the results can be different. For [kɨzlarɨn], the vowel in the genitive suffix remains [ɨ] because the Articulator node first spreads Dorsal from the root vowel to the plural giving [a], which then spreads its Dorsal feature to the plural. However for [pularɨn], the suffix is also [ɨn] and not [un]. Here the root vowel has a brancing Articulator node: Dorsal and Labial. But only Dorsal spreads because the plural suffix is specified for [low] and no low vowel in Turkish can have the feature Labial. Hence, from the plural, when the Articulator node spreads to the genitive suffix, the features are different from (9a ii) because only Dorsal spreads and the genitive suffix surfaces as [ɨ]. Notice, that the assumption is that each feature node is on a separate tier, although in the figure it looks as if the Articulator node passes through the Tongue Height node.

Until now we have only considered partial assimilations. Total assimilations can lead to gemination (long consonants) with the concomitant loss of one of the segments. In Bengali, [r] is totally assimilated to a following coronal obstruent. This process applies within a phonological phrase, both within and across word boundaries.

(10)   Total assimilation leading to gemination in Bengali
    (a)   bɔrda   >   bɔdda   elder brother
          kor+to   >   kotto   to do + 3P PAST
          ram+er ʤonno >   rameʤʤonno Ram+GEN for

    (b)   Spreading with delinking

       [cons]   [cons]

         r   o

            [cor]

In (10b), we have represented the assimilation process as spreading of the feature [coronal] leftwards to the preceding segment along with the deletion of the [r] which is indicated by delinking. Thus, as soon as we view assimilation as a spreading process, we are inherently attributing a nonlinear character to the phonological representation. This means that instead of assuming a one-to-one unstructured relation between segments and features, one piece of information can be spread over more than a single position. Notice that total assimilation can also be viewed as a compensatory lengthening process which leads to the lengthening of a segment due to the loss of an adjacent consonant. We will discuss more examples of compensatory lengthening in the next subsection.

Dissimilation, assimilation, and the OCP

Unlike assimilation, which creates similar segments, dissimilatory constraints lead to an avoidance of successive similar elements. In native Yamato vocabulary of Japanese, a combination of voiced consonants in a root is prohibited, as is seen in (11a) (Itô & Mester, 1986; Mester & Itô, 1989). There is another productive process known as Lyman's Law, which voices the initial obstruent in the second member of a compound. However, dissimilation is actively enforced in compounds (11b) preventing the initial stop in the second member of the compound *kami+kaze* from becoming voiced.

(11) Dissimilation and Lyman's Law in Japanese
- (a) futa   "lid"
  - fuda   "sign"
  - buta   "pig"   *buda
- (b) iro   +   kami   iro+gami   "coloured paper"
  - kami   +   kaze   kami+kaze   "divine wind"   *kami+gaze

Perhaps the most well-known example of dissimilation comes from Ancient Greek and Sanskrit where two aspirates were not tolerated in adjacent syllables and the first consonant was deaspirated. This phenomenon is particularly noticeable in the reduplicated verbs.

(12) Dissimilation in Greek and Sanskrit

	Greek		Sanskrit	
(a)	dōsō	I shall give	adāt	he gave
	didōmi	I give	dadāmi	I give
(b)	t^{h}ēsō	I shall put	ad^{h}āt	he put
	tit^{h}ēmi	I put	dad^{h}āmi	I put

The initial consonant in the reduplicated prefix is retained from the verb stem in the examples in (12a). In (12b), when the stem initial consonant is an aspirate, the reduplicated consonant is deaspirated. In Modern Greek we find a similar dissimilation process where a sequence of two stops or two fricatives tend to become a fricative plus stop cluster. The following examples are taken from Spencer (1996, p. 59).

(13) Dissimilation in modern Greek
- fθinos   >   ftinos   cheap
- sxolio   >   skolio   school
- epta   >   efta   seven
- okto   >   oxto   eight

Dissimilations involve avoidance of adjacent similar segments. These segments are not necessarily contiguous, but the similar features that are dissimilated are arguably represented on the same tier. Assimilations, on the other hand, appear to make two contiguous segments similar. However, when we consider assimilation to be spreading, the result is a multiple linking of two segments to a feature or a set of features. This statement is reminiscent of a constraint which arose from tonal phonology called the obligatory contour principle or OCP (originally due to Leben, 1973). It was tonal phonology that inspired phonologists to assume that linguistic units like tones are not part and parcel of vocalic segments, but that they were represented on separate tiers or levels (Goldsmith, 1976; see also Yip, 1995; Odden, 1995, and references therein). Tones could therefore have a many-to-one linking (multiple linking) with tone bearing units like vowels. The nonlinear feature representations that we discussed earlier stem from priniciples developed within the confines of tonal phonology. The OCP states that adjacent identical tones are prohibited from the lexical representation of a morpheme. Thus, if adjacent identical tones occur, on the surface, they must have arisen from a multiply linked single tone representation. The consequences of multiple linking can be seen from the following example from Margi (Hoffman, 1963; the present set of data from Kenstowicz, 1994, pp. 321–322). (The two accent marks on the vowels (for example, á and à) are shorthand methods of indicating a high (H) tone and a low (L) tone respectively. The diacritic ǎ indicates a sequence of a low and a high tone.)

(14)   Margi tones

ʔímí	ʔímyárì	water
kú	kwárì	goat
šèré	šèrérì	court
tóró	tórórì	three pence
ɔ́ncàlá	ɔ́ncàlárì	calabash
tì	tyǎrì	morning
hù	hwǎrì	grave
cédè	céděrì	money
fà	fǎrì	farm
làgù	làgwárì	road
màlà	màlárì	woman

In the above examples, when the definite suffix [árì] is added to a stem creating a V+ á sequence, the V becomes a glide if it is a high vowel (cf., làgwárì), the [a] of the suffix is deleted when the stem vowel is mid (cf., céděrì), and if the stem vowel is an [a] it is unclear which deletes (cf., ɔ́ncàlárì). In addition there is a tonal alternation in some instances. The alternations are easily explained if we assume nonlinear representations. When the high vowels become glides before the suffix vowel, and when the suffix [a] deletes after mid-stem vowels, the tone is freed and can associate according to the general principles of the language. Typically, the stranded tone gets associated with the vowel that triggered the loss of the earlier tone bearing unit. We then get the following derivations.

(15)   Tonal association

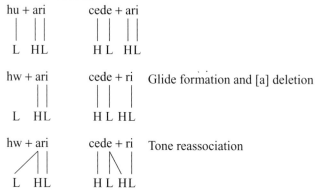

hu + ari   cede + ari

L   HL   H L   HL

hw + ari   cede + ri   Glide formation and [a] deletion

L   HL   H L HL

hw + ari   cede + ri   Tone reassociation

L   HL   H L HL

In the examples in (15), there are no identical sequences of tones. However, the derivation of [làgwári] from the stem [làgù] which has two identical tones, is unclear. There will be different consequences depending on whether there is a single low tone linked to two syllables or whether each syllable has a separate tone associated to it. The derivation of [làgwárì] supports the OCP constraint. In (16) we see the consequences of having two separate tones or a single tone multiply linked to the two stem vowels.

(16)   OCP and multiple linking

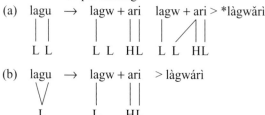

(a)   lagu   →   lagw + ari   lagw + ari > *làgwărì

L L   L L   HL   L L   HL

(b)   lagu   →   lagw + ari   > làgwárì

L   L   HL

If *làgù* is assigned two tones as in (16a), glide formation will lead to an unassociated tone which would then be associated with the suffix vowel leading to an incorrect contour tone. However, if the two vowels in *làgù* are multiply linked, glide formation simply delinks the tone from the vowel and there is no floating tone to be reassociated. Hence, *làgù* is best regarded as having a single tone and not two, obeying the OCP constraint.

There have been attempts to argue that OCP is present as a strong universal constraint on all lexical representations. McCarthy (1986) argues that a number of languages block deletion rules just so as to block tautomorphemic identical consonants from occurring together. However, granting that OCP is a marked configuration, it is not the case that languages automatically choose the same way to avoid a sequence of identical consonants. Some languages may choose epenthesis (as we will see in the next subsection) and others may prefer multiple linking. We want to draw attention to the fact that assimilation and dissimilation need not be seen as two competing processes. Rather assimilation is also one way of preventing similar sequences of adjacent consonants; since assimilation is spreading, it leads to multiple linking thereby preventing a X_iX_i configuration. Dissimilation, on the other hand, directly prevents such a sequence by deleting or changing a feature to make the adjacent segments less similar or not identical. Thus, again we see the connection between the OCP, and dissimilation and assimilation principles.

Phonological and phonetic underspecification

Within generative phonology, the question of contrastive segments and features has played a central role. If a feature is not contrastive, then it is usually assumed not to play a role in underlying representations. For instance, aspiration ([spread glottis]) is not lexically contrastive in English, although both [p^h] and [p] exist on the surface ([p^h]it vs. s[p]it). At the phonological level only voicing is distinctive ([b]in vs. [p]in). The difference can be exploited by stating that the voiceless stops are not specified for aspiration at the underlying lexical level. A context-sensitive rule assigns [spread glottis] at the beginning of stressed syllables (cf., pp. 202–203 on ambisyllabicity). Redundancy rules assigning context free features, like [sonorant] sounds being assigned [voiced], are common.

Later research, particularly feature geometry, made some of these rules unnecessary. If place of articulation features are monovalent or unary ([coronal], [labial], etc.), then a [p] does not have to be assigned [–labial] by default. There have been many proposals concerning the underspecification of features in lexical representations. The two opposing views, referred to as *radical underspecification* (Archangeli, 1988; Kiparsky, 1982) and *contrastive underspecification* (cf., Steriade, 1995 for a discussion of these issues) relate to whether minimal contrasts are represented in the lexical representation or not. According to the former, a feature value is not represented at all, even if it contrasts two segments, Universal Grammar assigning the default value to all segments. For instance, in Dutch, [k] and [g] do not contrast in underlying representation, but [p] vs. [b] and [t] vs. [d] do. Radical underspecification would claim that the underlying contrast for all segments are seen as [+voice] vs. [0 voice], [–voice] being assigned to all consonants by default. Contrastive underspecification would only assign [0 voice] to the velars, but the others would be assigned [+voice] or [–voice] in the lexical representation. The reasoning and arguments in support of one version over the other have depended largely on assimilation rules and blocking of such rules. If a feature is unspecified for a consonant, then assimilation can spread a feature across such a consonant without violating general principles of autosegmental phonology (see Kenstowicz, 1994, for a review).

In Kiparsky (1993) we find a more elaborate account of underspecification where he argues that the fact that certain rules are blocked in underived contexts in the lexical phonology (i.e., to the underlying morpheme without any affixation, or before any other rules having applied) is due to a proper account of underspecification. Blocking in underived contexts was an important consequence of the strict cyclicity effects in the earliest Lexical Phonology model. Rules like trisyllabic shortening were prevented from applying to underived monomorphemic words like *nightingale* because they were underived. Kiparsky (1993) argues that it is not cyclicity that blocks rules applying in underived contexts. Rather, the explanation lies in certain premises of underspecification which include that underlying representations are free of redundancy, and most important, underspecification may be context-sensitive. This aspect of context-sensitive underspecification had not been fully exploited earlier.

The central idea is that wherever possible phonological rules are structure building (rather than structure changing) which operate by changing [0F] to [±F]. Under this hypothesis, phonological alternations can also be accounted for by feature filling rules, where such rules can also fill in redundant information, but only in particular contexts. To understand this phenomenon, we will look at the following Finnish example:

(17) Context sensitive underspecification
       /vete/   >   [vesi]   "water"
       /vete + nä/   >   [vetenä]   "water" ESSIVE
       /äiti/   >   [äiti]   "mother"

The alternation of [vesi] (</vete/) vs. [äiti] seems to indicate that there is a contradiction in the appearance of a sibilant before a final [i]. The underlying /t/ in /vete/ becomes a sibilant (i.e., continuant) after the final vowel is raised to [i]. In contrast, an underlying word with a [t] plus [i] sequence remains unchanged. The facts can be accounted for by context dependent underspecification as given below. The underlying stems are /veTE/ and /äiti/, where the consonants and vowels in capitals indicate underspecification for the feature under discussion.

The feature [+high] is redundant in final position for front vowels, and [+continuant] is redundant for the opposition of /t/ vs. /s/ before [i]. Moreover, [−continuant] is the default for the obstruent /T/ because it occurs outside the context [i]. The derivations will be as follows:

(18)   Derivations

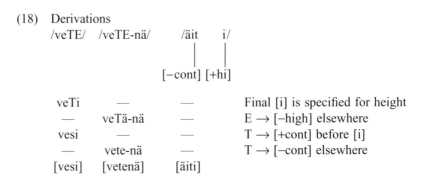

/veTE/	/veTE-nä/	/äit i/	
veTi	—	—	Final [i] is specified for height
—	veTä-nä	—	E → [−high] elsewhere
vesi	—	—	T → [+cont] before [i]
—	vete-nä	—	T → [−cont] elsewhere
[vesi]	[vetenä]	[äiti]	

The underlying /t/ in /veTE/ is unspecified for [continuant]. After the final vowel is assigned [+high], the /T/ is assigned [+continuant] before [i] and [−continuant] elsewhere. In contrast, the specification of /t/ in underlying /äiti/ is unpredictable, and therefore must be specified as [−continuant]. The default rule, making the [t] a sibilant before [i] therefore, will not apply. Underspecification successfully accounts for the presence of a sibilant in *vesi*, and presence of a coronal stop in *äiti*.

The place of articulation which has received the most attention in view of underspecification is [coronal]. There have been several reasons for assuming that coronals are special. Typologically, more contrasts exist within coronal consonants than in others. Within the coronal articulator (tip and blade of the tongue), several places of articulation can contrast phonemically (palatoalveolar, palatal, retroflex) within a single language. With respect to phonotactic restrictions, coronal consonants appear to be more lax in that they allow more combinations than other places of articulation. In addition, coronals appear to be the default place of articulation in many languages, and finally, coronals are more likely to assimilate to other places of articulation than the other way around. To account for this range of phenomena, phonologists have often assumed that coronals are underspecified for place (cf., Paradis & Prunet, 1991, for several papers on the special status of coronals). Such an assumption can fit in with the general assumptions of lexical phonology as well. For instance, in the case homorganic nasal place assimilation, either the nasal may match in place to a contiguous segment or it will remain coronal. In English, the prefix *iN*-assimilates to following labial nasals and stops (*immobile, impossible*), but not to labial fricatives (*infamous*). Since this is a lexical phonological rule, assimilation to labial fricatives would create segments like [ɱ], which would violate structure preservation. The default specification of the nasal appears instead, as it does before vowels.

Ghini (1999) has also argued strongly in favour of underspecification. Based on the dialect of Miogliola, Ghini shows that a complex pattern of vowel alternation which support not only the underspecification of vowel features, but also that two superficially similar dental nasals are underlyingly different—one specified for coronal, which surfaces always [n], and the other unspecified which surfaces as [ŋ] and [n] under prosodically defined conditions. The underspecification analysis has further support from language change. Latin single voiceless obstruents and fricatives became voiced fricatives in Miogliola ([p, b, f] > [v]; Latin *lupus*, Miogliola [lūv] "wolf"), but geminate obstruents simply degeminated ([pp, bb, ff] > [p, b, f], Latin *cippus*, Miogliola [tsæp] "tree stump"). In sonorants, there was no possibility of voicing, and hence, after degemination, there was a general neutralisation: [mm, m] > [m] (Latin *summa*, Miogliola [suma] "sum"). However, given the assumption of underspecification, the coronal nasal had the possibility of a dual pattern of change. And this is what happened:

(19)   Change of coronal nasals from Latin to Miogliola (Ghini, in press)
        Latin: distinction by LENGTH (both nasals are unspecified for PLACE)

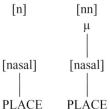

        Miogliola: distinction by PLACE, not LENGTH

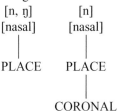

The original Latin single coronal nasal [n] remained unspecified for place, while the geminate [nn] degeminated, but became specified for place. As a result, the synchronic grammar of Miogliola shows surface neutralisations from two underlyingly different specifications. Latin *cinnus* became Miogliola [tsæn] SG., [tsænɪ] PLURAL "wink", but Latin *finus* became Miogliola [feŋ] SG. but [fena] PLURAL "fine".

Coronal underspecification has also been used to account for phonotactic constraints. Yip (1991) notes that many languages allow only homorganic clusters (clusters having only one specified place of articulation). Clusters with conflicting places of articulation invariably include a coronal consonant. If coronal is unspecified, these clusters are acceptable since they would not violate a constraint blocking different places of articulation. She observes that a similar constraint is also applicable for English monomorphemic roots which allow only the following clusters:

(20)   English root clusters
   (a)   Homorganic: nasal + stop   ba*n*quet, ga*n*der, tru*m*pet
   (b)   One member is a coronal liquid: no restrictions in place for the
           other consonant
                     liquid + stop, fricative gui*lt*, sha*rp*, su*lk*, coa*rs*e, su*lph*ur
                     stop, fricative + liquid su*ffr*age, a*tl*as, su*ppl*ant
   (c)   Restrictions on place

stop + stop	C_2 = t, d	a*bd*omen, ba*ct*eria, ru*pt*ure
stop + fricative	C_2 = s, z	a*x*is, syno*ps*is
stop + nasal	C_2 = n	sig*n*al
fricative + stop	C_1 = s, or C_2 = t, d	cla*sp*, a*ft*er
fricative + fricative	C_1 = s	a*sph*alt
nasal + fricative	C_1 = n	Wi*nds*or, pa*nth*er

If the constraint is that separate place nodes for adjacent consonants are not permitted, and if coronal is underspecified for place, all of these restrictions on root clusters follow. In (20a), all clusters share the same place. In (20b), one member is a liquid, and since liquids in English are coronal, the other consonant could have any place of articulation. For the last set, either C_1 or C_2 has to be a coronal consonant.

Other researchers, however, are not in favour of underspecification (other than redundant feature specifications). For instance, McCarthy and Taub (1992) argue that Coronal cannot be underspecified in underlying representations since it is required to be specified for phonotactic constraints which apply to an early stage of English phonology other than those that Yip mentions. The problem lies in the features which are dependent under the Coronal place node. If phonotactic constraints have to refer to [±anterior] (the difference between [ʃ] and [s]) which is dependent under Coronal, then the place node has to be specified. However, as Rice (1996) points out, if distinctions have to be drawn between consonants like [ʃ] and [s], these differences may be due to other features, leaving them free to remain unspecified for Coronal.

Rice (1996) has a particularly interesting proposal concerning place assimilation. She argues that there is enough evidence that Coronal is indeed phonologically absent. She addresses the issue that distributionally, languages appear to sometimes prefer coronals, and sometimes velars as the default place of articulation. This has raised doubts concerning the efficacy of Coronal being underspecified. However, the solution to this is that Coronal remains the unmarked consonantal place of articulation, and obtains specified coronal feature value in the phonetics. Rice shows that velars, on the other hand, obtain an apparent default specification, not due to default phonological marking, but due to a surface phonetic interpretation mechanism which assigns a velar place of articulation to a consonant lacking a phonological place or articulation. This fits into the hypothesis that segments can remain phonologically unspecified when they enter the phonetic level, as we will see in the next subsection.

Phonetic underspecification.   Keating (1988) proposed a provocative theory of underspecification in phonetics where she argued that "default" features need not necessarily surface at the end of the phonology. That is, at the point where phonology and phonetics interface, not all features may not be available for phonetic interpolation. Segments can remain underspecified such that phonetic interpolation will have three different types of articulatory transitions.

(21)   Possibilities of phonetic interpolation

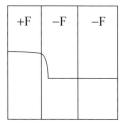
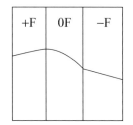

+F	−F	−F

+F	0F	−F		−F	0F	+F

All features specified
Rapid transition from
one state to another

Unspecified features
Cline: gradual transition

Building on this framework, Cohn (1990) differentiates between Sundanese and English nasal vowels, arguing that Sundanese has contrastive nasal vowels that are specified as [±nasal] in the phonological input to phonetics. Contrasting words like [ŋõbah] "change" and [ɲũliat] "stretch", Cohn shows that both nasal vowels show significant nasal airflow throughout. In [ŋõbah], the nasal vowel is followed by a [b], and there is a rapid transition from oral to nasal. Cohn claims that this supports the idea that [b] is specified as [−nasal]. In contrast, [l] is not specified as [0nasal] and there is a cline-like transition from the nasal vowel through the [l] to the following oral vowel. Unlike Sundanese, English vowels lack nasal specification, and presumably could exit the phonology with either [0nasal] or [−nasal] specification. Cohn's nasal airflow data suggests that vowels can remain unspecified throughout the phonology of English. The crucial results are as follows. Words like *den* and *Ned* both show cline-like transitions as compared to words like *men* or *none*, which show a plateau. In the two last words, where an oral vowel is flanked on both sides by nasals, the interpolation from one nasal consonant to another would walk straight through the vowel, but only if this vowel was unspecified for nasality. Had it been specified [−nasal], one would expect a rapid transition to orality and then another rise to the following nasal. In the words where a nasal consonant follows or precedes, the nasality gradually moves through the unspecified nasal vowel to the next oral target.

Thus, the phonetic underspecification studies seem to suggest that a three-way distinction of [+F], [−F], and [0F] specifications are possible at the point where the words enter the phonetics component from the phonology. Assuming monovalent features like [nasal] may require that the oral counterpart is contextually determined in the phonetics. The articulatory planning in language production will have to account for these different points of view. In any event, where [nasal] is concerned, both in the phonetics as well as in the phonology, it appears that the presence of nasality is more dominant than its absence.

Underspecification in language comprehension.   Some recent studies have incorporated the concept of underspecification in language comprehension (Gaskell & Marslen-Wilson, 1996; Gow, 1999; Lahiri, 1991; Lahiri & Marslen-Wilson, 1991; Lahiri & van Coillie, in press). Assuming that phonological lexical representations of words consist of underspecified featural representations (attached to segments as shown in the earlier discussion of feature geometry; see pp. 175–177), Lahiri and Marslen-Wilson argue the mapping process from the signal to the lexicon crucially depends on the absence and presence of features in the representations of words in the mental lexicon. The authors contrast vowel nasality in Bengali and English, where Bengali has underlying nasal vowels as well as contextual nasalisation ([kãdʰ] "shoulder" [kɑn] > [kãn] "ear"). Any nasality on a vowel in English comes from a neighbouring nasal consonant (see previous section). The authors argue that only underlying contrastive nasal vowels in Bengali are specified as [+nasal]; elsewhere, there is no nasality specified. Results show that indeed, the listener always interprets nasality on a vowel as being contrastively nasal even if the stimulus segment contained a vowel which was contextually nasalised. More strikingly, oral vowels in oral contexts, for both English and Bengali (English *bad*, Bengali [kʰɑd] "ditch"), are interpreted by listeners as having either a nasal or an oral context, depending on the distribution of the words in the language. That is, the vowel [a] in *bad* was equally likely to be interpreted as being part of *bad* or *ban*, showing that in both languages the oral vowels were represented as unspecified for nasality in spite of the fact that there may be surface phonetic nasalisation present in production of CVN words.

Thus, along with underspecification, a three-way matching process—perfect match, nonmismatch, and mismatch—is assumed which gives the asymmetry between coronals on the one hand and labials and dorsals on the other. If coronal is extracted from the signal, then it mismatches with labial (i.e., [n] mismatches with underlying /m/). It does not find a perfect match since /n/ is not specified for coronal, but it does not mismatch either—hence a nonmismatch situation occurs. If labial is retrieved from the signal, it matches perfectly with underlying /m/, but it also does not mismatch with /n/. This is not the best match, but it is a nonmismatch.

Lahiri and van Coillie (in press) provide further evidence for the underspecification of Coronal, and the efficacy of the three-way matching process.

They argue that medial coronal nasals in German which do not alternate in place of articualtion, are also underspecified. Using a lexical decision task with semantic priming, they show that a word like *Düne* "dune" primes its semantically associated word *Sand* "sand" just as well as nonwords made up with nonmismatching Labial or Dorsal nasals (as *Düme). In contrast, although *Himmel* "heaven" primes its semantic associate *Erde*, "earth", the nonword with a labial (*Hinnel) does not. The same holds for obstruents as well. The asymmetry again shows that when the feature Labial or Dorsal is extracted from the signal, it does not mismatch with the underlying unspecified Coronal, but an extracted Coronal does mismatch with Labial and Dorsal.

There have been later studies, involving coronal underspecification (Gaskell & Marslen-Wilson, 1996; Lahiri, 1997) and postlexical phonological assimilations (*lean bacon* > *lea[m] bacon*), in English and German. The most significant result is that when listeners hear part of a sentence like "*I would like some lea[m]/[n]*" (the right context is not available), both *lea[n]* and *lea[m]* equally prime a visually presented target LEAN. The "deviant" pronunciation of *lea[m]* leads to no inhibition. A difference in reaction times is observable if the context is viable or inappropriate. If the context is *gammon* rather than *bacon* (which would be expected after *lea[m]*), the subjects are slower in recognising the word LEAN. Gaskell and Marslen-Wilson explain the results by assuming both lexical featural underspecification (to account for the first set of results) as well as a process of inference which requires the listener to back-track after checking the context. Lahiri (1997), in contrast, argues that the results reflect not backtracking, but rather are a consequence of expecting a [labial] (extracted from the [m] in *lea[m]*), since this feature has not met with a complete match in the lexicon, and not finding it. The crucial point is that underspecification has to be appealed to, otherwise it is difficult to explain why both variants of *lean* are accepted when no context is provided. However, much more has to be done to understand the processing of postlexical assimilations and the consequences of the underspecified representations. In an attempt to model a system with an underspecified lexicon and a three-way matching process described previously, Lahiri and Reetz have developed an automatic speech recognition system that runs on these lines without using any statistical approaches (Lahiri, 1999; Reetz, 1998, 1999). The success of the system indicates that this approach is not entirely unreasonable. An overview of the processing models described above is given in Fitzpatrick-Cole and Wheeldon (1999).

Summary

In this section, we have sketched some of the central assumptions concerning the segmental and featural units of phonological representations, phonological processes, and constraints that operate on these units. Since lexical representations themselves, and the processes which operate on them, are crucial to a theory of language production accounting for access, planning, and encoding of online speech, the aim has been to address relevant issues that relate directly to the representations of words. The issue of underspecification and lack of redundancy in lexical representations has also been discussed. We should add a final caveat regarding the phonetics and phononology of underspecification. As we discussed earlier, phonological assimilation assumes spreading of features, regardless of whether it is a combination of delinking-cum-spreading, or spreading to node, unspecified for the relevant feature. What is crucial is that if it is phonological, there should be no effect of the original delinked feature available. If, on the other hand, the assimilation is partial, phonetic, and involves an overlapping of the gestures maintaining the original target as has been claimed for many of the English processes (*tenth* [tenθ], *lea[m] bacon*), the output of which is somewhere in between the two segments (cf., Browman & Goldstein, 1989; Nolan, 1992; Padgett, 1991, among others). Note however, that "partial" assimilation need not reflect "partial" perception. Problems concerning the extraction of the acoustic features from the speech stream and their mapping (for language comprehension) will be different for accounting for the phonetic planning in language production. If one assumes that the lexical representations that count for production and comprehension are the same, we have to deal with partial assimilations, underspecification, and mapping in very much the same way within a general framework of processing.

PROSODIC STRUCTURE AND PHONOLOGICAL PROCESSES

In general, shortening/lengthening and deletion/insertion processes are related to prosodic structure, i.e., syllables, feet, and the prosodic word (see Kenstowicz, 1994, for an overview). The prosodic hierarchy assumes that larger constituents are built on sequences of segments: syllables, then feet, and finally the prosodic (or phonological) word (see Nespor & Vogel, 1986; Wheeldon, this volume). We first discuss some of the properties of these constituents, particularly with respect to various phonological processes.

Syllable structure and related processes

The syllable has traditionally been assumed to consist of an onset followed by a rhyme, which is divided into a nucleus and a coda. The nucleus is the obligatory part of the syllable, while the onset and coda are optional. The most frequent syllable inventory in natural language consists of the following: V, CV, VC, CVC. The more complex syllable inventories arise from including more segmental material in the onset and the coda. Complex onsets and codas are generally governed by the *sonority scale*, which states that onset consonants increase in sonority and codas decrease in their sonority. The accepted sonority scale in terms of rising sonority is obstruents, nasals, liquids, glides, and finally vowels (cf., Blevins, 1995, for an overview).

The notions "closed" and "open" syllables play an important role in phonology. Closed syllables are those which are closed by a coda consonant, whereas open syllables end in a vowel (long or short) or a diphthong. To decide whether medial consonants are part of onsets or codas, the principle of maximisation of the onset is often evoked. That is, when there is more than one intervocalic consonant, whether all of them are part of the onset of the second syllable depends on whether the language permits "maximising the onset" based on sonority principles. Phonological processes can help determine whether consonants fall in the coda or not. We illustrate this with an example from German, which has a process of syllable final devoicing, familiar in many languages, including Turkish, Russian, Polish, Dutch, to mention just a few. The data are from Vennemann (1972). German has a rule of syncopation which allows for the following types of alternations:

(22) Syncope and syllable final devoicing in German
Standard German

	flirt	sail	go by bicycle
Infinitive	li:bəl+n	ze:gəl+n	ra:dəl+n
1SG. IND. PRES.	li:bl+ə	ze:gl+ə	ra:dl+ə

Standard German, Northern pronunciation

	li:bl+ə	ze:gl+ə	ra:tl+ə

After syncopation, the consonant clusters that are created are not equally accepted as onsets in the Standard German as compared to the Northern pronunciation. In Standard German, the sequence [dl] is accepted as an onset, and the maximisation of onset prevents the [d] being in the coda. Hence, coda devoicing does not apply. In contrast, the Northern pronunciation that allows [bl] and [gl] clusters, allows maximisation of consonants in these cases, but prevents [dl] from being part of an onset. As a result, coda devoicing applies and the surface form is [ra:t.lə] rather than [ra:.dlə].

Maximisation of the onset is closely related to the notion of a core syllable, or a CV syllable. There is a general tendency to avoid onsetless syllables such that in most languages, a VCV string is syllabified as [V.CV]. Resyllabification to prevent onsetless syllables is central to the analysis of German devoicing as well (cf., Giegerich, 1992; Rubach, 1990). The following alternations are relevant.

(23) Resyllabification in German

	believe		day		
2SG. IMP.	glaub	[p]	Tag	[k]	SG.
INF.	glaub-en	[b]	Tag-e	[g]	PL.
{-ly}	glaub-lich	[p]	täg-lich	[k]	{-ly}

As we have seen before, coda devoicing makes the word final consonants in the first column voiceless. A suffix vowel is added to the words in the second column. Here the medial sequence VCV is syllabified as [V.CV] forcing the medial consonant to be an onset, thereby blocking coda devoicing. Oddly enough, when the suffix begins with a sonorant consonant, and although the obstruent+liquid is a possible onset (as we saw in the previous example), resyllabification is blocked and coda devoicing applies. Obviously, resyllabification is sensitive to certain morphemes even if allowable onsets may arise. However, the crucial point is that when a vowel suffix follows, resyllabification is obligatory since German always requires a syllable with onset. Words or syllables without a surface consonant are always preceded by a glottal stop: cf., *Atmen* [ʔatmən] "breadth", *abteilen* "to separate" [ʔap-tailən], *mitarbeit* "to cooperate" [mɪt-ʔarbait], etc.

Once we accept the fact that languages have preferred syllable structures, any deviation from these preferences are repaired. Strategies for repairing them can differ. For instance, if affixation leads to unacceptable syllables, either epenthesis or syncope are invoked to maintain the preferred structures. In a language like Koryak (Spencer, 1996, pp. 63–64), the most complex syllable structure permitted is CVC. Hence, any affixation which leads to complex structures is resolved by schwa epenthesis.

(24)   Koryak schwa epenthesis
       Verb root /pŋlo/   ask
       Prefixes: *t-* 1SG. SUBJ., *mt-* 1PL. SUBJ., *na-* 3PL. SUBJ.
       (a)   t-pŋlo-n   təp.ŋo.lon   I asked him
       (b)   mt-pŋlo-n   mət.pəŋ.lon   we asked him
       (c)   na-pŋlo-n   nap.ŋo.lon   they asked him

If the segments are syllabified from left to right obeying the preferred CVC syllabic template, then the introduction of the schwa is entirely predictable. If we did not assume that epenthesis was syllable based, it would not be possible to account for the difference between the schwa insertions in the verb root in (24a) and (24b): *pŋəlo* vs. *pəŋl*.

Epenthesis is a one of the most frequent ways to resolve unwanted clusters and to obtain a preferred syllable template. Related languages often exhibit a difference in the acceptance of initial and final clusters. A striking example comes from certain final liquid+obstruent clusters in Germanic languages. English and German allow [l+obstruent] clusters in words like *milk* or *Milch*, but Dutch disallows such clusters and introduces a schwa as in *melek*.

Along with epenthesis, deletions are equally common in cluster simplification. In Bengali, the present progressive ending begins with a geminate affricate *-ʧʧʰ*, which is degeminated when added to a verb root ending in a consonant.

(25)   Bengali degemination as cluster simplification
  (a) ʃu-lɑm ʃu-ʧ ʧ ʰi   sleep 1P. PAST/1PRES. PROG.
  (b) boʃ-lɑm boʃ-ʧ ʰi *boʃ ʧ ʧ ʰi sit 1P. PAST/1PRES. PROG.

Bengali does not allow coda clusters. Since a geminate consonant belongs to the coda of one syllable and the onset of the following syllable, if the preceding syllable ends in a consonant, the geminate introduces a coda cluster and is degeminated to fit the syllable template of the language.

 Thus, both deletions and insertions are frequently found in languages, usually to obtain a preferred or an improved syllable. We have been focusing on the lexical level, but in postlexical phonology, and particularly in running speech, optional (partial) deletions and insertions do not always occur to rectify a syllable, but also to simplify difficult clusters (see also earlier, pp. 171–173). The final orthographic *d* of English *and*, and German *und* are frequently deleted in particular contexts: *and stuff* > *an' stuff*;[4] *acht und zwanzig* "eight-and-twenty" > *acht-en zwanzig*. Instances of reduction and augmentation also occur on the phrasal level, like phrase final lengthening. However, such processes are not connected to syllable weight and this is what we turn to in the next subsection.

Syllable quantity and weight

The moraic theory of representation views moras as phonological positions which intersect between prosody and segments (rooted in the feature tree). There appears to be general agreement that moras dominating vocalic segments project syllables. Further, long and short vowels, and long and short consonants are said to be differentiated by their moraic representation. Following Hayes (1989), we have the following representations:

(26)   Moraic representations

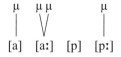

A single consonant is not assigned a mora in the lexical representation. It may or may not be assigned a mora depending on whether it is in the coda and whether the language treats closed syllables as heavy. If the coda is counted as heavy, then weight-by-position assigns a mora to the coda consonant. Geminates, on the other hand, are part of the onset of a syllable, but must close the preceding syllable as well, automatically adding weight to this syllable. Hypothetical syllabifications are given below; short vowels have one mora, long vowels have two moras, a single consonant has no moras, and a geminate consonant comes with one mora.

(27)   Syllable structure assignment

[ata]	[apta]	[atta]	[aːta]

μ μ   μ μ   μ μ μ   μ μ μ

a t a   a p t a   a t a   a t a

σ σ   σ σ   σ σ   σ σ

μ μ   μ μ   μ μ μ   μ μ μ

a t a   a p t a   a t a   a t a

σ σ   σ σ   σ σ   σ σ

μ μ   μ μ μ   μ μ μ   μ μ μ

a t a   a p t a   a t a   a t a

Just as languages often try to preserve preferred syllable structures, we often find processes that attempt to maintain the weight of a syllable. Bimoraic syllables are generally considered to be heavy, irrespective of whether they are closed syllables (the coda consonant adding weight to the syllable), or whether they have a long vowel. However, not all languages necessarily consider closed syllables to be heavy (cf., Lahiri & Koreman, 1989). Languages tend not to prefer trimoraic syllables although they do exist. We shall see more evidence of syllable weight when we consider stress.

Compensatory lengthening. Similar to deletions and insertions, shortening and lengthening processes are closely related to the syllable. As we mentioned earlier, a frequent process of lengthening is compensatory lengthening, where the loss of a segment is compensated by lengthening an adjacent segment. We have given one example of total assimilation in Bengali (see (10)) which can also be seen as an example of compensatory lengthening. Other common instances of compensatory lengthening involve the loss of a coda consonant which leads to the lengthening of the preceding vowel. If we compare the words for *five* in German, English, Dutch, and reconstructed Proto-Germanic, we find the following pattern.

(28)   Compensatory lengthening in Germanic

German	Dutch	English	Proto-Germanic
fünf	vijf	five	*fimfi
[ü]	[εɪ]	[ɑɪ]	[im]

The Proto-Germanic word had an initial short vowel followed by a nasal consonant. The nasal has been retained in German and the vowel is still short. The loss
of the nasal in Dutch and English, however, has led to a long vowel—an instance
of compensatory lengthening which we can represent in a nonlinear fashion. V
and N represent abstract vowels and nasals. Since long vowels are bimoraic,
delinking after the loss of the nasal and reassociation as in the case of tones,
gives us the desired result.

(29)   Compensatory lengthening as spreading

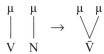

It is worth noting that when the loss of the consonant in such circumstances is closely
linked with the vowel lengthening, it is invariably confined to a particular syllable
position, and a similar loss elsewhere in the phonology of a language will not show
any concomitant lengthening. Consider the following examples in Latin (Hayes, 1989):

(30)   Compensatory lengthening in Latin
    (a)   *kasnus   →   kaːnus   grey
        *kosmis   →   koːmis   courteous
        *fideslia   →   fideːlia   pot
    (b)   *smereoː   →   mereoː   deserve—1 SG. PRES.
        *snurus   →   nurus   daughter-in-law
        *sluːbrikus →   luːbrikus   slippery

    (c)   CL as spreading onto a free mora

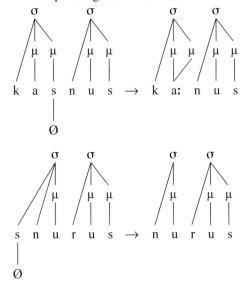

In (30a), the loss of the sibilant leads to the lengthening of the preceding vowel in the same syllable, as shown in (30c). The deletion of the sibilant frees a mora to which the vowel [a] then spreads leading to a long vowel. When the sibilant is lost in word initial position (30b), no mora is free since the onset does not have any mora and no lengthening occurs and the relevant words simply begin with a single onset (30c). Thus, compensatory lengthening can be viewed as maintaining the weight of a syllable.

Syllable weight, foot structure, and stress. Syllable weight often plays a crucial role in stress assignment. As we mentioned above, the weight of a syllable usually depends on whether it has a long bimoraic vowel or whether the coda of a closed syllable contributes a mora to the syllable. Vowel quality alone (front, back, or height) is never taken into account where syllable weight is concerned.

In general, syllables are considered to be grouped into metrical feet consisting of strong and weak syllables. The feet differ in terms of whether the head of the foot, i.e., the stressed position, occurs at the left or right edge. A left-headed foot is known as a trochee, and a right-headed foot is an iamb. Hayes (1995) argues that there are three basic foot types used in linguistic systems: a syllablic trochee, a moraic trochee, and an iamb. The syllabic trochee groups any two syllables together regardless of their weight. A moraic trochee and an iamb are weight sensitive. These three foot types are given below; the foot is demarcated between parentheses and the strong and weak branches are indicated by a [x] and a dot [.] respectively.

(31) Trochees and Iambs

    (a) Syllabic trochee (weight insensitive)

        (x   .)
        σ   σ

    (b) Moraic trochee: left headed (constructed over two light syllables or one heavy syllable; light syllable = σ, heavy syllable = σ̄)

        (x   .)   (x)
        σ   σ   σ̄
        | | /\
        μ   μ   μ μ

    (c) Iamb: right headed (constructed over a light plus a heavy syllable, two light syllables, or one heavy syllable)

        (x   .)   (.   x)   (x)
        σ   σ   σ   σ̄   σ
        | | | /\   /\
        μ   μ   μ   μ μ   μ μ

(d) Parsing the same sequence (left-to-right) into iambs and moraic trochees

```
MORAIC
TROCHEE   (x)          (x)  (x   .)   (x)
          μμ   μ       μμ   μ    μ    μμ
          σ̄    σ       σ̄    σ    σ    σ̄

IAMB      (x) (.       x)  (.   x)   (x)
          μμ   μ       μμ   μ    μ    μμ
          σ̄    σ       σ̄    σ    σ    σ̄
```

(e) Parsing the same sequence (right-to-left) into iambs and moraic trochees

```
MORAIC
TROCHEE         (x) (x   .)  (x   .)
          μ    μμ   μ    μ    μ    μ
          σ    σ̄    σ    σ    σ    σ

IAMB      (.    x) (.    x) (.    x)
          μ    μμ   μ    μ    μ    μ
          σ    σ̄    σ    σ    σ    σ
```

Note that on the basis of a single sequence of two light syllables, or only a single heavy syllable, it is not possible to distinguish between an iamb and a trochee. In (31d, e) we have two examples of parsing the same string of syllables into moraic trochees and iambs. In (31d), the parsing is from left-to-right and the second syllable is skipped by the moraic trochee since it could not be incorporated into the preceding of following foot. Both parsings give four feet, the difference being that the head of the third foot from the left is on different syllables. In (31e), the heads of the final and penultimate feet for the two parsings are on different syllables.

Although the moraic trochee and the iamb are both weight sensitive (i.e., the weak branch cannot be heavier than the strong branch), under Hayes' analysis these two feet are asymmetric. An iamb may have a [L(ight) H(eavy)] sequence, but a trochee is not permitted to have a branching head. However, this is not universally accepted. Others, such as Dresher and Lahiri (1991), Jacobs (1989), and Kager (1989), have claimed that asymmetric trochees incorporating heavy-plus-light syllable sequences are necessary as well. We are not in a position here to compare these various proposals. Rather we will provide brief examples of each type of foot to illustrate the effects of syllable weight.

In addition to the three basic foot templates, it is necessary to invoke the notion of extrametricality to understand some of the following stress patterns. Syllables or segments (usually consonants) at right edges are often extrametrical; that is, they behave as if they do not exist for footing and, therefore, not for stress. Further, feet may be constructed from right or left, and the foot on the rightmost or leftmost edge of the word obtains main stress (End Rule Right or

End Rule Left). Thus, there are four parameters to be taken into account: foot type, extrametricality, direction of foot parsing and the end rule. The following examples are from Hayes (1995).

(32) Examples of foot types
      Moraic trochee (with extrametricality: Cairene Arabic)[5] (Hayes, 1995, pp. 67–68)

Weight:	Long vowels and closed syllables are heavy
Extrametricality:	Final consonant of a word[6]
Foot construction:	Left to Right
Main stress:	End Rule Right

(x)	(x)	(x)	(x)	(x)	(x)
(x)	(x)	(x)	(x)	(x)(x .)	(x .)(x .)
μμ μ	μ μμ	μ μμ	μ μμμ	μ μμ μ μ	μ μ μ μ
béːta\<k\>	gatóː	katáb\<t\>	mudárri\<s\>	mudarrísi\<t\>	katabítu
your m.sg. house	cake	I wrote	teacher	teacher (f. construct)	she wrote it (m.)

Moraic trochee (Wargamay) (Hayes, 1995, p. 140)

Weight:	Long vowels are heavy
Foot construction:	Right to Left
Main stress:	End Rule Left

(x)	(x)	(x)	(x)
(x)	(x .) (x .)	(x .)	(x .) (x.)
μμ μ	μμ μ μ	μ μ μ	μ μ μ μμ
múːba	gíɟawùlu	gagára	ɟuɽágaymìri
stone fish	fresh water jew fish	dilly bag	Niagara-Vale-from

Iamb (Creek) (Hayes, 1995, pp. 64–65)

Weight:	Long vowels and closed syllables are heavy
Foot construction:	Left to Right
Main stress:	End Rule Right

(x)	(x)	(x)	(x)	(x)	(x)
(. x)	(. x)	(. x)(. x)	(. x)(. x)	(. x)	(x)(x)(x)
μ μ	μ μ μ	μ μ μ μ	μ μ μμ	μ μμ μ	μμμμ μμ
cokó	osána	apataká	anokicíta	kofócka	tiːniːtkíː
house	otter	pancake	to love	mint	thunder

(x)	(x)
(x) (. x)	(. x)(. x)
μμ μ μ μ	μ μμ μ μ
taːshokíta	tokhołhokíta
to jump (dual subj.)	to run (dual subj.)

Syllabic trochee (Pintupi) (Hayes, 1995, pp. 62–63)
Foot construction: Left to Right
Main stress: End Rule Left

(x)	(x)	(x)	(x)
(x .) (x .)	(x .) (x .)	(x .)(x .)(x .)	(x .)(x .) (x .)
σ σ σ σ	σ σ σ σ σ	σ σ σ σ σ σ	σσσσ σ σ σ
máḷawàṇa	púḷiŋkàlatʲu	tʲámulìmpatʲùŋku	tʲíḷiriŋulàmpatʲu
through from	we (sat) on	our relation	the fire for our benefit
behind	the hill		flared up

We will end with a very brief discussion of English (cf., Kager, 1989, for an exhaustive review and analysis). English stress is weight sensitive. Although pairs like *cóntrast–contrást* suggest that stress in English is not predictable, this is not the case. For instance, just as no native speaker of English would accept a nonsense word like *bnick* as a possible word of their language because the initial segmental sequence is not a word initial cluster, there are strong intuitions about what is a possible stress pattern. Bengali words like *Aditi*, *Darjeeling*, or *porishkar*, treated as nonsense words, would never be stressed initially in English. Any stress other than *Adíti*, *Darjéeling*, or *poríshkar*, would be perceived as foreign.

In general, final light syllables (syllables with lax vowels) in underived nouns are extrametrical. After syllable extrametricality, a moraic trochee placed on the right edge gives the desired stress pattern. We thus get words like *cíne<ma>*, *utén<sil>*, and *thrombó<sis>*. In the first word, there are two light syllables preceding the final extrametrical syllable, and a moraic trochee constructed on it gives the desired result. The last two words have a heavy penultimate syllable, and hence stress falls on that syllable. Verbs and underived adjectives behave differently with respect to extrametricality, because in these cases only a final consonant is extrametrical. Hence, final syllables with a long vowel, or a vowel followed by two consonants, attract stress. Examples include words like *astóni<sh>*, *compé<te>*, and *succínc<t>*. However, derived adjectives again allow syllable extrametricality: *signífi<cant>*, and not **significán<t>*.

These are, however, only the basic patterns. Cyclic stress assignment (as we saw in the case of *condensation* and *compensation* in the discussion of lexical phonology), as well as processes like "stress retraction", complicate matters. For instance, words like *húrricàne*, *ántelòpe*, *gúillotìne*, etc. have main stress apparently on the "wrong syllable". If the normal stress rules were observed, stress would be on the final syllable. One analysis is to assume that stress falls predictably on the last foot. Then the main stressed is "retracted" to the preceding foot: (hur) (ri) (cane) > [(hur)$_F$ (ri) (cáne)$_F$] > [(húr)$_F$ (ri) (càne)$_F$]. Note that the syllable which first bore main stress still retains secondary stress. There are many other complicating factors involved regarding English stress and the reader may consult Kager (1989) for a review. We want to emphasise once again, however, that stress in English is governed by a set of stress assignment rules and is not assigned randomly. Moreover, these rules are sensitive to syllable weight.

Ambisyllabicity.   We end this subsection with a brief discussion of syllable-based processes that are not necessarily related to weight effects. Earlier (pp. 192–195), we discussed processes such as German final devoicing and Koryak epenthesis in the context of well-formed syllable structures. Now, resyllabification frequently occurs in postlexical phonology, and since both allophonic and neutralising postlexical processes can be sensitive to syllable structure, words in isolation and words within a phrase can differ substantially in their pronunciation (see pp. 171–173 for discussion on postlexical assimilations). Here we focus on ambisyllabicity in conjunction with the processes of flapping and aspiration, which are much discussed phenomena in English (see Gussenhoven, 1986; Kahn, 1976).

Ambisyllabic consonants arise when a syllable attracts the first consonantal onset of a following unstressed syllable to form a coda unless this creates an impossible coda cluster. This consonant then becomes ambisyllabic, since it belongs to the coda of the first syllable and onset of the following syllable. This rule, which is foot internal, is known as Right Capture and its formulation is shown in (33a). A further process which also creates ambisyllabic consonants is Liaison which can apply across words (33b). By this process, any word-initial onsetless syllable acquires an onset from the preceding syllable.[7]

(33)   Ambisyllabicity
    (a)   Right Capture

    (b)   Liaison

Ambisyllabicity accounts for a number of postlexical phonological rules of American English like flapping, aspiration, glottalisation, etc. Flapping modifies coronal stops [t, d] to a flap [ɾ], when they are ambisyllabic. This accounts for why the coronal stops in *later*, *shouting*, *matter*, are subject to flapping, while those in *latex*, *bait*, *tail*, are not. In the latter set of words, the stops are either followed by a stressed syllable (cf., *látèx*), are only in the coda (cf., *bait*), or only in the onset (cf., *tail*), and hence none of them are ambisyllabic. Similarly, aspiration is also subject to ambisyllabicity. Aspiration of voiceless stops in American English occurs when in absolute syllable onset position, and ambisyllabic consonants cannot be aspirated (cf., Gussenhoven, 1986, who points out that in British English absolute onset position is not required for aspiration). Thus, words like *happy*, where the medial consonant is ambisyllabic, may be aspirated in British English, but never in American English. However, British English also requires ambisyllabicity as a structural possibility, since processes like weakening (which "weaken the oral closure of obstruents" in fast informal speech, Gussenhoven, 1986, pp. 125–126) can operate on the output of aspirated consonants. However, weakening only operates on ambisyllabic aspirated consonants, and those that are in absolute onset position are exempt.

Ambisyllabicity due to Liaison is not restricted to within words. In fact, flapping occurs easily across words, and indeed, is perhaps only bounded by utterances (cf., Nespor & Vogel, 1986). Thus, we have alternations in phrases like *set in* [sɛɾɪn] and *saw Tim* [sɒtʰɪm]. In the latter phrase, the proper noun has an onset, thereby blocking ambisyllabicity and hence blocking flapping. Instead, syllable initial aspiration occurs, leading to a voiceless aspirated [tʰ]. In the phrase *set in*, the [t] can be ambisyllabic and hence, it may be flapped.

One last point about resyllabification, clitics, and the prosodic word: Resyllabification across words in the postlexical phonology occurs most frequently between a content word and a clitic, which in many languages are a reduced form of a function word. The English example above, *set in* [sɛɾɪn], is a case in point. In Dutch, for example, *heb ik* (have I), would frequently become one prosodic word and be pronounced [hɛbək], without regular syllable final devoicing of the [b] in *heb* as in German (see earlier, pp. 192–195). This could also be an instance of ambisyllabicity, blocking devoicing in the coda. The formation of a single prosodic word is of great importance for a processing model since it may affect the unit of planning and encoding (see Wheeldon & Lahiri, 1997; Wheeldon, this volume). The point here is that phonological processes sensitive to the edges of syllable structure, onset and coda, are affected by resyllabification, ambisyllabicity, and prosodic word formation—all of which need to be incorporated within a language production model.

Prosodic word constraints: Minimal word

Until now, we have been looking at shortening and lengthening processes that strive to maintain preferred syllable structures. Another frequent lengthening process applies when words are smaller than the preferred size. Most languages have a minimal word requirement, usually phrased in terms of a prosodic constituent; for example, a word must have a long vowel or two. Lengthening can occur when a word has not met this requirement. In Bengali, for instance, a vowel in a monosyllabic word is always lengthened unless the vowel nucleus has a diphthong.

(34)   Vowel lengthening in Bengali
    (a)   ʧaː+∅   want+2P. FAMILIAR IMPERATIVE/tea
    (b)   ʧa+i   want+1P. PRESENT
    (c)   ʧaː=i   tea=ONLY
    (d)   naːk   nose
    (e)   nak+i   nose+ADJECTIVAL SUFFIX/nasal
    (f)   naːk=i   nose=ONLY

The morpheme /ʧa/ can be both a verb root "to want" or the noun "tea". The plus sign indicates a suffix, whereas the equals sign marks a clitic. The different suffixation and cliticised forms show the vowel length alternation. It should be noted that Bengali does not have contrastive vowel length. At first glance the lengthening of the vowel in (34f) seems to be a counterexample to structure preservation and to the claim that lengthening occurs in response to the minimal word requirement. In fact, (34e) shows that a derived word which is disyllabic does not lengthen a vowel as compared to the monosyllabic word in (34b). However, the final vowel in (34f) is not a suffix but a clitic, just as in (34c). Clitics are added to a word and hence, the minimal word requirement must be met before the clitic is added. We see a difference in (34b) and (34c) where the former is a suffixed word and the resulting diphthong satisfies the minimal word requirement. In (34c), however, the final vowel is a clitic and again, the initial vowel is lengthened.

These facts are not unusual. Many languages, including Germanic languages such as English, Dutch, and German, also have minimal word requirements. No content word of these languages can end with a single lax vowel: *[sɪ] or *[bɛ] would be completely impossible words in these languages. They should either have a long vowel as in sea/see [siː], or should be closed as in sit [sɪt]. The research of McCarthy and Prince (1990) demonstrates that the minimal word plays an important role in the prosodic morphology of languages. In their discussion of this phenomenon in Arabic, they give examples of a small number of nouns (usually related to body parts and kinship terms) which disobey the bimoraic, minimal word requirement (final consonants are extra-metrical and hence do not count for weight): [ʔab] "father", [ʔax] "brother", etc. However, when these nouns serve as the basis of regular word formation processes, they acquire an extra consonant, thus fulfilling the minimality require-ment: [ʔab] "father", but [ʔabaw-iy] "paternal"; cf., [maṣr] "Egypt", [maṣr-iy] "Egyptian".

Minimal word requirements are also often reflected in blocking the applica-tion of rules that may shorten a word beyond the minimum. For instance, Lardil has a disyllabic word minimum. Apocope applies freely to trisyllabic or longer stems, but it is blocked in disyllables since it would shorten a word beyond the acceptable minimal word requirement (Kenstowicz, 1994, p. 641). In the follow-ing examples we see that the final stem vowel is always deleted in the uninflected form, except in the last two words which are disyllabic.

(35) Lardil apocope

UNINFLECTED	INFLECTED	GLOSS
yalul	yalulu-n	flame
mayar	mayara-n	rainbow
karikar	karikari-n	butter-fish
mela	mela-n	sea
wiṭe	wiṭe-n	interior

Minimality constraints can also add a mora or a syllable when the base has less than the weight required to satisfy the minimum word requirements. Such a process is also evident in Lardil (Kenstowicz, 1994, p. 641).

(36) Addition of a mora in Lardil

UNINFLECTED	INFLECTED	GLOSS
kentapal	kentapal-in	dugong
yaraman	yaraman-in	horse
yaka	yak-in	fish
ṭera	ṭer-in	thigh

In the last two examples, the base forms are not disyllabic since the suffixation shows that they are consonant final stems (cf., the examples above). However, to meet the minimal word requirement, a final vowel is added to the base stem or the uninflected form to ensure that it surfaces as disyllabic.

Constraint-based approaches

Until now we have been assuming a derivational theory of phonology, where an underlying form can be transformed into its associated output. Implicitly, both representations and rules governing the transformation have been assumed to be constrained by both general and specific principles. To end this section, we will briefly touch on constraint-based approaches to phonology that have been of primary concern in recent years in phonological theory. The most influential model, Optimality Theory (OT), is explicated in various recent research articles (cf., McCarthy & Prince, 1993; Prince & Smolensky, 1993, etc.; for the most recent overview on OT see Kager, 1999). However, since the constraint-based theories have not explicitly addressed processing implications, we will only attempt to sketch the basic ideas.

In OT, the explanatory burden is shifted from processes to output candidates. The central claim is that universal grammar is made up of a set of constraints, all of which are available to a given language. The grammar generates a potentially infinite set of output candidates for each input, which are then evaluated based on the constraint system of the language. The candidate that best fits the constraint system is the victor. Languages differ in the way the constraints are ordered. One of the most interesting consequences is that it is possible for candidates to tie, either when all candidates fail the highest ranked constraint, or when more than one candidate equally satisfies the set of constraints. In a rule-based system, this conception is not easy to articulate. Since the model is explicated most clearly with respect to the prosodic aspects of phonology (alignment theory), we will illustrate how the system works by referring to the example of ambisyllabicity, which we discussed on pp. 202–203. There are three constraints, ranked accordingly, which are relevant for this discussion (based on McCarthy & Prince, 1993):

(37) Alignment constraints for English ambisyllabicity:
      ONSET>>ALIGN-LEFT>>FINAL-C
      ONSET: Align (σ, Left, Consonant, Left)
      ALIGN-LEFT: Align (Stem, Left, PrWd, Left)
      FINAL-C: A Prosodic Word (PrWd) ends in a consonant

The constraints should be read as follows. The constraint ONSET says that the left edge of a syllable should be aligned to a consonant. ALIGN-LEFT suggests that the left edge of a morphological stem should coincide with the left edge of a prosodic word. The final constraint, FINAL-C, states that a prosodic word must end in a consonant. The ordering given in (37) accounts for the ambisyllabicity and flapping facts of American English. Recall that ambisyllabicity depended on whether the following syllable was stressed or not. McCarthy and Prince compare the examples *sought Ed* [sɔrɛd] and *saw Ted* [sɔtʰɛd], where in the former phrase, the coronal stop is in word final position and can be ambisyllabic, whereas in the latter, the [t] can only be an onset. The interaction of the constraints are given in (38) and (39).[8]

(38) Optimal parse of *sought Ed*

Candidates	ONSET	ALIGN-LEFT	FINAL-C
(a) PrWd PrWd ... σ σ sought Ed	*!		
(b) ☞ PrWd PrWd ... σ σ sough t Ed		*	
(c) PrWd PrWd ... σ σ sough t Ed		*	*!

(39) Optimal parse of *saw Ted*

Candidates	ONSET	ALIGN-LEFT	FINAL-C
☞ (a) PrWd PrWd σ σ s a w T e d			*
(b) PrWd PrWd σ σ s a w **T** e d		*!	
(c) PrWd PrWd σ σ s a w **T** e d	*!	*	

The crucial difference lies between the alignment of the onset of the prosodic word and the onset of the syllable. Since ONSET is ranked higher than ALIGN-LEFT, when the second word has no onset (as in *Ed*), the language prefers to make the final consonant ambisyllabic, rather than leave a word onsetless, although the crisp edge matching between the stem and the word is thereby lost.

In more recent research within OT, more explicit correspondence between input and output, and between different output candidates have been proposed (McCarthy & Prince, 1993; see Kager, 1999 for an overview). There have been also extension of OT within the Lexical Phonology framework (Kiparsky, in press), arguing for independent levels of constraint ranking.

It is important to remember, that the constraints of a given language are there to evaluate output candidates. The constraints are independent and indeed, indifferent, to how these output candidates are generated. Within a processing model of language production, this basic tenet can play a crucial role, particularly after lexical access —in the planning and encoding stages. Although several open questions remain, since the theory makes explicit claims, the results are also empirically testable.

Summary

In this section, we have covered a wide range of facts involving prosodic structures, particularly syllables and feet. We have briefly discussed various phonological processes sensitive to prosodic structure, including shortening and lengthening processes, stress, segmental alternations, repair strategies for preferred syllables, etc. The aim was to demonstrate that phonological rules and phonetic processes do not only operate in local segmental contexts, but that hierarchical structures, such as syllables, feet, and minimal words, also constrain representations and processes.

"ACTION-AT-A-DISTANCE"

In this last section, we will address two important phonological phenomena that are relevant for the incremental planning as assumed by Levelt (1989) and Bock and Levelt (1994). Both are tonal phenomena, one concerning languages that contrast tones and the other concerns the mapping of tonal intonational tunes to utterances. The first is relevant only for tonal languages, but the intonational facts are valid for all languages.

The question here is how does a theory of phonological encoding deal with this type of lookahead. The lookahead proposed in Levelt (1989) is fairly local. The Prosody Generator is allowed to work on one word at a time. The facts discussed in the next section need to be seen in the light of a theory of incremental planning.

Long-distance tonal effects

In a seminal paper on Digo tonology, Kisseberth (1984) provides a detailed analysis of several complex tonal phenomena and their significance, both for morphological forms as well as syntactic phrases. We are interested here in tonal displacement effects across words, that is within phrases, and space limitations force us to limit ourselves to a cursory description of several interacting phenomena. The tonal symbols are the same as used for the earlier discussion on Margi on pp. 182–184. (´ = high tone (H), ` = low tone (L), ^ = falling tone (HL), and ˇ = rising tone (LH)). The four main tonal rules that are relevant for our purposes are as follows:

(40)   Morphological tonal rules in Digo
    (a)   High Displacement
    (b)   Leftwards High Spread
    (c)   Neutralisation
    (d)   Displacement-to-Stem

We will discuss these rules in turn. Kisseberth argues that certain morphemes (specific verb roots, tense, or subject prefixes among others) come with a high tone in the underlying form. The other morphemes are essentially toneless and acquire their surface tones from the spreading of tones from nearby constituents. Further, each utterance in Digo comes with two unassociated boundary low tones—an inital low tone and a final low tone. The following example shows the differences between verbs with underlying high tones and toneless verbs due to High Displacement and Leftwards High Spread.

(41) Verbs with underlying high tones and toneless verbs
  (a) ku-vugur-a   "to untie"   ku-vugurir-a   "to untie for/with"
       ku-tsukur-a   "to carry"   ku-tsukurir-a   "to carry for/with"
  (b) ku-fwinĭk-â   "to cover"   ku-fwinikĭr-â   "to cover for/with"
       ku-ezĕk-â   "to thatch"   ku-ezekĕr-â   "to thatch for/with"

The low tones are not marked here with any diacritic. The examples in (41a)
show that the addition of a derivational suffix like *-ir-/-er-* "for/with" does not
necessarily change the overall tonal pattern of the word. Clearly none of the
morphemes bear a high tone. However, in (41b) it is obvious that there is a
difference between the unsuffixed and the suffixed forms. There is a tonal displacement in the suffixed forms and the contour tones (falling–rising and rising–
falling) must come from an underlying high tone. High Displacement displaces
an underlying high tone to the final vowel of the word. Leftwards High Spread,
which follows High Displacement, links a high tone to a preceding vowel.
Kisseberth's analysis of how High Displacement and Leftwards High Spread
works is summarised below.

(42) High Displacement and Leftward High Spreading

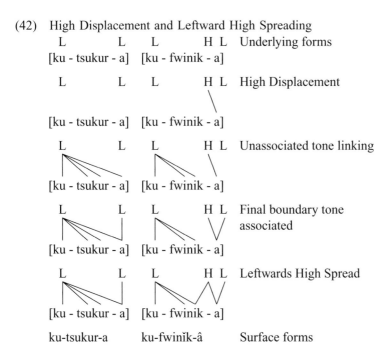

In the examples where the entire word has low tones (cf., *ku-tsukur-a*), it is not
possible to say in which direction the spreading occurs. The two boundary low
tones at each edge could have spread in either direction. Following Kisseberth,

we have spread the inital low rightwards and linked the final low to the last vowel since all tones must be linked. Universal well-formedness principles ensure that all the vowels will have the same tone. However, in the other examples (cf., *ku-fwinĭk-â*) the verb has an underlying high tone and there is a fixed sequence in which tonal association occurs. First, High Tone Displacement displaces the high tone from the verb to the final vowel which is the suffix [a]. Second, since all unassociated tones must link to a vowel, the initial boundary low tone spreads to the first three vowels. Third, after this the final low boundary tone is associated to the final vowel which is already linked to a high tone. Thus, a rising–falling contour tone results on the final vowel. Finally, by the rule of Leftwards High Spread, the high tone spreads to the preceding vowel, which then gives another contour tone on the penultimate vowel, this time a falling–rising tone.

That the high tone must be part of the verb root and not the suffix *-ir-/-er* is evident in the way the low-toned verb maintains level tone after suffixation, but High Tone Displacement forces a contour tone on the suffixed form of the verb root which has an underlying high tone: cf., [ku-tsukurir-a] and [ku-fwinikĭr-â]. The high tone of the verb is displaced to the final vowel and after Leftwards Spread of the high tone, the penultimate vowel, i.e., the vowel of the suffix [ir], gets the falling–rising tone.

The High Tone Displacement rule, which is a specific rule of Digo, associates an underlying high tone that comes with a morpheme, to a designated vowel. That it associates with the final vowel and not the penultimate vowel, as may be argued from the above example, comes from phrasal phonology. But before we come to phrasal phonology, we must discuss briefly the rule of Neutralisation which is restricted to a monosyllabic stem and is ordered after High Tone Displacement, which Kisseberth argues is restricted so that it may not apply to monosyllabic stems. The relevant comparisons are as follows.

(43)   Monsosyllabic stems, High Tone Displacement, and Neutralisation
    (a)   ku-chit-a   "to pierce"   ku-chitir-a   "to pierce with"
    (b)   ku-som-a   "to read"   ku-somĕr-â   "to read to/for/with"

The example in (43a) is similar to the polysyllabic verbs above (cf., 41). The verb root has a low tone and the suffixed form shows no difference in the level tone pattern. But the example in (43b) is a problem. Where does the high tone in the suffixed form come from? Kisseberth argues that there is an underlying high tone in these monosyllabic verb roots which are neutralised. Verbs like [chit] for example, may show up with a contour tone if a prefix with an underlying high tone precedes as in [ku-a-chĭt-â]. High Tone Displacement only occurs when it is not attached to the penultimate syllable of a word. The relevant derivations are as follows.

(44)   Derivations for [ku-som-a], [ku-somĕr-â], and [ku-a-chĭt-â]

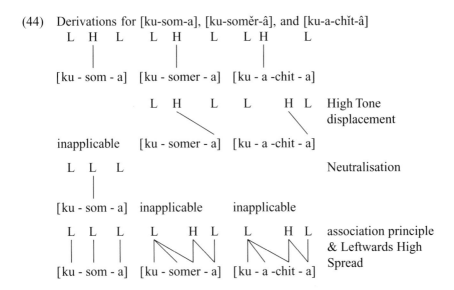

Having established the basic rules, we turn to phrasal phonology. Here we compare a sequence of a verb plus noun, where High Tone Displacement and Neutralisation interact. Recall that High Tone Displacement displaces a nonpenultimate high tone to the final vowel of a word. The rule of neutralisation lowers an H that is associated to a penultimate vowel in a word. We shall see that it is not really the word, but the phrase which is involved. There are two central claims in Digo phrasal phonology. First, High Tone Displacement works on the phrase level as well as on the word level. It applies cyclically, first on the word level and then extends its domain to the phrase. Second, in contrast, Neutralisation applies only on the phrase level. To see how this works, we must first consider the tonology of certain nouns to establish their underlying tonal associations.

(45)   Noun tonology (simple form and with the locative suffix)
   (a)   Nouns with low tones
          mu-hama   mu-hama-ni   "millet"
          goma   goma-ni   "drum"
   (b)   Nouns with high tones associated to the penult (subject to
          Neutralisation)
          vi-yogwe   vi-yogwĕ-nî   "sweet potatoes"
          ny-ungu   ny-ungŭ-nî   "pot(s)"
   (c)   Nouns with high tones not subject to neutralisation[9]
          ma-pĕmbâ   "maize"[10]
          chi-dăfû   "young coconut"

In both (45a) and (45b), the simple noun shows only a low tone throughout. In (45b), however, the underlying high tone which cannot be displaced by High Tone Displacement is removed by neutralisation. Now let us consider verb plus noun phrases with different patterns of underlying tones.

(46)   Tonal alternations in Verb plus Noun phrases
    (a)   Low-toned verbs plus low-toned nouns
        ku-sag-a mu-hama   "to grind millet"
        ni-na-pig-a goma   "I am beating a drum"
    (b)   Low-toned verb plus high-toned noun subject to neutralisation
        ku-takas-a ny-ungu   "to clean a pot"
        ni-na-jit-a bi-yoagwe   "I am cooking sweet potatoes"
    (c)   Low-toned verb plus high-toned noun subject to High Tone
        Displacement
        ku-sag-a ma-pěmbâ   "to grind maize"
        ni-na-tsor-a chi-dăfû   "I am picking a young coconut"

The data in (46) shows that after a verb which contains no high tone in its underlying structure, a noun is pronounced exactly as if it is pronounced isolation. That is, the noun is not affected by a preceding low-toned verb. The pattern is more complex when we compare verbs with underlying high tones. In the next set of examples, we find verbs with a high tone which are subject to neutralisation when spoken in isolation. These are followed by low-toned nouns. The verbs and nouns are given in their isolation forms followed by the verb plus noun phrase.

(47)   High-toned verbs (subject to Neutralisation) plus low-toned nouns
    ku-heg-a   n-guruwe ku-heg-a n-gurǔwê   "to trap a pig"
    ni-na-vug-a   w-ari   ni-na-vug-a w-ărî   "I am cooking rice"
    ku-ih-amu-ganga   ku-ih-a mu-gǎngâ   "to call a doctor"

In the isolated pronunciations, there are no tones in the noun or the verb. But as soon as the verb plus noun appears in a phrase, the high tone of the verb can displace to the final vowel of the noun. Kisseberth argues that the Neutralisation follows High Tone Displacement, for otherwise there would be no high tone to displace to the final vowel of the noun. Further, Neutralisation must be a phrase level rule since it fails to neutralise the penult high tone in the verbs when a noun follows. The following derivations illustrate the interaction, where word boundaries are marked with ω and phrase boundaries are indicated by φ.

(48)   Phrase-level interaction of High Tone Displacement and Neutralisation

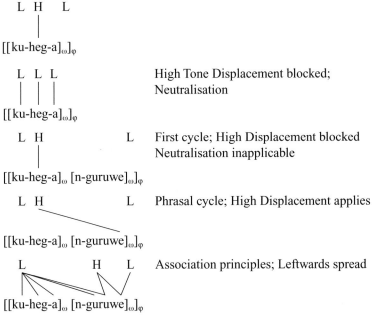

    L H   L

│

[[ku-heg-a]ₒ]φ

    L L L   High Tone Displacement blocked;
    │ │ │   Neutralisation

[[ku-heg-a]ₒ]φ

    L H   L   First cycle; High Displacement blocked
                                 Neutralisation inapplicable

│

[[ku-heg-a]ₒ [n-guruwe]ₒ]φ

    L H   L   Phrasal cycle; High Displacement applies

[[ku-heg-a]ₒ [n-guruwe]ₒ]φ

    L   H   L   Association principles; Leftwards spread

[[ku-heg-a]ₒ [n-guruwe]ₒ]φ

The point of this example is that Neutralisation is blocked in the inner cycle since it can apply only on the phrasal level; otherwise there would be no high tone left to be displaced to the noun. Hence, although the high tone of the verb is not displaced to the final vowel of the verb, it remains and gets displaced to the final vowel of the noun. To prevent neutralisation from applying, the knowledge must be available that the verb does not end the phrase but a noun follows it within the same phrase.[11]

A final example comes from a tonal pattern of phrases consisting of a verb with a single high tone followed by a noun that contains a H that does not neutralise. Other than the rules discussed above, another phrasal rule of Displacement-to-stem is required to account for these facts. This rule affects the first H before a stem (noun or verb) and displaces it to the first vowel of the stem that follows.[12] The following examples illustrate the tonal behaviour when both the noun and verb stems come with an underlying H tone.

(49)   Phrases consisting of verb plus noun, both with an underlying H
    (a)   a-na-sǔw-a   sahǎnî   a-na-suw-a-sáhánî
                                          "he is washing plates"
           ni-na-azǐm-â   chi-karǎngô   ni-na-azim-a chi-kárángô
                                          "I'm borrowing a frying-pan"

(b)   Derivation of [ni-na-azim-a chi-kárángô]

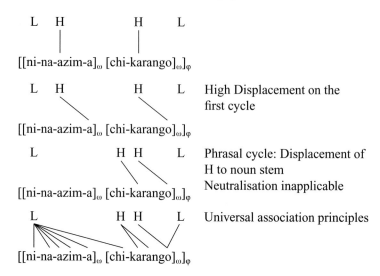

High Displacement on the
first cycle

Phrasal cycle: Displacement of
H to noun stem
Neutralisation inapplicable

Universal association principles

In sum, the phrasal tonal phenomena in Digo require knowledge of where the phrase ends to be able to correctly associate and spread the underlying tones which come with the morphemes and the boundary tones which mare the two edges of a phrase.

The prosody generator and phrasal tonology

We have to keep in mind the following points. First, recall that the two L boundary tones span a phrase and not individual words. The Prosody Generator, according to Levelt (1989) does not buffer large amounts of units to make decisions on upcoming words. It plans essentially word by word. The incremental assignment of prosodic structure in English requires no lookahead but it does require storing in memory the structure of previous stress assignments. The L boundary tones will not automatically be aligned to the boundaries of a word. It is only at the phrasal level that these tones will be assigned and associated after the underlying tones have undergone their various movements and associations. Second, the Prosody Generator has no problems incrementally adding a word at a time to construct a phrase. But the processing claim is that the prosodic pattern is assigned strictly left to right without checking later surface structure. It is unclear as to how this can be achieved for Digo tonal spreading.

Assume that each word comes with its underlying tone associated (or displaced) according to the cyclic rules. The Prosody Generator constructs a phrase, and must have enough lookahead to where the phrase ends, first to set the two L boundary tones and then to associate the H tone appropriately to the next noun, the last vowel of the phrase in [ku-heg-a n-gurǔwê], and the stem vowel of the noun in [ni-na-azim-a chi-kárángô] since there was already a final H on the final vowel of the phrase. In the instance where the noun has no underlying H, the H of the verb associates to the final vowel of the noun only if it is at the end of the domain that is being considered, which is a phrase. If [ku-heg-a] occurs in isolation, that is at the end of the phrase, Neutralisation deletes the underlying H tone. Thus, it seems that the Prosody Generator must (a) be minimally aware of where the phrase ends, and (b) be able to displace an already associated H from a verb to a following noun. There is some unclarity in what a lookahead involves. It appears from Levelt's discussion (p. 382) that in order to adjust the stress of *sìxtéen* to *síxtèen* in *síxtèen dóllars*, the Prosody Generator is allowed to preview the second word's metrical form. If the tonal pattern can be previewed as well, then in principle, the H tone from the verb could be spread to the noun according to its existing tonal structure.

Intonational phonology

The intonational structure of an utterance is closely tied to syntactic, semantic, and pragmatic factors, which dictate the choice of tune and affect tune-text alignment by determining which words are made prominent with phonological phrasing and/or stress. Following the theoretical framework for intonation of Hayes and Lahiri (1991), Pierrehumbert (1980), Pierrehumbert and Beckman (1986, 1988), Pierrehumbert and Hirschberg (1990), we assume the following hypotheses. Intonational contours can be analysed as tunes which are formal entities independent of the linguistic text. These tunes, which convey (often elusive) meanings, are decomposed and stored in an intonational lexicon. They are made of static tones (L(ow), H(igh)) specified for association to phonological phrasal structure (T^* to a stressed syllable; $T = T_p$ to an intermediate= phonological phrase boundary; $T\% = T_I$ to an intonational phrase boundary), following certain association principles. Based on research on Bengali (Fitzpatrick-Cole, 1994, 1996; Hayes & Lahiri, 1991; Lahiri & Fitzpatrick-Cole, 1999), we equate the intermediate phrase with the phonological phrase of the Prosodic Hierarchy (Hayes, 1989; Nespor & Vogel, 1986; Selkirk, 1986; Shattuck-Hufnagel & Turk, 1996, among others) since the phrasal domain for intonation is the same for segmental processes and reduplication.

In the discussion within a model of language production, it is important to see how intonational planning can be accounted for by incremental processes. Levelt (1989, pp. 401–403) discusses the assignment of a focus nuclear tone ("a step up or down to the nucleus", p. 401) and boundary tones. He argues that to set the nuclear tone the Prosody Generator requires no lookahead. However, the Prosody Generator has to know which nuclear stressed syllable is the last one in an intonational phrase to assign the nuclear tone. This can be done also without any lookahead, because according to Levelt, "the decision to break *creates* the intonational phrase boundary; it is in no way determined by it" (p. 402). Thus, the speaker can choose to assign pitch accented syllable, he can decide to nuclear tone and "then break at the next convenient break point". This works because Levelt assumes that boundary tones are all intonational boundary tones, and further, that they do appear to have more illocutionary and attitudinal roles rather than any grammatical function. In the next section, we discuss focus tunes and phrasing in Bengali, arguing that boundary tones can be assigned to the right edge of phonological phrases as well, and that they cannot be determined on the fly to be assigned at a convenient break option.

Bengali focused phrases and intonation.   We assume the general intonational terminology of dividing up the intonational phrase into a nucleus (the phrase containing main stress) and heads (all preceding phrases). Bengali nuclei tunes and the tune which associates with the head are given in (50) and (51). The subscripts $[_P]$ and $[_I]$ indicated whether the tones are linked to phonological phrases or intonational phrases.

(50)   Bengali intonational nuclei:
    (a)   Accents ("stems"):
          L*   neutral question accent
          H*   neutral declarative accent
          L* H_P focus accent
    (b)   Boundary tones ("suffixes"):
          L_I declarative
          L_I H_I continuation
          H_I offering
          H_I L_I yes/no

(51)   Bengali intonational head:[13]
    $L* H_P$

Before we discuss the alignment of text to tunes, we need to mention how phrasal prominence is assigned in Bengali. Word stress falls on the initial syllable. Under neutral focus, the first word of the last phonological phrase bears the maximal prominence. For narrow focus, the first word of the focused phrase bears the main prominence.

(52)   Phrasal prominence
    (a)   Neutral focus

```
                                      x
          x          x          x
     ((ω ω)ₚ    (ω ω ω)ₚ    (ω ω)ₚ)ᵢ
```

(b)   Narrow focus on the second P-phrase

```
                    x
      x       x           x
((ω ω)ₚ   (ω ω ω)ₚ   (ω ω)ₚ)ᵢ
```

The difference between neutral focus and narrow focus is illustrated in (53). Since pitch accents are always aligned to the strongest syllable of a P-phrase, the low pitch accent of the focus contour L* H$_P$ is aligned to the initial phonological word of the focused phrase. The high boundary tone attaches to the right edge of the P-phrase and not to any particular syllable.

(53)   (a)   Declarative, neutral focus

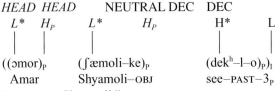

```
      HEAD HEAD       NEUTRAL DEC   DEC
       L*   H_P      L*      H_P      H*         L_I
       |    |        |       |        |          |

      ((ɔmor)_P      (ʃæmoli–ke)_P    (dekʰ–l–o)_P)_I
       Amar          Shyamoli–OBJ     see–PAST–3_P
      "Amar saw Shyamoli."
```

   (b)   Declarative, narrow focus

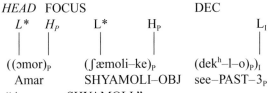

```
      HEAD   FOCUS                    DEC
       L*   H_P      L*      H_P                L_I
       |    |        |       |                  |

      ((ɔmor)_P      (ʃæmoli–ke)_P    (dekʰ–l–o)_P)_I
       Amar          SHYAMOLI–OBJ     see–PAST–3_P
      "Amar saw SHYAMOLI."
```

Intonational tunes can undergo phonological processes. In particular, Bengali obeys the Obligatory Contour Principle, which disallows a sequence of identical tones, hence there are no plateaus or hats, only single peaks. It applies in (53a) above (indicated by parentheses), and in (54) we see that the OCP can neutralise tunes on the surface. The H$_P$ of the focused phrase in (54b) is deleted because of the following H$_I$ of the yes/no question, neutralising it with the neutral focus version in (54a).

(54)   Deletion of H tone
   (a)   Yes/no question, neutral focus

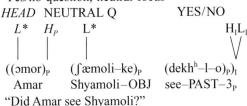

```
      HEAD   NEUTRAL Q               YES/NO
       L*   H_P    L*                H_I L_I
       |    |      |                  \ /

      ((ɔmor)_P   (ʃæmoli–ke)_P    (dekhʰ–l–o)_P)_I
       Amar        Shyamoli–OBJ     see–PAST–3_P
      "Did Amar see Shyamoli?"
```

(b) Yes/no question, narrow focus

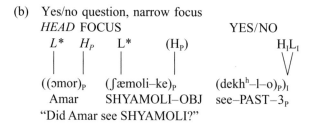

((ɔmor)ₚ   (ʃæmoli–ke)ₚ   (dekhʰ–l–o)ₚ)ᵢ
Amar   SHYAMOLI–OBJ   see–PAST–3ₚ
"Did Amar see SHYAMOLI?"

Although there is much variation in the formation of the P-phrase, particularly in left-branching structures, the most important points for us are the following. A P-phrase break is obligatory in two locations: immediately following a focused element (55a) and immediately preceding the verb, whether a simple verb or a complex predicate (55b).

(55) (a) FOCUS)ₚ
      (b) ₚ(V

To recapitulate, the focus tune is [L* Hₚ]. The L* is asigned to the first phonological word of the focused phrase, and the H boundary tone is aligned to the right edge of the string that is focused. The P-phrase break after the focused constituent is obligatory. Until now we have only seen a single word bearing the focused contour. However, an entire phrase can be focused as we see in the next example, where the same sequence of words are grouped together into different phonlogical phrases.

(56) Focusing phonological phrases

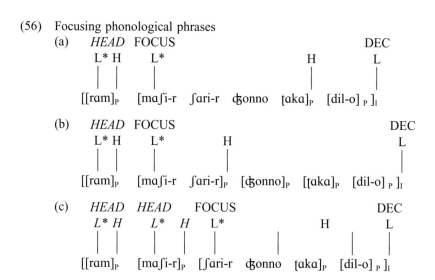

The sentence itself can have two readings: "Ram gave the money for aunt's saris" (57a, b) and "Ram gave aunt's money for the saris".

(57)   Dual reading
    (a)   money for aunt's saris   (b)   aunt's money for saris

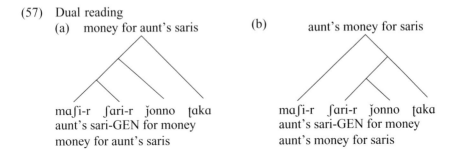

        maʃi-r ʃari-r jonno ʈaka   maʃi-r ʃari-r jonno ʈaka
        aunt's sari-GEN for money   aunt's sari-GEN for money
        money for aunt's saris   aunt's money for saris

Some of the focus possibilities overlap, but others do not. Note, that the focused sequence outlined by L* H$_P$, in (54 c), namely [ʃari-r ʤonno ʈaka] is unambiguous in its reading. It can only mean "aunt's money for saris", since in the other reading the sequence does not form a constituent and only constituents can be focused. Thus, with this intonation contour, the sentence is unambiguous.

    The above examples make two points. First, to obtain the correct reading the speaker must have an idea where to make the phrase break. The constituent [ʃari-r ʤonno ʈaka]$_P$ can only be focused if the speaker is talking about his/her aunt's money. Second, to get the correct constituent focused (not just a word), the speaker must know where the focused phrase ends to assign a high tone. Assigning the focus boundary high is not just a matter of looking for a convenient break point, as Levelt argued for intonational phrases. In fact, the question vs. declarative meaning must be part of the speaker's planning, otherwise a wrong boundary H will be added after the focused constituent. As shown above, and reiterated below, if a question follows, two H tones are not allowed and if an H is incorrectly added to the end of the focused constituent, the intonation contour would mean something else.

(58)   Focused phrase with a declarative and a question intonation.

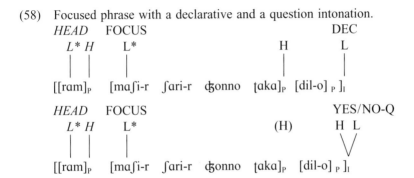

In the first example, the H_P tone marks the edge of the focused constituent. In the second example, although exactly the same constituent is focused, the H_1L_1 boundary tone of the question tune removes the H tone from the phrase.

Again, it appears that a certain amount of lookahead is necessary. The only global characteristics of intonation that are discussed by Levelt (1989) are declination, key, and register, and as he argues, effects such as declination do not necessarily suggest that the speaker needs to know the total length of the intonational phrase. However, for the examples given above, it seems that the speaker must be aware of the length of the focused constituent, as well as know the end of the intonational phrase to align the correct tones to the correct boundaries. Otherwise, the sentences would be entirely ambiguous.

A last point to be made here refers to segmental assimilations across words. In Bengali for instance, several phonological (optional) rules apply within a phonological phrase. For instance, the liquid [r] is totally assimilated to the following coronal consonant, but only within the phrase. Thus, if we take one of the above examples, the following segmental changes are observable.

(59)   Assimilations within a P-Phrase

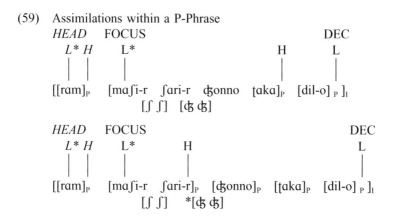

In the second example, the assimilation is blocked due to the phrase break. The assimilation processes that are discussed in the production literature appear to be restricted within the phonological word after cliticisation. But across word boundary assimilations are frequent even where the two words do not become a single phonological word (see pp. 171–173). The speaker, however, has to be aware of the phrase break, otherwise an ill-formed structure results.

Summary.   In this section on action-at-a-distance, our object was to draw attention to several factors concerning tonal spreading, or alignment of intonational tunes which involve phonological phrasing. The phenomena are rarely discussed in the literature concerned with the generation and planning of speech. The incremental model that has been advocated in several papers (Bock & Levelt, 1994;

Levelt, 1989, among others) has many advantages and it would be worthwhile to examine some of these complex phonological phenomena within this model.

CONCLUSION

We have demonstrated that the phonology of a language is not merely sequences of sounds or sequences of words without any internal structure and organisation. We have considered various types of morphophonological alternations, provided a typology of phonological processes, and discussed the relevance of distinct linguistic constituents. A model of language production is concerned with the representation, access, articulatory planning, and, finally, articulation of words and sentences. For such a model to account for crosslinguistic phonological generalisations, it must have a lucid account of phonological representations in the mental lexicon and must be able to account for phonological processes that apply within and across words. That is, to get to the articulation from representation, both phonological processes and phonological representations must play a central role in language production, for words in isolation as well as in sentences. Not everything is permissible within the phonology of a given language, and certainly there are universal preferences and constraints. In spite of the variability in the pronunciation across speakers, the child's competence in acquiring the phonological system, and the adult's ability to successfully communicate, suggests that the human processing system is able to cope with the confusion with apparent ease. To reconcile the phonologist's rendering of the grammar with a plausible processing model is perhaps a challenge, but, given the stability in the underlying system, surely not impossible.

ACKNOWLEDGEMENTS

This chapter has greatly benefited from comments from Jennifer Fitzpatrick-Cole, Frans Plank, Henning Reetz, and Linda Wheeldon. Special thanks go to Stefanie Shattuck-Hufnagel for her detailed comments on an earlier version of this chapter.

NOTES

1. We discuss prosodic structures in detail in a later section. Here it will suffice to note that a "foot" is a prosodic constituent built on syllables. Further, a constituent is extrametrical when it does not count towards building feet.
2. Postlexical processes are usually optional and the neutralisation may not always be phonetically complete. There is considerable phonetics literature on this topic. Readers may wish to consult the Laboratory Phonology series published by Cambridge University Press for various articles on this topic.
3. In the feature representation, A and TH are shorthand forms for the Articulator and Tongue Height nodes respectively. Since the nodes are assumed to be on separate tiers, the linear ordering of A and TH is irrelevant. In the last derivation of [pullarɨn], for instance, the order is switched only to make it easier to show the spreading.

4. This example comes from Stefanie Shattuck-Hufnagel.
5. We will consider here only the non-classical Arabic words.
6. Extrametrical elements are indicated within < >.
7. Kahn has a further rule of Left Capture which Gussenhoven argues to be not a rule of English.
8. The hand indicates the most successful candidate and * marks the violation of a constraint.
9. Kisseberth (1984, p. 161) argues that since High Tone Displacement can apply on these nouns, the underlying high tone cannot be associated to the penultimate vowel. He leaves the location of this high tone open, pointing out that the crucial bit is that these nouns have a high tone which displaces to the final vowel.
10. The locative forms are not given since Kisseberth points out that these are problematic and does not provide an analysis for them in this paper.
11. There are several other complicated examples which are not discussed here. The reader may refer to the original article.
12. There are restrictions based on voiced obstruents that we have left out of the discussion here.
13. In our examples we italicise the head in order to distinguish it for the reader from nuclear tones.

REFERENCES

Archangeli, D. (1988). *Underspecification in Yawelmani phonology and morphology*. New York: Garland Press.

Aronoff, M. (1976). *Word formation in generative grammar*. Cambridge, MA: MIT Press.

Beckman, M., & Pierrehumbert, J. (1986). Intonational structure in Japanese and English. *Phonology Yearbook, 3*, 255–309.

Blevins, J. (1995). The syllable in phonological theory. In J.A. Goldsmith (Ed.), *The handbook of phonological theory* (pp. 206–244). Cambridge, UK: Blackwell.

Bock, J.K., & Levelt, W.J.M. (1994). Language production: Grammatical encoding. In M.A. Gernsbacher (Ed.), *Handbook of psycholinguistics* (pp. 945–984). London: Academic Press.

Browman, C., & Goldstein, L. (1989). Articulatory gestures as phonological units. *Phonology, 6*, 201–251.

Carstairs, A. (1987). *Allomorphy in inflexion*. London: Croom Helm.

Carstairs-McCarthy, A. (1992). *Current morphology*. London: Routledge.

Cho, Y.Y. (1990). *Parameters of consonantal assimilation*. Unpublished PhD dissertation, Stanford University, CA.

Chomsky, N., & Halle, M. (1968). *The sound pattern of English*. New York: Harper & Row.

Clements, G.N. (1985). The geometry of phonological features. *Phonology Yearbook, 2*, 225–252.

Clements, G.N., & Hume, E. (1995). The internal structure of speech sounds. In J. Goldsmith (Ed.), *The handbook of phonological theory* (pp. 245–306). London: Blackwell.

Cohn, A. (1990). *Phonetic and phonological rules of nasalization* (Working papers in phonetics No. 76). Los Angeles: University of California.

Dresher, E., & Lahiri, A. (1991). The Germanic foot: Metrical coherence in Old English. *Linguistic Inquiry, 22*, 251–286.

Evers, V., Reetz, H., & Lahiri, A. (1998). Crosslinguistic acoustic categorization of sibilants independent of phonological status. *Journal of Phonetics, 26*, 345–370.

Fitzpatrick-Cole, J. (1994). *The prosodic domain hierarchy in reduplication*. Unpublished PhD dissertation, Stanford University, CA.

Fitzpatrick-Cole, J. (1996). Reduplication meets the phonological phrase in Bengali. *Linguistic Review*, *13*, 305–356.

Fitzpatrick-Cole, J., & Wheeldon, L.R. (1999). Phonology and phonetics in the psycholinguistic models of speech perception. In N. Burton-Roberts, P. Carr, & G. Doherty (Eds.), *Conceptual and empirical foundations of phonology*. Cambridge, UK: Cambridge University Press.

Gaskell, G., & Marslen-Wilson, W. (1996). Phonological variation and inference in lexical access. *Journal of experimental psychology: Human perception and performance*, *22*, 144–158.

Ghini, M. (1999). *Asymmetries in the phonology of Miogliola*. Unpublished PhD dissertation, University of Konstanz, Germany.

Ghini, M. (in press). Underspecification and feature assignment: Evidence from Miogliola. In T.A. Hall & U. Kleinhenz (Eds.), *Development in distinctive feature theory*. Berlin: Mouton.

Giegerich, H.J. (1992). Onset maximisation in German: The case against resyllabification rules. In P. Eisenberg, K.-H. Ramers, & H. Vater (Eds.), *Silbenphonologie des Deutschen* (Studien zur deutschen Grammatik No. 42). Tübingen, Germany: Gunter Narr Verlag.

Goldsmith, J. (1976). *Autosegmental phonology*. Unpublished dissertation, MIT.

Goldsmith, J. (Ed.). (1995). *The handbook of phonological theory*. London: Blackwell.

Gow, D. (1999). *Does phonological assimilation create lexical ambiguity?* Unpublished manuscript, Massachusetts General Hospital and Salem State College.

Gussenhoven, C. (1986). English plosive allophones and amibisyllabicity. *Gramma*, *10*(2), 119–141.

Gussenhoven, C., & van de Weijer, J. (1990). On V-place spreading vs. feature spreading in English historical phonology. *Linguistic Review*, *7*, 311–332.

Halle, M., & Clements, G.N. (1983). *Problem book in phonology*. Cambridge, MA: MIT Publishers.

Hayes, B. (1989). Compensatory lengthening in Moraic phonology. *Linguistic Inquiry*, *20*, 253–306.

Hayes, B. (1995). *Metrical stress theory: Principles and case studies*. Chicago/London: University of Chicago Press.

Hayes, B., & Lahiri, A. (1991). Bengali intonational phonology. *Natural Language and Linguistic Theory*, *9*, 47–96.

Hoffman, C. (1963). *A grammar of the Margi language*. London: Oxford University Press.

Itô, J., & Mester, R.A. (1986). The phonology of voicing in Japanese. *Linguistic Inquiry*, *17*, 49–73.

Jacobs, H. (1989). *Nonlinear studies in the historical phonology of French*. Unpublished PhD dissertation, University of Nijmegen, The Netherlands.

Jakobson, R., Fant, G., & Halle, M. (1952). *Preliminaries to speech analysis: The distinctive features and their correlates*. Cambridge, MA: MIT Press.

Kager, R. (1989). *A metrical theory of stress and destressing in English and Dutch*. Dordrecht, The Netherlands: Foris.

Kager, R. (1999). *Optimality theory*. Cambridge, UK: Cambridge University Press.

Kahn, D. (1976). *Syllable-based generalizations in English phonology*. Unpublished PhD dissertation, MIT, Cambridge, MA. (Distributed by Indiana University Linguistics Club.)

Keating, P. (1991). Coronal places of articulation. In C. Paradis & F. Prunet (Eds.), *The special status of coronals* (pp. 29–48). London: Academic Press.

Keating, P.A. (1988). Underspecification in phonetics. *Phonology*, *5*, 275–292.

Kenstowicz, M. (1994). *Phonology in generative grammar*. Cambridge, MA/Oxford, UK: Blackwell.

Kiparsky, P. (1982). From cyclic to lexical phonology. In H. van der Hulst (Ed.), *The structure of phonological representation*. Dordrecht, The Netherlands: Foris.

Kiparsky, P. (1985). Some consequences of lexical phonology. *Phonology Yearbook*, *2*, 83–138.

Kiparsky, P. (1993). Blocking in nonderived environments. In S. Hargus & E.M. Kaisse (Eds.), *Phonetics and phonology* (pp. 277–314). New York: Academic Press.

Kiparsky, P. (1996). Allomorphy or morphophonology? In R. Singh (Ed.), *Trubetzkoy's orphan: proceedings of the Montréal Roundtable "Morphonology: Contemporary responses"* (pp. 13–63). Amsterdam: Benjamins.

Kiparsky, P. (in press). Analogy as optimization: "Exceptions" to Sievers' Law in Gothic. In A. Lahiri (Ed.), *Analogy, levelling, markedness: Principles of change in phonology and morphology*. Berlin, Germany: Mouton de Gruyter.

Kisseberth, C. (1984). Digo tonology. In G.N. Clements & J. Goldsmith (Eds.), *Autosegmental studies in Bantu tone* (pp. 105–182). Dordrecht, The Netherlands: Foris.

Lahiri, A. (1991). Anteriority in sibilants. In *Proceedings of the 12th international congress of phonetic sciences* (Vol. 1, pp. 384–388). Aix-en-Provence, France: Comité d'Organisation du Congress.

Lahiri, A. (1997). *On resolving variation*. Unpublished manuscript, University of Konstanz, Germany.

Lahiri, A. (1999). Speech recognition with phonological features. In *Proceedings of the XIVth international congress of Phonetic Sciences (ICPhS 99), San Francisco* (Vol. 1, pp. 715–718). Berkeley, CA: Linguistics Department, University of California.

Lahiri, A. (Ed.). (in press). *Analogy, levelling, markedness: Principles of change in phonology and morphology*. Berlin, Germany: Mouton de Gruyter.

Lahiri, A., & Evers, V. (1991). Palatalization and coronality. In C. Paradis & F. Prunet (Eds.), *The special status of coronals* (pp. 79–100). London: Academic Press.

Lahiri, A., & Fikkert, P. (1999). Trisyllabic shortening. In English: Past and present. *English Language and Linguistics*, *3*(2), 229–267.

Lahiri, A., & Fitzpatrick-Cole, J. (1999). Emphatic clitics and focus intonation in Bengali. In R. Kager & W. Zonneveld (Eds.), *Phrasal phonology*. Dordrecht, The Netherlands: Foris.

Lahiri, A., & Koreman, J. (1989). *Proceedings of the 7th West Coast Conference on formal linguistics (WCCFL VII)*. Stanford, CA: The Center for the Study of Language and Information.

Lahiri, A., & Marslen-Wilson, W. (1991). The mental representation of lexical form: A phonological approach to the recognition lexicon. *Cognition*, *38*, 245–294.

Lahiri, A., & van Coillie, S. (1999). *Non-alternating underspecification in language comprehension*. Unpublished manuscript, University of Konstanz, Germany.

Leben, W. (1973). *Suprasegmental phonology*. Unpublished dissertation, MIT, Cambridge, MA.

Levelt, W.J.M. (1989). *Speaking: From intention to articulation*. Cambridge, MA: MIT Press.

Lombardi, L. (1991). *Laryngeal features and laryngeal neutralization*. Unpublished PhD dissertation, University of Massachusetts, Amherst.

McCarthy, J. (1986). OCP effects: Gemination and antigemination. *Linguistic Inquiry*, *17*, 207–263.

McCarthy, J., & Prince, A. (1990). Foot and word in prosodic morphology: The Arabic broken plural. *Natural Language and Linguistic Theory*, *8*, 209–284.

McCarthy, J., & Prince, A. (1993). Generalized alignment. In G. Booij & J. van Marle (Eds.), *Yearbook of morphology* (pp. 79–153). Dordrecht, The Netherlands: Kluwer.

McCarthy, J., & Taub, A. (1992). Review of Paradis and Prunet 1991. *Phonology*, *9*, 363–370.

Mester, R.A., & Itô, J. (1989). Feature predictability and underspecification: Palatal prosody in Japanese mimetics. *Language*, *65*, 258–293.

Myers, S. (1987). Vowel shortening in English. *Natural Language and Linguistic Theory*, *5*, 485–518.

Nespor, M., & Vogel, I. (1986). *Prosodic phonology*. Dordrecht, The Netherlands: Foris.

Nolan, F. (1992). The descriptive role of segments: Evidence from assimilation. In G.J. Docherty & D.R. Ladd (Eds.), *Papers in laboratory phonology: Vol. II. Gesture, segment, prosody* (pp. 261–289). New York: Cambridge University Press.

Odden, D. (1995). Tone: African languages. In J. Goldsmith (Ed.), *The handbook of phonological theory* (pp. 444–475). London: Blackwell.

Padgett, J. (1991). *Stricture in feature geometry*. Unpublished PhD dissertation, University of Massachusetts, Amherst.

Paradis, C., & Prunet, J.-F. (Eds.). (1991). *The special status of coronals: Vol. 2. Phonetics and phonology*. New York: Academic Press.

Pierrehumbert, J. (1980). *The phonetics and phonology of English intonation*. Unpublished dissertation, MIT, Cambridge, MA.

Pierrehumbert, J., & Beckman, M. (1988). *Japanese tone structure*. Cambridge, MA: MIT Press.

Pierrehumbert, J., & Hirschberg, J. (1990). The meaning of intonational contours in the interpretation of discourse. In P.R. Cohen, J. Morgan, & M.E. Pollack (Eds.), *Intentions and communication* (pp. 271–311). Cambridge, MA: MIT Press.

Prince, A., & Smolensky, P. (1993). *Optimality theory: Constraint interaction in generative grammar* (Tech. Rep.). Rutgers University, New Brunswick, NJ.

Reetz, H. (1998). *Automatic speech recognition with features*. Habilitationsschrift, University of Saarlandes, Germany.

Reetz, H. (1999). Converting speech signals to phonological features. In *Proceedings of the XIVth international congress of Phonetic Sciences (ICPhS 99), San Francisco* (Vol. 3, pp. 1733–1736). Berkeley, CA: Linguistics Department, University of California.

Rice, K. (1996). Default variability. *Natural Language and Linguistic Theory*, *14*(3), 493–543.

Rubach, J. (1990). Final devoicing and cyclic syllabification in German. *Linguistic Inquiry*, *21*, 79–94.

Sagey, E. (1990). *The representation of features and relations in nonlinear phonology*. New York: Garland Press.

Selkirk, E.O. (1986). On derived domains in sentence phonology. *Phonology Yearbook*, *3*, 371–405.

Shattuck-Hufnagel, S., & Turk, A.E. (1996). A prosody tutorial for investigators of auditory sentence processing. *Journal of Psycholinguistic Research*, *25*(2), 193–247.

Spencer, A. (1991). *Morphological theory*. Oxford, UK: Blackwell.

Spencer, A. (1996). *Phonology*. Oxford, UK: Blackwell.

Steriade, D. (1995). Underspecification and markedness. In J. Goldsmith (Ed.), *The handbook of phonological theory* (pp. 114–174). London: Blackwell.

Trommelen, M., & Zonneveld, W. (1979). *Inleiding In De Generatieve Fonologie*. Muiderberg, The Netherlands: Coutinho.

van der Hulst, H. (1989). Atoms of segmental structure: Components, gestures and dependency. *Phonology*, *6*, 253–284.

Vennemann, T. (1972). On the theory of syllabic phonology. *Linguistische Berichte*, *18*, 1–18.

Wheeldon, L.R., & Lahiri, A. (1997). Prosodic units in speech production. *Journal of Memory and Language*, *37*, 356–381.

Yip, M. (1991). Coronals, consonant clusters, and the coda condition. In C. Paradis & J.-F. Prunet (Eds.), *The special status of coronals: Vol. 2. Phonetics and phonology* (pp. 61–78). New York: Academic Press.

Yip, M. (1995). Tone in east Asian languages. In J. Goldsmith (Ed.), *The handbook of phonological theory* (pp. 476–494). London: Blackwell.

CHAPTER EIGHT

Morphological systems and structure in language production

Rachelle Waksler
Linguistics Program, San Francisco State University, USA

INTRODUCTION

Though the role of morphology in a model of language production has recently become a topic of interest, most investigations in the production literature have been focused on linguistic levels of speech other than morphology *per se*. Production models have usually used as examples the simplest morphological form of a word, the root, or sometimes the root with a single suffix or prefix, (e.g., Butterworth, 1989; Dell & O'Seaghdha, 1992; Levelt, 1989, 1992; Roelofs, this volume). Words with multiple affixes, different morphological types of affixes, and most of the different affixation processes used in languages have yet to be systematically examined in the production domain. As a result, only a small subset of the types of words in languages' lexical inventories have actually been considered.

For example, some languages build words by stacking multiple suffixes and/or prefixes onto roots and stems (e.g., Turkish, Swahili, Tamil, Maori). Other languages use infixes (e.g., Tagalog), circumfixes (e.g., German), incorporation (e.g., Greenlandic Eskimo), or reduplication (e.g., Indonesian), all morphological processes that need to be examined in psycholinguistic studies. Affixes in many languages encode various types of syntactic information, and the mechanisms proposed for obtaining that information in on-line language production need to be matched to the wide range of syntactically conditioned affixes found in languages. Furthermore, morphemes in many languages encode information from even higher levels of linguistic structure, such as marking the topic or focus of the discourse, which would mean that these higher levels of linguistic structure must also be able to inform the word formation processes.

In order to have a viable account of language production, we need to include all of the morphologically complex types of words used in languages. An examination of different morphological systems may well lead us to different types of mental lexical representations and different production processes than those envisaged so far. In this chapter, an outline of morphological systems and word formation processes in natural languages is provided, accompanied by questions regarding the various morphological types that will need to be addressed in a model of speech production.

The chapter is organised as follows. The first section contains a typology of morphological systems in languages of the world. The next section focuses on some of the categories of morphemes not yet examined in psycholinguistic studies and their potential contributions to research on the form of the lexical entry in the mental lexicon.[1] Issues that morphological systems in various languages bring to bear on inter- and intralevel organisation and processes in the production model are then raised. In the concluding section, the possibility of a production model including mechanisms for different systems of representation and process, activated differently by languages with different types of morphology, is discussed.

MORPHOLOGICAL TYPES OF LANGUAGE

Languages are divided into four major types with respect to word-formation: analytic, agglutinative, fusional, and incorporating. Typological categories are based on the average number of morphemes per word and the amount of information contained in each morpheme (Greenberg, 1954). The language typology is used as a guide to uncovering recurring structural patterns in languages of the world, rather than as a set of boxes into which individual languages will each fit perfectly. The relevance of the morphological typology to language production lies not in categorising the languages, but in gaining access to the structures of words found in each of the different language types. Next, the morphological types of languages are characterised and exemplified, and questions raised for production models are discussed.

Analytic languages

In analytic languages (e.g., Mandarin Chinese, Vietnamese), most words are monomorphemic. These languages use very few affixes. For example, number, case, gender, tense, and mood, which are often marked with inflectional agreement affixes in other languages, are either signalled by the semantics or not indicated at all in Mandarin. In these Mandarin sentences in (1), all words consist in a single morpheme (from Li & Thompson, 1990):

(1)   tā qù zhōngguó xué   zhōngguó huà
       3p go China   learn China   painting
       "S/he went to China to learn Chinese painting."

Note that there is no tense marked on the verb in (1). The past tense is inferred from the serial verb construction. The word for third person is used for both male and female referents. There is no morphological difference between the words for "China" and "Chinese". Subjects and objects are not morphologically differentiated; a Mandarin sentence with "he" or "she" as the object would use the same third person *tā* as is found in (1) as the subject.

Since most words are single root morphemes (or compounds built from two root morphemes) in analytic languages, issues of different combinations of affixes or different morpheme types usually do not come into play. The question of whether compounds are represented monomorphemically or compositionally in the mental lexicon can be fruitfully examined in these languages (e.g., Zhou & Marslen-Wilson, 1994), since there is very little other morphology which might interfere in the investigation.

Similarly, issues of other levels of linguistic structure, such as how tone is represented in the mental lexicon, would be easiest to investigate in analytic languages, since the contributions of morphological structure can be divorced from those of the other levels.

Agglutinative languages

Agglutinative languages (e.g., Hungarian, Luganda, Quechua, Swahili, Turkish) utilise highly productive affixes, each having a single syntactic or semantic function. These affixes may appear singly on root morphemes, or roots may be combined with affixes, forming stems, to which further affixes are added. The morphological boundaries in agglutinative languages are easily determined (as if the morphemes were "glued" together). For example, in Turkish, a root like *köy*, "village" can have a suffix attached to it, as in (2b, and 2c), or it can be the root portion of a stem, to which further affixes are added, as in (2d, and 2e):

(2) (a) köy   "village"   root
     (b) köy-e   "to a village"   root + affix
     (c) köy-den   "from a village"   root + affix
     (d) köy-jik-den   "from a little village"   [root + affix]$_{stem}$ + affix
     (e) köy-jik-ler-imiz-de   "in our little villages"   [[[root + affix]$_{stem}$ + affix]$_{stem}$ + affix]$_{stem}$ + affix

As expected in an agglutinative system, each suffix in the Turkish example bears a unique meaning: *–e* is the dative suffix, *–den* is the ablative suffix, *–jik* means "little", *–ler* is the plural suffix, *–imiz* means "our", and *–de* means "in". Each of these suffixes is fully productive, and each is clearly identifiable in the morpheme string.

Multiply affixed words like those in (2) raise the issue of morphological structure of the lexical entry. Are polymorphemic words listed as whole-word forms in the mental lexicon (e.g., Butterworth, 1983; Lukatela, Gligorijevic, Kostic, & Turvey, 1980; Segui & Zubizaretta, 1985; Stemberger, 1985), are all morphemes listed individually (e.g., Dell, 1986; Taft & Forster, 1975), or are both whole-word and individual morphemes available (e.g., Frauenfelder & Schreuder, 1992)? If words are listed as wholes, is the morphological constituency of a word like *köyjiklerimizde* available (in actual structure or via connections, depending on the framework), or are the morphological boundaries unavailable in the mental lexicon?

Hankamer (1989) argues convincingly that agglutinative languages could not be accounted for using a mental lexicon that lists each word as a whole form (with or without internal structure). In Turkish, over 200 billion entries would need to be stored, and there is not enough storage capacity in a human brain for such a large lexicon. (Though Hankamer's argument is directed towards lexical parsing, it holds equally well for production.) A production model that is able to account for words used in agglutinative languages such as Turkish, then, must have a morpheme storage and access system that is able to build words from their constituent morphemes, rather than one that can only access stored whole-word forms. Thus, the presence of agglutinative morphological systems in human languages argues against full-word listing models, and narrows the field of possibilities for lexical representation to either morphological decomposition models or dual-mechanism models, in which both morpheme listing and whole-word listing are available.

Fusional languages

In fusional languages (e.g., Greek, Latin, Spanish, Russian, French, Italian), stems and affixes are not as easily separated as those in agglutinative languages (i.e., the stems and affixes are "fused" together). Fusional languages also tend to encode more than one meaning into a single affix. For example, in Russian, a single affix, *–a*, added to a noun marks the noun as having feminine gender, singular number, and subject function. (In an agglutinative language, these three pieces of information would be marked by three separate morphemes.)

The fused nature of roots and affixes in fusional languages can complicate lexical representation because there is not always a clear cutting point for separate morphemes in polymorphemic words. For example, in Spanish, the following forms are found:

(3) habl*o*   "I am speaking"[2]   com*o*   "I am eating"
     habl*as*   "you (familiar) are   com*es*   "you (familiar) are eating"
                 speaking"
     habl*a*   "he/she is speaking"   com*e*   "he/she is eating"
     habl*amos* "we are speaking"   com*emos*   "we are eating"
     habl*an*   "they are speaking"   com*en*   "they are eating"

Spanish has three classes of verbs which differ in their vowel patterns in combination with tense suffixes. "Speak" belongs to a different verb class from that of "eat", and the different verb class vowels, *a* and *e*, respectively, are italicised in the second person familiar, third person singular, first person plural, and third person plural forms in (3).

If roots are separate entities in lexical entries (e.g., Dell, 1986; Lukatela et al., 1980; Taft & Forster, 1975), is the root for "eat" in the Spanish examples in (3) represented in the mental lexicon as *come–* or *com–*? An analysis using the root morphemes *habla–* and *come–* could use identical tense affixes for all verbs, but it would need a mechanism to delete the final root vowel before a vowel-initial suffix. Thus, for example, the root *come–* + the first person singular present tense affix *–o* would delete the stem-final vowel to yield *como* (and not **comeo*). Another analysis might have the roots *habl–* and *com–* and provide the vowels in the affixes (e.g., *–amos*, *–emos*). Such an analysis would not need the previously mentioned vowel deletion rule, but it would have different tense affixes for the different classes of verbs. Another hypothesis would have words with fusional morphology listed as whole-word forms in the mental lexicon. The linguistically viable analyses need to be examined in the experimental arena in order to posit representations for the mental lexicon. General criteria for determining the form of the lexical entry in words with fusional morphology need to be hypothesised and tested. Further, instances of analogous examples in different languages need to be compared in order to make sure that generalisations made using data from a single language are valid (in this linguistic domain and every other).

Incorporating languages

Incorporating languages (e.g., Ahtna Athabaskan, Cree, Chamorro, Zenzontepec Chatino, Chichewa, Greenlandic Eskimo, Samoan) allow the argument(s) of a predicate to be combined with the predicate's root and affixes into a single word. For a simplified example, the object, *sled*, of a verb, *stop*, could be combined with inflectional morphemes to get a single word meaning "he stopped the sled" or "he sledstopped". This morphological process has the effect of obtaining the meaning of an entire sentence in a single word. In Ahtna, an Athabaskan language spoken in Alaska's Copper River area, a verb template consists of the verbal root, at least one suffix, 27 distinct prefix positions, and a slot for possible incorporated arguments (Kari, 1992). Incorporated arguments in Ahtna can be subjects, manners, instruments, or objects. Examples of incorporation in Ahtna are shown in (4), with incorporated arguments underlined (from Kari, 1992, pp. 114–115):[3]

(4)　(a)　incorporated subject with intransitive verb
　　　　　na + *ta* + d + gh + n + ∅ + ∅ + taan + n
　　　　　down + *water* + thematic + mode + perfect + 3subject + classifier + drip + vb suffix
　　　　　natadghitaan　"water dripped down"

(b)   incorporated manner with intransitive verb
ti + *łi* + n + n + ∅ + ∅ + yaa + n
out + *dog* + mode + perfect + 3subject + classifier + hunt + vb suffix
tiłiniyaa   "he went out hunting with dogs"

(c)   incorporated instrument with intransitive verb
y + *qe* + z + ∅ + ∅ + ł + qay + ?
3object + *foot* + perfect + mode + 3subject + classifier + strike + vb suffix
iqełqas   "he struck him once with the foot, he kicked him once"

(d)   incorporated object with transitive verb
ni + *xał* + n + n + ∅ + ∅ + taan + n
stop + *sled* + mode + perfect + 3subject + classifier + handle elongated object + vb suffix
nixałnitaan   "he stopped the sled"

(e)   incorporated subject with transitive verb
qe + *ta* + y + d + z + ∅ + ∅ + ∅ + taan + n
ashore + *water* + 3object + gender + mode + perfect + 3subject + classifier + causes elongated object to move + vb suffix
qetaydeztaan   "water caused it (e.g., log) to drift ashore"

Incorporated forms are clearly identified as single words because word-level as opposed to phrase-level phonological rules apply. Moreover, incorporated forms behave like words (not like sentences) with respect to further morphological processes. (Note, for example, that the incorporated morphemes in (4) are preceded by prefixes.) Also, the semantics of incorporated forms is transparent (as opposed to compounds, which are often semantically opaque).

Languages with incorporation pose a dilemma for production (and/or processing) models which assume that all words are listed as wholes in the lexicon (e.g., Butterworth, 1989), and for models that treat derived forms as noncompositional, while inflections are added to roots or stems via composition rules (e.g., Sandra, 1994). Are the incorporated words like the Ahtna examples in (4) also represented as whole forms (with or without the inflections) in the lexicon? There would be a huge set of words analogous to (4a) alone (e.g., "milk dripped down", "honey dripped down", "cider dripped down", "ammonia dripped down", "salad dressing dripped down", etc., to say nothing of all the other verb roots that can be combined with this same set of incorporates). Because incorporation is a productive derivational process, languages of this type expand our view of noninflectional morphology. A production model that posited all whole word forms or one that posited all derived forms as whole-word forms would be untenable in a language with incorporation. In this way, including a wider variety of morphological types of languages illuminates properties of lexical representation, as well as the interactions between linguistic levels needed in word-formation processes for lexical access in a production model.

In this section, the major morphological types of language have been presented and exemplified, with some of the ramifications for production models pointed out. What is significant to mental representations and processes is not actually the typological category the language is ascribed to. As noted, many languages combine aspects of more than one type (e.g., Finnish is an agglutinative-fusional language). Rather, it is the differences in the words formed in each type of language described. The highly productive nature of agglutinative affixes, for example, might suggest a model in which each affix is represented separately in the mental lexicon, so that the enormous number of possible combinations can be combined, rather than stored as wholes. Words with fusional affixes raise questions of where one morpheme ends and another begins. No studies at all have looked at production of words with incorporation used in polysynthetic languages. Studies including languages from various typological categories will give a clearer picture of the nature of mental representations of morphemes, because the range of words examined will better reflect the range of words in human languages.

MORPHEME CATEGORIES AND THE LEXICAL ENTRY

Several categories of morphemes that have not yet been examined in the production arena raise questions regarding representation in the lexical entry. In this section, three such categories are presented, with their linguistic analyses and a discussion of the relevance of each morphological domain to issues regarding the form of the lexical entry in a model of production.

Reduplication

Many languages form polymorphemic words in which an affix is made up of phonological information cloned (or "reduplicated") from the root (e.g., Tagalog, Mokilese, Lardil, Yidin^y, Chamorro, Indonesian, Sudanese, Maori, Thai). The reduplicative affix has no specified segmental form of its own, as its sounds depend on the melodies of the root used as input.[4] For example, in Mokilese, an Austropolynesian language spoken in Micronesia, the progressive morpheme is a reduplicative one (data from Levin, 1985):

(5)	(a)	pɔdok	"plant"	pɔd-pɔdok	"planting"
	(b)	caak	"bend"	caa-caak	"bending"
	(c)	andip	"spit"	and-andip	"spitting"
	(d)	onop	"prepare"	onn-onop	"preparing"
	(e)	pa	"weave"	paa-pa	"weaving"
	(f)	wia	"do"	wii-wia	"doing"

It is clear from the data in (5) that there is no single phonological form for the morpheme carrying the progressive meaning in Mokilese. With the six different verbs in (5), there are six different instantiations of the progressive morpheme. Also note that in (5a–c) the first three melodies of the root appear in the prefix, but in (5d–f) reduplication yields a segmental concatenation not found in the roots. Rather, the reduplicative prefix has a melodically empty prosodic template, and melodic information from the root is transferred to this template. The reduplicative affix for the Mokilese data in (5) is analysed as a heavy syllable (i.e., a syllable that either contains a long vowel or a consonantal coda; McCarthy & Prince, 1990). When the melodic information of each root is associated to the reduplicative prefix (i.e., attached into the prosodic structure), the root-specific reduplicative morphemes shown in the data result. The single syllable of the reduplicative prefix means that only one vowel melody will appear (because another vowel would begin another syllable). The heaviness (bimoraicity) specified for the reduplicative affix accounts for the lengthening of the vowels or consonants in (5d–f).[5] Reduplication can be visualised as in (6):[6]

(6)   (a)   reduplicative affix for progressive morpheme

     (b)   reduplicative structures[7]
         for pɔdpɔdok "planting"   for paapa "weaving"

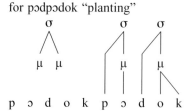

    (c)   surface representations (before erasure of unprosodised elements)

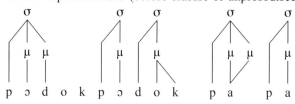

At this point, the unprosodised elements (i.e., those melodies not attached into the moraic or syllabic tree) are erased, and the forms in (5) are produced.

Reduplicative morphemes like the prefixes in (5) can inflectional or derivational, and they can be accompanied by other affixes, both inflectional and derivational. For example, in Tagalog, an Austropolynesian language spoken in the Philippines, words with a reduplicative prefix preceded by a regular prefix are found:

(7) root: ʔisda   "fish"
    future: ʔi-ʔisda   "will fish"
    agentive: maŋ-ʔi-ʔisda   "fisherman"

A reduplicative morpheme can appear as a prefix, as in these Mokilese and Tagalog examples, or a suffix, as in Kinande (Mutaka & Hyman, 1990), or an infix (i.e., an affix that is attached within the root rather than at the periphery), as in Levantine Arabic (Katamba, 1993). The positional subtype of the affix (i.e., prefix, suffix, infix) is relevant to the direction in which melodies are associated to the prosodic structure. Prefixes associate melodies to prosodic structure left-to-right, as in the earlier Mokilese examples. Suffixes associate from right-to-left, and infixes can be left-to-right or right-to-left, depending on the language.

The phenomenon of reduplication is particularly interesting to researchers of language production because its morphemes are quite unlike the melodically specified morphemes studied so far. For those production models which have the morpheme as the basic unit in the mental lexicon, either a reduplicative morpheme will have to be listed with as many forms as there are roots it attaches to (extremely unwieldy for language acquisition, since each member of the huge set of forms for the same meaning would have to be learned separately), or else a morpheme would need to be posited in the mental lexicon with prosodic structure but no melody. (I advocate this option, but note that it is unprecedented in models of production or processing.) If this latter tack were taken, a mechanism for filling in the appropriate melody and attaching it to the prosodic structure would also need to be posited.

Morphological code-switching (i.e., when a bilingual speaker combines morphemes from different languages into a single word) involving reduplicative forms can give us some inroad into how these morphemes are represented and produced. Waksler (1999) provides morphological code-switching from Tagalog to English (Waksler, 1999, p. 71):

(8) Saan si Jason? Nag-SWI-SWIMMING   siya.
    where det Jason   present-redup-SWIMMING he
    "Where is Jason? He's swimming."

The Tagalog root for "swim" is *languy*. The Tagalog present progressive is formed via reduplication of the root plus the prefix *nag–*. The form for "swimming" in Tagalog, then, is *nag-la-languy*, with the inflectional morpheme *nag–* prefixed to the reduplicated form of the root. In the code-switching example presented in (8), the Tagalog prefix *nag–* is attached to the reduplicated form of the English root *swimming*. Since English is not a language with reduplicative morphology, this code-switched form could not have been listed as a full-word form in the mental lexicon. Such examples suggest that the empty reduplicative template is represented as a separate morpheme in the mental lexicon of Tagalog speakers.

Nonconcatenative morphology

Languages such as Hebrew and ASL (American Sign Language) contain non-concatenative morphology, i.e., morphemes that are not added to their roots in sequential linear order. Nonconcatenative morphology can involve discontinuous morphemes, as are found in Semitic languages, or simultaneous morphemes, as are found in signed languages. Both types of nonconcatenative morphology have been linguistically analysed using separate morphological tiers for the morphemes (e.g., McCarthy, 1981, for Arabic; Sandler, 1993, for ASL). An analysis of discontinuous morphemes in Arabic is presented later.

The melodic elements of discontinuous morphemes, such as those found in Hebrew and Arabic derivational classes (called "binyanim"), are interspersed rather than concatenated.[8] For example, the root for "write" in Arabic consists of the three consonants *ktb*. When affixes are added to the root, their melodies separate and appear between the root consonants. Consider these (uninflected) examples in (9) (McCarthy, 1981):

(9) (a) katab   "write"
     (b) kaatab   "correspond" (habitual)
     (c) kattab   "cause to write"
     (d) ktatab   "write, be registered"
     (e) kitaab   "book"
     (f) kitaabat   "act of writing"

All of the examples in (9) share the *ktb* root morpheme "write". But when an affix is added to the root morpheme, neither the root nor the affix remains as a cohesive chunk. In (9e), for example, the morpheme consisting of the vowels *i* and *a* is added to the root for "write" to make the noun "book". (Vowel length will be discussed later.) The melodic elements of the affix are separated and inserted in between the *ktb* root consonants. The affix vowels must be inserted in a particular order (i.e., the *i* and then the *a*, and not the other way around). They also must be inserted between the root consonants in a particular pattern—the *i* melody after the first consonant and the *a* melody after the second. (Compare this form with (9d), in which no vowel is inserted after the first root consonant.)

McCarthy (1981) proposed a linguistic account of Arabic nonconcatenative morphology that uses different prosodic templates for the Arabic binyanim. When the melodies of a root are mapped onto different the prosodic templates, they yield different forms. McCarthy also hypothesised that each morpheme occupies a separate tier.[9] The template and morpheme tiers for (9a) are shown in (10):

(10)   a   (melody of affix)
       C V C V C   (skeletal template for appropriate binyan[10])
       ktb   (melody of root)

The template shown in (10) is made up of skeletal elements, C and V, representing timing units of consonants and vowels, respectively. Each skeletal element represents one unit of timing. A long vowel, then, is a vowel melody associated with two V-slots on the skeleton, and a geminate consonant is a consonant melody associated with two C-slots. The melodies are associated to the prosodic elements of the skeleton left to right,[11] one to one, with consonants mapped to C elements and vowels mapped to V elements. Each of the skeletal slots must be associated to a melody.

In (10a), there is only one vowel melody in the affix, but the binyan template has two V-slots that need to be associated to the melodic tier. That vowel melody spreads to fill both V-slots, as illustrated in (11):

(11)

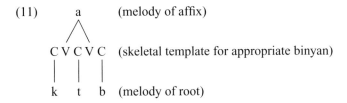

a   (melody of affix)

C V C V C   (skeletal template for appropriate binyan)

k   t   b   (melody of root)

In this way, even though the affixes in both (9a) and (9b) consist of the melody *a*, the different meanings in (9a) and (9b) are attributed to the different prosodic templates of the two binyanim. The template for the binyan in (9b) would have a CVVCVC skeleton, and then the *a* melody of the affix would be mapped to all three V-slots.

Many questions involving the mental representation of lexical entries arise for a production account of nonconcatenative morphology. The linguistic analysis posits a skeletal template, but the inclusion of sub-syllabic structure in a metrical frame is highly controversial in the production arena. For models that do not include sub-syllabic structure (e.g., Levelt, 1992; Roelofs & Meyer, 1998) how will non-concatenative morphology be represented? Are the roots and derivational affixes in forms like those in (9) represented separately in the mental lexicon? Or, are all the derived forms simply listed as whole words? Do morphologically related words in languages with nonconcatenative morphology exhibit the morphological family coherence in the mental lexicon that has been found in other languages (Marslen-Wilson, Tyler, Waksler, & Older, 1994)? If so, given that there is no uninterrupted string of melodies corresponding to the morphemes in the derived form, are morphological tiers (like those in (10), where each of the morphemes in the word are represented on separate levels) used in lexical entries?

Morphological code-switching found in languages with nonconcatenative morphology can again shed some light on morphological representation in these languages. Code-switching examples from Hebrew/English (Waksler, 1999, p. 72) such as those in (12) and (13) intersperse Hebrew nonconcatenative morphemes between the consonants of English roots.

(12) Aiza raiah tov,   tasmili.
      "What a good smell, smell [it]."
      root *sml* from English "smell" with Hebrew future, 2f nonconcatenative
      morphology

(13) dupaz
      "it was deposited"
      root *dpz* from English "deposit" with Hebrew -u-a
      nonconcatenative passive morphology

Because the nonconcatenative Hebrew inflectional morphemes are combined
with only the consonants of the English roots, such examples would suggest the
existence of a language-specific parameter which allows separate morpheme
tiers in lexical entries. Furthermore, examples like (12) and (13) argue against a
model with full-listing representations, since the code-switching data are not
words in either language.

Questions for future research in the production of languages with nonconcatenative morphology abound. What is the phonological form of the discontinuous
roots in these languages in the mental lexicon? (I.e., is a root represented as the
set of discontinuous consonants which would be phonologically ill-formed as a
word in that language, or is it represented in some phonologically well-formed
way?) Are there different patterns of speech errors for the nonconcatenative
morphemes and the standard concatenated prefixes and suffixes also found
in these languages? Do morphological speech errors in signed languages also
support the existence of different morphological tiers? Investigations directed
toward these empirical questions will bring important information about the
nature of lexical entries in a production model.

Inflections

Several researchers have proposed that the difference between inflections and
derivations is relevant to morphological representation in the mental lexicon
(e.g., Badecker & Caramazza, 1989; Sandra, 1994). But very few types of the
inflectional affixes in languages have been examined to date in the production or
processing literature. No infixes (affixes inserted within the root) or circumfixes
(affixes with two parts that surround the root) have been examined. In fact, all of
the prefixes in psycholinguistic studies have been derivational. It is precipitous
to assume that different representational or processing categories are based on
some particular property when that property has only been examined when
conflated with other properties.[12] Any or all of the morphological characteristics
such as position with respect to the root, predictability, productivity, frequency,
consistent semantics, morpheme type, and morphological system type might
contribute to categories of lexical representations. Here, data from an ergative

language with inflectional prefixes are presented, with a view of trying to expand the morphological set of inquiry, as well as to separate possible morphological properties that might be relevant to categories of lexical representation.

Tzotzil, a Mayan language of Mexico, is a highly inflected language that uses prefixes to encode information about aspect, person, and subject vs. object. (All data and analyses of Tzotzil in this section are from Aissen, 1987.) Prefixes are used to mark neutral, incompletive, and completive aspect, as illustrated in (14) (Aissen, 1987, pp. 41–42):

(14) (a)   neutral aspect: x-
           Mu x-   bat.
           not aspect-go
           He/she/it/they isn't/aren't going.
      (b)   incompletive aspect:[13] ta + x-
           Ta   x-   bat.
           aspect aspect-go
           particle
           He/she/it/they is/are going.
      (c)   completive aspect: ʔi-
           ʔi-   bat
           aspect-go
           He/she/it/they went.

In all of the languages examined in the production and processing literature to date, (regular) inflectional affixes are assumed to be a homogenous class of affixes suffixed to the root. But since several researchers have argued that suffixes and prefixes get different kinds of processing or representation in the mental lexicon (e.g., Cutler, Hawkins, & Gilligan, 1985), the presence of inflectional prefixes becomes relevant to the representation of inflections in the mental lexicon. With the inclusion of inflectional prefixes into the field of study, we would be able to separate the possible factors of position with respect to the root versus affix type as contributors to mental representations and processes.

Furthermore, the few languages that have been examined with respect to case inflections have had nominative/accusative case systems (e.g., Lukatela et al., 1980; Niemi et al., 1994). A nominative/accusative system is one that morphologically marks a distinction between subjects and direct objects. In a nominative/accusative system, subjects of both transitive and intransitive verbs are marked with morphemes from one morphological set (i.e., nominative), and objects of transitive verbs are marked with morphemes from another set (i.e., accusative), as shown in the English examples in (15):

(15) (a)   subject of intransitive verb: *I* sneezed.
      (b)   subject of transitive verb: *I* called Alex.
      (c)   object of transitive verb: Alex called *me*.

As seen in (15), subjects are marked with one set of pronouns in English, and objects are marked with another, e.g., first person singular as *I* in (15a, and b) vs. *me* in (15c). In English, the pronominal system holds the only surviving evidence of nominative/accusative case marking. Many languages (e.g., Turkish, Russian, Finnish, German, Serbo-Croatian) have a more robust nominative/accusative case-marking pattern, in which case is marked on nouns as well as pronouns. Furthermore, the first person case marking in English is not affixational, so the question of separate representation in the mental lexicon is moot; *I* and *me* must be represented as separate lexical entries because they do not share a morphological root. In most other languages, however, case marking is affixational, and the question of separate morphological entries for cases in the mental lexicon becomes relevant.

Tzotzil uses an ergative (or ergative/absolutive) case system. In this system, subjects of transitive verbs are marked with morphemes from one set (i.e., ergative), whereas subjects of intransitive verbs and objects of transitive verbs are marked with morphemes from another set (i.e., absolutive). An illustration of Tzotzil ergative marking is provided in (16) (ergative/absolutive case morphemes italicised) (Aissen, 1987, pp. 1–2):

(16) (a)   subject of intransitive verb
            L-*i*-tal-otik[14]
            completive-*1p abs*-come-1plural inclusive
            "We (inclusive[15]) came."
      (b)   object of transitive verb
            L-*i*-s-pet-otik
            completive-*1p abs*-3p erg-carry-1plural inclusive
            "He carried us (inclusive)."
      (c)   subject of transitive verb
            ʔi-*j*-pet-tik lok'el ti vinik-e.
            completive-*1p erg*-carry-1plural inclusive away the man-clitic
            "We (inclusive) carried away the man."

As shown in (16a, and b) the first person prefix for both subject of an intransitive verb and object of a transitive verb is *i*–, while the first person prefix for the subject of a transitive verb is *j*–. This morphological system represents a different grouping of grammatical relations from that shown in the nominative/accusative system.

Many of the world's inflected languages do not have nominative/accusative systems (e.g., many Native American languages of the US, Canada, and Mexico, like Yupik, Halkomelem, Tzotzil; most Australian languages, like Dyirbal, Diyari, Yidinʸ; some Asian languages like Tibetan; and other languages such as Basque, Tagalog, Avar). Linguistic evidence shows that nominative/accusative and ergative/absolutive are not simply different names or alignments of grammatical relations, but are separate entities with different properties (Woolford, 1997).

Until work is done in at least some of the languages that use an ergative case system, we will not know whether a difference in inflectional system type is relevant to morphological representation in the mental lexicon in models of language production or processing. Also, until languages using inflectional prefixes are examined, the separable properties of affix position (e.g., prefix/suffix) and inflection/derivation remain entangled.

INTER- AND INTRALEVEL ORGANISATION

In this section, morphological types that have not yet been examined in psycholinguistic studies are shown to have relevant information to contribute to queries of interaction between other linguistic levels and the lexicon, and the organisation of information in the lexicon itself. Interaction between the lexicon and phonological, syntactic, and/or semantic levels of representation has been proposed in various production models (e.g., Dell & O'Seaghdha, 1992; Levelt, 1989, 1992), and the level of discourse has been recognised as an important component in macroplanning (Levelt, 1989). But some languages exhibit morphological evidence that the discourse level must also enter into word-formation mechanism. Morphological markers of discourse topic and focus are found as affixes in these languages, demonstrating that information outside of the sentence must be available to word-formation processes or procedures.

Within a linguistic level, the organisation of information is a major area in which production models differ. For example, issues of whether prefixed forms are processed or produced differently from suffixed forms, whether lexical entries are organised around nuclei roots, whether categories of inflection vs. derivation are distinguished have all been seen to distinguish proposals in processing and/or production mentioned earlier. In this section, morphemes that can contribute to an expanded view of inter- and intralevel communication are presented.

Interlevel information: Topic marking

The topic of a discourse (i.e., what the discourse is about) is identified in some languages with word order and/or intonation (e.g., English, Italian, French), rather than with a topic-identifying morpheme. In other languages, however, topic is morphologically marked, or it is morphologically indicated whether the topic changes or remains the same in successive sentences. Because topic identity or change is a discourse-level phenomenon, its affixal marking in languages uncovers a level of information that has not yet been considered as contributing to word formation. Topic marking in Dyirbal is illustrated next. (All data and analyses of Dyirbal are from Dixon, 1972.)

In Dyirbal, an Australian language spoken in West Queensland, if a discourse contains two successive sentences, S_1 and S_2, with the same topic noun phrase, and the topic noun phrase in S_1 is in the ergative case, while the coreferent topic noun phrase in S_2 is in nominative case, then the verb(s) in S_2 take the suffix *–ŋura* instead of a regular tense ending. Examples are provided in (17) (Dixon, 1972, p. 77).

(17) (a)   separate sentences (not in discourse)
bala yugu baŋgul yaṯaŋgu madan
the stick the   man   threw
"The man threw the stick."
bala yaṯa wayɲḍin
the   man went uphill
"The man went uphill."

   (b)   same sentences, in discourse (–ŋura marking)
bala yugu baŋgul yaṯaŋgu madan bayi yaṯa wayɲḍiŋura
"The man threw the stick. The man went uphill."

The topic affix *–ŋura* also signifies that the event in the second sentence followed immediately after that in the first. This affix is only marked on sentences that meet all of the criteria described previously; if the noun phrases are not coreferent, or if the topic of the discourse changes from one sentence to the next, then the *–ŋura* affix is not used. This affix, then, depends on intersentential discourse information, providing evidence that the word-building mechanism in a production model must be able to encode discourse-level information. Affixes encoding discourse-level information are also found in Korean, Japanese, Hua, and Turkish (Croft, 1990), among other languages.

Intralevel organisation: Subcategorisation

Researchers agree that grammatical categories and syntactic subcategorisation specifications will need to be provided in the mental lexicon. Speech error evidence of word exchanges occurring between members of the same lexical category (Fromkin, 1971; Garrett, 1980) and evidence of different patterns of errors for different categories of affixes (Garrett, 1980) have been used to support the inclusion of categorial information in a production model. Data from agrammatic patients have revealed that the use of subcategorisation information, such as particular prepositions being subcategorised for by particular verbs, can be affected in production (Friederici, 1982). These realisations lead to two paths of intralevel investigation regarding organisation of subcategories on the lexical level: (a) What kinds of subcategorisation information are relevant to the production of language? and (b) When and how is subcategorisation information used in production? In order to address these questions, of course, it is necessary to obtain data from languages using a wide variety of subcategorised morphemes.

So far, the limited amount of production research that has been done in this area has centred on subcategorisation involving words from two lexical categories (e.g., verbs that subcategorise for certain prepositions, in Friederici, 1982).

However, many languages exhibit subcategorisation that affects morphological structures within a lexical category. For example, noun class systems (also called gender), in which different sets of nouns are distinguished using different agreement morphology, are found in Swahili, Japanese, Fijian, and Dyirbal, among many other languages. To illustrate, the following groupings are found in Swahili (class prefixes and their roots separated by "+") (from Katamba, 1993, p. 235):

(18)　(a)　*singular*　*plural*
　　　　　　m+tu　　　wa+tu　　　"person"
　　　　　　m+geni　　wa+geni　　"guest"
　　　　　　m+ke　　　wa+ke　　　"woman"
　　　(b)　m+ti　　　mi+ti　　　"tree"
　　　　　　m+ganda　mi+ganda　"bundle"
　　　　　　m+fereji　mi+fereji　"ditch"
　　　　　　m+to　　　mi+to　　　"river"
　　　　　　m+tego　　mi+tego　　"trap"
　　　(c)　ki+kapu　vi+kapu　　"basket"
　　　　　　ki+tabu　vi+tabu　　"book"
　　　　　　ki+oo　　vi+oo　　　"mirror"
　　　(d)　m+buzi　　m+buzi　　　"goat"
　　　　　　n+dege　　n+dege　　　"bird"
　　　　　　ŋ+guruwe　ŋ+guruwe　"pig"

In Swahili, the different noun classes take different prefixes that are attached to the nouns themselves as well as to any determiners or adjectives in the noun phrase (e.g., *m+toto m+moja m+dogo* "one small child"). The classes in Swahili are somewhat based on semantic features (e.g., nouns referring to humans are usually in separate noun classes from nouns referring to animals or inanimates), but the groups are not necessarily semantically determined. (E.g., *kijana*, the Swahili word for "youth" is in the class with the words for "basket" and "book".) Noun classes in some languages are more clearly associated with semantic properties (e.g., in Cherikawa Apache, Japanese), and in other languages more arbitrary (e.g., in Arapesh, a language of Papua New Guinea—Aronoff, 1994, French, German).

Processing and production research on noun class systems could provide information regarding a possible organisation of the different classes of nouns in the mental lexicon. In speech errors, do word exchanges tend to remain within noun class subcategories? In languages with semantically determined noun classes, do neologisms fall within predictable noun class groupings, or do they use a default noun class marker?

Morphological code-switching data from languages with noun class systems can be used to argue for the inclusion of class-marking morphemes as separate entities in the mental lexicon. Consider the Swahili/English code-switching data in (19) (data from Myers-Scotton, 1993, pp. 86 and 30, respectively):

(19) (a) ... ha-wa-end-i   ma-HOME ...
          neg-3P-Go-neg/FV cl.16-HOME
          "... they don't go home ..."
     (b) ... ni-ka-i-rub na kitambaa
          1s-consec-cl9 obj-RUB with cloth
          "and then I rubbed it with a cloth"

In (19a) the Swahili noun class prefix *ma–* is attached to an English noun in the code-switching example. In (19b), the Swahili object marker of a particular noun class (i.e., class 9) is attached to an English verb root. These examples suggest that the class-marking morphemes are listed separately in the mental lexicon, available for lexical access in production without being attached to a particular root.

CONCLUDING REMARKS

Because work in language production has been limited to a rather small number of languages, many of the morphological types and systems used in languages of the world have not yet been included in the field of study. Here, a typology of morphological systems has been provided, along with a selection of morphological processes that have particular repercussions for production models. The morphological areas of reduplication, nonconcatenative morphology, inflectional prefixes, ergative case marking, morphemes encoding discourse-level information, and noun class systems have been described and exemplified, with discussion of how each can bear relevant input to the representations and/or mechanisms used in a production model.

As humans are not born with a propensity for learning any one particular language, a model of language production is expected to be able to handle the linguistic constructions of any natural language. That is not to say, however, that the actual representations or mechanisms used to produce any particular language need to be universally used in producing every language. More and more evidence is being adduced to argue that the production model needs a dual system of representation or process for different areas of morphology (Frauenfelder & Schreuder, 1992; Pinker & Prince, 1991). That is, instead of a model being characterised by either whole-word listing or morpheme-by-morpheme construction in the mental lexicon, the model may need both types of representation. For example, Jaeger et al. (1996) provide neurolinguistic evidence that regular and irregular plurals in English are produced with different systems, as their production activates different areas of the cortex. Their positron emission tomographic study supports a model in which regular plurals are listed as separate morphemes, and irregular plurals are listed in whole-word forms.

A production model may include universal parameters or constraints[16] that are selectively activated or ordered as a language is acquired. Languages that have nonconcatenative morphology, for example, may use separate morphological tiers in lexical representations, whereas languages that do not have such morphology do not need such architecture. The model can have the option of using a particular mechanism or system of representation, as warranted by the input data from the language(s) being acquired,[17] but it is not preconstructed with it. To discover the types of structures and mechanisms that need to be available in a production model, it is necessary to include in our investigations all of the morphological constructions that languages use.

NOTES

1. Though I refer to "the mental lexicon" in this chapter, it should be noted that some researchers have argued for separate mental lexicons for processing and production (e.g., Niemi, Laine, & Tuominen, 1994). Under a separate lexicon system, reference to "the mental lexicon" in this chapter would apply to the production lexicon.
2. The Spanish present tense examples are translated into colloquially appropriate English. Spanish also has present progressive forms.
3. Glosses have been slightly adapted to suit the discussion. For example, roots are glossed per sentence here, though it is noted that the verb root "taan" is glossed differently when it has different themes. (In Kari, 1992, roots are unglossed.) This is a translation issue—English does not have a lexical counterpart to "taan". It is irrelevant to the morphological process being illustrated.
4. It is possible for a morpheme to be partially specified for some particular melody, and partially reduplicative, as in Saho, a Cushitic language spoken in North Africa (Katamba, 1993).
5. For an introduction to prosodic structures, see Lahiri (this volume).
6. Diagrams of reduplication like this one are proposed as linguistic accounts for the data. Since reduplication has not yet been studied with respect to production or processing, the mental representation of this morphological process has not yet been investigated.
7. Structures are simplified in areas that are irrelevant to the present discussion (e.g., extrametricality is ignored).
8. Detailed analyses of Hebrew and Arabic nonconcatenative structures include Aronoff (1994) for Hebrew, and McCarthy (1981) and McCarthy and Prince (1990) for Arabic.
9. McCarthy's proposals were made for the purposes of linguistic analysis. Whether morphemes are represented on separate tiers in the mental lexicon is an open question for psycholinguistic research.
10. Prosodic levels other than the skeleton will be omitted in these examples for simplicity.
11. The direction of association (left-to-right or right-to-left) for prosodic structures is language-specific.
12. Another issue complicating this hypothesis is that the categorial distinction between inflections and derivations is not uncontroversial. See Bybee (1985) for discussion.
13. The incompletive aspect is marked by a particle plus a prefix in Tzotzil. These may be combined by a phonological rule to ch-, e.g., ta x-bat > ch-bat.
14. Tzotzil also uses cross-referencing between prefix and suffix for 1p plurals.

15. Tzotzil has different morphemes for first person plural inclusive (including speaker, hearer, and others) vs. exclusive (including speaker and hearer, but excluding others).
16. All of the morphology in this chapter should be able to be handled by constraint-based or process-based theories. See Lahiri (this volume) for discussion of the theoretical distinction.
17. Production studies with data from bilingual subjects will be have an especially important contribution in this area of study.

REFERENCES

Aissen, J. (1987). *Tzotzil clause structure*. Dordrecht, The Netherlands: Reidel.

Aronoff, M. (1994). *Morphology by itself*. Cambridge, MA: MIT Press.

Badecker, W., & Caramazza, A. (1989). A lexical distinction between inflection and derivation. *Linguistic Inquiry, 20*, 108–116.

Butterworth, B. (1983). Lexical representation. In B. Butterworth (Ed.), *Language production* (Vol. 2, pp. 257–294). London: Academic Press.

Butterworth, B. (1989). Lexical access in speech production. In W. Marslen-Wilson (Ed.), *Lexical representation and process*. Cambridge, MA: MIT Press.

Bybee, J. (1985). *Morphology: A study of the relation between meaning and form*. Amsterdam: John Benjamins Publishing Company.

Croft, W. (1990). *Typology and universals*. Cambridge, UK: Cambridge University Press.

Cutler, A., Hawkins, J., & Gilligan, C. (1985). The suffixing preference. *Linguistics, 23*, 723–758.

Dell, G.S. (1986). A spreading-activation theory of retrieval in sentence production. *Psychological Review, 93*, 283–321.

Dell, G.S., & O'Seaghdha, P.G. (1992). Stages of lexical access in language production. *Cognition, 42*, 287–314.

Dixon, R. (1972). *The Dyirbal language of West Queensland*. Cambridge, UK: Cambridge University Press.

Frauenfelder, U., & Schreuder, R. (1992). Constraining psycholinguistic models of morphological processing and representation: The role of productivity. In G. Booij & J. van Marle (Eds.), *Yearbook of morphology 1991*. Dordrecht, The Netherlands: Foris.

Friederici, A. (1982). Syntactic and semantic processes in aphasic deficits: The availability of prepositions. *Brain and Language, 18*, 249–258.

Fromkin, V.A. (1971). The non-anomalous nature of anomalous utterances. *Language, 47*, 27–52.

Garrett, M. (1980). Levels of processing in sentence production. In B. Butterworth (Ed.), *Language production* (Vol. 1, pp. 177–220). London: Academic Press.

Greenberg, J.H. (1954). A quantitative approach to the morphological typology of languages. In R. Spencer (Ed.), *Method and perspective in anthropology*. Minneapolis, MN: University of Minnesota Press.

Hankamer, J. (1989). Morphological parsing and the lexicon. In W. Marslen-Wilson (Ed.), *Lexical representation and process*. Cambridge, MA: MIT Press.

Jaeger, J., Lockwood, A., Kemmerer, D., Van Valin, R., Murphy, B., & Khalak, H. (1996). A positron emission tomographic study of regular and irregular verb morphology in English. *Language, 72*, 451–497.

Kari, J. (1992). Some concepts in Ahtna Athabaskan word formation. In M. Aronoff (Ed.), *Morphology now*. Albany, NY: State University of New York Press.

Katamba, F. (1993). *Morphology*. New York: St Martin's Press.

Levelt, W.J.M. (1989). *Speaking: From intention to articulation*. Cambridge, MA: MIT Press.

Levelt, W.J.M. (1992). Accessing words in speech production: Stages, processes and representations. *Cognition, 42*, 1–22.

Levin, J. (1985). *A metrical theory of syllabicity*. Unpublished doctoral dissertation, MIT, Cambridge, MA.

Li, C., & Thompson, S. (1990). Chinese. In B. Comrie (Ed.), *The world's major languages*. New York: Oxford University Press.

Lukatela, G., Gligorijevic, B., Kostic, A., & Turvey, M.T. (1980). Representation of inflected nouns in the internal lexicon. *Memory and Cognition, 8*, 415–423.

Marslen-Wilson, W., Tyler, L., Waksler, R., & Older, L. (1994). Morphology and meaning in the English mental lexicon. *Psychological Review, 101*, 3–33.

McCarthy, J. (1981). A prosodic theory of nonconcatenative morphology. *Linguistic Inquiry, 12*, 373–418.

McCarthy, J., & Prince, A. (1990). Foot and word in prosodic morphology. *Natural Language and Linguistic Theory, 8*, 209–283.

Mutaka, N., & Hyman, L. (1990). Syllables and morpheme integrity in Kinande reduplication. *Phonology, 7*, 73–119.

Myers-Scotton, C. (1993). *Duelling languages*. Oxford, UK: Oxford University Press.

Niemi, J., Laine, M., & Tuominen, J. (1994). Cognitive morphology in Finnish: Foundations of a new model. *Language and Cognitive Processes, 9*, 423–446.

Pinker, S., & Prince, A. (1991). Regular and irregular morphology and the psychological status of rules of grammar. *Berkeley Linguistics Society, 17*, 230–251.

Roelofs, A., & Meyer, A.S. (1998). Metrical structure in planning the production of spoken words. *Journal of Experimental Psychology: Learning, Memory, and Cognition, 24*(4), 922–939.

Sandler, W. (1993). Sign language and modularity. *Lingua, 89*, 315–351.

Sandra, D. (1994). The morphology of the mental lexicon. In D. Sandra & M. Taft (Eds.), *Morphological structure, lexical representation and lexical access* (pp. 227–269). Hillsdale, NJ: Lawrence Erlbaum Associates Inc.

Segui, J., & Zubizarreta, J. (1985). Mental representation of morphologically complex words and lexical access. *Linguistics, 23*, 759–774.

Stemberger, J.P. (1985). *The lexicon in a model of language production*. New York: Garland Publishing.

Taft, M., & Forster, K. (1975). Lexical storage and retrieval of prefixed words. *Journal of Verbal Learning and Verbal Behavior, 14*, 635–647.

Waksler, R. (1999). Cross-linguistic evidence for morphological representation in the mental lexicon. *Brain and Language, 68*, 68–74.

Woolford, E. (1997). Four-way case systems: Ergative, nominative, objective, and accusative. *Natural Language and Linguistic Theory, 15*, 181–227.

Zhou, X., & Marslen-Wilson, W. (1994). Words, morphemes, and syllables in the Chinese mental lexicon. *Language and Cognitive Processes, 9*, 393–422.

CHAPTER NINE

Generating prosodic structure

Linda Wheeldon
School of Psychology, University of Birmingham, UK

INTRODUCTION

Research into speech production processes tends to divide into two main fields: research focusing on the generation of syntactic structure and research focusing on the generation of phonological form. While the former (not surprisingly) investigates the generation of whole utterances (Ferreira, this volume; Kempen & Hoenkamp, 1987), early models of phonological encoding have focused on the generation of single words (Dell, 1986, 1988). However, limiting the study of sound-form generation to single words means that a wide range of phonological phenomena that occur in connected speech production remain unaccounted for. The aim of this chapter is to introduce some of these phenomena and to argue that they arise during the generation of the prosodic (or rhythmic) structure of an utterance. The claim is that, following the generation of the syntactic structure of an utterance, an intervening prosodic structure is generated that groups words into prosodic units and that it is these prosodic units which guide the generation of the phonological form of the utterance.

The structure of this chapter is as follows. I will begin by introducing some speech phenomena that occur only during the production of fluent connected speech and that must be accounted for by any adequate theory of speaking. Many of these phenomena occur across word boundaries and cannot be explained with reference to lexical structure or to the nature of the immediately adjacent speech. Moreover, recent developments in linguistic theory suggest that the supralexical structures of syntactic theories also provide no account for many connected speech phenomena. Instead it has been proposed that many connected speech phenomena arise during the construction of the prosodic representation of an utterance. In the next section I will introduce the theory of the prosodic hierarchy, which divides an utterance into a nested hierarchy of prosodic units. These form the domains of application for many phonological rules (Inkelas & Zec, 1990; Nespor & Vogel, 1986; Selkirk, 1986).

As mentioned previously, most theories of speech production are restricted to explaining the production of single words. I will briefly review these models before discussion a theory of speech production in which prosodic units are given an explicit role. Levelt (1989, 1992) postulates a prosody generator that takes as input metrical information about the selected words, including their number of syllables and their weight (as well as phrasal and syntactic information), and combines them into prosodic units. This model generates a number of predictions concerning the time course of the production of prosody. Levelt, Roelofs, and Meyer (1999; Roelofs, 1997, this volume) present the WEAVER++ model which is a simulated version of aspects of this theory. The following section will review the few experimental studies which provide empirical data directly relevant to the production of prosody. A number of studies have used duration measurements as the independent variable (e.g., Ferreira, 1993; Gee & Grosjean, 1983; Meyer, 1994). These studies tested whether rhythmic structure in spoken sentences (i.e., duration of words and pauses) is best explained in terms of syntactic or prosodic phrasal structure. However, duration studies are limited in what they can tell us about the on-line generation of prosody. If prosodic units are indeed constructed during speech production processes, then it must also be possible to demonstrate effects of this computation on speech production *latencies*. There are a number of findings in the literature that are suggestive of such effects (Eriksen, Pollack, & Montague, 1970; Ferreira, 1991; Sternberg, Monsell, Knoll, & Wright, 1978; Sternberg, Wright, Knoll, & Monsell, 1980; Wheeldon & Lahiri, 1997). The final section will address the question of why we restructure lexical-phonological form into units that need not correspond to the lexical or syntactic units of an utterance. One purpose of this restructuring might be to prepare for articulation by producing strings of fluently pronounceable syllables (Levelt & Wheeldon, 1994). However, prosodic structure serves a number of other functions. Research in the fields of speech perception (Church, 1987; Cutler & Butterfield, 1992; Frauenfelder & Lahiri, 1989; Marslen-Wilson, Tyler, Warren, Grenier, & Lee, 1992; Speer, Crowder, & Thomas, 1993; Warren, Grabe, & Nolan, 1995) and language acquisition (Gerken & Ohala, 1991, this volume; Morgan & Demuth, 1996; Nazzi, Bertoncini, & Mehler, 1998) has begun to develop our understanding of how listeners and language learners make use of the prosodic information in speech.

SOME CONNECTED SPEECH PHENOMENA

Every time we produce the same word, in different contexts, it comes out differently. These differences can be as minor as minuscule alterations in the positioning of our tongue and lips as we produce the same sounds or can involve the articulation of entirely different constituent sounds and syllable structure. In addition, we can produce the same word with very different intonation pattern, duration, and amplitude. These changes are never random. Instead, they occur regularly in certain contexts but not in others. In this section, I will give a brief introduction to the range of connected speech phenomena that can occur. In the following section, a framework for the rules that govern these kinds of phenomena will be described.

Segmental structure

In connected speech the segmental content of words, as they are spoken in isolation, can be altered. In some contexts the nature of certain segments can be changed, in other contexts segments can be lost or added. For example in the following sentence (1a), the word final nasal of the word "ten" is produced as the alveolar /n/ when the word is pronounced in isolation but emerges as the bilabial /m/ in the sentence context given. In sentence (1b), the two-word sequence "do you" can be reduced to a single syllable in certain contexts. Finally, in sentence (1c), the word final /r/ of beer, which does not occur (in many dialects of British English) when the word is spoken in isolation, emerges in the context given. (See Nespor & Vogel, 1986, and Lahiri, this volume, for more examples.)

(1) (a) Change   "te*n* beers please"   [tɛm bɪəz]
     (b) Reduction   "what d*o you* want"   [dʒə]
     (c) Addition   "the bee*r* is cold"   [bɪər]

Syllable structure

The syllable structure of words in connected speech can also be changed such that syllable and word boundaries do not coincide. This restructuring occurs according to the Maximal Onset Principle (Selkirk, 1980). This principle states that, within a certain domain, a vowel will take as many of the consonants preceding it as possible that form a legal syllable onset of the relevant language. Consider the example (2). In each of these sentences a word-final segment resyllabifies to form the onset for the vowel in the following word.

(2) (a) the beer is cold   [bɪə-rɪz]
     (b) he has a cape on   [keɪ-pʰɔn]
     (c) she gave it to me   [geɪ-vɪt]

The Maximal Onset Principle applies throughout the world's spoken languages and evidence for it comes from a number of converging sources. For example, it is possible to see if segments behave like syllable onsets or offsets according to their phonetic structure. Phonetic rules can change the nature of segments in different syllable positions. In English, voiceless plosives like /k/, /p/, and /t/ are unaspirated or unexploded in syllable-final position but aspirated (followed by a small burst of air) when they occur stressed syllable-initially. Thus, in example (2b), the final /p/ of the word "cape" is unaspirated when the word is produced in isolation but becomes aspirated in the context given signalling its change to syllable onset position.

Stress and intonation structure

Words are produced with a particular stress pattern such that one of their syllables is often perceptually more prominent than others. However, the stress pattern of words when produced in isolation can change in some contexts. In example (3), the word-final stress on "kangaroo" becomes word-initial when followed by a stressed syllable.

(3)   kangaroó   →   A kángaroo's life

When a word is produced in context it is also produced within an appropriate rhythmic and intonation structure for the utterance. The rhythm of speech is realised by differences in the amplitude and duration of successive syllables (i.e., their level of stress) as well as the position and duration of periods of silence. Intonation is realised by changes in pitch. Although a given word can be produced with a wide range of absolute levels of stress and intonation, there is, nevertheless, a great deal of regularity in the relative values of these parameters assigned to a given utterance. For example, no speaker of English would produce the sentence, "I ate it", such that all words had equal levels of stress, and were separated by pauses of equal length. Instead there does seem to be a default structure and any deviation from this structure has consequences for the interpretation of the sentence. For example anyone hearing the sentence (4a) with stress on the capitalised word would understand that there was doubt about the person involved. Whereas, the same sentence produced with stress on the final word as in (4b) would indicate that there was doubt about the thing desired (Bartels & Kingston, 1994; Eady & Cooper, 1986; Eady, Cooper, Klouda, Mueller, & Lotts, 1986).

(4)   (a)   YOU want the car?
      (b)   you want the CAR?

Similarly, a great deal of information can be conveyed in the intonation contour that is imposed on an utterance. In English certain illocutionary acts such as making statements and asking questions are typically performed using certain intonation patterns. For example, a falling intonation on the final syllable of sentence (4b) would produce a statement, whereas a rising intonation on the same word would produce a question (Ladd, 1980, 1996).

In summary, a wide range of nonrandom phenomena exist in the sound form of connected speech that must be accounted for by an adequate model of speech production. These include changes in the canonical segmental content and syllable structure of words produced in different contexts, as well as changes in their stress and intonation patterns.

THE PROSODIC HIERARCHY

Recently, it has been argued that the phenomena described in the previous section arise during the generation of the prosodic (or rhythmic) structure of an utterance. The claim is that, following the generation of the syntactic structure of an utterance, an intervening prosodic structure is generated that groups words into prosodic units and that it is these prosodic units that guide the generation of the phonological form of the utterance. Prosodic theory has been developed by phonologists over the previous 20 years (Hayes, 1989; Inkelas & Zec, 1990; Nespor & Vogel, 1986; Selkirk, 1981, 1995). According to prosodic phonology, an utterance is divided into a nested hierarchy of units such that the units on a particular level are completely subsumed by the units at the level above and an utterance is exhaustively parsed at each level of prosodic units (see Figure 9.1). The smallest prosodic units are the mora, the syllable, and the foot.

The grouping of mora and syllables into feet is responsible for the rhythmic patterns of words in a language. However, because I am concerned with connected speech I'll limit myself to those prosodic units that are applicable to multiword utterances (see Chapters 7 and 10 of this volume for more on syllables and feet). The remaining units in the original prosodic hierarchy proposed by Selkirk (1981) are illustrated in Figure 9.1. In this hierarchy, an utterance (U), is divided into intonational phrases (IP), which divide into phonological phrases

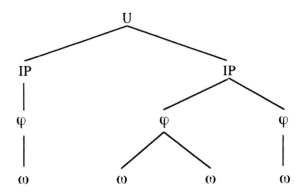

On tuesday   he measured   durations   carefully

Figure 9.1.   The prosodic hierarchy.

(φ), which in turn divide into phonological words (ω). Over the years several additional units have been proposed, including the clitic group above the phonological word (Hayes, 1989; Nespor & Vogel, 1986) and the splitting of the phonological phrase into major and minor components (Selkirk, 1986). However, my aim here is to give an introduction to the theory rather than an exhaustive account of it and I will restrict myself to the original units, all of which survive in a similar form in most current versions of the theory. For a detailed theoretical summary see Shattuck-Hufnagel and Turk (1996).

The prosodic hierarchy is a theory of domains, that is, each prosodic constituent serves as the domain of application of phonological rules and phonetic processes. The principles that define prosodic constituents draw on morphological, syntactic, and semantic information but, importantly, if a new level of representation is to be motivated, these constituents are not necessarily isomorphic with the constituents of these other domains. The arguments have mainly focused on the inability of syntactic domains to provide an account of many of these phenomena. For example, a phonological rule like voicing assimilation, which is common in natural languages of the world, does not apply *only* to noun phrases or applies in all syntactic phrases *except* prepositional phrases (see Lahiri, this volume, for a detailed discussion). An even stronger motivation for phonological constituents is that syntactic bracketing may not be the same as that required by phonology. The strong claim is that there exists a class of phonological rules which apply only to prosodic constituents and have no direct access to syntactic information about an utterance (Nespor & Vogel, 1986; see also Lahiri, this volume, for examples of these and other phonological rules). In what follows, I will discuss each unit of the prosodic hierarchy in turn and provide examples of phonological rules which operate within their domain.

The phonological word (ω)

The smallest unit in the prosodic hierarchy that can be larger than a word is the phonological word. The phonological word is minimally a stressed foot, such as (5a), and maximally a single lexical word combined with any associated unstressed function words such as auxiliaries, determiners, conjunctions, and prepositions (Booij & Lieber, 1993; Gussenhoven, 1989; Lahiri, Jongman, & Sereno, 1990; Selkirk, 1986, 1995).

In English, non-phrase-final unstressed items usually attach rightwards. This process is called cliticisation. Selkirk (1995) argues that these clitics are attached to a lexical phonological word but do not become part of one giving the following structure $[clitic[Lex]_\omega]_\phi$ for example (5b) and (5c) (but see Hayes, 1989; Nespor & Vogel, 1986). Clitics can, however also attach leftwards. This is called encliticisation and can occur in examples like (5d) where the final pronoun is cliticised to the preceding phonological word as $[[hit]_\omega \text{ 'm}]_\omega]_\phi$. Here the clitic attaches to the verb and becomes part of the phonological word.

(5) (a) jumping
     (b) for always
     (c) the day
     (d) hit him

Phonological word formation most often involves function words such as auxiliaries, pronouns, and conjunctions. If that is so, one might ask why we need to refer to constituents such as phonological words and not remain with the distinction of content words vs. function words. The reason is that a function word can also be a full phonological word. Under certain circumstances, a function word can bear stress and can therefore be minimally a foot and thereby a phonological word. For example, in some utterances a function word can receive focus, as in "I *can* eat it". Under no circumstances would a focused function word be cliticised to an adjoining word: It must be full a prosodic word. Thus, a content/function word distinction is insufficient to capture the grouping of a syntactic string into phonological words. Moreover a phonological word is not necessarily identical to any syntactic constituent like a noun phrase.

In a number of languages, the phonological word is the domain of syllabification. Consider these example sentences for Dutch (Wheeldon & Lahiri, 1997) and English where phonological word structure is given by the brackets.

(6) (a) [Ik heb een]$_\omega$ [laars]$_\omega$ [aan]$_\omega$ [laːrs-aːn]
           I have a   boot   on
     (b) [Ik heb een]$_\omega$ [laars te]$_\omega$ [koop]$_\omega$ [laːr-stə]
           I have a   boot to   sell

(7) (a) [he threw]$_\omega$ [a cape on]$_\omega$ [keɪ-pʰɔn]
     (b) [he threw]$_\omega$ [a cape]$_\omega$ [ON]$_\omega$ [keɪp-ʔɔn]

In sentence (6a) the final word *aan* comprises a heavy syllable which attracts stress and forms its own phonological word. In sentence (6b), however, the adverb *te* (to) is usually destressed and cliticises to the preceding noun *laars* (boot) to form a single phonological word (Lahiri et al., 1990). Within this phonological word, the final /s/ of *laars* resyllabifies to form the onset of the second syllable /ste/ (following the maximal onset principle; Selkirk, 1984). In sentence (6a), however, the phonological word boundary intervening between *laars* and *aan* prevents a similar resyllabification to *laar–saan*. Similarly, in English, in sentence (7a), the final preposition is destressed and cliticises to the preceding noun *cape*, to form a single phonological word. The rule of syllabification then applies across this unit such that the final /p/ of cape forms the onset of the following syllable. In sentence (7b) the preposition *on* receives focus and become a phonological word in its own right and the resyllabification of /p/ is blocked.

The phonological phrase (φ)

Phonological words combine to form phonological phrases up to and including the heads of syntactic phrases, which are nouns, verbs, or adjectives (e.g., sentence 8a). But phonological phrases are not necessarily identical to syntactic phrases. Other kinds of nonsyntactic information can influence their construction. For example, discourse information which gives focus to a word can cause a PP boundary to be placed immediately following the stressed word (as in sentence 8b). The length of the syntactic phrase is also important. Long syntactic phrases will also tend to be divided into more than one phonological phrase (sentence 8c).

(8) (a) [the happy man]$_φ$ [hugged his friend]$_φ$
     (b) [the happy man]$_φ$ [*hugged*]$_φ$ [his friend]$_φ$
     (c) [the happy man]$_φ$ [*hugged*]$_φ$ [his very best friend]$_φ$

Like the phonological word the phonological phrase is the domain of a number of phonological rules. I will restrict myself to one example. The English Rhythm Rule is a well-studied phenomenon which resolves the clash of two equally stressed syllables across words by shifting the main stress of a word demoting the main stress to secondary stress. The application of this rule is illustrated in the example sentences (9a–d), all of which comprise a single phonological phrase. The acute accent denotes main stress and the grave accent indicates secondary stress.

(9) (a) *phònológical*:   [I prefer a phónològical prócesses]$_φ$ [Adj+Noun]
     (b) *isomórphic*:   [It is not ísomòrphic with sýntax]$_φ$ [Adj+Prep Phrase]
     (c) *hìerárchically*: [This is híeràrchically órganised]$_φ$ [Adv+Verb]
     (d) *èvidéntly*:   [It is not évidèntly hím]$_φ$ [Adv+Pronoun]

As can be seen from these few examples, the rhythm rule can occur across many types of syntactic categories. There is no coherence regarding the type of syntactic phrase. We could perhaps say that the rhythm rule applies when a modifier precedes the head within a major syntactic phrase, but also if the head is fol-lowed by a complement (as in verb+prepositional phrase). But even this is not enough because as noted by many scholars, there is a constraint depending on whether the complement branches or not (Hayes, 1989; Nespor & Vogel, 1986). For instance, in the next examples, the rhythm rule applies in sentences (10a) and (11a) but not in sentences (10b) and (11b).

(10) (a) [She could not tolerate the nótoriety of bánkruptcy]$_\varphi$
       (b) [She could not tolerate the nòtoríety]$_\varphi$ [of bánkruptcy and divorce]$_\varphi$

(11) (a) [Given the chance rabbits réprodùce quíckly]$_\varphi$
       (b) [Given the chance rabbits reprodúce]$_\varphi$ [véry quickly]$_\varphi$

There are two points to be made from these examples. First the rhythm rule applies to several types of syntactic phrases, and, second, the rule is sometimes sensitive to the branchingness of the complement. Constraining the rule by describing the environment of the rule in terms of syntactic bracketing would not capture any generalisation at all. Instead, we could translate the various syntactic phenomena into a single unit by a phonological phrasing algorithm of English like the following (based on Hayes, 1989):

> In a configuration [... X° Y$_p$ ...] (a) an X° category would incorporate all other elements to the left of it within a P-phrase [φ]; Y$_p$ may be incorporated into the same [φ] if it does not branch.

Now the rule can be stated simply as applying within, but not across, phonological phrase boundaries.

The intonational phrase (I)

Phonological phrases combine to form intonational phrases. The intonational phrase is the largest prosodic unit within an utterance and is the domain over which intonation contours are planned. As with phonological phrases, syntactic factors play a role in the formation of intonational phrases as intonational phrase boundaries tend to coincide with the boundaries of major syntactic units. However, intonational phrases are also units of meaning or sense units within an utterance. In addition, semantic factors related to prominence, and performance factors such as rate of speech and style can affect the number of intonational phrases an utterance contains. Thus, there is a large degree of variability in the kinds of structures that can be intonational phrases and many utterances demonstrate a noncorrespondence between syntactic constituents and the domains of intonation contours. For example consider the embedded sentence under (12). The repeating syntactic unit is given by the bracketing in (12a), but the intonational structure is better represented by the bracketing in (12b) (Nespor & Vogel, 1986).

(12) (a) this is [$_{NP}$the cat that caught [$_{NP}$the rat that stole [$_{NP}$the cheese]]]
       (b) [this is the cat]$_I$ [that caught the rat]$_I$ [that stole the cheese]$_I$

However, there are some constructions that always seem to form intonational domains. Examples of some these are given in the next sentences: parenthetical expressions (13a), nonrestrictive relative clauses (13b), tag questions (13c), and expletives (13d).

(13)   (a)   Penguins [as you know]$_I$ can't fly.
       (b)   My dad[who loves a joke]$_I$.
       (c)   He's a nice guy [isn't he]$_I$.
       (d)   [Bloody Hell]$_I$ put that down.

Nespor and Vogel (1986) argue that these kinds of expressions *obligatorily* form intonational phrases and that, although they differ in form, they are all strings that are in some way external to the sentence they are associated with.

Intonational phrases, like other prosodic constituents, have only one main strong syllable. The position of the strong syllable of an intonational phrase varies and it cannot be structurally specified. It is determined by semantic factors such as focus and given and new information (semantic prominence). The assignment of stress within an intonational phrase depends on material found in previous utterances or on shared knowledge of a given situation that is not necessarily present in the linguistic context of the utterance in question. The strong syllable within an IP is called the nucleus and it is preceded (optionally) by a head and followed (optionally) by a tail. The nucleus is the element of high interest in the utterance—the one that should capture the interest of the listener. The head or prenuclear tune is less prominent than the nucleus and often contains given information in the conversation to which the focused nuclear information is to be added.

As with the other constituents of the prosodic hierarchy already discussed, the intonational phrase also forms the domain for a number of segmental rules. Nespor and Vogel (1986) discuss a number of sandhi rules for which the domain of application is the intonational phrase. For example, in Tuscan Italian the Goria Toscana (GT) rule changes the voiceless stops /p, t, k/ into the corresponding fricatives /ɸ, θ, h/ when they occur between [−consonantal] segments. This rule can apply within and across words but is blocked by an intonational phrase boundary.

The utterance (U)

This is the largest unit in the prosodic hierarchy and comprises at least a full grammatical sentence. However, it often applies to strings of words that are not generally recognised as sentences, such as "at five" and "over there", and may span more than one sentence, as has been argued by Nespor and Vogel (1986), Odden (1980), Selkirk (1980), and others.

An example of a phonological rule that takes the utterance as its domain of application is flapping in American English (Nespor & Vogel, 1986). This rule changes the alveolar stops /t/ and /d/ to the flap /ɾ/ when they occur between vowels. The rule can apply within words, e.g., (14a), and between words in a sentence, e.g., (14b).

(14)   (a)   water   →   wa[ɾ]er
       (b)   My brother bought a parrot last week   →   bough[ɾ]

The flapping rule occurs across any type of syntactic constituent. It is blocked only when a pause or interruption is introduced following the critical segment. Any rule that predicts the occurrence of flapping must define its domain of application and there are no syntactic boundaries defining domains that can do this. Thus, Nespor and Vogel (1986) argue that the utterance is the domain of this rule.

In summary, the domains of the prosodic hierarchy provide a structure for the application of rules that account for many of the segmental, stress, and intonational phenomena that occur during the production of connected speech. In the following section we will consider one model of speech production which postulates a process for the generation of prosodic structure.

PSYCHOLINGUISTIC MODELS OF SPEECH PRODUCTION

As mentioned in the Introduction, most work in the field of word-form encoding has focused on the production of single words. Most current models of word-form encoding make similar suggestions as to the levels of representation and processes involved (Dell, 1986, 1988; Garrett, 1980; Levelt, 1989, 1992; Levelt et al., 1999; Levelt & Wheeldon, 1994; Roelofs, 1997, this volume; Shattuck-Hufnagel, 1987, 1992; Stemberger, 1985; Wheeldon & Levelt, 1995). This standard model is discussed in detail by Meyer in Chapter 3 of this volume so I will be brief.

First, the morphemic/lexical representation associated to the activated (or selected) semantic/syntactic representation is activated. Activation (or selection) of this representation makes available two further types of form information: (a) the word's constituent phonemes, and (b) a frame for the shape of the word. A number of frame structures have been proposed: syllables (Dell, 1986), CVC slots (Dell, 1988), words (Shattuck-Hufnagel, 1987), and phonological words (Levelt, 1992). Whatever the proposed frame, a process is postulated that assigns the word's constituent phonemes to their positions in the frame. Various misfunctionings of this assignment process have been used to account for phonological speech errors (Dell, 1986, 1988; Shattuck-Hufnagel, 1987, 1992; Stemberger, 1985). Most models of speech production have been designed to explain how such errors occur. Despite the success of these models in explaining speech error data, the processes they postulate seem somewhat bizarre. Why take apart the form and content of the stored representation of a word simply in order to put it back together again—sometimes incorrectly? Levelt (1989, 1992) has argued that the motivation for this process was the production of connected speech. Given the vast number of possible articulatory tokens for a given word in different contexts, it is extremely unlikely that they each have individual stored representations. It is more likely that we store some abstract representation from which all the possible articulatory tokens can be computed by rule. (See Lahiri, this volume, for ideas about the underlying representations involved.) Levelt (1989, 1992) proposes a theory in which prosodic units are given an explicit role. He postulates a prosody generator that takes input from a number of sources and outputs prosodic units. According to Levelt, prosody generation requires information from three sources:

- The output from the grammatical encoder which is the unfolding surface syntactic structure of the utterance along with pointers to representations in the form lexicon.
- Phonological form information which has two aspects. First, the citation metrical structure of the words to be produced and, second, their segmental content.
- "Intonational meaning", which provides information about the illocutionary force of the utterance and of the emotions and attitudes of the speaker. This information has consequences for global aspects of the intonation pattern—for example, a high baseline pitch to express excitement.

The prosody generator uses the information from all components to restructure the citation metrical pattern of the retrieved word forms. A new metrical grid for the whole utterance is constructed (i.e., cliticisation, resyllabification, etc.), to which the segments are then attached in a left-to-right manner. The output from the prosody generator specifies for each successive syllable frame its duration, its amplitude, and its contribution to the pitch contour. As the segments for each syllable node are associated, they are used to retrieve stored syllable-sized, articulatory routines (following Crompton, 1982). When the articulatory routines for the entire phonological word have been retrieved, the phonetic plan is passed on to the articulator and is executed. Levelt et al. (1999; Roelofs, 1997, this volume) present the WEAVER++ model, which simulates at least part of this theory.

To summarise, there are three main claims that Levelt (1989, 1992) makes regarding the generation of prosody. Firstly, Levelt proposes that processing at all levels occurs in an incremental fashion. This requires that processing can occur from left to right in an utterance with minimal lookahead, i.e., what a processor is doing with a particular fragment of an utterance should not be dependent on information available in later fragments of the utterance. For example, intoning the first few syllables of a sentence should not be dependent on how the sentence will end. Secondly, for Levelt, the phonological word is the unit of phonological encoding. For example, to produce the sentence "I gave it to him", the citation form information of these words will be retrieved and restructured to form one phonological word with one main stress and a quite different syllable structure, e.g., /aɪ géɪ vɪ tɪm/. Thirdly, Levelt makes another claim concerning phonological words—that they are the minimal unit of articulation. In other words, during the production of connected speech the articulator waits until a whole phonological word has been constructed before beginning articulation. In the following section I review the experimental evidence available to test these claims.

GENERATING PROSODIC STRUCTURE: EXPERIMENTAL EVIDENCE

Few experimental studies provide empirical data directly relevant to the production of prosody. A number of studies have used duration measurements as the independent variable (e.g., Ferreira, 1993; Gee & Grosjean, 1983). These studies tested whether rhythmic structure in spoken sentences (i.e., duration of words and pauses) is best explained in terms of syntactic or prosodic phrasal structure. The tool used was the phenomena of phrase-final lengthening. Cooper and Paccia-Cooper (1980) found that a word and its following pause tend to have longer durations at the end of a syntactic phrase than in any other phrasal position. Thus, the word "black" and its following pause are longer in sentence (15a) than sentence (15b).

(15) (a)   The table that I thought was *black* tempted me
      (b)   The *black* table tempted me

However, more recently a number of studies have demonstrated that word and pause durations are predicted more successfully by a hierarchical prosodic representation than by a syntactic representation. In the previous example prosodic and syntactic structure are confounded. In the first sentence, the word "black" is at the end of both a subject-noun phrase and a phonological phrase. In the second sentence, "black" is the middle of both the syntactic and phonological phrase. Ferreira (1993) used contrastive stress in order to vary prosodic structure while keeping syntactic structure constant. For example, in sentences under (16), placing contrastive stress on "girl" results in the addition of a phonological phrase boundary immediately following it.

(16) (a)   [The girl left the room]$_\varphi$
      (b)   [The *girl*]$_\varphi$ [left the room]$_\varphi$

One problem with this method is that the word "girl" in both sentences is not matched for stress and duration. However, Ferreira found that not only the word but also its following pause was longer in the second version of the sentence. In another experiment syntactic structure was varied while prosodic structure was held constant.

(17) (a)   [The [friendliest]$_{Adj}$ [cop]$_{NP}$ saw the enterprising girls
      (b)   [The man [who's [[[a cop]$_{NP}$]$_{VP}$]$_S$]$_{S\text{-}bar}$]$_{NP}$ saw the enterprising girls
      (c)   [[[The [friendliest]$_w$ [cop]$_w$]$_\varphi$]$_{IP}$ saw the enterprising girls
      (d)   [[[The man]$_w$ [who's a cop]$_w$]$_\varphi$]$_{IP}$] saw the enterprising girls

In sentence (17a) the word "cop" is at the end of one syntactic constituent. In sentence (17b) it is at the end of five syntactic constituents. In contrast, the prosodic structures in (17c) and (17d) are identical. No significant difference was found between the two sentence types in the duration of "cop" or the pause following it.

   Ferreira explains her data in terms of an indirect model of the relationship between syntax and phonetic form, i.e., that while syntax can affect the generation of prosodic structure, only prosodic structure can affect phonetic form. Another finding allowed Ferreira to argue that the generation of prosodic structure is also independent of information about the segmental content of the words to be produced. In this experiment subjects produced sentences including words with long or short phonetic durations (as in 18a and 18b respectively).

(18) (a)   The table I thought was *green* tempted me
      (b)   The table I thought was *black* tempted me

Ferreira discovered that pauses were longer following short words like *black* than following long words like *green*. Interestingly, however, the total duration of word and pause was almost identical. Ferreira argued that the duration of a slot is calculated without knowledge of the segmental structure of the syllable that will fill it. Thus, a long syllable will be followed by a short pause to fill the slot assigned whereas a short word will require a longer pause. Ferreira goes on to propose a mechanism that predicts the phonetic durations of words and pauses in different prosodic structures. Her mechanism utilises a version of metrical grid theory (Liberman & Prince, 1977; Selkirk, 1984), according to which the rhythmic pattern of an utterance can be represented by a two-dimensional grid, such as in example (19).

(19)
```
                              x
                              x
              x               x
              x               x
              x               x
      x       x               x
      x      xxx            xxxxx
   [[[[the   child]w]φ  [[slept]w]φ]IP]U
```

The relative stress level of each syllable is encoded by the vertical axes such that the higher the column the more prominent a syllable is. Syllable duration is represented on the horizontal axes where each "x" represents an abstract timing unit. Ferreira claims that syllables obtain additional timing units when they occur at the edge of a prosodic constituent. Thus, the more prosodic boundaries that occur at the right edge of a syllable the more timing units it gets. Ferreira's model assigns each abstract timing unit a fixed duration (dependent on speech rate) and assumes that the total determines the duration of the syllable's "slot", i.e., the time between its onset and the onset of the following syllable. The duration of the syllable to be produced in the slot is then calculated based on the number and kinds of segments it comprises with some additional lengthening which is a fixed proportion of the duration of its slot. Finally, a pause is inserted to fill any remaining slot time.

Meyer (1994) tested Ferreira's theory in a series of experiments in Dutch. She systematically varied the segmental length of the vowels, onsets, and codas of monosyllabic words (see 20):

(20)   (a)   vowel   De groene *boon*/*bon* kleeft aan het bord
                    (The green bean/ticket stuck to the plate)
       (b)   onset   De rijke *boer*/*broer* koopt de gele bus
                    (The rich farmer/brother bought a yellow bus)
       (c)   coda   De houten *balk*/*bak* plonst in de vijver
                    (The wooden beam/tank fell into the pond)

Although Meyer (1994) also observed compensation between word duration and the length of the following pause, this compensation was not observed in all conditions and was only partial. She found that pause durations were affected by the length of the vowel and offset but not by the length of the onset. In addition, however, pause durations were shown to be affected by the length of the onset of the following word. In all conditions where compensation was observed, shorter words were followed by longer pauses and longer words were followed by shorter pauses. However, compensation was always partial such that total slot length also varied. Thus, slot length in these experiments was not independent of segmental content. Moreover slot length was affected by the segmental content of the following word. In Meyer's data the domain of compensation was vowel to vowel. Meyer suggests that the compensatory effect might not occur during phonological encoding but might occur during later articulatory processes. She argues that this may be an effect due to the tendency to produce vowels at regular intervals (Fowler, 1983).

The duration studies summarised here have provided good evidence that prosodic structures are generated during speech production. However, duration studies are limited in what they can tell us about the on-line generation of prosody. If prosodic units are indeed constructed during speech production processes, then it must also be possible to demonstrate effects of this computation on speech production *latencies*. Until recently, few studies have looked directly at this issue; however, one finding exists in the literature that may be attributable to the generation of prosodic structure.

Sternberg et al. (1978, 1980) used a prepared speech production task to investigate the retrieval and execution of stored motor programs. They presented subjects with random lists of one to six letters or digits or words. Subjects were given a few seconds to prepare to say the list as quickly and as fluently as possible as soon as they heard the go signal. Sternberg et al. then examined the effect of the number of words in the list on the temporal patterns of its production. The main result of interest here was that the latency to begin producing the list was found to increase linearly with list length, that is, the longer the list the longer it takes you to begin to say it. Interestingly the addition of unstressed words into a list did not alter the slope of the latency function they observed. In other words, the slope for the list BAY RUM MARK was the same as the slope for the list BAY AND RUM AND MARK.

Sternberg et al. concluded that production latencies in their task were a function not of the number of words in a list but of the number of stress groups—a stress group was defined as a unit of speech associated with one stressed syllable. Now this stress group looks very much like a phonological word. However, there is a problem with this work when it comes to relating it to normal sentence production. The bulk of the experiments examined list production. Lists have no syntactic structure and a very flat prosodic structure. They tend to consist of a series of concatenated intonational phrases. Because they have no structure its impossible to tell which unit is causing the effect. In addition, most of the results come from six highly trained subjects who received weeks of practice and were speaking as rapidly as possible, which also makes it difficult to relate the results to normal speech production processes. Monsell (1986) reports a series of experiments comparing the production of lists and sentence materials (e.g., *Barbara, Trixi, Arthur, Reuben, Dean*, and *Barbara tricks a rather rueful Dean*). The results for both types of materials are reported as being almost identical. However, the example sentence given is somewhat unusual and may also have elicited a list intonation prosodic structure.

Wheeldon and Lahiri (1997) used a technique similar to Sternberg et al. (1978) to examine the production of prosody directly. They looked for an effect on prepared sentence production latencies of the number of phonological words when number of syllables, syntactic words, and syntactic structure were held constant. The experiments were conducted in Dutch and made use of the processes of cliticisation. The cliticisations used were always leftwards (Berendsen, 1986; Booij & Lieber, 1993; Gussenhoven, 1989; Lahiri et al., 1990). In Dutch the cliticisation induces phonological word formation and has the following structure: $[[\text{Lex}]_\omega \text{ clitic}]_\omega]_\varphi$. The examples in (21) illustrate this cliticisation process.

(21) (a)   Ik [[[zoek]$_\omega$ het]$_\omega$]$_\varphi$ water   (I seek the water)
     (b)   Ik [[[drink]$_\omega$ de]$_\omega$]$_\varphi$ wijn   (I drink the wine)
     (c)   Ik [[[trap]$_\omega$ te]$_\omega$]$_\varphi$ hard   (I kick too hard)

The first experiment tested the delayed production of three sentence types, shown in (22).

(22) (a)   Ik [zoek het]$_\omega$ [water]$_\omega$ (I seek the water)
     (b)   Ik [zoek]$_\omega$ [vers]$_\omega$ [water]$_\omega$ (I seek fresh water)
     (c)   Ik [zoek]$_\omega$ [water]$_\omega$ (I seek water)

Sentence types (22a) and (22b) are matched for number of syntactic words, syntactic structure, and number of syllables. They differ, however, in their number of phonological words. In (22a) the word *het* is destressed and cliticises to the verb becoming a single phonological word that cuts across syntactic and phrasal structure. In contrast, in (22b) *vers* is stressed and forms an independent phonological word. If the latency effect is a function of the number of phonological words, then the latency to produce the clitic sentences like (22a) should be faster than the latency to produce the nonclitic sentences like (22b). Note, however, that the initial phonological word in the clitic sentences, e.g., [zoek het], has one more syllable than the initial phonological word in (22b), i.e., [Ik zoek]. It is possible therefore that any difference in latency due to number of phonological words may be reduced by an opposite effect due to the complexity of the initial phonological word to be retrieved. Therefore sentences of type (22c) were also included. These sentences are matched to (22a) for total number of phonological words but, like (22b) have only one syllable in the initial phonological word. Any effect of the length of the initial phonological word should be observable in a latency difference between (22a) and (22c).

In contrast to the procedure of Sternberg et al. (1978) a large number of relatively untrained subjects were tested and a more natural question–answer task was used to elicit the experimental sentences. All sentences were elicited from subjects using a question answer technique. Subjects read a noun phrase (e.g., vers water, fresh water) and then heard a question (e.g., "wat zoek je?"— "what do you seek?"). They then had approximately 4 seconds to fully prepare their response which they produced on cue. Production latencies for sentences comprising three phonological words were a significant 14 ms longer than for sentences comprising two phonological words. This 14 ms effect is similar in size to the slope of the Sternberg et al. (1978, 1980) function. In contrast, production latencies in the two two phonological word conditions did not differ.

Wheeldon and Lahiri's (1997) results provide evidence in favour of Levelt's (1989, 1992) claim that the phonological word is the unit of phonological encoding. But what of Levelt's claim that the phonological word is the minimal unit of articulation? In support of this claim Levelt (1989) sites the "syllable latency effect", which refers to the finding that the time taken to initiate production of a visually presented word increases with the number of syllables it contains (Eriksen et al., 1970). Latencies for three-syllable words (e.g., *cabinet*) were, on avererage, 23 ms longer than for one-syllable words (e.g., *cab*). This effect has been replicated using a digit reading task (e.g., 27 took longer than 26; Klapp, 1974) ruling out the possibility that the syllable latency effect could be due to perceptual factors to do with processing the number of letters in the word. A similar effect has been shown in picture-naming tasks (Klapp, Anderson, & Berrian, 1973) suggesting further that the effect is located in production rather than perceptual processes (but see Bachoud-Lévi, Dupoux, Cohen, & Mehler, 1998). The syllable latency effect dissapears in a simple reaction time task (Eriksen et al., 1970; Klapp et al., 1973) or when a yes/no categorisation response is required (Klapp et al., 1973). The effect therefore seems to be due to the programming of words rather than their selection and articulation. According to Levelt (1989), only plans for complete phonological words are delivered to the articulator, which must, therefore, wait for the whole phonological word before executing the first syllable's motor program.

However, the experiments reviewed here do not allow us to distinguish between phonological and syntactic words as the minimal unit required before articulation may commence. Wheeldon and Lahiri (1997) tested this claim using exactly the same sentences given in the previous example, but this time in an on-line speech production task. The experimental method was essentially the same as in prepared speech task except that subjects were requested to begin sentence production as soon as they could on hearing the question. In order to measure the sentence construction process, latencies were measured from the onset of the verb in the question. Levelt's model predicts that production latencies should now be a function of the size of the initial phonological word in the utterance rather than the number of phonological words it contains. The results support Levelt's model. In this experiment, production latencies in the clitic sentence condition were significantly longer than in the other two conditions, which did not differ. This finding also provides support for Levelt's claim of incremental processing, as on-line production latencies did not reflect the complexity of the sentence as a whole.

In summary, Levelt's (1989, 1992) main claims regarding the generation of prosodic structure are supported by the available experimental data. However, the claim of incrementality has not yet undergone any strong test. The results of Wheeldon and Lahiri's (1997) on-line experiment do not rule out the possibility of nonincremental generation of prosodic structure. The sentences to be produced were short and the boundaries of all prosodic units larger than the phonological word fell at utterance boundary. Moreover, all sentences were produced with the same declarative intonation pattern. Thus, prosodic encoding of these sentences required minimal processing with regard to larger prosodic structures and to intonation. It is therefore possible that with longer and more complex sentences, effects of whole sentence complexity may be observed in on-line sentence production latency. Lahiri (this volume) discusses data which present a challenge to strictly incremental models of phonological encoding.

THE FUNCTIONS OF PROSODY

So there is evidence that it is prosodic rather than syntactic structures that have consequences for the phonological and phonetic form of speech output. But why do we restructure lexical-phonological form so that sometimes the boundaries of syllabic and prosodic units no longer coincide with those of morphological and syntactic units? One motivation may have to do with articulatory constraints. Perhaps the aim of this restructuring is to generate strings of easily pronounceable syllables (Levelt & Wheeldon, 1994). But what are the consequences of this restructuring for the listener? Surely it must complicate the process of mapping the speech input onto representations in their mental lexicon. In the final two sections I will briefly review research in both speech perception and child language acquisition which investigates the role of prosody in the early stages of language processing. This research suggests that prosodic structure provides important information to the listener and to the language learner that can aid the processing of both lexical and syntactic structure.

Speech perception

As was argued at the beginning of this chapter, the units and structures of the prosodic hierarchy are not isomporphic with those of morphology and syntax (see also Beckman, 1996). Nevertheless both morphological and syntactic information play a role in the generation of prosodic structure. It is therefore possible that aspects of prosody may help in the recovery of both lexical and syntactic information from the speech stream.

A number of studies have shown that prosodic structure can help determine which syntactic structure is assigned to syntactically ambiguous sentences. For example, Nespor and Vogel (1986) carried out a study of 78 syntactically ambiguous Italian sentences for which syntactic differences were reflected in the prosodic structure in different ways or not at all. They demonstrated that successful disambiguation was dependent on a difference at the prosodic level of analysis between the possible interpretations. Speer et al. (1993) showed that prosodic structure determined which syntactic structure was assigned to the following sentences under (23).

(23)   (a)   they are *cooking* apples = NP
       (b)   they are cooking *apples* = VP

However, controversy exists about the exact nature of the role played by prosodic information during syntactic processing (see Cutler, Dahan, & van Donselaar, 1997, for a recent review). For example, it has been claimed that

prosodic information can resolve ambiguities early during the syntactic processing of speech and that prosodic cues to syntactic structure may even override
purely syntactic preferences in the assigning of structure (Marslen-Wilson et al.,
1992; Warren et al., 1995). However, others argue that prosodic information
may support but cannot constrain syntactic interpretation (Watt & Murray, 1996).

Research in speech perception has also shown that many prosodic structures
can provide relevant information for initial levels of processing in speech recognition. Many segmental changes can provide information to the listener about
the structure of the incoming speech signal. Also if we assume that the listener
has implicit knowledge about the phonological and phonetic rules of their language, then many of the changes that occur in connected speech provide clues to
the canonical word structure. Church (1987) proposes a parser that can make use
of allophonic variations in the pronunciation of spoken words to assist in their
identification. For example the parser would always assign an aspirated voiceless stop to a syllable-initial position. Frauenfelder and Lahiri (1989) discuss in
some detail the kinds phonological cues available in connected speech that can
help the listener to recover lost or changed segments in the speech stream. The
basic idea is that the listener has a great deal of knowledge about the phonological and phonetic rules of their language, which guides their parsing of the
incoming speech signal in particular ways. For example, in the reduced form of
the word *potato* (e.g., *p'tato*) the cluster [pt] is illegal in English. This violation
of a phonotactic constraint can be used as a signal for vowel deletion. However,
as with syntactic processing, controversy exists over exactly when certain kinds
of prosodic information play a role in the speech recognition process.

A number of researchers have suggested that prosodic representations form
the access units to the mental lexicon. Mehler, Dommergues, Frauenfelder, and
Segui (1981) demonstrated that sequences of sounds were monitored for faster
by French subjects when they matched the syllable structure of French words
(e.g., *bal*, *bal-con*) than when they did not (*ba*, *bal.con*). They argued that the
syllable was the unit of access to the mental lexicon, i.e., that the speech stream
is first segmented into syllable units prior to lexical access. However, Cutler,
Mehler, Norris, and Segui (1986) failed to replicate this finding using English
subjects monitoring both English and French words. Instead, they argued that
Mehler et al.'s syllable effect was the result of a segmentation strategy for identifying word boundaries and that listeners universally exploit whatever rhythmic
structure characterises their language in order to solve the problem of finding
word boundaries in continuous speech (Cutler, 1996; Cutler, Mehler, Norris, &
Segui, 1992; Cutler & Norris, 1988). For example, Cutler and Butterfield (1992)
argue that English listeners use a stressed syllable segmentation strategy in which
they treat strong syllables as likely to be the initial syllables of new (lexical)
words. The motivation for this strategy comes from the preferred stress pattern
for polysyllabic words in English—which is initial-syllable stress. Cutler and
Butterfield (1992) examined both spontaneous and laboratory induced segmentation errors that involved boundary misperceptions. As can be seen in example

(24), listeners erroneously insert boundaries before strong syllables but delete them before weak syllables.

(24) (a) she'll officially heard as → Sheila Fishley
      (b) how big is it   heard as → how bigoted

French, however, does not exhibit such opposition between strong and weak syllables and adopts a syllable segmentation strategy. Japanese on the other hand has a rhythmic structure based on the mora (a subsyllabic weight unit) and there is evidence for mora-based segmentation in Japanese (e.g., Cutler & Otake, 1994; Otake, Hatano, Cutler, & Mehler, 1993; see Cutler et al., 1997, for a recent review.)

Crucially, the segmentation strategy proposed by Mehler, Cutler, and colleagues is a prelexical process that analyses the speech signal into units (syllables, strong syllables, morae, etc.) prior to lexical access. An alternative view is that such prosodic units are not computed as an intermediate representation between the speech signal and the mental lexicon but that their role is confined to the parsing of the signal following lexical access (Frauenfelder, 1998; Frazier, 1987; Zwitserlood, Schriefers, Lahiri, & van Donselaar, 1993). The Featurally Under-specified Model of speech perception (the FUL model) incorporates a clear division of labour between lexical access and parsing (Lahiri, 1999; Lahiri & Jongman, 1990; Lahiri & Marslen-Wilson, 1991, 1992; Reetz, 1998). According to this model, lexical access is achieved by the direct mapping of phonetic features extracted from the acoustic signal onto the mental lexicon. Following the activation of lexical representations based on featural information, the set of lexical candidates is parsed using stored linguistic information of all types, e.g., semantic, syntactic, morphological, phonological, and prosodic information (see Fitzpatrick-Cole & Wheeldon, in press, for a review).

Language acquisition

Research investigating the role of prosody in child language acquisition has provided evidence that infants are sensitive to prosodic regularities in their native language (Nazzi et al., 1998). Infants will listen longer to speech that has been artificially segmented by pause insertions at the boundaries of syntactic units than to the same speech with pauses inserted phrase-internally (Hirsh-Pasek et al., 1987; Jusczyk et al., 1992). That prosody is important in language acquisition has also received some support from the finding that speech to children (so-called "motherese") has a richer prosodic structure than adult-directed speech (Fernald et al., 1989). There is also evidence that child-directed speech is not only prosodically richer but that it more reliably marks major syntactic units (Jusczyk et al., 1992). This has lead to the proposition that children use prosodic structure to gain access to important syntactic units such as clauses and phrases— the theory of prosodic bootstrapping (see Morgan & Demuth, 1996).

Prosodic information also seems to play a role in early lexical processing. There is evidence that, by 9 months, infants have acquired information about the lexical stress patterns of their language. For example, American infants prefer to listen to words with strong–weak patterns over words with weak–strong patterns (Jusczyk, Cutler, & Redanz, 1993) and also show a preference for stimuli in which pauses precede strong rather than weak syllables (Echols, Crowhurst, & Childers, 1997). Such findings have lead researchers to propose prosody-based speech segmentation strategies in infants similar to the adult strategies discussed in the previous section (Mattys, Jusczyk, Luce, & Morgan, 1999).

There is also evidence that very young children use prosodic units to organise their own utterances. By 10 months of age children will start to babble in rhythms consistent with the prosodic structure of their language (Levitt, 1993; Levitt & Wang, 1991). Moreover, Gerken (1991; Gerken & Ohala, this volume) demonstrates that young children often omit weak syllables in their production of words. However they don't just omit any weak syllables. They omit weak syllables that do not conform to the preferred stress pattern of their language. Thus, in English, children do not omit the word-final weak syllable of words with a strong–weak pattern, e.g., (25a) but frequently omit weak syllables that occur word-initially, e.g., (25b) and (25c).

(25) (a) *ze*bra   Sw
      (b) ba*nana*   wSS   →   nana
      (c) gi*raffe* wS   →   raffe

IN SUMMARY

Most cognitive models of speech production do not attempt to model the processes involved in the production of rhythmic connected speech. However, the development of prosodic theory within the field of theoretical phonology has major consequences for psycholinguistic models of language processing. In recent years experimental research has demonstrated that prosodic structure is generated during the production of connected speech and also plays an important role in language comprehension and language acquisition. Nevertheless, we are only beginning to understand the wealth of information carried by prosodic structure and the processes by which we generate it. The impressive state of current knowledge about single word production must now form the base for a concerted attack on the production of whole utterances.

REFERENCES

Bachoud-Lévi, A.C., Dupoux, E., Cohen, L., & Mehler, J. (1998). Where is the length effect? A cross-linguistic study of speech production. *Journal of Memory and Language, 39,* 331–346.

Bartels, C., & Kingston, J. (1994). Salient pitch cues in the perception of contrastive focus. In *Focus and natural language processing: Proceedings of a conference in celebration of the 10th anniversary of the Journal of Semantics: Vol. 1. Intonation and syntax* (pp. 1–10). Meinhard-Schwebda, Germany.

Beckman, M.E. (1996). The parsing of prosody. *Language and Cognitive Processses, 1,* 17–67.

Berendsen, E. (1986). *The phonology of cliticization.* Dordrecht, The Netherlands: Foris Publications.

Booij, G., & Lieber, R. (1993). On the simultaneity of morphological and prosodic structure. In S. Hargus & E.M. Kaisse (Eds.), *Phonetics and phonology: Vol. IV. Studies in lexical phonology.* San Diego: Academic Press.

Church, K. (1987). Phonological parsing and lexical retrieval. In U. Frauenfelder & L.K. Tyler (Eds.), *Spoken word recognition.* Cambridge, MA: MIT Press.

Cooper, W.E., & Paccia-Cooper, J.M. (1980). *Syntax and speech.* Cambridge, MA: Harvard University Press.

Crompton, A. (1982). Syllables and segments in speech production. In A. Cutler (Ed.), *Slips of the tongue and language production.* Berlin, Germany: Mouton.

Cutler, A. (1996). Prosody and the word boundary problem. In J.L. Morgan & K. Demuth (Eds.), *Signal to syntax: Bootstrapping from speech to grammar in early acquisition.* Mahwah, NJ: Lawrence Erlbaum Associates Inc.

Cutler, A., & Butterfield, S. (1992). Rhythmic cues to speech segmentation: Evidence from juncture misperception. *Journal of Memory and Language, 31,* 218–236.

Cutler, A., Dahan, D., & van Donselaar, W. (1997). Prosody in the comprehension of spoken language: A literature review. *Language and Speech, 40,* 141–201.

Cutler, A., Mehler, J., Norris, D., & Segui, J. (1986). The syllable's differing role in the segmentation of French and English. *Journal of Memory and Language, 25,* 385–400.

Cutler, A., Mehler, J., Norris, D., & Segui, J. (1992). The monolingual nature of speech segmentation by bilinguals. *Cognitive Psychology, 24,* 381–410.

Cutler, A., & Norris, D. (1988). The role of strong syllables in segmentation for lexical access. *Journal of Experimental Psychology: Human Perception and Performance, 14,* 113–121.

Cutler, A., & Otake, T. (1994). Mora or phoneme? Further evidence for language-specific listening. *Journal of Memory and Language, 33,* 824–844.

Dell, G.S. (1986). A spreading activation theory of retrieval in sentence production. *Psychological Review, 93,* 283–321.

Dell, G.S. (1988). The retrieval of phonological forms in production: Tests of predictions from a connectionist model. *Journal of Memory and Language, 27,* 124–142.

Eady, S.J., & Cooper, W.E. (1986). Speech intonation and focus location in matched statements and questions. *Journal of the Acoustical Society of America, 80,* 402–415.

Eady, S.J., Cooper, W.E., Klouda, G.V., Mueller, P.R., & Lotts, D.W. (1986). Acoustical characteristics of sentential focus: Narrow vs. broad and single vs. dual focus environments. *Language and Speech, 29,* 233–251.

Echols, C.H., Crowhurst, M.J., & Childers, J.B. (1997). Perception of rhythmic units in speech by infants and adults. *Journal of Memory and Language, 36,* 202–225.

Eriksen, C.W., Pollack, M.D., & Montague, W.E. (1970). Implicit speech: Mechanisms in perceptual encoding? *Journal of Experimental Psychology, 84,* 502–507.

Fernald, A., Taeschner, T., Dunn, J., Papousek, M., Boysson-Bardies, B., & Fukui, I. (1989). A cross-language study of prosodic modifications in mothers' and fathers' speech to preverbal infants. *Journal of Child Language, 16,* 177–501.

Ferreira, F. (1991). Effects of length and syntactic complexity on initiation times for prepared utterances. *Journal of Memory and Language, 30,* 210–233.

Ferreira, F. (1993). The creation of prosody during sentence production. *Psychological Review, 100,* 233–253.

Fitzpatrick-Cole, J., & Wheeldon, L.R. (in press). Phonology and phonetics in psycholinguistic models of speech perception. In N. Burton-Roberts, P. Carr, & G. Docherty (Eds.), *Conceptual and empirical foundations of phonology.* Oxford, UK: Oxford University Press.

Fowler, C.A. (1983). Converging sources of evidence on spoken and perceived rhythms of speech: Cyclic production of vowels in monosyllabic feet. *Journal of Experimental Psychology: General, 112*, 386–412.

Frauenfelder, U.H. (1998, December). *Units of speech processing.* Workshop on lexical representations in language comprehension, Maurach, Germany.

Frauenfelder, U.H., & Lahiri, A. (1989). Understanding words and word recognition: Can phonology help? In W. Marslen-Wilson (Ed.), *Lexical representation and process.* Cambridge, MA: MIT Press.

Frazier, L. (1987). Structure in auditory word recognition. *Cognition, 25*, 157–187.

Garrett, M.F. (1980). Levels of processing in sentence production. In B. Butterworth (Ed.), *Language production* (Vol. 1, pp. 177–220). London: Academic Press.

Gee, J.P., & Grosjean, F. (1983). Performance structures: A psycholinguistic and linguistic appraisal. *Cognitive Psychology, 15*, 411–458.

Gerken, L.A. (1991). The metrical bases for childrens' subjectless sentences. *Journal of Memory and Language, 30*, 431–451.

Gussenhoven, C. (1989). *Cliticization in Dutch as phonological word formation.* Unpublished manuscript, University of Nijmegen, The Netherlands.

Hayes, B. (1989). The prosodic hierarchy in meter. In P. Kiparsky & F. Youmans (Eds.), *Phonetics and phonology: Vol. 1. Phonology and meter* (pp. 201–260). San Diego: Academic Press.

Hirsh-Pasek, K., Kemler Nelson, D.G., Jusczyk, P.W., Wright Cassidy, K., Druss, B., & Kennedy, L. (1987). Clauses are perceptual units for young infants. *Cognition, 26*, 269–286.

Inkelas, S., & Zec, D. (1990). *The phonology–syntax connection.* Chicago: University of Chicago Press.

Jusczyk, P.W., Cutler, A., & Redanz, L. (1993). Infants' sensitivity to predominant stress patterns in English. *Child Development, 64*, 75–687.

Jusczyk, P.W., Hirsh-Pasek, K., Kemler Nelson, D.G., Kennedy, L.J., Woodward, A., & Piwoz, J. (1992). Perception of acoustic correlates of major phrasal units by young infants. *Cognitive Psychology, 24*, 252–293.

Kempen, G., & Hoenkamp, E. (1987). An incremental procedural grammar for sentence formation. *Cognitive Science, 11*, 201–258.

Klapp, S.T. (1974). Syllable-dependent pronunciation latencies in number naming: A replication. *Journal of Experimental Psychology, 102*, 1138–1140.

Klapp, S.T., Anderson, W.G., & Berrian, R.W. (1973). Implicit speech in reading reconsidered. *Journal of Experimental Psychology, 100*, 368–374.

Ladd, D.R. (1980). *The strucutre of intonational meaning.* Bloomington, IN: Indiana University Press.

Ladd, D.R. (1996). *Intonational phonology.* Cambridge, UK: Cambridge University Press.

Lahiri, A. (1999). Speech recognition with phonological features. In J. Ohala, Y. Hasegawa, M. Ohala, D. Granville, & A. Bailey (Eds.), *Proceedings of the XIVth international congress of Phonetic Sciences* (pp. 715–719). Berkeley, CA: University of California Press.

Lahiri, A., & Jongman, A. (1990). Intermediate level of analysis: Features or segments? *Journal of Phonetics, 18*, 435–443.

Lahiri, A., Jongman, A., & Sereno, J.A. (1990). The pronominal clitic [der] in Dutch: Theoretical and experimental approach. *Yearbook of Morphology, 3*, 115–127.

Lahiri, A., & Marslen-Wilson, W. (1991). The mental representation of lexical form: A phonological approach to the lexicon. *Cognition, 38*, 245–294.

Lahiri, A., & Marslen-Wilson, W. (1992). Lexical processing and phonological representation. In G.J. Docherty & D.R. Ladd (Eds.), *Papers in laboratory phonology: II. Gesture, segment, prosody* (pp. 229–254). Cambridge, UK: Cambridge University Press.

Levelt, W.J.M. (1989). *Speaking: From intention to articulation.* Cambridge, MA: MIT Press.

Levelt, W.J.M. (1992). Accessing words in speech production: Stages, processes and representations. *Cognition, 42*, 1–22.

Levelt, W.J.M., Roelofs, A., & Meyer, A.S. (1999). A theory of lexical access in speech production. *Behavioral and Brain Sciences*, *22*, 59–60.

Levelt, W.J.M., & Wheeldon, L.R. (1994). Do speakers have access to a mental syllabary? *Cognition*, *50*, 239–269.

Levitt, A.G. (1993). The acquisition of prosody: Evidence from French- and English-learning infants. In B. de Boysson-Bardies, S. de Schonen, P. Jusczyk, P. McNeilage, & J. Morton (Eds.), *Development neurocognition: Speech and face processing in the first year of life*. Dordrecht, The Netherlands: Kluwer.

Levitt, A.G., & Wang, Q. (1991). Evidence for language-specific rhythm influences in the reduplicative babbling of French- and English-learning infants. *Language and Speech*, *34*, 235–249.

Liberman, M., & Prince, A. (1977). On stress and linguistic rhythm. *Linguistic Inquiry*, *8.2*, 249–336.

Marslen-Wilson, W., Tyler, L.K., Warren, P., Grenier, P., & Lee, C.S. (1992). Prosodic effects in minimal attachment. *Quarterly Journal of Experimental Psychology*, *45A*, 73–87.

Mattys, S.L., Jusczyk, P.W., Luce, P.A., & Morgan, J.L. (1999). Phonotactic and prosodic effects on word segmentation in infants. *Cognitive Psychology*, *38*, 465–494.

Mehler, J., Dommergues, J., Frauenfelder, U., & Segui, J. (1981). The syllables role in speech segmentation. *Journal of Verbal Learning and Verbal Behavior*, *20*, 298–305.

Meyer, A.S. (1994). Timing in sentence production. *Journal of Memory and Language*, *33*, 471–492.

Monsell, S. (1986). Programming of complex sequences: Evidence from the timing of rapid speech and other productions. In C. Fromm & H. Heuer (Eds.), *Generation and modulation of action patterns*. Berlin, Germany: Springer.

Morgan, J.L., & Demuth, K. (1996). *Signal to syntax: Bootstrapping from speech to grammar in early acquisition*. Mahwah, NJ: Lawrence Erlbaum Associates Inc.

Nazzi, T., Bertoncini, J., & Mehler, J. (1998). Language discrimination by newborns: Towards an understanding of the role of rhythm. *Journal of Experimental Psychology: Human Perception and Performance*, *24*, 756–766.

Nespor, M., & Vogel, I. (1986). *Prosodic phonology*. Dordrecht, The Netherlands: Foris.

Odden, D. (1980). *The phrasal phonology of Kimatuumbi*. Unpublished manuscript, Yale University, New Haven, CT.

Otake, T., Hatano, G., Cutler, A., & Mehler, J. (1993). Mora or syllable? Speech segmentation in Japanese. *Journal of Memory and Language*, *32*, 358–378.

Reetz, H. (1998). *Automatic speech recognition with features*. Habilitation, University of the Saarland, Germany.

Roelofs, A. (1997). Syllabification in speech production: Evaluation of WEAVER. *Language and Cognitive Processes*, *12*, 657–693.

Selkirk, E.O. (1980). Prosodic domains in phonology: Sanskrit revisited. In M. Arnoff & M.L. Kean (Eds.), *Juncture* (pp. 107–29). Saratoga, CA: Anma Libri.

Selkirk, E.O. (1981). On prosodic structure and its relation to syntactic structure. In T. Fretheim (Ed.), *Nordic prosody II* (pp. 111–140). Trondheim, Norway: Tapir.

Selkirk, E.O. (1984). *Phonology and syntax: The relation between sound and structure*. Cambridge, MA: MIT Press.

Selkirk, E.O. (1986). On derived domains in sentence phonology. *Phonology Yearbook*, *3*, 371–405.

Selkirk, E.O. (1995). The prosodic structure of function words. In J. Beckman, L. Walsh Dickey, & S. Urbanczyk (Eds.), *Papers in optimality theory* (UMASS occasional papers in phonology). Amherst, MA: The Graduate Linguistic Society of Amhurst.

Shattuck-Hufnagel, S. (1987). The role of word onset consonants in speech production planning: New evidence from speech error patterns. In E. Keller & M. Gopnik (Eds.), *Motor and sensory processing in language*. Hillsdale, NJ: Lawrence Erlbaum Associates Inc.

Shattuck-Hufnagel, S. (1992). The role of word structure in segmental serial ordering. *Cognition*, *42*, 213–259.

Shattuck-Hufnagel, S., & Turk, A.E. (1996). A prosody tutorial for investigations of auditory sentence processing. *Journal of Psycholinguistic Research, 25,* 193–247.

Speer, S.R., Crowder, R.G., & Thomas, L.M. (1993). Prosodic structure and sentence recognition. *Journal of Memory and Language, 32,* 336–358.

Stemberger, J.P. (1985). An interactive model of language production. In W.W. Ellis (Ed.), *Progress in the psychology of language, Vol. 1.* Hillsdale, NJ: Lawrence Erlbaum Associates Inc.

Sternberg, S., Monsell, S., Knoll, R.L., & Wright, C.E. (1978). The latency and duration of rapid movement sequences: Comparisons of speech and typewriting. In G.E. Stelmach (Ed.), *Information processing in motor control and learning* (pp. 117–152). New York: Academic Press.

Sternberg, S., Wright, C.E., Knoll, R.L., & Monsell, S. (1980). Motor programs in rapid speech: Additional evidence. In R.A. Cole (Ed.), *The perception and production of fluent speech* (pp. 507–534). Lawrence Erlbaum Associates Inc.

Warren, P., Grabe, E., & Nolan, F. (1995). Prosody, phonology, and parsing in closure ambiguities. *Language and Cognitive Processes, 10,* 457–486.

Watt, S.M., & Murray, W.S. (1996). Prosodic form and parsing commitments. *Journal of Psycholinguistic Research, 25,* 291–318.

Wheeldon, L.R., & Lahiri, A. (1997). Prosodic units in speech production *Journal of Memory and Language, 37,* 356–381.

Wheeldon, L.R., & Levelt, W.J.M. (1995). Monitoring the time course of spoken word production. *Journal of Memory and Language, 34,* 311–334.

Zwitzerlood, P., Schriefers, H., Lahiri, A., & van Donselaar, W. (1993). The role of syllables in the perception of spoken Dutch. *Journal of Experimental Psychology: Learning, Memory and Cognition, 19,* 260–271.

CHAPTER TEN

Language production in children

LouAnn Gerken and Diane Ohala
*Department of Speech and Hearing Sciences, University of
Arizona, Tucson, USA*

INTRODUCTION

Studies of adult language production employ a variety of measures of adult
spontaneous and elicited utterances to infer the mechanism by which a message
is transformed into a perceivable signal and what (if any) intermediate representations are generated along the way. On the surface, this goal differs from that
of most studies of children's language production, which try to explain why child
forms deviate from adult forms. The aim of this chapter is to begin to close this
apparent gap between studies of child and adult production by drawing parallels
between child forms and several types of adult speech. Towards this end, we
provide examples from our own research illustrating the ways that some child
language researchers treat the relation between child and adult forms. We then
show that remarkably similar phenomena exist in both child and adult utterances.
Ultimately we suggest that these parallels should not be treated as coincidental,
but as evidence of the need for a single developmentally plausible model of
language production.

CHILDREN'S DEVIATION FROM ADULT MODELS

Before we discuss our research on children's early production, it is important to
discuss the reasons why we view children's deviations from adult forms as
relevant to a model of language production. In this section we will briefly review
and reject three interpretations of children's forms that do not share this view, as
well as offer a preview of our own approach.

Perceptual/representational accounts

One interpretation of children's deviations from adult forms is that they reflect which aspects of language children perceive and represent and which they do not (e.g., Echols, 1993; Echols & Newport, 1992; Pinker, 1984). For example, several researchers have suggested that young English speakers' omissions of sentential subjects reflect an immature or incorrectly configured grammar (e.g., Hyams, 1986; Hyams & Wexler, 1989, 1993; Mazuka, Lust, Wakayama, & Snyder, 1986; O'Grady & Peters, 1989). Similarly, a child who produces "fish" as "fis" might be thought of as unable to discriminate /ʃ/ from /s/, either at the level of perception or at the level of phonemic representation (e.g., Jakobson, 1941).

There are several types of evidence against such perceptual or representational accounts. First, a variety of perception studies suggest that children discriminate contrasts they do not produce. In addition, children distinguish between their own and adult versions of utterances (e.g., Smith, 1973) and demonstrate better comprehension for adult versions (e.g., Gerken & McIntosh, 1993; Shipley, Smith, & Gleitman, 1969). Second, children's deviations from an adult model typically involve omission or other types of simplification, suggesting that they are operating within a more limited system as opposed to simply an incorrect grammar (e.g., Donegan & Stampe, 1979; Stampe, 1969). Third, children's utterances often vary between more and less adult-like forms, suggesting that the less mature forms are not a result of the lack of an adult-like representation (Wijnen, Krikhaar, & den Os, 1994). Last, and most critical for the current discussion, parallels can be drawn between children's forms and particular types of adult forms, including cross-linguistic patterns, slips of the tongue, casual speech, and productions by impaired speakers like aphasics (Gerken, 1994b; Jakobson, 1941; Stampe, 1969; Stemberger, 1989, 1992). It is difficult to argue that all of these types of adult productions reflect deviant linguistic representations; therefore, their similarity to child forms casts doubt on such an interpretation of children's utterances.

Articulatory accounts

The evidence against perceptual/representational accounts of children's utterances suggest that children may have relatively adult-like perceptual abilities as well as adult-like representations of many linguistic forms and that their deviations from adult forms at least partially reflect constraints on language production (e.g., Gerken, 1993, 1994a,b, 1996; Menn, 1978, 1980; Stampe, 1969; Stemberger, 1992). The next two accounts of children's productions to be discussed assume such a framework, but differ as to the mechanisms by which an adult-like representation is produced as a child form. On one view, children are simply incapable of articulating the linguistic unit in question. Thus, a child who produces [s] instead of [ʃ] is not capable of producing the latter. There are several problems with such articulatory accounts. One shortcoming stems from cases in which a child produces a more adult-like form at Time 1 and apparently regresses to a less mature form at Time 2 (e.g., Leopold, 1947). Clearly the child's production at Time 2 cannot be due to a physical inability to produce the sound in question, since she/he was fully capable of doing so at Time 1. A second and related problem with purely articulatory accounts is illustrated by chain shifts, in which the child substitutes Sound A for Sound B, but then produces Sound B as a substitute for Sound C in another word (e.g., Smith, 1973). For example, a child might produce "duck" as "guck", but produce "truck" as "duck". Clearly the child is not physically incapable of producing /d/, although she/he may not be able to produce it in the proper circumstances. Finally, purely articulatory accounts fail to effectively explain cases in which a child alternates between adult-like and immature forms within a single session, unless one assumes that articulatory difficulties change from moment to moment.

Meaning-based accounts

On another view, children faced with production limitations might consciously or unconsciously "decide" to omit some part of an utterance that does not affect the meaning (e.g., Bates, 1976; Bloom, 1970). Thus, a child who produces "I want a cookie" as "Want cookie" preserves those sentential elements that maintain the core meaning of the intended utterances. The problem with this view is that it applies best to omissions, and even then, it does not apply well to omissions within words (Gerken, 1994a,b; Wijnen et al., 1994). Thus, reducing "hippopotamus" to [pamʌs] does not preserve the meaning or intelligibility better than saying [hɪpo], although children are more likely to produce the former (e.g., Kehoe, 1995; Klein, 1978).

The account of children's forms that we suggest here is similar to the two approaches just outlined, in that we believe children's deviations from adult models reflect constraints on language production. However, unlike other production-based accounts, we suggest that children's deviations do not reflect processes that are specific to immature talkers. Rather, child forms reflect the same properties of the language production system that are responsible for biases toward particular forms in cross-linguistic studies, slips of the tongue, and casual speech in normal adults, and characteristic patterns in aphasic speech.

THE RELATION OF CHILD AND ADULT FORMS: TWO EXAMPLES

In this section, we use our research on children's consonant cluster reduction and weak syllable omission to illustrate the types of child language phenomena that need to be explained and the kinds of explanations we have offered. In each case, we attempt to draw parallels between child forms and forms observed in other populations. In the last subsection, we offer a set of criteria by which to evaluate a developmentally plausible model of language production.

Sonority in children's consonant cluster reduction

Research on early speech clearly reveals young children's tendency to omit one consonant of a cluster (e.g., Kiparsky & Menn, 1977; Lewis, 1936; Oller, Weiman, Doyle, & Ross, 1976; Olmsted, 1971; Smith, 1973; Velten, 1943). For example, a child might produce "sky" as [kai]. There also exist many generalisations regarding which of two contiguous consonants a child is more likely to omit (Ingram, 1989; Locke, 1983). Although such generalisations are important for a complete understanding of the phenomenon, they do not explain why clusters reduce to one particular consonant. Early accounts make use of phonological rules (Kiparsky & Menn, 1977; Menn, 1978; Smith, 1973), but these can do no more than illustrate what the child does to achieve the simplified form (e.g., [sk] → [k]). In themselves, rules cannot why the child reduces a cluster in a specific way.

Insofar as any explanation is given in earlier rule-based accounts, it is hypothesised that the rules reflect articulatory ease. That is, [sk] reduces to [k], because [k] is easier to produce than [s]. It is obviously circular to argue that the consonant in a cluster that is preserved is the one that is easiest to produce. However, this circularity can be avoided to some extent by hypothesising that one singleton consonant is easier to articulate than another if it appears earlier in children's inventories. Figure 10.1 shows a typical order of appearance of singleton consonants and thus represents a potential ranking of articulatory ease (where [n] is the easiest).

An Articulatory Ease Hypothesis (AEH) predicts that clusters will reduce to whichever consonant is leftmost in the ranking shown in Figure 10.1. If two consonants are ranked together, the AEH predicts the production of both consonants equally. It is important to note that the AEH predicts that the ease of the consonant itself determines whether it will be preserved or omitted. Other factors external to the segment itself, such as the position of a cluster in a syllable or the order of consonants in a cluster, should not affect which member of the cluster is preserved.

In contrast, it is possible that children's cluster reductions reflect their adherence to more general principles governing language production in all speakers. Evidence for this hypothesis is that cluster reduction can be seen in adult slips of the tongue (Stemberger & Treiman, 1986), casual speech (e.g., Trudgill, 1974), and aphasic speech (Christman, 1994). Other evidence is that, across human languages, there are restrictions on whether or not consonant clusters are allowed, and if they are, the types of clusters that are possible. Like slips of the tongue, casual, and aphasic speech, such cross-linguistic data might at least partially

---

n > m p h f w ŋ > t k b g s > y d > l r > ǰ č > v > z ž > ð θ

Figure 10.1.   The order of acquisition of speech sounds (adapted from Locke, 1983, p. 73).

reflect the language production mechanism. In order to test the hypothesis that children's consonant cluster reduction is related to these apparently similar adult phenomena, it is necessary to make a finer grained examination of the parallels between child and adult forms.

A general principle that appears to govern the possible shapes that syllables can have across languages, and thus which (if any) clusters are allowed, is sonority (Clements, 1990; Selkirk, 1984; Steriade, 1982). In acoustic terms, Ladefoged (1975, p. 221) states that "the sonority of a sound is its loudness relative to that of other sounds with the same length, stress, and pitch". In articulatory terms, sonority has been described as the relative openness of the vocal apparatus (Price, 1980). Preferred syllables across languages are those whose sonority rises from the edge(s) inward, as in the syllable shape consonant–vowel (CV). Although there is conflict among linguists on how to precisely define sonority (i.e., whether sonority should be couched in featural or acoustic terms), most will agree that the notion can be used to rank sounds along these lines. Generally, sounds on the edges of syllables (consonants) tend to be less sonorous than sounds at the centre of syllables (vowels). Finer classification produces a Sonority Hierarchy, as in shown in Figure 10.2 ("<" indicates "is less sonorous than").

Clements (1990) further articulates these concepts and provides a definition of an optimal syllable. He notes that syllables prefer a particular sonority contour that includes a sharp rise in sonority from initial consonant to vowel and a minimal, or no, sonority descent. This defines the optimal syllable shape CV, where the C is a stop (e.g., [tɑ]). Syllables with other types of initial consonants (e.g., fricatives) would be less preferred (e.g., [sɑ]).

If children's cluster reductions are driven by considerations of sonority, then the consonant that is preserved should be the one resulting in the most optimal syllable. The Sonority Hypothesis (SH) predicts that initial clusters will reduce to whichever consonant creates a maximal sonority rise, and final clusters will reduce to whichever consonant creates a minimal sonority descent. For example, "sky" will reduce to [kɑi] and not [sɑi], because stops are less sonorous than fricatives and will provide a sharper sonority rise. However, "musk" will reduce to [mʌs] and not [mʌk] because fricatives are more sonorous than stops and will provide a minimal sonority descent. It is important to note that, unlike the AEH, the SH clearly predicts an effect of factors external to the segment itself, such as the position of the cluster in the word. The same cluster will reduce differently depending on whether it is initial or final (as previously shown with /sk/).

In order to compare the predictions of the SH with the AEH, English-speaking children ranging in age from 21 to 38 months were shown pictures of novel

Stops	<	Fricatives	<	Nasals	<	Liquids	<	Glides	<	Vowels
[t,d] <		[s,f]	<	[m,n]	<	[l,r]	<	[y,w]	<	[ɑ,i]

Figure 10.2. The sonority hierarchy.

TABLE 10.1
Sample Stimuli and Predictions

	Position	Type	Cluster	Sample item	Predictions	
					SH	AEH
a	Initial	F-S	/sk/	/skub/	S preserved	F, S preserved
b	Initial	F-N	/sn/	/snuf/	F preserved	N preserved
c	Final	F-S	/sk/	/fɪsk/	F preserved	F, S preserved
d	Final	F-S	/fp/	/mEpf/	F preserved	F, S preserved
e	Final	S-F	/pf/	/gɪfp/	F preserved	F, S preserved

animals and asked to imitate a nonsense name for each (Ohala, 1995, 1996, 1999).[1,2] The nonsense words were of the form CCVC or CVCC. Table 10.1 gives examples of clusters used in the two studies as well as the specific predictions of both theories with respect to each item. Clusters are modelled with associated nonsense words (F = Fricative, S = Stop, N = Nasal).

Table 10.1 illustrates three critical comparisons to be made among the predictions of the SH and the AEH. First, the SH, but not the AEH, predicts an interaction in children's cluster reductions between consonant type and cluster type in the initial fricative-stop and fricative-nasal clusters. In the initial fricative-stop clusters (a), the stop /k/ should be preserved, but in the initial fricative-nasal clusters (b), the fricative /s/ should be preserved. This is due to the fact that a stop at the edge of a syllable, having less sonority than a fricative, conforms better to notions of preferred syllables in the case of (a). However, a fricative at the edge of a syllable, having less sonority than a nasal, produces the more optimal syllable in the case of (b).

Second, the SH predicts an interaction between cluster position and consonant type in initial and final fricative-stop clusters. If the fricative-stop cluster is word-initial (a), the SH predicts the preservation of the stop /k/, but if the same cluster is word-final (c), the SH predicts the preservation of the fricative /s/. This reflects the fact that stops are preferred to fricatives in initial position, but fricatives are preferred to stops in final position. In contrast, the AEH, being based solely on characteristics of the individual phonemes, does not predict any such interaction.

Finally, the SH predicts that, since fricatives in final position produce a more optimal syllable contour than stops in final position, a juxtaposition of the order of these segments in a cluster will not affect children's reductions. Thus, the final fricative-stop cluster in (d) and the final stop-fricative cluster in (e) should both reduce to fricatives. The AEH also predicts in this case that the order of segments should not affect children's reductions, but differs from the SH by predicting that both consonants will be produced equally often.

All three predictions of the SH were borne out: Children reduced initial fricative-stop clusters to stops (e.g., /stig/ → /tig/), but reduced initial fricative-nasal clusters to fricatives (e.g., /snuf/ → /suf/). They also reduced final fricative-stop clusters to fricatives, and not stops as in initial position (e.g., /dust/ → /dus/). Additionally, they reduced both final /fp/ and /pf/ clusters to /f/.

In summary, children's pattern of consonant cluster reductions suggest that they are biased to produce syllables of particular types: those with a nonsonorous onset, followed by a sonority peak, followed by either no offset or one with relatively high sonority. As noted earlier, this pattern accords well with the most frequently observed syllable types seen in cross-linguistic surveys. Sonority has also been implicated in the pattern of syllable productions of jargon aphasics (Christman, 1994). Sonority is clearly a theory that bears on both child and adult production data and thus potentially provides a bridge between the fields. We will address this issue more thoroughly in the last subsection.

Prosodic structure in children's weak syllable omissions

Let us now turn to another example of child forms and what they reflect about the development of language production. Like consonant cluster reduction, weak syllable omission is common in the productions of young English speakers, who fail to produce syllables from multisyllabic words as well as weakly stressed morphemes from sentences. However, all weak syllables are not omitted with equal frequency. For example, the initial weak syllable in (1a) is likely to be omitted, while the final syllable in (1b) is not (e.g., Allen & Hawkins, 1980; Echols, 1993; Kehoe, 1995; Klein, 1978; capital letters indicate stressed syllables). Similarly, the sentence-initial pronoun and determiner in (2a) and (2b), respectively are omitted more frequently than their non-initial counterparts in (2c) and (2d) (Gerken, 1991, 1994b).

(1) (a) giRAFFE → RAFFE
     (b) MONkey → *MON

(2) (a) he KISSED JANE
     (b) the BEAR KISSED JANE
     (c) JANE KISSED him
     (d) JANE KISSED the BEAR

As in the case of consonant cluster reduction, a phenomenon similar to children's weak syllable omission can be seen in some types of adult productions, particularly in casual speech and agrammatic aphasic speech. Thus, in adult casual speech, the initial weak syllable of words like "opossum" and "potato" are sometimes omitted, as are sentence-initial pronouns and articles (e.g., "Having a great time. Wish you were here." or "Is this restaurant any good? Man over there seems to think so."). Similarly, agrammatic aphasics are more likely to omit word-initial syllables than others syllables of a word (Nickels, 1997). They are also more

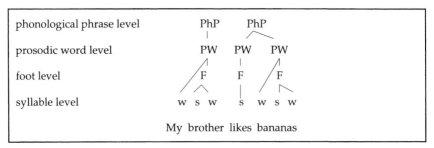

phonological phrase level	PhP	PhP
prosodic word level	PW	PW PW
foot level	F	F F
syllable level	w s w	s w s w

My brother likes bananas

Figure 10.3.   An example of prosodic structure; s = strong syllable, w = weak syllable.

likely to omit sentence-initial determiners than those occurring sentence-internally (Goodglass, Fodor, & Schulhoff, 1967).

The hypothesis offered here for the patterns of children's weak syllable omissions begins with the proposal that speakers organise their intended utterances into prosodically based planning units (Ferreira, 1993; Gee & Grosjean, 1983; Levelt, 1989; Lewis, 1995; Martin, 1970; Sternberg, Wright, Knoll, & Monsell, 1978; Wheeldon, this volume; Wheeldon & Lahiri, 1997). Syllables that do not fit into these planning units are susceptible to omission (Gerken, 1994b, 1996). Before considering this hypothesis further, let us review a current linguistic account of prosodic structure (also see Dresher, 1996; Hayes, 1989; Nespor & Vogel, 1986). In current linguistic theory, utterances comprise strings of syllables, which are contained within metrical feet, which are contained within prosodic words, which in turn are contained within phonological phrases (see Figure 10.3). Within linguistic accounts of prosody, it has been further proposed that prosodic structures are subject to an exhaustivity constraint, such that each smaller unit is completely subsumed by the next larger unit (e.g., Selkirk, 1996). The exhaustivity constraint appears not to be absolute, and there are a few specific cases in which it is violated. These violations figure importantly in the current proposal and will now be discussed in more detail.

Consider the prosodic structure in Figure 10.3. Syllables are joined into feet, comprising a strong syllable and (optionally) a weak syllable to its right. Thus, the lexical word "likes" forms a monosyllabic foot, "brother" forms a single s-w foot, as do the second and third syllables of "bananas". Note that the first syllable of "bananas" does not belong to any foot, but rather attaches to the next higher prosodic unit in the structure, the prosodic word, thereby violating the exhaustivity constraint described earlier. Prosodic words comprise one and only one lexical word plus adjacent function words. Thus, the function word "my" forms a prosodic word with the following lexical word "brother". Note that, like the first syllable of "bananas", "my" does not belong to a foot but attaches directly to a prosodic word and therefore also constitutes a violation of exhaustivity. Prosodic words contained within a single syntactic phrase are joined into phonological phrases.

Thus, the subject noun phrase and verb phrase each comprise a phonological phrase in Figure 10.3.

Let us now return to a discussion of children's weak syllable omissions. Data from several studies suggest that children not only omit utterance-initial weak syllables but also utterance-internal weak syllables. It appears that children, like adults, organise their intended utterances into prosodic structures like the one in Figure 10.3 (also see Demuth, 1996; Fee, 1996; Fikkert, 1994). From these intended utterances, they tend to omit syllables that violate the exhaustivity constraint, with more violations resulting in more omissions (Gerken, 1996). In the next examples, the word- and sentence-internal syllables that have an asterisk underneath violate exhaustivity by not belonging to a foot. Two-year-olds who were asked to imitate four-syllable nonsense words like the one in (3) omitted the second weak syllable (indicated by an asterisk) more than the first (Gerken, 1994b). Similarly, children who imitated the sentences in (4a–b) omitted the object article in (4b) more than in (4a) (Boyle & Gerken, 1997; Gerken, 1996). Such results suggest that feet are important units in children's utterance planning and production and that syllables that do not belong to feet are susceptible to omission.

(3)   ZAMpakaSIS
        S-w * S-(w)

(4)   (a)   TOM PUSHED the PIG
              S-(w)   S-w S-(w)
       (b)   TOM PUSHes the PIG
              S-(w)   S-w * S-(w)

Children's productions of other sentences suggest that they organise their utterances into prosodic words as well as feet. Compare sentences (5a–b) (which shows sentences (4a–b) bracketed into prosodic words) with (5c–d). Note that (5a) and (5c) have the same metrical pattern, as do (5b) and (5d). However, the weak syllable following the verb in (5a–b) is a function word, while in (5c–d), the weak syllable is part of a lexical word. Therefore, the object article in (5a) can form a foot and prosodic word with the preceding verb, but the first syllable of "Michele" in (5c) cannot. The different prosodic word arrangements in (5a–b) versus (5c–d) predict that, if children represent prosodic words as well as feet in their utterance planning, they should omit the object article in (5b) more than in (5a) (as discussed in the previous paragraph), but they should omit the first syllable of "Michele" equally frequently in (5c–d). This was in fact the pattern found in an imitation task with 28-month-olds (Gerken, 1996). Thus, children appear to organise their intended utterances into feet and prosodic words.

(5) (a) [TOM]$_{PW}$ [PUSHED the]$_{PW}$ [PIG]$_{PW}$
          S-(w)   S-w   S-(w)
     (b) [TOM]$_{PW}$ [PUSHes]$_{PW}$ [the PIG]$_{PW}$
          S-(w)   S-w   * S-(w)
     (c) [TOM]$_{PW}$ [PUSHED]$_{PW}$ [miCHELE]$_{PW}$
          S-(w)   S-(w)   * S-(w)
     (d) [TOM]$_{PW}$ [PUSHes]$_{PW}$ [miCHELE]$_{PW}$
          S-(w)   S-w   * S-(w)

Further evidence that children organise their utterances into prosodic words, and evidence that the number of violations of exhaustivity is related to the frequency of omissions can be seen by comparing (5a–b) with (6a–b). In (5b), the object article does not belong to a foot, but rather attaches to the prosodic word of the following noun, just as the determiner "my" did in Figure 10.3. Thus, it violates the exhaustivity constraint once. Although (6b) has the same syntactic structure as (5b), the object noun begins with a weak syllable. English words can begin with at most one weak syllable, and several researchers have proposed that this constraint is actually one applying to prosodic words, not lexical words (e.g., Hayes, 1982; McCarthy & Prince, 1993). If an English prosodic word can begin with only one weak syllable, the object article cannot be part of the prosodic word with the following noun in (6b) as it can in (5b). Thus, the object article in (6b) belongs neither to a foot nor a prosodic word, but only to the next unit in the prosodic hierarchy—the phonological phrase. On this analysis, the object article in (6b) violates the exhaustivity constraint twice and should be omitted more frequently than the article in (5b), while the articles in (5a) and (6a) should be omitted equally frequently. This was the pattern observed in young children's imitations of such sentences, suggesting that the degree to which a syllable fails to conform to a canonical prosodic structure determines how likely it is that children will omit it (Gerken, 1996).

(6) (a) [TOM]$_{PW}$ [PUSHED the]$_{PW}$ [giRAFFE]$_{PW}$
          S-(w)   S-w   * S-(w)
     (b) [TOM]$_{PW}$ [PUSHes]$_{PW}$ the [giRAFFE]$_{PW}$
          S-(w)   S-w   ** * S-(w)

Finally, children appear to organise their utterances into phonological phrases, as well as prosodic words and feet. Evidence for the phonological phrase in children's utterance planning can be seen in comparing sentences like (7a–b). In (7a), the object noun phrase is part of the phonological phrase containing the verb, and the object article can form a foot (and a prosodic word, see 5a) with the verb. In (7b), the verb bears contrastive stress. Linguistic and psycholinguistic investigations indicate that a phonological phrase is ended after a word receiving focal or contrastive stress (Ferreira, 1993; Vogel & Kenesei, 1990). Thus, the object article in (7b) cannot form a foot with the preceding verb and therefore does not belong to a foot at all. Consistent with the prosodic structures shown in (7a–b), children omitted the article more frequently in (7b) than (7a) (Gerken, 1996).

(7) (a) [TOM]$_{PhP}$ [PUSHED the PIG]$_{PhP}$
          S-(w)   S-w   S-(w)

     (b) [TOM]$_{PhP}$ **[PUSHED]**$_{PhP}$ [the PIG]$_{Ph}$
          S-(w)   S-(w)   * S-(w)

In summary, young English speakers appear to organise their intended utterances into prosodic units highly similar to those proposed for adults. Syllables that do not conform to these prosodic units are susceptible to omission, with greater failure to conform associated with more omissions. As in the case of consonant cluster reduction, child production phenomena have apparent parallels in adult casual and aphasic speech. We will discuss the implications of these parallels in the next section.

UNIFYING THE APPROACHES

The fields of child language and adult language production have much to offer each other. Perhaps the clearest contribution made by studies of adult language production seen in this volume and elsewhere is the basic notion that speech errors and other types of variation in performance can and should be ascribed to the language production system. This notion contrasts with a frequent assumption made in language acquisition research, namely that young children's utterances reflect only their developing grammar. Furthermore, studies of adult production take as their goal a detailed model of the production system integrated within a larger system of linguistic ability. Such models hold the potential to explain how factors such as attention, fatigue, and speaking rate affect production and therefore offer ways for understanding the incredible within-talker variability observed in studies of child production. Yet another contribution of adult language production research concerns the fact that these studies yield a much wider array of data types than have been heretofore examined in young children. For example, the slip induction technique developed by Baars and Motley (1974) has been extremely useful in testing hypotheses about the language production mechanism. Perhaps such a method might be modified to study developmental issues in language production (see Smith, 1990).

Studies of child language also have much to offer researchers who study adult production. In both of the examples of child production research presented here, the notion of an optimal or canonical form played a major role in our explanations of children's forms. Thus, we view consonant cluster reduction as influenced by the optimal stop-vowel syllable shape. Similarly, we view weak syllable omission as influenced by an optimal, perfectly alternating metrical pattern. The concept of optimal linguistic forms is at the heart of recent optimality theoretic approaches to child language (e.g., Barlow, 1997; Barnhardt & Stemberger, 1998; Demuth, 1996; Gnanadesikan, 1996; Ohala, 1995, 1996; Prince & Smolensky, 1993; also see Gerken, 1991, 1994b for a related view). However, to our knowledge, this notion has not played a role in models of adult language production *per se* (as distinct from formal accounts of linguistic data). A topic related to optimal forms that has played a major role in studies of child production is the observation that many child forms closely resemble frequently occurring cross-linguistic patterns. Although studies of adult language production have examined differences in error types and other aspects of production in speakers of different languages, little attention has been paid to more universal tendencies.

Clearly if we are to close the gap between studies of adult and child production, the possible role of optimal linguistic forms and cross-linguistic patterns must be further explored in both domains. Perhaps a framework for such investigations is a hypothesis that has been offered at different times and in different ways by several researchers (e.g., Donegan & Stampe, 1979; Stampe, 1969; Stemberger, 1989; Vihman & de Boysson-Bardies, 1994). On this view, the process of becoming a fluent speaker of one's native language is one in which universal tendencies (such as the one for CV syllables) gradually come to coexist with structural and typical properties of the target language (e.g., the grammaticality of initial /sp/ clusters in English). On such a view, canonical or optimal linguistic forms might play a role for both children and adults, perhaps with the patterns observed in adult casual and impaired speech reflecting a maximum adherence to optimal forms. Differences between children and adults might reflect the fact that children's optimal forms show a greater influence of universal tendencies, while adults' optimal forms show a greater influence of the grammar and of frequently produced patterns.

In summary, regardless of which framework ultimately proves most useful, the time has come when we must begin to see child and adult language production as part of a single, developing system. We have suggested two approaches to achieve this end. First, child language researchers must more frequently think in terms of production mechanisms that might be responsible for children's deviations from an adult model. Second, adult language researchers must look for influences of optimal cross-linguistic forms on language production. By employing these approaches, researchers in the two fields can begin to work together to create a developmentally plausible model of language production.

NOTES

1. A post-test was also run with each child in a separate session using the same procedure. The nonsense words used were designed to elicit the production of whichever consonant the child did not produce spontaneously in the first session. For example, if

the child produced /kub/ in response to /skub/, then the post-test would elicit the production of /sub/. The purpose of this was to ensure that the child had both of the sounds in a given cluster in his/her consonant inventory.

2. Only a subset of the clusters used in the two studies is shown here. See Ohala (1995, 1999) for a more detailed discussion.

REFERENCES

Allen, G., & Hawkins, S. (1980). Phonological rhythm: Definition and development. In G.H. Yeni-Komshian, J.F. Kavanagh, & G.A. Ferguson (Eds.), *Child phonology: Vol. I. Production* (pp. 227–256). New York: Academic Press.

Baars, B.J., & Motley, M.T. (1974). Spoonerisms: Experimental elicitation of human speech errors. *Catalog of Selected Documents in Psychology* (Vol. 4), 118.

Barlow, J. (1997). *A constraint-based account of syllable onsets: Evidence from developing systems.* Unpublished doctoral dissertation, Indiana University, Bloomington, IN.

Barnhardt, B., & Stemberger, J.P. (1998). *Handbook of phonological development.* New York: Academic Press.

Bates, E. (1976). *Language and context.* New York: Academic Press.

Bloom, L. (1970). *Language development: Form and function in emerging grammars.* Cambridge, MA: MIT Press.

Boyle, M.K., & Gerken, L.A. (1997). Effects of lexical familiarity on children's function morpheme omissions. *Journal of Memory and Language, 36,* 117–128.

Christman, S.S. (1994). Target-related neologism formation in jargonaphasia. *Brain and Language, 46,* 109–128.

Clements, G.N. (1990). The role of the sonority cycle in core syllabification. In J. Kingston & M.E. Beckman (Eds.), *Papers in laboratory phonology: I. between the grammar and physics of speech.* Cambridge, UK: Cambridge University Press.

Demuth, K. (1996). The prosodic structure of early words. In J. Morgan & K. Demuth (Eds.), *Signal to syntax: Bootstrapping from speech to grammar in early acquisition* (pp. 171–184). Mahwah, NJ: Lawrence Erlbaum Associates Inc.

Donegan, P., & Stampe, D. (1979). The study of natural phonology. In D.A. Dinnesen (Ed.), *Current approaches to phonological theory* (pp. 126–173). Bloomington, IN: Indiana University Press.

Dresher, B.E. (1996). Introduction to metrical and prosodic phonology. In J. Morgan & K. Demuth (Eds.), *Bootstrapping from speech to grammar in early acquisition* (pp. 41–54). Mahwah, NJ: Lawrence Erlbaum Associates Inc.

Echols, C.H. (1993). A perceptually-based model of children's earliest productions. *Cognition, 46,* 245–296.

Echols, C.H., & Newport, E.L. (1992). The role of stress and position in determining first words. *Language Acquisition, 2,* 189–220.

Fee, J. (1996). Syllable structure and minimal words. In B. Bernhardt, J. Gilbert, & D. Ingrom (Eds.), *Proceedings of the UBC international conference on Phonological Acquisition* (pp. 85–98). Somerville, MA: Cascadilla Press.

Ferreira, F. (1993). The creation of prosody during sentence production. *Psychological Review, 100,* 233–253.

Fikkert, P. (1994). *On the acquisition of prosodic structure.* Dordrecht, The Netherlands: Holland Institute of Generative Linguistics.

Gee, J.P., & Grosjean, F. (1983). Performance structures: A psycholinguistic and linguistic appraisal. *Cognitive Psychology, 15,* 411–458.

Gerken, L.A. (1991). The metrical basis for children's subjectless sentences. *Journal of Memory and Language, 30,* 431–451.

Gerken, L.A. (1993). *A slip of the tongue approach to language development.* Unpublished manuscript, State University of New York, Buffalo.

Gerken, L.A. (1994a). A metrical template account of children's weak syllable omissions from multisyllabic words. *Journal of Child Language, 21,* 565–584.

Gerken, L.A. (1994b). Young children's representation of prosodic phonology: Evidence from English-speakers' weak syllable productions. *Journal of Memory and Language, 33,* 19–38.

Gerken, L.A. (1996). Prosodic structure in young children's language production. *Language, 72,* 683–712.

Gerken, L.A., & McIntosh, B. (1993). Interplay of function morphemes and prosody in early language. *Developmental Psychology, 29,* 448–457.

Gnanadesikan, A. (1996). Child phonology in optimality theory: Ranking markedness and faithfulness constraints. In A. Stringfellow, D. Cahana-Amitay, E. Hughes, & A. Zukowski (Eds.), *Proceedings of the 20th annual Boston University conference on Language Development* (pp. 237–248). Somerville, MA: Cascadilla Press.

Goodglass, H., Fodor, I., & Schulhoff, C. (1967). Prosodic factors in grammar—evidence from aphasia. *Journal of Speech and Hearing Research, 10,* 5–20.

Hayes, B. (1982). Extrametricality and English stress. *Linguistic Inquiry, 13,* 227–276.

Hayes, B. (1989). The prosodic hierarchy in meter. In P. Kiparsky & G. Youmans (Eds.), *Phonetics and phonology: Rhythm and meter* (pp. 201–260). San Diego, CA: Academic Press.

Hyams, N. (1986). *Language acquisition and the theory of parameters.* Dordrecht, The Netherlands: Reidel.

Hyams, N., & Wexler, K. (1989, October). *Pro-drop: Some alternative accounts.* Unpublished paper presented at the Boston University Conference on Language Development.

Hyams, N., & Wexler, K. (1993). On the grammatical basis of null subjects in child language. *Linguistic Inquiry, 24,* 421–459.

Ingram, D. (1989). *First language acquisition: Method, description and explanation.* Cambridge, UK: Cambridge University Press.

Jakobson, R. (1941). *Kindersprache, aphasie und allgemeine lautgetze* [Child language, aphasia and phonological universals] (A.R. Keiler, Trans.). The Hague, The Netherlands: Mouton.

Kehoe, M. (1995). *An investigation of rhythmic processes in English-speaking children's word productions.* Unpublished doctoral dissertation, University of Washington, Washington DC.

Kiparsky, P., & Menn, L. (1977). On the acquisition of phonology. In J. MacNamara (Ed.), *Language learning and thought* (pp. 47–78). New York: Academic Press.

Klein, H.B. (1978). *The relationship between perceptual strategies and production strategies in learning the phonology of early lexical items.* Unpublished doctoral dissertation, Columbia University, OH.

Ladefoged, P. (1975). *A course in phonetics.* New York: Harcourt Brace Jovanovich.

Leopold, W. (1947). *Speech development of a bilingual child: A linguist's record: Vol. 2. Sound learning in the first two years.* Evanston, IL: Northwestern University Press.

Levelt, W.J.M. (1989). *Speaking: From intention to articulation.* Cambridge, MA: MIT Press.

Lewis, E. (1995). *The timing of prosodic units.* Unpublished manuscript, University of Arizona, Tucson.

Lewis, M.M. (1936). *Infant speech: A study of the beginnings of language.* New York: Harcourt, Brace.

Locke, J.L. (1983). *Phonological acquisition and change.* New York: Academic Press.

Martin, J.G. (1970). Toward an analysis of subjective phrase structure. *Psychological Bulletin, 74,* 153–166.

Mazuka, R., Lust, B., Wakayama, T., & Snyder, W. (1986). Distinguishing effects of parameters in early syntax acquisition. *Papers and Reports on Child Language Development, 25,* 73–82.

McCarthy, J., & Prince, A.S. (1993). Generalized alignment. In G. Booij & J. Van Marle (Eds.), *Yearbook of morphology, 1993* (pp. 79–153). Dordrecht, The Netherlands: Kluwer.

Menn, L. (1978). Phonological units in beginning speech. In A. Bell & J. Hooper (Eds.), *Syllables and segments* (pp. 157–171). Amsterdam: North-Holland Publishing Company.

Menn, L. (1980). Phonological theory and child phonology. In G.H. Yeni-Komshian, J.F. Kavanagh, & G.A. Ferguson (Eds.), *Child phonology* (Vol. 1, pp. 23–41). New York: Academic Press.

Nespor, M., & Vogel, I. (1986). *Prosodic phonology*. Dordrecht, The Netherlands: Foris.

Nickels, L.A. (1997). *Spoken word production and its breakdown in aphasia*. Hove, UK: Psychology Press.

O'Grady, W., & Peters, A. (1989). The transition from optional to required subjects. *Journal of Child Language, 16*, 513–529.

Ohala, D. (1995). Sonority-driven cluster reduction. *Papers and Reports on Child Language Development, 27*, 217–226.

Ohala, D. (1996). *Cluster reduction and constraints in acquisition*. Unpublished doctoral dissertation, University of Arizona, Tucson.

Ohala, D. (1999). The influence of sonority on children's cluster reductions. *Journal of Communication Disorders, 32*(6), 397–422.

Oller, D.K., Weiman, L.A., Doyle W.J., & Ross, C. (1976). Infant babbling and speech. *Journal of Child Language, 3*, 1–11.

Olmsted, D.L. (1971). *Out of the mouth of babes*. The Hague, The Netherlands: Mouton.

Pinker, S. (1984). *Language learnability and language development*. Cambridge, MA: Harvard University Press.

Price, P. (1980). Sonority and syllabicity: Acoustic correlates of perception. *Phonetica, 37*, 327–343.

Prince, A., & Smolenksy, P. (1993). *Optimality theory* (Tech. Rep.). New Brunswick, NJ: Rutgers University.

Selkirk, E.O. (1984). *Phonology and syntax*. Cambridge, MA: MIT Press.

Selkirk, E.O. (1996). The prosodic structure of function words. In J. Morgan & K. Demuth (Eds.), *Signal to syntax* (pp. 187–213). Hillsdale, NJ: Lawrence Erlbaum Associates Inc.

Shipley, E., Smith, C., & Gleitman, L. (1969). A study in the acquisition of language. *Language, 45*, 322–342.

Smith, B.L. (1990). Elicitation of slips of the tongue from young children: A new method and preliminary observations. *Applied Psycholinguistics, 11*, 131–144.

Smith, N.V. (1973). *The acquisition of phonology: A case study*. Cambridge, UK: Cambridge University Press.

Stampe, D. (1969). The acquisition of phonetic representation. *Chicago Linguistics Society, 5*, 443–451.

Stemberger, J.P. (1989). Speech errors in early child language production. *Journal of Memory and Language, 28*, 164–188.

Stemberger, J.P. (1992). A connectionist view of child phonology: Phonological processing without phonological processes. In C.A. Ferguson, L. Menn, & C. Stoel-Gammon (Eds.), *Phonological development: Models, research, implications* (pp. 165–189). Parkton, MD: York Press.

Stemberger, J.P., & Treiman, R. (1986). The internal structure of word-initial consonants. *Journal of Memory and Language, 25*, 163–180.

Steriade, D. (1982). *Greek prosodies and the nature of syllabification*. Unpublished doctoral dissertation, MIT, Cambridge, MA.

Sternberg, S., Wright, C.E., Knoll, R.L., & Monsell, S. (1978). Motor programs in rapid speech: Additional evidence. In R.A. Cole (Ed.), *Perception and production of fluent speech* (pp. 507–534). Hillsdale, NJ: Lawrence Erlbaum Associates Inc.

Trudgill, P. (1974). *Sociolinguistics: An introduction*. Harmondsworth, UK: Penguin.

Velten, H. (1943). The growth of phonemic and lexical patterns in infant speech. *Language, 19*, 281–292.

Vihman, M.M., & de Boysson-Bardies, B. (1994). The nature and origins of ambient language influence on infant vocal production and early words. *Phonetica, 51*, 159–169.

Vogel, I., & Kenesei, I. (1990). Syntax and semantics in phonology. In S. Inkelas & D. Zecs (Eds.), *The phonology-syntax connection* (pp. 339–363). Chicago: Chicago University Press.

Wheeldon, L.R., & Lahiri, A. (1997). Prosodic units in speech production. *Journal of Memory and Language, 37*, 356–381.

Wijnen, F., Krikhaar, E., & den Os, E. (1994). The nonrealization of unstressed elements in children's utterances: A rhythmic constraint? *Journal of Child Language, 21*, 59–83.

CHAPTER ELEVEN

Syntax in language production: An approach using tree-adjoining grammars

Fernanda Ferreira
*Department of Psychology, Michigan State University,
East Lansing, USA*

INTRODUCTION

Any utterance consisting of more than one word requires the speaker to make decisions about word order. In the most typical situation, the speaker constructs an utterance corresponding to a sentence—a combination of a verb, its arguments, and any optional modifiers, as in:

(1)   Simone was eating tuna yesterday.

Constraints concerning the words that may occur and their ordering arise from several sources. One is the lexical items making up the utterance. In the case of (1), the main verb *eating* requires both an appropriate subject and object. Another constraint comes from the general properties of the language (in this case English): The subject must occur before the verb and the object must occur after it. Other aspects of sentence form are less determined. For instance, grammatically the modifier *yesterday* may occur at the beginning or end of the sentence, and it is up to the speaker to choose a location. The theme of eating (*tuna*) can be the object of the sentence as it is in (1), or it can be the subject, in which case a passive structure would be required (*The tuna was eaten by Simone yesterday*). The choice of sentential position is based on a variety of factors, some of which will be reviewed in this chapter.

The syntactic information that provides the foundation for some of these decisions is consulted by speakers quickly and efficiently. The question for

291

psycholinguists interested in language production, of course, is how this speed and efficiency is accomplished. The challenges include at least the following: First, we need to develop an empirical base of knowledge concerning how syntactic decisions are made. For example, what caused the speaker of (1) to use the active form rather than the passive? How did the speaker manage to make the form of the auxiliary verb *to be* agree with the singular subject *Simone*? And, second, we need to develop theories that characterise how these decisions are made and suggest fruitful directions for conducting further work on syntactic production.

The goal of this chapter is to help the field of psycholinguistics meet some of these challenges by doing three things. First, I will review existing theories of syntactic production, focusing particularly on those motivated by human performance data such as speech errors, decisions about syntactic form, and reaction time performance. Second, I will describe an approach to syntax from the field of computational linguistics that provides an interesting perspective from which to view results in the production literature. This approach is known as tree-adjoining grammars (TAGs), and is associated with Aravind Joshi and his colleagues and students (Frank, 1992; Joshi, 1985; Joshi, Levy, & Takahashi, 1975; Kroch & Joshi, 1985). The important fundamental feature of this approach is that it assumes the existence of primitive, basic syntactic trees, which are combined in various constrained ways. This description of TAG will highlight the characteristics of elementary trees, the ways they may be combined, and the properties of the approach that are especially relevant to researchers interested in syntactic production. Third, I will then review some of the literature on syntactic production, focusing especially on (a) lexical influences on syntactic form, (b) syntactic priming, (c) computation of agreement (e.g., subject–verb agreement), and (d) evidence concerning the size and characteristics of syntactic "planning units". This presentation will be interlaced with discussions of how the results can be neatly captured using a TAG approach. I will conclude by describing a model of syntactic production that assumes the basic TAG machinery, and I will discuss the implications of this approach for the widely held assumption that language production is "incremental"—the assumption that the smallest chunks possible are passed from one processing level to another as an utterance is being constructed (Levelt, 1989).

MODELS OF SYNTACTIC PRODUCTION

As Bock (1995) points out, most researchers who work on language production assume that the formal grammatical structure linguists have proposed for different linguistic domains constitutes the knowledge that speakers consult when they create utterances. The psychologist's task, then, is to propose models of how such knowledge is put to use. Of course, matters become interesting when we take into account that the theories linguists have proposed are not all mutually compatible. For instance, in some theories (Chomsky, 1981), a phrase is sometimes described as having been "moved" from its canonical position, leaving behind a marker or "trace" of its previous location. According to these approaches, a passive sentence such as *The ball was kicked by the injured player* contains a trace after the word *kicked*, because *the ball* was moved from its original postverbal position to the front of the sentence. In other theories (e.g., Chomsky, 1981, 1986, 1995), the relation between an active and passive is captured lexically: It is assumed that the active and passive forms of the verb select for different syntactic arrangements of their arguments. The point, then, is that what a psycholinguist takes the content of the knowledge base to be will vary depending on what theory of linguistic structure he or she assumes.

But setting aside this complex issue, the most influential theories of syntactic production incorporate mechanisms for creating syntactic phrases, assigning grammatical functions to those phrases, and determining left-to-right order (Bock, 1982; Fromkin, 1971; Garrett, 1976). The standard architecture (see Bock & Levelt, 1995) uses two levels of processing to accomplish syntactic encoding in production, and these are generally referred to as the functional and positional levels of processing. At the stage at which a functional level representation is created, the syntactic and semantic aspects of a word's representation (so-called "lemmas") are selected and assigned grammatical roles such as subject and object. An error such as *I left my briefcase in my cigar* reveals what can occur when processing at this stage goes wrong: The lemmas for *briefcase* and *cigar* were accessed but their roles were misassigned. In the second stage of Garrett's model, word forms (the phonological representations of words) are assigned to their linear position within a phrase. Garrett proposed that the syntactic encoder accesses prestored phrasal frames and then inserts word forms into them. The frames come complete with closed class items and slots for the open class words. For instance, for the phrase *in my cigar*, the frame would include the items *in* and *my*, and a slot for *cigar*. If the noun had been plural, the plural morpheme would have been present as well. This architecture was proposed to account for a different class of speech errors, so-called "stranding errors" such as *It waits to pay* (from Garrett, 1976). Obviously, what was intended was *it pays to wait*. Notice that although the content words *pay* and *wait* were misaligned, the affix is in its correct position. It appears, then, that closed-class items such as function words and affixes are an intrinsic part of the phrasal frame, and so cannot move; the word forms for content words are then plugged into the slots in the frame, and under some conditions, can end up in the wrong locations. The result is an error such as *it waits to pay*.

Garrett assumed a modular organisation for syntactic analysis in production, and this is one of the points on which his theory has been challenged. In the original model, it should not be possible for phonological information to influence the syntactic shape of an utterance, because grammatical functions are decided before phonological information becomes available. This aspect of his theory has been challenged on a couple of grounds. One finding that compromises the modularity assumption is that, at least under some conditions, a phonologically primed word tends to occur late in a sentence, and the late placement may force an adjustment in the global syntactic organisation of a sentence. For example, Bock (1987b) found that if a speaker hears and repeats the word *trump* and then sees a picture of a truck towing a car, that person will tend to create a sentence in which the phonologically primed concept *truck* occurs later in the sentence. A second result that challenges the assumption of modularity concerns not so directly the syntactic procedures in production, but rather the proposal that lemma selection takes place during a distinct stage that is encapsulated from phonological information. The challenging finding is that words participating in errors such as substitutions are occasionally both semantically and phonologically related (Dell & Reich, 1981). Thus, it does not appear that lemma selection is discrete and isolated from access of word forms. (See Dell & O'Seaghdha, 1991, and Levelt et al., 1991, for further empirical and theoretical explorations of this controversial topic.)

Another aspect of Garrett's theory that has been questioned is the notion that positional level planning frames include both inflectional affixes and function words. Stemberger (1985) observed the occurrence of inflectional exchanges, an event that should not be possible according to the original Garrett architecture (that is, because inflections are intrinsic parts of the frame, it should not be possible for them to move). And using a syntactic priming technique (to be described in more detail in a later section), Bock (1989) reported that positional level frames with different prepositions (a particular type of function word) were interchangeable, indicating that they are not necessarily part of the frame.

Yet, despite these challenges, it is clear that more than just the outlines of Garrett's original architecture for language production are still widely assumed in current models. For example, the Bock and Levelt model (1995; see also Bock, 1995) consists of three main parts: a message level component, where the semantic intention behind an utterance is developed; a grammatical component, where the syntactic structure is encoded; and a phonological component, where the sound of the utterance is created. The grammatical component has two distinct subparts: A place where functional processing takes place, and a place where positional processing occurs. In the former module, lexical (lemma) selection occurs along with function assignment (establishment of grammatical roles such as subject and object). In the second module, lexical retrieval takes place (retrieval of word forms), together with constituent assembly (fleshing out of phrase-sized frames). Thus, clearly, the broad outlines and even many of the details of the original Garrett model survive even more than 25 years later.

Earlier, I made the point that not all linguistic theories of grammar are compatible, and that the theory a psycholinguist adopts has implications for the processing that is assumed to take place. (For example, if one's theory of grammar does not include traces of moved constituents, then one does not need a mechanism in processing to keep track of phrase-trace referential dependencies.) Here I will note that the influence perhaps might go the other way as well—that is, from production theories to assumptions about linguistic representation. What I have in mind is that many current and prominent theories of syntactic production assume that, at the functional-level stage of processing, grammatical roles such as subject and object are assigned to lemmas (and the constituents which they head). Interestingly, not all theories of linguistic analysis treat grammatical roles as primitives: Theories such as relational grammar and lexical-functional grammar do, but all the versions of generative grammar (the original Standard Theory, the Extended Standard Theory, Government and Binding Theory, and Minimalism) do not. Does the widespread adoption of grammatical roles as explanatory constructs for language production imply that they are indeed critical linguistic representations, such that any linguistic theory that eschews them is inadequate? In the next section, I will describe a computational model of grammar that follows generative grammars in not assuming that grammatical roles are representationally primitive. As will be seen, the structure-creating mechanisms allow lemmas (and associated syntactic structure) to be organised into positions in which they receive interpretations corresponding to subject, object, and so on, but this occurs without explicitly assigning those labels during processing. This approach has other interesting properties as well that make it perhaps appropriate as inspiration for a detailed model of syntactic encoding. I will now describe this computational model and offer proposals for how it can be adapted to explain normal language production.

TREE-ADJOINING GRAMMAR (TAG)

Despite what one might assume from the name "Tree-Adjoining Grammar", TAGs are really a formal meta-language in which to express syntactic generalisations (Frank, 1992). One can adopt the basic Principles and Parameters theory associated with Chomsky and his colleagues (Chomsky, 1986, 1991) or the more recent Minimalist framework (Chomsky, 1992, 1995), for example, and work with TAG as well. The reason for this is that a theory like Principles and Parameters or Minimalism provides the syntactic analyses, including information about the sorts of empty categories that exist and the constraints on their occurrence, as well as the structure of phrases and clauses. A computational grammar like TAG instantiates those analyses in a formal notation (which I will describe later). Thus, it is possible to use TAG and assume the Minimalist framework, a Lexical-Functional Grammar framework (Bresnan, 1982), or some other theoretical system for capturing syntactic analyses. It turns out that most computational linguists working with TAG have assumed a largely Principles and Parameters/Minimalist framework, and so the analyses I will examine will do so as well.

In the TAG approach, a grammar is a set of objects and a set of operations that manipulate those objects (Frank, 1992). The objects are termed *elementary trees*. Elementary trees are primitive syntactic units consisting roughly of a lexical head and the argument(s) the head licenses. For example, the following tree is an elementary tree:[1]

(2)

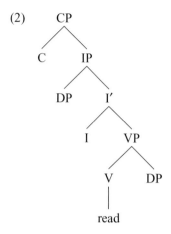

The verb *read* is the lexical head and it licenses two arguments—a subject and an object. Thus, elementary trees are prototypically clause-like. Indeed, they are often described as corresponding roughly to a simple clause (Kroch, 1987), and as being similar to Chomsky's (1955) original kernel sentences (Frank, 1992). The operations that manipulate elementary trees combine them in two different ways—by processes known as *substitution* and *adjoining*. Intuitively, substitution is similar to an appending operation: One elementary tree is attached to the bottom node of another elementary tree. The adjoining operation essentially inserts a special type of elementary tree inside another elementary tree.

More precisely, an elementary tree consists of a simple semantic predicate plus positions for its arguments. Frank (1992) has formalised this definition as the Condition on Elementary Tree Minimality (CETM): Every elementary tree consists of the extended projection of a single lexical head. The following tree gives an example:

(3)

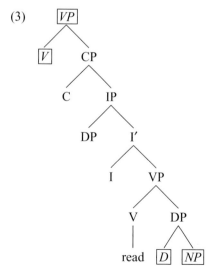

The nodes not in boxes are all part of the same elementary tree. Those nodes are allowed because of the notion *extended projection*. An extended projection of a head includes not just the nodes that the head obviously projects to (i.e., the VP node in the case of the lexical head V) but also its "functional projections"— nodes such as I(nflection) and its projections, C(omplementiser) and its projections, and depending on one's theory of clausal structure, A(greement), T(ense), and its projections (Chomsky, 1986; Pollock, 1993). The nodes in boxes are excluded from this elementary tree because their inclusion would not meet the CETM. The boxed VP and V nodes are excluded because the lexical head *read* does not license them; the boxed V takes the lower clause as its argument, not the other way around. The D and NP nodes at the bottom of the tree are excluded as well because the head *read* licenses the argument positions but does not license the internal content of those phrases. Thus, it should be clear at this point that inserting arguments into those argument positions will require some sort of grammatical operation (substitution, as it will turn out).

Elementary trees come in two basic types: auxiliary trees and initial trees. An example of an auxiliary tree is given in (4):

(4)

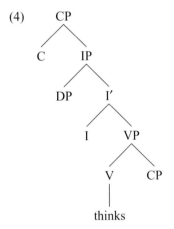

The important feature of this type of tree is that the root node (CP) is identical to one of the nonterminal nodes. This feature allows these trees to be recursive: The matrix clause takes a clause as complement to the verb. Of course, an auxiliary tree can be recursive on some other node—for example, the matching nodes might be NP, which would allow embedding of a noun phrase inside of another noun phrase. When I discuss the operation of adjoining later, the importance of this property will become clearer, above and beyond the obvious need for any grammar to provide a formalism to capture recursive embedding. Initial trees are simply all the elementary trees that are not auxiliaries. Initial trees do not by themselves permit recursion. An example of an initial tree was given in (2), which illustrates a transitive structure. Example (5) is of an initial tree with an intransitive structure:

(5)

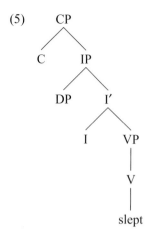

slept

Thus, these different basic syntactic frames correspond to different elementary trees—a transitive frame (2), an intransitive frame (5), a clausal complement frame (4)—and what determines the form of the frame is the lexical head (verb in each of these cases). One can view these trees, then, as bits of phrase structure appropriate for different lexical heads given their different argument-taking properties.

Although, as stated previously, the prototypical elementary tree is clausal (i.e., consists of a verb and its argument positions), clearly some tree types are required that are not. For example, as shown in (3), the actual content of a phrase such as the nominal argument of a verb is not specified in the tree that includes that verb, due to restrictions imposed by the CETM. Therefore, there must be elementary trees for such phrases, as shown in (6):

(6)

The lexical head is the determiner, D.

Adjunct phrases are also elementary trees. An example is given in (7), a structure that would correspond to a phrase such as *after Tom left* in the sentence *Mary closed the blinds after Tom left*:

(7)

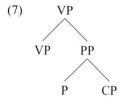

The lexical head in this case is the preposition, P. Note that this structure projects beyond just the PP all the way to VP. The justification for this degree of projection would take us too far afield here, but is assumed by Frank (1992) based on the work of Grimshaw (1991). Of course, an elementary tree for a clause could never include an adjunct phrase, because adjunct phrases are defined as phrases not licensed by a head (in this case, the verb). Therefore, the inclusion of any adjunct in a sentence requires a syntactic operation that combines a clausal elementary tree with another elementary tree for the adjunct.

So far, we've seen that TAG assumes the existence of elementary trees as primitive syntactic objects. The other component of TAG is the operations that manipulate those trees: substitution and adjoining. Substitution is straightforward: One elementary tree is inserted at the bottom of another tree. The restriction on this operation is that the root node of the tree to be inserted must match the label on the node at the insertion site. For example, the tree in (6) is labelled DP at its root, so it can be inserted into the tree given in (2) by substitution, yielding (8):

(8)

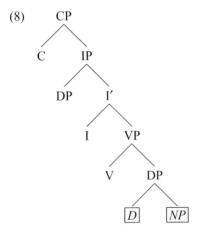

The nodes corresponding to the original (6) are surrounded by boxes. The term substitution highlights one feature of this operation: The DP node at the bottom of (2) is in some sense substituted with the root node from (6) (or vice versa). As stated previously, substitution is used to insert arguments into argument positions, including clausal complements as well as DPs such as *the book*.

The second operation is adjoining, which allows one tree to be inserted inside another. In (9) this operation is shown schematically:

(9)

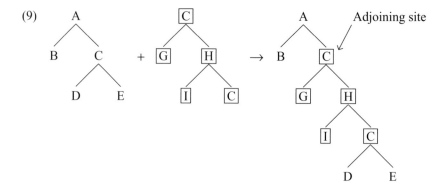

Adjoining is important because it allows a number of different sorts of syntactic structure to be created. One type is a structure including an adjunct phrase. Recall that an adjunct phrase has the structure shown in (7). Let's assume an elementary intransitive clause such as (5). To create a sentence such as *Bill slept after the party ended*, these two elementary trees would be adjoined as follows:

(10)

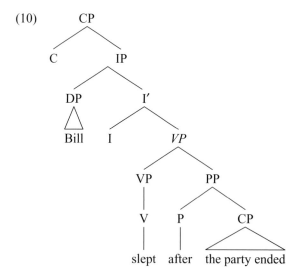

This structure now carries the critical information that the PP *after the party ended* is not an argument of the verb *slept*, because it is not sister to that head.

Adjoining is also the means for creating the so-called "raising" structure—sentences such as:

(11)   Pat is likely to leave.

The description of how this works will reveal not only how raising structures are derived, but will also begin to address the important question of how and to what extent empty categories are used in TAG. A sentence such as (11) is made up of two elementary trees, as shown next:

(12)

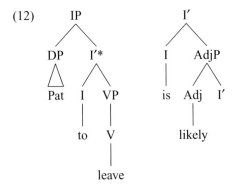

Following convention, the adjoining site has been indicated with an asterisk. Notice that the tree headed by *leave* represents the information that *Pat* is the subject of leaving. Now the two structures are adjoined at the asterisked node, and the result is given in (13):

(13)

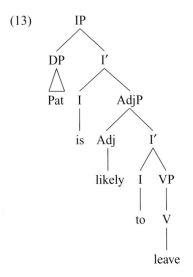

An intriguing effect of this operation, then, is that the raising structure can be represented without any sort of empty category. In theories of grammar that assume empty categories for this structure, the subject *Pat* would be co-indexed with the empty subject of the infinitive in order to maintain the thematic relationship between *Pat* and the action of leaving. In TAG, this representational tool is not necessary because the relationship is stated in the original elementary tree, and the operation of adjoining merely "stretches" the relationship. In the language of TAG, the "local structural relation between the subject and its associated clause has been stretched during the adjoining operation" (Frank & Kroch, 1995, p. 121). Thus, we see one important property of TAG: Fewer empty categories are used when a theory such as Principles and Parameters/Minimalism is translated into the meta-language of TAG.

In a similar vein, *wh-* movement also involves a more economic use of traces in TAG than in other syntactic theories. For example, a sentence such as:

(14)   What do you believe Tom dropped

is created by adjoining the two elementary trees shown in (15).

(15)

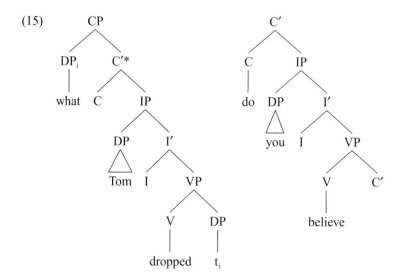

The result is (16):

(16)

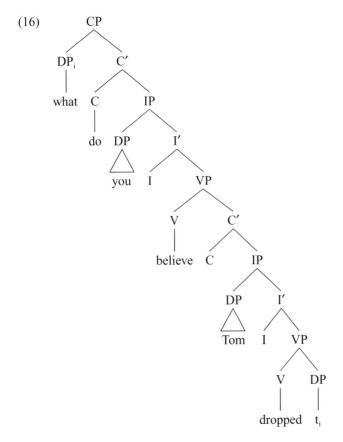

The tree on the left in (15) is an initial tree, and the adjoining site is indicated with an asterisk. The tree on the right is an auxiliary tree (recursive on C'). The initial tree uses an empty category to represent the thematic relationship between the *wh-* word *what* and the verb *dropped*. Thus, TAG does not eschew the use of traces entirely. However, when the trees are adjoined, there is no need for the intermediate traces employed in theories like Principles and Parameters/ Minimalism—just as in the case of raising structures, the local relation between the *wh-* word and the postverbal position is stretched when the two trees are combined. As Frank and Kroch (1995) point out, then, any computational burden associated with unbounded *wh-* structures (e.g., *Who did Mary say that Tom knew that Susan drove . . .*) comes not from the need to perform multiple instances of *wh-* movement, but rather comes from the need to perform several adjoining operations. An implication of this idea is that the computational burden associated with a sentence such as *Who did Mary say that Tom knew that Susan likes* is predicted to be no greater than for a similar sentence without *wh-* movement such as *Mary said that Tom knew that Susan likes eel.*

In summary, the TAG approach assumes the existence of a set of primitive syntactic objects—elementary trees—which have interesting properties that might be useful for a theory of syntactic production. Elementary trees are retrieved as a single chunk. Within this chunk are represented all dependency relations. For example, the relation between a *wh-* phrase and its thematic position is stated within a single syntactic chunk. Another important type of relation is the one that exists between a head such as a verb and its associated arguments, and these connections are also all included in an elementary tree. In addition, elementary trees contain information about what sorts of further syntactic entities they may take, because required positions are explicitly represented. For example, a tree such as (2) states the need for a DP to occur in subject position and another in object position. An auxiliary tree such as (7) makes clear that it requires a VP to which it can adjoin. The operations of substitution and adjoining also may be interesting from the point of view of a psychological theory of syntactic production. One useful aspect of these operations is that they obviate the need for some empty categories—intermediate *wh-* traces and traces in raising structures, for example. Another intriguing possibility is that the two operations might differ in how easily they can be performed—substitution might be easier than adjoining because it requires less effort to simply attach a tree to the bottom of another tree than to actually insert a tree into the middle of another. These and similar ideas will be explored further as we discuss the psychological literature on syntactic production. I turn to this topic next.

PRODUCTION OF SYNTAX

How do speakers make syntactic decisions? Addressing this question forces us to consider the psychological mechanisms that underlie our ability to combine words to form communicatively appropriate sentences. The types of syntactic decisions I will consider here include the following: First, I'll discuss how speakers arrive at a particular syntactic form for a sentence. Second, I'll consider speakers' ability to make two different constituents within an utterance agree properly. A third important question concerns the domain over which syntactic planning takes place. Here, I'll review the literature demonstrating that the planning unit for syntax appears to be roughly clausal. The goal of this section will be not just to review the existing literature but also to indicate how the results can be understood from the perspective of TAG.

Speakers' choice of syntactic form

Lexical influences

Most languages allow speakers to convey the same propositional content in more than one syntactic way. For example, consider the proposition that a particular adult human male named Tom quoted a particular adult human female named Mary. This idea may be expressed as either:

(17) (a) Tom quoted Mary
     (b) Mary was quoted by Tom.

Syntactic analysis has revealed the existence of these different structures—the active in the case of (17a) and the passive in the case of (17b)—and has provided important descriptions of their properties. (Of course, other ways to convey this same idea exist beyond the two shown here—for example, *It was Tom who quoted Mary*—but corresponding to the state of the empirical literature, we will limit our discussion to just a few basic syntactic forms, including actives, passives, and dative structures.) The question for psycholinguists is, given these options, what factors influence the decision to choose one of these structures during the on-line production of an utterance?

Bock and her colleagues have conducted a number of studies designed to address this question. To understand this work, it is important to begin with the way Bock reformulated the question to make it more amenable to a processing-based analysis: Instead of asking what factors determine the choice of syntactic form, Bock asked what factors influence the choice of entity to occupy the subject position of an utterance. This reconceptualisation of the problem is significant, because it changes the question from one that assumes a speaker has the communicative intention to select a particular syntactic structure to one that assumes the speaker makes a decision about just one constituent of that structure— the subject—with that decision then having consequences for the rest of the sentence's form. Linguists have long noted that the subject position of a sentence is privileged. For example, Keenan and Comrie (1977) argued for a hierarchy of grammatical positions, with subjects at the top, followed by direct objects, and then indirect objects (Bock & Warren, 1985). Correspondingly, psychologists have found evidence that the first-mentioned entity in a sentence is better remembered than entities in other sentential positions (Carreiras, Gernsbacher, & Villa, 1995; Gernsbacher & Hargreaves, 1988; for a review, see Gernsbacher, 1990), and that information shared between speaker and hearer tends to occur earlier than information that is new (Haviland & Clark, 1974). Thus, one might expect speakers to place known, available, and salient entities in subject position.

In numerous experiments, Bock has found evidence for just this tendency— concepts that are more prototypical, more concrete, more animate, and generally more activated tend to be syntactically encoded so as to occupy earlier syntactic positions (Bock, 1986a, 1987b; Bock & Warren, 1985; Kelly, Bock, & Keil, 1986; for a review, see Bock, 1987a). We will use the term "available" to capture all these different characteristics. With a regular agent-patient verb such as *quote*, for instance, if the agent is more available than the patient, the agent will grab the subject position of the sentence and the overall form will then be active; if the patient is more available, then it will take the subject position and the overall form will be passive. I will describe just one of the important studies illustrating this tendency. Bock (1986a) investigated whether semantically primed words would tend to occur earlier in a sentence. Participants were shown pictures demonstrating transitive actions such as lightning striking a church, and their task was to describe the picture. Before the picture was presented, one component of the action or the other (*lightning* or *church*) was primed with either a semantically or a phonologically related word (for example, for *lightning*, the prime was either *thunder* or *frightening*; for *church*, the prime was either *worship* or *search*). Results showed that speakers preferred to place the semantically primed word in subject position. As a consequence, if the word *thunder* were presented as a prime before the picture was shown, speakers tended to say *lightning was striking the church*; if the word *worship* were given as the prime, speakers tended to produce *The church was struck by lightning*.

Interestingly, the effect of the phonological prime was different—in Bock (1986a), the prime had little effect, although there was a nonsignificant tendency for the phonologically primed entity to occur late in the sentence. Bock (1987b) used a different sort of phonological prime (rather than priming with a word that rhymed, the prime began with the same initial phonemes as the target word) and found that the same tendency reached conventional levels of statistical significance —the phonologically primed word often occurred towards the end of the sentence. She concluded from this study that the phonological prime made the concept less available, and this inhibition caused the word to occur late in the sentence. She argued further that this result challenged the notion that the syntactic production system is organised with information flowing only from higher to lower levels of processing. Instead, it appears that a source of information from later in the information-processing sequence was able to influence a syntactic decision, a result that runs counter to certain views of information encapsulation (Fodor, 1983). A crucial assumption of Bock's account is that phonologically related words are connected by inhibitory links, as embodied in some connectionist models of the lexicon. However, a great deal of experimental evidence runs contrary to this assumption. For example, numerous studies have shown that the processing of a word is facilitated when it is preceded by one that is phonologically related (e.g., Collins & Ellis, 1992; Grainger & Ferrand, 1996; Hamburger & Slowiaczek, 1996; Radeau, Morais, & Segui, 1995; for a review see Lupker & Colombo, 1994). Therefore, it is not clear how viable Bock's account is. I will argue later in the chapter for a different explanation of the same effect.

In general, then, it appears that the availability of concepts influences syntactic form. A more available concept will tend to be a subject, and the rest of the sentence's structure will be adjusted appropriately. Another way to think about this is as follows: The speaker wishes to convey some propositional content. For some reason, one of the several components of that proposition is most available— for example, the patient is highly available because it is the topic of the discourse. The sentence production system begins working on this available piece right away, following the principle of incrementality. The grammatical encoder does the first thing it can do with an entity for a brand new utterance—it makes it a subject. The production system now has few options for encoding the rest of the utterance:

The verb must occur after the subject and the object must occur after the verb; and because the patient is the subject, the overall structure must be set up as a passive.

Can this sequence of events be described more precisely using TAG? I suggest that it can. Again, imagine a proposition in which someone named Tom in the past quoted someone named Mary. This representation may be captured as in (18), using the standard notation assumed in theories such as that of Kintsch (1974; Kintsch & van Dijk, 1978):

(18)   quote (Tom: agent, Mary: patient, PAST)

Now assume that the concept MARY is highly available. This concept can immediately be syntactically encoded. The nominal entity MARY is identified by the grammatical encoder as a determiner (see Levelt, 1989, for details concerning how this translation is effected), and a determiner is the lexical head of a determiner phrase. Thus, an elementary tree such as the one shown in (19) can be retrieved:

(19)

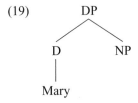

The propositional structure given in (18) is now used to retrieve the appropriate clausal frame for the utterance. The concept QUOTE constrains the grammatical encoder to select an elementary tree headed by the verb *quote*, and the information that the patient *Mary* has already been grammatically encoded as subject requires that the passive form of the verb be selected. Thus, the elementary tree that would be retrieved is one that includes the passive verb *quoted* as the lexical head:

(20)

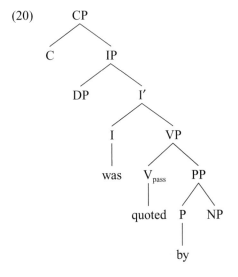

Now the elementary tree (19) can be inserted into the elementary tree in (20) by the operation of substitution. The DP node at the bottom of (19) is the same as the label on the root node of (18), and so substitution is legal. Because the passive structure requires a PP after the verb (for the agentive *by-* phrase), the DP could have substituted into the DP node serving as object of the preposition *by*. However, the principle of incrementality insures that the substitution will occur at the earliest position possible—the subject position. The result now is the tree shown in (21):

(21)

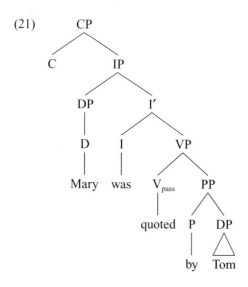

The last step is to retrieve an elementary tree for the object of the preposition in (21). A DP tree headed by the lexical head *Tom* is selected and then inserted into (21) by substitution. The syntactic representation for this sentence is now complete. Of course, as soon as the first NP for the sentence becomes available— that is, as soon as the DP *Mary* is inserted into the elementary tree for the clause and consequently encoded as subject—the phonological encoder began working on converting this syntactic structure into a format suitable for the articulators. This assumption follows from the principle of incrementality, which as defined in the introduction to this chapter states that different levels of processing can work on different pieces of an utterance at the same time. Thus, the phonological encoder can work on the early part of the clause while the syntactic encoder works on filling out what remains. As a result, once the syntactic representation for the sentence is done, its corresponding phonological representation is likely close to complete as well.

The view of syntactic production that has been outlined here has a number of interesting properties. First, because this model allows bits of syntactic structure to be retrieved complete with slots for functional elements, much of the work described in Levelt (1989) that is associated with creating slots for those elements is avoided. For example, Levelt describes a special procedure that fills in the slots for functional elements such as determiners. These special procedures are termed *functional procedures*, which contrast with what he terms *categorial procedures*—procedures that build syntactic structures based on activated lexical items. The model I am proposing does not require functional procedures because those functional elements are part of the elementary tree. Second, the model neatly captures a property Levelt refers to as resonance. In his model, the retrieval of a lexical head such as the verb *give* causes the information that an object should occur to be activated as well, and the NP slot is thus created. At the same time, once the lexical head of this object is known, it too builds an NP slot by projecting up from itself. As Levelt notes, then, there are two ways that a phrasal node may be created. A phrasal node such as DP after a verb could get made because the verb takes a DP, and so the verb predicts the existence of that DP slot; or, the DP slot could be built because the head of that DP "projects up" to its corresponding DP node. However, in the present model, both of these methods for creating phrasal nodes happen in parallel. Again, consider the case of a direct object slot after a verb. That DP slot would exist in a clause-sized elementary tree because the tree is retrieved on the basis of the verb, and that tree would include all the proper slots for arguments (by the CETM). At the same time, when the lexical head of that DP becomes available, it brings along its appropriate elementary tree. Then, the DP elementary tree is attached to the clausal elementary tree by substitution. Thus, the current model describes why these two ways of creating a phrasal node might occur, and also does not require the system to choose between them—both happen at the same time.

A final important property of this model of syntactic production is that it provides a critical role for the main verb of the sentence. Here, the model contrasts sharply with that of Levelt. According to Levelt, when an initial nominal element becomes activated, it projects not only to its N and NP nodes, but also to the sentence node. As a result, the grammatical encoder can create a subject tree (the nodes for the N, the NP, and the IP node dominating the NP) before the verb is even known. Indeed, the same process may occur with no more than a determiner—from the dominating D node the DP node can be built, and an IP node immediately above it. Furthermore, because sentence production is incremental, this unit consisting of just the subject may be phonologically encoded before the verb is made part of the syntactic representation. The model I have advocated here does not allow this degree of incrementality. There is no way for the NP or DP to encode the information that it is the subject of a sentence because of the CETM—the NP or DP node does not license the dominating IP node. Furthermore, there is no way for a nominal element to select for a particular verb at the same time, because again, a noun cannot take a verb as its argument. Thus, if a concept such as MARY becomes activated, a DP structure may be created, but no more—the creation of further syntactic structure must await the activation of the appropriate elementary tree headed by the verb.

This property, of course, can be viewed as either a strength or weakness of the model. Many researchers in language production such as Levelt and Bock have argued strongly for incrementality, and so it might seem a weakness that this model does not allow an initial DP or NP to be encoded grammatically as a subject until the verb for the sentence is known. However, whether this is indeed a weakness depends on what we know from empirical work on sentence production. It turns out that several studies provide evidence for the view described here. Ferreira (1994) found that whether a concept is encoded as a subject depends critically on the properties of the verb. Lindsley (1975) demonstrated that language production cannot begin until at least some information about the main verb of the utterance has been selected. Kempen and Huijbers (1983) drew conclusions similar to those of Lindsley. Finally, Meyer (1996) has obtained evidence that information about even the postverbal arguments of simple utterances are retrieved prior to articulation. We will review each of these studies in turn.

Ferreira (1994) investigated the possibility that the choice of active or passive syntactic form would be influenced by the properties of the sentence's main verb. Consider a verb such as *like*: In an active sentence such as *Mary liked Tom*, the experiencer *Mary* occurs before the theme *Tom*. Many theories of sentence meaning (Kintsch, 1974; Jackendoff, 1972, 1987, 1990) assume that thematic roles are organised in an ordered list, with agents and experiencers at the top and patients and themes at the bottom. Thus, the active structure might be favoured given a verb such as *like* because the active allows the thematic role higher in the hierarchy—the experiencer—to occur in the more prominent syntactic position—the subject. Now consider "theme-experiencer" verbs such as *frighten*. For these verbs, the active structure places the theme in subject position and the experiencer in object position, as in *The thunder frightened Tom*. Thus, the active structure demotes the more prominent thematic role. It might be expected, then, that the passive structure will be somewhat more preferred with theme-experiencer verbs than with normal verbs, because for the former the passive allows the more prominent thematic role to occur in the earlier syntactic position— the subject position. As evidence for this possibility, consider that the sentence *Tom was frightened by Mary* is much more natural than the sentence *Tom was liked by Mary*. This observation provides at least intuitive evidence that passive are better with theme-experiencer verbs than with normal verbs. In Ferreira (1994), I provided experimental evidence consistent with this intuition: Passives occurred on fewer than 5% of trials when the verb was normal, and this percentage did not differ depending on whether the two arguments of the verb were both animate or one animate and the other inanimate. In contrast, with theme-experiencer verbs, passives occurred on about 15% of trials when the two arguments of the verb were animate and about 30% when one was animate and the other inanimate.

In short, the decision whether to make a particular nominal concept a subject depends critically on the verb. Indeed, it is striking that with normal verbs, it made no difference whether a concept was animate or inanimate—speakers did not want to produce passives regardless of the animacy of the nominal concepts. But with theme-experiencer verbs, the animacy contrast exaggerated the tendency to create passives. This study demonstrates, then, that a nominal concept cannot by itself be encoded as the subject of a sentence. The concept may be encoded as a DP or an NP, but then that entire elementary tree can only be inserted into an elementary tree for a clause headed by a verb once the verb is accessed. The work done by the principle of incrementality is that it forces the DP to move into the earliest syntactic position possible—the subject position.

More specifically, assume that a concept such as TOM has become highly available, and imagine further that it is the experiencer of some action. This concept leads to retrieval of a DP elementary tree such as (19) (but with *Tom* as the head). This unit must now sit in a *syntactic buffer*—a structure proposed by Levelt (1989) for holding bits of syntactic structure that are waiting for units on which they are grammatically dependent. Now imagine that the concept corresponding to the main verb is activated, and that this verb is of the theme-experiencer variety—for example, the verb *frighten*. The propositional representation for the entire utterance shows that the experiencer has already been syntactically encoded. Given that entities higher on the thematic hierarchy like to occur in earlier syntactic positions, the passive form of the verb *frighten* is now likely to be activated so as to allow the experiencer to be the subject. An elementary tree for the passive structure will be retrieved, headed by *frighten*. Now the subject *Tom* is plugged into the tree by substitution, and the result is that the words *Tom was frightened* are grammatically encoded. This sequence may now be sent to the phonological encoder. At the same time, the remaining nominal concept is the basis for the retrieval of another DP, and that DP is inserted into the elementary tree headed by *frighten*. This tree includes the PP as well as the head *by* (those nodes are a part of the elementary tree because of the CETM), and so the DP is inserted, again by substitution. The rest of the sentence may now be phonologically encoded. The sequence of operations would not be much different given a normal verb such as *like*: If an experiencer became available first, a DP elementary tree would be retrieved, and then it would be substituted into an elementary tree headed by the normal verb. In this case the tree would be active, because that is the structure that permits the experiencer to occur in the subject position of the sentence.[2]

As stated earlier, Lindsley (1975) conducted a study that supports this view that an initial sentence NP cannot be phonologically encoded until the main verb of the sentence is known. Lindsley asked participants to respond as quickly as possible to a simple picture showing a transitive action (e.g., one person touching another). They were to produce utterances consisting of just the actor, just the action, or a combination of the actor and action. Initiation times for the utterances consisting of the actor plus action were longer than for utterances consisting of just the actor, but no longer than for utterances consisting of just the action. In a second experiment, Lindsley asked the participants again to describe transitive events, but they were to use utterances consisting of either just the actor and action or the actor, action, and object. These two types of utterances took participants the same amount of time to initiate. From these results, it appears that speakers begin to phonologically encode their utterances before they have syntactically encoded the object of a transitive action but not before they know the verb. These results are consistent with the model I have described—the syntactic encoder can represent some NP as a subject only once it has retrieved the elementary tree for the entire clause (headed by the verb) and substituted that NP into the clausal structure. At the same time, the content of the postverbal arguments is not relevant. Thus, the model assumes what we might term moderate incrementality: The production of the subject of a sentence depends on the particular verb but does not depend on the characteristics of the postverbal arguments.

Kempen and Huijbers (1983) conducted a study similar to Lindsley's, but they exploited an important and potentially useful property of Dutch: Utterances may take the form either of subject plus verb (as in English) or verb plus subject (which occurs rarely in English declaratives). The task of the speakers in their experiments was to describe simple displays of pictures with one utterance type or the other, and initiation times were recorded. A further manipulation involved changing the verb from one block of trials to another, in order to assess the effects of verb planning and retrieval on utterance preparation time. Kempen and Huijbers found that changing the verb increased latencies for both types of utterances, but more for the verb–subject than the subject–verb utterances. This pattern of results suggested an interpretation similar to the conclusion drawn by Lindsley: An utterance cannot be articulated until the subject as well as some aspects of the verb are computed. Kempen and Huijbers proposed that the verb's lemma (its semantic and syntactic features) must be retrieved, but articulation does not need to wait for information about the verb's phonological form. Again, it appears that only a moderate version of incrementality can be sustained: Speakers must have lemma information about the subject and its verb before beginning to speak. This empirically based conclusion is consistent with the model I have outlined here: Even if information about a DP is accessed early, that DP cannot be grammatically encoded as the subject of a sentence until the verb (and its elementary tree containing the subject slot) has been retrieved.

Meyer (1996) used a word distractor paradigm to examine how much information about the words of an utterance is accessed prior to articulation. In a couple of her experiments, speakers (of Dutch) produced simple utterances such as (the Dutch equivalents of) "the arrow is next to the bag". In addition, they were presented with a spoken distractor that was either semantically or phonologically related to either the first or second noun (*arrow* or *bag*). Meyer found that a semantic distractor for either noun increased initiation times, whereas a phonological distractor impaired performance only when it was related to the first noun. Meyer concluded that sentence production requires the retrieval of the semantic/syntactic information associated with most of the utterance, but only requires the retrieval of phonological information for the first word or phrase. Thus, Meyer's experiments provide evidence that grammatical encoding is even less incremental than the results reviewed earlier suggest: Speakers appear to encode information about both preverbal *and* postverbal material. Of course, no conclusions about the verb can be drawn given that distractors for the verb were not presented. The paradigm likely made it impossible to present such distractors, because it would have been difficult for speakers to avoid using any other verb besides "is", which is semantically and phonologically rather impoverished. In addition, it is possible that the simple nature of the utterances as well as the argument structures associated with the verb *is* led speakers to grammatically encode as far as the postverbal arguments in these experiments. Also, as Meyer argues, the circumstances of speaking might affect how carefully participants in experiments plan their utterances, and the conditions of her studies might have made participants careful (although it is important to note that participants were asked to begin to speak as quickly as possible). Still, the results of Meyer's experiments support the model of syntactic production based on TAG that I have described here, because they demonstrate that speakers need more than just the subject of a sentence before they can begin to produce their utterances.

Finally, Roelofs (1998) conducted seven experiments to test his model of language production. A critical assumption of this model is rightward incrementality —serial, left-to-right encoding of utterances. The Dutch participants were required to produce verb–particle constructions such as *opzoeken* ("to look up"), and the stimuli in a trial set either shared the initial, particle component of the utterance (as in the immediately preceding example) or the later, verb component. The logic was that if the production system is rightward incremental, then times to initiate the utterances should be facilitated in the former condition but not the latter. This prediction was confirmed, and the pattern of results was taken to support the notion that speech production is indeed incremental. But while these results are clearly important and intriguing, they do not necessarily bear on the issues under discussion here. First, it is important to note that the experiments most likely do concern speech production rather than creative sentence production, because the participants were retrieving small utterances from memory rather than formulating them. Second, the main question that has been examined in this section is whether a sentence can be initiated before the speaker knows the main verb. The Roelofs experiments do not speak to this issue, because the utterances consisted of just a single verb.

Syntactic priming

Speakers have a tendency to repeat a particular syntactic form. For example, if they have just described a transitive action using a passive structure, then they are likely to describe a subsequent transitive event also using the passive form. This effect was demonstrated by Bock (1986b), who had speakers listen to a sentence with a certain form, repeat that same sentence, and then describe a picture. For example, participants would receive a sentence such as *The referee was punched by one of the fans* and then a picture showing lightning striking a church. She found that speakers were more likely to say *The church is bring struck by lightning* in this case than in a condition in which they were primed with *One of the fans punched the referee*. The same effect held for prepositional and double-object dative structures: Speakers were more likely to say (for example) *The man is reading the boy a story* if they had just heard *A rock star sold an undercover agent some cocaine*. Bock also found that the priming effect was not enhanced by the semantic similarities between the prime sentence and the concepts shown in the pictures. In a follow-up study, Bock and Loebell (1990) found that the priming effect was no greater when prime and targets shared the same thematic role structures than when they did not. From these results, Bock concluded that there is a stage of sentence production where just the structural form of an utterance is decided, and that in addition, the structures created during production are frequency sensitive.

Another implication of these results that has not been addressed in the literature on language production is that they challenge extreme forms of incremental production. The priming results imply that there is a point during production where the entire syntactic form of a sentence is available to be influenced by its prior presentation. If a syntactic structure for a sentence is simply built up in little bits that are immediately converted into phonological units, then it is not clear when a representation containing the entire sentence's global syntactic form would be available to be primed. Thus, it appears that the syntactic priming effect obligates us to assume a point in syntactic encoding where a large chunk of syntactic structure is simultaneously available. Again, a model of grammatical encoding that is based on TAG may provide an explanation. Recall that, according to this model, when the main verb of a sentence becomes available it brings with it an elementary tree consisting of all of that verb's extended projections— that is, the entire clausal structure. Thus, even without having the content of all the arguments of the verb known, the availability of a verb also makes available the entire clause's overall syntactic form—whether it is active or passive, a prepositional or double-object dative, and so on. Furthermore, the finding that syntactic priming is independent of lexical (Bock, 1989), thematic (Bock & Loebell, 1990), and general semantic content (Bock, 1986b; Bock, Loebell, & Morey, 1992) is expected on this model as well: Recall that the elementary tree headed by a verb may not include the internal content of any of the arguments included in that tree. Thus, the priming effect could not be affected by these factors, because the type of tree available to be primed does not include any of that information. The only thing that may be primed is the number, configuration, and maximal projection labels of the verb's arguments, and Bock's studies demonstrate that this information is just what gets primed during sentence production.

A TAG-based model of syntactic production, then, provides an account of Bock's syntactic priming effect: Elementary trees can be primed. This conclusion suggests that not just clausal trees (i.e., trees headed by verbs) may be primed but other structures may be as well. This prediction is difficult to test in English because English has such a rigid word order, particularly at the level of phrases. However, it might be possible to test this prediction in languages with freer word orders. For example, the prediction that elementary trees can be primed implies that the presentation of a sentence with an adjective before a noun could lead a speaker to produce another sentence with the adjective and noun in the same order. Again, a language like English allows only prenominal adjectives, but languages such as French or Portuguese allow adjectives to occur either before or after the noun (with some corresponding slight changes in meaning, but this is no different than for the active/passive alternation, for example). Cross-linguistic research should allow this intriguing prediction to be tested. One interesting preliminary result comes from a recent study by Hartsuiker, Kolk, and Huiskamp (1999), which demonstrated that surface order in Dutch can be primed. Participants were presented either with "On the table is a ball" or "A ball is on the table", and Hartsuiker et al. found that the same order tended to be used in a picture description task. Notice that this finding does not necessarily show that within-phrase ordering can be primed (instead, what is at issue is the order of two large constituents with respect to each other), but it is useful for providing evidence that priming can occur even when the variations do not differ in grammatical relations. In addition, it is precisely what one would expect based on the TAG model I have presented, because, although both orders would be headed by *is*, each would have its own elementary tree.

Finally, Pickering and Branigan (1998) employed a novel paradigm for examining syntactic priming in production. Unfortunately, it relied on the creation of written rather than spoken utterances: Participants read a fragment of a dative sentence, which was to serve as a prime (or more than one, in some conditions), and their task was to complete it. For example, the participant might see *Mary gave the book* ____, and the most natural completion would be a prepositional phrase. Then, the same participant received just a subject and dative verb, and his or her task was to complete the sentence. Priming occurs when the form of this latter sentence matches that of the prime(s). Pickering and Branigan observed that the priming effect was smaller but still present when the prime and target sentences employed different verbs. In addition, the amount of priming was the same regardless of whether the verb in the prime and target were of the same tense, aspect, or number. These results can be accommodated by the TAG model I have presented, as long as we introduce a further, critical concept in the approach. TAG assumes that elementary trees are organised into what are termed "families". Families are clusters of related elementary trees. For instance, all elementary trees that are ditransitive and include a noun phrase and a prepositional phrase as postverbal arguments are part of the same family. Similarly, variations on the same basic tree headed by the same lemma (i.e., the differences associated with the same verb but in different tenses, and with different aspects) are also grouped together. Thus, one would expect that the priming effect is not just from trees that are identical to each other; instead, it makes sense that priming would occur across similar trees, and those similarity relations are captured by the notion of tree families.

Subject–verb agreement

Languages require different elements of a sentence to agree with one another. For example, in Portuguese, a phrase such as *O pequeno menino* ("the small boy") requires agreement among all three words—all must be singular and masculine. English uses inflectional morphology to a much lesser extent than many other languages and so overt agreement is not as prevalent. Still, the number of a determiner and noun must agree (i.e., *those boys* versus **those boy*), and the form of some verbs and their subjects must agree also. For example, if a phrase such as *The boys* is the subject of the verb *to have* or *to be*, the head noun and the verb must agree in number. This process becomes especially interesting given that the head noun may be indefinitely separated from the verb with which it must concur. For example, consider a phrase such as *The boys that Mary and Tom saw at the circus*. The head noun is *boys*, but several other nouns occupy the subject NP too. Does the speaker ever get distracted by those nouns and produce a sequence such as *The boys that Mary and Tom saw at the circus is . . .* ?

Bock has investigated this question in a number of experiments (Bock & Cutting, 1992; Bock & Eberhard, 1993; Bock & Miller, 1991). All employed the same paradigm: A spoken noun phrase such as *the keys to the cabinet* was presented to participants, and the participants' task was to repeat the phrase and complete the sentence. On many trials speakers produced a verb that requires overt agreement, and on some of those trials they made errors. Bock and Miller (1991) found that mistakes were rarely made, but those that did occur showed a particular pattern—errors were more frequent when the subject noun phrases contained a singular head noun and a plural distractor noun than when phrases contained a plural head noun and a singular distractor noun. Bock and Eberhard (1993) argued from this result that plurality is an explicitly marked feature while singularity is not. The overt plural feature on the distractor noun can become unbound from it and migrate up to the dominating NP (or DP) node. As a result, the speaker would produce an utterance with improper agreement between the subject and verb.

More relevant to the current discussion is the work of Bock and Cutting (1992), showing that agreement errors of this type are much less likely to occur if the head noun is separated from the verb by a clause rather than a prepositional phrase. Bock and Cutting contrasted agreement processes in phrases such as:

(22) (a) The report of the destructive fires
      (b) The report that they controlled the fires.

The phrase in (22a) includes a prepositional phrase, whereas the phrase in (22b) includes a relative clause. Recall from the discussion earlier that an elementary tree consists of a lexical head and all its extended projections. For (22a), the elementary tree for this DP would include the prepositional phrase, because the noun *report* takes the PP as its argument. In contrast, for (22b), the clause would not be included because it is merely a modifier of the head noun. Therefore, in (22a), the potentially interfering noun *fires* is part of the same elementary tree headed by the noun *report*; in contrast, in (22b), the potentially interfering noun *fires* is part of a different elementary tree (headed by *control*), which is inserted into the NP tree by the substitution operation.

Bock and Cutting (1992) found that agreement errors occurred more often given phrases such as (22a) compared with (22b). They argued that this result followed from the notion that clauses are in some sense independent planning units. The relative clause would be planned separately from the part of the phrase including the head, and so these two parts of the phrase would not be simultaneously present and so would not be available to interfere with one another. That is, even if the plural feature migrated from the final noun of the NP, it could not land on the head noun because the two are never copresent in memory. In contrast, the prepositional phrase and head noun would be simultaneously present and so the plural feature on the distractor noun *fires* could end up on the head noun. The approach I am advocating using TAG translates this account into an explanation invoking elementary trees. Because the phrase in (22a) is made up of one elementary tree headed by *report*, the head and local noun are part of the same structure and so are simultaneously available; but because the phrase in (22b) is made up of two elementary trees, one headed by *report* and the other by *control*, the two nouns are less likely to interact.

Not only does an account employing elementary trees provide an explanation of this result, it also leads to an interesting and highly testable prediction. The account depends critically on the notion that the noun *report* takes a prepositional phrase argument—that is, the PP is part of the elementary tree headed by *report* because it is an argument of *report*, and so its inclusion is required by the CETM. I would predict, then, that an experiment comparing agreement for NPs including PPs but differing in their argument/adjunct properties would show different results. Consider the phrases shown in (23):

(23) (a) The leader of the troops
      (b) The leader with the troops

The model using elementary trees predicts that agreement errors will occur less often for (23b) than for (23a), because the phrase *with the troops* is not an argument of *leader*, whereas the phrase *of the troops* is. This prediction does not follow from the account Bock and Cutting gave of their data, because their explanation relies entirely on the difference between PPs and clauses. Thus, I have outlined the basis for an experiment to distinguish between this proposal and the one given by Bock and Cutting, and I have shown that my explanation is not merely a translation of their terminology into the language of TAG.

Planning units

The issue to be addressed in this section is, what is the unit of syntactic encoding? In other words, how much of the syntactic information of an utterance must be available in parallel before the utterance can be spoken? This question came up earlier in this chapter in the section addressing how the activation levels of lexical items influence a speaker's choice of syntactic form. There I argued that although an available nominal concept might have an affinity for the subject position of a sentence, that assignment actually occurs in two steps. First, the nominal concept is translated into a noun, which leads to retrieval of an elementary tree headed by the noun. Second, the NP is inserted into the subject position of an elementary tree headed by a verb (by the operation of substitution). I provided empirical evidence for this view based on my own work as well as the experiments of Kempen and Huijbers (1983) and Lindsley (1975), all of which demonstrate that a sentence is not produced until the verb's lemma is accessed. Thus, according to this research, the "planning unit" for an utterance includes at least the sentence's verb and whatever argument(s) precede it.

Other sources of evidence suggest that the planning unit is larger—perhaps the size of an entire simple clause. For example, Garrett (1975, 1976, 1980) argued from word exchange errors such as:

(24) I left the briefcase in my cigar

that the syntactic structure of a sentence is planned over the domain of a verb together with its arguments. The evidence for this conclusion is that such errors involve words from different phrases (the arguments of the verb) but rarely from different clauses. And in several studies in which speakers talked freely about topics of interest to them, Ford and Holmes also found evidence for clause-sized planning units. Ford and Holmes (1978) asked participants to respond to tones as they spoke, and found that reaction times were longer for tones at the end of what they termed deep clauses (clauses consisting only of a verb and its arguments). Ford (1982) examined spontaneous speech for pauses longer than 200 ms and found that they preceded about 20% of deep clauses. She concluded that speakers plan an upcoming deep clause during the production of the last few syllables of the current clause; if that time is not sufficient for planning, then they hesitate. Because pause duration was unaffected by the number of upcoming deep clauses, Ford concluded that speakers planned no more than one deep clause. Holmes (1988) asked speakers to talk spontaneously on various topics and then asked another group of participants to read the utterances the former group produced. She found that pauses and hesitations occurred before complement and relative clauses in spontaneous but not read speech. This result provides further evidence for the conclusion that speakers plan in units roughly the size of a deep or simple clause: When speakers formulate their sentences they often pause not only at the start of a sentence but also before a clause that might be embedded inside that sentence. If participants are merely reading, then they pause much less often and almost never before embedded clauses.

Thus, the experimental work conducted by Ferreira (1994), Kempen and Huijbers (1983), and Lindsley (1975) suggests that speakers syntactically encode their utterances up to about a clause's main verb. The research examining spontaneous speech (both speech errors and pauses) indicates that speakers syn-tactically encode an entire simple clause. Although both types of studies support the notion that the planning unit for an utterance is larger than a word or phrase, they differ somewhat in what the size of that unit actually is. Can the results be reconciled? One important difference between the two types of studies is that the ones providing evidence for the smaller unit all employed experimental tasks in which speakers received the raw ingredients for some part of their utterances (a picture or a few critical words) and then produced sentences as quickly as possible. In this sort of paradigm, each utterance might be viewed by the particip-ant as a sort of performance, with a premium placed on reducing as much as possible the latency to initiate that performance. These circumstances might make the speakers less likely to take the time they normally would to plan their utterances. The nonexperimental studies do not impose these sorts of constraints on the speakers. Data from speech errors are obtained simply by noting the botched utterances when they are produced, and the pause data came from speakers who were constrained by no more than a discussion topic. It is possible, then, that in the normal case people grammatically encode over the domain of a simple clause, but if they are rushed they truncate planning at the earliest possible point—once the verb for the utterance is known.

What are the implications of these conclusions for the TAG-based model of syntactic planning I have been advocating in this chapter? To begin, let us recall that the elementary tree is the fundamental unit of TAG, and that each elementary tree is centred around its lexical head. Although there are therefore many different types of elementary trees (corresponding to the different types of heads), it is reasonable to propose that the type headed by the verb is pivotal for syntactic production, because such trees provide a global skeleton for the utterance. (Indeed, the earlier section describing the fundamentals of TAG points out that the clause is assumed to be the prototypical elementary tree.) The conclusion that speakers plan in units consisting of simple clauses can then be straightforwardly accounted for within the TAG framework: The critical syntactic chunk that must be retrieved for any utterance is the elementary tree headed by the verb. This entity provides the lexical head itself (intrinsically bound to the tree), the maximal projection labels for all the head's dependents, and any necessary traces. Retrieval of this unit takes some processing resources, and occasionally the time spent in articulation of a clause is not sufficient to allow retrieval of the elementary tree for the next. In those circumstances, a pause of some sort is required. A word exchange error such as (24) might occur when the clausal elementary tree is retrieved but the DP arguments of the verb are bound to the wrong argument positions. This view correctly predicts that verbs will not participate in word exchange errors, because they are an intrinsic part of the clause's skeleton and so can not be unbound from it. The actual content of the verb's arguments must be inserted into the tree, and so it is possible for the system to err by inserting the DP/NP elementary trees into the wrong argument positions. Finally, if the speaker is put into a situation in which he or she feels pressured to speak quickly (as in the standard experimental paradigm in which a stimulus is presented which the speaker must describe as quickly as possible), then planning will be limited to the smallest possible domain. The TAG approach to syntactic planning predicts that the smallest domain will have to include the verb, and so for English declarative sentences speakers may begin to speak once they know just the first NP and the main verb.

Not only does the TAG approach to syntactic production explain results already obtained, it also makes an intriguing prediction. Recall that in TAG, adjunct phrases are never part of an elementary tree for a clause. This restriction follows from the CETM, which specifies that an elementary tree may include only a head and its arguments. Thus, all adjunct phrases must be added by syntactic operations—operations to encode both their phrasal structure and their lexical content. One might expect, then, that adjuncts would be preceded by a pause more often than arguments. Ferreira (1988) compared pause durations before these two types of phrases and found support for this prediction. However, the speakers in these experiments did not produce the sentences spontaneously, and so the tendency to pause before adjuncts could be attributed to phonological or stylistic factors rather than to the need to plan. It is clear what needs to be done: Spontaneous speech should be examined to assess whether pauses occur more often before adjuncts than before arguments of comparable length and complexity.

SYNTACTIC PRODUCTION BASED ON TAG

In this section I will give an explicit description of how syntactic production takes place according to the TAG-based approach I have been advocating. In addition, I will contrast this model with one proposed by Levelt (1989), which is probably the most explicit and best-known in the area of language production. The critical representational assumption of the model I have proposed here is that syntactic structure is built up from primitive syntactic templates, each based on a single lexical item. A template is retrieved when its head is activated. The only primitive lexical content to the template is the head. All other material must be inserted by a syntactic operation, and so the other lexical items must be bound to their appropriate syntactic positions. It is reasonable to assume that this binding process requires resources, and that it can sometimes go awry (as in word exchange errors).

The production of an utterance begins with a message that is translated into a propositional representation—a formal representation of the utterance's meaning. The proposition specifies whether the utterance describes a state or an event; it is organised into a function–argument structure in which (usually) the main verb is the function and the rest of the proposition includes its arguments (including tense and aspect); it includes information about which argument is the topic (i.e., old information); and each nominal is specified in terms of definiteness, number, and thematic role. When a concept is activated, its corresponding lemma is activated as well. The lemma is translated into a syntactic head, and retrieval of that head brings along its associated elementary tree. The thematic role of any activated nominal concept that has been syntactically encoded determines which form of the verbal lemma becomes activated—active, passive, prepositional dative, double-object dative, and so on. Retrieval of the verb leads to retrieval of the syntactic skeleton for the whole clause. Any already constructed argument is inserted into the clause at the earliest possible point. This is the work the principle of incrementality does in this model—it ensures that the phrase is bound to the leftmost matching position (by substitution). At this point, the utterance could be sent to the phonological encoder and articulated. Meanwhile, any remaining arguments are grammatically encoded as well— the elementary trees based on each lexical item are retrieved and then inserted into the tree. If an adjunct phrase is part of the propositional representation (see Jackendoff, 1990, and Kintsch, 1974, for propositional notations that distinguish arguments from adjuncts) it is separately encoded and then inserted into the clausal elementary tree by the adjoining operation. The syntactic form is complete once each constituent of the propositional representation is grammatically encoded.

Let's take an example utterance: "The dog bit a flower". The propositional representation—expanded from the one shown in (18)—would look something like the following:

(25)   event: BITE(def/1/agent/topic: DOG; indef/1/patient: FLOWER; past)

According to this proposition, the topic is a definite, single dog. An event of biting took place in the past. The topic of the utterance is the agent of the action (the dog), and the thing bitten was an indefinite single flower. This proposition contains three concepts that can be translated into lexical heads: BITE, DOG, and FLOWER. Assume that the concept corresponding to DOG is activated first (a plausible assumption given that it is the topic of the sentence). Activation of that concept causes retrieval of a lemma for DOG that is a single, definite noun. Retrieval of that lemma brings along its associated elementary tree, an NP (or DP—it makes no difference for our purposes). The agent thematic role in the proposition can be checked off as grammatically encoded. The NP is placed into the syntactic buffer, where it awaits the retrieval of a clausal elementary tree.

Assume next that the concept corresponding to the verb is activated. The lemma for BITE is therefore retrieved. Because the proposition specifies that the action happened in the past, a past tense version of the verb will be accessed. And because the proposition also indicates that the agent has been grammatically encoded, the verb will also be in its active form. Retrieval of the past, active form of the verb brings along an elementary tree including the verb and instantiating a past tense, active syntactic structure. This tree contains two NP slots, so the NP in the syntactic buffer can be retrieved and inserted into the clausal elementary tree. The principle of incrementality makes it likely that the phrase will go into the leftmost NP slot, and so the NP *The dog* will be grammatically encoded as subject. At this point, because the first entity of the sentence is now grammatically encoded, a piece of the utterance (consisting of the subject plus verb) can be sent along for phonological encoding. What remains from the proposition is the patient of the action. The concept corresponding to FLOWER leads to retrieval of a lemma for FLOWER that is indefinite and singular, and this lexical head brings along an indefinite NP structure. This NP is bound to the only remaining NP slot in the clausal elementary tree, and the grammatical encoding of the utterance is now complete.

Let's consider another example. This one will illustrate the advantages of assuming only a moderate degree of incrementality. Imagine that someone wants to express the idea that a particular trunk (or boot of a car) was the location in which a particular singular male placed a body. The propositional representation would look something like the following:

(26)   event: PUT (def/1/agent: MAN; def/1/theme: BODY; def/1/location/
        topic: TRUNK; past)

Because the trunk is the topic, it is likely to be available first. Its conceptual features lead to retrieval of a singular, definite, noun lemma, and that brings along a corresponding elementary tree for a singular, definite NP headed by *trunk*. The thematic role LOCATION can be checked off as grammatically encoded. The NP is placed in the syntactic buffer. Now assume that the lemma for the action of putting becomes available. Because a location was grammatically encoded first, two lemmas for the action of putting will be retrieved (and their corresponding elementary trees): Both are past tense, but one is active and one passive. It's possible that the active structure is more activated because it is used more frequently,[3] but still two trees are available now in parallel. However, neither of the trees allows a location to be placed in subject position—the lexical semantics of the verb *put* are such that the argument corresponding to a location cannot be a subject. (*Put* contrasts with a verb such as *contain*, which does allow locations to be subjects, as in *The trunk contains the body*.) The system now has two options: One is to wait for another argument to be syntactically encoded. It will be either the agent or theme, both of which can occur in subject position. If the agent becomes available instead of the patient, it will move into the leftmost position (by incrementality) of the active syntactic structure; if the patient becomes available instead of the agent, it will move into the leftmost position of the passive syntactic structure. Whichever structure is not chosen will lose activation (either by passive decay or through a process of active inhibition; data sufficient to decide between these possibilities are not available) and the grammatical encoder will now have a single clausal elementary tree with the subject and verb slots filled.

Notice that if the system did not wait for the verb but instead immediately made nominal entities into subjects, it would attempt to create an utterance like "The trunk was put the body by the man", or something along those lines. Because the grammatical encoder waited for the verb, it received in time the information that the location argument could not be the subject of the utterance. Thus, the model I have presented here does not allow the system to create sentences violating the fundamental rules of the language. And, as Bock (1982) and Levelt (1989) have argued, any adequate theory of language production must explain how speakers produce sentences conforming to the language's syntactic constraints, as an overwhelming percentage of utterances are grammatically appropriate.

Another important characteristic of the model I have proposed here is that it assumes that syntactic encoding is not necessarily a serial process—instead, all syntactic structures compatible with a given lemma are activated at one time. As more information becomes available, competing lemmas drop out until only one structure is left by the time grammatical encoding is complete. Normally, activation of a nominal lemma together with a particular verb will uniquely determine a clausal elementary tree. However, the previous paragraph outlined one circumstance in which clausal trees could be activated in parallel. Another circumstance is one in which two nominal lemmas are equally available. In this case, the speaker might be disfluent at the beginning of the utterance, as the production system tries to choose between them (for example, by waiting for some other lemma to become available that forces the choice between the structures).

Is there evidence relevant to the question whether more than one syntactic tree is activated in parallel? At this point, only one study has been conducted to explore this question, and it appears to support a serial view of syntactic production. Victor Ferreira (1996) presented speakers with a sequence consisting of a nominative pronoun plus a verb, and then nouns that were to be used for the remainder of the utterance. The main manipulation was whether the verb permitted more than one arrangement of the postverbal nominal arguments—that is, either the verb was a dative such as *give* or a nonalternator verb such as *donate*. Participants were asked to produce sentences as quickly as possible using all the words they were provided on a computer monitor. Victor Ferreira found that participants produced utterances faster and with fewer errors when they were given an alternator verb.[4] He argued that the results were inconsistent with a model in which multiple syntactic structures for a verb are activated and compete. This conclusion is based on the assumption that competition takes time to resolve and should be reflected in longer and more error-prone responses. On this view, initiation times should have been longer in the alternator verb condition, because the alternator verbs would activate two syntactic structures, and resolution of the competition between them should have taken time. Instead, the alternator condition was faster than the condition in which only one syntactic structure could be grammatically produced. Victor Ferreira argued that these results support an incremental model of production: Speakers opportunistically select syntactic structures based on the activation states of lexical items, and so syntactic flexibility is helpful to the production system because choices allow it to quickly adjust to a particular lexical item's activation state.

On the face of it, this study appears to provide evidence against the model I have argued for here. Fortunately, it does not. The present model can account for the fact that activated words tend to occur early in sentences. The assumption of moderate incrementality states that an activated NP will sit in the syntactic buffer until a verb becomes available, but then it will move into the first syntactic position provided by the verb's elementary tree—the subject position. Thus, this model allows the activation states of lexical items to determine syntactic form quickly, as does the model Victor Ferreira assumes. Indeed, the Victor Ferreira study allows us to clarify some important properties of the present model. I assume that multiple syntactic structures will be available only when lexical activation states are not sufficient to uniquely specify a single structure. Under most typical speaking circumstances, lexical items will become available at different points and to different degrees, and so syntactic structures will be dynamically pruned away until only a single one remains. Thus, the results obtained by Victor Ferreira support the general model I have described here—a model that allows both moderate incrementality and the activation of multiple syntactic structures. Availability of lexical items influences syntactic positioning, which then leads to the immediate deactivation of syntactic forms not consistent with that positioning.

The TAG-based model can account for the effects of the various priming manipulations that have been used in experiments on language production—semantic, syntactic, and phonological. First, a semantic prime mimics the effect of some concept being a topic. Normally, the thing that is under discussion—the topic—will be the most available concept, and so it will be grammatically encoded first and will end up as the subject of the sentence (because of moderate incrementality). A semantic prime is simply an artificial way of making some concept active, as it would be if it were a topic. Second, a syntactic prime affects syntactic form because it affects which clausal elementary tree for a particular verb gets selected. Again, because most experiments do not provide any reason for making any particular concept a topic, speakers can do one of several things. Speakers may select randomly; they may use a heuristic such as making the leftmost entity in the picture the first constituent of a sentence; or they may default to the most frequent structure (typically an active clause). A syntactic prime minimises the chances that the speaker will choose any of these strategies, because it provides some activation for one of the competing syntactic forms. So if a participant in an experiment has just encountered a passive sentence and then has to describe a transitive action depicted on a computer monitor, he or she might produce the passive because it is activated by the prior retrieval of a passive. (Indeed, although the priming effect is statistically reliable, it is quite a small effect, suggesting that the other strategies described here are quite compelling.)

What about the phonological prime? Here I will make good on the promise I made earlier in the chapter to reinterpret Bock's (1986a, 1987b) finding that phonological primes under some conditions cause the primed word to occur late in a sentence. According to some interpretations of this effect (e.g., Bock, 1987b), this finding challenges modularity, because a source of information from late in the information processing sequence is able to affect syntactic form (which presumably is decided earlier). Bock's explanation of the effect of phonological primes is predicated on the notion that the links between phonologically related words are inhibitory rather than excitatory; and because the word is inhibited, it is not available to be encoded as an early constituent of the sentence. Therefore, there must be some feedback in the system, because the ultimate syntactic form of a sentence is responsive to the phonological states of one of the words.

However, the result could be taken to indicate that the system is not incremental, rather than that it is not modular. If the system were incremental in the extreme, then a phonologically primed word should occur early in a sentence—after all, it is highly available, and so if it were articulated the production system could get on with encoding the rest of the utterance. Instead, it appears that the language production system does not want to produce a word in the absence of any other information about the utterance. After all, the system does not know whether a determiner is required, whether the phrase is definite or indefinite, and of course it does not yet have the elementary clausal structure of the utterance (because the main verb is not yet known). Under these circumstances, the language production system might actively inhibit the word in order to prevent it from being produced, and that inhibitory state might cause the word to be the last one grammatically encoded. Under this view, the inhibition of the phonologically primed word is not attributed to passive spreading activation in a network in which phonologically related words are connected by inhibitory links (and indeed there is some evidence that phonological primes facilitate processing of the related word; Costa & Sebastian-Galles, 1998; Zwitserlood, 1996); instead, the word is actively inhibited by the language production system.

Implicit in the model I have outlined here are some critical attentional mechanisms. Attention plays a role in binding nonclausal elementary trees into the clausal elementary tree. Attention is used to monitor which thematic roles in the proposition have been grammatically encoded and which remain. And now we see that attention inhibits a word that becomes available for articulation too early. Clearly, an important next step in exploring whether this TAG-based model of production is viable is to specify explicitly what these attentional mechanisms are, how they work, and how they are related to the sorts of mechanisms about which a great deal is known in other areas of cognitive science (e.g., visual attention).

How does the model I have proposed here contrast with another well-known model of grammatical encoding, the one proposed by Levelt (1989)? Levelt's model assumes the existence of a propositional representation, and assumes that the activation levels of concepts that make up that proposition (as those activation states unfold in real time) determine the order in which lemmas are retrieved. The syntactic structure for a lemma is created as soon as a lemma becomes available, and the maximum amount of structure is created at that point. Levelt's model is lexically based—syntactic structure is projected from the lemmas themselves. Therefore, lemmas are inherently bound to their syntactic homes. Syntactic pieces are sent to the phonological encoder as soon as they are available, in accordance with the principle of incrementality. Therefore, rarely is the entire syntactic form for an utterance or its constituent lemmas available in working memory.

The model I have proposed here also assumes that an utterance is generated from a propositional representation. Concepts making up the proposition become differentially activated, but one important determinant of activation levels is whether one concept is marked as topic. If one is, it will be the most available concept and so will have a strong affinity for the subject position of the utterance. The verbal concept determines which verb lemma becomes available (active, passive, dative, and so on), and so which elementary tree(s) is(are) retrieved. All possible elementary trees compatible with a verbal lemma are accessed, with their activation levels depending on their frequency of use. As grammatical encoding unfolds, ultimately only one clausal elementary tree remains activated, and it determines the ultimate form of the sentence. Elementary trees for syntactic entities other than clauses must be inserted into the clausal tree, and the order of their insertion is determined by availability. Binding phrases to their appropriate clausal positions presumably takes resources, and errors may occur (if, for example, not enough resources are allocated to the task). All of the syntactic structure for a simple clause is simultaneously present; and even if an utterance is phonologically encoded at the earliest point possible (once the subject plus verb are available), the overall syntactic nodes for the verb's arguments will still be simultaneously present in working memory.

NOTES

1. Throughout this chapter, I use the following syntactic conventions and abbreviations. First, I assume the analysis of clauses presented in Chomsky (1986), according to which a clause is an Inflectional Phrase (abbreviated as IP), and a full clause including the node for a complementiser is a Complementiser Phrase (CP). I have not included clausal machinery involving tense or agreement, simply because those structures are not relevant to the discussion here. Finally, I assume Abney's analysis of noun phrases as Determiner Phrases (DPs). Other abbreviations are fairly standard: NP for noun phrase, PP for prepositional phrase, and VP for verb phrase.
2. Of course, this description assumes that important other factors are held constant—for instance, discourse. Clearly, the preferences that Ferreira (1994) uncovered can be overridden if a sufficient amount of context is provided.
3. As Bock (1986b) notes, one implication of syntactic priming is that the production of syntactic structure is frequency sensitive. The priming results show immediate and probably transient effects of frequency; however, it is likely that the overall frequency of use of some structure affects its accessibility during production.
4. A few other manipulations of syntactic choice were used by Victor Ferreira (1996). For example, he varied whether one of the nouns presented after the subject plus verb combination was marked as accusative. The logic is that the inclusion of the case-marked pronoun removes any syntactic flexibility afforded by the verb. As the results for all his flexibility manipulations were similar, I will focus just on the data from dative and nonalternator verbs.

REFERENCES

Bock, J.K. (1982). Toward a cognitive psychology of syntax: Information processing contributions to sentence formulation. *Psychological Review, 89*, 1–47.

Bock, J.K. (1986a). Meaning, sound, and syntax: Lexical priming in sentence production. *Journal of Experimental Psychology: Learning, Memory, and Cognition, 12*, 575–586.

Bock, J.K. (1986b). Syntactic persistence in language production. *Cognitive Psychology, 18*, 355–387.

Bock, J.K. (1987a). Coordinating words and syntax in speech plans. In A. Ellis (Ed.), *Progress in the psychology of language* (pp. 337–390). Hove, UK: Lawrence Erlbaum Associates Ltd.

Bock, J.K. (1987b). An effect of the accessibility of word forms on sentence structure. *Journal of Memory and Language, 26*, 119–137.

Bock, J.K. (1989). Closed-class immanence in sentence production. *Cognition, 31*, 163–186.

Bock, J.K. (1995). Sentence production: From mind to mouth. In J.L. Miller & P.D. Eimas (Eds.), *Speech, language, and communication: Handbook of perception and cognition* (Vol. II, 2nd ed., pp. 181–216). San Diego: Academic Press.

Bock, J.K., & Cutting, J.C. (1992). Regulating mental energy: Performance units in language production. *Journal of Memory and Language, 31*, 99–127.

Bock, J.K., & Eberhard, K.M. (1993). Meaning, sound, and syntax in English number agreement. *Language and Cognitive Processes, 8*, 57–99.

Bock, J.K., & Levelt, W.J.M. (1995). Language production: Grammatical encoding. In M. Gernsbacher (Ed.), *Handbook of psycholinguistics* (pp. 945–984). New York: Academic Press.

Bock, J.K., & Loebell, H. (1990). Framing sentences. *Cognition, 35*, 1–40.

Bock, J.K., Loebell, H., & Morey, R. (1992). From conceptual roles to structural relations: Bridging the syntactic cleft. *Psychological Review, 99*, 150–171.

Bock, J.K., & Miller, C.A. (1991). Broken agreement. *Cognitive Psychology, 23*, 45–93.

Bock, J.K., & Warren, R.K. (1985). Conceptual accessibility and syntactic structure in sentence formulation. *Cognition, 21*, 47–67.

Bresnan, J. (1982). *The mental representation of grammatical relations*. Cambridge, MA: MIT Press.

Carreiras, M., Gernsbacher, M.A., & Villa, V. (1995). The advantage of first mention in Spanish. *Psychonomic Bulletin and Review, 2*, 124–129.

Chomsky, N. (1955). *The logical structure of linguistic theory*. Bloomington, IN: Indiana University Linguistics Club.

Chomsky, N. (1981). *Lectures on government and binding*. Dordrecht, The Netherlands: Foris.

Chomsky, N. (1986). *Barriers*. Cambridge, MA: MIT Press.

Chomsky, N. (1991). Some notes on economy of representation and derivation. In R. Freidin (Ed.), *Principles and parameters in comparative grammar*. Cambridge, MA: MIT Press.

Chomsky, N. (1993). A minimalist program for linguistic theory. In K. Hale & S.J. Keyser (Eds.), *The view from Building 20: Essays in linguistics in honor of Sylvain Bromberger* (pp. 1–52). Cambridge, MA: MIT Press.

Chomsky, N. (1995). *The minimalist program*. Cambridge, MA: MIT Press.

Collins, A.F., & Ellis, A.W. (1992). Phonological priming of lexical retrieval in speech production. *British Journal of Psychology, 83*, 375–388.

Costa, A., & Sebastian-Galles, N. (1998). Abstract phonological structure in language production: Evidence from Spanish. *Journal of Experimental Psychology: Learning, Memory, and Cognition, 24*, 886–903.

Dell, G.S., & O'Seaghdha, P.G. (1991). Mediated and convergent lexical priming in language production: A comment on Levelt et al. (1991). *Psychological Review, 98*, 604–614.

Dell, G.S., & Reich, P.A. (1981). Stages in sentence production: An analysis of speech error data. *Journal of Verbal Learning and Verbal Behavior, 20*, 611–629.

Ferreira, F. (1988). *Planning and timing in sentence production: The syntax-to-phonology conversion*. Unpublished PhD thesis, University of Massachusetts, Amherst.

Ferreira, F. (1994). Choice of passive voice is affected by verb type and animacy. *Journal of Memory and Language, 33*, 715–736.

Ferreira, V.S. (1996). Is it better to give than to donate? Syntactic flexibility in language production. *Journal of Memory and Language, 35*, 724–755.

Fodor, J.A. (1983). *The modularity of mind*. Cambridge, MA: MIT Press.

Ford, M. (1982). Sentence planning units: Implications for the speaker's representation of meaningful relations underlying sentences. In J. Bresnan (Ed.), *The mental representation of grammatical relations*. Cambridge, MA: MIT Press.

Ford, M., & Holmes, V.M. (1978). Planning units and syntax in sentence production. *Cognition, 6*, 35–53.

Frank, R. (1992). *Syntactic locality and tree adjoining grammar: Grammatical, acquisition, and processing perspectives*. Unpublished PhD thesis, University of Pennsylvania.

Frank, R., & Kroch, A. (1995). Generalized transformations and the theory of grammar. *Studica Linguistica, 49*, 103–151.

Fromkin, V.A. (1971). The non-anomalous nature of anomalous utterances. *Language, 47*, 27–52.

Garrett, M.F. (1975). The analysis of sentence production. In G.H. Bower (Ed.), *The psychology of learning and motivation* (Vol. 9, pp. 133–177). New York: Academic Press.

Garrett, M.F. (1976). Syntactic processes in sentence production. In R.J. Wales & E. Walker (Eds.), *New approaches to language mechanisms* (pp. 231–256). Amsterdam: North-Holland.

Garrett, M.F. (1980). Levels of processing in sentence production. In B. Butterworth (Ed.), *Language production: Vol. 1. Speech and talk* (pp. 177–220). New York: Academic Press.

Gernsbacher, M.A. (1990). *Language comprehension as structure building*. Hillsdale, NJ: Lawrence Erlbaum Associates Inc.

Gernsbacher, M.A., & Hargreaves, D.J. (1988). Accessing sentence participants: The advantage of first mention. *Journal of Memory and Language, 27*, 699–717.

Grainger, J., & Ferrand, L. (1996). Masked orthographic and phonological priming in visual word recognition and naming: Cross-task comparisons. *Journal of Memory and Language, 35*, 623–647.

Grimshaw, J. (1991). *Extended projection*. Unpublished manuscript, Rutgers University, New Brunswick, NJ.

Hamburger, M., & Slowiaczek, L. (1996). Phonological priming reflects lexical competition. *Psychonomic Bulletin and Review, 3*, 520–525.

Hartsuiker, R.J., Kolk, H.H.J., & Huiskamp, P. (1999). Priming word order in sentence production. *Quarterly Journal of Experimental Psychology: Human Experimental Psychology, 52A*, 129–147.

Haviland, S.E., & Clark, H.H. (1974). What's new? Acquiring new information as a process in comprehension. *Journal of Verbal Learning and Verbal Behavior, 13*, 512–521.

Holmes, V.M. (1988). Hesitations and sentence planning. *Language and Cognitive Processes, 3*, 323–361.

Jackendoff, R.S. (1972). *Semantic interpretation in generative grammar*. Cambridge, MA: MIT Press.

Jackendoff, R.S. (1987). The status of thematic relations in linguistic theory. *Linguistic Inquiry, 18*, 369–412.

Jackendoff, R.S. (1990). *Semantic structures*. Cambridge, MA: MIT Press.

Joshi, A.K. (1985). How much context-sensitivity is required to provide reasonable structural descriptions: Tree adjoining grammars. In D. Dowty, L. Kartunnen, & A. Zwicky (Eds.), *Natural language parsing: Psychological, computational, and theoretical perspectives*. Cambridge, UK: Cambridge University Press.

Joshi, A.K., Levy, L., & Takahashi, M. (1975). Tree adjunct grammars. *Journal of the Computer and System Sciences, 10*, 136–163.

Keenan, E.L., & Comrie, B. (1977). Noun phrase accessibility and universal grammar. *Linguistic Inquiry, 8*, 63–99.

Kelly, M.H., Bock, J.K., & Keil, F.C. (1986). Prototypicality in a linguistic context: Effects on sentence structure. *Journal of Memory and Language, 25*, 59–74.

Kempen, G., & Huijbers, P. (1983). The lexicalization process in sentence production and naming: Indirect election of words. *Cognition, 14*, 185–209.

Kintsch, W. (1974). *The representation of meaning in memory*. Hillsdale, NJ: Lawrence Erlbaum Associates Inc.

Kintsch, W., & van Dijk, T.A. (1978). Towards a model of text comprehension. *Psychological Review, 85*, 363–394.

Kroch, A. (1987). Unbounded dependencies and subjacency in a tree adjoining grammar. In A. Manaster-Ramer (Ed.), *Mathematics of language*. Amsterdam: John Benjamins.

Kroch, A., & Joshi, A.K. (1985). *The linguistic relevance of tree adjoining grammar* (Tech. Rep. No. MS-CS-85-16). Department of Computer and Information Sciences, University of Pennsylvania.

Levelt, W.J.M. (1989). *Speaking: From intention to articulation*. Cambridge, MA: MIT Press.

Levelt, W.J.M., Schriefers, H., Vorberg, D., Meyer, A.S., Pechmann, T., & Havinga, J. (1991). The time course of lexical access in speech production: A study of picture naming. *Psychological Review, 98*, 122–142.

Lindsley, J.R. (1975). Producing simple utterances: How far ahead do we plan? *Cognitive Psychology, 7*, 1–19.

Lupker, S.J., & Colombo, L. (1994). Inhibitory effects in form priming: Evaluating a phonological competition explanation. *Journal of Experimental Psychology: Human Perception and Performance, 20,* 437–451.

Meyer, A.S. (1996). Lexical access in phrase and sentence production: Results from picture-word interference experiments. *Journal of Memory and Language, 35,* 477–496.

Pickering, M.J., & Branigan, H.P. (1988). The representation of verbs: Evidence from syntactic priming in language production. *Journal of Memory and Language, 39,* 633–651.

Pollock, J.-Y. (1993). Verb movement, universal grammar, and the structure of IP. *Linguistic Inquiry, 20,* 365–424.

Radeau, M., Morais, J., & Segui, J. (1995). Phonological priming between monosyllabic spoken words. *Journal of Experimental Psychology: Human Perception and Performance, 21,* 1297–1311.

Roelofs, A. (1998). Rightward incrementality in encoding simple phrasal forms in speech production: Verb-participle combinations. *Journal of Experimental Psychology: Learning, Memory, and Cognition, 24,* 904–921.

Stemberger, J.P. (1985). Bound morpheme loss errors in normal and agrammatic speech: One mechanism or two? *Brain and Language, 25,* 246–256.

Zwitserlood, P. (1996). Form priming. *Language and Cognitive Processes, 11,* 589–596.

CHAPTER TWELVE

Conceptual structures in language production

Mark Smith
School of Psychology, University of Birmingham, UK

What can the grammatical structure of a sentence, its lexemes, morphemes, syntax, and so on, tell us about the conceptual structure that underlies that sentence? Historically, there have always been two distinct approaches to this question—the empiricist and the rationalist approach. According to the empiricist, conceptual information is derived directly from an individual's experience of the world and as a result comes to inherit the idiosyncratic, indeterminate, analogue complexity of that experience. As such the empiricist is forced to deny that there can be any precise and comprehensive replication of conceptual information in the fixed, shared, digital structure of language. Instead, the empiricist envisions that grammatical structures constitute a recasting of conceptual structures into a simplified and impersonal form. In contrast, the rationalist argues that conceptual information has a transcendental origin and, consequently, an elegant structure which is impersonal, immutable, and universal in nature and which can be imposed on to the complex world around us thereby rendering it comprehensible. Consequently, the rationalist is able to argue that there is a natural affinity between conceptual and grammatical information with the digital structure of a sentence providing a faithful mirror of the order inherent in the concepts that underlie it.

In this chapter, the relation between conceptual and grammatical structures is considered in the context of speech production. Contemporary accounts of the relation between conceptual and grammatical structures in speech are wholly rationalist in outlook (Garrett, 1982; Levelt, Roelofs, & Meyer, 1999) and the essay begins by questioning the theoretical coherence of these accounts. In the next section of the essay, a diverse body of empirical data is presented that undermines the rationalist claim that conceptual and grammatical structures precisely replicate each other. In the third section, it is demonstrated that the speaker produces grammatical structures which simplify conceptual structures in order to reduce processing effort. In the fourth section, it is argued that the informational complexity of conceptual structures is such that they cannot be fully preserved in the simple, digital code of language. These four sections are drawn together in the final section of the chapter which concludes in favour of the empiricist view of the relation between conceptual and grammatical structures.

THE RATIONALIST VIEW OF CONCEPTUAL STRUCTURE

We are aware that our experience has a richness and continuity in its graded contents which far outstrips our capacity for linguistic description. Our thoughts, on the other hand, are just as digitalised as the sentences we use to express them. Indeed, since there often is . . . a one-to-one match between our thoughts and the natural language sentences which we use to express them, it is possible that we might come to confuse the thought itself with the natural language sentence

(Carruthers, 1996, p. 188)

Support for the rationalist claim that grammatical structures mirror conceptual structures typically comes not in the form of direct evidence but rather in the form of philosophical arguments that make indirect inferences about conceptual structures on the basis of certain observations about general properties of language use. Garrett (1982), for instance, has argued that both conceptual and grammatical structures must be composed of discrete, context independent bits of information (i.e. lexemes, concepts, syntactic structures) and that a model of speech production must solve the problem of how to get the bits in the conceptual structure to link up to the bits in the grammatical structure (cf., Fodor, 1987, for related language comprehension arguments). This "correspondence" problem leads Garrett to claim that all of the parts that a speaker uses in constructing a conceptual structure must be linked directly in a one-to-one relationship to parts in the speaker's grammatical system ("each simple surface vocabulary element corresponds to a conceptually simple entity at the message level", as Garrett, 1982, p. 26, puts it). If no such link existed, so the argument goes, then a speaker would run the risk of producing conceptual structures containing parts for which there existed no corresponding part in the speaker's own grammatical system. Clearly, if a speaker could not find a grammatical part corresponding to a conceptual part then this would block formulation. The fact, then, that speakers are able to formulate conceptual structures indicates, for Garrett, that all of the parts of a speaker's conceptual system must have a one-to-one link with parts in the speaker's grammatical system. In the view of speech which emerges from this argument, then, there is a precise equivalence between conceptual and grammatical structures; formulation in such a speech system always produces a single grammatical structure that is equivalent in both form and content to the conceptual structure underlying it.

In solving the correspondence problem, however, Garrett's rationalist approach gives rise to a number of other problems. Since in such a system a conceptual structure would be formally identical to its corresponding grammatical structure, for instance, there would be a danger that "we might come to confuse the thought itself with the natural language sentence". In such a system, it would thus be difficult to justify two separate stages of conceptual and grammatical planning. If formulating a grammatical structure only repeats what is already apparent within the conceptual structure, then why not get rid of the costly process of formulation and simply link the conceptual elements or tokens which feature in conceptual structures directly to phonological planning information? One reply to this is that there are conceptually uninformative elements specific to a language such as the gender of nouns in French which will not be apparent in the conceptual structure and which are added into a grammatical structure during formulation. It seems extremely unlikely, however, that such elements could by themselves justify all of the expense incurred by an extra processing stage.

A second problem resulting from the equivalence of conceptual and grammatical structures is that such a system leads to Whorfianism (Roelofs, 1992b). On such a view, the concepts expressed by different languages should be as different as the lexemes produced by them. However, the evidence for such language specific conceptual differences is so poor that few researchers now accept Whorfianism (Levelt, 1989). One way out of this problem, as Levelt has suggested, might lie with the ability to combine parts together to create novel phrases or sentences. Thus, if English speakers lack a lexeme and a lexical concept corresponding to the French term "La tisane" they can simply combine two lexemes together (i.e., "herb" and "tea"). Through such combinations, then, a speaker should, in theory, be able to generate sentences that are semantically equivalent to those of other languages. In practice, though, expressing a concept from a different language in our own would force us to constantly modify the concepts of our own language in order to capture such a concept precisely and this constant need for subtle adjectival, adverbial, and clausal modification would lead to extremely complex sentences. In reality, speakers try to minimise processing effort as much as possible and would thus tend to avoid such complex sentences (Kuiper, 1996). This drive towards processing efficiency, then, would constrain speakers to avoid expressing the concepts of other languages via the combination of parts from their own language and would instead lead them to achieve efficiency by limiting themselves to the conceptual and linguistic parts already given within their language. Although, then, a speech production system in which conceptual and grammatical structures are formally identical could allow us, in theory, to express the same conceptual structures as expressed by other languages and thus to escape Whorfianism, in practice, because this would involve excessive effort we would naturally gravitate towards those concepts directly expressible in our own language and thus to Whorfianism. The lack of evidence for Whorfianism, then, undermines the view that conceptual and grammatical structures are formally identical.

In sum, such theoretical arguments suggest that conceptual and grammatical structures are not equivalent and this is reinforced in the next section by empirical data demonstrating that the information contained within a grammatical structure does not precisely replicate that contained within a conceptual structure.

AGAINST PRECISE REPLICATION

> In our words we can never give more than an abstract of our thought and feeling, and this abstract can only be a weak outline. Human speech demands of the listener that he take careful note of the reality which it expresses, but which it cannot completely retain.
>
> (Schmaus, 1966, p. 194)

As argued earlier, Garrett's rationalist model of speech can produce only a single grammatical structure in response to a conceptual structure which precisely replicates that structure in terms of both content and form. Against this view, the following section highlights phenomena which demonstrate that grammatical formulation often gives rise not to a single but to multiple grammatical structures (cf., "mapping"), that information contained within conceptual structures is often not present in grammatical structures and vice-versa (cf., "content"), and that the form of information within a conceptual structure often differs from that in a grammatical structure (cf., "form").

Mapping

There are a number of phenomena that demonstrate that speakers will accept as a satisfactory formulation of a single conceptual structure a range of different grammatical structures. One such phenomenon is that of indirect election. As Levelt (1992, p. 8) puts it, indirect election shows that, "The selection of one word can depend on the selection of another word without there being conceptual reasons for this." Thus, as Levelt notes, in the phrases "strong air currents" and "high winds" the adjectives have the same conceptual function of serving to intensify the nouns. The adjectives if interchanged, however, may produce illegal phrases (i.e., *"high air currents") indicating that the selection of the adjective requires not only that it matches with the underlying conceptual chunk but also that it matches with other elements in the developing grammatical structure. Indirect election, then, shows that a single conceptual chunk can be satisfied by a number of different lexemes. More than this, though, it also indicates why it should be desirable that a single conceptual chunk should be able to be satisfied by several lexemes rather than one only: As we increase the set of lexemes that will satisfy an underlying conceptual chunk so we augment a speaker's ability to find a lexeme that both expresses the intended message and that fits into the lexical and syntactic environment into which it is being placed. In a speech system in which only a single lexeme ever corresponds to any given conceptual chunk, the potential for a clash between the selected lexeme and the colloca-tional restrictions of the grammatical structure into which it is being placed rise dramatically. Such a system would necessitate the constant revision of the developing lexical and syntactic environment in order to accommodate newly accessed lexemes.

Moreover, it is also the case that a single conceptual structure can be satisfied by a variety of grammatical structures that contrast with each other both in terms of their syntax and the lexemes they feature. Bierwisch and Schreuder (1992) point out that the German sentences "Stell dich hierhin!" and "Stellen Sie sich hierher!" though comprised of different numbers of lexemes seem to articulate the same underlying message, namely, the message expressed by the English sentence "Stand here!". Similarly, in reference to English, we might wonder whether different numbers of concepts underlie "can not" and "cannot" or "do not" and "don't". Clearly, though, if the number of units in a conceptual structure always corresponds to the number of lexemes in the grammatical sentence used to articulate it then we should not expect that a single conceptual message could be articulated via two grammatical sentences with different numbers of lexemes (interestingly, as Quine, 1981, points out, this argument was first developed by Bentham). However, contra the lexical concept view and in support of Bierwisch and Schreuder's intuition, the phenomenon of sentence blends provides direct evidence that they can (Brown, 1980; Fay, 1982). Sentence blends occur when two lexically and syntactically distinct grammatical structures are constructed in response to an underlying conceptual structure and the formulator is unable (usually because there are some features of the grammatical structures which are confusingly similar) to commit to a single grammatical structure and so merges the two structures into a single, frequently illegal, utterance:

(1)   And that is how I got interested into it.
        Intended: I got into it / I got interested in it (Fay, 1982)

Such blends clearly indicate that speakers are willing to articulate a conceptual structure with grammatical structures featuring varying quantities of lexemes and thus that it is not necessary for the number of units in the conceptual structure to correspond to the number of lexemes in the grammatical structure of an utterance. They emphasise that there is not a direct and rigid one-to-one correspondence between a conceptual structure and a single grammatical structure which articulates it but that instead there is a loosely yoked relationship between conceptual and grammatical structures such that a conceptual message can be satisfied by a number of distinct grammatical structures.

It is also true, however, that a single grammatical structure will often refer to a variety of conceptual structures. Thus, in a sentence such as "The occasional soldier walks by on the weekend", for instance, as Pustejovsky (1995) has pointed out, the quantity of the sentence that is actually conceptually modified by the adjective "occasional" is ambiguous. If we follow the grammatical structure which indicates that "occasional" is an adjective modifying the head element of the noun phrase (i.e., "soldier") we arrive at the conclusion that there is a soldier who is in some sense occasional—perhaps he is, for instance, a part-time soldier. On such a reading the sentence can be interpreted to mean "There is a part-time soldier who walks by on the weekend". In the more obvious reading of the sentence, however, the conceptual scope of "occasional" does not follow its syntactic scope in being restricted to the noun phrase but instead extends over the whole sentence so that it is the whole action of various soldiers walking by on the weekend which is modified as in "Occasionally, soldiers walk by on the weekend". In the latter interpretation, unlike the former, then, there are multiple soldiers none of whom are, necessarily, part-time. Such examples of scope ambiguity clearly illustrate that a single grammatical structure can give rise to a variety of different conceptual structures in which the various elements of conceptual meaning are configured in different ways (either according to the grammatical structure or not) to give rise to different meanings. Clearly, then, an utterance with a single syntactic structure may refer to a variety of different conceptual structures in which the conceptual information is configured in different ways.

In summary, then, it can be demonstrated that in language production a single underlying message can be satisfied by a range of grammatical structures which differ from each other in terms of lexemes or syntax, whereas a single grammatical structure may refer to multiple conceptual structures which differ from each other in terms of the conceptual elements they contain and the ordering of these elements. This undermines the view that there is a rigid one-to-one correspondence between conceptual and grammatical structures and argues for a more loosely yoked relation instead.

Content

As well as it being the case, however, that a single structure will often correspond to a multiple structures at another level, it is also the case that information featuring in the structure at one level will often not feature in the structure at a different level. It is apparent, for instance, that many features of a grammatical structure will arise during the process of grammatical formulation itself and will not be directly stipulated in the conceptual structure itself. As examples of this consider the following:

(2) (a) Make an effort!
     (b) *Put an effort into it!
     (c) *Make effort!
     (d) Put effort into it!
     (e) Make some effort!
     (f) Put some effort into it!

(3)   (a)   You can select positions so that either tactical or strategic aspects of the game are emphasised.

      (b)   You can select positions that/in order to emphasise either tactical or strategic aspects of the game.

Such data exemplifies the collocational restrictions evident in a language, which any speaker must conform to when formulating a grammatical structure. In (2), the presence or absence of the determiner and the type of determiner used is a function of both the noun (i.e., "effort") and the verb (i.e., either "make" or "put"). Thus when "put" and "effort" are selected we can select either the determiner "some" or leave out the determiner altogether, but the determiner "an" cannot be selected. In contrast, when "make" and "effort" are selected then the determiners "an" and "some" can both be selected but the determiner cannot be left out. In this particular instance, then, it is the grammatical formulator and not the conceptual planner which specifies the determiner. If the conceptual planner were to stipulate the conceptual equivalent of the determiner "an" alongside the verb "put" such information would simply be overridden during grammatical formulation because of its incompatibility with the collocational restrictions of English. In (3), the speaker's choice of closed class words such as "so that" and "in order" has dramatic effects on the speaker's subsequent formulation of the remainder of the sentence. In (3a) the speaker's selection of "so that" necessitates both the verb form "are emphasised" and a word order in which the verb occurs after the fragment "either tactical or strategic aspects of the game". In (3b), the selection of "in order" entails the selection of the verb form "emphasise" and the placing of the fragment "either tactical or strategic aspects of the game" after the verb. Again, then, major aspects of an utterance such as the tense of the verb and the word order which we might expect to be determined in the conceptual structure can instead be determined during grammatical formulation by the collocational restrictions imposed on such formulation by that part of the grammatical structure that has already been formulated. In effect, the information within the conceptual structure is rewritten during formulation in terms of language specific collocational restrictions so that much of the information in the grammatical structure arises during formulation and has no counterpart in the conceptual structure.

   It is also the case, moreover, that much information which is present in the conceptual structure produced by a speaker will not be manifested in the subsequent grammatical structure produced by a speaker. In the sentences "John landed the plane on the sea." and "John landed on the sea.", for instance, John lands on the sea by means of a plane (without the aid of at least some flying machine we would have to describe John as having landed *in* the sea rather than *on* it). The two sentences differ only in terms of emphasis; whereas the former sentence leads us to focus on the fact that it is the plane that is on the sea, the latter sentence leads us to focus on the fact that it is John who is on the sea. Yet, although the event underlying the two sentences is similar, what surfaces in the grammatical structures is very different. Thus, although the plane is present in the grammatical structure of the former sentence, it has vanished from the grammatical structure of the latter sentence. Clearly, such an example, where a conceptual element is both a necessary and salient component of the conceptual structure but is not manifested in the grammatical structure, shows that the conceptual structure will often contain information not present within the grammatical structure.

Crucially, this underspecification of the conceptual structure by the grammatical structure is not true simply of isolated examples but can be detected in most if not all of the sentences produced by speakers. In a study of English adjectives, for instance, Lahav (1989; cf., also Sedivy, Tanenhaus, Chambers, & Carlson, 1999) demonstrates that the types of conditions that determine how an adjective applies to a noun will change depending on the noun. Thus, a knife may be judged to be "good" on the basis of conditions such as its "sharpness" but such an applicability condition can hardly be said to be appropriate in evaluating whether paintings or houses are good. As Lahav argues, moreover, the notion that an adjective's applicability conditions are noun dependent is valid not only for evaluative adjectives such as "good" but for all adjectives including those typically thought to be the most noun independent, colour adjectives. Thus, as Lahav argues, whereas a red apple will be red only on its outside a red crystal will be red both inside and outside, and a red watermelon is red on the inside only. For a house to be described as red, however, it is necessary only that the outside of its walls be mostly red (and not its roof or door or windows), whereas for a car to be red it is necessary for its external surface excluding wheels, bumpers, lights, etc., to be red. Of course, such observations sit uneasily with rationalist models of speech such as Garrett's in which a single adjective will be connected to a single concept and suggest instead that language users constantly modify the meaning of adjectives by augmenting them with extra information from the surrounding context. Against this supposition, Fodor and Pylyshyn (1997) argue that when defined correctly adjectives do actually have a single, consistent meaning across a range of contexts. They thus argue that the adjective "good" means that a noun satisfies the relevant interest we have in it (i.e., a good book is good to read whereas a good chair is good to sit in, and so on). As Lahav argues, however, such an approach rather than solving the problem only pushes it one stage back since different objects will be interesting in different ways just as they will be good in different ways. Fodor and Pylyshyn's proposal, then, simply changes the problem of explaining the difference between a good knife and a good person from one in which objects are good in a variety of ways to one in which objects are interesting in a variety of ways. However we formulate the problem, then, applying an adjective to a noun gives rise to context dependent variability. As a consequence, it is inaccurate to view the meaning of an adjective–noun pair as a simple combination of two context-independent concepts; context dependence renders the whole meaning of an adjective–noun pair greater than the sum of its individual parts. Overall, then, Lahav's analysis demonstrates that, on a grammatical level, an adjective–noun pair, since it provides only the individual parts and not the whole, underspecifies the conceptual meaning which the language user must add in from context. This reinforces the notion that conceptual structures frequently contain information not directly present in grammatical structures contrary to strictly rationalist models of speech.

To summarise, then, it would appear that information occurring at the conceptual level is not always mirrored by information occurring at the grammatical level and vice versa. Specifically, though phenomena such as collocational restrictions indicate that aspects of a grammatical structure may not have any counterpart in the conceptual structure underlying it but may have arisen purely during formulation, phenomena such as the open-ended polysemy of adjectival modification indicate that more information must be present in a conceptual structure than can be marked within a grammatical structure. Overall, then, such data argues against the rationalist claim that grammatical structure precisely replicates conceptual structure.

Form

There are also a number of phenomena which suggest that the formal ordering of information at the conceptual level differs from that at the grammatical level. One such phenomenon, for instance, is grammatical incoherence (Brown, 1980; cf., also De Smedt, 1996, for a discussion of the related phenomenon of the apokoinu) which occurs when speakers, having drawn up a conceptual structure, find that they cannot generate a grammatical structure which articulates the conceptual structure both adequately and legally. Typically, in response to such a state, a speaker will not remain mute but will instead produce a sentence that is grammatically incoherent in being syntactically illegal (or at least extremely clumsy as in the next example) but which nevertheless still allows the hearer to retrieve the underlying conceptual message. Consider, for instance, the following text spoken live to camera by a journalist:

> If the bomb is found in Gaza then there could be big problems for Yasser Arafat politically. If the bomb is found to have come from within Israel then there will be less that Israel can do [pause] in the way of expecting Yasser Arafat to take action.
> (Mark Urban, *BBC 1 News at Six*, 19 October 1994)

Despite its grammatical awkwardness, the overall conceptual macrostructure behind the text can nevertheless be discerned (for a discussion of conceptual macrostructure, cf., Levelt, 1989). The first half of the first sentence hypothesises that the bomb originated in Gaza, and the second half of the sentence envisages the major consequences of this for Yasser Arafat. The second sentence has an identical logical structure to the first but contains diametrically opposing information. Thus, the first half of the second sentence hypothesises that the bomb originated in Israel (not Gaza), whereas the second half of the second sentence envisages the minor (not major) consequences of this for Yasser Arafat. Overall, then, the speaker's task is to formulate the simple and clearly defined conceptual macrostructure that has been mapped out. Despite the simplicity of the conceptual macrostructure, however, the speaker experiences difficulty during formulation and ends up producing a text which is syntactically clumsy and incoherent. This descent into grammatical incoherence stems from the selection of the phrase "then there will be less". Clearly, it is difficult to articulate the conceptual structure underlying the second half of the sentence with anything which is grammatically compatible with this phrase. Had the speaker chosen other phrases then simple and coherent formulations of this conceptual structure would have been possible (consider, for instance, ". . . then Israel cannot expect much action from Yasser Arafat" or ". . . then not much can be expected of Yasser Arafat"). Such incoherence is effectively, then, the sentential equivalent of the tip of the tongue state: We know precisely what it is that we have to say but still struggle to find adequate grammatical resources to articulate our intended message. Of course, if the conceptual structure were simply equivalent to the grammatical structure then grammatical incoherence should not occur—we should be able to follow the structure of the conceptual plan step by step and arrive at a grammatical structure that is as simple and coherent as the conceptual plan underlying it. The fact that grammatical incoherence does occur—that we as speakers and writers struggle to articulate our thoughts—is evidence that the conceptual structure does not precisely predetermine the structural form of the grammatical structure but that distinct problems of structural formulation peculiar to the grammatical structure arise during grammatical encoding.

The claim that there are substantial differences in the way information is structured during conceptual and grammatical processing is reinforced, moreover, by cross-linguistic differences in grammatical structure. One typical difference between these two forms of language is that the standard lexicon of a sign language will be much smaller than that of an isolating language such as English. Crucially, however, as Armstrong, Stokoe, and Wilcox (1995) argue, even though a deaf signer's lexicon of pre-stored terms is less complex than that of a language such as English, the variety, complexity and expressivity of lexical terms evident in the language production of deaf signers is comparable to that seen in a language such as English. Sign language users achieve such expressivity by exploiting certain natural features of their language such as temporality. As Armstrong et al. point out, lexemes in non-sign languages are spoken in a strict linear and temporal order. In sign languages, in contrast, the signs within a sentence often coexist simultaneously—the sign for the subject of a sentence may be present as the sign for the action that that subject undergoes is being produced. One consequence of this is lexical flexibility—a signer can actually change the sign for a subject over the course of a sentence as the action of the sentence has its effect upon that subject. More than this, though, the signer, as Armstrong et al. argue, achieves lexical richness by modulating a sign via other signs that are simultaneously present. Thus, when a signer appears to be reproducing the same sign repeatedly, he or she is often producing a series of lexemes distinguished by the subtle inflections provided by those signs they co-occur with. In short, then, the grammar of a sign language is often profoundly different from that of spoken languages. Yet we should not derive from this the conclusion that the conceptual structures produced by signers are fundamentally different to those produced by speakers. As Armstrong et al. argue, grammatical differences between sign and spoken languages do not reflect fundamentally different forms of cognition in the users of such languages—instead, the differences reflect simply aspects of the media (i.e., speech vs. gesture) in which the language user expresses the given conceptual structure. Such differences, then, originate during grammatical encoding and do not reflect aspects of the conceptual structure itself. The contrast between sign and spoken language, then, further reinforces the view that grammatical structure does not follow directly from conceptual structure, that the structuring of information during grammatical encoding may have characteristics which are peculiar to itself and which do not feature in conceptual planning in any way.

Of course, the same point can be made by cross-linguistic comparisons of spoken languages. In an incorporating language such as the Aboriginal language Tiwi, words and sentences are often coextensive in sharp contrast to an isolating language such as English where a sentence will be constituted by multiple, discrete lexemes (Comrie, 1989; cf., also Hankamer, 1989, on the related phenomenon of agglutinative languages). It seems highly unlikely, however, that the difference in the size and complexity of grammatical units in such languages reflects an equivalent difference in the size and complexity of the units featuring in the conceptual structures generated by speakers of these languages. If this were so, we might expect to see dramatic Whorfian-style differences in the cognition of speakers of an isolating language as compared to speakers of an agglutinative or incorporating language. But no evidence of such dramatic differences between speakers of these different types of languages exists, however, although a good deal of evidence has been provided that counters such relativism (Hadley, 1997). Agglutinative languages, for instance, are acquired by children at exactly the same rate as isolating languages (Hirsh-Pasek & Golinkoff, 1996). Yet if lexemes, and hence the conceptual units that underlie them, are larger and more complex in agglutinative languages than in isolating languages then it should be more difficult for children acquiring an agglutinative language to process the meaning of the input they receive and hence to acquire language than for children acquiring an isolating language. The fact that agglutinative languages are acquired at precisely the same rate as isolating languages, then, indicates that the conceptual structure is not divided up into a form which corresponds to the lexeme by lexeme structure of the final grammatical utterance (and more specifically, as I will argue later, that children and language users in general process meaning not in terms of lexical concepts but rather in terms of clausal units since the meaning of a clause in an agglutinative language will typically be no more complex than that in an isolating language). Again, then, such an absence of linguistic relativism indicates that cross-linguistic differences in grammatical structure simply reflect differences in the grammatical system that is used to formulate a given conceptual structure—it does not mean that such grammatical differences between agglutinative and isolating languages reflect differences in the form of the conceptual structure produced by speakers of these two types of language.

In summary, then, phenomena such as grammatical incoherence and cross-linguistic differences in syntax indicate that the structuring of information within a conceptual message is quite distinct from that within the grammatical structure used to formulate it. Again this undermines the rationalist notion of precise replication by showing, contrary to such a notion, that the structural form of the conceptual message is not replicated in the syntactic form of the grammatical structure.

General summary

In this section, then, a substantial body of data has been presented that undermines the rationalist claim that the form and content of each and every conceptual structure will always be precisely replicated by the form and content of a single grammatical structure. Contra the precise replication view, the data show that a single conceptual structure can correspond to multiple grammatical structures and vice versa and that the form and content of a conceptual structure may differ from that of a grammatical structure. Thus, the data argues against precise replication and suggests instead that there are fundamental dissimilarities between structures at the two levels. As yet, however, the data leaves unexplained why such dissimilarities might actually arise and it is this issue that is explored in the following sections.

THE EFFICIENCY OF GRAMMATICAL STRUCTURE

The first aim of language was to communicate our thoughts; the second to do it with despatch ... What wonder, then, that the invention of all ages should have been to add such wings to their conversation as might enable it, if possible, to keep pace in some measure with their minds.

(Horne-Tooke, 1786/1805, p. 15)

In the next section it is argued that differences between grammatical and conceptual structures arise as speakers try to minimise their own formulation costs and shift as much of the processing burden onto the listener as possible. To do this, the speaker generates a simplified grammatical structure which rather than exhaustively describing the conceptual structure merely provides sufficient information to enable the listener to reconstruct a conceptual structure. Such simplification is achieved both with respect to the grammatical structures produced by a speaker and the grammatical system that the speaker uses to produce those structures. The simplification of grammatical structures will be illustrated in terms of two themes—"preformulation", which concerns the tendency of speakers to build up grammatical structures using preformulated grammatical material, and "underspecification", which relates to the tendency of speakers to provide only minimal information about the conceptual structure in the grammatical structure. The simplification of the grammatical system will be illustrated in terms of "flexibility", which refers to the tendency of speakers to maximise the set of conceptual referents to which grammatical terms can be applied.

Preformulation

The term "preformulation" refers to those aspects of language use that allow a speaker to avoid formulation costs by producing language that has already been formulated on some prior occasion. Such preformulated material is very often drawn from recent speech with speakers recycling either the lexemes or syntax of their own recent utterances or those recently produced by their interlocutor. In a computer analysis of the London-Lund Corpus of Spoken English, for instance, Altenberg (1990; cf., also Sinclair, 1991) finds that roughly 70% of the speech we produce is made up of "recurrent word combinations", i.e., phrases made up from a small set of very frequent lexemes which are constantly repeated by speakers in their utterances. Such a finding gives the lie to the clichéd view that engaging in lexical access entails trawling through a massive lexicon with tens of thousands of individual entries. Instead it suggests that lexical access is generally a simple and rapid process because most lexemes in speech are extracted from a core lexicon composed of only a few hundred highly frequent lexemes. (Taking this further, if language users constrain lexical access in terms of word frequency so that the most frequent lexemes are always searched first, whereas the least frequent lexemes are searched last then the fact that more frequent lexemes are accessed more quickly than less frequent lexemes can be simply explained in terms of the fact that they involve searching through fewer lexemes).

Corpus analysis, moreover, has also been used to demonstrate structural repetition as well as lexical repetition. Thus, in an analysis of a large corpus of spoken English, Weiner and Labov (1983) give evidence of structural recycling with their finding that 72% of sentences which had been closely preceded by sentences featuring passives did themselves feature passives. Such observations have also been verified experimentally moreover. Levelt and Kelter (1982), for instance, recorded shopkeeper's responses to the questions "What time do you close?" and "At what time do you close?". They found that the latter question elicited significantly more responses featuring the lexeme "at" than the former question even though "at" made no semantic contribution to either the answer or the question. Such a finding, then, confirms the view that speakers draw upon the lexical and syntactic structure of recent speech as they generate their current utterance. They hypothesised, moreover, that such recycling serves to reduce processing effort on the part of the speaker. As they put it, "reusing previous discourse elements has the additional function of facilitating the fluency of the formulation process itself" (Levelt & Kelter, 1982, p. 105; cf., also Bock, 1986). Data supporting this hypothesis, moreover, has recently been provided by Smith and Wheeldon (1999b). In this study, participants produced simple sentences (i.e., "The dog and the house move up") in response to a visual display featuring moving pictures. Smith and Wheeldon found that when the syntax of the initial phrase of a sentence generated on a prime trial matched that of a sentence generated during the subsequent target trial onset latencies were a significant 50 ms faster than when there was no such match between the syntax of the prime and target trials. Further experiments indicated that this 50 ms facilitation could not be due to phonological, lexical, visual, or conceptual processing but must have reflected the syntactic planning of the first phrase of an utterance prior to speech onset. Clearly, if processing effort can be reduced by 50 ms for each phrase in a sentence then savings over the course of an entire sentence could be substantial—a fact in line with the view that speakers draw upon pre-formulated material from recent speech to reduce planning costs.

As well as exploiting recent speech for preformulated grammatical material, speakers also draw upon preformulated material that has been stored over long periods as part of the speaker's own grammatical system. Evidence of the presence of such preformulated material in the grammatical system of a speaker is provided by the phenomenon of noncompositional language. This phenomenon indicates that speakers do not always build up grammatical structures from discrete lexical and syntactic parts but draw upon larger, holistic units during formulation in which lexical and syntactic material has already been integrated. Consider, for instance, the following sentences:

(4) (a) By day, Montreal is a thriving city.
     (b) By night, Montreal is a thriving city.
     (c) *At day, Montreal is a thriving city.
     (d) At night, Montreal is a thriving city.

Clearly, such an example indicates that it is not enough for a speaker to be armed only with a separate syntactic system and lexicon. Syntactically, the illegal sentence (4c) must be perfectly acceptable since its syntax is identical to that of its legal counterparts, although lexically the illegal example would seem to be adequate since it makes as much sense in terms of its meaning as its legal counterparts. What such an example indicates is that a speaker must also be supplied with knowledge regarding the particular lexico-syntactic environments into which specific words must be placed enabling the speaker to produce "by day", for instance, and to avoid producing "at day". Inevitably, such knowledge would require the listing within the grammatical system of a speaker of preformulated grammatical units in which the lexemes and syntax are already integrated. We must thus list at some point in our grammatical system that "day" can combine with "by", for instance, but not with "at" in the formation of a prepositional phrase—without such knowledge the error in (4c) could not be avoided. Crucially, such preformulated units cannot be reduced to rules: As Gross (1979) argues, such units are simply idiosyncratic—they do not reduce to meaningful rules that can be generalised to other contexts. Clearly, then, speech is built not only from lexemes and syntax. If it were, speakers would be unable to cope with noncompositional language and would routinely produce illegal sentences similar to those listed in (4) (interestingly, such noncompositional language errors are very common in non-native speech).

As well as a syntactic system and a lexicon, then, a grammatical system must furnish a speaker with language formulas, i.e., holistic, preformulated units in which the lexemes and syntax are already integrated. Crucially, as Kuiper (1996) has shown, because the formulation of such holistic units has already been achieved within the grammatical system of the speaker their use entails little in the way of formulation costs—they involve no syntactic planning, for instance. In support of this claim, Kuiper has analysed the speech of auctioneers and sports commentators, the rate of which varies according to what kind of auction is being conducted or which kind of sport commentated upon. Kuiper observes that at slower rates the speech of commentators and auctioneers is similar to everyday speech. At quicker rates, however, such speech features an abnormally high proportion of "speech formulas", i.e., the pre-packaged clichés that a commentator or auctioneer will use to describe routine aspects of a situation. At the start of a horse race, for instance, one commentator might always deploy the formula "They're on their way", whereas another will always use "They're off and racing now". Because such formulas involve no syntactic planning they facilitate abnormally rapid speech.[1] The cost reductions afforded by such formulas would also be apparent in normal speech, moreover, and this serves to explain why they are so prevalent in normal speech (Van Lanckner, 1987).

In summary, then, the form of a grammatical structure often reflects the use of preformulated grammatical material rather than the conceptual structure *per se*. Using such material dramatically reduces the speaker's formulation costs.

Underspecification

Formulation costs can also be dramatically reduced simply by cutting down on the amount of information about the conceptual structure explicitly contained within the grammatical structure—that is, by ensuring the grammatical structure underspecifies to some degree the conceptual structure. Underspecification is such a significant feature of language use that the formal grammatical systems of most languages typically feature a number of grammatical terms that are dedicated solely to achieving it. Thus, as Halliday and Hasan (1976) show, languages typically feature linguistic terms which allow a simple, usually closed-class lexeme to be substituted for a more complex, open-class lexeme. Thus, in a text such as "Wash and core six cooking apples. Put them in an oven." the term "them" substitutes for the complex phrase "six cooking apples". Yet although "them" dramatically underspecifies the complex phrase it stands in for, the hearer can easily identify what the term refers to and generate a complete conceptual structure. As Halliday and Hasan note, such underspecification can also be achieved by ellipsis. Thus, in a sentence such as "Joan brought some carnations and Catherine some sweet peas" underspecification is achieved by ellipsing (i.e., removing) the verb "brought" from the second clause rather than by substituting a simpler term for it. By means of substitution and ellipsis, then, speakers reduce the information explicitly contained within the grammatical structure and thus underspecify the conceptual structure for the hearer.

Of course, underspecification, though it simplifies the grammatical structure and thus reduces the speaker's formulation costs, entails a concomitant increase in processing costs for the listener who has to fill in all the resultant gaps in the grammatical structure. Such filling in will be particularly expensive if the gap is ambiguous and capable of being filled by multiple lexemes, as in the sentence "Mary knows a taller man than Michael (is/knows)." Worse still for the listener, underspecification can also lead to what Kent Bach has termed "semantic indeterminacy" (Bach, 1987). As Bach notes, such indeterminacy differs from ambiguity in that whereas an ambiguous sentence has a determinate number of potential interpretations, which must be selected between, an indeterminate sentence has a potentially open-ended set of interpretations, which would clearly be too complex to calculate, much less select between. Thus, the sentence "Pepsi is better" could, as Bach notes, mean that Pepsi® is better than Coca-Cola® but it could also be used to mean that Pepsi® is better than an endless number of other drinks. It could also be taken to mean that Pepsi is better than all other beverages or some subset of beverages and so on. Clearly, then, there are potentially so many conceptual structures that correspond to the grammatical structure of that sentence that a hearer cannot arrive at the correct conceptual structure by laying out all of the potential conceptual structures and then selecting between them on the basis of contextual information. Instead, the grammatical structure of such a sentence should be thought of as specifying a single but incomplete conceptual structure which is filled in by the hearer on the basis of the relevant contextual information. Semantic indeterminacy, then, clearly illustrates the extent to which grammatical structures underspecify conceptual structures and gives some sense of the extra processing effort necessitated in listeners by the speaker's reduction of their own processing costs through underspecification.

Significantly, underspecification has also been confirmed experimentally. Thus, Olson (1970) hypothesised that in an object description task a speaker's expression would not fully specify the object it referred to but would instead give only as much information as the hearer needed in order to be able to discriminate the intended object from the set of objects in which it was contained. Along these lines, Clark and Wilkes-Gibbs (1986) set up an experiment in which pairs of subjects had to refer to irregular shapes from within a set of irregular shapes. In the experiment, speakers were observed trying to establish the mutual belief with their interlocutors that sufficient information had been given to allow the interlocutor to pick out the single intended referent as the following example shows:

(5)   A: Uh, person putting shoe on.
      B: Putting shoe on?
      A: Uh huh. Facing left. Looks like he's sitting down?
      B: Okay.

In this dialogue speaker A initially proposes a description, which speaker B then indicates is insufficiently informative to enable the shape to be chosen. Speaker A then responds by giving further information, which speaker B indicates is sufficient to allow the shape to be chosen. The dialogue, then, shows that in formulating a grammatical structure a speaker gives not an exhaustive but merely a sufficient description of the conceptual referent. Such a view is reinforced by a study by Pechmann (1984) in which participants were shown slides containing various objects of contrasting type, colour, or size. On each slide one object was marked with a star and the task was to describe the object to an imaginary listener who could see the slide minus the star marking. It was found that speakers do not describe the object exhaustively but instead produce a simplified description of it. Interestingly, however, speakers often provided the imaginary listener with more than the minimal amount of information necessary to discriminate the object. A speaker might say "the white bird", for instance, when the phrase "the bird" would actually suffice to discriminate the object. Why, then, did speakers, whilst simplifying their grammatical structures, not simplify them to the minimal amount? One possibility is that speakers supply hearers with more than enough information rather than a minimal grammatical structure because they want to avoid providing the hearer with so little information that the hearer is unable to form an adequate conceptual structure and must request more, thus forcing the speaker into the extra effort of reformulating the sentence. In avoiding this danger, then, speakers overcompensate by providing more than enough information in their grammatical structure. The redundancy observed in Pechmann's task could also be a product of lexical persistence, so that speakers producing the term "the white bird" are simply reproducing the grammatical structure produced on previous trials, knowing it to be (more than) adequate for current purposes rather than formulating a new grammatical structure such as "the bird". On this interpretation also, then, the speaker's ultimate goal is still the minimisation of formulation costs.

In short, then, languages always feature techniques for reducing grammatical structures and the costs involved in their formulation such as ellipsis and substitution. The resultant underspecification of the conceptual structure by the grammatical structure can lead to ambiguity or indeterminacy, which may require extra processing effort on the part of the hearer. As a result, speakers must ensure that the conceptual structure is not so underspecified that hearers are unable to reconstruct it.

Flexibility

It seems reasonable to claim that languages are fully expressive in the sense that they allow speakers to talk about any aspect of their experience of the world no matter how obscure or exotic (the existence of popular science books on quantum physics provides dramatic confirmation of this). Of course, a speaker's experience of the world involves an immeasurably complex body of information and it is no easy matter to devise a system which can articulate this. Potentially, there are three methods by which linguistic expressivity could be achieved. First, the grammatical system could feature a discrete lexeme for each concept needing to be expressed. Second, the grammatical system could feature a set of lexemes significantly smaller than the set of concepts needing to be expressed but achieve expressivity by combining lexemes together in a novel order. Third, the grammatical system could again feature a set of lexemes significantly smaller than the set of concepts needing to be expressed, but could achieve expressivity by associating each lexeme with not one single concept but with a very large number of different concepts instead. Each of these three approaches to the problem of expressivity has, quite obviously, its own unique flaw. The first approach (lampooned by Fodor, 1987, as a "phrasebook" approach to language processing) would not provide a practical solution to the problem of expressivity since it would require a grammatical system comprised of as many lexemes as there are concepts needing to be expressed by a speaker. Since a speaker needs to be able to express a massive quantity of concepts the phrasebook approach would involve an impractically complex grammatical system. The second approach (advocated by Fodor, 1987), involving the combination of a small set of lexemes into novel orders, would also be impractical because, as outlined earlier, it would give rise to hideously complex sentences. The third approach, involving associating a lexeme with a large number of conceptual referents, would also be unworkable. The massive amounts of concepts that a speaker needed to express in a language would mean that each lexeme would be attached to a massive amount of conceptual referents. As the number of conceptual referents to which a lexeme was attached increased so the difficulty of retrieving the intended conceptual referent of a lexeme would increase for a hearer. Eventually, expressivity would force a lexeme to be attached to so many conceptual referents that for the hearer its reference would become irretrievably opaque.

In their own way, then, each of these three approaches to expressivity fails. How then does language achieve expressivity? In fact, language achieves it by combining each of these three approaches and sharing the burden of expressivity between them. Thus, languages always have very large (if not impractically large) lexicons. Languages also always feature syntactic systems allowing speakers to combine words into novel orders. Finally, languages also always associate lexemes not with a single conceptual referent but with very large numbers of such referents. In combination, each approach lessens the burden on the other two approaches. Thus, associating a lexeme with multiple conceptual referents reduces the total number of lexemes required by a speaker and helps to prevent a speaker's grammatical system from becoming impractically complex (flexibility is thus a form of underspecification but, whereas underspecification leads to an underspecified grammatical structure, flexibility leads to underspecified grammatical system). In combination, then, the three approaches are practical and enable the expressivity problem to be solved.

In this section, the speaker's tendency to associate a lexeme with multiple conceptual referents (hereafter termed "flexibility") will be investigated because as a result of its role in enabling expressivity, it helps to simplify the grammatical system and shift processing costs away from the speaker to the hearer. The most familiar form of lexical flexibility is, of course, homonymy, where the same word is associated with two or more entirely unrelated meanings, the classic example being, of course, "bank". A second form of lexical flexibility is that of polysemy in which a single word will be associated with multiple meanings each of which are closely related to each other:

(6) (a) The newspaper is bulky.
     (b) The newspaper is worth reading.

In (6), as Nunberg (1979) points out, the noun "newspaper" has two discrete senses. Whilst in (6a) "newspaper" refers to a physical object, in (6b) it refers to a body of information. Yet, although these two senses can be distinguished, it is also the case that they overlap. It is, for instance, no mere accident that these two senses are both associated with the single lexeme "newspaper". It is this overlap in the senses of a polysemous word which distinguishes polysemy from homonymy and which leads, as Shanon (1996) points out, to differences in the syntactic behaviour of polysemous and homonymous words. Thus, for instance, the different polysemous meanings of a word can always be conjoined in an anaphoric relationship i.e.:

(7) Although the newspaper is bulky it is devoid of interest.

This contrasts sharply with homonymous meanings, which cannot be so conjoined. Sentence (8a) thus cannot legally be collapsed into sentence (8b):

(8) (a) The (monetary) bank is just by the (river) bank.
    (b) *The bank is just by it.

Such aspects of the behaviour of polysemous words have led to certain researchers arguing that the meanings of a polysemous word form a network of discrete senses each linked to one another via processes of metaphor and metonymy (Brugman & Lakoff, 1988; Kishner & Gibbs, 1998). Yet, though it is possible to distinguish certain of the polysemous meanings of a word from others, it is not the case that polysemous meanings form stable units that can simply be selected and retrieved whole in the way that homonymous meanings can. As Lahav's (1989) aforementioned study demonstrates, the adjective "red" has, for instance, a discrete polysemous meaning for virtually every context in which it occurs. The various polysemous meanings of a word will, then, be too numerous and the difference between them often too slight and trivial to warrant their being fully listed in the lexicon of a language user. Consequently, as Sweetser (1986; cf., also Caramazza & Grober, 1977) argues, the processing of polysemy requires not only the retrieval of different polysemous meanings but also the online modulation of these meanings to give a polysemous sense that is precisely tailored to its context (as both Sinclair, 1996, and Shanon, 1996, point out, moreover, it is precisely this process of creatively modulating and extending the senses of a word that allows words, through a process of diachronic evolution, to acquire such a rich array of polysemous meanings in the first place). What all of these studies illustrate, then, is that a single lexeme will not be linked to a single discrete concept but will rather allow a speaker to refer to a massive number of subtly different concepts by means of polysemy. Certainly, if a speaker were to employ a grammatical system which employed a different lexeme for each of these different concepts rather than simply a single lexeme the resultant system would be vastly more complex than those ordinarily employed by speakers and its operation would consequently incur inordinate processing costs. In this way, polysemy helps to reduce the speaker's processing costs to a reasonable level. In so doing, however, it also increases the costs incurred by the listener who in determining the specific meaning of a polysemous term is presented with a more complex task than that of simply retrieving a single invariant meaning.

Yet it is also the case that syntactic structures as well as lexemes can be flexible and have a variety of meanings (Goldberg, 1995). One example of this is scope ambiguity. Thus, as Fauconnier (1985) notes, a sentence such as "In Moldavia, the president is a tyrant." can be read as "The Moldavian president is a tyrant." or as "When the (non-Moldavian) president visits Moldavia he becomes a tyrant.". Of course, the speaker does not provide any syntactic information in the grammatical structure that enables the hearer to resolve this ambiguity: The hearer simply has to select between the possible conceptual structures on the basis of contextual knowledge. Just as a single lexeme, then, can be expressive of a range of different conceptual referents so a single syntactic structure can be associated with a range of different conceptual structures. Moreover, the net effect of such syntactic flexibility is similar to lexical flexibility: In both cases, flexibility serves to reduce the quantity of grammatical material of which a speaker's grammatical system need be comprised and thus to reduce the processing costs incurred by the speaker in operating that system. Moreover, the degree to which syntax is flexible (and thus the extent to which such flexibility reduces the operating costs of the grammatical system) should not be underestimated either. Studies of the machine parsing of sentences, for instance, often reveal that hundreds of different syntactic structures may be potentially associated with a single sentence (Bod, 1998). Presumably, syntactic flexibility like lexical flexibility is constrained only by the need to avoid rendering the conceptual reference so manifold as to make it opaque to the hearer. It is possible, then, that syntactic structures will exhibit the vast flexibility seen in polysemy. If this were so it would explain why linguists have been repeatedly defeated in their attempt to reduce the language produced by actual speakers to a finite and discrete set of syntactic structures. Certainly, there is a vast and seemingly unbridgeable gulf between the syntax actual speakers produce and the syntactic ability of even the most advanced machine parsing systems: "Perhaps the largest . . . Definite Clause Grammar anywhere . . . was able to parse completely and uniquely virtually no sentence chosen randomly from a newspaper" (Cunningham, Gaizauskas, & Wilkes, 1996). Perhaps the flexibility and creativity evinced in the production of syntactic structures by speakers is such that the attempt to determine the set of possible legal syntactic structures within a language is as futile as the attempt to determine all of the polysemous meanings of a word.

In sum, then, by flexibly attaching multiple conceptual referents to each grammatical term speakers reduce the complexity of their grammatical system and thus the cost of operating it. As such, phenomena such as polysemy and scope ambiguity emphasise that significant aspects of grammatical structure arise not from conceptual structure but from the need to minimise formulation costs.

General summary

The present section has provided support for the view that speakers strive to minimise formulation costs by generating grammatical structures which provide only sufficient, rather than exhaustive, information about the underlying conceptual structure. This cost reduction, it has been argued, can be achieved via underspecified or preformulated grammatical structures or by simplifying the grammatical system through flexibility and thus reducing its running costs. Such observations show that many aspects of grammatical structure do not reflect the precise replication of conceptual structure but simply the drive to minimise formulation costs.

THE COMPLEXITY OF CONCEPTUAL STRUCTURE

Thoughts die the moment they are embodied by words.

(Schopenhauer, 1851/1974, p. 508)

In the following section, empirical data and theoretical arguments are used to probe the nature of conceptual structures. First, it is argued that conceptual structures cannot be comprised of lexical concepts featuring semantic primitives since such digital structures fail to capture the complexity of information in a conceptual structure (cf., "Lexicalism"). Second, it is argued that conceptual structures are built up in chunks representing situations that correspond at the grammatical level not to lexemes but to clauses (cf., "Situations"). Finally, it is argued that formulation does not involve the matching of lexical concepts to lexemes but that instead clause-like conceptual structures are cut up into chunks during formulation rather than prior to it (cf., "Formulating conceptual structures"). Together, these three arguments demonstrate that conceptual structures, rather than reducing the speaker's experience to a simple, digital, language-like form, are comprised of informationally rich situations that preserve much of the analogue complexity of the world upon which that experience is based.

Lexicalism

If grammatical structures mirror conceptual structures then we might expect that, since grammatical structures are composed of lexemes, conceptual structures will be built up out of lexical concepts that encapsulate the meaning of the lexemes in the grammatical structure. In fact, such a position is, fundamentally, that which is advanced by the two notable theories of conceptual structure, the "nondecompositional" approach (Roelofs, 1992b) and the "decompositional" approach (Bierwisch & Schreuder, 1992). Both of these theories argue that lexical concepts are generated as a result of the progressive activation of semantic primitives (or "properties" as Roelofs, 1992b, calls them) equivalent to the component parts of the meaning of the lexical concept. The two theories also differ, however, insofar as the "decompositional" theory argues that semantic primitives are placed directly into the conceptual structure to form a cluster corresponding to a lexical concept, whereas the "nondecompositional" theory argues that a cluster of semantic properties triggers a "conceptual token", which is placed directly into the conceptual structure.

One problem with such theories, however, arises from the fact that the number of primitives needed to generate a lexical concept will vary depending on the specific lexical concept that is being generated. Thus, though in such theories a very simple lexical concept may well be comprised of a single semantic primitive (or triggered by a single semantic property) many lexical concepts involve inordinate quantities of semantic properties. The English lexeme "changeling", for instance, denotes the concept of ugly or stupid children given to families by fairies in compensation for the more gifted children which the fairies have stolen. This sense of the variability in the complexity of lexical concepts and thus in the number of semantic primitives needed to generate them is reinforced by cross-linguistic phenomena. French, for example, will often express in a single lexeme a concept which English requires multiple words to express (i.e., "la tisane"–"herb tea", "langer"–"to change a nappy", etc.). In such instances, it would appear that the quantity of semantic primitives that go to make up the concept expressed by the French lexeme is divided over several lexemes in the case of English and thus that the concepts expressed by the individual English lexemes are made up out of fewer semantic primitives than the French lexeme. Such observations, then, indicate that the quantity of semantic properties associated with a lexical concept is utterly unconstrained and will vary arbitrarily from lexeme to lexeme.

Crucially, the fact the number of semantic properties in a lexical concept varies arbitrarily undermines the speaker's attempt to build up a cluster containing the correct quantity of semantic properties corresponding to a lexical concept because it renders the speaker unable to determine how many semantic properties should be placed into the cluster. In essence, it leads to a halting problem. With no determinate number of properties to aim for, a speaker may generate a cluster featuring too few or too many semantic properties and this will profoundly disrupt lexical access. Thus, a cluster featuring too few primitives will either trigger the access of the wrong conceptual token or lexeme (i.e., if a speaker built up a cluster, which inappropriately featured the single primitive "parent" rather than the appropriate two primitives "male" and "parent", it would incorrectly trigger the token/lexeme "parent" rather than "father" as desired) or lead to the activation of no token or lexeme at all if the speaker possesses no token or lexeme corresponding to the cluster. Similarly, if a speaker were to build a cluster featuring an excess number of semantic primitives—perhaps by simultaneously activating the primitives belonging to separate conceptual tokens—it would again lead to the retrieval of an incorrect token or lexeme or to no token or lexeme at all.

We might imagine that a speaker must realise when the developing cluster of properties corresponds to the intended concept and terminate the development of the cluster at this point. Yet if a speaker can match the developing cluster of properties against the intended concept in order to check whether they correspond then the speaker must already possess the intended concept—in which case why bother to develop a cluster of properties? Also, it is necessary to ask how the speaker obtained this copy of the intended concept. It surely must have required a further copy of the intended concept against which it could itself have been matched and this opens up an infinite regress. We could also avoid the problem by rejecting the view that lexical concepts come into focus gradually through the activation of their semantic primitives and assuming that speakers can spontaneously alight on conceptual tokens but this is theoretically vacuous and undermined empirically by studies which reveal that conceptual information can lead to the simultaneous activation of semantically related competitor lexemes (i.e., Wheeldon, 1989). Crucially, the failure of these approaches to the problem indicates that in order to obviate this problem of arbitrary quantity it is necessary to abandon another of its key assumptions, namely the assumption that conceptual structures are built up in lexical chunks. As was argued earlier, it was the assumption that conceptual chunks correspond to lexical concepts that entailed that such chunks were comprised of an arbitrary quantity of semantic primitives and thus gave rise to the problem initially. If we drop the assumption that conceptual chunks must correspond to lexical concepts then the possibility arises that conceptual structures might be built up in conceptual chunks that, unlike lexical concepts, contain a quantity of conceptual information that can actually be specified in advance by the speaker. If we can find such a chunk (and in the next section I will suggest that we can) and substitute it for the lexical concepts employed in current speech production models then we can provide the speaker with a speech production system which successfully obviates the problem of arbitrary quantity.

A second problem associated with semantic primitives stems from their ability to cluster together in entirely novel combinations. Many researchers, of course, find the fact that semantic primitives can generate an open-ended set of semantic clusters and thus concepts extremely attractive. It helps to explain, for instance, the fact that we can generate novel concepts (a fact confirmed by phenomena such as neologisms; cf., Clark, 1981) and the fact that speakers can produce such a vast, seemingly open-ended range of concepts (as phenomena such as polysemy reveal; cf., Lahav, 1989). But such novelty engenders its own peculiar problems. Presumably, since the set of lexemes that a speaker uses is relatively small and limited then the set of lexical concepts that these lexemes represent is relatively small and limited also. It would seem, therefore, that a small and limited set of lexemes would be unable to articulate a vast and unconstrained set of concepts. Specifically, if a speaker produced a lexical concept that was novel in the sense of not corresponding exactly to any of the concepts represented by the lexemes in their vocabulary then the speaker would seem to lack a lexeme with which to articulate this novel concept. In order to overcome this problem, Bierwisch and Schreuder (1992) propose that not all of the semantic primitives within a conceptual chunk need to feature in the meaning of a word in order for that conceptual chunk to successfully trigger the access of that word. On such a view, then, a lexical concept need only correspond partially or loosely to the meaning of a lexeme and this enables a speaker to successfully trigger lexical access even on the basis of a novel concept that does not correspond exactly to any lexeme.

There are, however, severe problems with Bierwisch and Schreuder's partial correspondence approach to semantic primitives. One significant problem arises from the fact that although the model stipulates that only a portion of the primitives in a conceptual chunk need feature in the "semantic form" that represents a word's meaning, it fails to specify how a speaker could determine precisely which portion this might be. Thus, colour is often a criterial feature for certain animals—a zebra must be black and white, for instance. On the partial correspondence model, then, when the conceptual chunk for zebra is produced by a speaker the speaker must select a word with a semantic form featuring the primitives "black" and "white". If the speaker failed to realise that these primitives were necessary features of the conceptual chunk needing to be satisfied by the semantic form of the word chosen then such a speaker might incorrectly select the word "horse" in response to the conceptual chunk for zebra. The partial correspondence model, then, falls down because it has no way of marking primitives as necessary features needing to be satisfied in semantic form. More than this, though, the model has no way of determining which features are necessary features in the first place. Certainly, it would be futile to attempt to correct this flaw by marking certain semantic primitives within the common set of primitives as inherently necessary because there are no primitives which are necessary in all contexts. Rather, a specific feature, though it might be necessary in certain contexts, will be unnecessary in others. Thus, a man made object such as a car will be coloured, for instance, but it is not necessary that it be a particular colour—indeed, we might view an invisible car as a perfectly good car. Colour, then, although a defining feature for zebras is mostly not so for cars. The significance of a semantic feature for an object, then, differs according to the object it is placed in. To assess whether a primitive in a conceptual chunk, then, is a necessary feature needing to be satisfied in semantic form the speaker needs some sense of the whole object which the cluster of primitives is purporting to represent and the role played by the specific features within that object. That is, the speaker needs not only an understanding of the component parts of an object but also an understanding of the way in which those component parts are structured together to render the whole object. Only when the speaker realises the role played by a primitive within the object as a whole can he or she decide whether or not it is a necessary feature. But, of course, it is precisely this—the sense of how the components parts of an object connect with each other to form a whole object—that the speaker using a common set of semantic primitives lacks, for a set of semantic primitives contains no whole object information but only information about the possible parts of such objects. As a result of this lack, then, the relation of partial correspondence between lexical concepts and lexemes that Bierwisch and Schreuder propose could not be successfully effected on the basis of semantic primitives. This inability of semantic primitives to deal with the freedom and novelty that they create indicates that conceptual knowledge, then, cannot consist merely in a small set of context independent semantic primitives but rather that speakers must make use of whole object representations that detail not only the parts an object is composed of but also the manner in which these parts are put together in the context of each individual object.

Perhaps the most severe problem associated with semantic primitives, however, stems from the assumption that conceptual information naturally forms into stable concepts comprising a determinate body of information that can be defined quite independently of other such concepts. Such an assumption manifests itself in the very notion of the semantic primitive, which forms a discrete and self-sufficient atom of information quite independently of other semantic primitives (thus, the primitive "red" will denote the colour red irrespective of whether a speaker possesses related primitives such as "blue"). It also manifests itself, however, in the idea that we can define a lexical concept in terms of a simple and determinate set of semantic primitives. In fact, however, when we look at conceptual information we find that it is not made up of discrete, determinate, and self-sufficient atoms of information but rather that it has an altogether more complex structure. Specifically, concepts, rather than forming atoms, seem to constitute "open systems" (to appropriate a term more frequently associated with physics). As Rosen states, "The essence of an open system is the necessity of invoking an "outside" or an environment, in order to understand what is going on "inside". That is, we must go to a larger system and not to smaller ones to account for what an open system is doing" (Rosen, 1996, p. 181). Evidence for this view of conceptual information is provided by the notorious failure of work in AI such as Winograd's blockworlds (1972) or Schank's research on scripts (1975), which attempts to treat a body of conceptual information as a closed system, i.e., as a domain for which a comprehensive and self-sufficient description can be given without reference to any conceptual domains beyond it. Of course, as Dreyfus's (1997) ruthless Heideggerian critique of Schank's script detailing all of the knowledge necessary for eating in a restaurant establishes such a project is futile—knowledge from neighbouring conceptual domains will always leak into and enrich our understanding of a particular domain. Such cross-domain leakage is, moreover, crucial for our understanding of any one domain—our understanding of paying for the food in a restaurant will always be informed by our experience of paying in other contexts and it is precisely this cross-domain leakage that supports the conceptual flexibility so apparent in human thinking and so woefully absent in AI knowledge simulation systems.

Yet, although Dreyfus has primarily applied his critique of the "closed system" paradigm of conceptual information to concepts at the textual level, his argument applies with equal vigour to conceptual information at other scales such as the word-meaning level because, as Shanon (1996) has argued, there is fundamentally no difference in the conceptual information at these different scales. Thus, Fodor (1981) shows that a word's meaning is an open system so that when, for instance, we try to specify all of the conceptual information required for the correct usage of the verb "to paint" we quickly find that an endless series of specifications is necessary to describe the meaning exhaustively. Moreover, Levelt (1989) finds similar problems operating at the sublexical scale of the semantic primitive. Thus, as Levelt points out, when we try to define lexical meaning in terms of semantic primitives we are effectively doing nothing more than defining a single word in terms of a series of other words. Since the series of other words also need to be defined in terms of other words, however, this approach quickly opens up an infinite regress for us from which there is no escape except via some entirely arbitrary cut-off point. We thus never reach a stage at which the words we employ in our definitions do not themselves need to be defined. That is, we never find a point at which semantic primitives attain the status of closed systems. Indeed, as Winograd (1976) observes, the further we pursue our definitions of a word, the more likely we are to require the stipulation of features which are themselves highly complex semantically, perhaps more complex than the notions they purport to explain. Certainly, the failure of attempts to work out a common set of semantic primitives bears this pessimistic analysis out (i.e., Miller & Johnson-Laird, 1976).

In short, conceptual information is never atomic. Rather, at all scales, it forms an open system, i.e., a system that can only be made sense of in relation to some larger system or context. Indeed, as Searle (1980; cf., also Dreyfus, 1997; Heidegger, 1962) has argued, it is precisely because a concept is enmeshed in a broader conceptual "background" that the concept acquires meaning in the first place. It would seem, therefore, that though lexemes do form discrete, stable units (in isolating languages at least) to seek to break up their meanings into similarly discrete and determinate units via semantic primitives is to fundamentally mis-construe the nature of conceptual information. There is good reason to suspect that there are no such things as semantic primitives because conceptual information constitutes open rather than closed systems. Moreover, even if we were able to pin down a set of such primitives, it is unlikely that they could successfully be used to describe word meaning since word meaning seems itself to form an open system grounded in a complex body of real-world understanding.

Overall, then, problems arise when we attempt to model the information in conceptual structures around lexical concepts comprised of semantic primitives. Specifically, conceptual information resists being carved into chunks correspond-ing to lexemes and it resists being described in terms of a determinate set of semantic primitives. This resistance arises because in modelling conceptual information in a digital, linguistic form we reduce its rich complexity and thereby corrupt it. Ultimately, therefore, the failure of attempts to impose a language-like form upon conceptual information strengthens the view that conceptual information rather than having a simple, digital structure fully embodies our complex experience of the world around us.

Situations

If the lexicalist approach to conceptual information is, then, untenable what are we to replace it with? If conceptual structures are not built out of lexical chunks what kind of chunks are they built out of? In fact, questions of this sort have a long history in speech production research since they were asked by the founding father of modern speech production research, Wilhelm Wundt, in his influential work "Die Sprache" (1900; cf., Blumenthal, 1970, and Seuren, 1998, for discussion of this work; cf., also Lashley, 1951, for a related theory of speech production). Wundt's vision of the conceptual planning process stemmed initially from a fierce rejection of lexicalist approaches to conceptual structure then popular in the German linguistic circles of the time (cf., Schmidt, 1976, for a discussion of this). In large part, it was Wundt's awareness of the massive differences in word structures across language types as diverse as isolating languages, agglutinative languages, sign languages, and so on that led him to argue that the word was simply too arbitrary and variable a notion to be meaningfully imposed on conceptual structures. In place of the lexical concept, Wundt argued that a conceptual structure is built up out of a "Gesamtvorstellung" or "unified mental representation" (Blumenthal, 1970). When formulated, the "Gesamtvorstellung" yields a clause but, although a clause is built up incrementally according to Wundt in successive lexical/phrasal units, the "Gesamtvorstellung" must be built up not part by part but as a unified whole—that is, each of its component parts must be produced and exist simultaneously during the conceptual planning process. According to Wundt, then, speakers build up conceptual structures in chunks containing the various conceptual elements which form the basis for the grammatical formulation of the clause. Importantly, Wundt further argued that the whole of the "Gesamtvorstellung" must be fully constructed before incremental grammatical formulation could begin.

Is it the case, then, that speakers plan out conceptual structures not in lexical chunks but in much larger, clause-like chunks? In fact, support for such a claim is provided by the vast amount of psycholinguistic work both in language comprehension (i.e., Gernsbacher, Hargreaves, & Beeman, 1989; Stine, 1990; Van Petten, 1995) and production (i.e., Ford, 1982; Ford & Holmes, 1978; Garrett, 1982; Miller & Weinert, 1998; Smith & Wheeldon, 1999a), which supports the idea that the clause forms a key unit in language processing. Thus, Ford and Holmes (1978) found that whilst subjects talked freely on a given subject their responses to an auditory signal were significantly slower when the signal was presented near the end of a nonfinite clause, even when the end of that clause did not correspond to the end of a finite clause. Reinforcing this, a study of pausing in speech by Ford (1982) showed that pauses occur just as frequently prior to nonfinite clauses as to finite clauses and that the quantity of pausing that occurs prior to finite clauses is not significantly greater than that which occurs prior to nonfinite clauses. Thus, Ford and Holmes' work reveals that speakers plan their utterance a clause at a time and that nonfinite and finite clauses necessitate equivalent amounts of planning time. In English (the language employed in Ford and Holmes' experiments), nonfinite clauses are typically less complex grammatically than finite clauses but have an equivalent conceptual complexity; we may not mark out the subject of a nonfinite clause but we must understand who the subject is. The work of Ford and Holmes is compatible with the view, then, that at a prelinguistic, conceptual level planning is conducted in clause-like units but is incompatible with the view that a clausal processing scope is employed during grammatical encoding.[2] Wundt's claims are also put to the test in experiments by Smith and Wheeldon (1999a), which determine latencies to a wide variety of sentences using an on-line picture description task. This paradigm is further coupled with a picture preview period which removes the time dedicated to the processing of a lexeme prior to speech onset from the latencies thus allowing for an estimate of this time. Smith and Wheeldon found that equivalent amounts of time are dedicated to the processing of both nouns in a sentence featuring a complex initial phrase (i.e., "the kite and the house move up"). They reason that since the first noun must be accessed prior to speech onset the accessing of the second noun must also be completed prior to speech onset. They also find, however, that prior to speech onset some time is dedicated to elements far beyond the first phrase (though it is significantly less than that dedicated to elements within the first phrase). Thus, in producing the sentence "The dog which is next to the eye moves up", subjects dedicate a small amount of processing time prior to speech onset to the processing of the picture corresponding to the noun within the relative clause. Clearly, such a result in indicating that processing prior to speech onset is not restricted to the initial phrase but can extend far into the first clause is consistent with Wundt's theory which entails that conceptual planning must be conducted for the first clause of an utterance prior to speech onset.

Why, then, might speakers plan out conceptual structures in clausal rather than lexical chunks? To understand this it is necessary to understand what a clausal chunk would represent on a conceptual level. One theory which focuses on this issue is STV theory (Smith, 1999), which takes as its starting point the observation that all clauses in all languages contain three necessary and sufficient features (whether explicitly or in an ellipsed form)—a verb phrase, a noun phrase, and a subject phrase (for work arguing for the universal distribution of nouns, verbs and subject phrases, cf., Comrie, 1989; Langacker, 1987; Plank, 1979). The theory argues that, on a conceptual level, clauses prototypically refer to situations and that these three features are necessary and sufficient because they refer to the fundamental conceptual parameters that define a situation. Thus, on a conceptual level, a verb phrase refers to the single time period over which the situation occurs (Langacker, 1987; Menaugh, 1988), a noun phrase denotes an entity grounded in the single space in which the situation occurs (Smith, 1999), and a subject phrase refers to the single viewpoint from which the situation is subjectively experienced (Katagiri, 1991; Kuno, 1986). The three phrase types are necessitated at a grammatical level, then, because they articulate the three parameters of space, time, and viewpoint which create and delimit a situation at a conceptual level. Crucially, such a theory also provides suggestions as to why a speaker might plan out conceptual structures in holistic clausal chunks rather than lexical chunks. It is, for instance, impossible, as Kant realised, to imagine a timeless situation or a situation not grounded in space or a situation not experienced from a particular viewpoint. The conceptual interdependence of these three aspects of a situation, then, suggests that, during conceptual planning, they should be generated simultaneously and holistically rather than consecutively and incrementally. It is also possible that speakers plan out conceptual structures in holistic clausal chunks rather than lexical chunks because doing so might enable them to avoid the problem of arbitrary quantity. Whereas lexical concepts, as argued previously, contain an arbitrary or open-ended amount of information and thus give rise to a halting problem, it is possible that clause-like conceptual chunks, in always containing only a single situation's worth of information, do provide predetermined informational parameters.

The question remains, of course, as to what kinds of conceptual information such situations might be built out of if they are not built out of lexical concepts. One possibility is suggested by Nunberg in his classic paper "The non-uniqueness of semantic solutions: Polysemy" (1979). In it, it is argued that word use involves not the semantic determination of meaning but rather the pragmatic determination of reference. In such an approach, conceptual structures are built not from standardised word meanings but simply from our knowledge of the world (cf., also Haiman, 1980). Nunberg initiates his argument by drawing on polysemy to support the claim that a language user's lexicon will not specify in advance all of the distinct meanings that can attach to a word but rather that a lexicon necessarily "undergenerates the class of acceptable uses" (Nunberg, 1979, p. 153). He then considers the possibility that in response to such a state of affairs the lexicon might define a word in terms of a small set of prespecified word meanings from which other polysemous meanings are then pragmatically derived online. Subsequently, Nunberg denies that such a response is practicable. Specifically, he demonstrates repeatedly that in many instances of word use it is impossible to determine which of a lexeme's meanings are prespecified and "conventional" and which are derived pragmatically on the basis of these conventional meanings. That is, he demonstrates that in relation to word use it is impossible to determine where semantic meaning ends and pragmatic meaning begins. Thus, in a sentence such as "There are three trees on that island", for instance, the trees may be construed either as tree-types (i.e., oak, ash, and willow) or tree-tokens (i.e., three oak trees). As Nunberg demonstrates, however, designating either of these uses as the conventional one is an entirely arbitrary manoeuvre since "the pattern of use would be entirely rational no matter what the words conventionally designated: we could derive 'type' interpretations if words named classes of tokens and vice-versa" (Nunberg, 1979, p. 173). As a consequence of a variety of analyses along these lines, Nunberg concludes that word use involves not the semantic determination of meaning but rather the pragmatic determination of reference: "We do not have to know what a word means to be able to say what it is being used to refer to" (Nunberg, 1979, p. 177).

Nunberg then sets out to demonstrate how the pragmatic determination of a word's reference might be accomplished. In Nunberg's theory of the pragmatic determination of reference a word is thought of as a "demonstratum". By this term, Nunberg means to suggest that the word itself does not directly represent its referent but merely points to it indirectly. As a result, the hearer must determine in which direction and at what referent the word is pointing: That is, the hearer must correctly determine the nature of the relation between the "demonstratum" and the "referent". This relation is determined by the hearer, Nunberg argues, through the selection of a "referring function", which specifies the relation between "demonstratum" and "referent". As an example of this, if a speaker points to a sports car and says "He is a friend of mine" in such an instance the sports car assumes the role of demonstratum, whereas numerous referring functions such as "X is usually repaired by Y" and "X was designed by Y" suggest themselves. In determining the reference of the subject of the sentence, then, the hearer must work from the demonstratum (i.e., "sports car") to one of a range of potential referents (i.e., "the car's designer", "the car's mechanic") via the selection of one of a range of referring functions. Crucially, the selection of the referring function is a pragmatic process—specifically, a hearer will assume that a speaker intended the selection of that referring function which renders identification easiest. Since, for instance, it is generally easier to identify the designer of a sports car than its mechanic the referring function "X was designed by Y" would typically be preferred by a hearer over "X is usually repaired by Y". In Nunberg's view, then, a hearer does not respond to a word by first selecting a conventional meaning—the possible range of referents to which any given word may apply is simply too large and complex to be specified in a set of conventional meanings. Instead, according to Nunberg, a word can be used to refer to a wide range of things in the world or aspects of our world knowledge and a hearer must determine the intended reference by applying pragmatic assumptions to whatever demonstrata, linguistic or otherwise, the speaker has supplied the hearer with. Applied to speech production, Nunberg's view of meaning suggests that conceptual structures would not be built out of separate word meaning and world knowledge stores with lexical concepts forming the backbone of the conceptual structure and world knowledge being packed in around them. Instead, Nunberg's view suggests that speakers draw all of the information used in a conceptual structure from a single store of conceptual information that does not distinguish between semantic and pragmatic information. On such a view, conceptual structures are composed of world knowledge rather than lexical concepts.

Experimental evidence in support of Nunberg's view of conceptual information has been provided by studies investigating the processing of figurative and literal language. In a series of eye-tracking experiments, for instance, Frisson and Pickering (1999; cf., also Gibbs & Gerrig, 1989) compare times taken to process a word in its literal and metonymic senses. Thus, they compare reading times to the word "Vietnam" when it is used in its literal sense of location (as in "I grew up in Vietnam") and in its metonymic sense of event (as in "I grew up during Vietnam") and find that the word is comprehended as rapidly when used metonymically as when used literally. Clearly, if a word's meaning is derived first by accessing a prespecified, conventional meaning and then, if necessary, by modulating this meaning via world knowledge then we should expect the literal sense of a word to be comprehended more rapidly than its metaphoric sense since the former requires only the access of a conventional meaning, whereas the latter requires both the access of a conventional meaning and its subsequent pragmatic modulation. In contrast, Nunberg, in claiming that literal and figurative language are both comprehended through a single stage of pragmatic reference determination would predict that figurative language should be comprehended as rapidly as literal language as long as the reference of the figurative language is as easy to pragmatically determine on the basis of context as the reference of the literal language (on the role of context, cf., Gibbs & Gerrig, 1989; Onishi & Murphy, 1993; Van Petten, 1995). The fact, then, that a word can be comprehended as rapidly in its figurative sense as in its literal sense undermines the view that language processing makes use of a distinction between core semantic meaning and derived, figurative, or pragmatic meaning to generate conceptual structures composed of lexical concepts with world knowledge packed in around them and supports Nunberg's more elegant view that conceptual structures are composed wholly of world knowledge.

In summary, then, a number of studies indicate that conceptual structures are built up not in lexical chunks but in clausal chunks that represent situations. It is likely that the conceptual information featuring in such clausal chunks might be drawn not from separate stores of lexical concepts and world knowledge but from a single informational store embodying all of a speaker's conceptual knowledge.

Formulating conceptual structures

How does a speaker convert a conceptual structure into a grammatical structure? Typically, it is argued that conceptual structures comprise a string of chunks corresponding to lexical concepts and that grammatical formulation is a process of matching the chunks within a conceptual structure to chunks within the speaker's own grammatical system and thereby producing a string of lexemes and thus a sentence. It was argued earlier, however, that aspects of conceptual information such as the problem of arbitrary quantity indicate that conceptual structures cannot be comprised of chunks corresponding to lexical concepts but must instead be built up in clausal chunks denoting situations. Such a claim is reinforced by sentence blends (Brown, 1980; Fay, 1982), which, as argued previously, indicate that the number of lexemes in a grammatical structure does not result from there being a similar number of lexical concepts in the conceptual structure thus undermining the view that formulation involves matching a single lexeme to each conceptual chunk. (NB We cannot rescue the lexical concept view by arguing that speakers have the freedom to formulate a single lexical concept via multiple lexical chunks because this suggests that concepts are no longer constrained to match up with elements within the grammatical system and thus entails the correspondence problem.) Such problems are compounded, moreover, by the fact that the lexical concept view commits us to the Whorfian claim that the concepts produced by speakers of different languages are as varied as the lexemes produced by speakers of different languages. As noted earlier, however, there is little support for such a view. Moreover, such Whorfianism gives rise to a number of absurd implications. If we assume, for instance, that the chunking of a grammatical structure precisely reflects the chunking of the conceptual structure underlying it then this forces us to further assume that multilingual speakers have multiple stores of concepts—one for each language they speak. This is, of course, highly redundant since there would be a tremendous amount of overlap between much of the information contained within the various conceptual stores. Such inefficiency is surely incompatible, moreover, with the rapid, intrasentential code switching that multilingual speakers often demonstrate. It seems highly unlikely that such rapid code switching could result from speakers rapidly switching between a variety of different conceptual stores.

Perhaps the greatest challenge to the view that the chunking of a grammatical structure matches that of the conceptual structure that underlies it, however, is provided by formulaic language (Van Lanckner, 1987). In formulaic language, a conceptual structure will often be articulated via a single, formulaic, grammatical chunk. Thus, as Kuiper (1996) has observed, in order to describe the start of a race, a racing commentator will often deploy a stock formula such as "They're off and racing now", which is stored and accessed whole and unanalysed from the speaker's lexicon. Yet if we assume that the chunking of a grammatical structure matches that of the conceptual structure that underlies it, then we must also assume (as both Fodor, 1987, and Levelt, 1989, do) that such stock formulas correspond to single conceptual chunks. Such an assumption, however, gives rise to a number of problems. The conceptual chunk referred to by a speech formula such as "They're off and racing now" can presumably, if we subscribe to the notion of lexical concepts, be broken down into a number of smaller conceptual chunks (such as those referred to by the lexemes "They" and "racing", for instance), which will already be stored within the speaker's conceptual lexicon. Such a view of formulaic language, then, leads (once again) to a tremendous amount of redundancy within a speaker's conceptual store wherein a good deal of information is specified not once but repeatedly. Furthermore, it is surely the case that, since the lexical concepts into which a formulaic conceptual chunk can be divided contain less information than the formulaic conceptual chunk itself, the conceptual information necessary to trigger the access of such lexical concepts would always become available before the conceptual information necessary for the accessing of a formulaic conceptual chunk. As a result, the lexical concepts into which a formulaic conceptual chunk can be divided would always be selected before the formulaic conceptual chunk itself and this would mean that, in practice, formulaic chunks would never actually get selected. Since conceptual structures would always be built up in lexical concepts in preference to formulaic chunks this would further entail that grammatical structures would be built up in lexemes and thus that we should never encounter formulaic language. Finally, if we assume that conceptual chunks can correspond either to entire clauses or to single lexemes we further exacerbate the problem of the arbitrary quantity of information contained within conceptual chunks. Such an assumption provides a speaker with a set of conceptual chunks that are wildly imbalanced in terms of the quantity of information they refer to, with certain chunks referring to entire situations and others merely to single objects. Given all of these problems, it is perhaps not surprising that accounts of speech production that assume that the chunking of conceptual structures matches that of grammatical structures also tend, as Kuiper (1996) argues, to marginalise formulaic language and treat speech production as if it involved solely the production of lexemes.

Such linguistic phenomena illustrate, then, that a variety of severe and intractable problems arise when we make the assumption that conceptual structures are comprised of a string of chunks that encapsulate the meaning of the lexemes in grammatical structure. When coupled with the problem of arbitrary quantity such phenomena begin to make such an assumption appear extremely unattractive indeed and suggest the need for a different approach to the relation between conceptual structures and grammatical formulation. In fact, in order to account successfully for the above phenomena, we need to drop the view that conceptual structures are cut into chunks during conceptual planning that are matched up with lexemes during grammatical encoding and replace it with the view that a conceptual structure is comprised of an uncut clausal chunk that is subsequently cut up during grammatical formulation according to the grammatical resources available to the speaker. On such a view, formulation now gives the speaker the freedom to clump together bits of information into chunks that fit with whatever grammatical resources the speaker possesses. As a result of such freedom, phenomena such as different sentences with synonymous meanings and sentence blends are no longer a problem since we are no longer committed to the view that differences in grammatical structure must reflect differences in conceptual structures. Instead, such a view allows us to claim that different sentences with synonymous meanings and the various sentences that are combined together in sentence blends do result from a single underlying conceptual structure and reflect merely the fact that a speaker may have, on occasion, a variety of different grammatical resources that allow the conceptual structure to be cut up in a variety of different ways. Building conceptual structures out of clausal chunks also provides for a simple account of cross-linguistic differences in word structure. On such a view, such differences do not reflect differences in conceptual structure and thus in the set of conceptual chunks available to speakers of different languages. Instead, such differences simply reflect differences in the way that speakers of different languages cut up a given conceptual structure during grammatical formulation. Thus, the fact that French speakers use the verb "amerrir" where English speakers use the phrase "to land on the sea" no longer commits us to the view that the conceptual structures underlying their use must be built out of correspondingly different sets of conceptual chunks. Instead, we can simply argue that French and English speakers will cut the same conceptual structure into different-sized chunks during grammatical encoding because the French language uses a single word "amerrir" to cover a certain amount of information where the English language requires several to cover the same amount of information. Because, then, we are no longer committed to the view that cross-linguistic differences in word structure entail corresponding differences in the conceptual chunks available to speakers of different languages, we are no longer committed to Whorfianism. Consequently, it is, on such a view, no longer surprising that the massive differences in the grammatical structures produced by signers and speakers are not accompanied by correspondingly massive differences in conceptualisation. Building up conceptual structures in clausal chunks also allows us to provide a straightforward account of multilingualism. If we assume that conceptual structures are cut into lexical chunks, then, since such chunks differ across languages, we are committed to the view that grammatical structures in a multilingual speaker's first language must be based upon different conceptual structures to grammatical structures in a multilingual speaker's second or third language. In contrast to lexical chunks, however, the quantity of information contained within a clausal chunk will not be determined by and tied to a specific language but will instead, as argued earlier, always comprise a single situation irrespective of the language it is to be subsequently encoded in. As a result, it is no longer necessary to assume that a grammatical structure in a multilingual speaker's first language is built up from a different set of conceptual chunks to a grammatical structure in that speaker's second or third language, and it can be argued, instead, that the conceptual structure generated by a speaker provides a quantity of information which can be formulated equally effectively in any language.

Of course, a system that has the freedom to cut up a single conceptual structure into as many different grammatical structures as the grammatical resources of the speaker will allow naturally throws up the problem of how to decide between the various possible grammatical structures that may result. It seems reasonable to assume that, faced with a choice between two grammatical structures that convey equivalent amounts of conceptual information, speakers will generally prefer the grammatical structure with the least grammatical chunks since such a structure will, as Kuiper (1996) demonstrates, incur less formulation costs and so allow for more rapid and efficient speech production. Crucially, if speakers do actively select for the competing grammatical structure with the fewest grammatical chunks then we would naturally expect to see speech formulas flourish in language. Clearly, if a speaker can formulate a clausal chunk with the speech formula "They're off and racing now!" or with a grammatical structure built out of the equivalent lexemes then the speech formula would be preferred to the grammatical structure comprised of lexemes for the simple reason that it featured less grammatical chunks and so required less formulation costs. A speech system in which grammatical structures with the least number of grammatical chunks are always preferred also provides an elegant solution to the word-to-phrase synonymy problem (Roelofs, 1992b), which concerns the difficulty of selecting an appropriate single word (such as "father") in preference to an inappropriate phrase (such as "male parent"), which is synonymous with it. Being synonymous we can expect that the word "father" and the word "male parent" will cover equal portions of the conceptual structure. Again, though, as with formulaic language, the word "father" covers this portion in less grammatical chunks than the phrase "male parent" (i.e., the word covers it in a single chunk, whereas the phrase requires two chunks) and so is preferred to it because it reduces formulation costs and optimises processing efficiency.

Yet a system which allows speakers the freedom to pack as much or as little conceptual information into the grammatical chunks that feature in a grammatical structure would also give rise to the problem of how to decide between grammatical structures that feature an equivalent number of grammatical chunks but which convey different amounts of information. It seems reasonable to assume, as Grice (1975) argued, that speakers generally strive to be informative and that, consequently, when faced with a choice between two grammatical structures that feature equivalent numbers of chunks and thus incur similar processing costs, a speaker will generally prefer the most informative structure. Crucially, such an assumption provides for an elegant solution to the hypernym problem (Roelofs, 1992b). A hypernym, as Cruse (1986) notes, is a word whose meaning is contained within or implied by a second word (known as a hyponym). Thus "parent" is a hypernym of "father", whereas "father" is a hyponym of "parent" since a person who is a father is also a parent. Clearly, a hyponym will always contain more information than its hypernym since it both contains all of the information within the hypernym and adds in a little extra besides (i.e., "father" contains "parent" but adds in "male" also). When a conceptual structure contains all of the information necessary to trigger the access of a hyponym, therefore, it clearly also contains all of the information necessary to trigger the access of all of its hypernyms also. The hypernym problem, then, concerns the difficulty of selecting a hyponym such as "father" and avoiding selecting one of its hypernyms such as "parent". Of course, if speakers do prefer the most informative structure in a choice between grammatical structures featuring equivalent numbers of grammatical chunks then the hypernym problem simply disappears. In such a system, speakers will always select hyponyms in preference to hypernyms because, though both are comprised of a single grammatical chunk, the hyponym contains more information than the hypernym and so satisfies the speaker's desire to be informative.[3]

In summary, then, the assumption that conceptual structures are cut up into lexical chunks that are then matched to lexemes during formulation is inconsistent with phenomena such as sentence blends, cross-linguistic differences in word structure, and multilingualism. Such phenomena are, however, consistent with a system in which clausal conceptual structures are cut up into chunks during formulation according to the available grammatical resources. Moreover, adding in to such a system the assumptions that speakers strive to minimise the number of chunks in a grammatical structure and to maximise the informativeness of each of those chunks enables us to account for formulaic language, the word-to-phrase synonymy problem, and the hypernym problem.

General summary

In the present section, it has been argued that conceptual structures cannot be comprised of lexical concepts featuring semantic primitives since such an approach fails to capture the rich complexity of conceptual information. In place of lexical concepts, it was argued, conceptual structures should be seen as being built up in chunks representing situations that correspond at the grammatical level to clauses. Finally, it was argued that clause-like conceptual structures are cut up into lexeme-sized chunks during formulation rather than prior to it. Overall, then, such arguments suggest that conceptual structures, rather than possessing a simple, digital form similar to language, are comprised of informationally rich situations that preserve the analogue complexity of our experience of the world.

CONCLUSION

Proper expressions rise to the surface from the heat and fermentation of the mind, like bubbles on an agitated stream.

(Hazlitt, 1825, p. 143)

In this chapter, rationalist and empiricist approaches to the relation between conceptual and grammatical structure have been investigated. The chapter began by outlining the theoretical problems associated with the rationalist contention that grammatical and conceptual structures form precise replications of one another (i.e., Garrett, 1982). This line of attack was reinforced in the next section by empirical data demonstrating that there are, in fact, significant differences between conceptual and grammatical structures. Specifically, it was argued that information featuring in a conceptual structure may have no counterpart in a grammatical structure and vice versa, that the structural form of a conceptual structure is distinct from that of a grammatical structure and that many conceptual structures may map on to a single grammatical structure and vice versa. In all of these respects the available language data seriously undermines the rationalist claim that a grammatical structure will precisely replicate the conceptual structure that underlies it, and suggests that there is a far more complex relation between information at these two levels.

In the next section, it was argued that grammatical structures deviate from the conceptual structures that underlie them largely because speakers aim to produce simplified grammatical structures that incur minimal formulation costs. In support of this claim, it was shown that speakers simplify grammatical formulation by using preformulated grammatical material, by producing underspecified grammatical structures that contain minimal amounts of information, and by maximising the flexibility and thus efficiency of the grammatical system itself. In the fourth section, it was argued that the form and content of conceptual structures are significantly more complex than the simple, digital structure of language and resist all attempts to model them in language-like terms. In support of this claim, it was argued that breaking up conceptual structures into a lexicon-like store of discrete conceptual chunks radically underestimates the rich complexity of the information stored within those structures, that conceptual structures are comprised not of lexical concepts but of situations formed directly from world knowledge, and that lexical chunking is imposed on to conceptual structures during formulation rather than prior to it. Overall, then, these two sections provide unequivocal support for the empiricist view that conceptual structures preserve the analogue and open-ended complexity of the world experienced by the speaker and that grammatical structures rather than replicating this informational richness recast it in a greatly simplified form.

Significantly, such a view of speech production accords well with a view of information processing recently outlined by Tor Norretranders (1998). In Norretrander's view, human information processing is generally comprised of two discrete stages—an initial stage at which vast quantities of information are processed unconsciously and a subsequent stage at which this vast quantity of unconscious information is stripped down into a highly simplified but conscious representation. In support of this view, Norretranders cites a raft of psychophysical and neurological studies (i.e., Taylor & McCloskey, 1990; Zimmermann, 1989), which demonstrate that a far greater quantity of information is processed subliminally than ever passes into consciousness. He also draws on work by Benjamin Libet and colleagues (i.e., Libet, Gleason, Wright, & Pearl, 1983) demonstrating that we become conscious of a decision to engage in a simple action such as getting out of a chair or moving an arm approximately 350 ms after the unconscious cerebral activity that originates that activity has been initiated. Clearly, if the thesis advanced in this chapter is correct then we should treat conceptual planning as an example of Norretranders' first stage, since it generates immensely rich and complex informational structures, whereas we should link grammatical formulation to Norretranders' second processing stage, as it outputs comparatively simple digital structures. Support for this view is provided by studies linking conceptual structures to unconscious processing (as in the first stage) and grammatical structures to conscious processing (as in the second stage). Thus, as Wundt (1900) realised, although we are not directly aware of the conceptual structures we produce we do become directly aware of the grammatical structures we produce through our phonological representations of them. Reinforcing Wundt's claims, studies of priming in picture naming have shown that prime pictures exposed for subliminal durations prime only the conceptual planning of subsequent target pictures, whereas pictures exposed for longer, nonsubliminal periods influence the grammatical planning of the target picture as well (i.e., McCauley, Parmelee, Sperber, & Carr, 1980). A recent study of picture naming by Levelt, Praamstra, Meyer, Helenius, and Salmelin (1998), moreover, has shown that whereas conceptual planning is accomplished as rapidly as 150 ms after the onset of cerebral activity, the phonological word representations that form the basis of conscious activities such as self-monitoring (i.e., Wheeldon & Levelt, 1995) are not accessed until 350 ms after the onset of cerebral activity in line with Libet et al.'s estimate.[4] Linking the current analysis of language production to Norretranders' theory, then, suggests that the fact that we are conscious of grammatical but not conceptual structures provides further support for the view that conceptual structures are immensely complex informationally, in contrast to grammatical structures, which are comparatively simple. More generally it suggests that the tendency of rationalists to "confuse the thought itself with the natural language sentence" stems from mistaking the aspect of language production that we are conscious of for the whole of language production (or, to use Norretanders' terms, from mistaking the "I" for the "Me").

To conclude, then, this chapter has been sharply critical of rationalist approaches that try to model conceptual structures in terms of our understanding of the form of language. Instead, the chapter has provided support for the standard empiricist claim that conceptual and grammatical structure diverge sharply so that grammatical structure is effectively an interpretation of conceptual structure providing only a partial and indirect approximation to it. It has also provided support for the standard empiricist argument that, whereas conceptual structures are built out of information derived from and structured in terms of a speaker's experience of the world, grammatical structures are driven by the speaker's concern for the optimisation of processing costs. As such, the chapter suggests that the phenomenon of human language production is compatible with an empiricist account of thought and its relation to language. Of course, the present chapter only provides an account of this relation in the most broad and general terms— it cannot be said to provide a model of language production. Nevertheless, in emphasising the need for an empiricist rather than rationalist model of language production it is to be hoped that the present chapter does go some way towards indicating the direction in which such a model might be found.

ACKNOWLEDGEMENT

The preparation of this manuscript was supported by an ESRC research grant.

NOTES

1. Interestingly, the same lesson is now being learnt by programmers of computer languages who, increasingly, save time by building programs not from the ground up but from pre-assembled stretches of code. Moreover, such an approach leads to programs that are less concise and take longer to process, which neatly parallels the fact that when speakers reduce their own formulation costs it inevitably leads to a concomitant rise in processing costs for hearers.

2. It is an interesting matter to speculate whether the clause-by-clause processing of language is mirrored by the bar-by-bar processing of music. If the notes within a bar are processed as a holistic unit then presumably an experimental design similar to that employed by Ford and Holmes would yield evidence of slower responses to a signal presented near bar boundaries.

3. It is important to note that the nondecompositional approach (Levelt et al., 1999) does not solve the hypernym problem but simply relocates the problem so that it arises during conceptualisation rather than grammatical formulation. That is, it converts the standard problem of how to get from semantic primitives to lexemes into a new problem of how to get from semantic features to conceptual tokens. Roelofs (1992a) renames this relocated hypernym problem the "superordinate problem" and argues that speakers solve it by making use of an object's "entry point", which he defines as "the point at which contact is first made with semantic memory" (Roelofs, 1992a, p. 104). Such a solution fails, however, because it prevents speakers from accessing conceptual tokens that do not correspond to entry points and thus from producing lexemes with non-entry point conceptual tokens underlying them such as "robin". In general, it seems impossible to solve the hypernym problem whilst maintaining a lexicalist view of conceptual structure and, consequently, the hypernym problem is perhaps best understood as a critique of lexicalism.

4. Remarkably, Levelt et al.'s data also suggests that the phonological word representations that form the basis of self-monitoring are accessed 200 ms prior to speech onset, which parallels Libet et al.'s finding that the conscious awareness of a decision to move occurs 200 ms prior to the occurrence of the movement, thus allowing the movement to be vetoed before it occurs.

REFERENCES

Altenberg, B. (1990). Speech as linear composition. In G. Caie, K. Haastrup, A.L. Jakobsen, J.E. Nielsen, J. Sevaldsen, H. Specht, & A. Zetterstein (Eds.), *Proceedings from the Fourth Nordic Conference for English Studies*. Copenhagen, Denmark: Copenhagen University Press.

Armstrong, D.F., Stokoe, W.C., & Wilcox, S.E. (1995). *Gesture and the nature of language*. Cambridge, UK: Cambridge University Press.

Bach, K. (1987). *Thought and reference*. Oxford, UK: Clarendon Press.

Bierwisch, M., & Schreuder, R. (1992). From concepts to lexical items. *Cognition, 42*, 23–60.

Blumenthal, A.L. (1970). *Language and psychology: Historical aspects of psycholinguistics*. New York: John Wiley.

Bock, J.K. (1986). Syntactic persistence in language production. *Cognitive Psychology, 18*, 355–387.

Bod, R. (1998). *Beyond grammar: An experience-based theory of language*. Cambridge, MA: Cambridge University Press/CSLI Publications.

Brown, E.K. (1980). Grammatical incoherence. In H.W. Dechert & M. Raupach (Eds.), *Temporal variables in speech: Studies in honour of Frieda Goldman-Eisler* (pp. 28–38). The Hague, The Netherlands: Mouton.

Brugman, C., & Lakoff, G. (1988). Cognitive topology and lexical networks. In S. Small, G. Cotrell, & M. Tanenhaus (Eds.), *Lexical ambiguity resolution* (pp. 477–508). Palo Alto, CA: Morgan Kaufman.

Caramazza, A., & Grober, E. (1977). Polysemy and the structure of the subjective lexicon. In C. Rameh (Ed.), *Semantics: Theory and application (proceedings)*. Washington DC: Georgetown University Press.

Carruthers, P. (1996). *Language, thought and consciousness: An essay in philosophical psychology*. Cambridge, UK: Cambridge University Press.

Clark, E.V. (1981). Lexical innovations: How children learn to create new words. *Behavioural Development: A Series of Monographs, 7*, 299–328.

Clark, H.H., & Wilkes-Gibbs, D.L. (1986). Referring as a collaborative process. *Cognition, 22*, 1–39.

Comrie, B. (1989). *Language universals and linguistic typology*. Chicago: Chicago University Press.

Cruse, D.A. (1986). *Lexical semantics*. Cambridge, UK: Cambridge University Press.

Cunningham, H., Gaizauskas, R.J., & Wilkes, Y. (1996). *A general architecture for text engineering*. Unpublished manuscript, University of Sheffield, Department of Computer Science.

De Smedt, K. (1996). Computational models of incremental grammatical encoding. In T. Dijkstra & K. de Smedt (Eds.), *Computational psycholinguistics* (pp. 279–307). London: Taylor & Francis.

Dreyfus, H.L. (1997). From micro-worlds to knowledge representation: AI at an impasse. In J. Haugeland (Ed.), *Mind design 2: Philosophy, psychology and artificial intelligence* (pp. 143–182). Cambridge, MA: MIT Press.

Fauconnier, G. (1985). *Mental spaces*. Cambridge, MA. MIT Press.

Fay, D. (1982). Substitutions and splices: A study of sentences blends. In A. Cutler (Ed.), *Slips of the tongue and language production*. Berlin, Germany: Mouton.

Fodor, J.A. (1981). *Representations*. Cambridge, MA: MIT Press.

Fodor, J.A. (1987). *Psychosemantics*. Cambridge, MA: MIT Press.

Fodor, J.A., & Pylyshyn, Z. (1997). Connectionism and cognitive architecture: A critical analysis. In J. Haugeland (Ed.), *Mind design 2: Philosophy, psychology and artificial intelligence* (pp. 351–377). Cambridge, MA: MIT Press.

Ford, M. (1982). Sentence planning units: Implications for the speaker's representation of meaningful relations underlying sentences. In J. Bresnan (Ed.), *The mental representation of grammatical relations* (pp. 797–827). Cambridge, MA: MIT Press.

Ford, M., & Holmes, V.M. (1978). Planning units in sentence production. *Cognition, 6*, 35–53.

Frisson, S., & Pickering, M. (1999). The processing of metonymy: Evidence from eye movements. *Journal of Experimental Psychology: Learning, Memory and Cognition, 6*, 1–18.

Garrett, M.F. (1982). Production of speech: Observations from normal and pathological language use. In A.W. Ellis (Ed.), *Normality and pathology in cognitive functions* (pp. 19–76). London: Academic Press.

Gernsbacher, M.A., Hargreaves, D.J., & Beeman, M. (1989). Building and accessing clausal representations: The advantage of first mention versus the advantage of clause recency. *Journal of Memory and Language, 28*, 735–755.

Gibbs, R.W., & Gerrig, R.J. (1989). How context makes metaphor comprehension seem special. *Metaphor and Symbolic Activity, 3*, 145–158.

Goldberg, A.E. (1995). *Constructions: A construction grammar approach to argument structure.* Chicago: University of Chicago Press.

Grice, H.P. (1975). Logic and conversation. In P. Cole & J.L. Morgan (Eds.), *Syntax and semantics: Vol. 3. Speech acts.* New York: Academic Press.

Gross, M. (1979). On the failure of generative grammar. *Language, 55,* 859–885.

Hadley, G. (1997). Lexis and culture: Bound and determined? *Journal of Psycholinguistic Research, 26,* 483–496.

Haiman, J. (1980). Dictionaries and encyclopaedias. *Lingua, 50,* 329–357.

Halliday, M.A.K., & Hasan, R. (1976). *Cohesion in English.* London: Longman.

Hankamer, J. (1989). Morphological parsing and the lexicon. In W. Marslen-Wilson (Ed.), *Lexical representation and process* (pp. 392–407). Cambridge, MA: MIT Press.

Hazlitt, W. (1825). *The plain speaker, or, opinions on books, men and things.* Paris: Galignani.

Heidegger, M. (1962). *Being and time* (J. Macquarrie & E. Robinson, Trans.). New York: Harper & Row.

Hirsh-Pasek, K., & Golinkoff, R.M. (1996). *The origins of grammar: Evidence from early language comprehension.* Cambridge, MA: MIT Press.

Horne-Tooke, J. (1805). *The diversions of purley.* London: Author. (Original work published 1786)

Johnson-Laird, P.N. (1983). *Mental models.* Cambridge, UK: Cambridge University Press.

Katagiri, Y. (1991). Perspectivity and the Japanese reflexive "zibun". In J. Barwise, J.M. Gawron, G. Plotkin, & S. Tutiya (Eds.), *Situation theory and its applications, Vol. 2.* Stanford, CA: CSLI Publications.

Kishner, J.M., & Gibbs, R.W. (1998). The polysemy of "just". *Language and Speech, 39,* 19–37.

Kuiper, K. (1996). *Smooth talkers.* Mahwah, NJ: Lawrence Erlbaum Associates Inc.

Kuno, S. (1986). *Functional syntax—anaphora, discourse and empathy.* Chicago: University of Chicago Press.

Lahav, R. (1989). Against compositionality: The case of adjectives. *Philosophical Studies, 57,* 261–279.

Langacker, R. (1987). Nouns and verbs. *Language, 63,* 53–94.

Lashley, K.S. (1951). The problem of serial order in behavior. In L.A. Jefress (Ed.), *Cerebral mechanisms in behavior.* New York: John Wiley.

Levelt, W.J.M. (1989). *Speaking: From intention to articulation.* Cambridge, MA: MIT Press.

Levelt, W.J.M. (1992). Accessing words in speech production: Stages, processes and representations. *Cognition, 42,* 1–22.

Levelt, W.J.M., & Kelter, S. (1982). Surface form and memory in question answering. *Cognitive Psychology, 14,* 78–106.

Levelt, W.J.M., Praamstra, P., Meyer, A.S., Helenius, P., & Salmelin, R. (1998). An MEG study of picture naming. *Journal of Cognitive Neuroscience, 10,* 553–567.

Levelt, W.J.M., Roelofs, A., & Meyer, A.S. (1999). A theory of lexical access in speech production. *Behavioral and Brain Sciences, 22,* 1–75.

Libet, B., Gleason, C.A., Wright, E.W., & Pearl, D.K. (1983). Time of conscious intention to act in relation to onset of cerebral activity (readiness-potential). *Brain, 106,* 623–642.

McCauley, C., Parmelee, C.M., Sperber, R.D., & Carr, T. (1980). Early extraction of meaning from pictures and its relation to conscious identification. *Journal of Experimental Psychology: Human Perception and Performance, 6,* 265–276.

Menaugh, M. (1988). A mechanistic model for the English verb. *Linguistic Analysis, 18,* 3–60.

Miller, G.A., & Johnson-Laird, P.N. (1976). *Language and perception.* Cambridge, MA: Harvard University Press.

Miller, J., & Weinert, R. (1998). *Spontaneous spoken language: Syntax and discourse.* Oxford, UK: Clarendon Press.

Norretranders, T. (1998). *The user illusion: Cutting consciousness down to size.* New York: Penguin Viking.

Nunberg, G. (1979). The non-uniqueness of semantic solutions: Polysemy. *Linguistics and Philosophy*, *3*, 143–184.

Olson, D.R. (1970). Language and thought: Aspects of a cognitive theory of semantics. *Psychological Review*, *77*, 257–273.

Onishi, K.H., & Murphy, G.L. (1993). Metaphoric reference: When metaphors are not understood as easily as literal expressions. *Memory and Cognition*, *21*, 763–772.

Pechmann, T. (1984). *Uberspezifizierung und Betonung in referentieller Kommunikation*. Unpublished doctoral dissertation, Mannheim University, Germany.

Plank, F. (1979). Ergativity, syntactic typology and universal grammar: Some past and present viewpoints. In F. Plank (Ed.), *Ergativity: Towards a theory of grammatical relations* (pp. 3–39). London: Academic Press.

Pustejovsky, J. (1995). *The generative lexicon*. Cambridge, MA: MIT Press.

Quine, W.V.O. (1981). *Theories and things*. Cambridge, MA: Harvard University Press.

Roelofs, A. (1992a). *Lemma retrieval in speaking: A theory, computer simulations and empirical data* (NICI Tech. Rep. No. 92-08). University of Nijmegen, The Netherlands.

Roelofs, A. (1992b). A spreading-activation theory of lemma retrieval in speaking. *Cognition*, *42*, 107–142.

Rosen, R. (1996). The Schrodinger question: What is life? Fifty years later. In P. Buckley & F.D. Peat (Eds.), *Glimpsing reality: Ideas in physics and the link to biology* (pp. 168–190). Toronto, Canada: University of Toronto Press.

Schank, R. (1975). Using knowledge to understand. In B. Nash-Webber & R. Shank (Eds.), *Proceedings of the first theoretical issues in natural language processing conference (TINLAP 1)*. Ohio: Math. Social Sciences Board.

Schmaus, M. (1966). *The essence of Christianity*. Chicago: Scepter.

Schmidt, S.J. (1976). German philosophy of language in the late nineteenth century. In H. Parret (Ed.), *History of linguistic thought and contemporary linguistics* (pp. 658–684). Berlin, Germany: Walter de Gruyter.

Schopenhauer, A. (1974). *Parerga and paralipomena: Short philosophical essays* (E.F.J. Payne, Trans.). Oxford, UK: Clarendon Press. (Original work published 1851)

Searle, J.R. (1980). The background of meaning. In J.R. Searle & M. Bierwisch (Eds.), *Speech act theory and pragmatics* (pp. 221–232). Dordrecht, The Netherlands: D. Reidel.

Sedivy, J.C., Tanenhaus, M.K., Chambers, C.G., & Carlson, G.N. (1999). Achieving incremental semantic interpretation through contextual representation. *Cognition*, *71*, 109–147.

Seuren, P.A.M. (1998). *Western linguistics: An historical introduction*. Oxford, UK: Blackwell.

Shanon, B. (1996). *The representational and the presentational: An essay on cognition and the study of mind*. New York: Harvester.

Sinclair, J.M. (1991). *Corpus, concordance and collocation*. Oxford, UK: Oxford University Press.

Sinclair, J.M. (1996). The empty lexicon. *International Journal of Corpus Linguistics*, *1*, 99–116.

Smith, M.C. (1999). *Reflexives, pronouns and the clause*. Manuscript in preparation.

Smith, M.C., & Wheeldon, L.R. (1999a). High level processing scope in spoken sentence production. *Cognition*, *73*, 205–246.

Smith, M.C., & Wheeldon, L.R. (1999b). *An on-line study of syntactic persistence*. Manuscript submitted for publication.

Stine, E.L. (1990). On-line processing of written texts by younger and older adults. *Psychology and Aging*, *5*, 68–78.

Sweetser, E. (1986). Polysemy versus abstraction: Mutually exclusive or complementary? In V. Nikiforidou, M. van Clay, M. Niepokuy, & D. Feder (Eds.), *Proceedings of the 12th annual meeting of the Berkeley Linguistics Society* (pp. 528–538). Berkeley, CA: Berkeley Linguistics Society.

Taylor, J.L., & McCloskey, D.I. (1990). Triggering of preprogrammed movements as reactions to masked stimuli. *Journal of Neurophysiology*, *63*, 439–446.

Van Lanckner, D. (1987). Non-propositional speech: Neurolinguistic studies. In A.W. Ellis (Ed.), *Progress in the psychology of language* (Vol. 3, pp. 49–118). Hillsdale, NJ: Lawrence Erlbaum Associates Inc.

Van Petten, C. (1995). Words and sentences: Event related potential measures. *Psychophysiology, 32*, 511–525.

Weiner, E.J., & Labov, W. (1983). Constraints on the agentless passive. *Journal of Linguistics, 19*, 29–58.

Wheeldon, L.R. (1989). *Priming of spoken word production.* Unpublished doctoral dissertation, Cambridge University, UK.

Wheeldon, L.R., & Levelt, W.J.M. (1995). Monitoring the time course of phonological encoding. *Journal of Memory and Language, 34*, 311–334.

Winograd, T. (1972). Understanding natural language. *Cognitive Psychology, 1*, 1–191.

Winograd, T. (1976). Towards a procedural understanding of semantics. *Revue Internationale de Philosophie, 26*, 260–303.

Wundt, W. (1900). *Die Sprache.* Leipzig, Germany: Kroner.

Zimmermann, M. (1989). The nervous system in the context of information theory. In R.F. Schmidt & G. Thews (Eds.), *Human physiology.* Berlin, Germany: Springer-Verlag.

CHAPTER THIRTEEN

Coordinating spontaneous talk

Jean E. Fox Tree
Psychology Department, University of California, Santa Cruz, USA

Traditional accounts of language production rarely reach the level of describing coordinated talk among people engaged in conversations. Many models explain various aspects of what goes one in an individual's mind as speaking occurs. But what happens when two minds are involved? A distinguishing characteristic of two minds is that talk cannot be planned in advance the way it might be with the production of preset words, phrases, or sentences, and that the talk needs to be coordinated between conversational participants. Both these elements—spontaneity and coordination—have been relatively under-researched in comparison to single-speaker, planned production. Correspondingly, in the current chapter I will focus on different issues from other, more often explored aspects of production. I will lay out the problems that conversations present and some of the tools participants have to overcome them. My hope is that the information provided here will aid researchers in expanding current production models to include the elements necessary for real-life, real-time conversations.

INTRODUCTION

The way we talk to old friends over a cup of coffee is different from the way we talk in front of the mirror as we rehearse colloquium addresses. Compare the following spontaneously told story with the segment of a political speech after it (adapted from Svartvik & Quirk, 1980, 1.3.788–1.3.801 and from a Martin Luther King Jr. speech transcribed by Atkinson, 1984, p. 109; asterisks indicate overlapped speech, periods indicate brief pauses, and dashes indicate longer pauses):

(1)   A: and conversation . went like this . this sort of conversation um - - -
            have you noticed president . that . um - - the boiled eggs at Sunday
            *breakfast * - always hard - -
      B: *(- laughs)*
      A: and president said - ah well - the simple truth is that . if you're
            going to boil eggs . communally - they must be hard *(- - - laughs)*
      B: *(- - - laugh)*

(2)   King: and he's allowed me to go up to the mountain.
      Audience: go a*head*
      King: *and* I've looked over and I've seen . the promised *land*
      Audience: *holy* holy *holy holy*
      King: *I may* not get there with you but I want you to know
                  tonight that we as a *people*
      Audience: *yeah*
      King: will get to the promised land

The two forms of speech share some important features; in both, speakers plan
for particular audiences, decide what to say, and decide how to say it. But
spontaneous and prepared talk differ in several key ways. Conversations are not
planned in advance, they are not rehearsed, and they always involve the mutual
cooperation of two or more people. These factors influence the way we express
ideas spontaneously.

One of the most noticeable ways spontaneity affects talk is by causing an
increased number of repetitions of words or phrases, *um*s, restarted ideas, words
like *you know* and *well*, and long pauses. Though these phenomena are sometimes found in prepared speech, such as dialogue in novels, they are most common in everyday talk. A quick mental comparison of TV commercials provides
a ready example of the naturalness of imperfect speech. Those advertisements
featuring slick and rehearsed actors are recognised as staged. But those that
contain a variety of naturalistic speech phenomena such as disfluencies, *well*s,
and *um*s create the impression of spontaneous enthusiasm.

The phenomena that are the hallmark of spontaneous talk have often been
thought of as unwanted elements of speech, unfortunate by-products of speaking
on the fly. However, another way of viewing these phenomena is as an integral
part of the communicative enterprise. In this chapter, I will show how these
elements are used to get around some of the problems inherent to the communication medium of spontaneous speech.

In all speaking situations, we have one overarching goal that governs everything that we say: making sure that we have been understood by our listeners.
Participants in conversations are engaged in a continual process of achieving
mutual understanding, which includes collaborating on what's said and checking
that intentions have been understood. In the first part of the chapter, I will
discuss how speakers and listeners achieve grounding by monitoring each other's

states of understanding. I will also discuss how spontaneous speech differs from other communication mediums because it lacks the ability to be revised in private before production and it lacks the ability to be reviewed as a whole after production. The lack of these features has implications for how grounding proceeds in spontaneous talk.

In the second section, I will discuss how conversations are structured, how conversational turns are coordinated, and what happens when turns are not co-ordinated. The need to carefully time turns has implications for how speech is produced. Speakers do not have the luxury to carefully prepare their utterances before taking a turn, to privately revise them after they've started speaking, or to review a record of the conversation up to that point.

In the third section, I will discuss devices that developed in spontaneous speech to handle the lack of reviewability. Without reviewability, speakers face a challenge in coherently organising their hierarchical ideas to conform to the linear nature of speech. *Discourse markers* are one tool speakers use to help them represent a multilayered discourse. Discourse markers are words such as *well*, *you know*, *like*, *oh*, and some uses of connectives such as *and* and *but anyway*, which are found frequently in spontaneous speech but not in prepared speech. They are a kind of vocal activity that doesn't contribute to the propositional content of utterances but instead relates ideas at the level of organising talk (Schiffrin, 1987). Addressees also contribute to communicative success by building bridging inferences between utterances. I will discuss both the use of discourse markers and the building of bridging inferences, and show how speakers' uses of discourse markers can control the bridging inferences that are built.

In the fourth and final section, I will discuss how the lack of preproduction revisability is handled in spontaneous speech. Turn-taking constraints and problems in speech production lead all speakers to make speech disfluencies or lexical or pragmatic errors at some time or other. But a number of devices exist in spontaneous speech that help minimise the impact of disfluencies and speed the process of revision. So, though speakers cannot fully revise their talk before they speak, they can and do speak in such a way that their spontaneous revisions lead to the least possible comprehension difficulty for their addressees.

Participants in conversations are engaged in a continual process of achieving mutual understanding, which includes collaborating on what they say, checking that their utterances and intentions have been understood, and minimising the impact of errors and revisions. The way we talk in spontaneous conversation helps us fulfil these communicative goals.

GROUNDING IN CONVERSATIONS

Spontaneous face-to-face talk is a universal communication medium. Many cultures are not literate and have no access to telephones or more recent communication mediums such as email. But in every culture people use face-to-face conversation as their primary means of communication. Spontaneous talk can come in many forms, including storytelling, where one speaker has the floor and speaks in a monologue, verbal instruction, where a speaker gives directions that are confirmed by addressees, and ritualised teasing, where people take turns ribbing each other. The most common form of talk, however, is conversation. Conversations share certain underlying principles with all forms of communication, but they also have their own particular problems and tools for resolving problems.

No matter how varied the medium or format of communication, all communication has in common the ultimate goal of achieving understanding between communicative participants. In conversations, we check that we have been understood by noting whether our interlocutors nod their heads, say *mhm*, or reply appropriately to what's been said. Even when the discourse is a one way street, as in monologues or lectures, we still check for understanding. In giving a speech, we monitor understanding by checking for alert faces, head nods, or quizzical expressions. When we can't make out faces, as in a large crowd or on a stage in a darkened room, we monitor audience comprehension by noticing whether people laugh or clap at appropriate moments. If our addressees make no reply to what we've said, or our audience fails to respond, we may be facing communicative failure. Communicative failure in conversations can arise for two reasons: One is that something necessary for communicative success in general is missing, and the other is that something necessary for communicative success in conversations is missing. I'll first discuss what's necessary for communicative success in general, and then I'll discuss the special case of conversations.

What does is take to be understood? To achieve understanding, speakers cannot just vocalise what is on their minds. Saying *I'd like a cup of coffee* communicates nothing if the statement isn't heard. Clark and Schaefer identified four *states* that an utterance must go through before understanding is reached. They are listed below, with S representing the speaker, A the addressee, and *u* the utterance (adapted from Clark & Schaefer, 1987, p. 22):

State 0.   A didn't notice that S uttered any *u*.
State 1.   A noticed that S uttered some *u* (but wasn't in state 2).
State 2.   A correctly heard *u* (but wasn't in state 3).
State 3.   A understood what S meant by *u*.

In understanding every utterance, addressees need to go through each of these states. They need to notice that they are being spoken to, they need to hear the utterance correctly, and they need to interpret the utterance correctly. Likewise, speakers need to check that addressees are paying attention, that they have heard the utterances, and that the words heard have conveyed a meaning appropriate to the conversational goals. Without feedback from addressees, speakers would not know if the communication succeeded or failed, and ultimately whether or not their conversational goals would be met.

How do speakers gauge addressees' states of understanding? One way they could do this would be to assume that the addressees have attended, heard, and understood unless the addressees say otherwise. That is, speakers could rely on *negative evidence* of mishearing and misunderstanding, such as an addressee's request for clarification, or an addressee's saying *I didn't hear you* (Clark & Brennan, 1991). But relying on negative evidence is unlikely to be the norm for two reasons. First, it won't work for assessing whether addressees are in state 1. If addressees don't know that they are being spoken to, they will not be able to respond that they haven't been attending. Second, it won't work in many cases of misunderstanding where the misunderstanding is not recognised by the addressee. It turns out that speakers do not consider negative evidence a sufficient gauge of understanding (Clark & Brennan, 1991). Instead, they seek *positive evidence* of understanding, in the form of positive feedback from addressees that they are attending, hearing, and understanding what's being said.

Let's illustrate the seeking of positive evidence with the shift from state 0 to state 1, or from not noticing that someone has spoken, to noticing that they've said something. How do speakers know that they are being attended to? The most direct positive evidence an interlocutor could supply would be responding to the speaker's utterance with *I'm listening, go ahead*, a precise description of the addressee's being in state 1. But *I'm listening, go ahead* leaves the exact state ambiguous; the addressee may or may not be in state 2, because they may or may not have understood. To supply precise information about their state of understanding, addressees would have to say something like *What did you say?* This question shows not only that addressees are attending and have heard something, but they do not know what it is; that is, they are in state 1 but not state 2.

In addition to direct evidence of attention, interlocutors can also use indirect means to demonstrate that they've heard that something was said. They can turn their head in the direction of the speaker, meet the speaker's gaze, or lay open their hands in a gesture of offering the floor to the speaker. These movements indicate that the interlocutor is listening without directly saying so. Another indirect means that interlocutors can use to demonstrate that they are attending is by supplying information that they are in a higher state. If they show that they are in state 2, then they must have been in all earlier states. Addressees can nod or utter *backchannels* like *mhm*, providing evidence that the speaker has been heard, and also, logically, that the speaker has been attended to. Note that backchannels do not imply that the speaker has been heard correctly; to do that the addressee would have to say *I heard you say such and such* or to reply in a way that the speaker could judge whether the hearing was correct. Addressees on their own cannot determine their states. It takes both participants in the conversation to assess whether the hearing and understanding were correct.

Direct and indirect evidence can also be used by speakers in checking that their interlocutors have reached the other states. The action of getting up and closing a door in response to the utterance *it's cold in here* implies that the door-closer has reached each component state leading to understanding: attending, hearing, and understanding. The action, if appropriate to the speaker's intentions, is indirect evidence of the addressee's having reached state 3 in interpreting the speaker's utterance. But the action might also demonstrate that the addressee has not reached state 3: If *it's cold in here* were meant merely as an opening line to a story about surviving a New England winter (. . . *but it's not as cold as it was back in '76*), then the addressee who closed the door would only have achieved state 2.

To achieve understanding, each interlocutor participates in a constant process of checking that the other interlocutor is attending, hearing what's been said, and understanding what's been said. Seeking negative evidence with the passive process of waiting for an addressee's signal of confusion does not do the job. By seeking positive evidence, speakers increase the amount of work they need to do to in the conversation, but they also ensure more accuracy in evaluating comprehension. They have a moment-by-moment picture of exactly where the addressees are in their understanding process.

But what counts as understanding in the final state? Do addressees need to have a complete picture of exactly what the speaker is thinking, or only of the direction the speaker is headed towards? Clark and Schaefer describe the final state as the point where conversational participants have achieved the *grounding criterion*: that "the contributor and the partners mutually believe that the partners have understood what the contributor meant, to a criterion sufficient for current purposes" (1989, p. 262). The necessary level of understanding is that at which the conversational goals can be met. These goals could be any desired outcome of a conversation, such as conveying directions, explaining a decision, or sharing gossip. So it isn't necessary to exhaustively analyse every word a speaker utters, just to understand enough to realise the goals of the conversation.

Both speakers and addressees are responsible for checking that the grounding criterion is reached with every utterance. This mutual responsibility leads to a system of trade-offs between the amount of effort required to formulate an utterance compared to the amount of effort required to understand the utterance. These trade-offs have been formalised as the *principle of least collaborative effort* (Clark & Wilkes-Gibbs, 1986), which has been summarised as "[i]n conversation, the participants try to minimise their collaborative effort—the work that both do from the initiation of each contribution to its mutual acceptance" (Clark & Brennan, 1991, p. 135).

Together, the grounding process and the principle of least collaborative effort lead to certain predictions about language use. One prediction is that as interlocutors become accustomed to each other's way of thinking, they will cut down on the words used to convey an idea. Because they know each other, fewer words are needed to reach criterion. Another prediction is that people will be very good at determining just how much information is needed to reach the necessary level of understanding. Because the grounding process is necessary for every linguistic interaction, people have a lot of practice at achieving the grounding criterion with diverse conversational partners.

Both phenomena have been observed in the speech produced in *referential card tasks*. In one version of this task, one person, the *director*, describes a set of ordered abstract figures to another person, the *matcher*, who tries to put an identical set of scattered figures in the same order. People cannot see each other, so success or failure of placement can confidently be related to verbal communication. When describing a figure, people start off with long descriptions, but then shorten them upon recurrent references to the figure. What started out as "a person who's ice skating, except they're sticking two arms out in front" became on later reference "the person ice skating, with two arms" and then became simply "the ice skater" (Clark & Wilkes-Gibbs, 1986, p. 12). At first, a long explanation was necessary to describe exactly which figure the director meant, but afterwards the same figure could be referred to by a shorter label. When interlocutors have different levels of expertise, they are very good at determining exactly how much information is needed to achieve the grounding criterion. In a referential card task using postcards of New York City, directors adjusted for the expertise of the matchers by the time the first quarter of the cards had been described (Isaacs & Clark, 1987). If people did not try to reach a grounding criterion or to minimise their collaborative effort, each referential description would be equally long no matter how much the interlocutors had discussed the figure, and interlocutors would speak in the same way to each other no matter what their expertise.

As with the referential card task, conversational participants monitor each other's states of understanding to ensure that the grounding criterion is reached with each utterance, while following the principle of least collaborative effort. A similar process exists for all other communicative mediums as well, such as telephone conversations, scripted interviews, and email. In all settings, the ultimate goal of grounding is the same: understanding sufficient for current purposes. But how grounding is achieved differs across mediums.

To illustrate these differences, let us consider Clark and Brennan's sample of eight factors that differ across different mediums (adapted from 1991, p. 141):

- Copresence: A and B share the same physical environment.
- Visibility: A and B are visible to each other.
- Audibility: A and B communicate by speaking.
- Cotemporality: B receives at roughly the same time as A produces.
- Simultaneity: A and B can send and receive at once and simultaneously.
- Sequentiality: A's and B's turns cannot get out of sequence.
- Reviewability: B can review A's messages.
- Revisability: A can revise messages for B.

As Clark and Brennan discuss, the presence and absence of any of these factors will influence how grounding takes place.

Consider letter writing. The fact that there's no copresence or cotemporality means that letter writers cannot get immediate positive evidence from their addressees that they have been understood. Consequently, they put more time into expressing their ideas carefully, and take care to review and revise their messages before sending them off. More thought goes into each letter writer's turn than into each turn of a conversational participant. Furthermore, the lack of copresence and cotemporality affects the type of information supplied in a turn. Letter writers might need to remind each other of what was said in prior letters. This isn't necessary in conversations because speaking turns are not separated by days or weeks and the same discourse record is immediately available to all participants, assuming everyone has roughly the same memory capacity.

The absence of a factor can be thought of as incurring costs for the communicative process, the goal of which is to minimise the costs across communicative partners. For example, the absence of cotemporality can incur the letter writer a cost of not knowing how much is enough when writing down information. But the presence of revisability allows the writer to make up for this absence by writing more clearly, and correcting what was written until it expresses just what was meant. At the same time, the fact that letter writers have the opportunity to revise means that if writers make errors that do not get corrected before the letters are sent, they will be held more accountable for their mistakes than they would have been for errors in talk. The politician who declares that calling an opponent a "drunk" was a slip of the tongue would have much more serious problems were the word the result of a slip of the pen.

Spontaneous speech has its own cost trade-offs. Because spontaneous speech is cotemporal, it doesn't incur the cost of not knowing how much is enough. The interlocutor can readily provide feedback about when to stop talking or when to elaborate. However, cotemporality does incur a cost for delaying. Because the other interlocutor is actively waiting for the speaker to continue, if the speaker delays speech, this has immediate ramifications. This cost doesn't exist with letter writing.

But there is one special kind of writing that does occur a waiting cost: writing with the *talk* facility on Unix. With talk, two people can write to each other on a computer with a split screen where one person's writing appears on the top of the screen and the other's writing appears on the bottom. The writing takes place in real time. Like letter writing, talk writers are not copresent, not visible to each other, not audible to each other, and they have some amount of reviewability (at least a half-screen full). But like speaking, the talk writers are cotemporal, can send simultaneous messages, take sequential turns, and cannot revise their writing in private. Correspondingly, talk writers incur the costs of cotemporality and have been observed to use the same devices that speakers use in speech (as will be discussed later) to minimise these costs, such as writing *um*.

In spontaneous speech, interlocutors have the first six of Clark and Brennan's factors, which are exactly the factors letter writers do not have. Interlocutors talk to each other while in the same environment, while visible and audible to each other, and in sequence. Each speaker also knows that they are being heard at the same time as they are speaking, without a time delay between production and receiving of the production, and that they can overlap in speech with their interlocutors. What spontaneous speech does not have is reviewability and (private) revisability. The effervescence of talk means that there isn't a record available for both people to review after something has been said. Short-term memory can only briefly store the most recent speech in both interlocutors' minds. The cotemporality of talk also means that it cannot be revised after it is spoken without all participants being aware of the revision. This awareness makes public revision different from private revision. With public revision, other speakers hear what's being revised and can jump in to help or even change the revision. Private revision, where speakers revise their speech plan mentally before uttering anything, is difficult to accomplish in spontaneous talk because it requires long moments of silence that disrupt the conversation and that create gaps where interlocutors could take the floor.

This doesn't mean that reviewability and revisability are impossible in spontaneous speech. We can imagine situations where these factors are present. It's possible to record conversations and then play them back as the discussion develops, and it's also possible to set an accepted standard where people could be silent for longer periods without risking losing their turns. But both possibilities would entail different grounding procedures. In the first case, speakers might take longer to say something that they knew was being taped. In the second, there would need to be some way other than the existence of a long pause to indicate a turn exchange, such as a system where the person holding a stick gets to talk, or the words *I'm done* must be said before someone else can take the floor.

In spontaneous speech, the lack of reviewability and revisability affects grounding in predictable ways. The lack of reviewability means that listeners incur a cost in not being able to check exactly what had been said up to that point in the conversation. This may lead speakers to repeat information, or to argue about who said what in a debate. This wouldn't happen with letter writers; indeed, a letter writer who repeated information several times would seem strange. Likewise, the lack of repetition of instructions in a letter would not be noticed as bizarre, but a single list of verbal instructions without repetition would seem strange, as if the speaker assumed the addressee had a taperecorder for a brain. To balance this cost of not having reviewability, conversations are structured so that participants can keep a good representation of the discourse in memory.

This trade-off in the grounding process helps maintain interlocutors' least collaborative effort in communicating.

The lack of revisability means that speakers may end up saying something they will later need to adjust. The reasons people speak before they are ready is that it is costly to delay a message in order to revise it. A delay could open the floor for another person to start talking, or could send social signals to the other conversational participants implying a lack of interest in the conversation (Clark & Brennan, 1991; Smith & Clark, 1993) There might also be a cost to addressees in waiting. Addressees might be less able to connect ideas to those preceding after a long delay, or their attention may wander in a long break. These waiting costs to speakers and addressees don't exist with other mediums like letter writing, where revision time has no implications for either communicator.

But once again, the costs of not being able to carefully prepare talk has its own benefits in comparison to other mediums. Revising on the fly has fewer ramifications in speech than in other mediums because people expect formulation problems in speech. Readers do not expect unprepared sentences in letters, so a revision is much more difficult to achieve. It is easier to correct a misspoken word than a miswritten one.

The communicative trade-offs among grounding process factors have been demonstrated in studies of conversations. In interviews, people will pause longer and talk more when the interviewer is absent rather than when the interviewer is present (Siegman & Reynolds, 1983). This is considered to be a direct result of the trade-off between the time pressure posed by a ready and waiting listener and people's ability to organise their thoughts and decide what to say. Without the cotemporal constraint, interviewees can think more about what to say, and review messages for a longer period of time in their heads before talking. The absence of simultaneity had marked effects on the amount of speech people needed to complete a referential card task. When the dyads couldn't communicate in both directions, the amount of speech used to convey the card positions varied greatly (372 words to 1830 words); when they could communicate, speech was much more constrained (641 words to 1280 words; Fox Tree, unpublished research). Like in letter writing, without feedback from matchers, directors could not tell how much information was enough.

Conversational participants are constantly working towards achieving mutual understanding. They check that their utterances have been attended to, heard, recognised, and understood well enough to carry out the goals of the communication. They also deal with a number of problems that are not present in other forms of communication. In this chapter, I will focus on the lack of reviewability, the lack of revisability, and the devices that interlocutors use to achieve grounding despite these handicaps. But before I discuss how spontaneous speech is designed to help fulfill the overarching goal of being understood despite the inherent constraints of conversations, I will first discuss the structure of conversations themselves.

COORDINATING CONVERSATIONAL TURNS

Conversations can be described as an incremental build-up of units called *contributions* (Clark & Schaefer, 1987). Contributions consist of a *presentation phase* and an *acceptance phase*. In the presentation phase, speakers present an assertion, request, or question to their interlocutors. In the acceptance phase, the interlocutors either accept the presentation or work to revise the presentation so that it is acceptable. Each phase must achieve the grounding criterion before it is accepted. As described in the previous section, interlocutors check that they have achieved the highest state of understanding by monitoring each other's acceptances.

To make sure that the presentation phase has been accepted and that participants have grounded their contributions requires either nonverbal feedback or taking turns speaking. If people said important things simultaneously, it would be hard to determine what each contributor thought about each other's presentation because their own simultaneous utterances would not necessarily be taken as replies, and as such could not be taken as indirect evidence of acceptance. The grounding process would grind to a halt.

Though it is true that one or more conversational participants can speak at the same time, overlapped speech is usually different in quality from nonoverlapped speech, with overlapped speech being less informative (Atkinson, 1984; Clark, 1996; Sacks, Schegloff, & Jefferson, 1974). In fact, one person's overlapping another can be purposefully done to demonstrate that additional information is unnecessary (Jefferson, 1973). In cases of nonintentional overlap, interlocutors choose to treat overlapped speech either such that one person's contribution were not said, or such that both people's contributions were said sequentially, with the first person to talk after the overlap determining which utterance would be taken as having been said first (Jefferson, 1973). When information needs to be conveyed, only one speaker has the floor. The regularity in turns is essential to ensure that each partner in a conversation has the opportunity to both make a presentation and to accept the interlocutor's presentation so that grounding can be achieved.

Turn-taking is a precisely timed activity. People begin to speak just as their interlocutors finish (Sacks et al., 1974). Precision timing is perhaps best demonstrated by the fact that addressees can complete speakers' sentences without any intervening pause (Jefferson, 1973). How do people coordinate their utterances so precisely?

One way is by using gaze, facial expressions, and body language to identify turn units. Turning gaze away and putting on a "thinking face" is one way speakers can signal to listeners when to enter a conversation in the situation where speakers need help completing their thoughts (Goodwin & Goodwin, 1986, p. 57). People can also use other nonverbal cues. Addressees can indicate their desire to take the floor by turning their heads away from the speaker or using hand gestures (Duncan & Niederehe, 1974). Likewise, speakers can signal the desire to end a turn by stopping gesturing (Duncan, 1972). When conversational participants can see either each other's eyes or each other's bodies, they can synchronise their talk better (Argyle, Lalljee, & Cook, 1968).

Another way to synchronise turn units is by using special words and phrases to signal either a desire to gain access to the floor or a willingness to give up a turn (Erman, 1987; Erman & Kotsinas, 1993; Holmes, 1986; Jefferson, 1973; Schegloff, 1987; Schiffrin, 1987; Schourup, 1985; Stenström, 1990). The evidence for these claims, as well as for the claims in the following sections, comes by and large from corpora analyses. This empirical technique starts with a written-out transcript of spontaneous talk including every vocalisation made by the conversational participants. Transcriptions vary in detail, such as how pronunciations and prosody are represented (Edwards, 1993). Often with the help of a computer, researchers search their corpora for every example of a particular phenomenon, such as the word *oh*. They then identify ways the phenomenon is used, sometimes tallying the number of times the use occurred in their data source. Phenomena can be analysed in a myriad of ways, including where they fall in an utterance or a turn, where they fall syntactically, how they are pronounced, what type of other phenomena precede or follow them, and how they are used pragmatically. Researchers have gained a lot of mileage with this technique, and I will review some of the findings. At the end of the next section, I will also review the few experimental tests that have been done.

To start in on a turn, speakers can use words like *well, but, and* or *so*. These words can be used to orient backwards to what was already said in the discourse and can indicate a desire to start in on a turn even before the turn itself has been planned (Clark, 1983; example adapted from Svartvik & Quirk, 1980, 3.5.914–3.5.916):

(3)   A: it's necessary for the best kind of tragedy I think,
      B: so you think that uhw u:h Romeo and Juliet, is an inferior kind of
           tragedy

Here speaker B uses *so* to take over the floor, initiating the turn before the utterance is completely ready, as evidenced by the stumbling before the words *Romeo and Juliet*. Speakers can also grab the floor with a word like *now*, which shifts attention to upcoming talk (Schiffrin, 1987; example adapted from Svartvik & Quirk, 1980, 3.5.999–3.5.1003):

(4)   A: that u:h i it is . related . to the . image . that he's chosen - I think it - - -
      B: now, let's go back to Hamlet then

Here speaker B's *now* helps to both change turns and to shift attention away from what speaker A said and towards what speaker B is going to say.

In order to end a turn, speakers can use tag questions like *don't you think so?* or *didn't it?*. These devices indicate that the turn is finished, and orient forwards towards choosing the next speaker (Clark, 1983; Sacks et al., 1974; example adapted from Svartvik & Quirk, 1980, 1.3.1190–1.3.1195):

(5)   A: m - - but she . at the same time she seems, . unusual, . doesn't she,
      B: . yes, - yes, and everybody notices that she's unusual

Here speaker B pauses for a brief moment before picking up on the cue and taking over the floor. Speakers can also use other phrases like *but uh* and *or something* to show that they've completed their turns (Duncan, 1972).

Still other words, like *then*, can be used to hold the floor and prevent inter-locutor interruption (Redeker, 1991; example adapted from Svartvik & Quirk, 1980, 1.3.557–1.3.571):

(6)   A: I mean I just insisted very firmly, on calling her Miss Tillman, but
           one should really call her president. - - and . um then, . a bell rang,
           - - and - millions of feet, . ran, . along corridors, you know, and
           then they . it all died away, it was like like sound effects from the
           Goon Show, . you *know,* - and then there was a, - tap on the
           door, -
      B: *m*

Here the speaker is relating a long story and uses *then* to maintain her turn while she tells it. *Anyway* can also help speakers keep their turns. One researcher found that addressees don't take over the floor after a speaker says *anyway* even when *anyway* is followed by a pause (Bublitz, 1988). Using a signal of desire to keep the floor is particularly important in cases where a long pause might run the risk of signalling the end of a turn; to counteract this effect of the pause, the speaker can say *then* to block the interlocutor's taking the floor.

The more nonverbal and verbal cues for turn exchange, the more likely a successful turn exchange will occur (Duncan, 1972). Overlapped speech can be viewed as a result of interlocutor error; either the speakers inadvertently sup-plied turn-yielding signals, or the addressees took the floor without signals, which is perceived as an interruption (Duncan, 1972). Turn-taking cues are also important in resolving overlap that occurs when two interlocutors try to take the floor at the same time; whoever has provided the most positive cues for taking the floor will be the one to win the turn (Duncan & Niederehe, 1974).

So conversational participants have a lot of tools available to them to estimate what their conversational partners want to do. They can use gaze, gesture, and special words and phrases to carefully interleave their conversational turns with minimal overlap. But why are turns so carefully timed? Consider what happens when they aren't, as in the following two constructed exchanges:

(7)   A: Did you have a good time in Boston?
      B: It was great.

(8)   A: Did you have a good time in Boston?
      B: (3 s delay) It was great.

In the second exchange, speaker A will infer that the question posed was not an easy one to answer, that there were some misgivings about the trip to Boston, or that something happened that B did not want to say to A. B would be expected to give some explanation for the long pause, if only to say *I don't want to talk about it*. Turns are carefully timed because responses that are too quick or too slow carry weight and have meaning for the interlocutors. A slow response to a question can cause a speaker to be seen as "uncooperative, ignorant, poor in judgment, or slow-witted" (Smith & Clark, 1993, p. 36). Pauses of three or more seconds are particularly undesirable, and there is some evidence that frequently producing such lapses is interpreted as having poor social skills (McLaughlin & Cody, 1982).

These judgements are made because at every moment in the conversation, each interlocutor is monitoring what the other is saying (Clark, 1996; Clark & Brennan, 1991; Smith & Clark, 1993). If a pause occurs, it is a contribution to the discourse and will be interpreted. Pauses have been shown to not only be used differently, but to actually be interpreted differently. For example, pauses can reflect the state of understanding that people are in. In answering questions, people pause longer when they think they know the answer but can't think of the word than when they know they don't know the answer (Smith & Clark, 1993), and listeners interpret these pauses accordingly (Brennan & Williams, 1995). Of course, not all pauses are interpreted in a negative light as a sign of uncooperativeness or of lack of knowledge. If speakers are talking while driving, abrupt stops in conversations might be expected, especially coinciding with difficult manoeuvring of the car. Interlocutors take pragmatic circumstances into account when estimating acceptable pause length or inter-turn intervals. But in every situation, there is only so much pausing that is acceptable given the circumstance. When left without a situational excuse in a conversation, such as visible evidence of doing something else that precludes talking, interlocutors come up with other explanations for too-long pauses. But because nonsituational pauses are sometimes necessary to organise ideas or decide what to say next, there are several devices speakers can use to control the interpretations that are made.

To prevent their conversational partners from interpreting the wrong things, people can supply information about what is causing time delays in their responses. Sometimes this information is a direct explanation, such as saying *let me get my thoughts straight*, or, in answering questions, saying "shoot hang on a minute (1 s pause) this one has potential" (Smith & Clark, 1993, p. 36). Speakers can also signal the length of their upcoming pause by using either an *um* or an *uh*, with *um*s signalling longer pauses and *uh*s shorter (Smith & Clark, 1993). By using one of these words, speakers can control the interpretations interlocutors make and save face. In answering questions, speakers can punctuate a pause with an *um* or an *uh* to show that they are not generally ignorant, they just can't recall the answer at that time (Smith & Clark, 1993). In general, not more than one second goes by before speakers do some activity like guess at a sought-after word or utter an *um* or an *uh* (Jefferson, 1989). There is also some evidence that if a pause does become longer than a second, a correspondingly more noteworthy expression will be used, such as *oh gee* (Jefferson, 1989).

Conversational participants need to coordinate turns in order to achieve the grounding criterion. Conversations are structured as a series of presentation and acceptance phases which together make up a conversational unit. Interlocutors take turns presenting and accepting information in their accumulating discourse representation. The timing of turns has implications for how talk is interpreted. By saying *well, but, didn't it?, um,* or *oh gee* speakers can help to coordinate turns and they can provide information about how pauses should be interpreted. We will now turn to how interlocutors handle the absence of the two grounding factors, reviewability and revisability. I'll discuss reviewability first.

COORDINATING IDEAS

Planning speech while speaking poses a number of problems for conversational participants. One is to be able to utter a smooth passage of speech while monitoring the way the thoughts are being expressed, maintaining interlocutor's interest, checking for understanding, and other constraints, such as making sure there is time to say what needs to be said in the time available for the conversation to take place. How are all these complexities of the everyday speaking situation maintained in a coherent way?

Because speakers need to keep several layers of information in mind as they're speaking, they sometimes experience difficulty in saying what they mean to say. Speakers start talking before they are fully prepared, and then later revise or qualify what they've said, as in the following example (adapted from Svartvik & Quirk, 1980, 1.5.416–1.5.421):

(9) but what functions, do people variously fill, I mean are you . all members of a research . project, or just a group, I mean is . Marilyn, . uh: uh assistant le uh I mean is she a lecturer?

In this example, the speaker paused, said *uh*, and restarted several times before finally getting to the question *Is Marilyn a lecturer?*. Speakers also sometimes mention information out of order, and have to return to an earlier part of their discourse to clarify, as in the following example from a corpus collected by Herbert Clark:

(10)   uh I believe there are two people talking Susan and Kevin she is a tv
       broadcaster or something and he's a journalist and they're discussing
       Gary Hart and the Miami Herald story about his- his supposed affair
       with Donna Rice and um she asks him where he was when he heard
       about it and he says he was in Denver oh he was apparently canvassing
       for Hart and um she asked him if feel- if he felt angry about it

In this example, the speaker is prepared to relate the information about the TV
broadcaster's question about whether the journalist felt angry, but realises that
a crucial piece of information is missing, namely that the journalist was also
canvassing for Hart. So the speaker says *oh* and retraces the temporal order of
her narrative to add the missing information.

The difficulty in ordering ideas in a discourse arises because of the inherent
problem in having sequential or linear speech and yet nonlinear ideas. Ideas
frequently have many levels, such as a primary goal with several subgoals.
Despite their layering, the constraints of speech are such that the ideas have to
be expressed one at a time. This has been called the *linearisation problem*
(Bestgen & Costermans, 1994; Levelt, 1989). On top of this problem there is the
additional problem of expressing the relationship between the ordered ideas.
Some ideas might be more or less closely related to each other. For example,
collections of ideas might work together as a unit, and we might want to express
the different relationship between the ideas in the collection versus between
the units (Bestgen & Costermans, 1994). In dealing with these two problems,
speakers often find themselves making asides or shifting focus as they talk,
which further reduces the local coherency of adjacent utterances (Jucker, 1993).

Understanding conversations involves more than a sentence by sentence analysis of incoming speech. In the face of the linearisation problem, the problem of
expressing relationships between ideas, and the potential inconsistencies between
utterances, how do conversational participants manage to build an integrated
picture, while coordinating their speech with each other? One way they do this is
by using discourse markers and other devices found frequently in spontaneous
speech but not in prepared speech or written text. In the rest of this section, I
will discuss the general inference making process, the types of problems that
arise in spontaneous speech to thwart the inference making process, and how
speakers deal with these problems in such a way that they preserve maximum
coherency.

One problem that addressees face in all communicative mediums is how to
connect one sentence to its following sentence, or how to build *bridging inferences* (Clark & Haviland, 1975). The difficulty of building a bridging inference
between two sentences varies depending on how much information needs to be
inferred. Clark and Haviland (1975) found that *The beer was warm* took less
time to read after *Horace got some beer out of the trunk* than after *Horace was
especially fond of beer*. This is because in the first case, some particular beer

was in mind to connect with the concept *warm*, but in the second case, there was no particular beer in mind. In the second case a larger bridging inference had to be constructed between Horace's generally liking beer and a particular beer that was warm.

In spontaneous speech, inferences between successive utterances can often require a large leap. Speakers do not always have enough time to put their thoughts in order and to check that each idea follows from the previous idea. Speakers can also change their speech plans on the spur of the moment to add asides or to switch topics. But speakers do have tools available to them to help listeners make the correct bridging inferences at these difficult transition points. We'll discuss how interlocutors deal with the problem of time pressure first, and then we'll talk about the problem of change of plans.

One way of dealing with the lack of time to prepare orderly utterances is by using techniques to gain time while still holding the floor. One technique is the use of stock phrases such as "this is the point" (Schiffrin, 1987, p. 328) or "They're away and racing" in a racetrack commentary (Kuiper, 1996, p. 17). Although it's not always possible to determine what is a stock phrase and what is not, most speech has some more or less formulaic aspects (Kuiper, 1996). Formulaic phrases may aid speech production by providing the opportunity to access larger than one-word chunks directly from memory, and thereby freeing processing resources (Kuiper, 1996). They may also aid comprehension by "making speech more predictable" and spreading out the resources necessary to understand a stretch of speech (Kuiper, 1996, p. 98). Single words such as *bueno* (*good* in Spanish), *well*, *then*, or *um* are also thought to free processing resources by maintaining the floor while speakers plan their upcoming utterance (Brody, 1987; Jucker, 1993; Redeker, 1991). The here-and-now nature of talk puts pressure on the language processing system to operate quickly while conforming to the short-term memory constraints that arise out of the lack of reviewability of speech.

Gaining time is one technique speakers can use to get their ideas straight, but it is not always effective. Time pressure can cause speakers to speak before they're fully prepared, which can result in speakers' belated realisation that they've omitted some crucial information. When ideas get out of order, interlocutors face the problem of determining how to correct the discourse to represent the accurate order of information, given linear utterances and turn taking. One way speakers do this is by using a speech signal such as *oh* or explicit phrases like *oops I forgot something* to indicate to listeners that the upcoming speech won't fit in to what's just been said, but rather fits in to an earlier stretch of discourse (Fox Tree & Schrock, 1999; Redeker, 1991; Schiffrin, 1987). That is, the signals inform listeners not to build bridging inferences between these out-of-order utterances. People's natural inclination is to assume continuity between sentences in the absence of evidence to the contrary (Segal, Duchan, & Scott, 1991). Without a signal to halt bridge building, people will always try to bridge adjacent ideas.

Even when speakers do have enough time to organise their ideas and are able to correct organisation errors, they can still suddenly decide to alter their speech plans. That is, speakers can have said what they needed to without omitting background information but decide spontaneously and intentionally to change their conversational focus. But as with the time-crunch problems, speakers have tools available to them to change speech plans on the spur of the moment while maintaining continuity for the listener. The main way they do this is with discourse markers.

Discourse markers have been described as unwanted particles of speech that interrupt the speakers' message (Adams, 1982; Johnson, 1961; Levin, Silverman, & Ford, 1967). One reason that they might have been viewed as extraneous is because people don't need to have them in order to understand language. Think of any newspaper article or slick radio advertisement: Written words and rehearsed orations pose no problem for the comprehension system. So in some sense, discourse markers are superfluous to the understanding of language. But at the same time, discourse markers are not empty words. They cannot occur at any point in a conversation, as pointed out rhetorically by Schourup (1985, p. 162): "Did anyone, except the critics, ever really say 'Like Hi!'." James (1972, pp. 164–165) offers many other examples, including "*With a hammer . . . well . . . Bill hit Fred" and "*I'll throw the dinner I just ate . . . oh . . . up." Discourse markers can also not be substituted for each other (Redeker, 1991, p. 1165, adapted from Schiffrin, 1987, p. 93):

(11)   Henry: Do you know where Abe's is?
       Debby: Yeh I know where Abe's is.
       Henry: Right across the street.
       Debby: *Oh* (**Well*) it's that way.*

They only occur at certain points in a conversation and for certain reasons.

Analysts have identified a wide array of functions discourse markers might serve, such as to show politeness, to make a conversational setting less formal and more intimate, to play down interpersonal difficulty, and to identify with a social group (Bernstein, 1962; Brody, 1987; Jucker, 1993; Kotthoff, 1993; Maschler, 1994; Östman, 1981; Stubbe & Holmes, 1995). We will be concerned with the use of discourse markers in facilitating the grounding process. Discourse markers help interlocutors get around the lack of reviewability that can cause disorganised ideas and thwart the inference making process, and, as will be discussed in the next section, they also help interlocutors get around the problem of the inevitable occurrence of speech disfluencies, a result of the lack of revisability.

Discourse markers like *oh, then, actually, now,* and *well* can help listeners deal with speakers' shifts of topic and focus by indicating when a topic shift will occur (Aijmer, 1988; Bestgen & Costermans, 1994; Heritage, 1984; Schiffrin,

1987), as in the following two examples (adapted from Svartvik & Quirk, 1980, 2.7.187–2.7.199 and 2.8.431–2.8.435):

(12)   A: I think it's a snotty place the the Academy - .
       B: oh, . from the point of view of non-smoking, I find it marvelous, says she, strikes a match - - . actually they've got a film, . on now, that . was on at dhiː festival, - just opened at the Academy

(13)   A: the reason it was quiet before, nineteen sixty-eight, was because . you can argue, is because . the British - didn't . didn't stir up the Northern aiuhr uh um the Ulster Protestants,
       B: well it wasn't entirely quiet

Because grounding is a continual process of updating a discourse with each new contribution, it will sometimes happen that speakers have built up a background that doesn't match what they next want to say (Jucker, 1993). Discourse markers can signal the need to alter prior assumptions, helping listeners to build bridging inferences between utterances.

Other markers can be used to show the return to a prior topic of conversation. *Anyway* and variants like *but anyway* and *anyway be that as it may* can be used to mark the end of a digression and the return to the prior topic, as can be seen in the following example after the brief digression *you know what getting up Sunday's like* (Bublitz, 1988, p. 118; Takahara, 1998; example adapted from Svartvik & Quirk, 1980, 2.7.41–2.7.48):

(14)   A: I had some people to lunch on Sunday, and . they turned up half an hour early,
       B: really
       A: I mean you know what g getting up Sunday's like, anyway, and - . I'd - I was behind in any case, . and I'd said to them one o'clock

Stock phrases like *as I was saying* can also be used to signal the return to an earlier topic (Bublitz, 1988).

Two superficially similar discourse markers, *and* and *then*, can be used in contrasting ways to indicate either topic continuity or topic shift in text comprehension, and might serve similar functions in listening. *And* is used to show continuity and *then* is used to show that a new idea will come up (Bestgen & Costermans, 1994). The choice between one or the other provides very specific information to the reader, and very likely the listener as well, about what to expect next. Removing either of them from the discourse would eliminate the forewarning of a new idea, which is potentially useful information for building bridging inferences.

So, to deal with the two main ways inference making can be thwarted, by having disorganised ideas or by suddenly shifting focus, speakers can use a number of carefully placed discourse markers. But even when inference making is not thwarted, there is still the problem of expressing the relationship between ideas so that it is clear to listeners which ideas go together and how groups of ideas relate to one another. Here too speakers can use discourse markers to move between different layers of talk and to indicate different kinds of perspective shifts. Speakers can indicate shifts at a register level, such as moving from joking back to seriousness, with the marker *I mean* (Redeker, 1991). They can indicate shifts between speakers' stances, such as moving from statements to evaluation of those statements, with the word *well* (Schiffrin, 1987). And they can indicate shifts between the speakers themselves and the characters in the speakers' narratives, as in the following where the critical discourse markers are italicised:

(15)   and I said well what does she want it for, he said . *oh* I I don't know, but Ella needs it, she called for it (adapted from Svartvik & Quirk, 1980, 2.13.1244–2.13.1247)

(16)   Both sides of the street can hear her yelling at us and she's *like* "Come in here and have a beer" you know? (adapted from Schourup, 1985, p. 43)

(17)   But the twins in the family say *well* they were so surprised that of all the people, that she had the twins (adapted from Schiffrin, 1987, p. 125)

Well, *like*, and *oh* have been thought to mark shifts between the speakers' talk and the talk of the character in a story the speaker is telling, introducing both direct and indirect quotes (Jucker, 1993; Redeker, 1991; Schiffrin, 1987; Schourup, 1985). In addition to forewarning a shift between the perspective of the speaker versus that of the character, these discourse markers help limit the confusion about who said what in a storytelling situation, so that it is clear whether a speaker's *I* refers to the speaker or to the character; in example (15), the *I* of *he said oh I don't know* refers to the *he* who is talking, not to the narrator of the story.

Discourse markers might also be used to indicate shifts between major and minor idea breaks. The different kinds of breaks are associated with different temporal markers in writing (Bestgen & Costermans, 1994), and these markers might be used in the same way in conversations. *Anchorage markers*, such as *in the afternoon*, are markers of precise time and tell exactly when an event occurred for later events to refer back to. *Sequence markers*, such as *afterwards*, show the relative organisation of events. In written text, anchorage markers are used at major idea breaks and sequence markers at minor breaks (Bestgen & Costermans, 1994). These discourse markers keep the flow of ideas coherent by providing information about how to relate sentences.

In addition to forewarning perspective shifts, another way speakers help listeners interpret the relationship among ideas in a discourse is by providing information about what they are thinking. Because speakers are driven to express ideas in a brief amount of time and with limited elaboration to comply with the constraints of turn-taking and least collaborative effort, their contributions might end up vague or not well thought out; it is to both speakers' and addressees' advantage if addressees can predict where speakers' ideas are headed.

Discourse markers can serve this function is by indicating a mismatch between what's said and what's intended or by indicating that speakers have not completely filled out their intentions, inviting addressees to complete the ideas (Jucker & Smith, 1998; Schourup, 1985). Researchers argue that *like, I mean, sort of,* and *kind of* indicate what's said is not exactly what's intended, that *you know* indicates that what's said is incomplete, and that *well* and *oh* indicate that speakers are choosing between alternatives for what to say next, as in "another guy comes in, a little more heavy-set guy, and uh mmh *ohh* a banker of some sort" (Redeker, 1991, p. 1154; see also Jucker, 1993; Schourup, 1985; Stubbe & Holmes, 1995). Speakers can also use *um* and *uh* to indicate that their answers to questions might not be correct; with an *um* or *uh*, answers are perceived as less likely to be correct than had the speaker used a pause of the same length (Brennan & Williams, 1995). By marking their utterances as equivocal, speakers can inform listeners that they may need to do more work to interpret the speakers' meaning. Having information about the speakers' knowledge states and being able to predict upcoming utterances aids in the grounding process and helps maintain least collaborative effort in an exchange. Addressees can use the information in evaluating the speakers' contributions and planning their own.

The multifunctionality of some discourse markers may seem to threaten a functional account. After all, if they can do so many things, how can a listener know which use to apply in a given instance? One reassuring observation is that markers can be uniformly interpreted enough to be used deceptively. *Well* can be used to get listeners to believe that the next statement is relevant when it may not be (Schiffrin, 1982). *You know*'s use in getting addressees to take what's said to be common ground (Östman, 1981) can be used to elicit agreement from addressees in an argument, or "as a subtle means of getting the hearers to admit to the validity of a premise" (Watts, 1989, p. 218). *Incidentally* and *by the way*, which mark temporary digression, can be exploited to permanently steer conversations away from topics the speaker doesn't want to discuss (Bublitz, 1988). *Oh* can be used to show information is new when it isn't, or withheld to show it's not new when it is (Fox Tree & Schrock, 1999; Heritage, 1984). The deceptive use of discourse markers is only possible because speakers can reliably count on their being interpreted in particular ways.

Another way of approaching the worrisome multifunctionality issue is by arguing that a particular function of a discourse marker arises out of a combination of an underlying function and a particular pronunciation, position in turn, syntactic placement, or pragmatic environment (Erman, 1987; Östman, 1981; Schiffrin, 1987; Stenström, 1990).

A third way of exploring multifunctionality is by directly measuring what's understood. Although evidence using experimental approaches is sparse in comparison to corpora analyses, it is a useful direction for future studies. Evidence from reading experiments has supported the claims that discourse markers are used in predictable ways and are beneficial to discourse processing. When connectives such as *because* and *although* linked two sentences, the second sentence was read more quickly and integrated better, as measured by accuracy on comprehension questions, than when the connectives were absent (Millis & Just, 1994). When *then*, *and*, *so*, *because*, and *but* were used to link sentences, the relationships between sentences were interpreted differently from when the connectives were absent; for example, readers were more likely to agree that two sentences were temporally related when a marker was present than when it was absent (Segal et al., 1991). Listeners may use markers like readers do. But they also may not. As discussed earlier, the problems listeners face are different from the problems readers face, so markers may function differently in the two modalities. This is on top of a perhaps more basic problem in extrapolating reading findings to listening: Different discourse markers are used in writing and speech (Flowerdew & Tauroza, 1995; Stenström, 1990).

Direct tests of how spoken discourse markers affect listeners' interpretations have supported the idea that discourse markers are beneficial. A videotaped lecture containing markers was understood better than the same lecture with the markers edited out, as measured by the amount of lecture material recalled and the accuracy of responses to a test on the material (Flowerdew & Tauroza, 1995). As another example, overhearers can complete a referential card task better when there are discourse markers than when there aren't (Fox Tree, 1999). But in this study, it is unclear whether it is the number of markers or other co-occurring factors such as the number of differing perspectives that is driving the effect (Fox Tree, 1999). Finally, other experimental tests using *word monitoring* tasks (Fox Tree & Schrock, 1999) and *semantic verification* tasks (Fox Tree & Schrock, 1999; Gernsbacher & Jescheniak, 1995) have also demonstrated the beneficial contribution of discourse markers and other spontaneous speech signals to language comprehension.

In word monitoring, people listen for the occurrence of a particular word in an utterance and press a button if they hear the word. The speed at which they press the button is related to the comprehensibility of the utterance up to that point (Fox Tree, 1995; Marslen-Wilson & Tyler, 1980). In a study on the use of the discourse maker *oh*, researchers found that listeners were faster at detecting a word in an utterance after they had heard an *oh* than they were at detecting the same word when the *oh* had been digitally removed, demonstrating the on-line beneficial effects of *oh* to language comprehension (Fox Tree &

Schrock, 1999). *Oh* can signal addressees to halt the building of bridging inferences or to expect an updating of earlier information, and addressees benefit from this signal.

In semantic verification, people see a word appear on a computer screen as they are listening to an utterance, and they press a button corresponding to whether or not the word they saw had been said in the utterance they heard (Fox Tree & Schrock, 1999; Gernsbacher & Jescheniak, 1995). The discourse marker *oh* was found to have a predictable effect with this task as well; people were faster at verifying that a word had been said when the visual target was presented after an *oh* than when it was presented at the same point in the utterance but with the *oh* excised, once again demonstrating the usefulness of *oh* in on-line language comprehension (Fox Tree & Schrock, 1999). Stressing a word and using *this* cataphorically, as in "So a man walks into a bar with *this* parrot on his shoulder", was also found to improve the incorporation of upcoming information into the discourse model (Gernsbacher & Jescheniak, 1995, p. 26). For example, listeners were faster at confirming that the word *ashtray* had been said when the utterance was "she just had to buy this ashtray" than when it was "she just had to buy an ashtray" (Gernsbacher & Jescheniak, 1995, p. 44).

Other evidence that discourse markers are important to interpretation comes from observing second language learners. Omitting discourse markers can cause the speech of nonnative speakers to sound odd (Stubbs, 1983), as can using them incorrectly. After living in the US for 17 months, some people learning English still had not mastered the pragmatic use of *and* as a temporal marker instead of as a logical conjunction (Bouton, 1994). When given the information "Sandy went to Philadelphia and stole a car", these speakers had difficulty determining if one act preceded another or if the two were simultaneous (Bouton, 1994, p. 162); native English speakers agreed that going to Philadelphia came first. Interpreting discourse markers correctly is a skill that has to be learned.

The spontaneous speech phenomena we have just discussed, including discourse markers, stock phrases, and cataphoric *this*, are all used regularly by conversational participants. They play a role in coordinating discourse, achieving grounding, and expressing attitudes among conversational participants. They constrain interpretations between utterances and the types of bridging inferences that are built. In their absence, people make a greater variety of interpretations about the relationship between two ideas (Segal et al., 1991). They help coordinate spontaneous talk by creating connections between the sometimes disparate utterance productions that can result from the lack of sufficient planning time in speaking. And when all else fails, they can be used to show that what's being said is not exactly what's meant, or what would have been said had there been enough time to plan. Without them, information would be lost; listeners would not have forewarning about an impending need to adjust grounding assumptions, they would not have signals that they should hold a certain concept in mind for future reference, and they would not have information about how to organise or evaluate speakers' talk. Discourse markers not only have clear functions in spontaneous speech, which can be used to promote understanding or exploited for deceptive ends, but they can also be required.

Discourse markers are not unwanted interruptions but devices that are purposefully used to overcome grounding problems that arise with the communicative medium of spontaneous speech. They are important precisely in those communicative situations where they occur, where language is not written down or prepared in advance but is produced on the fly in spontaneous discourse. We now turn to another by-product of speaking on the fly—disfluencies.

COORDINATING REPAIRS

In order to maintain turns in a conversation and speak in a timely manner while ensuring moment-by-moment interlocutor comprehension, speakers often find themselves either speaking before they're ready or needing to adjust what they've said on the fly based on addressees' feedback. These problems arise because of the absence in spontaneous speech of one of the grounding factors described earlier, the lack of private revisability. How do listeners follow speech with errors, restarts, revisions, or the sudden insertion of out-of-order information? Several devices exist to help interlocutors maximise understanding in the face of speech disfluencies and errors.

The terms *disfluency* and *error* cover a wide range of problems in spontaneous speech. These include (a) leaving long silent gaps between words, (b) slips of the tongue, such as saying *knoor dob* instead of *door knob*, (c) mispronunciation, such as pronouncing Yosemite as /yo-seh-mayt/ instead of /yo-seh-mi-tee/, (d) repaired speech, as in *the house- the red house*, and (e) pragmatic errors, such as a clerk's answering a customer's question *What time is it?* with *We close at seven* when the question was asked with the intention of finding out the actual time and not as an indirect way to find out what time the shop closed. These categories are not mutually exclusive: Slips of the tongue can be repaired and a pragmatic error can contain long silent gaps.

A problem in speech can be either *repaired* or *unrepaired*. Repaired and unrepaired disfluencies and errors pose different problems for interlocutors. Unrepaired errors either result in communicative breakdown, which we are not concerned with here in our investigation of how interlocutors successfully navigate problematic speech, or they result in no threat to communicative success, such as with some misplaced word accents (Cutler, 1983). Disfluencies and errors are repaired when interlocutors feel it is important to do so for communicative success. The repair poses problems for both speakers and addressees. Speakers need to make repairs that clearly indicate what is to be removed from the discourse record and what is to be retained. Addressees need to follow these repairs so that they can piece together what the speakers' intended utterance is.

Repairs can be categorised into two main types: *self-repairs* and *other-repairs*. In self-repairs, speakers notice and correct problems without recourse to other conversational participants. With other-repairs, speakers and interlocutors work together to resolve problems, as in the following example (adapted from Svartvik & Quirk, 1980, 1.13.613–1.13.614):

(18)   A: this is one that's Milligan tsh uh . *fire bone china*
       B: *Milligan china*

While speaker A searched for the way to express the type of dishware, speaker B jumped in to complete the partial noun phrase that began with *Milligan* by saying *Milligan china*. Both interlocutors work to resolve the word-finding problem. We'll talk about self-repairs first, and then other-repairs.

Self-repairs can be broken down into three main types. One is *repetition*, as in "well I'll I'll get them through . quickly" (Svartvik & Quirk, 1980, 1.1.220). Repetitions can be of words or phrases, as in "I mean it isn't just . it isn't just this morning" (Svartvik & Quirk, 1980, 3.3.814). A second type of self-repair is a *restart*, where speakers start to say something, but then restart their utterances, as in "but it's far more than . well it lasts quite a time" (Svartvik & Quirk, 1980, 1.4.937). A third is midway between a repetition and a restart, where some aspects of the information are repeated, and some are not, as in "they had no . riuh they had never they had no plans whatever" (Svartvik & Quirk, 1980, 2.3.120). These will be called *replacements*.

Self-repairs are common in spontaneous speech because speakers are constantly monitoring what they say. This means checking both that they are making sense and that what they are saying is appropriate to the situation. If there is a problem, they need to fix it as they speak. In other language production situations, such as writing emails or letters, people don't make as many errors because they have time to review their words before addressees receive the information. Although revising talk publicly is a necessary component of speaking spontaneously, the revision process has also developed so that it is less burdensome to listeners.

One way that speakers help listeners recoup after a stumble is by starting repairs with words that are systematically related to the speech they replace. This relatedness can be exploited in determining exactly what the intended utterance was. In interpreting repairs, listeners can use either the *word-identity convention* or the *category-identity convention* (Levelt, 1989, p. 493):

(19)   The word-identity convention
       If the first word of the repair is identical to some word *w* of the original utterance, the repair is to be interpreted as a continuation of the original utterance from *w* on. (If there is more than one such word in the original utterance, take the last one.)

(20)   The category-identity convention
        If the syntactic category of the first word of the repair is identical to the
        syntactic category of some word *w* of the original utterance, the repair
        is to be interpreted as a continuation from *w* on, with the first repair
        word replacing *w*. (If there is more than one such word in the original
        utterance, take the last one.)

Listeners can use one or both of these conventions to accurately determine
where to attach the repair syntactically. The word-identity convention allows for
a replacement with a lead-in word, such as the word *to* in "Right to yellow, uh
to white", the category-identity for replacements without lead-ins, as in "From
the green disc to up to a pink ... , orange disk" (Levelt, 1983, p. 90; italics
removed). In a corpus of route descriptions, there were few violations of these
conventions; by the first word of the repair, listeners had enough information to
connect repairs to earlier aborted speech (Levelt, 1989, p. 495).

By systematically relating the first word of the repair to an earlier word in the
utterance, speakers can indicate to listeners where to begin a repair. They can
also signal how far back in the speech stream the correction lies by the *editing
expressions* they use between the *reparandum* and the *repair*. Editing expressions are words or phrases like *um*, *I mean*, *sorry*, and "oh, that's impossible; I
will start again, ok?" (Levelt, 1989, p. 482). Reparandums are the stretches of
the speech that are to be replaced, and repairs are the stretches that do the
replacing. Saying *uh* or *um* before the repair signals that the reparandum is likely
to be only a short distance back, around 1.7 syllables; saying *sorry* or *that is*
signals that the reparandum is likely to be further back, around 4.3 syllables
(Levelt, 1989, p. 484).

Editing expressions might also be used to distinguish between two categories
of repairs: *error* repairs, where a wrong word or phrase is used, and *appropriateness* repairs, where an inappropriate or imprecise word or phrase is used (Levelt,
1983, 1989). In the route description corpus, 62% of error repairs had editing
expressions, compared to 28% of appropriateness repairs (Levelt, 1989, p. 483).
The choice of editing device might further distinguish the kind of repair taking
place. In Dutch, *uh* or *no* were used for error repairs, and *so* was used for
appropriateness repairs (Levelt, 1989, p. 483). This systematicity allows listeners
to predict whether a replacement or an adjustment will follow after an editing
expression is heard.

Nonexperimental observations of the use of *um* and *uh* support the hypothesis
that these words are informative. With an *um* or an *uh*, speakers can indicate
"not just the unavailability of a word, but a *relevant* unavailability—one that
impedes the ongoing development of the talk in progress" (Goodwin & Goodwin, 1986, pp. 55–56). That is, speakers are indicating not just that a word is not
immediately accessible, but that finding the word is imperative for communicative success. When they can't find a word but also don't need to find the word,

speakers don't say *um*; instead they do something else, like saying *something or other* in place of an unaccessible last name in the example "what the hell was her name. Karen. Right. Karen. her name was Karen something or other" (adapted from Goodwin & Goodwin, 1986, p. 54). These observations support the claim that *ums* and *uhs* are not said randomly but instead supply information.

Experimental observation also supports the hypothesis that at least *uhs* are informative. People are faster to identify words after *uh* than they are to identify the same words when the *uh* is digitally excised, both in English and in Dutch (Fox Tree, 1997). People are also faster to identify which object is being described when the description is in its original form, *uh* plus repair, than when *uh* and repair have been edited out (Brennan & Schober, 1997).

So both corpora analyses and experimentation support the idea that editing expressions are useful in listeners' recovering from repairs. But editing expressions are infrequent with one kind of repair, restarts. Only 6% of restarts contained the editing expressions *um* or *uh* (Levelt, 1989, p. 494). When speakers completely restart what they are saying, the repair shares little or nothing in common with the reparandums, so it's possible that editing expressions' potential benefit in signalling how far back the correction lies or what kind of correction it is, is just not useful enough.

Without the benefit of self-repair conventions or editing expressions, how do listeners recover from restarts? The answer is they don't recover as easily from restarts as from other repairs. A restart that requires figuring out what information to excise from the discourse record and what to retain will slow listeners down in comprehending spontaneous speech, but a different kind of repair, a repetition, will not (Fox Tree, 1995). It takes longer to monitor for the word *looks* in *and the next figure, that has- it looks a little like a uh like a hammer* than it does to monitor for it in *and the next figure, it looks a little like a uh like a hammer*, the identical sentence with the false start *this has* digitally excised. In contrast, monitoring for the word *shield* in *and the inner part that looks like a uh like the shape of a of a shield or a weapon* is not slowed down by the presence of the repetition *of a* (Fox Tree, 1995). Fortunately, there is reason to believe that if a speaker is to make a repair, restarts are a last resort. In a sample of 607 repaired noun phrases beginning with *the* in the Svartvik and Quirk corpus (1980), about 36% contained repetitions, but only 11% contained restarts (Fox Tree & Clark, 1997).

Restarts cause noticeable trouble and are unlikely to be forewarned by editing expressions. But there are alternative forewarning tools speakers may use. One of these is pronouncing words preceding trouble in marked ways. For example, in noun phrases the determiners *the* and *a* may be pronounced in elongated form as *thee* and *ay* instead of *thuh* and *uh* (Fox Tree & Clark, 1997). In one analysis, when *thee* was used instead of the unmarked pronunciation *thuh*, 81% of the time the determiner was immediately followed by a suspension of speech, such as a pause, *um* or *uh*, or a repair. For comparison, only 7% of *thuh*s were immediately followed by suspensions (Fox Tree & Clark, 1997). *Thee* also signalled to listeners that the suspension was likely to be relatively severe. For example, looking only at *the* noun phrases with suspensions, 76% of restarts were after *thee* (24% after *thuh*) compared to 42% of replacements (58% after *thuh*; Fox Tree & Clark, 1997). So although there may be fewer editing expressions before restarts, there are still other signals of impending trouble, such as marked pronunciations of the words preceding the restarts. Forewarning can mitigate the effects of speaker revisions by alerting listeners that they should pay more attention to the upcoming speech because it is likely to require a repair.

In addition to forewarning repairs and making repairs in particular ways, speakers may also aid listeners in recovering from speech suspensions by continuing to speak after suspensions in ways that preserve continuity (Clark & Wasow, 1998). For example, speakers may choose to repeat what they said before the suspension after the suspension, as in "I uh I wouldn't be surprised at that", instead of merely continuing after the suspension, as in "I uh wouldn't be surprised at that" (Clark & Wasow, 1998, p. 236). In this view, repetitions are not problems as much as they are solutions. Disrupting the continuity of phonological phrases can lead to slower recognition of words in speech (Fox Tree, 1995); preserving continuity may do the opposite and aid processing.

Evidence of listeners' active work in creating successful repairs is demonstrated by the existence of other-repairs, which contrast with the repairs within a speaker's own speech discussed up to now. If listeners were not actively engaged in the communicative process, other-repairs would not exist. One common kind of other-repair is pragmatic repair. Unlike disfluencies, which can often be described at the word level or at most the sentence level, pragmatic errors are errors that span several sentences as in the following constructed example where the boldface utterance is disjointed from the rest of the passage (Kreuz & Roberts, 1993, p. 244):

(21)　A:　Would you believe I got *another* speeding ticket today?
　　　B:　Not again! What happened this time?
　　　A:　Same thing as always. They have this speed trap I have to drive through to get to work, and I was late again, so . . .
　　　B:　You should find some other way to get to work. Why don't you try using that exit at Washington Street?
　　　A:　**Don't the police have anything better to do?**
　　　B:　Well, what's wrong with the Washington exit?
　　　A:　They've got it blocked off for the next few months. I think they're paving it.
　　　B:　Oh. That doesn't leave you too many options, does it?

In this example, the line "Don't the police have anything better to do?" introduces the pragmatic error, but the whole discourse is necessary for the line to be interpreted as an error.

Pragmatic repairs have different effects on overhearers from lexical or phonological repairs. Spoken passages containing pragmatic errors were compared to the same passages with lexical or phonological errors substituted for the pragmatic errors; in the above example, "Don't the police have anything better to do?" was replaced with "They've got Jefferson, I mean, Washington blocked off for the next few months", with the subsequent dialogue altered accordingly (adapted from Kreuz & Roberts, 1993, p. 244). Both kinds of repairs caused the personality of the speaker of the problematic sentence to be rated more negatively than in passages without repairs. But in contrast to lexical or phonological errors, with pragmatic errors, the addressees were also rated more negatively than without the error. Though the utterer of a lexical or phonological error seems to be solely responsible for those mistakes, both interlocutors seem to be responsible for pragmatic errors. Overhearers treat the resolution of pragmatic errors as a mutual task where both interlocutors can be held accountable. Addressees have a recognised responsibility in avoiding and resolving communicative breakdowns.

The idea of achieving repair by mutual work helps explain why not all errors are corrected. When a correction is not necessary to achieve mutual understanding, errors can be left unrepaired. When a word is pronounced with a mistaken stress that preserves vowel quality, such as "You think it's sarCASm, but it's not", speakers don't correct the word; but when the mispronunciation leads to a distortion of the word that might threaten comprehension, it is corrected (Cutler, 1983, pp. 85–86). Likewise, when sentence accent is anomalous but doesn't lead to an interpretation different from its intended interpretation it isn't corrected, as in "The only trouble WITH it—[pause]—is the hood is too small"; but when the accent does affect the meaning, it is corrected, as in "and what I'M saying— what I'm SAYing is" (Cutler, 1983, pp. 86–87). The driving force behind whether or not talk will get corrected is whether or not the correction is necessary for understanding.

When people need to adjust what they're saying, they don't just stop what they're saying and say what they really mean. Instead, they adjust their speech in ways that help listeners successfully correct their discourse model to accommodate the repair. By (a) preserving continuity, (b) using editing expressions and elongation to forewarn the presence and type of upcoming repairs, and (c) making repairs that follow the conventions about relating the first word of the repair to the reparandum, speakers can help listeners identify errors and make corrections smoothly. It is in speakers' best interest to make repairs that help listeners to follow along, and in listeners' best interest to use all available information to process speech.

CONCLUSION

In this chapter, I discussed the use of timing, discourse markers, editing expressions, and other devices in resolving the problems that arise in the communicative medium of spontaneous speech. The main obstacles discussed were the effervescence of speech, which leads to an inability to review the discourse record, and the cotemporality of the interlocutors, which limits private revisability and creates a pressure to speak before being fully prepared, resulting in speech errors and disfluencies.

Speaking on the fly—in unplanned, unrehearsed conversation—leads to the production and use of specialised words, phrases, and pronunciations in order to achieve the grounding criterion, coordinate turns, organise ideas, correct errors, and warn listeners of upcoming speech production trouble. The nonessential words and phrases of spontaneous speech are not so nonessential after all. Instead, these hallmarks of conversations need to be attended to on a moment-by-moment basis as discourse is building up. They cannot be ignored even for one moment, or else one person risks being misinterpreted by a conversational partner.

REFERENCES

Adams, M.R. (1982). Fluency, nonfluency, and stuttering in children. *Journal of Fluency Disorders*, *7*, 171–185.

Aijmer, K. (1988). "Now may we have a word on this": The use of "now" as a discourse particle. In M. Kytö, O. Ihalainen, & M. Rissanen (Eds.), *Corpus linguistics, hard and soft: Proceedings of the 8th international conference on English Language Research on Computerized Corpora*. Amsterdam: Rodopi.

Argyle, M., Lalljee, M., & Cook, M. (1968). The effects of visibility on interaction in a dyad. *Human Relations, 21*, 3–17.

Atkinson, M. (1984). *Our master's voices: The language and body language of politics*. New York: Methuen.

Bernstein, B. (1962). Social class, linguistic codes and grammatical elements. *Language and Speech*, *5*, 221–240.

Bestgen, Y., & Costermans, J. (1994). Time, space, and action: Exploring the narrative structure and its linguistic marking. *Discourse Processes, 17*, 421–446.

Bouton, L.F. (1994). Conversational implicature in a second language: Learned slowly when not deliberately taught. *Journal of Pragmatics, 22*, 157–167.

Brennan, S.E., & Schober, M.F. (1997). *When do speech disfluencies help comprehension?* Unpublished paper presented at the 38th annual meeting of the Psychonomic Society, Philadelphia.

Brennan, S.E., & Williams, W. (1995). The feeling of another's knowing: Prosody and filled pauses as cues to listeners about the metacognitive states of speakers. *Journal of Memory and Language, 34*, 383–398.

Brody, J. (1987). Particles borrowed from Spanish as discourse markers in Mayan languages. *Anthropological Linguistics, 29*(4), 507–521.

Bublitz, W. (1988). *Supportive fellow-speakers and cooperative conversations: Discourse topics and topical actions, participant roles, and "recipient action" in a particular type of everyday conversation*. Philadelphia: John Benjamins Publishing Company.

Clark, H.H. (1983). Language use and language users. In G. Lindzey & E. Aronson (Eds.), *Handbook of social psychology* (3rd ed.). Reading, MA: Addison-Wesley.

Clark, H.H. (1996). *Using language*. New York: Cambridge University Press.

Clark, H.H., & Brennan, S.E. (1991). Grounding in communication. In L.B. Resnick, J.M. Levine, & S.D. Teasley (Eds.), *Perspectives on socially shared cognition*. Washington, DC: American Psychological Association.

Clark, H.H., & Haviland, S.E. (1975). Comprehension and the given-new contract. In R.O. Freedle (Ed.), *Discourse production and comprehension*. Norwood, NJ: Ablex.

Clark, H.H., & Schaefer, E.F. (1987). Collaborating on contributions to conversations. *Language and Cognitive Processes*, *2*(1), 259–294.

Clark, H.H., & Schaefer, E.F. (1989). Contributing to discourse. *Cognitive Science*, *13*, 259–294.

Clark, H.H., & Wasow, T. (1998). Repeating words in spontaneous speech. *Cognitive Psychology*, *37*, 201–242.

Clark, H.H., & Wilkes-Gibbs, D.L. (1986). Referring as a collaborative process. *Cognition*, *22*, 1–39.

Cutler, A. (1983). Speakers' conceptions of the function of prosody. In A. Cutler & D.R. Ladd (Eds.), *Prosody: Models and measurements*. New York: Springer-Verlag.

Duncan, S., Jr. (1972). Some signals and rules for taking speaking turns in conversation. *Journal of Personality and Social Psychology*, *23*(2), 283–292.

Duncan, S., Jr., & Niederehe, G. (1974). On signalling that it's your turn to speak. *Journal of Experimental Social Psychology*, *10*, 234–247.

Edwards, J.A. (1993). Survey of electronic corpora and related resources for language researchers. In J.A. Edwards & M.D. Lampert (Eds.), *Talking data: Transcription and coding in discourse research*. Hillsdale, NJ: Lawrence Erlbaum Associates Inc.

Erman, B. (1987). *Pragmatic expressions in English: A study of you know, you see, and I mean in face-to-face conversation*. Stockholm: Almqvist & Wiksell International.

Erman, B., & Kotsinas, U.-B. (1993). Pragmaticalization: The case of *ba'* and *you know*. In J. Falk, K. Jonasson, G. Melchers, & B. Nilsson (Eds.), *Stockholm studies in modern philology* (Vol. 10, pp. 76–93). Stockholm: Almqvist & Wiksell International.

Flowerdew, J., & Tauroza, S. (1995). The effect of discourse markers on second language lecture comprehension. *Studies in Second Language Acquisition*, *17*, 455–458.

Fox Tree, J.E. (1995). The effects of false starts and repetitions on the processing of subsequent words in spontaneous speech. *Journal of Memory and Language*, *34*, 709–738.

Fox Tree, J.E. (1997). *Listeners' uses of* ums *and* uhs *in on-line speech processing*. Poster presented at the 38th annual meeting of the Psychonomic Society, Philadelphia.

Fox Tree, J.E. (1999). Listening in on monologues and dialogues. *Discourse Processes*, *27*, 35–53.

Fox Tree, J.E., & Clark, H.H. (1997). Pronouncing "the" as "thee" to signal problems in speaking. *Cognition*, *62*, 151–167.

Fox Tree, J.E., & Schrock, J.C. (1999). Discourse markers in spontaneous speech: Oh what a difference an oh makes. *Journal of Memory and Language*, *40*, 280–295.

Gernsbacher, M.A., & Jescheniak, J.D. (1995). Cataphoric devices in spoken discourse. *Cognitive Psychology*, *29*, 24–58.

Goodwin, M.H., & Goodwin, C. (1986). Gesture and coparticipation in the activity of searching for a word. *Semiotica*, *62*(1/2), 51–75.

Heritage, J. (1984). A change-of-state token and aspects of its sequential placement. In J.M. Atkinson & J. Heritage (Eds.), *Structures of social action: Studies in conversation analysis*. Cambridge, UK: Cambridge University Press.

Holmes, J. (1986). Functions of *you know* in womens' and men's speech. *Language in Society*, *15*, 1–22.

Isaacs, E.A., & Clark, H.H. (1987). References in conversation between experts and novices. *Journal of Experimental Psychology: General*, *116*(1), 26–37.

James, D. (1972). Some aspects of the syntax and semantics of interjections. *Papers from the Eighth Regional Meeting*. Chicago: Chicago Linguistics Society.

Jefferson, G. (1973). A case of precision timing in ordinary conversation: Overlapped tag-positioned address terms in closing sequences. *Semiotica*, *9*, 47–96.

Jefferson, G. (1989). Preliminary notes on a possible metric which provides for a "standard maximum" silence of approximately one second in conversation. In D. Roger & P. Bull (Eds.), *Conversation: An interdisciplinary perspective*. Philadelphia: Multilingual Matters.

Johnson, W. (1961). Measurements of oral reading and speaking rate and disfluency of adult male and female stutterers and nonstutterers. *Journal of Speech and Hearing Disorders*, *7*, 1–20.

Jucker, A.H. (1993). The discourse marker "well": A relevance theoretical account. *Journal of Pragmatics*, *19*, 435–452.

Jucker, A.H., & Smith, S.W. (1998). And people just you know like "wow": Discourse markers as negotiating strategies. In A.H. Jucker & Y. Ziv (Eds.), *Discourse markers: Descriptions and theory*. Amsterdam: John Benjamins.

Kotthoff, H. (1993). Disagreement and concession in disputes: On the context sensitivity of preference structures. *Language in Society*, *22*, 193–216.

Kreuz, R.J., & Roberts, R.M. (1993). When collaboration fails: Consequences of pragmatic errors in conversation. *Journal of Pragmatics*, *19*, 239–252.

Kuiper, K. (1996). *Smooth talkers: The linguistic performance of auctioneers and sportscasters*. Mahwah, NJ: Lawrence Erlbaum Associates Inc.

Levelt, W.J.M. (1983). Monitoring and self-repair in speech. *Cognition*, *14*, 41–104.

Levelt, W.J.M. (1989). *Speaking: From intention to articulation*. Cambridge, MA: MIT Press.

Levin, H., Silverman, I., & Ford, B.L. (1967). Hesitations in children's speech during explanation and description. *Journal of Verbal Learning and Verbal Behavior*, *6*, 560–564.

Marslen-Wilson, W., & Tyler, L.K. (1980). The temporal structure of spoken language understanding. *Cognition*, *8*, 1–71.

Maschler, Y. (1994). Metalanguaging and discourse markers in bilingual conversation. *Language in Society*, *23*, 325–366.

McLaughlin, M.L., & Cody, M.J. (1982). Awkward silences: Behavioral antecedents and consequences of the conversational lapse. *Human Communication Research*, *8*(4), 299–316.

Millis, K.M., & Just, M.A. (1994). The influence of connectives on sentence comprehension. *Journal of Memory and Language*, *33*, 128–147.

Östman, J.-O. (1981). *You know: A discourse functional approach*. Amsterdam: John Benjamins.

Redeker, G. (1991). Linguistic markers of discourse structure. *Linguistics*, *29*, 1139–1172.

Sacks, H., Schegloff, E.A., & Jefferson, G. (1974). A simplest systematics for the organization of turn taking for conversation. *Language*, *50*, 696–735.

Schegloff, E.A. (1987). Recycled turn beginnings: A precise repair mechanism in conversation's turn-taking organisation. In G. Button & J.R.E. Lee (Eds.), *Talk and social organisation* (Vol. 1, pp. 70–85). Clevedon, UK: Multilingual Matters.

Schiffrin, D. (1982). *Discourse markers: Semantic resources for the construction of conversation*. Unpublished PhD dissertation, University of Pennsylvania.

Schiffrin, D. (1987). *Discourse markers*. New York: Cambridge University Press.

Schourup, L.C. (1985). *Common discourse particles in English conversation*. New York: Garland.

Segal, E.M., Duchan, J.F., & Scott, P.J. (1991). The role of interclausal connectives in narrative structuring: Evidence from adults' interpretations of simple stories. *Discourse Processes*, *14*, 27–54.

Siegman, A.W., & Reynolds, M.A. (1983). Speaking without seeing, or the effect of interviewer absence on interviewee disclosure time. *Journal of Psycholinguistic Research*, *12*(6), 595–602.

Smith, V.L., & Clark, H.H. (1993). On the course of answering questions. *Journal of Memory and Language*, *32*, 25–38.

Stenström, A.-B. (1990). Lexical items peculiar to spoken discourse In J. Svartvik (Ed.), *The London-Lund corpus of spoken English: Description and research*. Lund, Sweden: Lund University Press.

Stubbe, M., & Holmes, J. (1995). *You know, eh* and other "exasperating expressions": An analysis of social and stylistic variation in the use of pragmatic devices in a sample of New Zealand English. *Language and Communication*, *15*(1), 63–88.

Stubbs, M. (1983). *Discourse analysis: The sociolinguistic analysis of natural language*. Oxford, UK: Basil Blackwell.

Svartvik, J., & Quirk, R. (Eds.). (1980). *A corpus of English conversation*. Lund, Sweden: CWK Gleerup.

Takahara, P.O. (1998). Pragmatic functions of the English discourse marker *anyway* and its corresponding contrastive Japanese discourse marker. In A.H. Jucker & Y. Ziv (Eds.), *Discourse markers: Descriptions and theory*. Amsterdam: John Benjamins.

Watts, R.J. (1989). Taking the pitcher to the "well": Native speakers' perception of their use of discourse markers in conversation. *Journal of Pragmatics*, *13*, 203–237.

Author Index

Subject Index